7

IMPRINT

PROJECT MANAGEMENT
Florian Kobler, Cologne

COLLABORATION
Harriet Graham, Turin

PRODUCTION
Thomas Grell, Cologne

DESIGN
Sense/Net, Andy Disl
and Birgit Eichwede,
Cologne

GERMAN TRANSLATION
Kristina Brigitta Köper and
Holger Wölfle, Berlin

FRENCH TRANSLATION
Jacques Bosser, Paris

© **VG BILD-KUNST**
Bonn 2010, for the works
of Santiago Calatrava and
Dominique Perrault

PRINTED IN ITALY
ISBN 978–3–8365–1736–2

© **2010 TASCHEN GMBH**
Hohenzollernring 53
D–50672 Cologne
www.taschen.com

ARCHITECTURE NOW!

Architektur heute / L'architecture d'aujourd'hui
Philip Jodidio

TASCHEN

CONTENTS

INTRODUCTION

NO TWILIGHT IN SIGHT

In the fall of 2008, the world stopped turning. Or so commentators would have had it. Swimming in a sea of toxic assets, banks and businesses saw their figures drop precipitously, as governments rode to the rescue with untold billions in aid. With the economy in a tailspin, how could architecture possibly go anywhere but down? It didn't take long for *Time* magazine critic Richard Lacayo to review the previous volume in this series in a piece entitled "The End of the World as We Know It": "*Architecture Now! 6* is part of the series that the German publisher TASCHEN produces periodically to round up interesting buildings from the preceding year or two. This volume was being wrapped up last year, sometime just before or after Lehman Brothers imploded in September and took the Dow with it. Looking over the 70-plus projects that were included—plus a few artworks with architectural implications—it was hard not to wonder whether Philip Jodidio, the architecture historian who presides over the series, hadn't inadvertently produced a book that should have been called 'Twilight of the Gods: The Last Moments of the Great 21st-Century Architecture Boom.'" After listing some of the more spectacular buildings of the past few years, Lacayo concludes: "…more than any other art form, architecture is linked to prosperity. Even poor artists can scrape together the money to buy supplies, but architects need clients. Now the money has dried up and so have the projects, and it may take a while before things bounce back. So you can't help but look at this gorgeous compilation as a snapshot of an era that has come to a close, or at least to an extended pause. You turn the pages and think, well, it was beautiful while it lasted."[1]

THERE'S THE EMERALD CITY

The moment to compile *Architecture Now! 7* came around and, guess what? The world was still turning, and architects were still building. Granted, some projects published in this book were quite far along when the economy suffered its greatest shock in decades. One shining example of this truth is the tallest building in the world, the Burj Khalifa (Dubai, UAE, 2004–10, SOM, Adrian Smith, page 432). Topped out at an astonishing 828 meters, this spindly tower may well have been completed at the end of 2009, and yet many other ambitious projects in Dubai have come to a grinding halt, at least for the time being.

Adrian Smith, the designer of the Burj Khalifa tower, admits that he was inspired by the towers of the Emerald City in the film version of *The Wizard of Oz*. "That was in my mind as I was designing Burj Khalifa," Smith says, "although in a subliminal way." "I didn't research the way it looked. I just remembered the glassy, crystalline structure coming up in the middle of what seemed like nowhere. The funny thing is, I didn't remember it being green." The classic 1939 film based on L. Frank Baum's book *The Wonderful Wizard of Oz* of course chronicles the voyage of Dorothy, a young girl from Kansas, played by Judy Garland in the movie, to the Emerald City, residence of the Wizard of Oz. Accompanied by a Lion, a Scarecrow, and a Tin Woodsman, Dorothy first sees gleaming green towers at the edge of a forest. "There's Emerald City," she says. "Oh, we're almost there at last, at last! It's beautiful, isn't it? Just like I knew it would be. He really must be a wonderful Wizard to live in a city like that." But the great and powerful Wizard of Oz turns out to be no more than a fraud, a "humbug," and the Emerald City the product of poppy-induced hallucinations. It would be difficult to invent the rapport between such a source of inspiration and the reality of today's Dubai.

1
SOM/Adrian Smith, Burj Khalifa,
Dubai, UAE, 2004–10

There was no doubt a good deal of excess in the world of architecture, closely related, as Richard Lacayo notes, to the casino economy of the first years of the 21st century. Then, too, remarkable advances in computer technology have permitted the design and construction of buildings that would have remained imaginary just a few years ago. These advances, not only in computer-assisted design (CAD) but also in manufacturing through computer numerical controlled (CNC) machine tools, will remain useful, no matter what the state of the economy. Indeed, CAD/CNC-designed and manufactured buildings should logically cost less than their counterparts of an earlier era.

Architects, even the most high-flying amongst them, have long voiced concern for the significance of cost savings in their designs. To name but one example, Rem Koolhaas/OMA have used inexpensive materials in many of their buildings for many years. Whether the budgets of famous architects are frequently so reasonable remains a contentious issue.

PASSIVELY YOURS

The point here is that the need to save money does not condemn architecture to the "end of the world as we know it." A brief glance at the projects in this book will suffice to respond to the critic's fears. Architecture, even post-bubble architecture, remains vital and inventive. New issues have surfaced rapidly in recent years, whether because of the crisis or before it. One of these is clearly the need to make architecture "greener" than it was in the heady days of the design of the Burj Khalifa tower. Even the casual observer will note that more and more buildings, both public and private, boast their "green" credentials and that architects now seek out the slightest potential for reduction of their infamous carbon footprints. This entails aesthetic changes, too, but the time when a "green" building had to look green has long since passed. The technology has evolved and "passive" techniques for energy savings, such as using the orientation or cladding of a building to reduce solar gain, are hardly visible as ecological gestures, even when they are quite effective.

What may be a prescient response to a downturn that had not yet begun is a series of inventive, small buildings such as the Juvet Landscape Hotel (Gudbrandsjuvet, Norway, 2007–09, Jensen & Skodvin Architects, page 262). Located in northwestern Norway, this hotel is conceived essentially as a series of small individual houses set up on 40-millimeter steel rods that can be removed without any serious damage to the natural setting. Here tourists admire natural scenery in an ecologically sound building that is clearly the work of accomplished designers. "Today's concern for sustainability in architecture focuses almost exclusively on reduced energy consumption in production and operation," state the architects. "We think that conservation of topography is another aspect of sustainability which deserves attention." Others have turned to a more radical approach to urban construction that may well carry lessons for times of difficulty. RDF181 (Brussels, Belgium, 2007, page 400) was conceived by the nonprofit organization Rotor as a form of parasitic "legal squatting," occupying part of a site that was awaiting planning permission for more permanent construction with a 60-square-meter temporary office. As planning permission was never requested for this office, used by Rotor for one year, and only waste materials were used in construction, RDF181 certainly represents a slap in the face for authorities who tend to complicate building more than they encourage it, particularly in urban settings. Like the similar efforts spearheaded by Santi Cirugeda in Spain, this type of parasitic temporary structure can, indeed, be seen as architecture for dark times, even if the horizon in late 2009 already seemed a bit brighter than one year before.

2

Big architectural offices in the United States, the United Kingdom, and other countries have certainly downsized in more difficult economic times, but inventive architecture is precisely about adapting to new conditions, be they financial or material. Calling on recycled products or seeking to reduce energy consumption for monetary or ecological reasons need not crimp the style of architects, quite the contrary. What do you do when the rallying call of the times is no longer "higher, bigger, madder"? *Architecture Now! 7* should hardly be a disappointment after *Architecture Now! 6*. The world has not stopped turning and architects have not stopped inventing new forms and new ideas.

It is no secret that artists and architects have long maintained a relationship both in shared realizations, and in shared ambitions. Clearly put, many architects long to be artists, just as Frank Gehry did in his early years, and artists, too, long for the space that a building can occupy. It might well be mutual jealousy that fuels some of the more interesting and creative works in both domains. This is the reason that *Architecture Now! 7*, like the previous volumes, contains a number of artworks, or perhaps works by architects that resemble art, for example the Lusatian Lakeland Landmark (Senftenberg, Germany, 2008, Architektur & Landschaft, page 70). This 30-meter tower made of Corten steel resembles nothing so much as an outside work by a sculptor such as Richard Serra. The designers evoke the typical bridges used in this former mining area, but they sought to create a "landmark" symbolizing the will of the region to transform itself. In another sense, this tower might well be termed a monument to past glories, thus rendering its affinity to sculpture clearer. It is no accident that Richard Serra, like Architektur & Landschaft, also bends his massive sheets of Corten steel in a shipping yard—no other industrial facility is capable of this kind of manipulation. "The difference between art and architecture," says the American sculptor, "is that art serves no purpose." If a set of stairs and a viewing platform constitute a purpose, then the Lusatian Lakeland Landmark might not be a pure work of art, but it is certainly on the cusp between the two disciplines.

LIKE RUINS FROM A LOST CIVILIZATION

Giacomo Costa is by no means an architect. He is rather a photographer with an eye for urban chaos of a sort. His computer-enhanced photographic images, published recently under the title *The Chronicles of Time* (2009, page 140), might well offer visions of an apocalyptic future, one that would frighten even the bears of Wall Street. The architect Lord Foster writes: "These portrayals of the city occur not only post-9/11, but in a period in which the terrorist threat lurks behind our everyday normality. In these unsettling times our pundits conjecture if and when hidden forces might unleash the Armageddon of a nuclear strike or biological attack out of the blue. Giacomo Costa's visions, with their infinite perspectives and limitless horizons, are like ruins from a lost civilization, which could be our civilization. Through his powerful vision they remind us above all of the fragility of our built world and the civic premises that have so far underpinned it."[2] Costa is not the only artist to have been inspired in some sense by the destruction unleashed on September 11, 2001, in New York, but his ruins are odder still, since they are almost always punctuated by great, enigmatic structures that have not been leveled by the same violence as all that surrounds them. This, too, might be architecture of a foreboding sort, great buildings with enigmatic purposes—food for thought in times of darkness.

Another artist who has clearly transgressed the normal limits between sculpture, installation art, and architecture is Tadashi Kawamata. Kawamata's structures, inspired originally by the apparently chaotic and ephemeral nature of Tokyo, are almost always made of wood—

pieces of recycled wood gathered and put together by local volunteers or laborers. Each piece is a commentary on its architectural environment, but also on architecture and art themselves. Made to be dismantled just weeks or months after they are created, these installation pieces can sometimes be walked on or through, and sometimes not. The latter is the case of his recent Tree Huts installed in trees near the medieval Donjon de Vez, 70 kilometers from Paris (France, 2009, page 40). Unlike children's tree houses, these high-perched structures could not be visited. Rather their enigmatic presence was like a reminder of a distant, even primitive past. Where visitors came in good part to admire the seemingly eternal stones of the Donjon de Vez, the Japanese artist created a counterpoint in bits and pieces of wood, willfully ephemeral and seemingly disordered, serving no apparent purpose, yet also signifying the earliest shelters.

SEARCHING FOR THE IDEAL PALACE

Another Japanese artist, Shinro Ohtake, has just finished new public baths (2009, page 338) for the Island of Naoshima in the Inland Sea of Japan. Naoshima is the location of numerous projects designed by Tadao Ando, but also of a series of "art houses" created by noted artists, including James Turrell, in an old fishing village on the island. Ohtake, who admits to being inspired by David Hockney, or Adolf Wölfli (1864–1930), one of the first artists to be associated with the Art Brut movements, also refers to Ferdinand Cheval (1836–1924), also known as the Facteur Cheval, who spent 33 years of his life building a remarkable work of naive art and architecture called Le Palais Idéal (the "Ideal Palace") in Hauterives, France. Using a great variety of found objects, including colored tiles, an aircraft cockpit, the bottom of a ship, a statue of a small elephant from a museum of erotica, he also planted pine trees on the roof of this bathhouse. In this instance, a work of art (the bathhouse) does, indeed, have a purpose. Used by the town's people and visitors and operated like a traditional Japanese hot bath, Shinro Ohtake's structure with its décor represents a decided contrast to the strong, minimal structures by Tadao Ando that dot the island. Ohtake's work in this instance underlines the fact that much contemporary architecture is, indeed, shifting away from any version of minimalism and toward what might be termed a decorative and complex period.

HERE COMES AGRI-TECTURE

Another discipline that clearly verges on architecture is that of landscape design, if only because landscape tends to be associated with buildings or groups of buildings. It might be noted in passing that more traditional architecture books tend to draw a line between landscape and buildings, just as they might decline to include works of art in a survey of contemporary architecture. Be that as it may, one of the more remarkable projects carried out in New York recently concerns a very clear interaction between planted spaces and the built, urban environment. The High Line (USA, 2006–09, Section 1, James Corner Field Operations/Diller Scofidio + Renfro, page 256) is a disused elevated railway spur running about 2.5 kilometers from the Jacob Javits Convention Center in New York to Gansevoort Street in the Meatpacking District of Manhattan's Lower West Side. The first phase of this project, completed in 2009, involved an architecture firm (DS+R) associated with a landscape group (James Corner Field Operations). The latter firm even coined a word to describe this intervention: "By changing the rules of engagement between plant life and pedestrians, our strategy of agri-tecture combines organic and building materials into a blend of changing proportions that accommodate the wild, the cultivated, the intimate, and the hyper-social." Although "agri-tecture" may not become a standard term, in this instance, by planting the surface of the elevated train line and opening it to the public, the firms have stimulated new construction around what used to be an eyesore and a source of potential criminality. It is precisely through the integration of landscape design and architecture that this result is achieved—in fact, in this case, the two apparently different disciplines become almost impossible to dissociate.

A second landscape project featured in this volume is *Towards Paradise* (Venice Architecture Biennale, Venice, Italy, 2008, Gustafson Porter/Gustafson Guthrie Nichol, page 182). Located at the exit of the Arsenale, along the Porta Nova and the Rio delle Vergine, this work was created in a largely abandoned garden located in the grounds of the former Convento delle Vergini, founded in 1239 and demolished in 1830. Although the landscape architects had rather high-minded explanations for their installation ("Remember—The Store Room; Nourish—Abundance; and Enlighten—Contemplation"), the fact is that Towards Paradise above all brought an almost forgotten part of Venice back into the public domain. Although the old brick buildings in the area are mostly abandoned and overgrown with dense vines, the organizers of the Biennale have progressively occupied more and more of the space with installations. Though the space might well have been used without the intervention of Gustafson Porter, it is a fact that landscape design here brought architecture back to life, revealing it and investing its "romantic ruins" with a new public persona.

RUSTIC, VOLUPTUOUS, AND PLAYFUL

Just as art and landscape have their links to contemporary architecture, so, too, does design. Projects published here show the approach to design practiced by an architect and also that of a designer vis-à-vis architecture. The architect is none other than Greg Lynn, one of the leading lights of thought and innovation in the area in the United States. Lynn's Blobwall and Toy Furniture published here (2007–08, page 296) take a modular, computer-assisted approach to the creation of space dividers that are almost infinitely variable. Building on his own childhood experience and the work of his father, who was with a plastics firm, Greg Lynn writes of his system: "In the Renaissance, palaces were designed to have a mixture of the opulent and the base, the elegant and the rustic. Stones were hewn so that they had planar faces for stacking and bonding but their outward faces expressed on their façades were left cloven and rustic. The recycled toy constructions are rustic, curvaceous, globular, molded, voluptuous, and playful; they are toys after all." The link he creates with the architecture of the past is interesting, if not entirely convincing, but there is a message here nonetheless. With his bright, quirky objects, Greg Lynn surely crosses the barriers that may exist between design (furniture, interiors) and architecture itself: with these plastic building blocks, he seeks a new method and variety in the standardized world of construction.

CRYSTALS IN THE FOREST

A second, equally intriguing figure is the designer Yoshioka Tokujin. Widely published and yet little visited, his Waterfall Bar (Tokyo, Japan, 2005–06, page 468) is made of 4.2-meter-long blocks of glass—the sort of glass used in precision telescopes. Tokujin is something of a magician of space and materials, and glass is one of his favorite "building blocks," if one can seize on the analogy referred to by Greg Lynn.

3
James Corner Field Operations/
Diller Scofidio + Renfro, The High
Line (Section 1), New York, NY, USA,
2006–09

Tokujin's Swarovski Ginza store (Tokyo, Japan, 2006–08, page 462), makes an even more ample use of glass, around a retailing concept he created for the Austrian luxury goods firm. "I looked to the forest as a key element of my inspiration. I intended to design a new retail architecture, which makes the visitor wonder, from the moment of stepping into the boutique, whether he/she is in the forest, jeweled with crystals and pieces of jewelry, rather than proposing an ordinary interior design." Here, too, distinctions and barriers dissolve. Tokujin refers to "retail architecture" but also to "interior design." Though it is true that architects and others have often relegated interior design to a somehow inferior rung of creativity, some, like this Japanese designer, seem to willfully break the rules and to make the mastery of space and light their domain, at whatever scale.

TEMPORARY CONTEMPORARY

Architecture, at least that commented on by John Ruskin and others, has always had the ambition to be more permanent than other forms of creativity. Monuments, even in ruin, speak of centuries past, of products of human imagination and engineering that can withstand the time that makes all else disappear. And so, too, the great architect creates for eternity, or so the "legend" would have it. Contemporary architecture has differed from that of the past in its warm embrace of the ephemeral. Cities like Tokyo or Los Angeles are built not to last but to constantly morph into new iterations, and their architecture has logically come to be considered more and more impermanent. These two cities, of course, have in common earthquake-prone locations, a fact that emphasizes their vulnerability, and the inevitability of change. The Prada Transformer (Seoul, South Korea, 2008–09, page 344), by OMA*AMO/Rem Koolhaas, is precisely the kind of ephemeral structure that contemporary design and construction have rendered possible. Given that Prada is in a business where constant change is requisite, it seems only natural to create a building for them that cannot only be moved, but can also transform itself through a series of programmed rotations that change its shape and potentially its functions. For all the talk of "flexible" buildings and space that has long filled architecture journals, this is one of the first buildings that can actually move and change forms.

It is only logical that a Tokyo firm, SANAA, should have a taste for the ephemeral, and their very recent Serpentine Gallery Pavilion (Kensington Gardens, London, UK, 2009, page 412), of 550 square meters and meant to last only one summer, proves their capacity to deal with such work. One of an ongoing series of such pavilions designed by the elite of contemporary architecture, their structure was made essentially of a 26-millimeter-thick aluminum roof supported by random 50-millimeter steel columns. The polished surfaces and varying heights of this undulating roof made reflections and distortions of space the norm. Within the pavilion, the visitor was left to wonder where "reality" and reflection ended or began. This kind of visual and spatial ambiguity is a strength of SANAA, as they showed in their 21st Century Museum of Art (Kanazawa, Ishikawa, Japan, 2002–04). SANAA was completing their new building, the Rolex Learning Center, for the EPFL (Lausanne, Switzerland, 2007–09, see page 418), as this book was in the making. There, too, uninhibited, undulating space on a much larger scale experiments with the frontiers between what is in movement and what is fixed, or permanent. The EPFL building has almost no internal walls, only full-height glazing around its perimeter, an idea that stretches both technical aspects of the architecture and its very use as a student space. In their apparently gentle way, the architects of SANAA are challenging some of the most basic ideas of contemporary architecture.

4
*Zaha Hadid, JS Bach/ Zaha Hadid
Architects Music Hall, Manchester,
UK, 2009*

The London-based architect Zaha Hadid, winner of a 2009 Praemium Imperiale Award, has long been interested in design and, indeed, in temporary structures. Her JS Bach / Zaha Hadid Architects Music Hall (Manchester, UK, 2009, page 196) is based on the deployment of a "voluminous ribbon" that "swirls within the room, carving out a spatial and visual response to the intricate relationships of Bach's harmonies." Made up of a translucent fabric membrane around an internal steel structure, the ribbon is complemented by clear acrylic acoustic panels suspended above the stage. Programmed lighting and musical recordings outside the hours of performance are also part of the installation. Intended to be transportable and installable in similar locations, this work carries forward Hadid's bold efforts to stretch the possibilities of contemporary architecture beyond the fixed, rectilinear forms that seemed so characteristic of new buildings just a few years ago. Her work is about a "fluidification" of space, making volumes flow into one another in an uninterrupted manner. Zaha Hadid has also carried out projects, such as her recent bar for Home House (London, UK, 2007–08), within existing spaces. In that case, it was a Georgian décor that was the theater for the installation of a resin, fiberglass, and fabric bar that literally transforms the space. "A unique dichotomy is realized within Home House between this new formal language of morphology," say the architect, "and the dynamic forces and characteristic orthogonal programming of its Georgian envelope." Like Kazuyo Sejima, her counterpart at SANAA, Zaha Hadid has reached the highest levels of international architecture and has brought a new vision to design and even construction. It would be inappropriate to suggest that these two women engage in what might be called a "feminine" architecture, and yet, the subtlety, ambiguity, and fluidity of their work do somehow break with a world of contemporary architecture that also engendered the Burj Khalifa tower.

UNDERGROUND MOVEMENT

Two projects in this book make unexpected use of underground spaces. The temptation to recycle disused parts of cities may well be a sign of the times, but so too is the voluntary reshaping of parts of an industrial or historical heritage to make contemporary what had lost all utility. Rand Elliott is something of an exception in *Architecture Now!*, because he is based in a state that rarely produces stunning contemporary architecture—Oklahoma. Indeed, his firm has received ten National AIA Honor Awards and is the only architecture firm in Oklahoma ever to receive this distinction. His Underground (Oklahoma City, Oklahoma, USA, 2007, page 146) is a 3900-square-meter remake of a series of tunnels that connect 23 buildings in downtown Oklahoma City. Built beginning in 1931, these tunnels had fallen into disrepair, and Elliott's renovation—featuring music, colored lights, and historically themed photo galleries—has made them usable again. Though the distinction between architecture and interior decoration may be difficult to make in this instance, it is true that sound and light have made their way into the vocabulary of contemporary buildings in new ways. Underground, where natural lighting is not, or hardly available, space can also be defined and shaped with such immaterial tools. Though the Underground need not be compared to a work of art, it is true that artists like James Turrell have rendered those attentive to his art sensitive to the fact that light can be an almost palpable material that can find new uses in contemporary architecture.

The Bahnhof Pionen (Stockholm, Sweden, 2007–08, page 158) by French-born architect Albert France-Lanord represents a very different approach to a quintessentially underground space—a nuclear bomb shelter 30 meters below the granite underlying the Vita Berg Park.

5
Rand Elliott, Underground,
Oklahoma City, OK, USA, 2007

The client is an Internet service provider, and the space is used for server halls and offices. The architect sought to bring as much variety to the lighting as possible in order to avoid the claustrophobic feeling that such a setting might easily have given. The result is intentionally like something out of a James Bond movie, a curious space isolated from its urban context and with more than a hint of Cold War era intrigue. Albert France-Lanord states: "It has been very exciting to work with a space which at first didn't offer one square angle: the rock. The main room is not a traditional space limited by surfaces but, rather, is defined by the emptiness inside a mass."

Curiously, underground spaces seem related to industrial architecture more than to the kind of willful shaping of volumes that characterizes most high-quality contemporary architecture. Even in a city such as Tokyo, with its maze of largely uninspired underground stations and shopping malls, some progress has been made with projects like Tadao Ando's Tokyu Toyoko Line Shibuya Station (Shibuya-ku, Tokyo, Japan, 2006–08, page 29). This 27 725-square-meter egg-shaped station was made with a Glass Fiber Reinforced Concrete (GFRC) shell and boasts natural ventilation despite being buried deep beneath the Japanese capital. Other examples of this sort abound and show that contemporary architects are continuing to make inroads into areas from which they had been largely excluded in the past. This rhymes with a realization that architects are capable of making space attractive and usable, whereas the kind of engineers usually in charge of subway stations think mainly of how to move a train, or a crowd, through the least space possible at the lowest cost.

THE ART IN BUILDINGS

It is probably true that economic circumstances will bring expenses on museums and other art-related structures down. This, in a field that had provided the most visible and stunning opportunities for architects, from Zaha Hadid to David Chipperfield, to create places for art that have marked the popular imagination. Frank Gehry's Guggenheim Bilbao remains the reference when it comes to architecture that sings and dances, and draws in crowds as well, but the boom in museum building all over the world might well have calmed even if Lehman Brothers had not gone out of business. There are only so many new museums that a country like Japan can build, after all, and other countries such as the United States had already reached a certain maturity in the field as well. With this word of caution, it is nonetheless possible to point out numerous new institutions created recently. The New York-based architect Steven Holl has been particularly active in museum design and in 2009 he opened two cultural buildings of note in Scandinavia—HEART: Herning Museum of Contemporary Art (Herning, Denmark, 2007–09, page 216) and the Knut Hamsun Center (Hamarøy, Norway, 2006–09, page 222). The first combines facilities for the visual arts and for music and shows the usual subtle complexity that the architect has come to be known for. Steven Holl has also frequently been involved in the landscape design around his buildings, so for the Herning Center, he created 3700 square meters consisting in a "bermed landscape of grass mounds and pools" that conceals parking and service areas. The Knut Hamsun Center concerns one of Norway's best-known writers and is located above the Arctic Circle near the farm where the author grew up. Calling on Norse churches for formal inspiration, and making the most of local lighting conditions, Holl created a building that honors not only the work of an author, but also the numerous movies inspired by his books.

The Artfarm (Salt Point, New York, USA, 2007–08, page 210) by the Swiss architects HHF in collaboration with the Chinese artist Ai Wei Wei is an entirely different matter from the larger museums that have marked the chronicles of contemporary architecture for so many years.

6

6
*IROJE KHM Architects, Island House,
Gapyung-gun, Gyeonggi-do,
South Korea, 2007–09*

Conceived as a hermetically closed volume, with white shiny PVC insulation, the building is really a sophisticated shed, designed to resist the large fluctuations in temperature between summer and winter in New York State. Inspired in part by industrial architecture, the Artfarm demonstrates that cutting-edge architectural design can be quite simple in appearance and even in terms of how its volumes are defined. The place is really left to the Chinese art that is intended to be displayed here and that, too, represents a more mature response to the relationship between art and architecture than some billowing clouds of titanium that have marked more than one landscape in recent years.

On a similar scale to that of the Artfarm, Rudy Ricciotti's Villa Navarra (Le Muy, France, 2007, page 384) represents another take on how a building can be used for the purpose of displaying works of art. In this instance, Ricciotti and his son, the engineer Romain Ricciotti, have experimented with a remarkable cantilevered roof made up of 17 panels of Ductal concrete (each 9.25 x 2.35 meters in size) that is just three centimeters thick. Ductal is a fiber-reinforced concrete made by Lafarge capable of withstanding the kinds of stress that a 7.8-meter cantilevered roof engenders. Having also used this material for bridge design, Ricciotti seems comfortable with it and able to create designs that are certainly unusual and innovative. Another unusual aspect of this place for the exhibition of art is that it will not be open to the public, but will, instead, be used for Internet-based exhibitions.

The Los Angeles architect Eric Owen Moss has always taken a sculptural or artistic approach to the buildings he has designed and renovated in Culver City, California. His most recent structure there is the Gateway Art Tower (USA, 2007–09, page 320), a 22-meter-high information facility located at the intersection of Hayden Avenue and National Boulevard, at the entry to the area of Culver City that he has done much to redevelop over the years. The Tower is meant to display cultural and local event information. Made up of five stacked circular steel rings about nine meters in diameter, the Tower is to have translucent acrylic projection screens at each level. Viewing decks for visitors are provided at each level. In the spirit of the Lusatian Lakeland Landmark referred to above, this sculptural structure might almost be considered a work of art in itself. Moss has often taken material from neighboring warehouse buildings and turned it into sculptural extrusions, giving an artistic and dynamic appearance and reality to formerly ordinary structures. The Art Tower takes this sculptural approach a step further, creating a new building that is a kind of monument to the work that the architect and the promoter (Samitaur Constructs) have done to bring Culver City back to life, after its former identity as an early center of the movie industry.

BIG IN ASIA

Private houses remain a mainstay for the creative impulse of architects around the world, in particular where economic conditions have allowed certain individuals to accumulate sufficient funds to allow themselves something out of the ordinary. For sometime, South Korea has shown promising signs in contemporary architecture, with a number of home-grown talents coming to international attention. One of these is Byoung-soo Cho, born in 1957 in Seoul. Though he is based today in Seoul, Byoung-soo Cho attended Montana State University (Bozeman, Montana, B.Arch, 1986), and obtained his M.Arch and M.Arch in Urban Design from the Harvard University GSD in 1991. His 494-square-meter Three Box House (Paju, Gyeonggi-do, South Korea, 2005–06, page 122) shows a refined sense of simplicity. Comprising three concrete boxes connected by a horizontal wooden screen and decks, this house is based on a strict composition of rectangles, but with a sense of

*7
IROJE KHM Architects, Purple Hill
House, Youngin, Gyeonggi-do,
South Korea, 2009*

7

aesthetics and a capacity to juxtapose opaque and transparent blocks that seems truly new. The architect says: "This project is simple and straightforward; drawing from the industrial/agricultural materiality of Montana," and yet it would seem to have little to do with the sparse architectural inventiveness of the American state.

Where Byoung-soo Cho is well versed in the strengths of a relatively minimal vocabulary, another of his countrymen, HyoMan Kim, a graduate of DanKook University (Seoul, 1978), seeks to create works where "architectural nature is a place of recreation." His Island House (Gapyung-gun, Gyeonggi-do, South Korea, 2007–09, page 238) is a surprising riverfront residence with a large, water-filled courtyard that looks something like a boat from a distance. Though straight lines are the rule here, the plan of the house and its appearance are somewhat irregular, echoing the architect's desire to integrate the house into its natural setting but also somehow to make it part of that setting. Another residence by HyoMan Kim is the smaller Purple Hill House (Youngin, Gyeonggi-do, South Korea, 2009, page 15) with its form that evokes nearby GwangGyo Mountain. Turning the house toward the northwest for reasons of its relation to the site and the view, the architect knowingly condemned the residence to receiving relatively little direct sunlight—a problem he resolved with a series of glass light boxes that penetrate the volume. Here, as with the Island House, HyoMan Kim shows a propensity for complexity that is expressed using a crystalline composition that clearly favors straight lines juxtaposed in complex patterns.

Though stylistically different, with Byoung-soo Cho preferring relatively simple plans and aesthetics and HyoMan Kim opting for multifaceted designs, both of these architects are representatives of a new, strong national school that may eventually rival the inventiveness of neighboring Japan. This trend, of course, has been fueled by a long economic rise punctuated by a certain number of passing financial difficulties. Again, though, it would seem that what really matters is the capacity of architects to invent new forms. Should they be obliged to spend less and to build smaller structures, such creative figures will surely remain architects to be reckoned with in the years to come.

Another Asian architect of considerable capacities is Sou Fujimoto, born in 1971 and educated in Tokyo. Fujimoto is one of the most prolific and talented of the younger generation of Japanese architects, and his structures often deal with fundamental issues, such as the real borders between a house and a city. His House H (Tokyo, Japan, 2008–09, page 176) was imagined like a tree house, with walls, floors, and ceilings opening onto each other with a system of glazed surfaces. "Using artificial materials and geometric order," says Fujimoto, "the succession of voids in connectivity engenders a greater field of relationships. This concept of a residence akin to a large tree, with a treelike ambiguity in its connectivity with the exterior, propounds a prototypical dwelling/city of the future." Fujimoto's recent Final Wooden House (Kumamura, Kumamoto, Japan, 2007–08, page 33) was conceived through the "mindless" stacking of 350-millimeter-square pieces of lumber. "I envisioned the creation of new spatiality that preserves primitive conditions of a harmonious entity before various functions and roles differentiated," he says. There are no separations, no floors, no real walls or ceilings in this house, allowing visitors to "distribute themselves three-dimensionally in space." Floors become walls, or chairs, as he says, causing visitors to rethink the entire idea of the building. "Rather than just a new architecture," Fujimoto concludes, "this is a new origin, a new existence." Though House H is intended to be inhabited and the Final Wooden House is not, Fujimoto is exploring the limits of residential space, and questioning fundamentals in a way that architects from other countries have rarely done. He is an architect to be watched in the future.

8

8
Susanne Nobis, Walls in the Land-scape, Grossburgwedel, Germany, 2007–09

QUE SERRA SERRA

Half a world away, Susanne Nobis, born in 1963 and educated in London and Munich, has just completed the Walls in the Landscape residence in Grossburgwedel (Germany, 2007–09, page 324). An asymmetric composition of rectangular plan forms, this house is marked by a series of high walls made of Corten steel. Such sheets of steel inevitably bring to mind the imposing sculptures of Richard Serra, and, indeed, despite its relatively minimal design, the house has a brute strength contrasting with a gentle and glazed rapport with its natural setting. The point of describing this design is that there is still no set logic or style in contemporary houses. Their aesthetics and functionality are a function of the great variety of styles that are being concurrently practiced all over the world. Though strict minimalism may no longer be in fashion, and an almost extravagant complexity is on the rise, in Asia in particular, other approaches remain equally valid. Susanne Nobis worked in the Renzo Piano Building Workshop (Genoa, 1992–93), and with Herzog & de Meuron (Munich, 1994–95), before creating her own office. Both of these firms have approached modernity with a similar pragmatism. Piano's Beyeler Foundation in Riehen (Basel, Switzerland, 1991–97) operates a similar contrast between strong (stone-clad) walls and high glazing facing the fields that run from the Foundation toward the German border. There is a kind of classical logic in the Walls in the Landscape residence that makes it almost timeless in its modernity.

SOON IN THE CLOUDS

Recent developments in computer technology have led to what has been dubbed "the Battle of the Clouds." Firms like Microsoft or Google are seeking to dominate computing as a service that will be offered over the Internet, "where documents, e-mails and other data will be stored online, making them accessible from any PC or mobile device."[3] It is interesting to note that the racing development of technology has also had an impact on the creation of loosely defined firms or organizations that can no longer be readily classified. This is the case of Supersudaka, based in Talca, Chile, but also stretching, in its related websites—www.supersudaka.cl and www.supersudaca.org—across borders and disciplines. Supersudaca (with a "c") bills itself as a "think tank for architecture and urban investigation," while the website of Supersudaka (with a "k") starts with the phrase: "We don't want to change the world with architecture, we want to change architecture with the world." The Kiltro House (Talca, Chile, 2006–08, page 450) published here is one of the completed works of this group, headed in Chile by Juan Pablo Corvalán and Gabriel Vergara. Kiltro is Chilean slang for a "cross-breed dog," although their house appears to have been bred with a certain refinement and logic. The faceted wooden design of the house might recall the plans of HyoMan Kim, albeit in a very different setting and materiality. At this point in time, although national characteristics still play an essential role in many architectural designs, the era of architectural "cloud" with contributions from all over the world is upon us. For reasons of their own, Supersudaka lists only Juan Pablo Corvalán's Talca University mailing address, no tangible office with rows of black-dressed young architects here, but rather an active group of participants who may be just about anywhere.

9
*Cecil Balmond, UPENN Weave Bridge,
Philadelphia, PA, USA, 2008–09*

BRIDGES TO THE OTHER SIDE

Just as the limits between architecture and other disciplines, such as art or design, appear to be dissolving, so, too, the often unbridgeable gap between architects and engineers may be closing. A number of projects published in *Architecture Now! 7* are the work of engineers or rely heavily on their direct knowledge. A well-known figure in both fields, Santiago Calatrava recently completed his spectacular Liège-Guillemins TGV Station (Liège, Belgium, 1996–2009, page 132) on the line that links Paris, Brussels, and Cologne. The Spanish-born architect-engineer created a 200-meter-long passenger terminal, built symmetrically along a northwest-southeast axis. The arched roof of the terminal building extends over the five platforms for another 145 meters. A monumental vault made of glass and steel allows the station to be completely open to the city. Pedestrian bridges and a walkway under the tracks allow for fluid communication between the two sides of the station. Calatrava had previously designed futuristic railway stations for Lisbon and Lyon-Saint Exupéry Airport, but this station brings a formerly rather run-down part of the European rail network very much into the 21st century.

One of the best-known engineers in the world, Cecil Balmond, Deputy Chairman of the multidisciplinary engineering firm Arup since 2004 and founder of the Advanced Geometry Unit (AGU) at Arup, completed his UPENN Weave Bridge in Philadelphia in 2009 (Pennsylvania, USA, page 88). A particularity of this bridge is that it appears rather straightforward, while in fact it employs an innovative load-bearing structure in the form of a double helix. Part of a master plan that Balmond is working on to improve movement on the University of Pennsylvania campus, this bridge shows that sometimes the most inventive of structures can appear to be relatively unsurprising to the layman. Then, too, it may be that 2009 was a time for architecture (and engineering) to put on more modest clothes, after a long period of extravagant novelties.

Actually, extravagant buildings continue to rise across the globe, and the Guangzhou TV and Sightseeing Tower (Guangzhou, China, 2005–10, page 228) by the Dutch firm Information Based Architecture is tangible proof of this fact. At a height of 610 meters, it may not surpass the Burj Khalifa tower, but it certainly is tall. The twisting, tapering tube form of the structure is, if anything, a feat of engineering, and it will be a recognizable beacon for the planned 2010 Asian Games to be held nearby. While engineering plays an undeniable role in the design of such a structure, it can be argued that the reasons for going so high in such a visible manner did not have to do only with the mechanics of television broadcasting, though height remains an advantage in such cases. There is surely an element of hubris in the thoughts of the client, and, why not, in the mind of the architects as well. My tower is bigger than yours…

50 BELOW AND NO CARBON EITHER

Engineering of a different sort has played a fundamental role in the design of the surprising Princess Elisabeth Antarctica ice station (Utsteinen, 71°57'S–23°20'E, Dronning Maud Land, East Antarctica, 2007–09, page 232). The work of the International Polar Foundation, the station marks the Belgian presence in Antarctica in a convincing and thoroughly modern way. Located at an altitude of 1300 meters in a place where temperatures vary between -50°C and -5°C, with wind gusts that can reach 250km/hour, the station is the first of its kind to boast zero carbon emissions. The Princess Elisabeth facility operates with renewable energy sources and advanced energy efficiency protocols. Though it is above all a technical object, this structure shows a good deal of aesthetic sense as well, in its silvery presence at the bottom of the world.

MAKE IT RIGHT

Exploration of the polar ice caps is surely a worthy pursuit, particularly in these times of global warming, but it is true that contemporary architecture of quality may only rarely serve those who would need good design most. A notable exception to this rule is the work of the South African architect Peter Rich, whose two most recent projects, the Alexandra Heritage Center (Johannesburg, Gauteng, South Africa, 2004–09, page 390) and the Mapungubwe Interpretation Center (Mapungubwe National Park, Limpopo, South Africa, 2007–09, page 396) are published in this volume. Peter Rich was born in 1945 in Johannesburg, South Africa, and was a full-time Professor at the University of the Witwatersrand for 30 years. He has studied indigenous African iconography and architecture, in particular that of the Ndebele. The Alexandra Center is located opposite a former residence of President Nelson Mandela, but above all it is a building intended to showcase the arts, culture, and heritage of the area in a dignified and modern way. Given the poverty that surrounds it, this building stands out from its environment and yet also fits into it in a remarkable way. Peter Rich states: "The project builds a sense of community and provides poverty relief through training inhabitants in tourism and heritage; nurturing small enterprises; and by showcasing the arts, culture and heritage of Alexandra." Connected directly to the street by ramps, the building also makes use of a courtyard plan that seeks to use every available square meter of land even as it evokes local traditions. The adaptability of the work of Peter Rich can be seen in the Mapungubwe Center as well. Its thin shell vaults are intended to echo the "archeological revelation of past cultures" that the National Park in which it is situated celebrates. Peter Rich is not engaged in the creation of a pastiche here, but rather in adapting local materials and forms to a very contemporary use, giving dignity and accessibility to cultures that have not always enjoyed such attention.

The barriers that separate contemporary architecture from other disciplines, from design to engineering, are coming down. Some might argue that such barriers never existed since landscape architecture or art have been an implicit part of architecture for centuries. Though the founders of Germany's Bauhaus actively sought to create a "total work of art" (*Gesamtkunstwerk*), the reality of modern times has been different, with academic circles often firmly separating such obviously related disciplines as architecture and engineering. Figures like Santiago Calatrava, who is also an artist, have done a great deal to make it clear that creativity is most natural when it does not respect divisions that are artificially put in place for the benefit of some. Architecture magazines or art magazines still tend clearly to make a distinction between what is architecture and what is art, as do many creative individuals. Indeed, one has to be trained to design buildings, while artists have an innate freedom that some such as Frank Gehry longed for in his early years. Gehry, too, helped to bring down barriers even when his buildings gave more attention to aesthetics than to practicality.

GREEN AND LEAN

The facts of architecture require relatively long building cycles, in particular where large structures are concerned. Thus *Architecture Now! 7* cannot fully take into account any impact of the economic crisis of 2008. Trends may be emerging that lead architects, and above all their clients, to seek to create smaller, less expansive structures. Other existing trends, such as the need to control carbon emissions and to reduce energy consumption, have surely been reinforced by the downturn. Reducing energy use also cuts electricity bills, therefore it is likely

10
*Peter Rich, Mapungubwe
Interpretation Center, Mapungubwe
National Park, Limpopo, South Africa,
2007–09*

10

to be a more and more significant factor in architecture in the years to come. Technological advances mean that sources of power such as photovoltaic cells are improving their efficiency and their ability to be discreetly inserted into windows or other parts of buildings. Some of the best ecologically responsible buildings are hardly visible as such today, unlike the early "green" buildings that tended to look like something out of a late 1960s commune. Green is here to stay and contemporary architecture will take ecological consciousness into its mainstream even more fully than it has to date.

It may well be true that buildings as extravagant as the Burj Khalifa tower are a thing of the past, at least for the moment. Such soaring monuments are the fruit of times of economic euphoria and they may not ultimately make much practical sense either. Symbols will abide and will continue to be created, no matter what, even if they are more modest than the sky-piercing tower imagined by Adrian Smith. And even if most of the buildings in *Architecture Now! 7* had their origins in a time of euphoria, they are sufficiently convincing to give a clear response to the critic who fears that "it was beautiful while it lasted."[4] The advances now clearly integrated into contemporary architecture include an ability to design and produce unique parts with computer-assisted design and machinery. This fact in itself will continue to make possible buildings that could only have been dreamt of by architecture critics in the good old times of conspicuous consumption. Architecture Now is still alive.

Philip Jodidio, Grimentz, Switzerland, October 21, 2009

[1] http://lookingaround.blogs.time.com/2009/04/29/the-end-of-the-world-as-we-know-it/, accessed on October 20, 2009.
[2] Norman Foster, "Foreword," *The Chronicles of Time*, Damiani, Bologna 2008.
[3] "Battle of the Clouds," *The Economist*, October 17, 2009.
[4] http://lookingaround.blogs.time.com/2009/04/29/the-end-of-the-world-as-we-know-it/, accessed on October 20, 2009.

EINLEITUNG

DIE DÄMMERUNG BLEIBT AUS

Im Herbst 2008 hat die Welt aufgehört, sich zu drehen. So und ähnlich lauteten die Kommentare. Banken und Unternehmen schwammen in einem Meer aus Giftpapieren, ihre Kurse stürzten ins Bodenlose, und die Regierungen traten mit unvorstellbaren Milliardenhilfen als Retter in der Not auf. Angesichts einer solchen Talfahrt der Wirtschaft, wie hätte es da der Architektur anders ergehen sollen? Wenig später erschien eine Rezension des *Time*-Autors Richard Lacayo zum Vorgängerband der *Architecture-Now!*-Serie. Unter dem Titel *Das Ende der Welt wie wir sie kennen* hieß es da: „*Architecture Now! 6* ist Teil einer Buchreihe, die der deutsche TASCHEN Verlag in regelmäßiger Folge produziert, um interessante Bauwerke aus den vergangenen ein oder zwei Jahren zu präsentieren. Der vorliegende Band entstand im vergangenen Jahr, kurz vor oder nach dem Zusammenbruch von Lehman Brothers im September und dem Absturz des Dow Jones. Schaute man sich die gut 70 Architekturprojekte – nebst einigen künstlerischen Arbeiten mit architektonischem Bezug – an, so drängte sich die Frage auf, ob der für die Reihe verantwortliche Architekturhistoriker Philip Jodidio nicht unbeabsichtigt ein Buch zusammengestellt hatte, das eher den Titel ‚Götterdämmerung: Die letzten Augenblicke des großen Architekturbooms des 21. Jahrhunderts' verdient hätte." Nach Aufzählung von einigen der spektakuläreren Bauten jüngeren Datums kommt Lacayo zu dem Schluss: „… stärker als jede andere Kunstform ist die Architektur an wirtschaftliche Prosperität geknüpft. Während selbst arme Künstler noch das Geld für ihr Arbeitsmaterial zusammenkratzen können, sind Architekten auf Auftraggeber angewiesen. Mit dem Versiegen des Geldflusses sind nun auch die Projekte ins Stocken geraten, und es dürfte eine Weile dauern, bis die Dinge sich wieder erholen. Insofern muss diese prachtvolle Zusammenstellung zwangsläufig wie die Momentaufnahme einer Ära wirken, die an ihr Ende gekommen oder zumindest in ein langes Pausenstadium eingetreten ist. Man blättert durch die Seiten und denkt: Das war zwar alles schön, aber jetzt ist es Geschichte."[1]

DA IST DIE SMARAGDSTADT

Als es an der Zeit war, *Architecture Now! 7* zusammenzustellen, da – man stelle sich das vor – drehte die Welt sich noch immer, und noch immer gab es für Architekten etwas zu bauen. Zugegeben, als die Wirtschaft ihre größte Krise seit Jahrzehnten erlebte, waren einige der im Folgenden vorgestellten Projekte schon recht weit fortgeschritten. Ein perfektes Beispiel dafür ist das höchste Bauwerk der Welt, der Burj Khalifa (vormals Burj Dubai, VAE, 2004–10, SOM/Adrian Smith, Seite 432). Der bis zur obersten Spitze 828 m hohe spindelförmige Turm wurde zwar noch zum Jahresende 2009 fertig, doch die Arbeiten an zahlreichen anderen ehrgeizigen Projekten kamen jäh und für unbestimmte Zeit zum Erliegen.

Der für den Entwurf des Burj Khalifa verantwortliche Architekt Adrian Smith gesteht, dass bei seinem Konzept die Türme der Smaragdstadt aus der Filmversion des „Zauberers von Oz" Pate gestanden haben. „Das hatte ich im Kopf, als ich am Entwurf für den Burj Khalifa arbeitete", erzählt Smith, „wenn auch eher unterbewusst". „Ich habe nicht recherchiert, wie [die Smaragdstadt] aussieht. Ich erinnere mich nur an die gläserne, kristalline Struktur, die scheinbar aus dem Nichts heraus in die Höhe wuchs. Das Seltsame ist, dass ich mich offenbar nicht daran erinnert habe, dass die Stadt grün war." Der nach L. Frank Baums Buchvorlage *The Wonderful Wizard of Oz* entstandene Filmklassiker

11
Jensen & Skodvin Architects,
Juvet Landscape Hotel, Gudbrandsjuvet,
Norway, 2007–09

aus dem Jahr 1939 erzählt bekanntlich von den Abenteuern der kleinen Dorothy, des im Film von Judy Garland verkörperten Mädchens aus Kansas, auf dem Weg zum Anwesen des Zauberers von Oz. Als Dorothy in Begleitung eines Löwen, einer Vogelscheuche und eines Blechmanns schließlich die leuchtend grünen Türme am Waldrand erblickt, sagt sie: „Das muss die Smaragdstadt sein. Oh, endlich, endlich sind wir da, endlich. Es ist wundervoll, ja? So hab ich's in Gedanken gesehen. Er muss schon ein mächtiger Zauberer sein, wenn er so eine Stadt hat." Wie sich jedoch herausstellt, ist der so berühmte und mächtige Zauberer von Oz ein bloßer Aufschneider, ein Blender, und seine smaragdene Stadt nichts als eine durch Mohnblüten hervorgerufene Halluzination. Die Realität des heutigen Dubai vor Augen würde man wohl kaum darauf kommen, aus welcher fantastischen Inspirationsquelle Smiths Entwurf sich gespeist hat.

Dass es in der Architekturwelt eine Unmenge an Übertreibungen gegeben hat, steht außer Frage – Übertreibungen, die, wie Richard Lacayo bemerkt, eng mit dem Kasinokapitalismus des frühen 21. Jahrhunderts verbunden sind. Außerdem ermöglichten die beeindruckenden Fortschritte der Computertechnologie Entwürfe und Gebäudekonstruktionen, die vor wenigen Jahren undenkbar gewesen wären. Auf diese technischen Neuerungen – nicht nur das computergestützte Entwerfen (CAD), sondern auch die Herstellung von Bauteilen mittels computergesteuerter Werkzeugmaschinen (CNC) – wird man auch künftig nicht mehr verzichten, egal wie es gerade um die Wirtschaft steht. Dabei wäre es allerdings logisch, wenn mithilfe von CAD und CNC entstandene Gebäude weniger kosteten als ihre Vorläufer aus früherer Zeit.

Schon seit Langem zeigen Architekten ein verstärktes Interesse an der Frage, wie sie in ihren Entwürfen Kosten einsparen können. Das gilt auch für die erfolgreichsten unter ihnen, so etwa – um nur ein Beispiel zu nennen – für Rem Koolhaas und OMA, die bei einem Großteil ihrer Gebäude schon seit vielen Jahren preiswerte Baustoffe verwenden. Doch auch ob das Budget berühmter Architekten immer angemessen ist, bleibt ein viel diskutiertes Thema.

MIT PASSIVSTEN EMPFEHLUNGEN

Die Notwendigkeit von Kosteneinsparungen bedeutet für die Architektur nicht automatisch „das Ende der Welt wie wir sie kennen". Ein flüchtiger Blick auf die Projekte in diesem Buch reicht aus, um Lacayos Befürchtungen etwas entgegenzuhalten. Auch im Postblobstadium bleibt die Architektur vital und einfallsreich. In den vergangenen Jahren sind neue Themen in den Vordergrund getreten, sei es aufgrund oder trotz der Krise. Eines davon ist in jedem Fall die Notwendigkeit, die Architektur „grüner" zu machen als zu den großen Tagen des Entwurfs des Burj Khalifa . Auch wer sich nur am Rand für Architektur interessiert, wird mitbekommen, dass immer mehr Gebäude – im öffentlichen wie im privaten Sektor – für ihr „grünes Bewusstsein" gerühmt werden und Architekten nach jeder erdenklichen Möglichkeit suchen, um die berühmt-berüchtigte CO_2-Bilanz von Bauwerken zu verbessern. Damit gehen zugleich ästhetische Veränderungen einher – auch wenn die Zeiten, als ein „grünes" Gebäude auch „grün" aussehen musste, längst vorbei sind. Der Stand der Technik ist heute ein völlig anderer, und sogenannte passive Techniken zur Energieeinsparung, etwa die richtige Ausrichtung von Gebäuden oder die Nutzung der Fassadenverkleidungen zur Verringerung der Sonneneinstrahlung, sind bei aller Wirksamkeit kaum noch als ökologische Maßnahmen sichtbar.

12
Architektur & Landschaft,
Lusatian Lakeland Landmark,
Senftenberg, Germany, 2008

12

Die kleinen Gebäudeeinheiten, die zum Juvet Landscape Hotel gehören (Gudbrandsjuvet, Norwegen, 2007–09, Jensen & Skodvin Arkitektkontor, Seite 262), wirken wie eine Reaktion auf einen vorausgeahnten Konjunkturrückgang, der noch gar nicht eingesetzt hatte. Das im Nordwesten Norwegens gelegene Hotel besteht im Wesentlichen aus mehreren kleinen Einzelhäusern, die auf Stahlstützen von 40 mm Durchmesser aufgeständert sind und sich wieder abbauen lassen, ohne Schaden in der Natur zu hinterlassen. Den Gästen bieten die ökologisch verträglichen Häuser, die unverkennbar ein Werk versierter Designer sind, einen wunderbaren Ausblick auf das Naturpanorama. „Das heutige Interesse an Nachhaltigkeit richtet sich fast ausschließlich auf einen niedrigen Energieverbrauch während des Baus und beim späteren Betrieb", stellen die Architekten fest. „Wir verstehen demgegenüber auch die Rücksichtnahme auf den jeweiligen Standort als einen Nachhaltigkeitsaspekt, der Aufmerksamkeit verdient." Im städtischen Umfeld stößt man mitunter auf radikalere Positionen, aus denen sich Lehren für schwierige Zeiten ziehen lassen. So wurde etwa RDF181 (Brüssel, Belgien, 2007, Seite 400) von der Non-Profit-Organisation Rotor für eine „legale Hausbesetzung" konzipiert: ein 60 m² großes temporäres Büro auf einem Teil eines Grundstücks, für das die Baugenehmigung für eine dauerhaftere Bebauung noch ausstand. Dass Rotor für das ein Jahr lang betriebene RDF181 eine Baugenehmigung gar nicht erst beantragte und das Gebäude außerdem ausschließlich aus Material vom Sperrmüll bestand, kam jedenfalls einer Ohrfeige für die Behörden gleich, die speziell das Bauen im städtischen Raum für gewöhnlich eher erschweren als fördern. Wie auch die ähnlich gearteten Unternehmungen von Santi Cirugeda in Spanien könnte man solche parasitären temporären Bauten als Architektur für düstere Zeiten verstehen, mag der Horizont Ende 2009 auch schon wieder etwas heller erscheinen als noch ein Jahr zuvor.

Große Architekturbüros in Großbritannien und den Vereinigten Staaten haben ihre Aktivitäten in wirtschaftlich schwierigeren Zeiten zurückgefahren, doch genau darum geht es bei innovativer Architektur: um die Fähigkeit, sich auf neue Erfordernisse einzustellen, seien sie ökonomischer oder materieller Natur. Die Verwendung von Recyclingprodukten oder das Bemühen um einen niedrigen Energieverbrauch – ob aus ökologischen oder finanziellen Gründen –, muss sich nicht negativ auf den Stil eines Architekten auswirken. Ganz im Gegenteil, denn was soll man tun, wenn das Motto der Zeit nicht mehr „höher, größer, verrückter" lautet? *Architecture Now! 7* dürfte im Vergleich zu seinem Vorgängerband nicht als Enttäuschung ausfallen. Schließlich hat die Welt nicht aufgehört sich zu drehen, und die Architekten haben nicht aufgehört, neue Formen und Ideen zu entwickeln.

Es ist kein Geheimnis, dass zwischen Künstlern und Architekten seit Langem eine gewisse Verwandtschaft besteht, sowohl hinsichtlich der Ambitionen als auch der Umsetzungen. Deutlicher ausgedrückt, gibt es viele Architekten, die gerne Künstler wären (so wie Frank Gehry in seiner Frühzeit), und umgekehrt Künstler, die gerne einmal so viel Platz zur Verfügung hätten, wie ihn ein Gebäude beansprucht. Es könnte durchaus gegenseitiger Neid sein, der in beiden Domänen für manche der interessanteren und kreativeren Arbeiten verantwortlich ist. Deshalb enthält *Architecture Now! 7* wie schon die vorangegangenen Bände auch eine Reihe von Kunstwerken oder eben Werken von Architekten, die an Kunst erinnern. Ein Beispiel dafür ist die Landmarke Lausitzer Seenland (Senftenberg, 2008, Architektur & Landschaft, Seite 70), ein 30 m hoher Turm aus Corten-Stahl, der große Ähnlichkeit mit den Skulpturen eines Richard Serra hat. Mit ihrer Arbeit verweisen die Designer auf die für das ehemalige Tagebaugebiet typischen Brücken, legen jedoch zugleich Wert darauf, ein Wahrzeichen zu schaffen, das den in der Region herrschenden Willen zum Wandel symbolisiert. Ebenso wird man den Turm aber auch als Denkmal für eine ruhmvolle Vergangenheit verstehen dürfen, was seine Nähe zur Skulptur noch deutlicher macht. Es ist kein Zufall, dass Architektur & Landschaft ihre massiven Stahlplatten wie Richard Serra in einer Werft biegen lassen, gibt es doch keine anderen Fertigungsstätten für eine solche Bearbeitung. „Der Unterschied zwischen Kunst und Architektur", so der amerikanische Bildhauer, „besteht darin, dass die Kunst keinem bestimmten Zweck dient." Wenn also eine Reihe von Treppen und eine Aussichtsplattform einen Zweck darstellen, wäre die Landmarke Lausitzer Seenland kein reines Kunstwerk – aber sie steht sicher auf der Grenze zwischen den beiden Disziplinen.

WIE RUINEN EINER UNTERGEGANGENEN ZIVILISATION

Giacomo Costa ist mitnichten Architekt. Eher könnte man ihn als Fotografen mit einem Blick für eine seltsame Art von urbanem Chaos bezeichnen. Seine jüngst unter dem Titel *The Chronicles of Time* (2009, Seite 140) erschienenen digital bearbeiteten Fotografien wirken wie die Visionen einer apokalyptischen Zukunft, die noch die Bären der Wall Street das Fürchten lehren würde. Der Architekt Norman Foster schreibt über die Arbeiten des Italieners: „Costas Stadtporträts tauchen nicht einfach in der zeitlichen Folge des 11. September auf, sondern in einer Epoche, in der unser ganz normaler Alltag von terroristischen Bedrohungen überschattet ist. In einer Zeit der Verunsicherung, in der unsere Experten darüber spekulieren, ob und wann im Verborgenen agierende Kräfte durch einen Angriff mit biologischen Waffen oder Atombomben ohne jede Vorwarnung eine Katastrophe unvorstellbaren Ausmaßes heraufbeschwören könnten. Giacomo Costas Visionen mit ihren ins Unendliche gerichteten Perspektiven und ihren schrankenlosen Horizonten wirken wie die Ruinen einer untergegangenen Zivilisation, die die unsere sein könnte. Costas gewaltige Fantasieprodukte erinnern uns vor allem an die Zerbrechlichkeit der von uns erbauten Welt und zugleich der gesellschaftlichen Voraussetzungen, die dieser bislang noch zugrunde liegen."[2] Costa ist nicht einzige Künstler, den die Zerstörungen vom 11. September 2001 in New York auf die eine oder andere Weise künstlerisch angeregt haben, nur dass seine Ruinen noch um einiges befremdlicher sind, werden sie doch fast immer von großen rätselhaften Gebilden durchzogen, die offenbar nicht von derselben Gewalt getroffen wurden wie alles andere um sie herum. Auch so könnte eine Architektur von vorausahnender Natur aussehen: imposante Bauten, die rätselhaften Zwecken dienen – Denkanstöße in düsteren Zeiten.

Auch Tadashi Kawamata ist ein Künstler, der die gängigen Grenzen zwischen Skulptur, Installation und Architektur überschreitet. Seine Bauten, deren Grundidee auf die scheinbar chaotische und flüchtige Natur der Stadt Tokio zurückgeht, bestehen fast immer aus Holz, aus gebrauchten Brettern und Balken, die der Künstler von freiwilligen Helfern vor Ort oder sonstigen ungelernten Hilfskräften zusammensetzen lässt. Die einzelnen Bauwerke sind sowohl Kommentar zur jeweiligen Architektur ihrer unmittelbaren Umgebung als auch zu Architektur und Kunst allgemein. Manchmal sind die Installationen, die nur für ein paar Wochen aufgebaut und dann wieder abgerissen werden, begehbar, manchmal nur zum Anschauen gemacht. Letzteres war der Fall bei den Baumhütten, die Kawamata in den Bäumen der 70 km vor Paris gelegenen mittelalterlichen Burganlage Donjon de Vez (2009, Seite 40; später im Jahr auch in Berlin) errichtete: Im Gegensatz zu Baumhäusern,

13
*Gustafson Porter + Gustafson
Guthrie Nichol*, Towards Paradise,
*Venice Architecture Biennale,
Venice, Italy, 2008*

13

wie Kinder sie lieben, konnte man zu diesen Hütten nicht hinaufgelangen. Ihre rätselhafte Anwesenheit wirkte vielmehr, als gemahnten sie an eine ferne, eine primitive Vergangenheit. An einem Ort, den die Besucher in erster Linie wegen der scheinbar ewigen Steine des Donjon de Vez schätzen, schuf der japanische Künstler einen Kontrapunkt in Form von hölzernen Brettern und Balken, bewusst vergänglich und scheinbar ungeordnet, der keinem ersichtlichen Zweck dient, außer dem einen, auf menschliche Behausungen aus frühester Vorzeit zu verweisen.

AUF DER SUCHE NACH DEM IDEALEN PALAST

Der ebenfalls aus Japan stammende Künstler Shinro Ohtake hat vor kurzer Zeit auf der Insel Naoshima in der japanischen Seto-Inlandsee ein öffentliches Badehaus (2009, Seite 338) errichtet. Auf Naoshima ist neben zahlreichen, auf der gesamten Insel verteilten Bauten Tadao Andos in einem alten Fischerdorf eine Reihe von „Kunsthäusern" zu finden, die von so bekannten Künstlern wie James Turrell gestaltet wurden. Shinro Ohtake verweist nicht nur auf den Einfluss der Arbeiten von David Hockney oder Adolf Wölfli (1864–1930), eines der ersten mit dem Begriff Art Brut in Verbindung gebrachten Künstler, , sondern ebenso freimütig auf Ferdinand Cheval (1836–1924), der, auch bekannt als Facteur Cheval (Briefträger Cheval), im französischen Hauterives 33 Jahre seines Lebens auf den Bau seines persönlichen Palais Idéal verwandte, einem als naive Kunst wie als Architektur gleichermaßen außergewöhnlichen Werk. Als Baumaterialien für sein Badehaus verwendete Ohtake die unterschiedlichsten Fundstücke, darunter farbige Fliesen, ein Flugzeugcockpit, ein Schiffsrumpf und die Statue eines kleinen Elefanten aus einem Museum für Erotica, und bepflanzte das Dach anschließend mit Pinien. Hier nun hat das Kunstwerk – das Badehaus – sehr wohl einen Zweck. Ohtakes Haus mit seinem Schmuck, das von Dorfbewohnern wie von Besuchern genutzt und wie ein traditionelles japanisches Badehaus betrieben wird, bildet einen entschiedenen Kontrast zu den massiven, minimalistischen Bauten Tadao Andos, die die Insel regelrecht überziehen. Damit unterstreicht auch Ohtakes Arbeit den Umstand, dass ein Großteil der zeitgenössischen Architektur sich vom Minimalismus, egal welcher Prägung, abwendet und sich in eine Richtung bewegt, die man vielleicht als komplexe, dekorative Phase bezeichnen könnte.

VORHANG AUF FÜR AGRI-TEKTUR

Eine weitere Disziplin, die unmittelbar an die Architektur angrenzt, ist die Landschaftsgestaltung, und sei es nur, weil man bei „Landschaft" oft automatisch einzelne Gebäude oder Gebäudegruppen mit einbezieht. Dabei sei kurz angemerkt, dass traditionellere Architekturbücher gerne genauso deutlich zwischen Landschaftsgestaltung und Architektur trennen, wie sie auch die Aufnahme von Kunstwerken in einen Überblick über aktuelle Architektur ablehnen. Wie dem auch sei, eines der interessanteren jüngst in New York entstandenen Projekte beschäftigt sich mit der unmittelbaren Wechselbeziehung zwischen begrünten Flächen und ihrer gebauten städtischen Umgebung. The High Line (2006–09, Abschnitt 1, James Corner Field Operations/Diller Scofidio + Renfro, Seite 256) ist der Name einer nicht mehr in Betrieb befindlichen Hochbahntrasse, die auf einer Länge von knapp 2,5 km vom Jacob K. Javits Convention Center in New York bis zur Gansevoort Street im Meatpacking District in der Lower West Side Manhattans verläuft. Im Rahmen der ersten, 2009 abgeschlossenen Projektphase taten sich ein Architekturbüro (DS+R) und ein Team von Landschaftsgestaltern (James Corner Field Operations) zusammen, wobei Letztere auch gleich den

14
Greg Lynn FORM, Blobwall
and Toy Furniture, various locations,
2007–08

14

passenden Begriff zur Beschreibung der Intervention parat hatten: „Mit unserer Strategie der ‚Agri-Tecture' verändern wir die üblichen Bezie-
hungsverhältnisse zwischen Fußgängern und städtischer Vegetation, indem wir Bepflanzung und Bebauung in proportional unterschiedlichen
Anteilen zueinander kombinieren, sodass Raum für Natur und Kultur, Ruhe und Geselligkeit entsteht." Auch wenn „Agri-Tecture" vielleicht
kein Standardbegriff wird, ist es seinen Erfindern mit der Begrünung der Bahntrasse und ihrer Öffnung für das Publikum jedenfalls gelungen,
in einer Gegend, die ehedem als Schandfleck und Nährboden für Kriminalität galt, die allgemeine Bautätigkeit anzuregen. Ein Ergebnis, das
gerade aufgrund der Verquickung von Landschaftsgestaltung und Architektur zustande gekommen ist – wobei die beiden Disziplinen sich hier
kaum mehr voneinander unterscheiden lassen.

Eine weitere landschaftsgestalterische Arbeit, die in diesem Band vorgestellt werden soll, ist das von Gustafson Porter und Gustafson
Guthrie Nichol für die Architektur-Biennale in Venedig entwickelte Projekt Towards Paradise (Italien, 2008, Seite 182). Angelegt wurde die Ar-
beit an der Zufahrt zum Arsenale zwischen Porta Nova und Rio delle Vergini auf einem weitgehend ungenutzten Gartengrund, der einst zum
Convento delle Vergini gehörte, das sich hier vom Gründungsjahr 1239 bis zu seinem Abriss im Jahr 1830 befand. Die etwas hochtrabenden
Titel, die die Landschaftsarchitekten den einzelnen Abschnitten ihrer Installation gegeben haben („Erinnern – Der Vorratsraum; Ernähren –
Überfluss; Erleuchtung – Kontemplation") ändern nichts an der Tatsache, dass sie mit Towards Paradise einen schon fast in Vergessenheit ge-
ratenen Teil Venedigs wieder zu Gemeingut gemacht haben. Von den größtenteils leer stehenden und dicht mit Wein überwachsenen alten
Backsteingebäuden des Geländes haben die Organisatoren der Biennale sich nicht abhalten lassen, Stück für Stück einen immer größeren Teil
der Fläche mit Installationen zu bespielen. Womöglich hätte sich auch ohne den Eingriff von Gustafson Porter eine Verwendung für das Gelände gefunden, dennoch muss man feststellen, dass erst die Landschaftsgestaltung auf die vorhandene Architektur aufmerksam gemacht, sie
wieder zum Leben erweckt und so den „romantischen Ruinen" zu neuem öffentlichen Ansehen verholfen hat.

RUSTIKAL, SINNLICH UND VERSPIELT

Genauso wie es Verbindungen zwischen der Kunst oder der Landschaftsgestaltung und der Gegenwartsarchitektur gibt, steht es auch
mit dem Design. Ein besonderes Verständnis von Design zeigen die folgenden Arbeiten eines Architekten, der der Architektur jedoch wie ein
Designer gegenübertritt. Dieser Architekt ist kein anderer als Greg Lynn, einer der in den Vereinigten Staaten führenden kreativen Köpfe auf
diesem Gebiet. Seine hier vorgestellten Blobwall und Toy Furniture (2007–08, Seite 296) sind keine einfachen Raumtrennwände, sondern
mithilfe des Computers entwickelte Modulgebilde mit unendlich vielen Variationsmöglichkeiten. Unter Verweis auf Erinnerungen an die eigene
Kindheit und an die Arbeit seines Vaters bei einer Kunststofffirma schreibt Lynn über sein System: „In der Renaissance wurden Paläste als
Kombination aus Opulenz und Einfachheit gestaltet, aus Eleganz und Rustikalität. Steine wurden so behauen, dass einige Seiten flach waren,
um sie stapeln und mit Mörtel bestreichen zu können. Die an der Fassade sichtbare Schauseite wurde jedoch grob und rustikal belassen. Die
recycelten Spielzeugkonstruktionen sind derb, geschwungen, kugelig, thermisch geformt, üppig und verspielt – schließlich sind es Spielzeuge." Die von Lynn hergestellte Verbindung zur Architektur der Vergangenheit überzeugt vielleicht nicht restlos, reizvoll ist sie allemal – und die

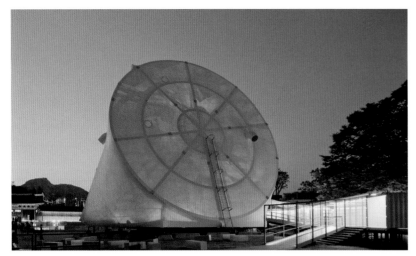

15
OMA*AMO/Rem Koolhaas,
Prada Transformer, Seoul,
South Korea, 2008–09

15

Botschaft ist klar. Mit seinen skurrilen bunten Objekten überschreitet Greg Lynn in jedem Fall die Grenzen, die zwischen Design (im Sinne von Möbeln und Interieur) und Architektur anscheinend nach wie vor bestehen; er zeigt mit seinen Bausteinen aus Plastik neue Methoden und Möglichkeiten für eine Welt des standardisierten Bauens auf.

KRISTALLE IM WALD

Eine ähnlich faszinierende Figur wie Lynn ist der Designer Yoshioka Tokujin. Seine trotz großen Medienechos kaum besuchbare Waterfall Bar (Tokio, 2006, Seite 468) besteht aus 4,2 m langen Glaskuben, die aus einer Glassorte gefertigt sind, wie sie in Hochleistungsteleskopen verwendet wird. Tokujin versteht mit Räumen und Materialien umzugehen wie ein Zauberer, wobei einer seiner bevorzugten „Bausteine" – um nochmals den im Zusammenhang mit Greg Lynn gewählten Begriff aufzugreifen – eben Glas ist. Bei seinem für die Tokioter Ginza-Filiale des österreichischen Luxusgüterherstellers Swarovski (2006–08, Seite 462) entwickelten Ladenkonzept ging Tokujin sogar noch verschwenderischer mit dem Material um. „Ich habe mich vor allem von der Idee des Waldes anregen lassen. Anstatt auf ein gewöhnliches Innendesign zu setzen, wollte ich eine neuartige Ladenarchitektur entwerfen, bei der der Kunde sich beim Betreten des Geschäfts fragt, ob er in einen mit Kristallen und Juwelierarbeiten geschmückten Wald geraten ist." Auch bei diesem Beispiel lösen sich gängige Unterscheidungen auf, Tokujin bezieht sich sowohl auf „Ladenarchitektur" als auch „Innendesign". Es mag zwar sein, dass Architekten – und nicht nur sie – im Innendesign ein geringeres Maß an Kreativität vorzufinden meinen, doch es gibt eben auch Vertreter wie Tokujin, die gezielt mit den Regeln brechen und sich als Fachleute in puncto Beherrschung von Licht und Raum ausweisen, in jeder beliebigen Größenordnung.

ZEITWEILIG ZEITGENÖSSISCH

Die Architektur, zumindest jene, mit der John Ruskin und andere sich befasst haben, zeigt von jeher das Bestreben, beständiger zu sein als andere Formen der Kreativität. Monumente, und seien es nur noch Ruinen, erzählen von vergangenen Jahrhunderten, als Resultate menschlichen Erfindungsgeistes und technischen Geschicks, die die Zeiten zu überdauern vermögen, während alles andere verschwindet. Und so schaffen denn auch große Architekten Werke für die Ewigkeit – so jedenfalls will es die „Legende". Von der Baukunst der Vergangenheit unterscheidet sich die Gegenwartsarchitektur durch ihre ausgesprochene Offenheit gegenüber dem Vergänglichen. Städte wie Tokio oder Los Angeles werden nicht für die Ewigkeit gebaut, sondern bilden immer neue Wiederholungsmuster ihrer selbst aus, sodass ihre Architektur zwangläufig immer unbeständiger wird. Beiden Metropolen gemeinsam ist ihre erdbebengefährdete Lage, was ihre Anfälligkeit und die Unvermeidlichkeit des Wandels noch verstärkt. Der Prada-Transformer (Seoul, Südkorea, 2008–09, Seite 344) von OMA*AMO/Rem Koolhaas entspricht genau jener Art von kurzlebiger Gebäudekonstruktion, die erst durch die heutigen Entwurfs- und Fertigungsmethoden möglich geworden ist. Angesichts des von permanentem Wandel bestimmten Geschäftsfelds, für das der Name Prada steht, erscheint der Entwurf eines Bauwerks, das nicht nur mobil ist, sondern überdies durch verschiedene programmierbare Drehbewegungen seine Gestalt und seine Einsatzmöglichkeiten verändern kann, nur konsequent. So lange in Architekturmagazinen nun schon von „flexiblen" Gebäuden die Rede ist, ist der Prada-Transformer doch immer noch eines der ersten, das Standort und Gestalt wirklich verändern kann.

16
SANAA, Rolex Learning Center,
EPFL, Lausanne, Switzerland,
2007–09

16

Dass ein Tokioter Architekturbüro wie SANAA eine besondere Vorliebe für das Vergängliche hat, erscheint nur logisch, und wie gut SANAA das Metier beherrschen, beweist ihr 550 m² umfassender Pavillon für die Serpentine Gallery (Kensington Gardens, London, 2009, Seite 412), der für nur einen einzigen Sommer errichtet wurde. Der Bau ist Teil einer fortlaufenden Serie von Pavillons, die von der zeitgenössischen Architekturelite entworfen werden, und bestand im Grunde nur aus einem 26 mm dicken Aluminiumdach, das von 50 mm starken, nach dem Zufallsprinzip angeordneten Stahlpfeilern getragen wurde. Die polierten Oberflächen des in der Höhe variierenden wellenförmigen Dachs sorgten für permanente Spiegelungen und Verzerrungen. Im Innern des Pavillons durfte der Besucher darüber nachsinnen, wo die „Wirklichkeit" aufhört und wo das reflektierte Bild anfängt. Diese Form der visuellen und räumlichen Zweideutigkeit ist eine Stärke von SANAA, wie sie auch mit ihrem Museum für die Kunst des 21. Jahrhunderts zeigten (Kanazawa, Ishikawa, Japan, 2002–04). Während der Produktion dieses Buchs stellten SANAA ihr neues Gebäude, das Rolex Learning Center für die École Polytechnique Fédérale de Lausanne (EPFL) fertig (Lausanne, Schweiz, 2007–09, Seite 418). Der wellenförmige Raum des EPFL-Neubaus ist ein noch größer dimensioniertes Experiment mit den Grenzen zwischen Bewegung und Starre bzw. Dauerhaftigkeit. Auf Innenwände wurde fast vollständig verzichtet, nach außen ist der Bau durchgehend verglast – eine Konzeption, die sowohl die technische Seite der Architektur als auch ihren genuinen Zweck als Einrichtung für Studenten hervortreten lässt. Auf gewohnt elegante Weise hinterfragen die Architekten von SANAA damit manches Grundprinzip der zeitgenössischen Architektur.

Die mit ihrem Büro in London ansässige Zaha Hadid, Trägerin des Praemium Imperiale 2009, interessiert sich seit Langem für Design und – nicht zu vergessen – für temporäre Bauten. Das bestimmende Element der Johann Sebastian Bach Chamber Music Hall von Zaha Hadid Architects (Manchester, 2009, Seite 196) ist ein „voluminöses Band", das sich „durch den Raum schlängelt und zum räumlichem und visuellen Pendant der kunstvoll ineinandergreifenden Bach'schen Harmonien wird". Das aus einem Stahlrahmen und einer darübergespannten durchscheinenden Stoffmembran bestehende Gebilde wird ergänzt durch Akustikpaneele aus klarem Acryl, die oberhalb der Bühne angebracht sind. Außerdem gehören zu der Installation eine vorprogrammierte Beleuchtungsanlage nebst Musikaufnahmen, die in der aufführungsfreien Zeit zum Einsatz kommen. Die transportable und an ähnlichen Orten immer wieder neu installierbare Arbeit zeugt einmal mehr von Hadids Anspruch, der zeitgenössischen Architektur neue Gestaltungsmöglichkeiten zu eröffnen, die nichts mehr mit jenen starren rechtwinkligen Formen zu tun haben, die noch vor wenigen Jahren für neue Bauwerke so charakteristisch waren. Kennzeichnend für Hadids Œuvre ist eine „Verflüssigung" des Raums, bei der einzelne Gebäudekörper ungehindert ineinanderfließen. Dieser Ansatz erstreckt sich auch auf Arbeiten, die in bereits bestehende Räume eingebettet werden, so wie in jüngerer Zeit ihre Installation für das Home House in London (2007–08): Das georgianische Dekor des Klubs bildet die Bühne für eine Bar, bei der Fiberglas, Kunstharz und Textilien verwendet wurden und die den Raum vollständig verwandelt. „Im Home House ging es um die Herstellung einer ganz eigenen Dichotomie zwischen der hier gewählten neuartigen Formensprache der Morphologie", so die Architektin, „und den dynamischen Kräften der georgianischen Hülle mit ihrer typisch rechtwinkeligen Programmatik." Wie ihre SANAA-Kollegin Kazuyo Sejima hat Zaha Hadid es im internationalen Architekturgeschäft zu den höchsten Weihen gebracht und dabei nicht allein das Design, sondern auch das Feld der Baukonstruktion um neue Einsichten bereichert. So

17

unangebracht die Bezeichnung „weibliche Architektur" für das Schaffen der beiden Architektinnen sicherlich wäre, zeigt sich in der Subtilität, der Vieldeutigkeit, dem fließenden Element ihrer Arbeiten doch ein gewisser Bruch mit jener zeitgenössischen Architekturwelt, die Bauten wie den Burj Khalifa hervorbringt.

UNTERGRUNDBEWEGUNG

Zwei der im vorliegenden Band vorgestellten Projekte befassen sich auf ungewöhnliche Weise mit der Nutzung unterirdischer Räume. Die Versuchung, ausgediente Stadträume komplett umzukrempeln, mag kennzeichnend sein für die Gegenwart, doch ebenso charakteristisch ist die freiwillige Wiedernutzbarmachung von Industriebauten oder historischen Gebäuden, die ihre ursprüngliche Funktion verloren haben. Rand Elliott ist im Rahmen von *Architecture Now!* insofern eher eine Ausnahmeerscheinung, als das von ihm geführte Architekturbüro seinen Sitz in einem Bundesstaat hat, der nicht unbedingt für aufregende junge Architektur bekannt ist – in Oklahoma. Elliotts Firma allerdings hat nicht nur bereits zehn National AIA Honor Awards erhalten, sondern ist auch die bislang einzige, der in Oklahoma derartige Ehren überhaupt zuteil wurden. Der Name Underground (Oklahoma City, Oklahoma, USA, 2007, Seite 146) steht für Elliotts Neugestaltung eines insgesamt 3900 m² umfassenden Tunnelsystems, das im Zentrum von Oklahoma City 23 Gebäude miteinander verbindet. Durch Elliotts Renovierung unter Einbeziehung von Musik, farbigem Licht und Fotogalerien mit historischen Themen wurden die mit der Zeit baufällig gewordenen unterirdischen Passagen, deren Ursprünge bis ins Jahr 1931 zurückreichen, wieder voll nutzbar. Wenngleich sich bei diesem Beispiel Architektur und Innendesign nicht klar auseinanderhalten lassen, ist allgemein festzustellen, dass Licht und Klang in der zeitgenössischen Baukunst einen neuen Stellenwert erlangt haben. Gerade unterirdischen Räumen, in die kein oder nur wenig Tageslicht einfällt, lassen sich mit derartigen immateriellen Gestaltungsmitteln neue Qualitäten und Nutzungsmöglichkeiten abgewinnen. Man muss Underground nicht gleich mit einem Kunstwerk vergleichen, kann aber in diesem Zusammenhang auf Künstler wie James Turrell verweisen, der dem für seine Arbeiten empfänglichen Publikum die Erfahrung vermittelt, dass Licht ein nahezu gegenständliches Medium sein kann, für das sich in der zeitgenössischen Architektur neue Einsatzmöglichkeiten bieten.

Für einen völlig anderen Umgang mit unterirdischem Raum steht der Bahnhof Pionen (Stockholm, Schweden, 2007–08, Seite 158) des in Frankreich geborenen Architekten Albert France-Lanord: Es handelt sich um einen in 30 m Tiefe unter dem Granitfels des Vitabergparks angelegten atombombensicheren Stollen. Der Bauherr ist ein Internetprovider, der den Ort für Büros und Räume für die Server nutzt. Der Architekt versuchte, so abwechslungsreiche Beleuchtung wie möglich zu verwenden, um ein Gefühl von Klaustrophobie zu vermeiden, das in solch einer Umgebung leicht entstehen kann. Nicht ganz zufällig wirkt das Ergebnis wie die Kulisse aus einem James-Bond-Film: ein eigenartiger, von der urbanen Außenwelt isolierter Raum, der an die Machenschaften des Kalten Kriegs anspielt. Albert France-Lanord bemerkt dazu: „Es war sehr spannend, mit einem Raum zu arbeiten, in dem es zunächst keinen einzigen rechten Winkel gab, nur Fels. Der Hauptsaal ist kein im üblichen Sinn durch klare Flächen begrenzter Raum, sondern wird vielmehr von der Leere im Innern einer Masse bestimmt."

18
Tadao Ando, Shibuya Station,
Shibuya-ku, Tokyo, Japan, 2006–08

18

Interessanterweise scheinen unterirdische Räume stets mehr mit Industriearchitektur zu tun zu haben als mit jener bewussten Art der Formgebung, die den größten Teil der anspruchsvollen Gegenwartsarchitektur auszeichnet. Doch selbst in einer Stadt wie Tokio mit ihrem Labyrinth aus meistenteils einfallslosen Metrostationen und Shoppingcentern zeigen sich Fortschritte, etwa in Form von Projekten wie Tadao Andos Station Shibuya (Shibuya-ku, Tokio, 2006–08, siehe oben) für die Linie Tokyu Toyoko. Die eiförmige U-Bahn-Station, die eine Gesamtfläche von 27 725 m² umfasst, besteht aus einer glasfaserverstärkten Betonhülle und bietet den Luxus der Frischluftversorgung, obwohl sie sich tief im Bauch der japanischen Hauptstadt befindet. Viele weitere Beispiele dieser Art zeigen, dass zeitgenössische Architekten immer häufiger in Aufgabengebiete vordringen, von denen sie früher größtenteils ausgeschlossen waren. Diese Entwicklung korrespondiert mit der Einsicht, dass es Architekten gelingt, solche Räume attraktiv und nutzbar zu machen, bei denen die normalerweise mit der Konzeption von Metrostationen betrauten Ingenieure sich vor allem Gedanken darüber machen, wie sie einen Zug bzw. große Menschenmengen durch einen möglichst kleinen und preiswerten Raum schleusen können.

DIE KUNST IN DER BAUKUNST

Man wird wohl davon ausgehen können, dass die Ausgaben für Museen und andere Bauten mit Kunstbezug aufgrund der wirtschaftlichen Gesamtlage zurückgehen werden – auf einem Feld also, das Architekten wie Zaha Hadid oder David Chipperfield fantastische, nämliche maximale Aufmerksamkeit versprechende Voraussetzungen bot, um Orte zu schaffen, die sich rasch ins öffentliche Bewusstsein einschreiben sollten. Frank Gehrys Guggenheim-Museum in Bilbao ist und bleibt *die* Referenz, wenn es um eine Architektur geht, die gleichsam singt und tanzt und nicht zuletzt die Zuschauer herbeiströmen lässt; wobei der weltweite Boom auf dem Gebiet des Museumsbaus wohl auch dann nachgelassen hätte, wenn Lehman Brothers nicht pleite gegangen wären. Ein Land wie Japan kann auch nur eine begrenzte Zahl an neuen Museen bauen, während andere Länder wie die Vereinigten Staaten in dieser Beziehung bereits einen gewissen Sättigungsgrad erreicht haben. Trotz dieser Einschränkung gibt es einige in jüngerer Zeit neu gebaute Institutionen, die man hervorheben sollte. 2009 wurden gleich zwei bedeutende skandinavische Kultureinrichtungen eröffnet, deren Entwürfe von dem besonders als Museumsarchitekt aktiven New Yorker Steven Holl stammen: das Museum für zeitgenössische Kunst im dänischen Herning, HEART (2007–09, Seite 216), sowie das Knut Hamsun Center im norwegischen Hamarøy (2006–09, Seite 222). Das erstgenannte vereint Räumlichkeiten für Kunstausstellungen und Konzerte und zeigt einmal mehr jene subtile Komplexität, mit der sich der Architekt einen Namen gemacht hat. Wie schon häufiger hat Steven Holl auch in Herning zusätzlich die Gestaltung der Grünflächen rund um das Gebäude übernommen; dieses Mal schuf er ein 3700 m² großes „geböschtes Gelände mit grasbewachsenen Hügeln und Wasserbassins", unter dem sich die Servicebereiche und eine Tiefgarage befinden. Das zu Ehren eines der bekanntesten Schriftsteller Norwegens entstandene Knut Hamsun Center liegt nördlich des Polarkreises in der Nähe des Gehöfts, auf dem Hamsun aufwuchs. Mit seinen formalen Anklängen an den norwegischen Kirchenbau und bestmöglich auf die Lichtverhältnisse nordischer Breiten abgestimmt, erweist Holls Gebäude nicht nur dem Namensgeber seine Reverenz, sondern auch den zahlreichen Filmen, die nach Hamsuns Büchern entstanden sind.

19
HHF, Artfarm, Salt Point, New York,
NY, USA, 2007–08

Die von den Schweizer Architekten HHF in Zusammenarbeit mit dem chinesischen Künstler Ai Wei Wei entworfene Artfarm (Salt Point, New York, 2007–08, Seite 210) beschreitet einen ganz anderen Weg als die größeren Museen, die über viele Jahre die zeitgenössische Architektur geprägt haben. Gleichsam ein technisch avancierter Schuppen, ist das Gebäude als hermetisch abgeschlossener, mit weißen PVC isolierter Baukörper gezielt darauf ausgelegt, mit den großen Temperaturunterschieden zwischen Sommer und Winter, wie sie im US-Bundesstaat New York typisch sind, zurechtzukommen. Der nicht zuletzt von Industriebauten beeinflusste Artfarm-Entwurf demonstriert, dass innovatives Gebäudedesign nicht nur in seiner äußeren Erscheinung, sondern genauso in seiner räumlichen Anlage ausgesprochen schlicht sein kann. Die Räumlichkeiten sollen allein der zur Ausstellung geplanten chinesischen Kunst dienen, womit sie gleichzeitig für einen reiferen Umgang mit der Beziehung von Kunst und Architektur stehen als manche der wabernden Titanwolken, die seit einigen Jahren in vielen Gegenden das Bild prägen.

Rudy Ricciottis Villa Navarra (Le Muy, Frankreich, 2007, Seite 384) ist ähnlich wie die Artfarm dimensioniert, zeigt aber eine andere Herangehensweise an die Frage, wie ein Gebäude für die Ausstellung von Kunstwerken konzipiert sein kann. Ricciotti und sein Sohn, der Ingenieur Romain Ricciotti, haben mit einem beeindruckenden Kragdach experimentiert, das aus 17 Ductal-Betonplatten (je 9,25 x 2,35 m) von jeweils nur 3 cm Stärke besteht. Die außerordentliche Tragfähigkeit dieses faserverstärkten Betons, eine Entwicklung der Firma Lafarge, ermöglichte die Konstruktion eines Dachs, das 7,8 m weit vorspringt. Nach offensichtlich positiven Erfahrungen mit dem Material bei seinen früheren Brückenentwürfen beweist Ricciotti hier, dass er es auch für Bauten zu nutzen versteht, die erst recht ungewöhnlich und innovativ sind. Ein weiterer außergewöhnlicher Aspekt der Villa Navarra besteht darin, dass sie nicht für Publikum geöffnet ist, sondern für Online-Ausstellungen genutzt werden soll.

Der in Los Angeles gebürtige Architekt Eric Owen Moss verfolgt bei seinen Gebäudeentwürfen und -renovierungen für das kalifornische Culver City von jeher einen skulpturalen oder künstlerischen Ansatz. Seine bislang letzte in Culver City realisierte Arbeit ist der Gateway Art Tower (USA, 2007–09, Seite 320), ein 22 m hohes Informationszentrum, das an der Kreuzung Hayden Avenue, National Boulevard steht, gleich am Ortseingang der Gemeinde, für deren Sanierung Moss in den letzten Jahren viel getan hat. Die Konstruktion besteht aus fünf aufeinandergesetzten Stahlringen von jeweils rund 9 m Durchmesser und besitzt auf jeder Ebene Infoscreens aus mattem Acrylglas, die auf Kulturveranstaltungen und sonstige lokale Ereignisse hinweisen. Zusätzlich gibt es auf allen Ebenen Aussichtsplattformen für Besucher. Der skulpturartige Bau stellt – vergleichbar der oben vorgestellten Landmarke Lausitzer Seenland – eigentlich schon für sich ein Kunstwerk dar. Wiederholt hat Moss auf Materialien aus Lagerhäusern der Umgegend zurückgegriffen und aus den zuvor gewöhnlichen Objekten skulpturale Gebilde von kunstvollem, dynamischem Ausdruck geschaffen. Der Art Tower führt diese bildhauerische Vorgehensweise noch einen Schritt weiter und präsentiert sich als eine Art Dokument für den Einsatz, den Architekt und Bauherr (Samitaur Constructs) geleistet haben, um Culver City nach dem Verlust seiner einstigen Identität als frühes Zentrum der Filmindustrie zu neuem Leben zu erwecken.

20
Eric Owen Moss, Gateway Art Tower,
Culver City, CA, USA, 2007–09

20

STARS IN FERNOST

Privathäuser sind für Architekten nach wie vor ein ideales Terrain, um kreative Vorstellungen zu verwirklichen. Das gilt zwar weltweit, insbesondere aber dort, wo Auftraggeber über das nötige Kapital verfügen, um sich Wünsche abseits der Norm verwirklichen zu können. Seit einiger Zeit empfiehlt sich Südkorea auf dem Gebiet zeitgenössischer Architektur als ein aufstrebender Akteur, dessen einheimische Talente inzwischen auch internationale Aufmerksamkeit erlangen. Eines dieser Talente ist der 1957 in Seoul geborene Byoung-soo Cho. Der heute wieder in Seoul ansässige Architekt besuchte zunächst die Montana State University (Bozeman, Montana, B.Arch 1986), um 1991 seinen Master of Architecture nebst einem weiteren Masterabschluss mit Schwerpunkt Städtebau an der Graduate School of Design der Harvard University zu erwerben. Chos 494 m² Grundfläche umfassendes Three Box House (Paju, Gyeonggi-do, Südkorea, 2005–06, Seite 122) zeichnet sich durch eine raffinierte Schlichtheit aus. Bei aller Strenge der rechtwinkligen Grundkomposition, die sich aus drei einzelnen, durch einen horizontalen Holzschirm und hölzerne Stege verbundenen Baukörpern zusammensetzt, zeigt sich in dem Gebäude ein besonderes Gespür für Ästhetik; seine Gegenüberstellung von opaken und transparenten Blöcken wirkt tatsächlich neuartig. Würde nicht der Architekt selbst erklären, dass „die Schlichtheit und Schnörkellosigkeit" seines Projekts vom „industriell und landwirtschaftlich geprägten Erscheinungsbild Montanas" herrühre, käme man wohl kaum auf die Vermutung, dass es in einem Zusammenhang mit diesem nicht gerade für seine architektonische Innovationsgabe berühmten US-Bundesstaat steht.

Während Byoung-soo Cho sich erfolgreich auf die Stärken einer recht minimalistischen Formensprache besinnt, geht es seinem Landsmann HyoMan Kim, der sein Studium an der DanKook Universität in Seoul abgeschlossen hat (1978), um Werke, deren „architektonische Beschaffenheit sie zu Orten der Erholung macht". Kims Island House (Gapyung-gun, Gyeonggi-do, Südkorea, 2007–09, Seite 238) ist eine originelle, direkt am Ufer des Hangang gelegene Residenz mit einem großen Außenbassin, die aus der Entfernung ein wenig an ein Boot erinnert. Zwar herrschen gerade Linien vor, dennoch sind Grund- und Aufriss mehr oder weniger unregelmäßig und lassen so das Anliegen des Architekten erkennen, das Haus einerseits in seine natürliche Umgebung einzubetten, es aber zugleich von ihr abzuheben. Ein anderes von HyoMan Kim entworfenes Wohnhaus ist das etwas kleinere Purple Hill House (Youngin, Gyeonggi-do, Südkorea, 2009, Seite 14), in dessen Form sich der Umriss des unweit aufragenden Bergs Gwanggyo doppelt. Der Aussicht und der Grundstücksbeschaffenheit halber hat der Architekt das Haus nach Nordwesten ausgerichtet, womit er in Kauf nahm, dass nur wenig direktes Sonnenlicht einfällt. Das Problem löste er durch den Einbau mehrerer Lichtkästen, die in das Gebäude hineinragen. Wie schon beim Island House zeigt HyoMan Kim einen Hang zur Komplexität, der sich hier in einer kristallartigen Komposition äußert, in der abermals seine bevorzugten geraden Linien in einer vielschichtigen Gesamtstruktur aufgehen.

Ungeachtet ihres unterschiedlichen Stils – Byoung-soo Cho mit seiner Präferenz für verhältnismäßig schlichte Konzepte, HyoMan Kim mit seinem Faible für sehr facettenreiche Entwürfe – sind beide Architekten Repräsentanten einer neuen nationalen Schule, die über kurz oder lang dem für seine Innovationskraft bekannten Nachbarn Japan Konkurrenz machen könnte. Gestützt wird dieser Trend durch einen seit

21
Sou Fujimoto, House H, Tokyo,
Japan, 2008–09

21

geraumer Zeit anhaltenden wirtschaftlichen Aufstieg, dem auch zeitweilige Schwierigkeiten keinen Abbruch tun konnten. Letztlich aber sollte es vor allem darauf ankommen, welches kreative Potenzial jeder einzelne Architekt vorzuweisen hat. Wer sich auch dann als kreativ erweist, wenn er zu Sparsamkeit und zum Entwerfen kleinerer Bauwerke angehalten ist, mit dem dürfte in den kommenden Jahren noch zu rechnen sein.

Ein weiterer asiatischer Architekt, der mit einer enormen Erfindungsgabe glänzt, ist der 1971 geborene Sou Fujimoto, der in Tokio ausgebildet wurde. Der zu den produktivsten und talentiertesten Vertretern der jüngeren japanischen Architektengeneration zählende Fujimoto befasst sich häufig mit grundsätzlichen Fragestellungen wie etwa der nach den eigentlichen Grenzen zwischen Wohnhaus und Stadt. In seinem House H (Tokio, 2008–09, Seite 176), das sich an der Idee eines Baumhauses orientiert, sind Wände, Decken und Böden durch ein System aus verglasten Flächen zueinander geöffnet. „Mithilfe künstlicher Materialien und einer streng geometrischen Anordnung", erklärt Fujimoto, „ergab sich ein Schema aus miteinander korrespondierenden Durchlässen, die ein erweitertes Beziehungsgefüge entstehen lassen. Ein Haus, das wie ein großer Baum aufgebaut ist, dessen Eingebundenheit in sein direktes äußeres Umfeld sich nie eindeutig bestimmen lässt, könnte ein Prototyp für das Wohnen beziehungsweise die Stadt der Zukunft sein." Fujimotos kurz zuvor realisiertes Final Wooden House (Kumamura, Kumamoto, Japan, 2007–08, Seite 33) entstand durch das „planlose" Übereinanderstapeln von 350 mm starken Kanthölzern. „Meine Vorstellung ging dahin, eine neue Art von Räumlichkeit zu entwerfen, in der sich jene primitiven Bedingungen von harmonischer Einheit wiederfinden, wie sie herrschten, als sich noch keine gesonderten Funktionen und Aufgaben herausgebildet hatten", erklärt der Architekt. Im Final Wooden House gibt es weder Raumaufteilungen noch Böden oder herkömmliche Wände oder Decken, stattdessen erlaubt es dem Benutzer „sich ganz nach Belieben in dem dreidimensionalen Raum einzurichten". Wo Böden zu Wänden oder Wände zu Sitzplätzen werden, ist der Besucher angehalten, so Fujimoto, das klassische Konzept des Wohnhauses neu zu überdenken. „Es ist mehr als bloß ein neues Stück Architektur", stellt Fujimoto fest, „es ist ein neuer Anfang, eine neue Daseinsweise." Ob nun das Final Wooden House dazu gedacht ist, so wie das House H wirklich bewohnt zu werden oder auch nicht – mit jedem seiner Projekte lotet Fujimoto die Grenzen von Wohnarchitektur neu aus; vermeintliche Grundregeln stellt er auf eine Weise infrage, wie man es bei seinen Kollegen aus anderen Ländern bislang selten gesehen hat. Fujimoto ist ein Architekt, den man im Auge behalten sollte.

QUE SER(R)A SER(R)A
Auf der anderen Seite des Globus hat die 1963 geborene Susanne Nobis, die ihr Architekturstudium in London und München absolviert hat, vor Kurzem die Arbeiten am Haus H. (auch „Walls in the Landscape") in Großburgwedel (Deutschland, 2007–09, Seite 324) abgeschlossen. Das als asymmetrische Komposition aus rechteckigen Grundrissfeldern angelegte Haus wird äußerlich durch hohe Wandelemente aus Cor-Ten-Stahl bestimmt. Die Stahlplatten lassen unweigerlich an die imposanten Skulpturen Richard Serras denken, und das Haus hat denn auch trotz seiner recht minimalistischen Anlage einen kraftvoll-wuchtigen Gestus. Den Kontrast dazu bildet die elegante harmonische Verbindung, die es durch seine Verglasung mit der umgebenden Natur unterhält. Die Präsentation dieses Entwurfs zeigt, dass zeitgenössische

22
Sou Fujimoto, Final Wooden House,
Kumamura, Kumamoto, Japan,
2007–08

22

Wohnarchitektur nach wie vor keiner starren Logik, keinem festen Stil folgt. Ihre jeweilige Ästhetik und Funktionalität leiten sich aus einer immensen Vielfalt unterschiedlicher Stile ab, die rund um den Globus gleichberechtigt nebeneinander praktiziert werden. Auch wenn ein strenger Minimalismus aus der Mode gekommen sein mag, bleibt er als Position ebenso gültig wie die geradezu extravagante Komplexität, die sich derzeit insbesondere in Asien auf dem Vormarsch befindet. Vor ihrem Schritt in die Selbstständigkeit arbeitete Susanne Nobis für den Renzo Piano Building Workshop (Genua, 1992–93) und anschließend für Herzog & de Meuron (München, 1994–95), beides Architekturbüros, die einen ähnlich pragmatischen Umgang mit der klassischen Architekturmoderne pflegen. Pianos Fondation Beyeler in Riehen (Basel, Schweiz, 1991–97) schöpft wie Nobis aus dem Kontrast von natursteinverkleideten Außenwänden und einer deckenhohen Verglasung, die aus dem Gebäudeinnern den Blick auf die Felder in Richtung der deutsch-schweizerischen Grenze freigibt. Die Wände von Nobis' Haus H. zeugen von einer Art klassischen Auffassung, die dem Entwurf etwas geradezu zeitlos Modernes gibt.

AUF NEUEN WOLKEN

Die jüngsten Entwicklungen der Computertechnologie haben zu einer Situation geführt, die bereits als „Battle of the Clouds" bezeichnet wird: Firmen wie Microsoft oder Google kämpfen um die Vormachtstellung auf dem Gebiet des via Internet erfolgenden „Cloud Computing", „bei dem man Dokumente, E-Mails und andere Daten online ablegt, um anschließend von jedem beliebigen Computer oder mobilen Endgerät aus auf sie zugreifen zu können."[3] Interessant ist hierbei, dass der rasante technologische Fortschritt sich auch auf die Entstehung lose organisierter Firmen oder Gruppen auswirkt, die sich nicht mehr in bisheriger Form klassifizieren lassen. So etwa im Fall des Unternehmens Supersudaka, das zwar im chilenischen Talca ansässig ist, dessen Aktivitäten im Zusammenhang mit seinen Webseiten www.supersudaka.cl und www.supersudaca.org jedoch an keine Landes- oder Disziplinengrenzen gebunden sind. Supersudaca (mit „c") beschreibt sich selbst als „Thinktank für Architektur und Stadterforschung", während die Webseite von Supersudaka (mit „k") überschrieben ist mit der Devise: „Wir wollen die Welt nicht durch Architektur verändern, wir wollen die Architektur durch die Welt verändern." Zu den realisierten Projekten der Gruppe, die in Chile von Juan Pablo Corvalan und Gabriel Vergara angeführt wird, gehört u. a. die hier vorgestellte Casa Kiltro (Talca, Chile, 2006–08, Seite 450). „Kiltro" ist ein chilenischer Slangausdruck für einen Mischlingshund, wobei das Supersudaka-Haus wie eine Kreuzung aus besonderer Raffinesse und innerer Logik anmutet. Die facettierte Holzverkleidung des Baus erinnert an die Entwürfe HyoMan Kims, wenn auch in einer ganz anderen Umgebung und Materialität. So groß die Bedeutung nationaltypischer Kennzeichen in Architekturentwürfen meist noch ist, sind wir nun in eine Ära eingetreten, in der auch in der Architektur „Clouds" entstehen, mit Beiträgen aus aller Welt. Aus naheliegendem Grund führt Supersudaka ausschließlich Juan Pablo Corvaláns E-Mail-Adresse von der Universidad de Talca auf; statt mit einem klassischen Büro mit schwarz gewandeten Jungarchitekten hat man es hier mit einer flexiblen Gruppe zu tun, deren Mitglieder von überall aus operieren können.

VERBINDUNGSSTIFTER

So wie sich die Grenzen zwischen Architektur und anderen Disziplinen wie Kunst oder Design offenbar immer mehr auflösen, beginnt sich nun auch die oftmals unüberbrückbar erscheinende Kluft zwischen Architekten und Ingenieuren zu schließen. Jedenfalls sind einige der im vorliegenden Band von *Architecture Now!* versammelten Projekte wenn nicht das Werk von Ingenieuren selbst, so doch oft nur dank ihrer Fachkenntnisse entstanden. Als Architekt wie als Ingenieur gleichermaßen renommiert ist Santiago Calatrava, der in Lüttich unlängst den Bahnhof Liège-Guillemins (Belgien, 1996–2009, Seite 132) an der TGV-Strecke Paris-Brüssel-Köln fertiggestellt hat. Entlang einer von Nord-west nach Südost verlaufenden Achse schuf der gebürtige Spanier ein 200 m langes symmetrisches Reiseterminal, dessen gewölbtes Dach auf einer Breite von 145 m fünf Bahnsteige überspannt. Die gewaltige Kuppel aus Stahl und Glas ist so konzipiert, dass der Bahnhof sich zur Stadt hin komplett öffnet. Fußgängerbrücken und eine unter den Gleisen hindurchführende Passage bilden eine direkte Verbindung zwischen den beiden Bahnhofseiten. Nach seinen futuristischen Bahnhofsentwürfen für Lissabon und dem Flughafen Saint Exupéry in Lyon hat Cala-trava in Lüttich einen Bahnhof geschaffen, der einen vor Kurzem noch recht vernachlässigten Abschnitt des europäischen Eisenbahnnetzes direkt ins 21. Jahrhundert befördert.

Einer der weltweit bekanntesten Bauingenieure ist Cecil Balmond, seit 2004 stellvertretender Vorsitzender des auf unzähligen Feldern engagierten Ingenieurbüros Arup sowie Gründer der dortigen Advanced Geometry Unit (AGU). Unter Balmonds Leitung entstand 2009 die UPENN Weave Bridge in Philadelphia (Pennsylvania, USA, Seite 88). Eine Besonderheit dieser Brücke besteht darin, dass sie, trotz ihrer un-komplizierten Gestalt, auf einer einfallsreichen Tragwerkkonstruktion in Form einer Doppelhelix beruht. Die Brücke ist Teil eines Masterplans, den Balmond zur Verbesserung der Verkehrswege auf dem Campus der University of Pennsylvania erarbeitet, und zeigt, dass auf den Laien manchmal selbst die innovativsten Entwürfe ziemlich gewöhnlich wirken können. Zudem war es 2009 für die Architektur wie für das Ingeni-eurwesen wohl auch an der Zeit, sich nach einer langen Phase der Extravaganzen wieder ein wenig mehr in Bescheidenheit zu üben.

Dass natürlich weiterhin auf der ganzen Welt ungewöhnliche Bauwerke in die Höhe wachsen, führen Projekte wie der von dem nieder-ländischen Büro Information Based Architecture entworfene Fernseh- und Aussichtsturm von Guangzhou (China, 2005–10, Seite 228) ein-drucksvoll vor Augen. Er überragt zwar nicht den Burj Khalifa, mit einer Höhe von 610 m ist er aber auch nicht gerade klein. Die verdrehte Doppelkegelstruktur des Bauwerks ist eine ingenieurstechnische Meisterleistung, die ein prägnantes Wahrzeichen für die 2010 ganz in der Nähe stattfindenden Asienspiele abgeben dürfte. Man wird jedoch – ohne damit die Bedeutung des ingenieurstechnischen Anteils bei der Entstehung eines solchen Bauwerks abzuwerten – auch fragen dürfen, ob die Gründe, derart hoch und auffällig zu bauen, allein in den tech-nischen Erfordernissen des Fernsehrundfunks zu suchen sind, so wichtig die Höhe hierbei auch ist. Die Wünsche der Auftraggeber sind si-cherlich nicht frei von Hybris, genauso wenig – und was spricht auch dagegen? – wie der Ehrgeiz der Architekten, ganz nach dem Motto: Mein Turm ist größer als deiner …

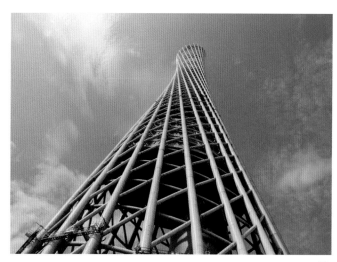

23
Information Based Architecture,
Guangzhou TV and Sightseeing Tower,
Guangzhou, China, 2005–10

NULL SCHADSTOFFAUSSTOSS BEI 50 GRAD MINUS

Eine ganz andere Art der Ingenieursleistung bereichert seit Kurzem den Südpol: die von der International Polar Foundation entwickelte Prinzessin-Elisabeth-Polarstation (Utsteinen, 71° 57' S, 23° 20' Ost, Königin-Maud-Land, Ostantarktis, 2007–09, Seite 232), ein so modernes wie überzeugendes Aushängeschild für das Engagement Belgiens in der Antarktisforschung. Obwohl sich ihr Standort in 1300 m Höhe befindet, wo Temperaturen von minus 5 bis minus 50 Grad Celsius und Windgeschwindigkeiten von bis zu 250 km/h herrschen, ist sie die erste Einrichtung ihrer Art, bei der keine CO_2-Emissionen anfallen. Der Betrieb der Prinzessin-Elisabeth-Station erfolgt so energieeffizient wie irgend möglich und auch ausschließlich mit erneuerbaren Energien. Und obwohl es sich in erster Linie um eine technische Einrichtung handelt, ist das Bauwerk am untersten Ende des Globus in seiner silbrigen Erscheinung auch unter ästhetischen Gesichtspunkten ausgesprochen reizvoll.

MIT GUTEM BEISPIEL VORAN

So sinnvoll die Erforschung der Pole zweifelsohne ist, zumal angesichts der zunehmenden Erderwärmung, muss man andererseits feststellen, dass anspruchsvolle neue Architektur nur in wenigen Fällen jenen zugutekommt, die sie eigentlich am dringendsten benötigen. Eine bemerkenswerte Ausnahme von dieser Regel bildet das Werk des südafrikanischen Architekten Peter Rich, dessen letzten beiden Projekte, das Alexandra Heritage Center (Johannesburg, Gauteng, Südafrika, 2004–09, Seite 390) und das Mapungubwe Interpretation Center (Mapungubwe National Park, Limpopo, Südafrika, 2007–09, Seite 396) wir hier vorstellen wollen. Der 1945 in Johannesburg geborene Rich studierte indigene afrikanische Ikonografie und Architektur, unter besonderer Berücksichtigung des Volksstamms der Ndebele, und unterrichtete 30 Jahre lang als ordentlicher Professor an der Witwatersrand-Universität. Das gegenüber einem ehemaligen Wohnhaus von Nelson Mandela errichtete Alexandra Center dient vor allem dazu, regionale Geschichte, Kunst und Kultur auf angemessene, moderne Weise zu vermitteln. Dazu Peter Rich: „Das Projekt ist gemeinschaftsstiftend und trägt zur Armutsminderung bei, indem es die Anwohner in den Bereichen Tourismus und Kulturerbe ausbildet, kleine Unternehmen fördert und auch der Kunst, der Kultur und dem kulturellen Erbe von Alexandra ein Forum bietet." So deutlich das Zentrum aus seiner ärmlichen Umgebung heraussticht, so erstaunlich gut fügt es sich zugleich in sie ein. Über Rampen ist das Gebäude direkt mit der Straße verbunden, außerdem verfügt es über einen Innenhof, in dem – ganz im Sinne lokaler Bautraditionen – jeder verfügbare Quadratmeter so sinnvoll wie möglich ausgenutzt ist. Wie anpassungsfähig Richs Arbeit ist, zeigt auch das Mapungubwe Center, dessen dünnschalige Kuppeln nach dem Vorbild der „archäologischen Zeugnisse vergangener Kulturen" konstruiert sind, denen der Nationalpark, in dem das Informationszentrum sich befindet, gewidmet ist. Dabei verfällt Rich nie in die Herstellung von Pastiches, sondern nimmt die lokalen Bauformen und -materialien auf und passt sie ganz an ihre aktuellen Verwendungszwecke an. Auf diese Weise macht er auf respektvolle Weise Kulturen zugänglich, denen eine derartige Aufmerksamkeit lange nicht vergönnt war.

Die Schranken, die zeitgenössische Architektur von anderen Disziplinen – vom Design bis hin zum Ingenieurwesen – trennen, sind im Verschwinden begriffen. Der Einwand, dass derlei Schranken eigentlich nie bestanden hätten, insofern Landschaftsarchitektur oder Kunst seit Jahrhunderten ein fester Bestandteil von Architektur seien, ist schwer zu halten. Denn obwohl die Gründer des Bauhauses in Deutschland sich um die Schaffung eines „Gesamtkunstwerks" bemüht haben, sah die Realität in der Moderne anders aus. Trotz der offensichtlichen Verwandtschaft zwischen Architektur und Ingenieurwesen wurde in akademischen Kreisen häufig strikt zwischen den Disziplinen unterschieden. Heute tragen kreative Köpfe wie Santiago Calatrava, der ebenso sehr Künstler wie Architekt ist, in hohem Maß zu der allgemeinen Erkenntnis bei, dass Kreativität da am selbstverständlichsten entsteht, wo man keine Rücksicht auf künstliche Unterscheidungen zu nehmen hat, die zum bloßen Nutzen einiger weniger getroffen wurden. Architektur- wie Kunstzeitschriften neigen immer noch dazu, eine Trennlinie zwischen Architektur und Kunst zu ziehen, und selbst bei vielen Kreativen ist es nicht anders. Selbstverständlich muss jemand, der Gebäude entwerfen will, eine entsprechende Ausbildung besitzen, wohingegen bildende Künstler ihrem inneren Schaffensdrang folgen können, so wie es sich ein Frank Gehry in jungen Jahren ersehnt hat. Derselbe Gehry hat später das Seine zum Niederreißen mancher Schranken beigetragen, wenn er bei seinen Gebäuden das Ästhetische stärker in den Vordergrund stellte als ihre Nutzbarkeit.

GRÜN UND GUT

Dass Architektur nicht von heute auf morgen entsteht, liegt in der Natur der Sache, zumal wenn es um Großbauten geht. Von daher kann der vorliegende siebte Band der Reihe *Architecture Now!* den Auswirkungen der 2008 eskalierten Wirtschaftskrise auch nur zum Teil Rechnung tragen. Die Entwicklung scheint jedoch dahin zu gehen, dass Architekten, und erst recht ihre Auftraggeber, sich künftig stärker um kleinere und kostengünstigere Projekte bemühen. Andere, bereits bestehende Trends, etwa hin zu einer notwendigen Begrenzung des Schadstoffausstoßes und des Energieverbrauchs, sind durch die Rezession sicherlich noch verstärkt worden. Da ein geringerer Verbrauch auch die finanziellen Aufwendungen für Energie senkt, wird dieser Faktor in den kommenden Jahren vermutlich immer stärker berücksichtigt werden. Technischer Fortschritt bedeutet konkret, dass Anlagen zur Energieerzeugung wie etwa Fotovoltaiksysteme immer effizienter werden und sich zudem immer unauffälliger in Fenster oder andere Gebäudeteile integrieren lassen. Heutzutage entstehen Gebäude, denen man kaum noch ansieht, dass sie den höchsten Umweltstandards entsprechen, ganz anders als die ersten Ökohäuser, die häufig aussahen, als seien sie das Werk einer Kommune aus den späten 1960er-Jahren. „Grüne" Standards werden künftig nirgendwo mehr wegzudenken sein, und auch in der zeitgenössischen Architektur wird ökologisches Verantwortungsbewusstsein noch stärker als bisher selbstverständlich werden.

Über die Maßen extravagante Bauwerke wie der Burj Khalifa gehören möglicherweise der Vergangenheit an. Solche Monumente, die in immer neue Höhen vorstoßen, sind Früchte wirtschaftlicher Euphoriephasen, und ob sie letztlich besonders sinnvoll sind, ist nicht ausgemacht. Symbole freilich sind beständig, und es gibt keinen Grund, warum solche nicht auch künftig geschaffen werden sollten, mögen sie auch ein wenig bescheidener ausfallen als der von Adrian Smith entworfene Megawolkenkratzer. Doch auch wenn der Großteil der hier besprochenen Bauten auf eine Phase der Euphorie zurückgeht, besitzen sie allesamt genügend Überzeugungskraft, um die Befürchtungen des

24
International Polar Foundation, Princess Elisabeth Antarctica, Utsteinen, 71°57′S–23°20′E, Dronning Maud Land, East Antarctica, 2007–09

24

oben angeführten Kritikers zu zerstreuen, dem zufolge alles zwar schön gewesen, aber nun Geschichte sei.[4] Was eben noch neu war, wie die mittels rechnergestützter Entwurfs- und Fertigungsverfahren mögliche Herstellung von Spezialbauteilen, ist längst ein selbstverständlicher Bestandteil der zeitgenössischen Architektur. Allein dieser Umstand ermöglicht auch künftig die Entstehung von Gebäuden, von denen Architekturkritiker in der guten alten Zeit des Geltungskonsums nur hätten träumen können. Architecture Now ist vital wie eh und je.

Philip Jodidio, Grimentz, 21. Oktober 2009

[1] http://lookingaround.blogs.time.com/2009/04/29/the-end-of-the-world-as-we-know-it, Stand vom 20. Oktober 2009.
[2] Norman Foster, „Foreword", *The Chronicles of Time*, Damiani, Bologna 2008.
[3] „Battle of the Clouds", *The Economist*, 17. Oktober 2009.
[4] http://lookingaround.blogs.time.com/2009/04/29/the-end-of-the-world-as-we-know-it, Stand vom 20. Oktober 2009.

INTRODUCTION

PAS DE CRÉPUSCULE EN VUE

Le monde se serait arrêté de tourner à l'automne 2008 ... ou du moins, certains commentateurs le voient ainsi. Perdues sur un océan de créances toxiques, les banques et les grandes entreprises ont vu leurs performances chuter tandis que les gouvernements se précipitaient à leur secours pour les sauver à grand renfort de milliards de dollars. L'économie étant acculée, comment l'architecture aurait-elle pu ne pas en ressentir les effets ? Il ne fallut guère de temps pour que le critique d'architecture du magazine *Time*, Richard Lacayo, ne commente le précédent volume de cette collection dans un article intitulé « La fin du monde tel que nous le connaissons » : « *Architecture Now! 6* fait partie d'une collection périodique publiée par l'éditeur allemand TASCHEN, chaque volume présente une sélection de constructions intéressantes réalisées un ou deux ans plus tôt. Ce sixième volume a été préparé l'an dernier, juste avant ou après l'implosion de Lehman Brothers en septembre qui entraîna le Dow Jones dans sa chute. Quand on regarde les plus de 70 projets que l'ouvrage contient – en dehors de quelques projets artistiques à aspects architecturaux – on ne peut que se demander si Philip Jodidio, l'historien de l'architecture qui préside à cette collection, n'avait pas par inadvertance publié un livre qui aurait dû s'intituler " Le crépuscule des dieux : les derniers moments du grand essor de l'architecture du XXIe siècle ". » Après avoir dressé la liste de quelques-unes des réalisations les plus spectaculaires des années passées, Lacayo conclut : « ... plus que toute autre forme d'art, l'architecture est liée à la prospérité. Même les artistes les plus pauvres peuvent se débrouiller pour trouver de l'argent et acheter leur matériel, mais les architectes ont besoin de clients. Aujourd'hui les sources de financement se sont asséchées de même que les projets et il faudra sans doute attendre un certain temps avant que la situation ne rebondisse. On ne peut s'empêcher de prendre cette superbe compilation comme la photographie instantanée d'une ère qui vient de s'achever, ou du moins de se mettre sur pause longue. En tournant ces pages, vous ne pouvez vous empêcher de penser que tout ceci fut magnifique ... tant que ça a duré. »[1]

LA CITÉ D'ÉMERAUDE

Lorsque le moment arriva de préparer *Architecture Now! 7*, devinez quoi ? Le monde tournait encore et les architectes construisaient toujours. Certes, quelques projets publiés dans cet ouvrage étaient déjà très engagés lorsque l'économie tomba victime de la plus sérieuse commotion subie depuis des décennies. Un exemple particulièrement brillant est le plus haut immeuble du monde, le Burj Dubaï, aujourd'hui renommé Burj Khalifa (EAU, 2004–10, SOM, Adrian Smith, page 432). Stoppée à la stupéfiante hauteur de 828 mètres, cette flèche tirée vers le ciel a bien été achevée fin 2009, même si de nombreux autres projets ambitieux de Dubaï ont été soudainement mis en sommeil, du moins pour un temps.

Adrian Smith, concepteur de la tour Burj Khalifa admet qu'il a pu être inspiré par les tours de la Cité d'émeraude de la version filmée du *Magicien d'Oz* : « Je ne suis pas allé voir à quoi tout cela ressemblait. Je me souvenais seulement de constructions cristallines s'élevant au milieu de nulle part. La chose amusante est que je ne me rappelais pas la couleur verte. » Ce grand film classique de 1939 d'après le livre éponyme de L. Frank Baum raconte les pérégrinations de Dorothy, une petite fille du Kansas (interprétée par Judy Garland dans le film) vers la Cité d'émeraude, résidence du Magicien d'Oz. Accompagnée d'un lion, d'un épouvantail et d'un homme en fer-blanc, elle aperçoit de la

25
Rotor, RDF181, Brussels,
Belgium, 2007

lisière de la forêt des tours vertes étincelantes : « C'est la Cité d'émeraude », dit-elle, « nous sommes presque arrivés, enfin, enfin! C'est splendide, n'est-ce pas? Exactement comme je savais que ce serait. Ce doit être vraiment un merveilleux magicien pour vivre dans une cité comme celle-ci! Mais le grand et puissant Magicien d'Oz se révèle être un charlatan et la Cité d'émeraude le produit d'hallucinations provoquées par des pavots. Il serait difficile d'inventer un rapport entre une telle source d'inspiration et la réalité du Dubaï d'aujourd'hui. Comme le note Richard Lacayo, il est certain que beaucoup d'excès ont été commis dans le monde de l'architecture, très lié à l'économie de casino des premières années du XXIe siècle. Mais il est tout aussi vrai est que les remarquables progrès des technologies informatiques ont permis la conception et la construction d'immeubles qui n'auraient pu que rester dans les cartons ou les imaginations il y a quelques années encore. Ces progrès, comme dans la conception assistée par ordinateur (CAD) ou la fabrication par machines-outils à pilotage numérique (MOCN) restent utiles quel que soit l'état de l'économie. Les technologies nouvelles devraient permettre de concevoir et de réaliser des projets normalement moins coûteux qu'avant leur invention.

Les architectes, même les plus grands d'entre eux, ont depuis longtemps exprimé leurs préoccupations sur le sens des réductions de coûts dans leurs projets. Pour n'en donner qu'un exemple, Rem Koolhaas et l'OMA utilisent des matériaux bon marché dans beaucoup de leurs réalisations depuis des années. En revanche, que les budgets des architectes célèbres soient toujours raisonnables reste un point à discuter.

PASSIVEMENT VÔTRE

Économiser ne devrait pas pour autant condamner l'architecture à la « fin du monde tel que nous le connaissons ». Un bref coup d'œil aux projets présentés dans cet ouvrage suffit à répondre aux craintes du critique de *Time*. L'architecture, même celle d'après l'explosion de la bulle financière, reste inventive et bien vivante. De nouveaux enjeux sont apparus dans ces dernières années que ce soit du fait de la crise ou avant elle. L'un d'entre eux est à l'évidence le besoin de produire une architecture « plus verte » qu'elle n'était dans la période enfiévrée de conception du Burj Khalifa. Même l'observateur peu averti notera que de plus en plus de réalisations, aussi bien privées que publiques, affichent leurs qualités écologiques et que les architectes sont à la recherche de la moindre possibilité de réduire l'infâme empreinte carbone. Ceci peut entraîner des changements esthétiques, mais l'époque où un immeuble « vert » devait avoir l'air franchement « vert » est passée depuis longtemps. La technologie a évolué et les techniques d'économie d'énergie dites « passives », telles que l'orientation ou le parement d'une façade pour réduire le gain solaire, ne sont plus guère perçues comme des gestes écologiques, même s'ils sont efficaces.

Une éventuelle réponse anticipée à un retournement qui n'a pas encore commencé est une série de projets de petites réalisations comme le Juvet Landscape Hotel (Hôtel-paysage du ravin, Gudbrandsjuvet, Norvège, 2007–09, Jensen & Skodvin Arkitektkontor, page 262). Situé dans le nord-ouest de la Norvège, cet établissement prend la forme d'un ensemble de petites maisons individuelles dressées sur des pilotis de 40 millimètres de côté qui peuvent être donc déplacées sans dommage sérieux à l'environnement naturel. Les touristes découvrent ainsi le paysage naturel à partir d'une résidence écologique qui est l'œuvre de praticiens accomplis. « Le souci actuel de durabilité en architecture se concentre presque exclusivement sur la réduction de la consommation d'énergie dans la production et le fonctionnement », expli-

26

quent les architectes. « Nous pensons que la conservation de la topographie est un autre aspect de la durabilité qui mérite notre attention. » D'autres se sont tournés vers une approche plus radicale du bâti urbain qui fournit peut-être d'autres leçons en cette période de difficultés. RDF181 (Bruxelles, 2007, page 400) est un bureau temporaire de 60 mètres carrés conçu par l'association à but non lucratif Rotor comme une forme de « squat légal » occupant une partie d'un site en attente de permis de constructions plus permanentes. Comme aucun certificat d'urbanisme n'a été demandé pour ce bureau, utilisé par Rotor pendant un ans et que des matériaux de récupération ont servi à sa construction, RDF181 représente certainement un désaveu pour ces autorités qui tendent à compliquer l'acte de construire plutôt que de l'encourager, en particulier dans les villes. De même que les efforts similaires déployés en Espagne par Santi Cirugeda, ce type de structure temporaire parasite peut être considéré à juste titre comme de l'architecture pour époque troublée, même si début 2010, l'horizon semble un peu plus dégagé qu'un an auparavant.

Les grandes agences américaines, britanniques et autres ont certainement réduit leurs effectifs, mais l'architecture inventive ne porte-t-elle pas précisément sur la capacité de s'adapter à de nouvelles conditions, qu'elles soient matérielles ou financières ? S'appuyer sur des produits recyclés ou chercher à réduire la consommation d'énergie pour des raisons écologiques ou financières ne devrait pas être une contrainte stylistique pour les architectes, bien au contraire. Que faites-vous quand le leitmotiv du moment n'est plus « plus haut, plus gros, plus fou » ? *Architecture Now! 7* ne devrait pas décevoir les lecteurs d'*Architecture Now! 6*. Le monde ne s'est pas arrêté de tourner et les architectes n'ont pas cessé d'inventer de nouvelles formes et de nouveaux concepts.

Ce n'est un secret pour personne que les artistes et les architectes ont longtemps entretenu une collaboration aussi bien dans leurs ambitions que dans leurs réalisations. Clairement, de nombreux architectes rêvent d'être des artistes, comme Frank Gehry au début de sa carrière, et les artistes eux aussi réfléchissent aux espaces qu'un bâtiment génère. Une certaine envie mutuelle nourrirait-elle quelques-unes des plus intéressantes créations actuelles dans ces deux domaines ? C'est une des raisons pour lesquelles *Architecture Now! 7*, comme les précédents volumes, contient un certain nombre d'œuvres artistiques ou mieux d'œuvres d'architectes proches de l'art, comme par exemple le Monument du lac de Lusatie (Senftenberg, Allemagne, 2008, Architektur & Landschaft, page 70). Cette tour de trente mètres de haut en acier Corten fait beaucoup penser à l'œuvre d'un sculpteur comme Richard Serra. Ses concepteurs évoquent les ponts typiques de ce vieux pays minier mais ont cherché à créer un « monument » symbolisant la volonté de transformation de cette région. Dans un autre sens, cette tour pourrait aussi être un monument à des gloires passées, ce qui rend son affinité avec la sculpture encore plus claire. Ce n'est pas un hasard si Richard Serra, comme Architektur & Landschaft, fait lui aussi travailler ses épaisses tôles d'acier Corten dans un chantier naval : aucune autre installation industrielle ne serait capable de mener à bien ce type d'intervention. « La différence entre l'art et l'architecture », explique le sculpteur américain, « est que l'art n'a pas de but. » Si une volée de marches et une plate-forme d'observation constituent un but, alors le Monument du lac de Lusatie ne serait pas une pure œuvre d'art mais se situerait certainement à la frontière entre l'art et l'architecture.

27

COMME LES RUINES D'UNE CIVILISATION DISPARUE

Giacomo Costa n'est en aucun cas un architecte. C'est plutôt un photographe qui sait observer le chaos urbain. Ses images photographiques transformées numériquement et récemment publiées sous le titre *The Chronicles of Time* (2009, les Chroniques du temps, page 140) offrent les visions d'un futur apocalyptique qui pourrait effrayer même les piliers de Wall Street. L'architecte Norman Foster a écrit : « Ces portraits de la ville n'apparaissent pas seulement dans l'après 11 septembre, mais dans une période où la menace terroriste reste tapie derrière la normalité de tous les jours. En ces temps troublés, nos pontifes se demandent si et quand ces forces cachées déchaîneront l'Armageddon d'une frappe nucléaire ou d'une attaque biologique. Les visions de Giacomo Costa, dans leurs perspectives infinies et leurs horizons sans limite, sont comme les ruines d'une civilisation disparue qui pourrait être la nôtre. Cette vision puissante nous rappelle par-dessus tout la fragilité de notre univers construit et les bases civiques qui l'ont soutenu jusque là. »[2] Costa n'est pas le seul artiste à s'être inspiré d'une manière ou d'une autre des destructions déchaînées par les événements du 11 septembre 2001 à New York, mais ses ruines semblent encore plus étranges car presque toujours ponctuées de grandes structures énigmatiques qui n'ont pas été anéanties par la violence comme ce qui les entoure. Ce pourrait être aussi une architecture de mauvais augure. En cette période sombre, ces grands immeubles aux fonctions énigmatiques font réfléchir.

Tadashi Kawamata fait également partie de ces artistes qui transgressent les limites habituelles entre sculpture, installation artistique et architecture. Ses constructions, inspirées à l'origine du caractère chaotique et éphémère apparent de Tokyo, sont presque toujours faites de bois et de morceaux de bois recyclé réunis et assemblés par des ouvriers ou des bénévoles locaux. Chacune de ses pièces est un commentaire sur l'environnement architectural, mais aussi sur l'architecture et l'art. Prévues pour être démontées quelques semaines ou mois après leur création, ces installations peuvent parfois se parcourir, se traverser, ou non. Ce dernier cas est illustré par ses récentes Huttes dans les arbres, installées non loin du donjon médiéval de Vez à 70 kilomètres de Paris (2009, page 40). À la différence des cabanes d'enfants, ces structures haut perchées ne pouvaient se visiter. Leur présence énigmatique était comme le rappel d'un passé lointain et même primitif. Alors que les visiteurs venaient surtout pour voir les pierres intemporelles du donjon de Vez, l'artiste japonais avait créé un contrepoint de bric et de broc en bois, volontairement éphémère et apparemment désordonné, sans but apparent, mais représentant néanmoins une des premières formes d'habitat.

À LA RECHERCHE DU PALAIS IDÉAL

Un autre artiste japonais, Shinro Ohtake, vient tout juste d'achever un établissement de bains publics (2009, page 338) dans l'île de Naoshima en Mer intérieure du Japon. Naoshima est le site de nombreux projets de Tadao Ando mais aussi d'une série de « maisons d'art » créées par des artistes connus, dont James Turrell, dans un vieux village de pêcheurs. Ohtake, qui admet avoir été inspiré par David Hockney ou Adolf Wölfli (1864–1930), l'un des premiers artistes rattachés à ce que l'on a appelé l'art brut, se réfère également à Ferdinand Cheval (1836–1924), plus connu sous le nom du Facteur Cheval qui consacra trente-trois années de sa vie à la construction d'une étonnante œuvre d'art et d'architecture naïve appelée le Palais idéal à Hauterives en France. Se servant de toutes sortes d'objets trouvés ou récupérés comme

28

28

28
Yoshioka Tokujin, Waterfall,
Tokyo, Japan, 2005–06

des carreaux de couleur, un cockpit d'aéroplane, un fond de coque de bateau, une statue de petit éléphant venu d'un musée d'érotisme, il planta également des pins sur le toit de sa maison de bains, œuvre d'art qui possédait néanmoins une fonction précise. Utilisée par les habitants de la ville et les visiteurs et gérée come une traditionnelle maison de bains japonaise, la structure édifiée par Ohtake et son décor forment un contraste frappant avec les constructions minimalistes de Tadao Ando qui parsèment l'île. L'œuvre nouvelle souligne le fait qu'une grande partie de l'architecture contemporaine se détache des formes minimalistes pour s'orienter vers une période que l'on pourrait qualifier de complexe et décorative.

VOICI L'AGRI-TECTURE

Une autre discipline qui converge à l'évidence vers l'architecture est celle de l'architecture paysagère, ne serait-ce que parce que le paysage tend à être de plus en plus lié à des constructions ou des groupes de constructions. On peut noter en passant que les livres d'architecture plus traditionnels ont tendance à marquer la frontière entre le paysage et le bâti, de même qu'ils refusent éventuellement d'inclure des œuvres d'art dans leurs panoramas de l'architecture contemporaine. Néanmoins, un des plus remarquables projets récemment réalisés à New York repose sur l'interaction entre un espace planté et son environnement urbain bâti. La High Line (États-Unis, 2006–09, Section 1, James Corner Field Operations/Diller Scofidio + Renfro, page 256) est une ancienne voie ferrée surélevée qui court sur environ 2,5 kilomètres entre le Jacob Javits Convention Center et Gansevoort Street dans le quartier du Meatpacking du Lower West Side de Manhattan. La première phase de ce projet, achevée en 2009, a été confiée à une agence d'architecture (DS+R) associée à une structure spécialisée dans l'aménagement du paysage (James Corner Field Operations). Cette dernière a même inventé un terme pour décrire son intervention : « Modifiant les règles des rapports entre le monde végétal et les piétons, notre stratégie d'agri-tecture combine des matériaux organiques et de construction en un mélange de proportions changeantes qui réunit le sauvage, le cultivé, l'intime et l'hypersocial. » Si ce terme « agri-tecture » risque de ne pas devenir d'emploi fréquent, la plantation de cette voie ferrée et son ouverture au public ont stimulé de nouvelles constructions autour de ce qui était une verrue et une source potentielle de criminalité urbaine. C'est précisément par l'intégration de la conception paysagère et de l'architecture que ce résultat a pu être atteint. Ces deux disciplines, apparemment différentes, sont devenues ici presqu'indissociables.

Un second projet de paysage présenté dans ce volume est Towards Paradise (Vers le paradis, Biennale d'architecture de Venise, 2008, Gustafson Porter/Gustafson Guthrie Nichol, page 182). Installée à la sortie de l'Arsenal, le long de la Porta Nova et du rio delle Vergini, cette œuvre a été créée dans un jardin en grande partie abandonné situé sur le domaine de l'ancien couvent delle Vergini fondé en 1239 et démoli en 1830. Si les architectes paysagistes fournissent des explications assez intellectuelles à leur installation (« Souvenir – le grenier ; Nourrir – abondance ; Éclairer – contemplation »), il reste qu'elle a permis de réintégrer dans le domaine public une partie oubliée de Venise. Alors que les vieux bâtiments de brique du quartier sont presque abandonnés et recouverts d'une dense végétation grimpante, les organisateurs de la Biennale ont peu à peu de plus en plus occupé cet espace à travers leurs installations. S'il aurait pu être également utilisé sans l'intervention de Gustafson Porter, il est certain que ce projet paysager a revitalisé l'architecture, l'a fait redécouvrir et a investi ces « ruines romantiques » d'une nouvelle personnalité publique.

29
*Yoshioka Tokujin, Swarovski Ginza,
Tokyo, Japan, 2006–08*

29

RUSTIQUE, VOLUPTUEUX, LUDIQUE

De même que l'art et l'architecture, le design entretient également des liens avec l'architecture contemporaine. Les projets publiés ci-dessous montrent certaines approches relevant du design pratiquées par un architecte mais aussi celles de designers qui empruntent à l'architecture. L'architecte n'est personne d'autre que Greg Lynn, l'une des stars de la pensée et de l'innovation dans ce domaine aux États-Unis. Son Blobwall et son Toy Furniture (Mobilier en jouets recyclés) publiés ici (2007–08, page 296) s'appuient sur une approche modulaire et la CAO. Ils permettent des divisions spatiales pratiquement variables à l'infini. S'inspirant de son enfance et de la profession de son père qui travaillait pour une entreprise de plastiques, Greg Lynn explique ainsi son système : « À la Renaissance, les palais mélangeaient l'opulence et le basique, l'élégant et le rustique. Les pierres étaient taillées de façon à présenter des faces planes pour assurer un bon appareillage mais leur face extérieure, qui s'exprimait en façade, était rustiquée. Les constructions en jouets recyclées sont rustiques, tout en courbes, globuleuses, moulées, voluptueuses et ludiques. Ce sont des jouets après tout. » Le lien qu'il trace avec l'architecture du passé est intéressant et véhicule un certain message, même s'il n'est pas entièrement convaincant. À travers ces objets bizarres de couleurs éclatantes, Greg Lynn franchit certainement les barrières qui existent encore entre le design (mobilier, aménagements intérieurs) et l'architecture. Avec ces blocs de construction en plastique, il cherche une méthode et une diversité nouvelles dans l'univers standardisé de la construction.

DES CRISTAUX DANS UNE FORÊT

Autre personnage tout aussi intrigant : le designer Yoshioka Tokujin. Très publié mais peu visité son Waterfall Bar (Bar de la cascade, Tokyo, 2006, page 468) se compose de blocs de 4,2 mètres de long taillés dans un type de verre réservé aux télescopes de précision. Tokujin est une sorte de magicien de l'espace et des matériaux et le verre est l'un de ses « blocs de construction » favoris par analogie avec Greg Lynn. Le magasin Swarovski qu'il a récemment conçu à Ginza (Tokyo, 2008, page 462) utilise encore mieux le verre dans le cadre d'un concept de vente imaginé pour la firme de produits de luxe autrichienne. « J'ai recherché dans les forêts l'élément-clé de mon inspiration. J'ai voulu créer une architecture commerciale nouvelle qui fait qu'au moment où il entre dans la boutique, le visiteur se demande s'il ne se trouve pas dans une forêt ornementée de cristaux et de pièces de joaillerie, plutôt que dans un aménagement intérieur de boutique ordinaire. » Là encore, distinctions et barrières se dissolvent. Tokujin se réfère à l'architecture commerciale mais aussi à la « décoration intérieure ». S'il est vrai que les architectes et d'autres ont souvent considéré la décoration comme une forme de création inférieure, certains, comme ce designer japonais semblent vouloir rompre avec cette règle et reprendre la maîtrise de l'espace et de la lumière, qu'elle qu'en soit l'échelle.

TEMPORAIRE CONTEMPORAIN

L'architecture, du moins telle qu'elle a été commentée par John Ruskin et d'autres, a toujours tendu vers davantage de permanence que d'autres formes de création. Même en ruines, les monuments nous parlent encore des siècles passés. Ce sont des productions de l'imagination et de l'ingéniosité des hommes qui ont résisté au temps destructeur. Le grand architecte crée lui aussi pour « éternité », du moins si l'on en croit les légendes. L'architecture contemporaine diffère de celle du passé par son ralliement enthousiaste à l'éphémère. Des villes comme Tokyo ou Los Angeles ne sont pas édifiées pour durer mais pour se modifier et s'adapter sans cesse. Logiquement, leur architecture en est venue à être de plus en plus pensée comme temporaire. Ces deux villes partagent le risque d'être édifiées sur des zones sismiques, ce qui renforce leur vulnérabilité et l'inévitabilité de leur changement. Le Prada Transformer (Séoul, Corée du Sud, 2008–09, page 344) de OMA*AMO/Rem Koolhaas est précisément le type de structure éphémère que le design et les techniques de construction contemporains ont rendu possible. Étant donné que Prada est une entreprise pour laquelle le changement est une condition d'existence, il paraît naturel d'avoir créé pour elle une structure qui non seulement peut se déplacer mais aussi se transformer grâce à des rotations qui modifient sa forme et éventuellement ses fonctions. Par rapport à tous les articles sur les constructions et espaces «flexibles» qui emplissent depuis longtemps les colonnes des journaux d'architecture, voici le premier immeuble réellement capable de se déplacer et de changer de forme.

Il est tout aussi logique qu'une agence de Tokyo, SANAA, ait elle aussi le goût de l'éphémère et son très récent pavillon pour la Serpentine Gallery (Kensington Gardens, Londres, 2009, page 412) de 550 mètres carrés prévu pour ne durer qu'un été montre sa capacité à maîtriser ce type de projet. Dernier avatar d'une série de pavillons conçus par l'élite de l'architecture contemporaine, cette structure se présente essentiellement sous la forme d'un toit de 26 millimètres d'épaisseur en aluminium soutenu par des colonnes d'acier de 50 millimètres de diamètre apparemment implantées au hasard. Les plans découpés et les hauteurs variées de cette toiture ondoyante provoquent des reflets et des distorsions de l'espace. À l'intérieur, le visiteur peut se demander ou commence la «réalité» ou le reflet. Ce type d'ambiguïté visuelle et spatiale est une des marques de SANAA, comme le montre aussi son Musée d'art du XXIe siècle (Kanazawa, Ishikawa, Japon, 2002–04). Elle achevait un nouveau chantier pour l'École polytechnique fédérale de Lausanne en Suisse, au moment de mettre ce livre sous presse. Là encore, un espace ondoyant sans contraintes et de beaucoup plus grande échelle qu'à Londres se joue des les frontières entre ce qui est fixe et permanent ou en mouvement. L'immeuble de l'EPFL ne possède presqu'aucun mur intérieur mais des vitrages toute hauteur en périphérie, concept qui bouscule à la fois les aspects techniques de l'architecture et son usage par les étudiants (Rolex Learning Center, EPFL, Lausanne, Suisse, 2007–09, page 418). À leur façon apparemment pleine de douceur, les architectes de SANAA remettent en cause certaines des idées les plus basiques de l'architecture contemporaine.

L'architecte basée à Londres Zaha Hadid, qui a remporté en 2009 le Praemium Imperiale, s'intéresse depuis longtemps au design mais aussi aux structures temporaires. Son JS Bach/Zaha Hadid Architects Music Hall (Manchester, Grande-Bretagne, 2009, page 190) consiste en un «volumineux ruban» qui «se déroule à travers la salle, pour offrir une réponse visuelle et spatiale aux relations complexes des harmonies de Bach». Composé d'une membrane en tissu translucide tendue sur une structure en acier, ce «ruban» se complète de panneaux acoustiques en acrylique transparent suspendus au-dessus de la scène. Un éclairage et des enregistrements sonores diffusés hors des heures des concerts font également partie de l'installation. Prévue pour être transportée et installée dans des lieux similaires, cette réalisation manifeste une fois de plus les audacieux efforts de Zaha Hadid pour développer les possibilités de l'architecture contemporaine au-delà des formes fixes et rectilignes qui caractérisaient encore toute nouvelle construction il y a quelques années. Son travail porte sur la «fluidification» de l'espace. Ses volumes sont des flux qui s'interpénètrent sans rupture apparente. Zaha Hadid a également réalisé des projets, comme son récent bar pour Home House (Londres, 2007–08) dans des espaces existants. Là, il s'agissait d'une salle à décor de style géorgien dont

30
SANAA/Kazuyo Sejima + Ryue
Nishizawa, Serpentine Pavilion,
Kensington Gardens, London, UK,
2009

l'espace a été transformé par l'implantation d'un bar en résine, fibre de verre et tissu. « Une dichotomie se produit dans Home House, entre ce nouveau langage formel morphologique », explique l'architecte, « et les forces dynamiques de la programmation orthogonale caractéristique de son enveloppe géorgienne. » Comme Kazuyo Sejima, son équivalent chez SANAA, Zaha Hadid a atteint au plus haut niveau de l'architecture internationale et apporté une nouvelle vision du projet et même de la construction. Il serait sans doute inapproprié de parler « d'architecture féminine » et pourtant la subtilité, l'ambiguïté et la fluidité présentes dans leur travail rompt d'une certaine façon avec l'univers architectural qui a pu engendrer la tour de Burj Khalifa.

MOUVEMENT SOUTERRAIN

Deux projets présents dans cet ouvrage utilisent le sous-sol de façon inattendue. La tentation de recycler les zones inutilisées d'une ville est peut-être un signe des temps, mais c'est aussi l'occasion de reformuler l'usage d'un patrimoine industriel ou historique qui a perdu son sens. Rand Elliott est une sorte d'exception pour *Architecture Now!*, car il vit dans un État américain – l'Oklahoma – qui ne produit guère d'architecture contemporaine remarquable. Son agence a reçu dix prix d'honneur nationaux de l'AIA et reste la seule en Oklahoma à avoir jamais reçu cette distinction. Son Underground (Souterrain, Oklahoma City, Oklahoma, 2007, page 146) est une rénovation de 3900 mètres carrés d'une série de tunnels qui relie 23 immeubles du centre de la ville. Creusés en 1931, ils étaient pratiquement abandonnés et l'intervention d'Elliott – à base de musiques, de lumières et de galeries de photo historiques à thème – leur a redonné une utilité. Si la distinction entre architecture et décoration est peut-être délicate à établir dans cet exemple, il est vrai que le son et la lumière ont fait une entrée remarquée dans le vocabulaire des immeubles contemporains. Les espaces souterrains, où l'éclairage naturel n'est pas ou peu disponible, peuvent aussi se voir définis et reformulés par des outils immatériels. Même si cet Underground n'a pas à être comparé à une œuvre d'art, il est vrai que des artistes comme James Turrell ont montré que la lumière pouvait devenir un matériau quasi palpable, en mesure de trouver de nouveaux emplois dans l'architecture contemporaine.

Le projet Bahnhof Pionen (Stockholm, 2007–08, page 158) de l'architecte français Albert France-Lanord représente une approche très différente pour un espace là aussi essentiellement souterrain, ancien abri anti atomique creusé à 30 mètres sous le parc de Vita Berg. Le client est un fournisseur des services Internet qui y a installé ses salles d'informatique et ses bureaux. L'architecte a cherché à varier autant que possible les sources lumineuses pour éviter le sentiment de claustrophobie qu'un tel cadre aurait pu provoquer. Cet espace curieux, isolé de son contexte urbain, non sans quelques allusions à la Guerre froide, fait penser au décor d'un film de James Bond. « Ce fut une expérience passionnante de travailler sur un espace qui, au départ, n'offrait pas un seul angle droit mais du rocher. La salle principale n'est pas un volume traditionnel limité par des surfaces, mais plutôt un vide dans une masse », explique l'architecte.

Curieusement, les espaces souterrains semblent davantage reliés à l'architecture industrielle qu'au type de mise en forme de volumes qui caractérise l'architecture contemporaine de qualité. Même dans des villes comme Tokyo, dans son labyrinthe souterrain de gares et de centres commerciaux traité en grande partie sans inspiration, certains progrès ont été accomplis à travers des projets comme la gare de Shibuya de la ligne de métro Tokyu Toyoko (Shibuya-ku, Tokyo, 2006–08, page 29). Cette gare souterraine de 22 725 mètres carrés en forme

31
Steven Holl, HEART: Herning Museum
of Contemporary Art, Herning,
Denmark, 2007–09

31

d'œuf en béton renforcé de fibre de verre (GFRC) bénéficie d'une ventilation naturelle bien qu'elle soit profondément enfouie sous le sol de la capitale japonaise. D'autres exemples de cette sorte abondent et montrent que les architectes contemporains ne cessent de faire des incursions dans des domaines d'où ils avaient été en grande partie exclus dans le passé. On a compris que les architectes peuvent créer des espaces attractifs et pratiques alors que les ingénieurs généralement en charge des stations de métro pensent principalement en termes de gestion des déplacements de trains et de foules dans des espaces les plus réduits et les moins coûteux à réaliser.

L'ART ET LE BÂTI

Il est sans doute probable que les circonstances économiques amèneront à réduire les investissements dans les constructions de musées et autres installations liées à la vie culturelle. Et pourtant, ce domaine a offert aux architectes, de Zaha Hadid à David Chipperfield, les plus belles et plus étonnantes opportunités de créer des lieux qui ont marqué l'imagination populaire. Le Musée Guggenheim de Frank Gehry à Bilbao reste la référence lorsque l'on pense à une architecture « qui chante et qui danse » et qui attire également les foules, mais l'essor de la construction de musées dans le monde s'est peut-être calmé. Il existe tant de nouveaux musées qu'un pays comme le Japon ou d'autres comme les États-Unis ont atteint un certain niveau de maturité, ou de saturation. Néanmoins, on peut encore noter de nombreuses institutions nouvelles qui ont récemment ouvert leurs portes. L'architecte new-yorkais Steven Holl a été particulièrement actif dans le domaine des musées et a achevé en 2009 deux bâtiments culturels remarquables en Scandinavie, le HEART (Musée d'art contemporain d'Herning, Danemark, 2007–09, page 216) et le Knut Hamsun Center (Hamarøy, Norvège, 2006–09, page 222). Le premier associe divers équipements pour les arts plastiques et la musique et illustre la complexité subtile pour laquelle l'architecte s'est fait connaître. Steven Holl est également fréquemment intervenu sur le paysage autour de ses réalisations. Pour le musée Herning, il a créé 3700 mètres carrés de « paysage de bermes de monticules d'herbe et de bassins » qui dissimulent un parking et des installations techniques. Le Knut Hamsun Center a été édifié en souvenir d'un des plus célèbres écrivains norvégiens. Il se trouve au-dessus du cercle polaire près de la ferme ou il a grandi. S'appuyant sur l'exemple des églises de la région et utilisant au mieux les conditions particulières de l'éclairage naturel, l'architecte a créé un bâtiment qui honore à la fois l'œuvre de l'auteur et les nombreux films inspirés par ses livres.

L'Artfarm (Ferme d'art, Salt Point, New York, États-Unis, 2007–08, page 210) des architectes suisses HHF en collaboration avec l'artiste chinois Ai Wei Wei est de nature entièrement différente de celle des grands musées qui ont marqué la chronique de l'architecture contemporaine depuis tant d'années. Conçu sous forme d'un volume hermétiquement clos recouvert de PVC d'isolation blanc brillant, le bâtiment est en fait un hangar sophistiqué, conçu pour résister aux importantes fluctuations de température saisonnières de l'État de New York. Inspiré en partie de l'architecture industrielle, l'Artfarm montre qu'une architecture d'avant-garde peut être d'apparence assez simple, même en termes de définition des espaces. Le lieu est d'abord conçu pour l'art chinois qu'il contient, ce qui représente, là aussi, une réponse plus mature aux relations entre l'art et l'architecture que certains gros nuages de titanes qui ont marqué le paysage muséal de ces dernières années.

D'une échelle similaire, la Villa Navarra de Rudy Ricciotti (Le Muy, France, 2007, page 384) illustre une autre approche de la façon dont un bâtiment peut servir à exposer des œuvres d'art. L'architecte et son fils, l'ingénieur Romain Ricciotti, ont ici fait l'expérience d'un remar-

32
*Steven Holl, Knut Hamsun Center,
Hamarøy, Norway, 2006–09*

32

quable toit en porte-à-faux constitué de 17 panneaux de béton Ductal de 9, 25 x 2, 35 mètres chacun et de 3 centimètres d'épaisseur. Le Ductal est un béton renforcé de fibres fabriqué par Lafarge et qui résiste aux tensions qu'un tel toit en porte-à-faux doit affronter. Ayant déjà utilisé ce matériau dans un projet de pont, l'architecte maîtrise ses possibilités et s'en sert pour ses projets inhabituels et novateurs. Un autre aspect étonnant de ce lieu d'art est qu'il ne sera pas ouvert au public, mais utilisé pour des expositions liées à l'Internet.

L'architecte de Los Angeles Eric Owen Moss a toujours emprunté une démarche sculpturale ou artistique dans ses projets de rénovation pour Culver City en Californie. Il vient d'y réaliser tout récemment une Art Tower (Tour d'art, 2007–09, page 320), équipement de 22 mètres de haut dressé à l'intersection de Hayden Avenue et du National Boulevard à l'entrée de la partie de Culver City pour laquelle il a tant fait depuis des années. La tour affiches des informations évènementielles culturelles et locales. Faite de cinq anneaux d'acier empilés de neuf mètres de diamètre environ, elle est équipée d'écrans acryliques de projection à chaque niveau, où des plates-formes accueillent également les visiteurs. Dans l'esprit du Monument du lac de Lusatie cité plus haut, cette structure sculpturale pourrait pratiquement être considérée comme une œuvre d'art en soi. Moss a souvent emprunté ses matériaux aux entrepôts voisins dont il a fait des sortes d'extrusions en leur donnant un aspect dynamique et artistique décalé par rapport aux structures préexistantes banales. La Tour d'art est un pas supplémentaire dans cette démarche : faire une nouvelle construction qui est en quelque sorte un monument à l'œuvre que l'architecte et le promoteur (Samitaur Consructs) réalisent pour revitaliser Culver City, un des anciens centres de l'industrie cinématographique.

À SUIVRE EN ASIE

La résidence privée reste un passage préféré pour la créativité des architectes partout dans le monde, en particulier là où les conditions économiques permettent à certains d'accumuler suffisamment de richesse pour s'offrir une maison qui sorte de l'ordinaire. Depuis quelque temps, la Corée du Sud a montré des signes prometteurs dans le domaine de l'architecture à travers les réalisations d'un certain nombre de talents formés sur place qui ont attiré l'attention internationale. L'un d'entre eux est Byoung-soo Cho, né à Séoul en 1957. Installé à Séoul il a étudié à la Montana State University (Bozeman, Montana, B.Arch en 1986) et a obtenu deux mastères en architecture et en urbanisme à la GSD d'Harvard en 1991. Sa Three Box House de 494 mètres carrés (Maison en trois boîtes, Paju, Gyeonggi-do, Corée du Sud, 2005–06, page 122) témoigne d'un sens raffiné de la simplicité. Reposant sur un concept de trois boîtes réunies par un écran horizontal et des terrasses en bois, cette maison respecte une composition stricte en rectangles mais avec un sens de l'esthétique et une habileté dans la juxtaposition de blocs opaques et transparents qui semblent authentiquement nouveaux. Pour l'architecte : « Ce projet est simple et direct, il s'inspire de la matérialité industrielle et agricole du Montana » même si l'on ne voit pas beaucoup de rapports avec l'inventivité architecturale assez discrète de cet État américain.

Alors que Byoung-soo Cho paraît sensible à la force d'un vocabulaire relativement minimaliste, un de ses concitoyens, HyoMan Kim, diplômé de l'Université de Dankook (Séoul, 1978), cherche à créer des œuvres dont la « nature architecturale est d'être un lieu de récréation ». Son Island House (Maison-île, Gapyung-gun, Gyeonggi-do, Corée du Sud, 2007–09, page 238) est une étonnante résidence en bordure d'une rivière, dotée d'une vaste cour noyée d'eau et qui fait presque penser de loin à un bateau. Bien que la ligne droite y règne, le plan et

33
Rudy Ricciotti, Villa Navarra,
Le Muy, France, 2007

33

l'aspect général sont assez irréguliers en écho au souhait de l'architecte d'intégrer la maison dans son cadre naturel mais aussi d'une certaine façon d'en faire un élément de ce cadre. Du même architecte, mais moins grande, la Purple Hill House (Maison de la colline pourpre, Youngin, Gyeonggi-do, Corée du Sud, 2009, page 14) dont la forme évoque celle des montagnes voisines de GwangGyo. L'orientant vers le nord-ouest pour des raisons tenant au site et à la vue, l'architecte a condamné sa maison à ne recevoir qu'une faible lumière directe, problème résolu par une série de boîtes de verre qui pénètrent dans son volume. Ici, comme dans la Island House, HyoMan Kim montre une propension à la complexité qui s'exprime dans cette composition cristalline de lignes droites juxtaposées selon des rapports complexes.

Bien que stylistiquement différents – Byoung-soo Cho préférant les plans et une esthétique relativement simples et HyoMan Kim ayant opté pour des compositions à facettes – ces deux architectes sont représentatifs d'une nouvelle et dynamique école internationale qui pourrait rivaliser avec l'inventivité du Japon voisin. Cette tendance est alimentée par une longue période de croissance économique malgré certaines crises financières passagères. Là encore, cependant, ce qui compte réellement est la capacité des architectes à inventer des formes nouvelles. Même s'ils sont contraints à dépenser moins et à réaliser des projets moins importants, des personnalités aussi créatives seront certainement des architectes avec qui compter dans les années à venir.

Un autre architecte asiatique de capacités remarquables est Sou Fujimoto, né en 1971 et formé à Tokyo. C'est l'un des plus prolifiques et plus talentueux membres de la nouvelle génération des architectes japonais et ses réalisations s'attaquent souvent à des enjeux fondamentaux comme les limites entre la maison et la ville. Sa House H (Maison H) (Tokyo, 2008–09, page 176) a été pensée comme une maison dans un arbre, les murs, les sols et les plafonds s'ouvrant les uns dans les autres par un système de plans vitrés. « Grâce à des matériaux artificiels et à un ordre géométrique strict », explique Fujimoto, « la succession de vides en connexion engendre un champ de relations plus important. Ce concept de maison est proche de celui d'un grand arbre, développe une ambiguïté de nature arboricole dans sa connexion avec l'extérieur, et propose un prototype d'une solution d'habitat/ville pour le futur. » Sa récente Final Wooden House (Maison de bois définitive, Kumamura, Kumamoto, 2007, 08, page 33) est un empilement « sans ordre » de pièces de bois de section carrée de 35 centimètres de côté. « J'ai recherché une spatialité nouvelle qui préserve les conditions primitives d'une entité harmonieuse avant de prendre en compte les diverses fonctions et la différenciation des rôles », précise-t-il. On ne trouve ni séparations, ni sols, ni vrais mur ou plafonds dans cette maison qui laisse ses habitants « se distribuer eux-mêmes dans les trois dimensions de l'espace ». Les sols deviennent des murs, ou des sièges, dit-il amenant les visiteurs à repenser l'idée même de maison. « Plutôt qu'une simple architecture nouvelle », conclut-il, « c'est une nouvelle origine, une nouvelle existence. » Bien que la Maison H soit réellement conçue pour être habitée et que la Maison en bois définitive ne le soit pas, Fujimoto explore les limites de l'espace résidentiel et remet en cause ses fondamentaux d'une façon rarement pratiquée par les architectes d'autres pays. C'est décidément un architecte à suivre.

QUE SER(R)A SER(R)A

À l'autre bout du monde, Susanne Nobis, née en 1963 et formée à Londres et Munich, vient d'achever la résidence Walls in the Landscape (Murs dans le paysage) à Grossburgwedel (Allemagne, 2006–07, page 324). Composition asymétrique de formes de plan rectangulai-

34
Supersudaka, Kiltro House,
Talca, Chile, 2006–08

34

re, cette maison se caractérise par de grands murs en acier Corten. Ces tôles d'acier rappellent inévitablement les imposantes sculptures de Richard Serra et en fait, malgré ses dimensions relativement réduites, elle possède une force brutale qui contraste avec de grandes parois vitrées et son cadre naturel. L'intérêt critique de ce projet est d'illustrer qu'il n'existe ni logique ni style dans les maisons contemporaines. Leur esthétique et leur fonctionnalisme dépendent de la très grande variété de styles pratiquée actuellement dans le monde. Si un minimalisme strict semble être passé de mode, et qu'apparaît une complexité presque extravagante, en Asie en particulier, d'autres approches conservent leur valeur. Susanne Nobis a travaillé au Renzo Piano Building Workshop (Gênes, 1992–93) et avec Herzog & de Meuron (Munich, 1994–95) avant de créer sa propre agence. Ces deux agences approchent la modernité par un pragmatisme de nature similaire. La Fondation Beyeler de Piano à Riehen (Bâle, Suisse, 1991–97) organise un contraste similaire entre de puissants murs parés de pierre et des grands plans vitrés qui font face aux champs s'étendant entre la Fondation et la frontière allemande. On observe une certaine logique classique dans ces Walls in the Landscape qui rend leur modernité presque intemporelle.

BIENTÔT DANS LES NUAGES

De récents développements dans les technologies de l'informatique ont conduit à ce que l'on a appelé « La bataille des nuages ». Des entreprises comme Microsoft ou Google cherchent dominer les service offerts par Internet « où les documents, les e-mails et autres données seront stockés en ligne, les rendant accessible de n'importe quel PC ou appareil mobile ».[3] Il est intéressant de noter que cette course à la puissance des technologies exerce également un impact sur la création de firmes ou d'organisations que l'on ne sait plus comment classer. C'est le cas de Supersudaka, basée à Talca au Chili, mais qui s'étend à travers ses sites au-delà des frontières et des disciplines (www.super-sudaka.cl et www.supersudaca.org). Supersudaca (avec un « c ») se présente comme un « groupe de réflexion sur l'architecture et la recherche urbaine », tandis que Supersudaka (avec un « k ») accueille par cette prise de position : « Nous ne voulons pas changer le monde par l'architecture, nous voulons changer l'architecture par le monde. » La maison Kiltro (Talca, Chili, 2006–08, page 450) est l'une des réalisations de ce groupe dirigé au Chili par Juan Pablo Corvalán et Gabriel Vergara. Kiltro est un mot d'argot chilien qui signifie « chien bâtard », même si cette maison semble faire preuve de logique et de quelque raffinement. Les plans à facettes et le bois peuvent rappeler l'œuvre de HyoMan Kim, bien que dans un cadre et avec une matérialité très différents. À cet instant, bien que les caractéristiques nationales jouent encore un rôle essentiel dans de nombreux projets architecturaux, nous sommes entrés dans l'ère du « nuage » architectural, qui regroupe des contributions venues du monde entier. Pour des raisons qui lui sont propres, Supersudaka ne donne que l'adresse électronique de Juan Pablo Corvalán à l'université de Talca. Pas de bureaux où s'alignent de jeunes architectes tous vêtus de noir, mais plutôt un réseau de participants actifs qui peuvent se trouver n'importe où.

UN PONT VERS L'AUTRE RIVE

De même que les limites entre l'architecture et d'autres disciplines comme l'art ou le design semblent se dissoudre, le fossé souvent infranchissable entre architectes et ingénieurs va peut-être se refermer. Un certain nombre de projets publiés dans *Architecture Now! 7* sont

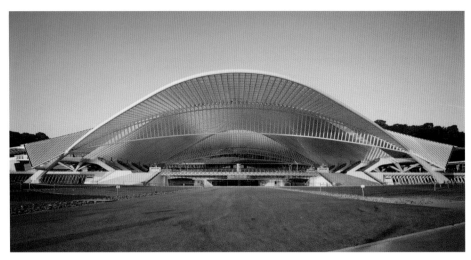

35

l'œuvre d'ingénieurs ou s'appuient fortement sur leur participation directe. Une personnalité aussi à l'aise dans un domaine que dans l'autre que Santiago Calatrava a récemment achevé une spectaculaire gare de TGV, celle de Liège-Guillemins (Liège, Belgique, 1996–2009, page 132) sur la ligne entre Paris, Bruxelles et Cologne. L'architecte-ingénieur d'origine espagnole a créé un terminal pour passagers de 200 mètres de long implanté symétriquement par rapport à un axe nord-ouest/sud-est. Le toit voûté du bâtiment s'étend au-dessus de cinq quais sur 145 mètres supplémentaires. Une voûte monumentale en verre et acier permet à cette gare de s'ouvrir entièrement sur la ville. Des passerelles piétonnières et un passage sous les voies facilitent la fluidité de la communication entre les deux côtés de la gare. Calatrava avait auparavant déjà conçu des gares futuristes pour Lisbonne et l'aéroport de Lyon-Saint Exupéry et cette nouvelle implantation fait entrer dans le XXIe siècle une partie du réseau ferré européen un peu délaissée.

L'un des plus célèbres ingénieurs du monde, Cecil Balmond, président de l'agence d'ingénierie multidisciplinaire Arup depuis 2004 et fondateur de l'Advanced Geometry Unit AGU, Agence de géométrie avancée au sein d'Arup, a récemment achevé le UPENN Weave Bridge (pont tissé) à Philadelphie en 2009 (Pennsylvanie, États-Unis, page 88). Une des particularités de cet ouvrage est d'apparaître comme assez simple alors qu'il fait appel à une structure porteuse toute nouvelle en forme de double-hélice. Élément d'un plan directeur sur lequel Balmond est intervenu pour dynamiser le campus de l'Université de Pennsylvanie, ce pont montre que les structures les plus inventives peuvent parfois paraître relativement banales aux yeux du non-initié. Peut-être aussi, cela tient-il à la période : l'architecture (et l'ingénierie) doivent faire montre de plus de modestie après une longue période de nouveautés extravagantes.

En fait, des constructions extravagantes continuent à s'élever à la surface du globe et la Tour d'observation et de télévision de Guangzhou (Guangzhou, Chine, 2005–10, page 228) due à l'agence néerlandaise Information Based Architecture en est une preuve tangible. D'une hauteur de 610 mètres, elle ne surpasse cependant pas celle du Burj Khalifa. Sa forme effilée et torsadée est un festival d'ingénierie et sera le signal des Jeux d'Asie prévus non loin en 2010. Si l'ingénierie joue un rôle indiscutable dans la conception d'une telle construction, on peut dire que les raisons de s'élever aussi haut n'étaient pas seulement liées aux nécessités de la diffusion de la télévision même si la hauteur présente des avantages dans ce domaine. Il y avait certainement une part d'orgueil dans la pensée de ce client et, pourquoi pas, également dans celle des architectes. Ma tour est plus haute que la tienne …

50°C AU-DESSOUS DE ZÉRO ET PAS DE CARBONE

Une ingénierie d'un type différent a joué un rôle fondamental dans la conception de la surprenante station antarctique princesse Elizabeth (Utsteinen, 71°57'S–23°20'E, Dronning Maud Land, Antarctique oriental, 2007–09, page 232). Œuvre de la Fondation polaire internationale, cette station marque la présence belge dans l'Antarctique de façon convaincante et profondément moderne. Située à une altitude de 1300 mètres en un lieu où les température varient entre -50°C et -5°C et où les vents atteignent 250 km/h, la station est la première de ce type à afficher zéro émission de carbone. Elle opère grâce à des sources d'énergie renouvelable et des protocoles d'efficacité énergétique particulièrement affûtés. Bien que ce soit avant tout un objet technique, cette structure n'est pas sans aspects esthétiques par sa présence scintillante au bout du monde.

35
Santiago Calatrava, Liège-Guillemins
TGV Station, Liège, Belgium,
1996–2009

UNE ARCHITECTURE JUSTE

L'exploration de la calotte glaciaire polaire est certainement un objectif valable, en particulier en ces temps de réchauffement global, mais il est vrai que l'architecture contemporaine de qualité n'est que rarement mise au service de ceux qui en auraient le plus besoin. Une exception notable à cette règle nous est offerte par l'œuvre de l'architecte sud-africain Peter Rich, dont les deux plus récents projets, le Centre d'héritage d'Alexandra (Johannesburg, Gauteng, Afrique du Sud, 2004–09, page 390) et le Centre d'interprétation de Mapungubwe (Parc national de Mapungubwe, Limpopo, Afrique du Sud, 2007–09, page 396) sont publiés dans ce volume. Peter, Rich, né à Johannesburg en 1945, a été professeur à l'Université du Witwatersrand pendant 30 ans. Il a étudié l'iconographie et l'architecture africaines et en particulier celles des Ndebele. Le Centre d'Alexandra est situé face à une ancienne résidence de Nelson Mandela mais est d'abord une vitrine des arts, de la culture et du patrimoine de la région présentée ici de façon digne et moderne. Étant donnée la pauvreté environnante, le bâtiment se détache de son environnement mais s'y adapte de façon remarquable dans le même temps. Peter Rich explique : « Le projet participe à la construction d'un sentiment communautaire et apporte des solutions à la pauvreté en proposant aux habitants des formations au tourisme et au patrimoine, en encourageant de petites entreprises et en présentant les arts, la culture et le patrimoine locaux. » En liaison directe avec la rue par des rampes, le plan à cour du bâtiment cherche à utiliser chaque mètre carré du terrain tout en évoquant les traditions locales. L'adaptabilité de l'œuvre de Peter Rich se constate également dans son centre de Mapungubwe. Ses voûtes en coque mince font écho à « la révélation de cultures du passé » que le parc national dans lequel il se trouve est chargé de protéger. Peter Rich ne s'est pas engagé dans la création d'un pastiche mais plutôt dans l'adaptation de matériaux et de formes locaux à un usage très contemporain pour redonner dignité et accessibilité à des cultures qui n'avaient pas bénéficié d'une telle attention depuis longtemps.

Les barrières qui séparent l'architecture contemporaine d'autres disciplines comme le design ou l'ingénierie, s'abaissent. Certains peuvent dire qu'elles n'ont jamais vraiment existé puisque l'architecture du paysage ou l'art ont fait implicitement partie de l'architecture depuis des siècles. Si les fondateurs du Bauhaus ont activement cherché, eux aussi, à créer « une œuvre d'art totale » (Gesamtkunstwerk), la réalité des temps modernes a été différente, les cercles académiques séparant souvent avec fermeté des disciplines aussi objectivement liées que l'architecture et l'ingénierie. Des figures comme Santiago Calatrava, qui est aussi un artiste, ont beaucoup fait pour prouver que la créativité est à son sommet quand elle se moque des divisions artificielles établies au bénéfice de quelques-uns. Les magazines d'art ou d'architecture, comme de nombreux créateurs, tendent encore clairement à faire la distinction entre ce qui est architecture et ce qui est art. On doit en effet être formé pour concevoir des constructions alors que les artistes disposent d'une liberté innée que certains, comme Frank Gehry à ses débuts, ont mis en pratique. Gehry, lui aussi, a contribué à abaisser ces barrières, même lorsque ses réalisations semblent plus attentives à l'esthétique qu'à la fonction.

VERT ET BEAU

L'architecture suit des cycles de construction relativement longs, en particulier pour les projets importants. Ainsi *Architecture Now! 7* ne peut pas entièrement prendre en compte l'impact de la crise économique récente. Peut-être émergeront des tendances qui conduiront les

36
Peter Rich, Alexandra Heritage Center, Johannesburg, Gauteng, South Africa, 2004–09

37
Rand Elliott, Underground, Oklahoma City, Oklahoma, USA, 2007

36   37

architectes, et d'abord leurs clients, à réfléchir à des constructions plus petites et moins coûteuses. D'autres, comme la nécessité de contrôler les émissions de CO_2 et de réduire la consommation d'énergie, ont certainement été renforcées par le retournement économique. Réduire la consommation d'énergie diminue du même coup les factures d'électricité et deviendra donc sans doute un facteur de plus en plus important dans les années à venir. Les progrès technologiques vont améliorer l'efficacité de sources d'énergie comme les cellules photovoltaïques et la possibilité à les insérer discrètement dans des fenêtres ou d'autres parties des bâtiments. Certains des bâtiments les plus « durables » dissimulent cette qualité alors que beaucoup de constructions « vertes » des débuts semblaient tout droit sorties de l'imagination de communautés hippies des années 1960. La préoccupation écologique est là pour longtemps et l'architecture contemporaine l'intègrera bientôt dans le gros de sa production, plus encore qu'elle ne l'a fait à ce jour.

Il est peut-être vrai que des immeubles aussi extravagants que le Burj Khalifa appartiennent déjà au passé, du moins pour l'instant. Ces monuments sont le produit d'une époque d'euphorie économique, mais n'ont peut-être pas vraiment de valeur pratique. Les symboles demeureront et d'autres seront créés, quels qu'ils soient, même s'ils sont plus modestes que le « perce-ciel » imaginé par Adrian Smith. Et même si la plupart des réalisations présentées dans *Architecture Now! 7* ont pris naissance dans une période d'euphorie, elles sont suffisamment convaincantes pour répondre au critique pour lequel « ce fut magnifique tant que ça a duré ».[4] Les progrès que l'on voit aujourd'hui de plus en plus souvent intégrés à l'architecture contemporaine comprennent la capacité à concevoir et à produire des pièces ou éléments uniques grâce à la CAO et à la MOCN. Ce fait en soi rend possible la construction de bâtiments dont les critiques d'architecture ne pouvaient que rêver au bon temps d'une consommation sans entrave. L'architecture reste bien vivante. Now !

Philip Jodidio, Grimentz, 21 octobre 2009

[1] http://lookingaround.blogs.time.com/2009/04/29/the-end-of-the-world-as-we-know-it/ consulté le 20 octobre 2009.
[2] Norman Foster, « Avant-propos, » *The Chronicles of Time*, Bologne, Damiani, 2008.
[3] « Battle of the Clouds », *The Economist*, 17 octobre 2009.
[4] http://lookingaround.blogs.time.com/2009/04/29/the-end-of-the-world-as-we-know-it/ consulté le 20 octobre 2009.

EMILIO AMBASZ

Emilio Ambasz & Associates, Inc.
200 West 90th Street, Suite 11A, New York, NY 10024, USA
Tel: +1 212 580 3263 / Fax: +1 212 580 3218
E-mail: info@ambasz.com / Web: www.ambasz.com

EMILIO AMBASZ was born in 1943 in Argentina, and studied at Princeton University. He completed the undergraduate program in one year and received an M.Arch from the same institution the next year. He taught at Princeton University's School of Architecture, was a Visiting Professor at the Hochschule für Gestaltung in Ulm, Germany, and has lectured at several American universities. Ambasz served as Curator of Design at the Museum of Modern Art in New York (1970–76) and was a two-term President of the Architectural League (1981–85). Founded in 1976, Emilio Ambasz & Associates, Inc., offers a full range of design services, including building design, consulting, lighting, landscape, exhibition, graphic, and product design. Ambasz states: "It is my deep belief that design is an act of invention. I believe that its real task begins once functional and behavioral needs have been satisfied. It is not hunger, but love and fear, and sometimes wonder, which make us create. Our milieu may change from generation to generation, but the task, I believe, remains the same: to give poetic form to the pragmatic." His projects include Nichii Obihiro Department Store (Hokkaido, Japan, 1987, unbuilt); Lucille Halsell Conservatory at the San Antonio Botanical Center (San Antonio, Texas, USA, 1988); Mycal Sanda Cultural and Athletic Center (Hyogo Prefecture, Japan, 1990–94); and Fukuoka Prefectural International Hall (Fukuoka, Japan, 1995, winner of the 2001 DuPont Benedictus Award). More recently, he has built the Nuova Concordia Residential and Hotel Complex in Apulia (2001–03); the Casa de Retiro Espiritual (Casa de Cordoba, Seville, Spain, 1975/2003–05); an Advanced Ophthalmological Research Laboratory (Banca dell'Occhio, Venice-Mestre, 2003–08, published here); and a 680-bed hospital (Ospedale dell'Angelo, Venice-Mestre, 2005–08, also published here), all in Italy unless stated otherwise.

Der 1943 in Argentinien geborene **EMILIO AMBASZ** studierte Architektur in Princeton, wo er binnen eines Jahres sein Grundstudium absolvierte und bereits im Jahr darauf mit dem M.Arch abschloss. Ambasz lehrte an der School of Architecture der Princeton University, war Gastprofessor an der Hochschule fur Gestaltung in Ulm und lehrte an verschiedenen amerikanischen Universitäten. Von 1970 bis 1976 war Ambasz Kurator für Design am Museum of Modern Art in New York, zweimal amtierte er als Präsident der Architectural League of New York (1981-85). Sein 1976 gegründetes Büro Emilio Ambasz & Associates, Inc. offeriert die unterschiedlichsten Dienstleistungen in Sachen Design, vom Entwurf und der Architekturberatung über Landschaftsgestaltung, Lichtkonzeption und Ausstellungsplanung bis hin zu grafischen Konzepten und Produktdesign. Ambasz selbst erklärt: „Ich bin davon überzeugt, dass Design vor allem mit Erfinden zu tun hat. Ist die Anforderung nach Funktionalität und Handhabbarkeit erfüllt, beginnt in meinen Augen erst die eigentliche Aufgabe des Designs. Nicht der Hunger, sondern die Liebe und die Angst – und manchmal das Staunen – machen uns kreativ. Unsere Unwelt mag sich in jeder Generation verändern, aber die Aufgabe bleibt meiner Ansicht nach stets die gleiche: dem Praktischen eine poetische Form zu verleihen." Zu Ambasz' Projekten gehören das Kaufhaus Nichii Obihiro (Hokkaido, Japan, 1987, nicht realisiert), das Lucille-Halsell-Gewächshaus im Botanischen Garten von San Antonio (Texas, USA, 1988), das Kultur- und Sportzentrum Mycal Sanda (Präfektur Hyogo, Japan, 1990–94) und die Fukuoka Prefectural International Hall (Fukuoka, Japan, 1995), für die Ambasz 2001 den DuPont Benedictus Award erhielt. Zuletzt entstanden die Wohn- und Hotelanlage Nuova Concordia in Apulien (Italien, 2001–03), die Casa de Retiro Espiritual bei Sevilla (Spanien, 1975/2003–05) und die beiden hier vorgestellten Bauten in Venedig-Mestre (Italien), die Banca dell'Occhio, ein Forschungsinstitut für Augenheilkunde (2003–08) und das 680-Betten-Krankenhaus Ospedale dell'Angelo (2005–08).

Né en 1943 en Argentine, **EMILIO AMBASZ** a étudié à Princeton University. Il y a accompli ses études de licence en un an et obtenu son mastère en architecture l'année suivante. Il a enseigné à l'École d'architecture de Princeton, a été professeur invité à la Hochschule für Gestaltung d'Ulm (Allemagne), et a donné des cours dans plusieurs universités américaines. Conservateur pour le design au Musée d'art moderne de New York (1970–76), il a présidé l'Architectural League pendant deux mandats (1981–85). Fondée en 1976, l'agence Emilio Ambasz & Associates, Inc. offre une gamme complète de services en conception architecturale, consultance, éclairage, aménagement du paysage, expositions, graphisme et design produit. Ambasz a déclaré : « Je crois profondément que le design est un acte d'invention. Je crois que sa vraie tâche débute une fois les besoins fonctionnels et comportementaux satisfaits. Ce n'est pas la faim, mais l'amour, la peur et parfois l'émerveillement qui nous font créer. Notre milieu peut évoluer de génération en génération, mais la tâche reste pour moi la même : donner une forme poétique au pragmatique. » Parmi ses projets : le grand magasin Nichii Obihiro (Hokkaido, Japon, 1987, non construit) ; la serre Lucille Halsell au San Antonio Botanical Center (San Antonio, Texas, 1988) ; le Mycal Sanda Cultural and Athletic Center (préfecture de Hyogo, Japon, 1990–94) ; le Hall international de la préfecture de Fukuoka (Fukuoka, Japon, 1995) qui a remporté le prix DuPont Benedictus 2001. Plus récemment, il a réalisé l'hôtel et ensemble résidentiel Nuova Concordia dans les Pouilles (Italie, 2001–03) ; la Casa de Retiro Espiritual (Casa de Cordoba, Seville, Espagne, 1975/2003–05) ; un laboratoire de recherches avancées en ophtamologie (Banca dell'Occhio, Venise-Mestre, 2003–08, publié ici) et un hôpital de 680 lits (Ospedale dell'Angelo, Venise-Mestre, 2005–08, également publié ici).

BANCA DELL'OCCHIO

Venice-Mestre, Italy, 2003–08

Address: Nuovo Ospedale di Mestre, Via Don Tosatto 147, 30174 Mestre, Venice, Italy,
+39 41 965 71 11, www.nuovospedalemestre.it
Area: 5000 m². Client: Regione Veneto. Cost: € 26 million
Collaboration: Studio Altieri (Architect of Record, Alberto Altieri, Principal)

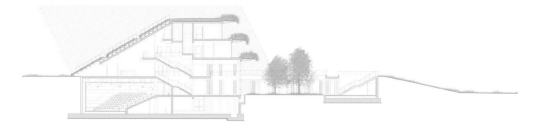

A general exterior view of the
Banca dell'Occhio showing its
dramatic slanted outer walls.

Gesamtansicht der Banca
dell'Occhio mit ihren dynamisch
geneigten Außenwänden.

Vue d'ensemble de l'extérieur
de la Banca dell'Occhio et de ses
spectaculaires murs inclinés.

This facility was designed to house a surgery area, but also spaces for stem-cell research, administrative offices, and educational facilities for the EIDON Foundation, including a 450-seat auditorium. Built on a triangular, 2.8-hectare site across the street from a hospital also designed by the architect (page 60), the **BANCA DELL'OCCHIO** features two 12-meter-high walls set at right angles to each other and clad in copper. Landscaped terraces rising in steps to a roof garden were created between these walls. Educational facilities are located below grade, with natural light provided by a circular courtyard. The courtyard is bisected by a two-story glass wall forming the building's lobby. Administrative, research, and surgery areas are housed in the three levels above grade. Planting on the terraces is designed to reduce solar gain, although all interior spaces receive natural light. Parking and mechanical facilities are underground, allowing the environment of the Banca dell'Occhio to remain as green as the architect's basic design for the structure.

Emilio Ambasz' **BANCA DELL'OCCHIO** ist kein reines Forschungsinstitut, sondern umfasst neben Räumlichkeiten für die Stammzellforschung auch einen Operationsbereich sowie Verwaltungsbüros und Lehrräume für die EIDON-Stiftung (einschließlich eines Hörsaals mit 450 Plätzen). Das auffälligste Merkmal des Gebäudes, das vis-à-vis einem ebenfalls von Ambasz entworfenen Krankenhaus (Seite 60) auf einem dreieckigen, 2,8 ha großen Grundstück errichtet wurde, sind seine beiden 12 m hohen, kupferverkleideten Wände, die im rechten Winkel aufeinander zulaufen. Zwischen diesen hat der Architekt begrünte Terrassen angelegt, die stufenförmig ansteigen bis hinauf zu einem Dachgarten. Die ins Untergeschoss verlegten Räume für Lehrveranstaltungen werden über einen runden Innenhof mit Tageslicht versorgt. Eine zweigeschossige Glaswand teilt den Hof in zwei Hälften, von denen eine das Eingangsfoyer bildet. Die Verwaltungs-, Forschungs- und Operationsbereiche verteilen sich auf die drei oberirdischen Ebenen. In sämtliche Innenräume fällt Tageslicht ein, einer allzu starken Sonneneinstrahlung beugt die Terrassenbepflanzung vor. Da der Architekt die Betriebsanlagen und die Parkmöglichkeiten unter die Erde verlegt hat, wird das rundum grüne Erscheinungsbild der Banca dell'Occhio durch nichts beeinträchtigt.

Ce bâtiment a été conçu pour accueillir un service de chirurgie, des installations de recherches sur les cellules souches, des bureaux administratifs et des locaux d'éducation pour la fondation EIDON, dont un auditorium de 450 places. Édifié sur un terrain de 2,8 hectares face à un hôpital (page 60) également conçu par l'architecte, la **BANCA DELL'OCCHIO** se caractérise par deux énormes murs de 12 mètres de haut dressés à angle droit et habillés de cuivre. Des terrasses paysagées s'étagent jusqu'à un jardin en toiture qui s'étend entre les grands murs. Les installations destinées à l'enseignement sont en sous-sol, néanmoins éclairées par la lumière naturelle grâce à une cour circulaire. Celle-ci est coupée à un certain moment par un mur de deux étages de hauteur pour constituer le hall d'entrée de l'immeuble. L'administration, la recherche et la chirurgie sont logées dans les trois niveaux à l'air libre. Les plantations des terrasses devraient réduire le gain solaire, bien que tous les volumes intérieurs bénéficient de la lumière naturelle. Les parkings et les installations techniques sont souterrains, ce qui a permis l'aménagement d'un environnement immédiat aussi vert que la structure elle-même.

Another exterior façade view shows a less surprising façade of the Banca dell'Occhio with its planted terraces.

Die Außenansicht der anderen Gebäudeseite der Banca dell'Occhio zeigt die etwas herkömmlichere Fassade mit den begrünten Terrassen.

Une vue de l'autre façade, constituée de balcons plantés mais moins impressionnante, de la Banca dell'Occhio.

A plan (right) shows the triangular form of the structure and its main entrance (top).

Der Grundriss (rechts) zeigt die Dreiecksform des Baus; oben: der Haupteingang.

À droite, le plan triangulaire du bâtiment. Ci-dessus, l'entrée principale.

OSPEDALE DELL'ANGELO

Venice-Mestre, Italy, 2005–08

Address: Nuovo Ospedale di Mestre, Via Don Tosatto 147, 30174 Mestre, Venice, Italy, +39 41 965 71 11, www.nuovospedalemestre.it
Area: 92 903 m². Client: Regione Veneto. Cost: €500 million
Collaboration: Studio Altieri (Architect of Record, Alberto Altieri, Principal)

This is a 680-bed facility billed as the "world's first green general hospital." It features an entrance hall 200 meters in length and 30 meters high, conceived as a "veritable winter garden." Fully half the patients have a view of this garden from their rooms, and lounges placed on each floor also overlook it. The other rooms have plant-covered containers outside their windows. The basic plan of the facility is rectangular, but its sloping façades and its emphasis on green elements make the structure both inviting and pleasant to look at, quite the contrary of most hospital architecture. The project took almost 40 years to realize, with three other architectural firms having been involved before Emilio Ambasz took on the task. Service facilities, parking, laboratories, and operating rooms are covered with earth and plants on three sides and their roof space so as not to interfere with the agreeable central areas containing the rooms. The hospital is located across a street from the Banca dell'Occhio (page 56) by the same architect.

Das **OSPEDALE DELL'ANGELO** wird nicht umsonst „als die erste grüne Klinik der Welt" gepriesen: Ist da doch zunächst einmal seine 200 m lange und 30 m hohe Eingangshalle, die als „veritabler Wintergarten" angelegt ist. Dessen Grün lässt sich nicht nur von den auf jeder Ebene eingerichteten Lounges aus genießen – nicht weniger als die Hälfte der Patienten hat in ihren Zimmern direkten Blick auf den Garten. Vor den Fenstern der übrigen Zimmer sind großzügig begrünte Pflanzenkübel angebracht. Mag der Grundriss des Gebäudes auch schlicht rechteckig sein, bietet sich dank der schrägen Fassaden und der Betonung naturgrüner Elemente ein ungewohnt positiver, ja einladender Anblick – ganz im Gegensatz zu den meisten sonstigen Krankenhäusern. Die Umsetzung des Projekts hat sich über beinahe 40 Jahre hingezogen; bevor Emilio Ambasz die Sache endlich in die Hand nahm, hatten sich bereits drei andere Architekturbüros daran versucht. Die Parkplätze, Haustechnik, Labore und Operationssäle sind so in den Erdraum eingelassen, dass nur ihre Vorderseite freiliegt, uneinsehbar für den Zentralbereich mit den Patientenzimmern, dessen angenehme Atmosphäre somit ungestört bleibt. Gleich gegenüber der Klinik befindet sich auf der anderen Straßenseite Ambasz' Banca dell'Occhio (Seite 56).

Cet hôpital de 680 lits, qualifié de « premier hôpital général écologique du monde », s'ouvre par un hall d'entrée de 200 mètres de long et 30 mètres de haut conçu comme un « véritable jardin d'hiver ». La moitié des patients bénéficient d'une vue sur ce jardin de leur chambre comme des salons aménagés à chaque étage. Les autres chambres sont dotées de jardinières plantées devant leurs fenêtres. Le plan d'ensemble est rectangulaire, mais l'inclinaison des façades et l'importance accordée à la verdure rendent le bâtiment accueillant et agréable à regarder, contrairement à l'architecture habituelle de la plupart des hôpitaux. Le projet a mis plus de quarante années avant de naître, trois autres agences d'architecture s'y étaient succédé avant l'intervention d'Ambasz. Les services, les parkings, les laboratoires et les salles d'opérations sont recouverts de terre et de plantationssur trois côtés et leur toiture, ce qui les isole de la zone centrale qui regroupe les chambres. L'hôpital est séparé de la Banca dell'Occhio (page 56) du même architecte par une avenue.

The Ospedale dell'Angelo shares with its neighbor, the Banca dell'Occhio, surprising slanted façades. Right, the glazed surface of the hospital.

Das Ospedale dell'Angelo besitzt ähnlich wie sein Nachbar, die Banca dell'Occhio, ungewohnt schräge Wände. Rechts gut zu erkennen die Fassadenverglasung.

L'Ospedale dell'Angelo partage avec la Banca dell'Occhio voisine, d'étonnantes façades inclinées. À droite, la façade de verre de l'hôpital.

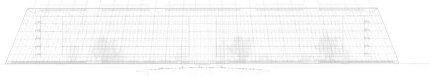

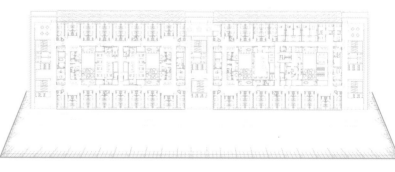

Interior views of the hospital emphasize its "green" aspect, with the kind of generous planting that is frequent in the work of Emilio Ambasz.

Die Innenansichten der Klinik führen die „grüne" Gestaltung des Baus vor Augen. Die großzügige Integration von Pflanzen ist ein häufig wiederkehrendes Merkmal in Emilio Ambasz' Arbeiten.

Ces vues intérieures de l'hôpital mettent en valeur l'aspect écologique de cette réalisation. On y retrouve les généreuses plantations fréquentes dans l'œuvre d'Emilio Ambasz.

ALEJANDRO ARAVENA

Alejandro Aravena Architects/
Ricardo Torrejón (Associated Architect)
Av. Los Conquistadores 1700, 25th Floor
Providencia, Santiago
Chile

Tel: +56 2 753 3000 / Fax: +56 2 753 3016
E-mail: info@elementalchile.cl
Web: www.alejandroaravena.com

ALEJANDRO ARAVENA graduated as an architect from the Universidad Católica de Chile (UC) in 1992. He studied history and theory at the IUAV in Venice, Italy (1992–93). Aravena was a Visiting Professor at Harvard University (2000–05) and has been a Professor at UC since 1994. He created Alejandro Aravena Architects in 1994. Since 2006, he has been the Elemental Copec Professor at UC and Executive Director of Elemental, described as a "Do Tank affiliated to the Pontificia Universidad Católica de Chile and COPEC, its focus is the design and implementation of urban projects of social interest and public impact." His professional work includes the Mathematics (1998–99), Medical (2002–04), and Architecture (2004) Schools at UC (Santiago); Pirehueico Lake House (2003–04); Quinta Monroy Social Housing (Iquique, 2003–04, XV Santiago Biennale Grand Prix); and the Siamese Towers at UC (Centro Tecnológico, San Joaquin Campus, Santiago, 2003–06), all in Chile. In 2006, he was chosen as the architect for the new facilities of Saint Edward's University in Austin (Texas, USA, 2007–08, with **RICARDO TORREJÓN**, published here). Ongoing projects include VITRA, the new children's workshops and exhibition hall for Vitra (Weil am Rhein, Germany); a Villa in the Ordos 100 Project (Inner Mongolia); and the Metropolitan Promenade for the Chilean Bicentennial. Alejandro Aravena became a member of the Pritzker Prize Jury in 2009.

ALEJANDRO ARAVENA schloss 1992 sein Architekturstudium an der Universidad Católica de Chile (UC) in Santiago ab und vertiefte seine Ausbildung anschließend in den Bereichen Architekturtheorie und Architekturgeschichte am Instituto Universitario di Architettura di Venezia (Italien, 1992–93). Seit 1994 ist Aravena Lehrstuhlinhaber an der UC, 2000–05 war er Gastprofessor an der Harvard University. 1994 gründete er seine Firma Alejandro Aravena Architectos. Seit 2006 ist er Geschäftsführer von Elemental, einem an die Pontificia Universidad Católica de Chile angeschlossenen „Do Tank", der sich mit Unterstützung des Energieunternehmens COPEC „der Gestaltung und Durchführung von sozialpolitisch verantwortungsbewussten und öffentlichkeitswirksamen Stadtentwicklungsprojekten widmet"; die parallel dazu eingerichtete Elemental Copec-Professur an der UC hält Aravena ebenfalls seit 2006. Zu seinen Arbeiten als Architekt gehören die Fakultäten für Mathematik (1998–99), Medizin (2002–04) und Architektur (2004) der UC, ein Wohnhaus am Pirihueico-See (Chile, 2003–04), die Sozialwohnanlage Quinta Monroy in Iquique (Chile, 2003–04, ausgezeichnet mit dem Großen Preis der 15. Biennale von Santiago) und die „Siamesischen Zwillingstürme" des Centro Tecnológico auf dem San Joaquin Campus der UC (Santiago, 2003–06). 2006 wurde Aravena zusammen mit **RICARDO TORREJÓN** als Architekt für die neuen Universitätsbauten der Saint Edward's University im texanischen Austin ausgewählt (2007–08, hier vorgestellt). Zu seinen derzeit laufenden Projekten gehören ein Gebäudeprojekt für Kinder-Workshops und Ausstellungen auf dem Vitra-Campus in Weil am Rhein, eine Villa im Rahmen des Projekts Ordos 100 in der Inneren Mongolei, und eine Promenade im Parque Metropolitano de Santiago für die Zweihundertjahrfeier Chiles. 2009 wurde Aravena zum Jurymitglied für die Vergabe des Pritzker-Preises ernannt.

ALEJANDRO ARAVENA est diplômé d'architecture de l'Universidad Católica du Chili (1992). Il a également étudié l'histoire et la théorie de l'architecture à l'Istituto Universitario di Architettura di Venezia (Italie, 1992–93). Il a été professeur invité à Harvard University (2000–05) et enseigne à l'Universidad Católica (UC) du Chili depuis 1994. Il a créé l'agence Alejandro Aravena Architectos en 1994. Depuis 2006, il est Elemental Copec Professor à UC et directeur exécutif d'Elemental, un « Do Tank » dépendant de la Pontificia Universidad Católica du Chili et de la Copec, qui a pour objet « la conception et la mise en œuvre de projets urbains d'intérêt public à impact social ». Parmi ses réalisations figurent les collèges de mathématiques (1998–99), de médecine (2002–04), et d'architecture (2004) à UC (Santiago) ; la maison du lac de Pirehueico (2003–04) ; les logements sociaux de la Quinta Monroy (Iquique, 2003–04, Grand prix de la XVᵉ Biennale de Santiago) et les tours siamoises de UC (Santiago, 2003–06, publiées ici), le tout au Chili. En 2006, il a été choisi pour concevoir les nouvelles installations de Saint Edward's University à Austin ((Texas, États-Unis, 2007–08, avec **RICARDO TORREJÓN**, publiées ici). Parmi ses projets actuels : le nouvel atelier des enfants et hall d'exposition de Vitra (Weil am Rhein, Allemagne) ; une villa pour l'Ordos 100 Project (Mongolie intérieure) et la Promenade métropolitaine pour le bicentenaire du Chili. Alejandro Aravena est devenu membre du jury du prix Pritzker en 2009.

SAINT EDWARD'S UNIVERSITY
Residence and Dining Hall, Austin, Texas, USA, 2007–08

Address: 3001 South Congress Avenue, Austin, TX 78704, USA, +1 512 448 8400, www.stedwards.edu
Area: 30 000 m² (10 000 m² dormitories, 20 000 m² parking). Client: Saint Edward's University, Austin, Texas. Cost: not disclosed
Collaboration: Ricardo Torrejón (Associated Architect), Cotera + Reed (Partner Architects)

The architects were commissioned by the University to create new dormitories (300 beds), dining facilities, and other student services, as well as a large parking garage. The architect declares: "We thought that a dorm is like a monastery: it's about how to organize a collection of repetitive small cells ... and how to relate them with the refectory and chapel. Here it was about the rooms and the dining hall and common facilities. Both of them have to do with old atavist situations: sleeping, studying and eating. Or to put it in a more suggestive way: feeding the body and the soul and digesting." Referring to Alvar Aalto's Baker House (MIT, Cambridge, Massachusetts, 1947–49) and to Louis Kahn's Erdman Hall (Bryn Mawr, Pennsylvania, 1960–65), Alejandro Aravena resolved to increase the footprint of the building, allowing each room to have natural light and a view. He also carefully examined the "appropriate architectural language" vis-à-vis the rest of the campus. Commenting on his first project outside Chile, Aravena states: "Today many architects build around the globe as if it was a natural thing; for me, it's not. I've had to design in English not in Spanish. I've had to learn to think in inches and feet instead of meters. I've had to transit from a culture of scarcity to a culture of abundance (where I want tightness, my clients may see meanness; where I want compression, users may see invasion). But mainly I had to go from the third world to the first one and lead a project there."

Alejandro Aravenas Büro erhielt den Auftrag, ein neues Wohnheim für 300 Studenten inklusive Mensa und weiterer studentische Einrichtungen sowie einer gro-ßen Parkgarage zu entwerfen. Der Architekt erläutert: „Uns fiel auf, dass ein Studentenwohnheim viel von einem Kloster hat: Geht es dort darum, eine Vielzahl identischer Schlafzellen in ein sinnvolles Gefüge zu bringen und sie an das Refektorium und die Kapelle anzubinden, galt hier dasselbe für die Zimmer, den Speisesaal und die sonsti-gen Einrichtungen. Beide Modelle haben mit ganz ursprünglichen Tätigkeiten zu tun, dem Schlafen, Lernen und Essen – oder um es etwas bedeutungsvoller klingen zu lassen: dem Nähren von Körper und Seele. In Bezug auf Alvar Aaltos Baker House (MIT, Cambridge, Massachusetts, 1947–49) und Louis Kahns Erdman Hall (Bryn Mawr, Pennsylvania, 1960–65) beschloss Aravena, die Größe der Gebäudegrundfläche so zu wählen, dass in jedem Zimmer ein vernünftiger Tageslichteinfall und eine gute Aussicht gewährleistet sind. Darüber hinaus setzte er sich eingehend mit dem Campus auseinander, um eine „dazu passende Formensprache" zu entwickeln. Dass es sich um sein erstes Projekt außerhalb Chiles handelt, kommentiert Aravena so: „Viele Architekten verwirklichen Projekte in aller Welt, als wäre das eine völlig normale Sache. Für mich war das nicht der Fall. Ich musste meinen Entwurf erstmals nicht auf Spanisch, sondern auf Englisch anlegen, also lernen, in Fuß und Inches zu denken statt in Metern. Aus einer Kultur kommend, die von Mangel gekennzeichnet ist, musste ich mich in eine Kultur des Überflusses hineinfinden (wo es mir um Sparsamkeit geht, könnten meine Auftraggeber Geiz sehen; was ich als Verdichtung verstehe, könnte künftigen Nutzern als Eingriff in die Privatsphäre vorkommen). Die Welt, in der ich nun ein Projekt zu realisieren hatte, war nicht mehr die dritte, sondern die erste Welt."

La commande portait sur de nouveaux logements pour étudiants (300 lits), un restaurant, divers services pour étudiants et de vastes parkings. « Nous avons pensé qu'un foyer d'étudiants est comme un monastère : il s'agit d'organiser un ensemble répétitif de petites cellules […], et de trouver comment les relier au réfectoire et à la chapelle. Ici, il s'agissait plutôt de chambres, d'un restaurant universitaire et d'installations communes. Tout est en relation avec de très anciennes situations : dormir, étudier et manger. Ou, de façon plus imagée : nourrir le corps et l'esprit et digérer », commente l'architecte. Se référant à la Maison Baker d'Alvar Aalto pour le MIT (Cambridge, Massachusetts, 1947–49) et à l'Erdman Hall de Louis Kahn (Bryn Mawr, Pennsylvanie, 1960–65), Alejandor Aravena a choisi d'accroître l'emprise au sol de chaque bâtiment pour que chaque chambre dispose d'un éclairage naturel et d'une vue. Il a également étudié de façon approfondie « un langage architectural approprié » en relation avec le reste du campus. Commentant ce premier projet réalisé hors du Chili, il précise : « Aujourd'hui, beaucoup d'architectes construisent partout dans le monde comme si c'était une chose naturelle. Pour moi, ça ne l'est pas. Je devais concevoir ici en anglais, pas en espagnol. Je devais apprendre à penser en inches et en pieds et non pas en mètres. Je devais faire le saut entre une culture de la rareté et une culture de l'abondance (lorsque je veux quelque chose de modeste, mes clients peuvent y voir de la mesquinerie, là où je veux de la compression, ils peuvent ressentir une invasion). Mais surtout, je devais passer du tiers-monde au monde développé et mener à bien mon projet. »

The relative austerity of the façades is alleviated by the irregular window patterns, with higher windows at ground level and a staggered pattern above.

L'austérité relative des façades est allégée par la composition irrégulière des ouvertures. Elles sont plus hautes au rez-de-chaussée et disposées selon un certain rythme dans les étages.

Damit die Fassaden nicht allzu nüchtern wirken, wurden die Fenster unregelmäßig angeordnet: etwas höher im Erdgeschoss, in den darüberliegenden Geschossen bilden sie ein gestaffeltes Muster.

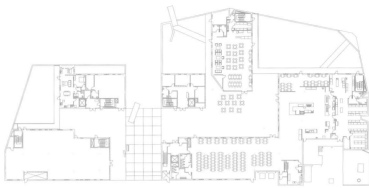

Inner volumes of the complex reveal glazed surfaces and, above all, bright colors. The stone severity of the exterior yields here to a more lively concept.

Wird die Außenseite der Anlage von steinerner Nüchternheit bestimmt, folgen die Innenfassaden der einzelnen Trakte einem lebendigeren Konzept: Hier herrschen verglaste Fassaden und kräftige Farben vor.

L'intérieur du bâtiment est animé de grandes parois de verre et surtout par des plans de couleurs vives. La sévérité minérale de l'extérieur cède la place à une plus grande diversité.

ARCHITEKTUR & LANDSCHAFT

Architektur & Landschaft
Preysingplatz 2
81667 Munich
Germany

Tel: +49 89 54 64 66 73
Fax: +49 89 41 17 57 97
E-mail: giers@architekturundlandschaft.de
Web: www.architekturundlandschaft.de

STEFAN GIERS was born in 1967 in Bonn, Germany. He attended the University of Innsbruck (Austria, 1987–90) and the University of Darmstadt (Germany, 1991–94). He worked in numerous offices, including that of Herzog & de Meuron (Basel, 1995), and is currently a Research Assistant at the Technical University in Munich. **SUSANNE GABRIEL** was born in Salzburg, Austria, in 1970. She attended the University of Vienna, where she studied art history and philosophy (1989–90), and the University of Berlin (1990–97), where she received her M.A. degree as a landscape architect. She has worked in numerous architectural offices since that time, and most recently with the architects Keller & Damm (Munich, 2006–). Giers and Gabriel have worked together on a courtyard design for a residential building (2006–07); the Lusatian Lakeland Landmark (Senftenberg, Germany, 2008, published here); and the Infopavilion at the Lusatian Lakeland Landmark (2008–09), all in Germany.

STEFAN GIERS, geboren 1967 in Bonn, absolvierte sein Studium an der Universität Innsbruck (1987–90) und der Universität Darmstadt (1991–94). Anschließend arbeitete er in mehreren Architekturbüros, u. a. bei Herzog & de Meuron (Basel, 1995). Derzeit ist Giers als Forschungsassistent an der Technischen Universität München tätig. **SUSANNE GABRIEL**, 1970 in Salzburg geboren, nahm zunächst ein Studium der Kunstgeschichte und Philosophie an der Universität Wien (1989–90) auf, um anschließend an der Universität Berlin zu studieren (1990–97) und ihren Magistertitel als Landschaftsarchitektin zu erwerben. In der Folgezeit war sie Mitarbeiterin in verschiedenen Landschaftsarchitekturbüros, seit 2006 arbeitet sie für das Münchner Büro Keller & Damm. Gemeinsam mit Stefan Giers hat Susanne Gabriel unter anderem die Hofgestaltung für ein Wohnhaus in München (2006–07) übernommen und die Landmarke Lausitzer Seenland in Senftenberg (2008, hier vorgestellt) sowie den dazugehörigen Infokiosk (2008–09) realisiert.

STEFAN GIERS, né en 1967 à Bonn (Allemagne), a étudié à l'Université d'Innsbruck (Autriche, 1987–90) et à l'Université de Darmstadt (Allemagne, 1991–94). Après avoir travaillé dans de nombreuses agences dont celle d'Herzog & de Meuron (Bâle, 1995), il est actuellement assistant de recherches à l'Université polytechnique de Munich. **SUSANNE GABRIEL**, née à Salzburg (Autriche) en 1970, a étudié l'art et la philosophie à l'Université de Vienne (1989–90) et à l'Université de Berlin (1990–97, M.A. d'architecte paysagiste). Elle a travaillé dans de nombreuses agences et plus récemment pour Keller & Damm à Munich (2006–). Giers et Gabriel ont élaboré ensemble un projet de cour pour un immeuble résidentiel (2006–07) ; le signal du lac de Lusatie (Senftenberg, Allemagne, 2008, publié ici) et l'Infopavillon de ce même signal monumental (2008–09).

LUSATIAN LAKELAND LANDMARK

Senftenberg, Germany, 2008

Address: Lake Sedlitz, Senftenberg, Germany, www.iba-see.de
Area: 250 m². Client: Stadt Senftenberg, IBA Fürst-Pückler-Land. Cost: € 1 million
Collaboration: Seeberger, Friedl und Partner (Structural Engineers)

The areas around Senftenberg are known for extensive coal mining. Various plans have been put forth for the reuse of the abandoned open pit mines in the area, such as turning them into interconnected lakes. Architektur & Landschaft won the 2005 international competition to design a landmark structure symbolizing the will of the region to transform itself. The designers made a tower of Corten steel that recalls the typical bridges used in the mine area. With its observation platform set at a heights of 30 meters, the structure is intended to make a resonating noise as visitors use its stairs. One hundred and eleven tons of six- and ten-millimeter-thick steel was used for the structure. Using principles similar to those employed in the shipping industry, the designers created the largest prefabricated elements possible to avoid extensive on-site welding to the greatest extent possible. Two sides of the tower are made up of blank, hollow walls with cross bracing, while the third façade reveals the sculptural stairway, with its nine flights of stairs and eight landings.

Die Gegend rund um Senftenberg ist bekannt für den Braunkohleabbau. Um die verbliebenen offenen Tagebaugruben neuen Zwecken zuzuführen, wurden verschiedene Konzepte in Anschlag gebracht, deren Kern die Schaffung einer ausgedehnten zusammenhängenden Seenlandschaft vorsieht. Im Jahr 2005 gewannen Architektur & Landschaft einen europaweiten Planungswettbewerb für eine Landmarke, die symbolisch den in der Region herrschenden Willen zum Wandel verkörpern sollte. Susanne Gabriel und Stefan Giers entwarfen einen Stahlturm, der an die für das ehemalige Tagebaugebiet typischen Brücken erinnert. Unter Verwendung von 111 t sechs- und zehn mm starken Corten-Stahls entstand ein dreieckiges Gebilde mit zwei geschlossenen glatten Fassaden aus hohlen, durch Querverstrebungen verstärkten Wänden. Die dritte, offene Seite gewährt den Zugang zu einer stählernen Treppe aus neun versetzt angeordneten Läufen und acht Absätzen, die zu einer in 30 m Höhe angelegten Aussichtsplattform hinaufführt. Erklimmt man die Stufen, ertönt ein schwingender Metallklang. Zur Konstruktion ihres Turms griffen die Designer auf Techniken zurück, die in ähnlicher Weise im Schiffsbau genutzt werden. Um umständliche Schweißarbeiten vor Ort weitestgehend zu vermeiden, verwendeten Gabriel und Giers Bauelemente, die sie im größtmöglichen Format vorfabrizieren ließen.

La région de Senftenberg est connue pour ses importantes activités minières. Divers plans ont été établis pour la réutilisation des anciennes mines à ciel ouvert, en les transformant, par exemple, en un réseau de lacs. Architektur & Landschaft a remporté, en 2005, le concours international pour la conception d'une structure-signal symbolisant la volonté de la région de se transformer. L'agence a réalisé une tour en acier Corten qui rappelle celles typiques des puits de mine de la région. Sa plateforme d'observation, installée à 30 mètres de haut, est desservie par un escalier que fera résonner les pas des visiteurs. La structure a nécessité 111 tonnes de tôle d'acier d'un centimètre d'épaisseur. Utilisant des principes constructifs similaires à ceux des chantiers navals, les architectes ont dessiné des éléments préfabriqués les plus grands possible pour limiter autant que nécessaire le travail de soudure *in situ*. Deux côtés de la tour de plan triangulaire sont des murs aveugles à contreventements, tandis que la troisième façade est occupée par l'escalier à neuf volées de marches et huit paliers.

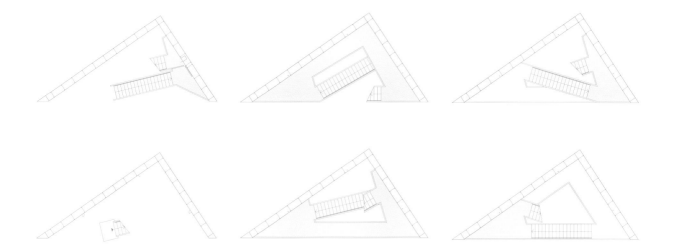

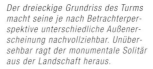

A triangular plan implies that the exterior appearance of the tower varies according to the angle from which it is viewed. Isolated in its setting, the tower has a decided monumentality about it.

Der dreieckige Grundriss des Turms macht seine je nach Betrachterperspektive unterschiedliche Außenerscheinung nachvollziehbar. Unübersehbar ragt der monumentale Solitär aus der Landschaft heraus.

Le plan triangulaire fait que la tour change d'aspect selon l'angle de vue du spectateur. Isolée dans le paysage, elle possède une présence réellement monumentale.

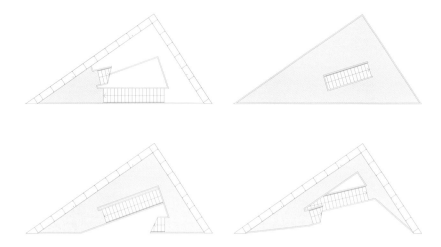

The landscape around the tower seems to correspond well to the metallic harshness of the architecture, as much sculpture as it is a building.

Die Architektur des Turmes, gleichermaßen Skulptur und nutzbares Bauwerk, und die Naturkulisse ringsumher stehen in einem wirkungsvollen Zusammenspiel.

Le paysage environnant semble répondre à la brutalité métallique de cette architecture qui relève autant de la sculpture que du bâtiment.

The stairway leading up the tower is patterned differently at each level, as the drawing to the right and the photos above demonstrate.

Wie die Zeichnung rechts und die Fotos oben demonstrieren, sind die zur Aussichtsplattform hinaufführen Treppenläufe von Ebene zu Ebene unterschiedlich angeordnet.

Chaque palier de l'escalier est de forme différente, comme le montrent ce plan (à droite) et ces photos (ci-dessus).

ASYMPTOTE

Asymptote Architecture
11–45 46th Avenue
Long Island City, New York 11101
USA
Tel: +1 212 343 7333 / Fax: +1 718 937 3320
E-mail: info@asymptote.net / Web: www.asymptote.net

HANI RASHID received his M.Arch degree from the Cranbrook Academy of Art, Bloomfield Hills, Michigan. He is presently a Professor of Architecture at Princeton University. **LISE ANNE COUTURE** received her B.Arch degree from Carlton University, Canada, and her M.Arch degree from Yale. Couture currently holds the Davenport chair at Yale University School of Architecture and teaches at Cornell. As cofounders and principals of Asymptote Architecture, they are leading architectural practitioners of their generation with innovative work and academic contributions that have received international recognition. Since Asymptote's founding, in 1988, key projects include their 1988 prize-winning commission for the Los Angeles West Coast Gateway; a virtual trading floor for the New York Stock Exchange; and the Guggenheim Virtual Museum, a multimedia project aimed at creating an online museum. Built works include the HydraPier, a public building housing technology and art located near Schiphol Airport (Harlemmermeer, the Netherlands, 2002); the Carlos Miele Flagship Store on West 14th Street in Manhattan (New York, USA, 2003); the design of the 2004 Venice Biennale of Architecture, *Metamorph*; a new theater for the Hans Christian Andersen festival in Odense (Denmark, 2004); Beukenhof Crematorium and Memorial Chapel in Rotterdam (The Netherlands, 2004); the Alessi Flagship store in the SoHo area of Manhattan (New York, USA, 2006); and The Yas Hotel (Abu Dhabi, UAE, 2008–09, published here). Current work includes the Strata Tower (Abu Dhabi, UAE, 2006–13); World Business Center Solomon Tower (Busan, South Korea, 2007–13); and Guggenheim Contemporary Art Pavilions (Saadiyat Island, Abu Dhabi, UAE, 2006–).

HANI RASHID erwarb seinen M.Arch an der Cranbrook Academy of Art in Bloomfield Hills, Michigan. Gegenwärtig ist er als Professor für Architektur an der Princeton University tätig. **LISE ANNE COUTURE** erhielt ihren B.Arch an der Carlton University in Kanada, den M.Arch erwarb sie an der Yale University. An letzterer hat Couture derzeit die Davenport-Professur für Architektur inne, außerdem lehrt sie an der Cornell University. 1988 gründeten Rashid und Couture ihr Architekturbüro Asymptote, mit dem sie sich auf der internationalen Bühne einen Ruf als richtungsweisende Protagonisten ihrer Architektengeneration erworben haben. Zu Coutures und Rashids herausragenden Projekten gehören ihr 1988 preisgekrönter Entwurf für den Los Angeles West Coast Gateway, ein virtuelles Börsenparkett für die New York Stock Exchange sowie das Guggenheim Virtual Museum, ein Multimediaprojekt zur Online-Ausstellung von Kunstwerken. Baulich realisiert wurden ihr unweit des Flughafens Schiphol errichteter HydraPier, ein Ausstellungspavillon für Kunst und Technik (Harlemmermeer, Niederlande, 2002), der Carlos Miele Flagshipstore in der West 14th Street in Manhattan (New York, USA, 2003), ihr Beitrag zur Gestaltung der unter dem Motto „Metamorph" ausgerichteten Architektur-Biennale Venedig 2004, ferner ein neues Theatergebäude für das Hans Christian Andersen Festival in Odense (Dänemark, 2004), das Krematorium und die Gedenkkapelle Beukenhof in Rotterdam (Niederlande, 2004), der Alessi Flagshipstore im Bezirk SoHo in Manhattan (New York, USA, 2006) und das Yas-Hotel (Abu Dhabi, VAE, 2008–09, hier vorgestellt). In der Entstehungsphase befinden sich ihr Strata Tower (Abu Dhabi, VAE, 2006–13), das World Business Center Solomon Tower (Busan, Südkorea, 2007–13) und die Guggenheim Contemporary Art Pavilions (Saadiyat Island, Abu Dhabi, VAE, 2006–).

HANI RASHID, M. Arch. de la Cranbrook Academy of Art (Bloomfield Hills, Michigan), est actuellement professeur d'architecture à Princeton University. **LISE ANNE COUTURE**, née à Montréal en 1959, est B. Arch. de Carlton University (Canada) et M. Arch. de Yale. Elle est actuellement titulaire de la chaire Davenport de l'École d'architecture de Yale University. Cofondateurs et dirigeants d'Asymptote Architecture, ils font partie des grands praticiens de leur génération, internationalement reconnus pour leurs approches novatrices et leurs contributions universitaires. Parmi leurs projets les plus célèbres depuis la création de l'agence en 1988 figurent la commande primée de la Los Angeles West Coast Gateway, une salle des marchés virtuelle pour le New York Stock Exchange et le Musée virtuel Guggenheim, projet multimédia de musée en ligne. Ils sont les auteurs notamment de : HydraPier, un bâtiment public pour l'art et les technologies près de l'aéroport de Schiphol (Harlemmermeer, Pays-Bas, 2002) ; du magasin « amiral » de Carlos Miele, West 14th Street à Manhattan (New York, 2002) ; du concept « Metamorph » présenté à la Biennale d'architecture de Venise 2004 ; d'un nouveau théâtre pour le festival Hans Christian Andersen (Odense, Danemark, 2004) ; du crématorium et de la chapelle du souvenir du Beukenhof (Rotterdam, 2004) ; du magasin principal d'Alessi à SoHo dans Manhattan (New York, 2006) ; et du Yas Hotel (Abou Dhabi, EAU, 2008-09, publié ici). Actuellement, parmi leurs projets en cours de réalisation figurent la tour Strata (Abou Dhabi, EAU, 2006–13) ; la World Business Center Solomon Tower (Pusan, Corée du Sud, 2007–13) et les pavillons d'art contemporain Guggenheim (île de Saadiyat, Abou Dhabi, EAU, 2006–).

THE YAS HOTEL

Abu Dhabi, UAE, 2008–09

Address: P.O. Box 131808, Abu Dhabi, UAE, +971 2 656 0000, www.theyashotel.com
Area: 85 000 m². Client: Aldar Properties PJSC. Cost: not disclosed

The Yas Hotel, located at the heart of Yas Island, not far from Abu Dhabi Airport, sits atop a Formula 1 racetrack and next to a marina, seen below.

Quer durch das gleich am Yachthafen im Herzen der Insel Yas, nicht weit vom Abu Dhabi Airport, gelegene Yas-Hotel verläuft eine Formel-Eins-Rennstrecke.

Le Yas Hotel, au cœur de l'île de Yas, non loin de l'aéroport d'Abou Dhabi, est implanté au-dessus d'un circuit de Formule Un, en bordure d'une marina.

This 500-room hotel is located in the large Yas Marina development area, which includes a Formula 1 raceway circuit. The architects declare: "Asymptote envisioned an architectural landmark embodying various key influences and inspirations ranging from the aesthetics and forms associated with speed, movement, and spectacle to the artistry and geometries forming the basis of ancient Islamic art and craft traditions." The most striking element of the exterior design is a 217-meter curving grid shell made of steel with 5800 pivoting glass panels. The shell wraps around two hotel towers and a monocoque steel link bridge. Abu Dhabi, unlike neighboring Dubai, has carried forward its ambitious architectural projects despite the world economic situation, and **THE YAS HOTEL** is one of the most outstanding current examples of an effort that is transforming the Emirate into a must-see location for fans of contemporary architecture.

Das mit nicht weniger als 500 Zimmern aufwartende **YAS-HOTEL** liegt in dem neu geschaffen Yachthafen-Areal der Insel Yas, zu dem auch ein Motorsportrennstrecke gehört. Zur Entstehung ihres Projekts erklären die Architekten: „Wir wollten ein architektonisches Wahrzeichen schaffen, in dem verschiedene bedeutsame Einflüsse und Impulse zum Ausdruck kommen sollten. Die Bandbreite reicht von ästhetischen Elementen und Formen, die für Geschwindigkeit, Bewegung und Spektakel stehen, bis hin zu jener Art von Kunstfertigkeit und geometrischen Formen, die die Grundlage alter islamischer Kunsthandwerkstraditionen bildet." Die äußere Erscheinung des Komplexes wird bestimmt von einer beeindruckenden, 217 m langen facettierten Hülle aus Stahlverbindungen und rund 5800 neigbaren Glaspaneelen. Das Freiformdach überspannt die beiden Hoteltürme und eine als Halbschalenkonstruktion aus Stahl angefertigte Verbindungsbrücke. Im Gegensatz zu seinem Nachbarn Dubai hat Abu Dhabi die Verwirklichung seiner ehrgeizigen Architekturprojekte trotz der Weltwirtschaftskrise weiterverfolgt. Das Yas-Hotel gehört zu jenen herausragenden Beispielen für die in der jüngeren Zeit vollbrachten Bauleistungen, die das Emirat zu einem Muss für Fans zeitgenössischer Architektur zu machen.

Cet hôtel de 500 chambres est situé dans la vaste zone d'aménagement de la Yas Marina qui comprend par ailleurs un circuit de Formule 1. «Asymptote a imaginé un signal architectural qui incarne diverses influences et sources d'inspiration allant de l'esthétique et de formes liés à la vitesse, au mouvement et au spectacle, à l'approche artistique et géométrique de l'art et des traditions islamiques anciennes», expliquent les architectes. L'élément le plus frappant est une coque tramée de 217 mètres de long constituée de 5800 panneaux pivotants. Elle recouvre les deux bâtiments de l'hôtel et la passerelle monocoque en acier qui les relie. À la différence de ses voisins de Dubaï, Abou Dhabi poursuit ses ambitieux projets architecturaux malgré la crise économique internationale. Le **YAS HOTEL** est un des exemples les plus remarquables de transformation de l'Émirat en lieu de destination pour amateurs d'architecture contemporaine.

The architects were responsible for some of the interior spaces, which emphasize the continuity with the exterior design of the hotel.

Die Architekten zeichnen auch für einen Teil der Interieurs verantwortlich, in denen sich die Außengestaltung des Hotels fortsetzt.

Les architectes sont également intervenus en partie sur les aménagements intérieurs, qui reprennent l'esprit du dessin des façades de l'hôtel.

Sitting literally atop the Formula 1
racetrack, the hotel is divided into
two volumes, linked by a bridge and
the overarching roof structure.

Das Hotel ist unmittelbar auf die
Formel-Eins-Rennstrecke aufgesetzt;
die beiden Gebäudetrakte sind durch
die gewölbte Dachkonstruktion sowie
durch eine Brücke miteinander
verbunden.

Littéralement construit au-dessus
d'un circuit de compétition automobile, l'hôtel est divisé en deux volumes
reliés par une passerelle et la
structure de la couverture.

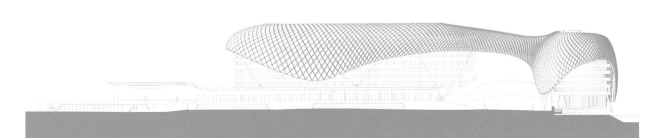

ATELIER-DEN / INAHARA ARCHI-LAB

Atelier-Den
205, 3–14–8 Higashishinkoiwa
Katsushika-ku, Tokyo 124–0023
Japan

Tel: +81 3 3693 9081
Fax: +81 3 3696 6414
E-mail: info@atelier-den.com
Web: www.atelier-den.com

Inahara Archi-Lab
25–3 Ohmiya-cho Fujinomiya
Shizuoka 418–0066
Japan

Tel: +81 54 422 8082
Fax: +81 54 426 4163
E-mail: matsuya1615@ybb.ne.jp

Hideya Tanaka of **ATELIER-DEN** was born in 1966 in Kyoto. He graduated from Kyoto University with an M.Arch degree in 1992 and began working the same year for Akira Kuryu Architect & Associates. He established Atelier-Den in 1998 and is an Adjunct Professor of Architecture at Chiba University. Works of Atelier-Den include a House in Sekimachi (Tokyo, 2005), and an Apartment in Koiwa (Tokyo, 2009) in Japan. Ken Inahara was born in Tokyo in 1967 and graduated from Kyoto University in 1990, when he began working for Shimizu Corporation. His firm, **INAHARA ARCHI-LAB**, has completed the Totoro-Box House (Fujinomiya, Shizuoka, 2008) and the 2+4 Box House (Hachioji, Tokyo, 2009) in Japan. Together they completed the Sano Clinic Therapy Square (Fujinomiya, Shizuoka, Japan, 2008, published here).

Hideya Tanaka vom **ATELIER-DEN** wurde 1966 in Kyoto geboren. 1992 schloss er sein Architekturstudium an der Universtität Kyoto mit dem Mastertitel ab und begann noch im selben Jahr für Akira Kuryu Architect & Associates zu arbeiten. Parallel zur Leitung seines 1998 gegründeten Atelier-Den ist Tanaka als außerplanmäßiger Professor für Architektur an der Universität Chiba tätig. Zu seinen Arbeiten gehören ein Wohnhaus in Sekimachi (Tokio, 2005) und ein Apartment in Koiwa (Tokio, 2009). Der 1967 in Tokio geborene Ken Inahara schloss sein Studium an der Universität Kyoto im Jahr 1990 ab und begann im Anschluss für das Architekturbüro Shimizu Corporation zu arbeiten. Mit seinem eigenen Büro **INAHARA ARCHI-LAB** hat er das Totoro-Box House (Fujinomiya, Shizuoka, Japan, 2008) und das 2+4 Box House (Hachioji, Tokio, 2009) realisiert. Tanakas und Inaharas Gemeinschaftsprojekt, der Sano Clinic Therapy Square, wurde 2008 fertiggestellt (Fujinomiya, Shizuoka, Japan, hier vorgestellt).

Hideya Tanaka de l'**ATELIER-DEN**, né en 1966 à Kyoto, est M. Arch de l'Université de Kyoto (1992) et a commencé à travailler la même année pour l'agence Akira Kuryu Architect & Associates. Il a créé l'Atelier-Den en 1998, et est professeur adjoint d'architecture à l'Université Chiba. Parmi ses réalisations : une maison à Sekimachi (Tokyo, 2005) et un appartement à Koiwa (Tokyo, 2009). Ken Inahara, né à Tokyo en 1967, est diplômé de l'Université de Kyoto (1990), puis a travaillé pour la Shimizu Corporation. Son agence, **INAHARA ARCHI-LAB**, a réalisé la Maison Totoro-Box House (Fujinomiya, Shizuoka, 2008) et la Maison 2+4 Box (Hachioji, Tokyo, 2009). Ils ont construit ensemble la Sano Clinic Therapy Square (Fujinomiya, Shizuoka, 2008, publiée ici).

SANO CLINIC THERAPY SQUARE

Fujinomiya, Shizuoka, Japan, 2008

Area: 431 m². Client: not disclosed. Cost: not disclosed

As the architects have pointed out, this clinic has a good view of Mount Fuji, an important fact in Japan. They proposed the expansion of a clinic both in terms of physical size but also in terms of its "healing" functions. They used blue, green, pink, and a wood color, in accordance with the psychological effects of the colors: "Blue, concentration; Green, relaxation; Pink, comfort; and Wood, healing." The interior spaces of the building are not closed off, giving a "sense of relaxation and unity" to the whole. Holes corresponding to various functions, all of the same size, are another unifying element in the design—one use of these openings is a "double ventilation system" that handles both interior and exterior air circulation.

Nach den Besonderheiten ihrer Klinik befragt, verweisen die Architekten als Erstes auf die ausgezeichnete Aussicht auf den nehegelegen Fuji, der für jeden Japaner von besonderer Bedeutung ist. Aber auch sonst gingen Tanaka und Inahara über die üblichen Vorstellungen von einer Klinik hinaus, sowohl im Hinblick auf die räumliche Gestaltung des Baus als auch auf die ihm eigene „heilende Komponente". Letztere betonten die Architekten durch den Einsatz verschiedener Farbtöne, die jeweils mit einer bestimmten psychologische Wirkung assoziiert werden: „Blau steht für Konzentration, Grün für Enspannung, Rosa für Behaglichkeit, ein Holzton für Heilung". Die einzelnen Abschnitte im Innenbereich des Gebäudes sind zueinander geöffnet und lassen so „einen Gesamteindruck von Einklang und Entspannung" entstehen. Die zahlreichen gleichformatigen Wand- und Deckenöffnungen stiften indes nicht nur eine visuelle Einheitlichkeit, sondern dienen auch praktisch-technischen Zwecken wie dem Luftaustausch zwischen Innen und Außen.

Les architectes précisent que cette clinique bénéficie d'une vue intéressante sur le Mont Fuji, avantage particulièrement apprécié au Japon. Ils ont proposé de développer l'établissement en termes de dimensions, mais aussi de fonctions thérapeutiques. Par exemple, ils ont choisi le bleu, le vert, le rose et une couleur boisée, pour les effets psychologiques de ces couleurs : « Bleu, la concentration ; vert, la relaxation ; rose, le confort ; et la couleur bois, la guérison. » Les espaces intérieurs ne sont pas fermés, ce qui génère un « ressenti de détente et d'unité ». Les ouvertures et découpes, toutes de la même taille, correspondant aux différentes fonctions, donnent un sentiment d'unité du projet. Elles participent également au « système de double ventilation » qui contrôle la circulation de l'air extérieur et intérieur.

The irregular pattern of openings in the building renders its interior structure impossible to understand from the outside, while admitting color and light.

Die Öffnungen in den Außenfassaden sorgen für Helligkeit und farbliche Akzente im Gebäudeinneren, gleichwohl lässt sich anhand ihrer unregelmäßigen Anordnung schwerlich auf die Gestaltung des Innenbereichs schließen.

La composition irrégulière des ouvertures fait qu'il est impossible de comprendre la structure intérieure vue de l'extérieur. Elles apportent la lumière et, en même temps, multiplient les effets chromatiques.

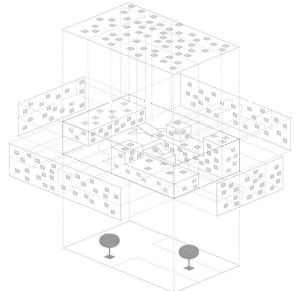

Characterized by its multiple square
or rectangular openings, the building
is also suffused with points of color.

Caractérisé par ses multiples ouvertures de forme carrée ou rectangulaire, l'immeuble est également constel-
lé de points colorés.

Mit ihrer Farbsymbolik verleihen
die zahlreichen quadratischen und
rechteckigen Öffnungen dem Gebäude
seine besondere Charakteristik.

UPENN Weave Bridge ▶

CECIL BALMOND

Arup
13 Fitzroy Street, London W1T 4BQ, UK
Tel: +44 20 77 55 42 48 / Fax: +44 20 77 55 29 94
E-mail: webmail@arup.com / Web: www.arup.com

Born and educated in Sri Lanka, **CECIL BALMOND** went to London for postgraduate studies and joined Arup in 1968. He is an internationally recognized designer, structural engineer, and author, and Deputy Chairman of the multidisciplinary engineering firm Arup since 2004. He founded the Advanced Geometry Unit (AGU) at Arup. His interest lies in the genesis of form, using numbers, music, and mathematics as vital sources. His notable books include *Number 9: The Search for the Sigma Code* (Prestel, 1998) and *Informal* (Prestel, 2002), which explores structure as a catalyst in architecture. He is an external examiner at the Architectural Association (AA) in London, and Senior Design Fellow at the London School of Economics. His interest in architecture and design has led to successful collaborations with a number of major international architects. He worked with the Dutch architect Rem Koolhaas on the Kunsthal (Rotterdam, The Netherlands, 1994); Grand Palais (Lille, France, 1994); Seattle Central Library (Seattle, Washington, USA, 2004); Casa da Musica (Porto, Portugal, 2005); and the Serpentine Pavilion (London, UK, 2006). He worked with Álvaro Siza on the Portuguese National Pavilion for Expo '98 in Lisbon (Portugal); with Daniel Libeskind on the latter's ill-fated World Trade Center projects (New York); and with the artist Anish Kapoor on the sculpture *Marsyas*, presented in the Turbine Hall of London's Tate Modern in 2002. Other projects include the redevelopment of Battersea Power Station (London, UK, since 1999); Coimbra Footbridge (Coimbra, Portugal, 2006); the design of the new Centre Pompidou-Metz (Metz, France, 2006–10, with Shigeru Ban); the CCTV Headquarters building in Beijing (China, 2005–08, again with OMA/Rem Koolhaas, page 352); *Temenos*, the first of the Tees Valley Giants sculptures, with Anish Kapoor (Middlehaven, UK, 2008–09); and UPENN Weave Bridge (Philadelphia, Pennsylvania, USA, 2008–09, published here).

Der in Sri Lanka geborene und ausgebildete **CECIL BALMOND** kam zu weiterführenden Studien nach London und schloss sich 1968 dem Büro Arup an. Balmond ist ein international bekannter Designer, Bauingenieur, Autor und seit 2004 stellvertretender Vorsitzender des multidisziplinären Ingenieurbüros Arup, wo er die Advanced Geometry Unit (AGU) begründete. Er interessiert sich für die Genese von Formen durch Zahlen, Musik und Mathematik als wesentliche Quellen. Zu seinen wichtigen Büchern gehören *Number 9 – The Search for the Sigma Code* (Prestel, 1998) oder *Informal* (Prestel, 2002)), in dem er sich mit Baukonstruktion als Katalysator in der Architektur beschäftigt. Sein Interesse an Architektur und Design führte zur erfolgreichen Zusammenarbeit mit einer Reihe von international bedeutenden Architekten. Gemeinsam mit dem niederländischen Architekten Rem Koolhaas entstanden die Kunsthal in Rotterdam (Niederlande, 1994), der Grand Palais in Lille (Frankreich, 1994), die Seattle Central Library (Washington, USA, 2004), die Casa da Musica in Porto (Portugal, 2005) und der Serpentine Pavilion in London (2006). Balmond war ebenso beteiligt an Daniel Libeskinds vom Unglück verfolgten Planungen für das World Trade Center (New York) wie an Álvaro Sizas Portugiesischem Pavillon für die Expo '98 in Lissabon oder der im Jahr 2002 in der Turbinenhalle der Londoner Tate Modern ausgestellten Skulptur *Marsyas* des Künstlers Anish Kapoor. Weiterhin wirkte Balmond mit an der Umgestaltung der Battersea Power Station in London (seit 1999), an den von Shigeru Ban geleiteten Planungen für den neuen Centre Pompidou-Metz (Metz, Frankreich, 2006–10) und an den Arbeiten für die Zentrale von CCTV in Peking (2005–08; wiederum mit OMA/Rem Koolhaas, Seite 352). Als Gemeinschaftsprojekt mit Anish Kapoor entstand in Middlehaven *Tenemos*, der erste Beitrag für das Skulpturenprojekt Tees Valley Giants (Großbritannien, 2008–09). Als Eigenprojekte entwickelte Balmond eine Fußgängerbrücke im portugiesischen Coimbra (2006) sowie die UPENN Weave Bridge in Philadelphia (Pennsylvania, USA, 2008–09, hier vorgestellt).

Né et formé au Sri Lanka, **CECIL BALMOND** est venu à Londres pour y poursuivre des études supérieures, et a rejoint l'agence Arup en 1968. Concepteur, ingénieur structurel et auteur de notoriété internationale, il est, depuis 2004, vice-président de l'agence d'ingénierie multidisciplinaire Arup au sein de laquelle il a fondé une Unité de géométrie avancée (AGU). Parmi ses écrits notables figurent *Number 9, The Search for the Sigma Code* (Prestel, 1998), et *Informal* (Prestel, 2002) qui explorent la structure en tant que catalyseur d'architecture. Il est examinateur invité à l'Architectural Association de Londres et Senior Design Fellow de la London School of Economics. Son intérêt pour l'architecture et la conception l'a conduit à des collaborations applaudies avec quelques-uns des plus grands architectes mondiaux. Il a collaboré avec l'architecte néerlandais Rem Koolhaas sur le Kunsthal de Rotterdam (1994) ; le Grand Palais à Lille (1994) ; la bibliothèque centrale de Seattle (Washington, 2004) ; la Casa da Musica à Porto (2005) ; et le Serpentine Pavilion (Londres, 2006). Il a travaillé avec Álvaro Siza sur le projet du Pavillon national portugais pour Expo '98 à Lisbonne, et avec Daniel Libeskind sur des projets inaboutis pour le World Trade Center à New York. Il a également assisté l'artiste Anish Kapoor pour la sculpture *Marsyas* installée dans le Turbine Hall de la Tate Modern à Londres en 2002. Parmi ses autres projets : la restructuration de la Battersea Power Station, Londres (depuis 1999) ; la conception, aux côtés de Shigeru Ban, du Centre Pompidou Metz (Metz, 2006–10) ; la passerelle de Coimbra (Coimbra, Portugal, 2006) ; le siège de la chaîne de télévision chinoise CCTV à Pékin (2005–08, avec OMA/Rem Koolhaas, page 352) ; *Temenos*, la première des sculptures des Géants de la Tees Valley avec Anish Kapoor (Middlehaven, Royaume-Uni, 2008–09) ; et l'Uppen Weave Bridge (Philadelphie, Pennsylvanie, 2008–09, publié ici).

UPENN WEAVE BRIDGE

Philadelphia, Pennsylvania, USA, 2008–09

Address: University of Pennsylvania, 3451 Walnut Street, Philadelphia, PA 19104-6243, USA, +1 215 898 5000, www.upenn.edu
Span: 50 m. Client: University of Pennsylvania. Cost: not disclosed
Collaboration: Daniel Bosia, Director of AGU

This bridge crosses over rail lines and links the University of Pennsylvania with its sports area. The "weave" referred to in the name of the bridge is a double helix form of steel girders coiling over the tracks. Cecil Balmond states: "The project is not about engineering a new type of bridge structure per se. It is about treating the bridge as architectural space: a space of passage in a master plan that is not unlike a major corridor or link in a large building complex." Although it looks like a conventional bridge in many respects, the load-bearing structure of the **UPENN WEAVE BRIDGE** has never been used in a bridge before. It is part of a larger plan devised by Cecil Balmond to connect the campus to its sports areas more fully. The designers state: "The bridge itself was built as a single element off site and lifted into place over the live railway lines. Glazed panels provide good views out from the bridge, while negating the requirement for handrails, which would spoil the architectural form of the bridge."

Die **UPENN WEAVE BRIDGE** überspannt eine Gleisstrecke, die das Gelände der University of Pennsylvania von den universitätseigenen Sportanlagen trennt. Der in dem Brückennamen enthaltene Begriff des Gewebes (weave) bezieht sich auf die Stahlträger, die sich in Form einer Doppelhelix über das Gleisbett erstrecken. Es geht für Cecil Balmond „bei dem Projekt nicht um einen neuen Typus von Brückenkonstruktion als solcher. Die Brücke sollte vielmehr wie ein architektonischer Raum behandelt werden, als ein in einen Gesamtplan integriertes Passagenelement, ähnlich einem Hauptkorridor in einem großen Gebäudekomplex." Die Konstruktion sieht zwar in mancher Hinsicht wie die einer konventionellen Brücke aus, doch tatsächlich wurde die Tragwerkkonstruktion der Weave Bridge noch nie zuvor im Brückenbau eingesetzt. Das Bauwerk ist Teil eines umfassenderen von Balmond entwickelten Konzepts, das auf eine sinnvollere Anbindung der Sportstätten an den Universitätscampus abzielt. „Die Brücke selbst wurde nicht vor Ort gebaut, sondern komplett montiert auf Schienen zu ihrem Bestimmungsort tranportiert. Die großflächige Verglasung bietet eine hervorragende Aussicht und machte zugleich Handläufe überflüssig, die ansonsten die formale architektonische Geschlossenheit der Brücke gestört hätten."

Cette passerelle de franchissement de voies ferrées, relie l'Université de Pennsylvanie à ses terrains de sports. Le « tressage » auquel renvoie son nom évoque la forme constructive constituée de poutres d'acier en double hélice. Pour Balmond : « Ce projet n'est pas l'ingénierie d'un nouveau type de structure de pont en soi. Il s'agit de traiter le pont comme un espace architectural : un espace de passage dans un plan directeur, qui n'est pas très différent d'un grand corridor ou d'un lien à travers un vaste complexe de constructions. » Bien que l'ouvrage ressemble à de nombreux égards à un pont conventionnel, ce type de structure porteuse n'avait jamais été utilisé pour un pont auparavant. Il fait partie d'un plan plus important mis au point par Cecil Balmond pour établir une meilleure liaison entre le campus et ses installations sportives. « La passerelle elle-même a été construite hors site, puis mise en place par levage au-dessus des voies ferrées en fonctionnement. Des panneaux vitrés libèrent la vue du pont et rendent inutile la présence de garde-corps qui auraient gâché la forme architecturale. »

Drawings show the "double-helix form" of the bridge better than most photographs. Right, a site plan shows the thin bridge crossing over the rail lines, linking different parts of the campus.

Auf Zeichnungen lässt sich die „Doppelhelixform" der Brücke besser erkennen als auf den meisten Fotos. Der Geländeplan (rechts) zeigt die Bahnstrecke und den Verlauf der quer hinüberführenden schmalen Brücke, die die beiden Campusteile miteinander verbindet.

Les dessins illustrent plus clairement que les photographies la forme en double hélice du pont. À droite, un plan d'ensemble montre la passerelle légère qui franchit les voies ferrées et relie différentes parties du campus.

Although Cecil Balmond's main area of interest is engineering, he has sought to bring this bridge closer to the notion of architectural space than a pure engineer might have—as is visible in the photo above.

Cecil Balmonds Hauptbetätigungsfeld ist zwar die Baukonstruktion, das Foto oben zeigt jedoch, dass er versuchte, der Brücke das Erscheinungsbild eines architektonischen Raums zu geben – anders als ein reiner Ingenieur vielleicht vorgegangen wäre.

Bien que le principal centre d'intérêt de Cecil Balmond soit l'ingénierie, il a plus traité ce pont comme un espace architectural qu'un ouvrage d'ingénieur, ainsi que le montre la photo ci-dessus.

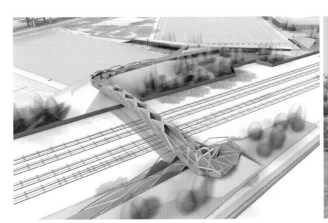

CHARLES BARCLAY

Charles Barclay Architects
74 Josephine Avenue
London SW2 2LA
UK

Tel: +44 20 86 74 00 37
Fax: +44 20 86 83 96 96
E-mail: cba@cbarchitects.co.uk
Web: www.cbarchitects.co.uk

CHARLES BARCLAY was born in London in 1962. He graduated from North London University (now Metropolitan) in 1994 and created Charles Barclay Architects in 1996. He worked previously for Rick Mather, Mark Guard, and John Winter in London, for Peter Eisenman in New York, and for Sarvodaya in Sri Lanka. Charles Barclay writes about architecture and design, and is a guest critic at Metropolitan University's Department of Architecture. The work of Charles Barclay Architects ranges from houses to remodeling of inner London schools. Their highest-profile commission to date is the Kielder Observatory, won in competition in 2005 and completed in May 2008 (Kielder, Northumberland, UK, published here). Ongoing projects include the Grafton and Vittoria Schools (Islington, London, UK); a Ranch House (Buenos Aires, Argentina); and an African Eco-House (Entebbe, Uganda).

CHARLES BARCLAY wurde 1962 in London geboren. Nach seinem Abschluss an der North London University (heute London Metropolitan University) im Jahr 1994 gründete er 1996 Charles Barclay Architects. Zuvor hatte er bereits für die in London ansässigen Architekturbüros von Rick Mather, Mark Guard und John Winter gearbeitet sowie für Peter Eisenman in New York und für Sarvodaya in Sri Lanka. Charles Barclay betätigt sich auch als Autor zu Architektur- und Designthemen und ist Gastkritiker am Department of Architecture der Metropolitan University. Die Projektbandbreite von Charles Barclay Architects reicht von Wohnhausentwürfen bis hin zur Modernisierung von Londoner Schulen. Die bis dato meiste Aufmerksamkeit erlangte das Büro mit ihrem Entwurf für das Kielder Observatory, das als Siegerbeitrag aus einem im Jahr 2005 entschiedenen internationalen Wettbewerb hervorgangen war und im Mai 2008 fertiggestellt wurde (Kielder, Northumberland, Großbritannien, hier vorgestellt). Zu den gegenwärtigen Projekten des Büros gehören zwei Schulumbauten in London (Grafton School und Vittoria School, Islington, Großbritannien), ein Ranch-haus in Buenos Aires (Argentinien) und ein Öko-Haus in Entebbe (Uganda).

CHARLES BARCLAY, né à Londres en 1962, est diplômé de la North London University (aujourd'hui Metropolitan University) en 1994 et a fondé Charles Barclay Architects en 1996. Auparavant, il avait travaillé pour Rick Mather, Mark Guard et John Winter à Londres, pour Peter Eisenman à New York et pour Sarvodaya au Sri Lanka. Il écrit sur l'architecture et le design, et est critique invité au département d'architecture de la Metropolitan University. Son travail couvre aussi bien des maisons indivi-duelles que la rénovation d'écoles londoniennes. Son projet le plus remarqué à cette date a été l'Observatoire de Kielder, remporté à l'issue d'un concours en 2005 et achevé en mai 2008 (Kielder, Northumberland, G.-B., publié ici). Parmi ses projets en cours figurent les écoles Grafton et Vittoria (Islington, Londres) ; une maison de ranch (Buenos Aires, Argentine) et une écomaison en Afrique (Entebbe, Uganda).

KIELDER OBSERVATORY

Kielder, Northumberland, UK, 2008

Address: Kielder, Northumberland NE48 1ER, UK, +44 78 05 63 84 69, www.kielderobservatory.org
Area: 235 m². Client: Forestry Commission. Cost: €450 000

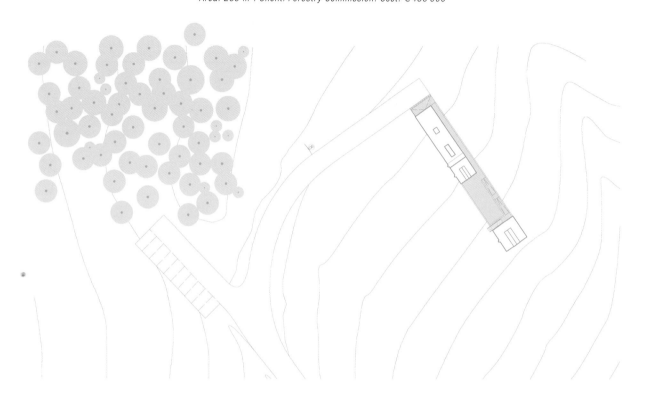

Charles Barclay Architects won the 2005 international competition with over 230 entries to build an astronomical **OBSERVATORY IN THE KIELDER WATER AND FOREST PARK** in Northumberland near the Scottish border. This commission is part of an ongoing initiative entitled "Art and Architecture at Kielder" that has seen the construction of other small structures in the park, such as James Turrell's *Kielder Skyspace*. The program called for a structure intended to house two telescopes with a view of the southern sky and a room for amateurs or scientific research. An open deck joining the two telescopes allows all-comers to set up their own equipment for "star-gazing events." The building is designed to be removed from the site after 25 years with minimal damage to the ground. "We wanted the experience of being on the observatory to feel like being on a vessel at sea in this rough, open landscape, with an amazing array of stars overhead," states the architect. Siberian larch was used for its "low-carbon" profile and to make a concerted contrast with high-tech observatories. A 2.5kW wind turbine and photovoltaic panels provide energy.

2005 gewannen Charles Barclay Architects den international ausgeschriebenen Wettbewerb mit mehr als 230 Beiträgen für den Bau einer **STERNWARTE IM WATER AND FOREST PARK VON KIELDER** in Northumberland, nahe der Grenze zu Schottland. Die Ausschreibung erfolgte im Rahmen der seit 1999 bestehenden Initiative „Art and Architecture at Kielder", durch die bereits einige kleinere Projekte wie etwa James Turrells *Kielder Skyspace* in dem Naturpark realisiert wurden. Verlangt war ein Gebäudeentwurf, der die Aufstellung von zwei Teleskopen zur Beobachtung des Südhimmels sowie einen für die Nutzung von Hobbyastronomen wie von Forschern gedachten Raum berücksichtigen sollte. Zwischen den beiden Aufbauten für die Teleskope befindet sich eine Plattform, auf der jeder Besucher seine eigene Ausrüstung zur Sternenbeobachtung aufstellen kann. Die gesamte Konstruktion ist so angelegt, dass sie nach 25 Jahren wieder abgebaut werden kann, ohne nennenswerte Spuren zu verlassen. „Unsere Idee war, dass man sich beim Besuch des Observatoriums in der rauen weiten Landschaft fühlen sollte, als sei man – Abertausende von Sternen über sich – an Bord eines Schiffes auf dem Meer", erklärt der Architekt. Um den Bau möglichst ressourcenschonend zu errichten, wurde sibirische Lärchen verwendet, die zugleich für einen bewussten visuellen Kontrast zu den üblichen Hightech-Observatorien sorgt. Die benötigte Energie wird mithilfe einer 2,5-KW-Windturbine und einer Solarstromanlage erzeugt.

Charles Barclay Architects a remporté, parmi 230 participants, le concours international organisé en 2005 pour la construction d'un **OBSERVATOIRE ASTRONO-MIQUE DANS LE KIELDER WATER AND FOREST PARK** (Northumberland), près de la frontière écossaise. Cette commande fait partie d'un programme en cours de développement intitulé «Art et architecture à Kielder» qui est à l'origine de la présence d'autres petites constructions comme le *Kielder Skyspace* de James Turrell. La demande portait sur une structure contenant deux télescopes et une salle pour chercheurs, amateurs ou scientifiques. Une terrasse relie les deux télescopes et permet aux astronomes de disposer leur propre équipement pour leurs séances d'observation des étoiles. Le bâtiment est conçu pour être démonté dans vingt-cinq ans, en laissant le minimum de traces au sol. «Nous voulions que les utilisateurs de l'observatoire aient le sentiment de se trouver dans un navire en pleine mer au milieu de ce paysage naturel, tourmenté et ouvert, sous une étonnante voûte étoilée», explique l'architecte. Le mélèze de Sibérie a été choisi pour sa faible empreinte carbone et pour renforcer le contraste avec les observatoires d'allure plus généralement high-tech. Une éolienne de 2,5 kW et des panneaux photovoltaïques fournissent l'énergie nécessaire.

The long, thin wooden structure is set on progressively higher pilotis in order to maintain its horizontality on the sloping site.

Um die Abschüssigkeit des Geländes auszugleichen, wurde die lange schmale Holzkonstruktion auf unterschiedlich lange Pfeiler gesetzt.

La longue et fine construction en bois repose sur des pilotis de plus en plus hauts qui compensent la pente du terrain.

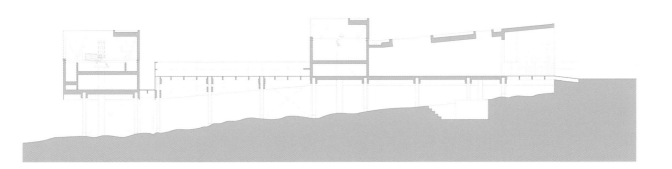

Above, Charles Barclay's sketch of the structure as seen from the opposite angle of the photo below. The wooden structure blends in with its beige setting in these pictures taken shortly after construction.

Die obige Zeichnung des Architekten und das Foto unten zeigen das Bauwerk aus entgegengesetzten Winkeln. Die kurz nach der Errichtung entstandenen Aufnahmen zeigen den farblichen Einklang zwischen Holz und sandfarbenem Untergrund.

Ci-dessus, un croquis de l'architecte représente l'observatoire sous un angle opposé de celui de la photographie ci-dessous. Habillée de bois, la construction se fond dans le cadre terreux de ces images de fin de chantier.

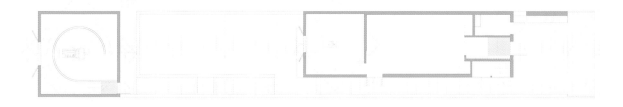

The simple, rectangular floor plan seen above culminates in the square observatory space visible in the photo above (and left on the plan).

Das Foto zeigt den hinteren Aufbau der schlichten rechteckigen Konstruktion, den eigentlichen, größeren der beiden quadratischen Teleskopräume (auf der Grundrisszeichnung links).

La simplicité du plan rectangulaire culmine dans la forme carrée de l'observatoire (à gauche sur le plan et photo ci-dessus).

BARKOW LEIBINGER ARCHITECTS

Barkow Leibinger Architekten
Schillerstr. 94, 10625 Berlin, Germany
Tel: +49 30 315 71 20 / Fax: +49 30 31 57 12 29
E-mail: info@barkowleibinger.com / Web: www.barkowleibinger.com

REGINE LEIBINGER was born in 1963 in Stuttgart, Germany. She studied architecture in Berlin (Diploma, Technical University, 1989) and at Harvard University (M.Arch, 1990). She created a joint office with Frank Barkow in 1993. She has been a Visiting Professor at the Architectural Association (AA) in London (Unit Master, 1997–98), Cornell University, and Harvard University, and, since 2006, a Professor for Building Construction and Design at the Technische Universität Berlin. **FRANK BARKOW** was born in 1957 in Kansas City, USA, and studied architecture at Montana State University (B.Arch, 1982) and at Harvard University (M.Arch, 1990). He has been working with Regine Leibinger in Berlin since 1993. Barkow has been a Visiting Professor at the AA in London (Unit Master, 1995–98), Cornell University, Harvard University, and at the State Academy of Art and Design in Stuttgart. Their recent work includes Pavilions for Research and Production (Grüsch, Switzerland, 2001; 2004); a house in Berlin-Karlshorst (2007); a Gatehouse (Stuttgart, Ditzingen, 2007); Campus Restaurant (Ditzingen, 2006–08); and the Marcus Prize Pavilion (Menomonee Valley, Milwaukee, Wisconsin, USA, 2008, published here), all in Germany unless stated otherwise. Current work includes the high-rise Total Tower (Berlin, Germany, 2012). Kyle Talbott, the professor in charge of the Marcus Prize Pavilion with the architects, was born in 1967 and received his M.Arch degree from Texas A&M University (1993). He led a digital technology research-and-development unit for the international firm NBBJ in the late 1990s, and is now an Associate Professor of Architecture at the University of Wisconsin in Milwaukee.

REGINE LEIBINGER, geboren 1963 in Stuttgart, studierte Architektur an der Techischen Universität Berlin (Diplom 1989) und der Harvard University (M.Arch 1990). 1993 gründete sie mit Frank Barkow ein Gemeinschaftsbüro in Berlin. Leibinger war Gastprofessorin an der Architectural Association (AA) in London (Unit Master, 1997–98) sowie an den Universitäten Cornell und Harvard, seit 2006 ist sie Professorin für Baukonstruktion und Entwerfen an der TU Berlin. **FRANK BARKOW**, geboren 1957 in Kansas City in den USA, erwarb 1982 seinen B.Arch an der Montana State University und 1990 seinen M.Arch an der Harvard University. Wie Leibinger war Barkow Gastprofessor an der AA in London (Unit Master, 1995–98) und den Universitäten Cornell und Harvard, außerdem lehrte er an der Staatlichen Akademie der Bildenden Künste Stuttgart. Zu den jüngeren Arbeiten des Gespanns gehören zwei Forschungs- und Produktionspavillons für eine Maschinenfabrik im schweizerischen Grüsch (2001; 2004), ein Wohnhaus in Berlin-Karlshorst (2007), die Hauptpforte der Firma Trumpf (2007) und ihr Betriebsrestaurant (2006-08) in Ditzingen bei Stuttgart und der Marcus Prize Pavilion (Menomonee Valley, Milwaukee, Wisconsin, USA, 2008, hier vorstellt). Gegenwärtig arbeiten Barkow Leibinger an den Planungen für den TOTAL Tower in Berlin, der 2012 fertiggestellt sein soll. Kyle Talbott, der als Professor gemeinsam mit den Architekten die Entstehung des Marcus Prize Pavilion betreute, wurde 1967 geboren. Seinen M.Arch erwarb er 1993 an der Texas A&M University. Ende der 1990er-Jahre arbeitete Talbott für das international tätige Architekturbüro NBBJ als Leiter einer Abteilung für digitale Forschung und Entwicklung, derzeit lehrt er als Associate Professor of Architecture an der University of Wisconsin in Milwaukee.

REGINE LEIBINGER, née en 1963 à Stuttgart (Allemagne) a étudié l'architecture à Berlin (diplômée de la Technische Universität, 1989) et à Harvard University (M. Arch, 1990). Elle a créé son agence en association avec Frank Barkow en 1993. Elle a été professeure invitée à l'Architectural Association (AA) de Londres (Unit Master, 1997–98), Cornell University et Harvard University, et, depuis 2006, est professeure de conception et de construction à la Technische Universität de Berlin. **FRANK BARKOW**, né en 1957 à Kansas City (États-Unis), a étudié l'architecture à la Montana State University (B. Arch, 1982) et Harvard University (M. Arch, 1990). Il travaille depuis 1993 avec Regine Leibinger à Berlin. Barkow a été professeur invité à l'AA de Londres (Unit Master, 1995–98), Cornell University, Harvard University et l'Académie d'État d'art et de design à Stuttgart. Parmi leurs récents travaux : des pavillons pour la recherche et la production (Grüsch, Suisse, 2001–04) ; une maison à Berlin-Karlshorst (2007) ; un pavillon d'entrée (Ditzingen, Stuttgart, 2007), un restaurant de campus (également à Ditzingen, Stuttgart, 2007) et le pavillon du prix Marcus (Menomonee Valley, Milwaukee, Wisconsin, États-Unis, 2008, publié ici). Kyle Talbott, professeur chargé de ce projet de pavillon avec les architectes, est né en 1967. Il est M. Arch de la Texas A&M University (1993). Il a dirigé une unité de recherche et de développement pour l'agence internationale d'architecture NBBJ à la fin des années 1990, et est maintenant professeur associé d'architecture à l'Université du Wisconsin à Milwaukee.

MARCUS PRIZE PAVILION

Menomonee Valley, Milwaukee, Wisconsin, USA, 2008

www.renewthevalley.org
Area: 23 m². Client: Menomonee Valley Partners. Cost: $35 000
· Collaboration: Professor Kyle Talbott and 16 students from the University of
Wisconsin—Milwaukee's School of Architecture and Urban Planning

The Marcus Prize is given for "emerging talent in architecture." Barkow Leibinger won the award in 2007, and taught for a semester at the University of Winconsin-Milwaukee's School of Architecture and Urban Planning. Working with Professor Kyle Talbott, Frank Barkow and Regine Leibinger participated in a community design-build project in a studio with 16 students. The project was carried out with the nonprofit organization Menomonee Valley Partners, which focuses on revitalizing an industrial area near downtown Milwaukee, with the intention of providing a meeting place, a location for informal classes, and storage for landscaping equipment. Students were asked to study local leaves, flowers, and ferns to identify possible roof structures. The group was divided into four sections concerning skin, materials, site, and structure. Their study resulted in "a leaf-shaped roof structure made of plywood and glued-laminated beams that is supported by a system of V-shaped steel column clusters" that was erected beneath the 35th Street viaduct. The group used a digital model followed by digital shop drawings and templates to make a series of unique elements for the design. Transparent corrugated polycarbonate was used for the rooftop. Recycled stones and black locust wood were employed in the structure as well.

Im Jahr 2007 erhielten Barkow Leibinger den in regelmäßiger Folge an „verheißungsvolle Talente auf dem Gebiet der Architektur" verliehenen Marcus Prize und unterrichteten ein Semester lang an der Winconsin-Milwaukee School of Architecture and Urban Planning. Gemeinsam mit dem dort lehrenden Kyle Talbott und 16 studentischen Teilnehmern eines Werkstattprojekts erarbeiteten Frank Barkow und Regine Leibinger einen Entwurf, der anschließend realisiert werden sollte. Ausgeführt wurde das Projekt mit Unterstützung der gemeinnützigen Organisation Menomonee Valley Partners, die sich der Wiederbelebung eines in Milwaukee in Stadtzentrumsnähe gelegenen Industriegebiets widmet, in dem ein Kommunikationszentrum mit Räumlichkeiten für freien Unterricht und zur Unterbringung von Equipment zur Landschaftsgestaltung entstehen soll. Die Studenten waren aufgerufen, auf dem betreffenden Areal wachsende Blätter, Blumen und Farne unter die Lupe zu nehmen und auf Strukturen hin zu untersuchen, die sich zum Bau eines Daches eignen könnten. Anschließend wurden vier Gruppen eingeteilt, die sich mit der Gebäudeverkleidung, Baumaterialien, dem Standort und der Konstruktion auseinandersetzen sollten. Aus diesen Untersuchungen ergab sich der Entwurf für „eine blattförmige Dachstruktur aus Sperrholz und Brettschichtträgern, die von einem System aus V-förmig angeordneten Pfeilergruppen getragen wird". Ausgehend von einem Computermodell entstanden digitale Fertigungszeichnungen und Templates zur Anfertigung der einzelnen Spezialbauteile. Neben einer Dachabdeckung aus durchsichtigem gewelltem Polykarbonat kamen auch natürliche Materialen – wiederverwertete Steine und Robinienholz – zum Einsatz. Der fertige Pavillon wurde unterhalb der Überführung der 35th Street aufgestellt.

Le prix Marcus est destiné à des « talents émergents en architecture ». Barkow Leibinger l'a remporté en 2007 et tous deux ont enseigné pendant un semestre à l'École d'architecture et d'urbanisme de l'Université de Wisconsin-Milwaukee. En collaboration avec le Professeur Kyle Talbott, Frank Barkow et Regine Leibinger ont travaillé sur ce projet dans le cadre d'un atelier de conception collective avec seize étudiants. Il a été mené à bien grâce au soutien d'une association à but non lucratif, les Menomonee Valley Partners, qui a pour objectif de revitaliser une zone industrielle proche du centre de Milwaukee, et souhaitaient créer un lieu de réunions où pourraient être donnés des cours et stocké du matériel d'entretien paysager. Les participants ont été chargés d'étudier les feuillages, les fleurs et les fougères locales dans le cadre d'une recherche sur la structure de la toiture. Le groupe a été divisé en quatre sous-groupes : peau, matériau, site, structure. Leur étude a abouti à « une structure de toit en forme de feuilles, faite de poutres en lamellé-collé et contreplaqué, soutenue par un ensemble de colonnes d'acier en forme de V » qui a été mise en place sous le viaduc de la 35e Rue. L'atelier a réalisé une maquette en images de synthèse, puis a réalisé des plans et des modèles sur ordinateur pour préparer la fabrication des éléments spécifiques du projet. Le toit utilise aussi des panneaux de polycarbonate ondulé transparent. On remarque dans la structure des pierres et du bois de caroubier noir de récupération.

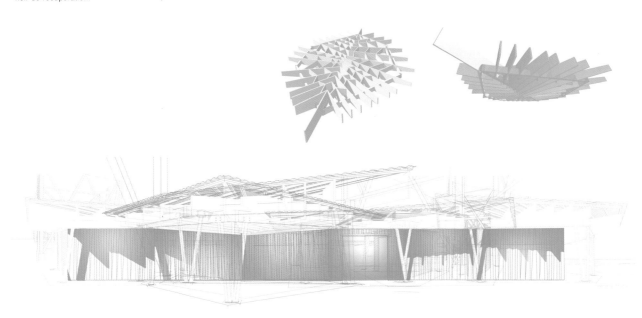

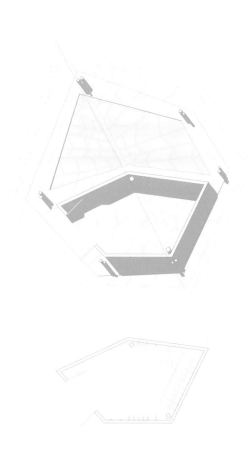

Seen left in its situation below the 35th Street viaduct, the Marcus Prize Pavilion is a lightweight, largely wooden structure. Plans and drawings on this double page reveal its full forms.

Der Marcus Prize Pavilion, links eine Fotografie seines Standortes unter der Überführung der 35. Straße, ist eine leichte, vornehmlich aus Holz bestehende Konstruktion. Die Konstruktionszeichnungen oben und auf der gegenüberliegenden Seite zeigen den Gesamtaufbau.

Vu à gauche en situation, sous le viaduc de la 35e Rue, le Pavillon Marcus Prize est une construction légère en grande partie en bois. Les plans et les dessins de cette double-page explicitent sa forme.

BAUMSCHLAGER EBERLE

Baumschlager Eberle
Lochau ZT GmbH
Lindauer Str. 31
6911 Lochau
Austria

Tel: +43 557 44 30 79-0
Fax: +43 557 44 30 79-30
E-mail: office@be-lochau.com
Web: www.baumschlager-eberle.com

CARLO BAUMSCHLAGER was born in 1956 in Bregenz, Austria. He studied at the University of Applied Arts in Vienna under Hans Hollein, Oswald M. Ungers, and Wilhelm Holzbauer, graduating in 1982. He worked at Baumschlager-Eberle-Egger (1984–85), before creating his current firm in 1985. **DIETMAR EBERLE** was born in Hittisau, Austria, in 1952. He completed his studies at the Technical University in Vienna in 1978 and participated in the working group Cooperative with Markus Koch, Norbert Mittersteiner, and Wolfgang Juen (1979–82), before creating his current association with Carlo Baumschlager in 1985. Their recent work includes the Lohbach Residential Project (Innsbruck, Austria, 2000); Munich Re Office Building (Munich, Germany, 2001); Hohlstrasse Office Building (Zurich, Switzerland, 2004); Moma (Beijing, China, 2005); CUBE Savognin (Savognin, Switzerland, 2005); Eichgut Residential Building (Winterthur, Switzerland, 2005); Molkereistrasse Student Residence (Vienna, Austria, 2005); WHO-UNAIDS Administration Building (Geneva, Switzerland, 2007); Nordwesthaus (Fussach, Vorarlberg, Austria, 2007–08, published here); VIE Skylink (Vienna-Schwechat, Austria, due for completion 2011); and the AZ Groeninge Hospital (Kortrijk, Belgium, due for completion 2018).

CARLO BAUMSCHLAGER, geboren 1956 im österreichischen Bregenz, studierte an der Universität für angewandte Kunst Wien bei Hans Hollein, Oswald M. Ungers und Wilhelm Holzbauer (Abschluss 1982). Von 1984 bis 1985 gehörte er dem Architekturbüro Baumschlager-Eberle-Egger an, 1985 rief er mit dem 1952 im österreichischen Hittisau geborenen **DIETMAR EBERLE** das gemeinsame Büro Baumschlager Eberle ins Leben. Eberle schloss sein Studium 1978 an der Technischen Universität Wien ab, anschließend gehörte er von 1979 bis 1982 zusammen mit Markus Koch, Norbert Mittersteiner und Wolfgang Juen der Baukünstlerbewegung in Voralberg an. Zu den jüngeren Arbeiten des Büros Baumschlager Eberle gehören das Innsbrucker Wohnbauprojekt Wohnen am Lohbach (Österreich, 2000), ein Bürohaus für die Münchener Rück in München (2001), das Bürohochhaus Hohlstrasse in Zürich (Schweiz, 2004), die Moma-Wohntürme in Peking (China, 2005), das CUBE-Hotel in Savognin (Schweiz, 2005), die Wohnanlage Eichgut in Winterthur (Schweiz, 2005), das Studentenwohnheim Molkereistrasse in Wien (Österreich, 2005), das Genfer Verwaltungsgebäude für die WHO-UNAIDS (Schweiz, 2007), das Nordwesthaus in Fussach (Vorarlberg, Österreich, 2007–08, hier vorgestellt), die Flughafenerweiterung VIE Skylink in Wien-Schwechat (Österreich, geplante Fertigstellung 2011) und das AZ Groeninge Krankenhaus in Kortrijk (Belgien, geplante Fertigstellung 2018).

CARLO BAUMSCHLAGER, né en 1956 à Bregenz (Autriche), est diplômé (1982) de l'Université des arts appliqués de Vienne où il a étudié auprès d'Hans Hollein, Oswald M. Ungers et Wilhelm Holzbauer. Il a travaillé pour l'agence Baumschlager-Eberle-Egger (1984–85), avant de créer son agence en 1985. **DIETMAR EBERLE**, né à Hittisau (Autriche) en 1952, a terminé ses études à l'Université polytechnique de Vienne en 1978 et a participé au groupe de travail Cooperative avec Markus Koch, Norbert Mittersteiner et Wolfgang Juen (1979–82) avant de s'associer dans la structure actuelle avec Carlo Baumschlager en 1985. Parmi leurs réalisations récentes : le projet résidentiel Lohbach (Innsbruck, Autriche, 2000) ; un immeuble de bureaux pour Munich Re (Munich, 2001) ; un immeuble de bureaux Hohlstrasse (Zurich, 2004) ; le Moma (Pékin, Chine, 2005) ; le CUBE de Savognin (Savognin, Suisse, 2005) ; l'immeuble d'appartements Eichgut (Winterthur, Suisse, 2005) ; la résidence pour étudiants de la Molkereistrasse (Vienne, Autriche, 2005) ; l'immeuble administratif de WHO-UNAIDS (Genève, Suisse, 2007) ; la Nordwesthaus (Fussach, Vorarlberg, Autriche, 2007–08, publiée ici) ; le VIE Skylink (Vienne-Schwechat, Autriche, prévu pour 2011) et l'hôpital AZ Groeninge (Courtrai, Belgique, prévu pour 2018).

NORDWESTHAUS
Fussach, Vorarlberg, Austria, 2007–08

Address: Hafenstr. 18, 6972 Fussach, Bregenz, Vorarlberg, Austria
Area: 180 m². Client: Hafen Rohner GmbH und CoKG. Cost: not disclosed

Intended as a meeting point for the local sailing community, this structure is set in the port of Fussach. An unusual irregular concrete web is juxtaposed with rectangular sheets of glass. A random decorative pattern on the glass "avoids too sharp a contrast between the core and the envelope," controlling natural light within the building at the same time. Interior lighting is supplemented by illumination of the concrete support structure that gives the building a notable nighttime presence as well. A boat area is set at water level while an 8.8 meter high event room sits above the marina. With its unusual compact form and design, the building provides an architectural counterpoint to the usual activities of a port, enabling visitors to watch the changing interplay of light on the undulating concrete structure over the course of the day.

Direkt am Wasser des Yachthafens Fussach liegt das als Treffpunkt für die örtliche Seglergemeinde errichtete Nordwesthaus, dessen Erscheinungsbild von der Wechselwirkung zwischen unregelmäßig strukturierten Betonelementen und rechteckigen Glastafeln bestimmt wird. Die nach dem Zufallsprinzip entstandene Ornamentik des Glases „verhindert allerdings, dass Hülle und Kern in ihrer Systematik zu scharf kontrastieren", und kontrolliert zugleich den Lichteinfall ins Gebäude. Die Innenraumbeleuchtung wird ergänzt durch die in die Tragstruktur integrierte Illumination, die im Dunkeln zudem für eine interessante Außenerscheinung des Gebäudes sorgt. Auf Wasserspiegelniveau befindet sich die „Bootbox", und oberhalb dieser der 8,8 m hohe Clubraum. Bildet die kompakte Gestalt des Entwurfs ohnehin einen architektonischen Kontrapunkt zum üblichen Hafengeschehen, entfaltet sie außerdem durch den steten Wandel des Tageslichts eine immer wieder andere Wirkung auf den Betrachter.

Point de rencontre destiné aux amateurs de sports de voile locaux, ce petit bâtiment se dresse dans le port de Fussach sur le lac de Constance. Sa trame en béton de dessin irrégulier est gainée de panneaux de verre rectangulaires. Un motif décoratif imprimé sur le verre « évite un contraste trop fort entre le cœur du bâtiment et son enveloppe », et contrôle dans le même temps la pénétration de la lumière naturelle. L'éclairage intérieur est complété par l'illumination de la structure de béton ce qui assure à l'ensemble une forte présence nocturne. Au ras de l'eau se trouve un espace technique pour les bateaux. La salle de réceptions de 8,8 mètres d'hauteur est au-dessus du lac. Par sa forme compacte inhabituelle, ce petit bâtiment fournit un contrepoint architectural aux activités classiques du port et offre à ses utilisateurs des vues évoluant avec les changements de la lumière qui jouent sur le dessin sinueux de la structure en béton.

The architects' intention to avoid too great a correspondence between the core and the envelope of the structure is perfectly illustrated in the image above and the photo on the left page.

Die Abbildung oben und das Foto auf der gegenüberliegenden Seite bringen hervorragend den von den Architekten beabsichtigten Kontrast zwischen dem Kern und der Hülle des Gebäudes zur Geltung.

L'intention de l'architecte d'éviter une trop grande correspondance formelle entre le cœur et l'enveloppe de la structure s'illustre parfaitement dans la photo ci-dessus et celle de la page de gauche.

The coloring of the volume can be varied with its artificial lighting, as seen in the green and red variants above.

Dank eines speziellen Beleuchtungskonzepts lässt sich der Clubraum in verschiedene Farben tauchen, hier die grüne und die rote Variante.

Un éclairage artificiel permet de faire varier la couleur du volume, ici en rouge et en vert.

On the left page, a broad view of the external glass envelope and the intervening irregular concrete structure emphasizes the contrast between geometric rigor and a more organic design.

Die Großansicht der gläsernen Außenhülle und der unregelmäßig strukturierten Betonkonstruktion (gegenüberliegende Seite) hebt das Wechselspiel von geometrischer Strenge und einer eher organischen Komponente hervor.

Page de gauche : contraste entre la composition organique de la structure de béton et la rigueur géométrique de l'enveloppe externe en verre.

BIG

BIG
Bjarke Ingels Group
Nørrebrogade 66d, 2nd Floor
2200 Copenhagen N
Denmark

Tel: +45 72 21 72 27
Fax: +45 35 12 72 27
E-mail: big@big.dk
Web: www.big.dk

Bjarke Ingels was born in 1974 in Copenhagen. He graduated from the Royal Academy of Arts School of Architecture (Copenhagen, 1999) and attended the ETSAB School of Architecture (Barcelona). He created his own office in 2005 under the name **BJARKE INGELS GROUP (BIG)**, after having cofounded PLOT Architects in 2001 and collaborated with Rem Koolhaas at OMA (Rotterdam). In 2004, he was awarded the Golden Lion at the Venice Biennale for the Stavanger Concert House. His latest completed project, The Mountain (Copenhagen, Denmark, 2006–08, published here), has already received numerous awards, including the World Architecture Festival Housing Award, Forum Aid Award, and the MIPIM Residential Development Award. Jakob Lange is an Associate of BIG and has been collaborating with Bjarke Ingels since 2003. He was born in 1978 in Odense, Denmark, and also attended the Royal Academy of Arts School of Architecture. He was the project leader for The Mountain. BIG has recently won competitions to design the National Library of Astana (Kazakhstan) and Tallin Town Hall (Estonia). Their Danish Pavilion for Expo 2010 (Shanghai, China) and the Danish Maritime Museum (Elsinore, Denmark, 2011) are amongst numerous ongoing projects that make BIG one of the most carefully watched young architecture firms in the world.

Bjarke Ingels, geboren 1974 in Kopenhagen, schloss 1999 nach zwischenzeitlichem Besuch der Escola Tècnica Superior d'Arquitectura in Barcelona sein Studium an der Architekturschule der Königlich Dänischen Kunstakademie ab. Nach seiner Mitgründung von PLOT Architects im Jahr 2001 und der Zusammenarbeit mit OMA/Rem Koolhaas, rief er 2005 sein eigenes Büro unter dem Namen **BJARKE INGELS GROUP (BIG)** ins Leben. 2004 erhielt er bei der Venedig-Biennale den Goldenen Löwen für seine Konzerthalle Stavager. Sein zuletzt abgeschlossenes Projekt, „The Mountain" (Kopenhagen, Dänemark, 2006–08, hier vorgestellt) wurde bereits mit zahlreichen Preisen ausgezeichnet, darunter der World Architecture Festival Housing Award, der Forum Aid Award und der MIPIM Residential Development Award. Jakob Lange gehört zu den Partnern von BIG und arbeitet seit 2003 mit Ingels zusammen. Lange, geboren 1978 in Odense, besuchte ebenfalls die Architekturschule der Königlich Dänischen Kunstakademie. Für „The Mountain" übernahm Lange die Projektleitung. In jüngster Vergangenheit hat BIG die Architekturwettbewerbe für den Entwurf der Nationalbibliothek von Astana (Kasachstan) und für das Rathaus von Tallin (Estland) gewonnen. Der Dänische Pavillon für die Expo 2010 in Shanghai und das dänische Schifffahrtsmuseum in Elsinore (Fertigstellung geplant für 2011) sind nur eine Auswahl aus zahlreichen weiteren Projekten eines der wichtigsten jungen Büros weltweit, das man im Auge behalten sollte.

Bjarke Ingels, né en 1974 à Copenhague, est diplômé de l'École d'architecture de l'Académie royale des arts (Copenhague, 1999) et a également étudié à l'ETSAB de Barcelone. Il a créé son agence en 2005 sous le nom de **BJARKE INGELS GROUP (BIG)**, après avoir été parmi les fondateurs de PLOT Architects en 2001 et collaboré avec Rem Koolhaas à OMA (Rotterdam). En 2004, il a reçu le Lion d'or de la Biennale de Venise pour la salle de concerts de Stavanger. Sa dernière réalisation achevée, « the Mountain » (Copenhague, Danemark, 2006–08, publiée ici), a déjà reçu de nombreux prix, dont le World Architecture Festival Housing Award, le Forum Aid Award, le MIPIM Residential Development Award. Jakob Lange est un des associés de BIG et collabore avec Bjarke Ingels depuis 2003. Né en 1978 à Odense (Danemark), il a également étudié à l'École d'architecture de l'Académie royale des arts de Copenhague. Il a été architecte de projet pour « the Mountain ». BIG a récemment remporté des concours pour la Bibliothèque nationale d'Astana (Kazakhstan) et l'hôtel de ville de Tallin (Estonie). Son pavillon danois pour Expo 2010 (Shanghaï) et le Musée maritime danois (Elsinore, Danemark, 2011) font partie de ces projets en cours qui font que BIG est l'une des jeunes agences les plus attendues sur le marché mondial de l'architecture.

THE MOUNTAIN
Copenhagen, Denmark, 2006–08

Address: Ørestads Boulevard 55, 2300 Copenhagen, Denmark, www.vmbjerget.dk
Area: 33 000 m². Client: Høpfner A/S, Danish Oil Company A/S. Cost: € 36 million
Collaboration: Jakob Lange (Project Architect), JDS

"How do you combine the splendors of the suburban backyard with the social intensity of urban density?", ask the architects. Their response is based in part on a program that called for two thirds of the space in the building to be devoted to parking (480 spots) and just one third to living (80 apartments). They decided to use the parking garages as a base on which to build terraced housing, creating a "symbiotic" relationship between the two elements. With a sloping elevator and ceiling heights that rise to 16 meters in certain places, even the garage is an architectural experience. The garden terraces that flow over the building provide the architects with the suburban lifestyle that they had aimed for while retaining urban density. A watering system ensures the survival of the balcony plants, while only a glass door separates each apartment from its terrace. Perforated aluminum plates are used for cladding on the north and west façades, allowing light and air into the parking areas. The perforations in the façade are intended to "form a huge reproduction of Mount Everest."

„Wie kombiniert man die Annehmlichkeiten eines Reihenhausgartens mit der sozialen Intensität städtischer Dichte?", lautete bei diesem Projekt die Ausgangs-frage der Architekten. Die Lösung fiel wie folgt aus: Zwei Drittel des gesamten Gebäudevolumens sollten von einem Parkhaus (mit 480 Plätzen) und nur ein Drittel von Wohnraum eingenommen werden. In symbiotischer Beziehung zwischen den beiden Elementen war der Parkbereich als Fundament gedacht, auf dem in treppenförmiger Stufung 80 Apartments aufgesetzt werden sollten. Ein diagonal verlaufender Aufzug und bis zu 16 m hohe Decken machen hier selbst die Benutzung eines Parkhauses zu einem architektonischen Erlebnis. Die kaskadenartige Anlage von Bungalows und Gartenterrassen erfüllt die geforderte Verquickung von suburbanem Wohnstil und dich-tem urbanen Nebeneinander. Ein spezielles Bewässerungssystem sorgt für eine ausreichende Wasserversorgung der begrünten Terrassen – ein Schritt durch die Glastür, schon steht man im eigenen blühenden Garten. Die Nord- und die Westfassade des Baus sind mit perforierten Aluminiumplatten verkleidet, durch die Licht und frische Luft in den Parkhausbereich gelangen. Zugleich hält die Fassadenperforation ein metaphorisches Element bereit, fügen sich die Löcher doch zu einem „übergroßen Abbild des Mount Everest" zusammen.

« Comment combiner les splendeurs de la cour de la maison de banlieue et l'intensité sociale de la densité urbaine ? » se sont demandés les architectes. Leur réponse consiste en partie en un programme qui réserve les deux tiers de l'espace construit aux parkings (480 emplacements) et un tiers seulement aux logements (80 appartements). Ils ont décidé de se servir des parkings comme d'une base sur laquelle édifier des appartements en terrasses en créant une relation « symbiotique » entre les deux éléments. En dehors de l'ascenseur incliné et des hauteurs de plafond qui atteignent jusqu'à 16 mètres à certains endroits, le garage devient lui aussi une nou-velle expérience architecturale. Les terrasses-jardins qui cascadent en façade offrent ce style de vie de banlieue que les architectes souhaitaient tout en conservant un certain sentiment de densité urbaine. Un système d'arrosage assure la survie des plantations et l'appartement n'est séparé de sa terrasse que par une porte de verre. Des plaques d'aluminium perforé habillent les façades nord et ouest, laissent entrer un éclairage naturel et permettent l'aération du parking. Les perforations des façades dessinent une « énorme reproduction de l'Everest ».

Despite the fundamental regularity of
its units, as seen in the drawing
(right), the complex assumes something of an organic aspect due to the
angling and irregular external outline
of the whole.

*Trotz der streng einheitlichen
Ausführung der einzelnen Bungalows,
deutlich erkennbar auf der Zeichnung
rechts, bekommt die Anlage durch
ihren komplexen, vielwinkeligen
Umriss etwas Organisches.*

*Malgré le plan régulier des apparte-
ments, le complexe n'en présente pas
moins un aspect organique provoqué
par son inclinaison en gradins et son
profil extérieur irrégulier (dessin à
droite).*

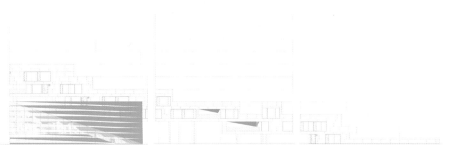

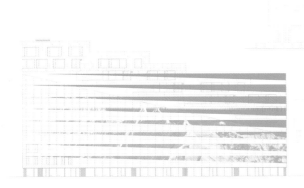

A liberal use of wood and lattice-work surfaces contributes to the "natural" aspect of the project, in contrast with the substantive rectangular volumes revealed by the elevations seen here.

Die großzügige Verwendung von Holz zur Wand- und Bodenverschalung unterstützt den „Naturaspekt" des Projekts und bildet ein Gegengewicht zur bestimmenden Rechtwinkeligkeit, die in den Aufrissen oben deutlich wird.

La généreuse utilisation du bois et de lattis de bois contribue à donner au projet un aspect « naturel » qui contraste avec l'importance de ses volumes parallélépipédiques (élévations ci-dessus).

STEFANO BOERI

Stefano Boeri Architetti
Via Donizetti 4
Milan 20122
Italy

Tel: +39 2 55 01 41 01
Fax: +39 2 55 01 36 93
E-mail: boeristudio@boeristudio.it
Web: www.stefanoboeri.net

STEFANO BOERI was born in 1956, studied architecture in Milan, and in 1989 received his Ph.D from the IUAV in Venice, Italy. Since September 2007, he has been the Editor-in-Chief of the magazine *Abitare*. From 2004 to 2007, he was Editor-in-Chief of *Domus* magazine. He is Professor of Urban Design at the Milan Polytechnic Institute, and has taught as Visiting Professor at Harvard GSD, MIT, and at the Berlage Institute in Amsterdam, amongst others. Boeri is the founder of Multiplicity, an international research network focused on the transformation of European urban areas. Based in Milan, Italy, Stefano Boeri Architetti's recently completed projects include the refurbishment of Italy's oldest mall (Cinisello Balsamo, Milan, 2008); a housing project on the outskirts of Milan (Seregno, 2009); the renovation of the former Arsenale in La Maddalena (Sardinia, 2008–09, published here); and the new RCS—Corriere della Sera Headquarters (work is now under way on the remaining buildings of the competition master plan, Milan), all in Italy. The design for a multifunctional building for the PACA Region on the Marseille Waterfront (La Villa, France) and two eco-compatible residential towers (Il Bosco Verticale) in Milan, the constuction of which is scheduled to start at the beginning of 2010. Boeri is part of the Advisory Board in charge of developing the guidelines for the urban transformations to be implemented within the frame of the 2015 Milan Architecture Expo.

STEFANO BOERI, geboren 1956, wurde nach seinem Architekturstudium in Mailand 1989 an der Università IUAV in Venedig promoviert. Von 2004 bis 2007 war Boeri Chefredakteur des Architekturmagazin *Domus*, seit 2007 besetzt er selbigen Posten bei der Zeitschrift *Abitare*. Boeri lehrt als Professor für Stadtplanung am Politecnico di Milano, als Gastprofessor war er u. a. an der Harvard Graduate School of Design, am Massachusetts Institut of Technology und am Amsterdamer Berlage Institute tätig. Des Weiteren hat Boeri das internationale Forschungsnetzwerk Multiplicity gegründet, das sich mit der Umwandlung von europäischen Stadtflächen befasst. Mit Stefano Boeri Architetti, seinem in Mailand ansässigen Büro, hat das Multitalent zuletzt unter anderem Italiens älteste Einkaufsmall modernisiert (Cinisello Balsamo, Mailand, 2008), eine Sozialwohnanlage am Stadtrand von Mailand realisiert (Seregno, 2009) und das ehemalige Arsenale in La Maddalena neugestaltet (Sardinien, 2008–09; hier vorgestellt), alle in Italien. In den kommenden Monaten wird der Bau des neuen Mailänder Hauptsitzes der RCS MediaGroup (Rizzoli–Corriere della Sera) fertiggestellt sein. Die Umsetzung der Entwürfe für einen Vielzweckbau in der Region Provence-Alpes-Côte d'Azur an der Küste von Marseille (La Villa) und für zwei ökologisch ausgerichtete Wohnhochhäuser (Il Bosco Verticale) in Mailand soll ab Anfang 2010 erfolgen. Darüber hinaus gehört Boeri dem Beratungsgremium an, das mit der Richtlinienentwicklung für die im Rahmen der Expo 2015 in Mailand umzusetzenden Stadtentwicklungmaßnahmen betraut ist.

STEFANO BOERI, né en 1956, a étudié l'architecture à Milan, et a passé son doctorat à l'IUAV à Venise. Depuis septembre 2007, il est rédacteur en chef du magazine *Abitare* après avoir été celui de *Domus* de 2004 à 2007. Il enseigne l'urbanisme à l'Institut polytechnique de Milan et a été professeur invité à l'Harvard GSD, au MIT et à l'Institut Berlage à Amsterdam, entre autres. Boeri est fondateur de Multiplicity, réseau de recherche international qui se consacre au phénomène de transformation des zones urbaines. Installé à Milan, Stefano Boeri Architetti a récemment mené à bien divers projets dont la restauration du plus ancien centre commercial italien (Cinisello Balsamo, Milan, 2008) ; des logements à la périphérie de Milan (Seregno, 2009) ; la rénovation de l'ancien arsenal de La Maddalena (Sardaigne, 2008–09, publié ici) et le nouveau siège social de RCS – Corriere della Sera à Milan (travaux en cours). Le projet d'un immeuble multifonction pour la région PACA sur le front de mer de Marseille (La Villa) et le chantier de deux tours résidentielles écocompatibles (Il Bosco Verticale) à Milan devraient débuter en 2010. Boeri fait partie du Conseil consultatif en charge de mettre au point des stratégies pour les transformations urbaines prévues dans le cadre de la Milan Architecture Expo en 2015.

FORMER ARSENALE LA MADDALENA

House of the Sea, La Maddalena, Sardinia, Italy, 2008–09

Address: La Maddalena, 07020 Palau, Sassari, Sardinia, Italy
Area: 2230 m². Client: Regione Sardegna and Dipartimento Protezione Civile
Cost: not disclosed. Collaboration: Michele Brunello, Davor Popovic

This project was designed to host the 2009 G8 Summit, but also to revitalize tourism in an area long marked by a military presence. The overall project concerns the two kilometers of new quays, a Conference Center, a hotel, and the reuse of other existing structures. The former Arsenal harbor can accommodate up to 700 boats, and covers an area of 155 000 square meters. The Conference Hall is cantilevered six meters over the water. A "modular beehive-like façade made of opaline glass characterizes the new landmark that reinterprets, in contemporary key, the relation between the power of the surrounding natural elements and the rigorous forms of Italy's traditional military architecture." Next to the Conference Center, granite arcade spaces have been restructured and are marked by a 10 000-square-meter white "sail-like roof suspended 10 meters above the ground and equipped with photovoltaic panels."

Die Neugestaltung des ehemaligen Arsenale erfolgte anlässlich des 2009 in La Maddalena ausgerichteten G8-Gipfels. Gleichzeitig diente das Projekt der Wiedererschließung des – lange der militärischen Nutzung vorbehaltenen – Areals für den Tourismus. Die Gesamtkonzeption sah einen 2 km langen Abschnitt aus neuen Kaianlagen, ein neues Kongresszentrum, einen Hotelneubau und die Umnutzung bereits bestehender Bauten vor. Der ehemalige Arsenale-Hafen umfasst eine Fläche von 155 000 m² und bietet Ankerplatz für 700 Boote. 6 m weit kragt die neu entstandene Konferenzhalle über das Hafenbecken aus. Eine „Wabenfassade aus Opalglas als hervorstechendes Merkmal des neuen Wahrzeichens, das unter zeitgenössischem Vorzeichen das Verhältnis zwischen der eindrucksvollen umgebenden Naturkulisse und den strengen Formen der traditionellen italienischen Militärarchitektur neu interpretiert." In direkter Nachbarschaft zu der Konferenzhalle wurden alte Granitarkaden einer neuen Bestimmung zugeführt und zusammen mit neuen Gebäudeelementen mit einem weißen, 10 000 m² großen „segelartigen Dach überspannt, das in 10 m Höhe aufgehängt und mit großen Solarzellen-Paneelen bestückt ist."

Ce projet a été conçu pour accueillir le sommet du G8 en 2009, mais aussi pour aider à faire renaître le tourisme dans une zone marquée par la longue présence de la marine italienne. Le projet concerne deux kilomètres de quais nouveaux, un centre de conférences, un hôtel et la rénovation de constructions existantes. L'ancien port de l'Arsenal, d'une surface de 155 000 mètres carrés peut recevoir jusqu'à 700 bateaux. Le centre de conférences est en porte-à-faux à six mètres au-dessus de l'eau. « Une façade modulaire en nid d'abeille faite de verre opalin caractérise ces nouvelles installations, qui réinterprètent, selon une clé contemporaine, la relation entre la force des éléments naturels environnants et les formes rigoureuses de l'architecture militaire italienne traditionnelle », précise l'architecte. Près de ce centre de conférences, des espaces à arcades de granit ont été restructurés et sont signalés par un « toit en forme de voile de 10 000 mètres carrés, suspendu à 10 mètres au-dessus du sol, et équipé de cellules photovoltaïques ».

These structures were realized for a
G8 meeting that was moved, at the
last moment, to another location. The
architect Rem Koolhaas found this an
adequate topic for a widely
published essay.

Stefano Boeris Bauten entstanden für
den G8-Gipfel 2009, der im letzten
Moment an einen anderen Ort verlegt
wurde – eine Entwicklung, der Rem
Kohlhaas einen kritischen und viel re-
zipierten Essay widmete.

Ces bâtiments ont été réalisés pour
une réunion du G8 qui a été transfé-
rée au dernier moment dans une
autre région. L'architecte Rem
Koolhaas en a fait le thème d'un
essai largement publié.

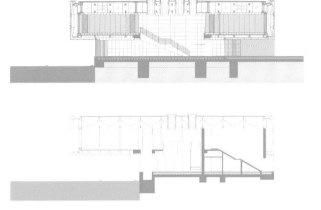

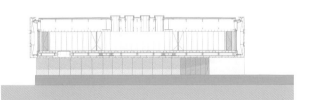

The simplicity of the lines of the architecture is contrasted to some extent with the preserved stone arches, or the kind of round openings seen in the image below left.

Als Kontrapunkte zur Schlichtheit der architektonischen Linien treten die erhaltenen Granitarkaden oder runde Deckenöffnungen auf, wie sie auf dem Bild unten links zu sehen sind.

La simplicité des lignes architecturales contraste dans une certaine mesure avec la conservation d'arcs de pierre anciens ou la présence d'ouvertures circulaires (image ci-dessous).

The architect's elegant lightness offers open views to the sea. Below, stone walls echo the former Arsenale, punctuating the otherwise white spaces.

Der leichte elegante Entwurf des Architekten bietet freien Ausblick auf das Meer. Die Granitmauern im Bild unten erinnern an das einstige Arsenale und setzen Akzente in den ansonsten weiß gehaltenen Räumen.

La légèreté lumineuse recherchée par l'architecte s'exprime aussi dans les immenses ouvertures donnant sur la mer. Ci-dessous, des vestiges de murs de pierre rappellent l'ancien arsenal et ponctuent ces espaces uniformément blancs.

BYOUNG-SOO CHO

BCHO Architects
Sil Building (3rd Floor)
57 Banpo-4-dong, Seocho-ku
Seoul
South Korea

Tel: +82 2 537 8261
Fax: +82 2 537 8201
E-mail: bc@bchoarchitects.com
Web: www.bchoarchitects.com

BYOUNG-SOO CHO was born in 1957 in Seoul, South Korea. He attended Montana State University (Bozeman, Montana, USA, B.Arch, 1986), obtained his M.Arch and M.Arch in Urban Design from Harvard University GSD in 1991, having spent 1990 at the ETH in Zurich on an exchange program. He has taught at Harvard (Visiting Critic, 2006), Montana State University (Associate Professor, 1999–2006), and at Yonsei University in Seoul (1997–99, 2004). His educational buildings include the Pai-chai University, College of Fine Arts and Architecture Building (Daejeon, 2004); and the Be-Twixt Building-BIPS Kindergarten (Cheongdamdong, 2006). In the residential design area, where he has been quite active, Byoung-soo Cho has completed the Three Box House (Paju, Gyeonggi-do, 2005–06, published here); and is currently completing the Jedong Ranch Guesthouse (Jeju-do). He has recently completed the Hanil Cement Information Center and Guesthouse (Pyeongdong-ri, Danyang-gun, 2008–09, also published here); while the Hanil TT Tower (Jongno); the Heyri Theater and Hotel (Heyri Art Valley); and KISWIRE Headquarters (Tokyo, Japan, 2007–) are all currently under construction, all in South Korea unless stated otherwise.

BYOUNG-SOO CHO wurde 1957 in Seoul, Südkorea geboren. Nach seinem ersten Abschluss an der Montana State University (Bozeman, Montana, USA; B.Arch 1986) erwarb er 1991 seinen Master of Architecture sowie einen Masterabschluss in Urban Design an der Graduate School of Design der Harvard University; im Jahr 1990 hatte er als Teilnehmer eines Austauschprogramms an der ETH Zürich studiert. Von 1997 bis 1999 sowie 2004 unterrichtete Byoung-soo Cho an der Yonsei Universität in Seoul, von 1999 bis 2006 war er Associate Professor an der Montana State University, 2006 außerdem Visiting Critic in Harvard. Zu seinen Entwürfen für Bildungseinrichtungen gehören u. a. das Gebäude des College of Fine Arts and Architecture an der Universität Pai Chai (Daejeon, 2004) und der Kindergarten des Be-Twixt Building-BIPS (Cheongdamdong, 2006). Auf dem Gebiet der Wohnarchitektur ist Byoung-soo Cho ebenfalls regelmäßig tätig; das hier vorstellte Three Box House (Paju, Gyeonggi-do) wurde 2005–06 fertiggestellt, gegenwärtig entsteht ein Gästehaus für die Jedong Ranch (Jeju-do). Des Weiteren entstanden in jüngerer Zeit das Informationszentrum sowie das Gästehaus für das Unternehmen Hanil Cement (Pyeongdong-ri, Danyang-gun, 2008–09, ebenfalls hier vorgestellt). Derzeit im Bau sind der Hanil TT Tower (Jongno), das Heyri Theater und Hotel (Heyri Art Valley) und der Hauptsitz der Firma KISWIRE (Tokio, Japan, 2007–). Bis auf letzteres befinden sich alle genannten Projekte in Südkorea.

BYOUNG-SOO CHO, né en 1957 à Seoul (Corée du Sud), a étudié à la Montana State University (Bozeman, Montana, B. Arch, 1986), et a obtenu son M. Arch en urbanisme de la Harvard University GSD en 1991, après un séjour d'un an, en 1990, à l'ETH de Zurich dans le cadre d'un programme d'échanges. Il a enseigné à Harvard (critique invité, 2006), à Montana State University (professeur associé, 1999–2006) et à l'Université Yonsei de Séoul (1997–99, 2004). Il a réalisé des bâtiments destinés à l'enseignement comme celui du Collège des beaux-arts et de l'architecture de l'Université Paichai (Daejeon, 2004) et le jardin d'enfant du Be-Twixt Building-BIPS (Cheongdamdong, 2006). Dans le domaine résidentiel, où il est assez actif, il a réalisé la Three Box House (Paju, Gyeonggi-do, 2005–06, publiée ici) et achève la maison d'hôtes du Jedong Ranch (Jeju-do). Il a récemment terminé le chantier du Centre d'informations et la maison d'hôtes de Hanil Cement (Pyeongdong-ri, Danyang-gun, 2008–09, également publiée ici) et réalise en ce moment la tour Hanil TT (Jongno); le théâtre et hôtel Heyri (Heyri Art Valley) et le siège de KISWIRE (Tokyo, Japan, 2007–).

THREE BOX HOUSE

Paju, Gyeonggi-do, South Korea, 2005–06

Area: 494 m². Client: not disclosed. Cost: not disclosed
Collaboration: Youngmook Cho, Yoon-hee Kim, Dong-hyun Koh, Young-jin Kang

As its name suggests, this residence is made up of three concrete boxes connected by a horizontal wooden screen and decks. Two of the boxes are set in the earth and the third is set up on steel columns, forming an enclosed courtyard space. According to the architect, this space "provides comfort and protection from surrounding developments and serves as a common space, important in Korean culture." The overall intention of the project is to emphasize a rapport between architecture and nature, and details such as a hand-woven wire mesh that covers five areas of the house make it decidedly unexpected in the context of contemporary architecture. Although his background explains the reference, some might find it surprising to hear that according to Byoung-soo Cho: "This project is simple and straightforward; drawing from the industrial/agricultural materiality of Montana."

Wie schon sein Name verrät, besteht dieser Wohnhausentwurf aus drei einzelnen Kuben; miteinander verbunden sind die Betonkörper durch einen seitlichen Lamellenschirm sowie mehrere Plattformen aus Holz. Während zwei der Kuben ebenerdig errichtet sind, ist der dritte Kubus auf Säulen aufgeständert, wodurch ein umschlossener Hofbereich entsteht. Wie der Architekt erörtert, bietet der Bereich „eine vor dem Geschehen ringsumher geschützte, behagliche Atmosphäre. Seine Zweckbestimmung als Gemeinschaftsraum ist in der koreanischen Kultur von großer Bedeutung." Vor allem ging es bei dem Projekt darum, die Verbindung zwischen Architektur und Natur zu betonen; Details wie der handgefertigte Maschendraht, der fünf Abschnitte des Hauses abdeckt, sind im Kontext der sonstigen zeitgenössischen Architektur schon ausgesprochen ungewöhnlich. Auch wenn sich der entsprechende Verweis mit dem Background des Architekten erklärt, mag es für manchen doch überraschend klingen, dass laut Byoung-soo Cho „die Schlichtheit und Schnörkellosigkeit des Projekts von dem industriell und landwirtschaftlich geprägten Erscheinungsbild Montanas herrührt".

Comme son nom le suggère, cette résidence se compose de trois boîtes en béton reliées par un écran de bois et des terrasses. Deux de ces boîtes sont enfoncées dans le sol, la troisième repose sur des colonnes d'acier qui forment une cour fermée. Selon l'architecte, cet espace « offre le confort et la protection des développements extérieurs et sert d'espace commun, ce qui est important dans la culture coréenne ». L'intention générale de ce projet est de mettre en valeur le rapport entre l'architecture et la nature. Certains détails comme un treillis de fil de fer façonné à la main, qui recouvre cinq zones de la maison, surprennent dans le cadre d'une architecture contemporaine. Bien que le contexte explique cette référence, on peut être surpris d'entendre Byoung-soo Cho affirmer : « Ce projet est simple et direct, il s'inspire de la matérialité industrielle et agricole du Montana. »

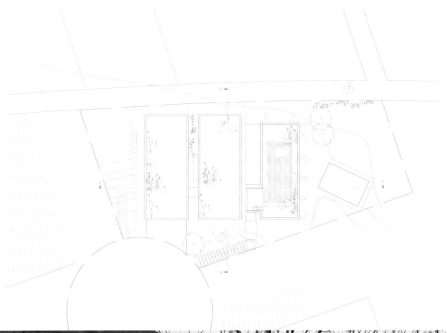

Through recently planted trees and
its natural setting, the house contrasts fairly rigid geometric volumes
with openings and movement that
make it an integral part of its site.

*Großflächige Öffnungen und freie
Blickachsen mildern den Kontrast der
strengen Kubatur zu der umgebenden
Natur und den neu gepflanzten Bäumen und integrieren das Gebäude in
das Gelände.*

*Contrastes entre les volumes géomé-
triques assez rigides de la maison,
ses ouvertures, le rythme de sa composition et la plantation d'arbres qui
la rapprochent de son site naturel.*

The house opposes wood-clad upper volumes with glazed or fully open ones at ground level in the image above, explained more fully by the plan below.

Den mit Holz verkleideten Gebäudeteilen der oberen Ebene stehen auf der unteren Ebene verglaste oder komplett offene Volumina gegenüber (Foto oben), deren Anordnung der Aufriss unten nachvollziehbar macht.

La maison oppose des volumes supérieurs bardés de bois à un rez-de-chaussée vitré ou entièrement ouvert (image ci-dessus et plan ci-dessous).

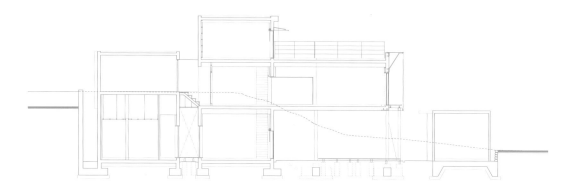

Again, rectilinear severity is juxtaposed with the forms of trees and the
opening to the site through broad
glazing or voids.

*Die Formen der Bäume und der
Ausblick durch verglaste oder offene
Fronten auf die Umgebung bilden ein
Gegengewicht zu der geradlinigen
Strenge des Hauses.*

*Là encore la sévérité rectiligne des
constructions vient en juxtaposition
avec de jeunes arbres et des ouvertures sur l'environnement à travers de
grands panneaux vitrés ou des vides.*

HANIL CEMENT INFORMATION CENTER AND GUESTHOUSE

Pyeongdong-ri, Danyang-gun, South Korea, 2008–09

Area: 1031 m². Client: Hanil Cement.
Cost: not disclosed. Collaboration: Youngmook Cho,
Nick Locke, Young-jin Kang, Mark West

The purpose of this project is to educate visitors about the potential for recycling concrete, which is the primary building material in South Korea. Several different techniques were used to recycle concrete for the construction of this building, and the intention of the architect and the client is to continue to make changes as new techniques become available. Translucent and opaque tiles, and the fabric-formed concrete façade of the structure, are made of recycled materials. Adjacent to Mount Sorak National Park, the site is near the Hanil Cement factory. The architect sought to revive the natural setting, damaged by heavy equipment and trucks. "We applied canvas-like concrete walls to the east façade, evoking images of the forest behind the building," states Byoung-soo Cho. "There are four openings in the eastern wall and long vertical windows have been created in their in-between spaces. Through the windows, one can see how concrete is produced at the factory. Behind the two larger openings, one can see the courtyard of the Visitors' Center and the cafeteria next to the courtyard, which is encircled by a water garden."

Das Hanil Cement Informationszentrum dient dem Zweck, Besucher mit dem Recyclingpotential von Beton, dem in Korea meistverwendeten Baustoff, bekannt zu machen. Auch das Gebäude selbst besteht aus Recyclingbeton, der mithilfe verschiedener technischer Verfahren aufbereitet wurde; erklärtermaßen beabsichtigen Architekt wie Auftraggeber auch künftig neue Wege zu gehen und neu entwickelte Recyclingmethoden zu nutzen. Neben den vorfabrizierten Fassadenelementen aus Beton wurden auch die Fliesen für das Informationszentrum, ob opak oder durchscheinend, aus Recyclingstoffen hergestellt. Das Gebäude steht unweit der Hanil-Betonfabrik in direkter Nachbarschaft zum Seoraksan Nationalpark, weshalb der Architekt nach der Errichtung Wert darauf legte, die durch Lastwagen und schweres Gerät in der Natur entstandenen Schäden wieder rückgängig zu machen. „Die Ostfassade besteht aus leinwandartigen Betonwänden, deren Erscheinung einen Bezug zu dem hinter dem Gebäude liegenden Wald herstellt", erklärt Byoung-soo Cho. „Die Wand auf der Ostseite besitzt an vier Stellen Öffnungen, in deren Zwischenräumen große vertikale Fenster eingesetzt wurden, durch die man dabei zuschauen kann, wie im Innern der Fabrik der Zement produziert wird. Hinter den beiden größeren Öffnungen sieht man den Innenhof des Besucherzentrums sowie die Cafeteria, die neben dem von einem Wassergarten umschlossenen Hof eingerichtet ist."

L'objectif de ce projet est l'éducation des visiteurs au potentiel de recyclage du béton, premier matériau de construction en Corée. Plusieurs techniques différentes ont été mises en œuvre pour obtenir les bétons recyclés utilisés dans la construction de ce bâtiment, et l'intention de l'architecte et de son client est de pouvoir y apporter des modifications au fur et à mesure que de nouvelles techniques deviendront disponibles. Les carrelages translucides et opaques et la façade en béton moulé dans du tissu du bâtiment sont en matériaux recyclés. L'ensemble se dresse près de la cimenterie Hanil, en bordure du Parc national du Mont Sorak. L'architecte a cherché à redonner vie au cadre naturel, endommagé par les camions et les équipements lourds. « Sur la façade Est, les murs sont à effet de tissage, pour évoquer des images de la forêt qui s'étend derrière le bâtiment », précise Byoung-soo Cho. « Le mur est percé de quatre ouvertures et d'étroites fenêtres en hauteur entre elles. À travers ces fenêtres, on peut voir la production du béton à l'usine. Par les deux ouvertures les plus importantes, on aperçoit la cour du Centre des visiteurs et son jardin aquatique ainsi que la cafétéria.

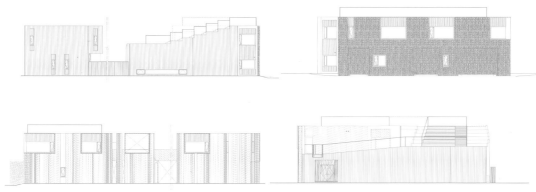

Here again, the architect orchestrates the contrast between rather severe, full forms with voids and varied surfaces.

Auch hier inszeniert der Architekt den Kontrast zwischen recht strengen, massiven Formen einerseits und Öffnungen und unterschiedlichen Oberflächen andererseits.

L'architecte a orchestré le contraste entre des formes pleines assez sévères et des vides ou des surfaces travaillées.

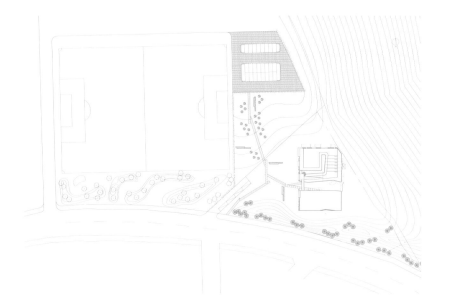

Despite its apparent hardness,
the facility has a subtle variety of
surfaces and spaces—some of
which are visible in these images.

Obschon von massiver Erscheinung,
wartet das Informationszentrum mit
einer raffinierten Palette unterschiedlicher Oberflächen und Raumformen
auf, die hier in Auswahl zu sehen
sind.

Malgré leur rudesse apparente, ces
installations présentent une variété
subtile de surfaces et de volumes,
comme le montrent les photos de
cette double-page.

SANTIAGO CALATRAVA

Santiago Calatrava SA
Parkring 11
8002 Zurich
Switzerland

Tel: +41 1 204 50 00
Fax: +41 1 204 50 01
E-mail: admin.zurich@calatrava.com
Web: www.calatrava.com

Born in Valencia, Spain, in 1951, **SANTIAGO CALATRAVA** studied art and architecture at the ETSA of Valencia (1968–73) and engineering at the ETH in Zurich (doctorate in Technical Science, 1981). He opened his own architecture and civil engineering office the same year. Santiago Calatrava received the American Institute of Architects (AIA) 2005 Gold Medal. His built work includes Gallery and Heritage Square, BCE Place (Toronto, Canada, 1987); the Torre de Montjuic (Barcelona, Spain, 1989–92); the Kuwait Pavilion at Expo '92, Seville, and the Alamillo Bridge for the same exhibition (Seville, Spain); the Lyon-Saint Exupéry TGV Station (Lyon, France, 1989–94); the Oriente Station in Lisbon (Portugal, 1998); the Valencia City of Science and Planetarium (Valencia, Spain, 1996–2000) and the Valencia Opera in the same city (2004); the Sondica Airport (Bilbao, Spain, 1990–2000); and a bridge in Orléans (France, 1996–2000). Other work includes Tenerife Auditorium (Santa Cruz, Canary Islands, 2003); Milwaukee Art Museum extension (Milwaukee, Wisconsin, USA, 2003); Athens Olympic Sports Complex (Athens, Greece, 2004); the Quarto Ponte sul Canal Grande (Fourth Bridge on the Grand Canal, Venice, Italy, 1999–2006); three bridges in Reggio Emilia (Italy, 2002–07); Jerusalem Light Rail Train Bridge (Jerusalem, Israel, 2002–08); and Liège-Guillemins TGV Station (Liège, Belgium, 1996–2009, published here). He is currently working on the Transportation Hub for the new World Trade Center site in New York.

SANTIAGO CALATRAVA, geboren 1951 Valencia, Spanien, studierte an der dortigen ETSA Kunst und Architektur (1968–73) sowie Bauingenieurwesen an der ETH Zürich, wo er 1981 promoviert wurde. Im selben Jahr gründete er sein Architektur- und Ingenieurbüro. 2005 wurde Calatrava mit der Goldmedaille des American Institute of Architects (AIA) ausgezeichnet. Zu seinen realisierten Bauten gehören der Gallery and Heritage Square, BCE Place in Toronto (Kanada, 1987), die Torre de Montjuïc (Barcelona, Spanien, 1989–92), der Kuwait-Pavillon und die Alamillo-Brücke für die Expo '92 in Sevilla, der TGV-Bahnhof des Flughafens Lyon-Saint-Exupéry (Frankreich, 1989–94), der Oriente-Bahnhof in Lissabon (Portugal, 1998), die Ciudad de las Artes y de las Ciencias (1996–2000) sowie das Opernhaus Palau de les Arts Reina Sofía in Valencia (2004), der Flughafen Sondica in Bilbao (Spanien, 1990–2000) und eine Brücke in Orléans (Frankreich, 1996–2000). Des Weiteren verwirklichte er das Tenerife Auditorio in Santa Cruz (Teneriffa, Spanien, 2003), die Erweiterung des Milwaukee Art Museum (Wisconsin, USA, 2003), mehrere Bauten für die Olympia-Sportanlage in Athen (Griechenland, 2004), den Quarto Ponte sul Canal Grande (Venedig, 1999–2006), drei Brückenbauten in Reggio Emilia (Italien, 2002–07), eine Brücke für die Jerusalemer Stadtbahn (Israel, 2002–08) und den TGV-Bahnhof Liège-Guillemins (Lüttich, Belgien, 1996–2009, hier vorgestellt). Gegenwärtig arbeitet Calatrava an der Planung für einen U-Bahnhof auf dem World-Trade-Center-Gelände in New York.

Né à Valence (Espagne) en 1951, **SANTIAGO CALATRAVA** a étudié l'art et l'architecture à l'ETSA de Valence (1968–73) et l'ingénierie à l'ETH de Zurich (doctorat en sciences techniques, 1981). Il a ouvert son agence d'architecture et d'ingénierie civile la même année. Il a reçu la médaille d'or de l'American Institute of Architects (AIA). Parmi ses réalisations : le Gallery and Heritage Square, BCE Place (Toronto, Canada, 1987) ; la tour de Montjuïc (Barcelone, 1989–92) ; le pavillon du Koweit et le pont de l'Alamillo pour Expo '92 (Séville) ; la gare de TGV de l'aéroport de Lyon-Saint Exupéry (Lyon, 1989–94) ; la gare de l'Orient à Lisbonne (1998) ; la Cité des sciences et le planétarium de Valence (1996–2000) ; l'opéra de Valence (2004) ; l'aéroport de Sondica (Bilbao, 1990–2000) et un pont à Orléans (France, 1996–2000). Ses autres réalisations comprennent l'auditorium de Tenerife (Santa Cruz, Iles Canaries, 2003) ; l'extension du Milwaukee Art Museum (Milwaukee, Wisconsin, USA, 2003) ; le complexe olympique d'Athènes (Athènes, 2004) ; le Quarto Ponte sul Canal Grande (Quatrième pont sur le Grand Canal, Venise, 1999–2006) ; trois ponts à Reggio Emilia (Italie, 2002–07) ; le pont du train léger de Jérusalem (Israël, 2002–08) et la gare de TGV de Liège-Guillemins (Liège, Belgique, 1996–2009, publiée ici). Il réalise actuellement la plate-forme d'échanges du nouveau World Trade Center à New York.

LIÈGE-GUILLEMINS TGV STATION

Liège, Belgium, 1996–2009

Address: Place de Guillemins 2, 4000 Liège, Belgium
Area: not disclosed. Client: Euro Liège TGV. Cost: not disclosed

For a number of years, the French rapid trains (TGV) bound for Cologne in Germany passed through the Belgian city of Liège at a pace that recalled the 19th century more than the 21st. In addition to the inevitable modernization of the train lines concerned, it was also necessary to update the stations along the line from Belgium to Germany. Santiago Calatrava received the commission to design the new **LIÈGE-GUILLEMINS TGV STATION** largely because of his experience in the field, in projects such as Lyon-Saint Exupéry and the Oriente Station in Lisbon. Much as he had in Lisbon, he conceived the station as a link between two distinct areas of the city of Liège, which previously had been separated by the railroad tracks. On the north side of the site is a rundown urban area, laid out in a typical 19th-century scheme. On the south side, on the slopes of the Cointe Hill, is a less dense, landscaped residential area. Calatrava's design bridges these two areas with a 200-meter-long passenger terminal, built symmetrically along a northwest-southeast axis. The arched roof of the terminal building extends over the five platforms for another impressive 145 meters. A monumental vault made of glass and steel allows the station to be completely open to the city. Pedestrian bridges and a walkway under the tracks allow for fluid communication between the two sides of the station. Particular attention was paid to the architectural detailing of these spaces. Basing his design on the open transition from interior to exterior, Calatrava resolutely rejected the monumental façade that has traditionally characterized railway stations. Given the need to keep the station functioning throughout construction, techniques learned from building bridges were employed to install the main elements at night.

Jahrelang durchquerte der TGV der Linie Brüssel–Köln die Stadt Lüttich mit einer Geschwindigkeit, die eher in das 19. als in das 21. Jahrhundert gehörte. Im Zuge der unumgänglichen Modernisierung des betreffenden Streckenabschnitts wurde auch die Erneuerung der an die Linie angeschlossenen Bahnhöfe nötig. Mit dem Entwurf des neuen **BAHNHOF LIÈGE-GUILLEMINS** wurde Santiago Calatrava vor allem deshalb beauftragt, weil er seine Erfahrungen auf dem Gebiet bereits mit Projekten wie dem Bahnhof Lyon-Saint Exupéry und dem Oriente-Bahnhof in Lissabon eindrucksvoll unter Beweis gestellt hatte. Ähnlich wie er es schon in Lissabon unternommen hatte, entwarf er den Lütticher Bahnhof als verbindendes Element zwischen zwei Stadtgebieten, die zuvor durch die Bahnstrecke scharf voneinander getrennt waren und sich deutlich unterscheiden. Die auf der Nordseite des Bahnhofs gelegene Gegend zeigt eine typische Bebauungsstruktur aus dem 19. Jahrhundert und ist recht heruntergekommen. Auf der südlichen Seite dagegen liegt in den Ausläufern des Hügels von Cointe eine weniger dicht bebaute Wohngegend mit Grünflächen. Zwischen diesen Gebieten schlägt Calatrava mit seinem 200 m langen Terminal, das parallel zu einer von Nordwest nach Südost verlaufenden Achse errichtet ist, eine Brücke. Das gewölbte Dach des Terminals überspannt auf einer Breite von 145 m fünf Bahnsteige. Dank eines Bogens von gewaltiger Größe ist der Bahnhof zur Stadt hin vollkommen offen. Über Fußgängerbrücken und durch eine unter den Geleisen hindurchführende Passage gelangt man mühelos von einer Bahnhofsseite auf die andere. Calatrava wandte sich mit der grundlegenden Idee eines offenen Übergangs zwischen Innen- und Außenbereich entschieden gegen den Entwurf einer monumentalen Fassade, wie sie für Bahnhöfe aus früheren Zeiten charakteristisch ist. Da der Bahnverkehr auch während der Bauphase aufrechterhalten bleiben musste, griff man auf Konstruktionsmethoden aus dem Brückenbau zurück, um die Hauptelemente während der Nacht zu montieren.

Pendant un certain nombre d'années, les trains à grande vitesse français en route pour Cologne traversaient la ville de Liège à une allure qui évoquait plus le XIXe siècle que le XXIe. La modernisation des voies devait inévitablement entraîner celle des gares le long de la ligne entre la Belgique et l'Allemagne. Santiago Calatrava a reçu la commande de la nouvelle **GARE DE LIÈGE-GUILLEMINS** en grande partie pour son expérience dans ce domaine, illustrée en particulier à Lisbonne (gare de l'Orient) et à Lyon (gare de l'aéroport de Lyon-Saint Exupéry). Comme à Lisbonne, il a conçu la gare belge comme un lien entre deux quartiers de la ville, naguère complètement séparés par les voies ferrées : au nord, une zone urbaine délabrée organisée selon un plan typique du XIXe siècle ; au sud, un quartier résidentiel moins dense implanté sur les flancs de la colline de Cointe. Le projet de Calatrava fait un pont entre ces deux quartiers par un bâtiment de 200 mètres de long, édifié symétriquement de part et d'autre d'un axe nord-ouest/sud-est. Sa toiture voûtée se prolonge au-dessus des cinq quais sur 145 mètres supplémentaires. La voûte monumentale en verre et acier permet à la gare de s'ouvrir complètement sur la ville. Des passerelles piétonnières et un passage sous les voies facilitent une communication fluide entre les deux côtés de la gare. Une attention particulière a été portée à la réalisation architecturale de ces espaces. Organisant ses plans sur ce principe de transition ouverte entre l'intérieur et l'extérieur, Calatrava a volontairement rejeté toute idée de façade monumentale à l'image de celle des gares du passé. Comme le trafic ferroviaire ne pouvait s'interrompre, des techniques empruntées à la construction des ouvrages d'art ont été utilisées pour la mise en place nocturne des principaux composants.

Quite contrary to the rather staid
image that one might have of a
Belgian provincial city, the Liège-
Guillemins Station adds a note of
excitement and surprising form to an
otherwise gray train line.

Wer Lüttich für eine eher langweilige
belgische Provinzstadt hält, wird
zumindest in einem Punkt eines Bes-
seren belehrt: An einer ansonsten
tristen Bahnstrecke setzt der Bahnhof
Liège-Guillemins einen ungewöhnlichen und faszinierenden Glanzpunkt.

Assez étonnante au cœur d'une ville
provinciale belge assez traditionnelle,
la gare de Liège-Guillemins a su faire
d'installations techniques qui
auraient pu être banales un spectacle
esthétique.

Having previously designed railway stations in Zurich, Lyon, and Lisbon, Calatrava masters the technical and spatial requirements of such facilities.

Dank der Erfahrung mit seinen früheren Bahnhofsentwürfen – für Zürich, Lyon und Lissabon – weiß Calatrava die technischen und räumlichen Anforderungen derartiger Einrichtungen ausgezeichnet zu erfüllen.

Auteur de gares à Zurich, Lyon et Lisbonne, Calatrava maîtrise les aspects techniques et architecturaux de ce type d'équipement.

With his surprising, sweeping forms in Liège, Calatrava appears to be reaching a new high point in his art, going beyond his earlier, more anthropomorphic designs.

Mit den aufregend schwungvollen Formen scheint Calatravas Kunst in Lüttich einen neuen Höhepunkt zu erreichen, der über die früheren, stärker anthropomorphen Entwürfe des Architekten noch hinausweist.

À travers cette étonnante voile gonflée, Calatrava semble atteindre un nouveau sommet de son art et va au-delà de ses projets antérieurs d'esprit plus biomorphique.

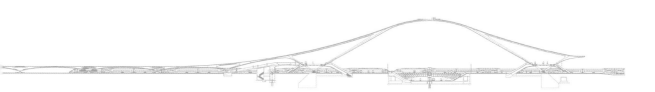

The extreme simplicity of the structure with its great arched form is visible in the section drawing above. Here, Calatrava's talents as both an architect and an engineer come together with an obviously elegant result.

Die extreme Schlichtheit der Grundstruktur mit ihrer weiten gebogenen Form wird im Aufriss oben deutlich. Hier vereinen sich Calatravas Talente als Architekt und Ingenieur mit einem offensichtlich eleganten Resultat.

La coupe ci-dessus met en valeur l'extrême simplicité de la structure et de son arc gigantesque. Les talents d'architecte et d'ingénieur de Calatrava se fondent en une création d'une indéniable élégance.

Calatrava's ribbed forms and openings, with frequent doses of daylight, animate the interior space and give it a surprising degree of movement, beyond the daily movement of travelers.

Die von Calatrava entworfene Rippenstruktur, deren Öffnungen beständig von Tageslicht durchstrahlt werden, macht das Bahnhofsinnere noch lebendiger, als es durch das Kommen und Gehen der Reisenden ohnehin ist.

Les formes nervurées, les ouvertures et l'abondance des percées de lumière naturelle, animent les espaces intérieurs et font naître un étonnant sentiment de mouvement, qui va bien au-delà de celui du déplacement des voyageurs.

GIACOMO COSTA

Guidi&Schoen
Vico Casana 31r
16123 Genoa
Italy

Tel/Fax: +39 010 253 05 57
E-mail: info@guidieschoen.com
Web: www.guidieschoen.com / www.giacomocosta.com

GIACOMO COSTA was born in Florence, Italy, in 1970; he entered a humanities-oriented secondary school but abandoned it in 1986 to dedicate himself to motorcycle racing and mechanics. In 1990, having finished studies as an external student, he moved to the Alps to climb, spending time at the Rifugio Torino and near the Mont Blanc. He also started to take landscape photographs. After an accident he went back to Florence where he started to work as a commercial photographer. In 1994 he set aside this activity to start his own artistic research. Two years later, he began to mix photography with digital techniques. Beginning with his "megalopolises" in 2002, Giacomo Costa abandoned traditional photography in favor of images created with the computer. Working part-time as a paramedic in an ambulance service in Florence, Costa also finds time to ski, sail his boat, and participate in motorcycle races. Recent exhibitions include "2009, Secret Gardens" (Guidi&Schoen Arte Contemporanea, Genoa, Italy, 2009) and "The Chronicles of Time" (Galerie Clairefontaine, Luxembourg, 2009). His work was also presented in the Italian Pavilion of the 2009 Art Biennale (Venice, Italy).

GIACOMO COSTA, geboren 1970 in Florenz, besuchte zunächst ein humanistisches Gymnasium, brach seine schulische Laufbahn jedoch 1986 ab, um sich Motorradrennen zu widmen und als Mechaniker zu arbeiten. Nach Abschluss eines Fernstudiums (1990) verbrachte Costa einige Zeit zum Bergsteigen in den Alpen, unter anderem im Rifugio Torino in der Nähe des Mont Blanc. In dieser Zeit wandte er sich auch der Landschaftsfotografie zu. Nach einem Unfall ging er zurück nach Florenz, wo er als Werbefotograf zu arbeiten begann. Diese Tätigkeit gab er 1994 auf, um einen eigenen künstlerischen Ausdruck zu finden. Zwei Jahre später begann er, Fotografie mit digitalen Verfahren zu kombinieren. In seiner Serie "megalopolises" aus dem Jahr 2002 verzichtete er ganz auf die analoge Fotografie und präsentierte stattdessen ausschließlich am Computer entstandene Bilder. Neben seiner Teilzeitbeschäftigung als Rettungsassistent findet Costa genügend Zeit, um Ski zu fahren, zu segeln und an Motorradrennen teilzunehmen. Zu seinen jüngeren Ausstellungen gehören „2009, Secret Gardens" (Guidi&Schoen Arte Contemporanea, Genua, Italien, 2009) und „The Chronicles of Time" (Galerie Clairefontaine, Luxemburg, 2009). 2009 wurden Costas Arbeiten zudem im Rahmen der Kunstbiennale in Venedig im Italienischen Pavillon gezeigt.

GIACOMO COSTA est né à Florence en 1970. Il étudie dans un lycée classique qu'il abandonne en 1986 pour se consacrer aux courses et à la préparation technique des motos. En 1990, après avoir terminé ses études hors d'un cadre scolaire, il s'installe dans les Alpes pour pratiquer l'alpinisme, séjourne au refuge Torino dans le massif du Mont-Blanc et commence à prendre des photos de montagnes. Après un accident, il revient à Florence où il entame une carrière de photographe qu'il met de côté en 1994, pour se livrer à des recherches artistiques personnelles. Deux ans plus tard, il commence à mêler la photographie et des interventions numériques. Il commence sa série des *megalopolises* en 2002, puis abandonne la photo traditionnelle pour l'image de synthèse. Travaillant à temps partiel en qualité d'assistant médical dans un service d'ambulance florentin, il trouve le temps de faire du ski, de la voile et de participer à des courses de moto. Parmi ses expositions récentes : « 2009, Jardins secrets » (Guidi&Schoen Arte Contemporanea, Gênes, Italie, 2009) et « The Chronicles of Time » (Galerie Clairefontaine, Luxembourg, 2009). Son œuvre a été présentée sur le pavillon italien de la Biennale de Venise 2009.

THE CHRONICLES OF TIME

*Agglomerato n.1 (1996); Aqua n.4 (2007); Atto n.3 (2006); Atto n.4 (2006);
Atto n.9 (2007); Private Garden n.7 (2009); Prospettiva n.7 (2003);
Scena n.21 (2004)*

Giacomo Costa's recent monograph **THE CHRONICLES OF TIME** (Damiani, 2009) has a preface written by Lord Norman Foster that reads in part: "I never discussed the imagery of these pages with the author, but they evoke science fiction, doom-laden prophecies and man-made disasters. They have an eerie quietness, mostly bereft of life and deeply foreboding. Although destruction and decay permeates so many of these works there is often the counterpoint of some other-worldly intervention with an alien, futuristic geometry—the remnants of a later and more idealized urbanity. The monumentality of these interventions recalls the heroic visions of a Boullée or Soleri." Costa blends photography with digital manipulation in ways that make it difficult to separate fiction from reality, but in the midst of his ruins there are, indeed, often prescient architectural presences, somehow inspired by buildings that might well feature in *Architecture Now!* but which are out of place and time, lost in a sea of urban excretions, "destruction and decay," as Foster says. Decidedly "post-9/11," as the English architect states, Costa's visions of the future may well be closer to reality than even he suspects. For the most part, the works produced here are C-prints on aluminum, measuring up to three meters in width.

In seinem Vorwort zu Giacomo Costas jüngstem Fotoband, **THE CHRONICLES OF TIME** (Damiani, 2009), schreibt Lord Norman Foster: „Costas Werke auf den folgenden Seiten, über die ich mich mit dem Autor persönlich nicht ausgetauscht habe, beschwören Science-Fiction-Stimmungen, Untergangsszenarien, menschengemachte Katastrophen. Sie wirken wie unheilvolle Prophezeiungen, denen eine unheimliche Ruhe innewohnt, als seien sie praktisch jeglichen Lebens beraubt. Während aber viele der Arbeiten von Zerstörung und Verfall durchdrungen sind, ist in ihnen oft auch ein Kontrapunkt in Gestalt merkwürdig fremder, futuristischer Gebilde wie aus einer anderen Welt eingeschaltet – den Überresten einer kommenden, einer idealisierteren Form von Urbanität. Die Monumentalität dieser hereinragenden Fremdkörper erinnert an die gewaltigen Visionen eines Boullée oder eines Soleri." Costa kombiniert Fotografie und digitale Manipulation auf eine Weise, die es schwierig macht, Fiktives und Reales zu unterscheiden, doch könnten die inmitten seiner Ruinenvisionen auftauchenden und scheinbar auf irgendetwas Kommendes vorausdeutenden architektonischen Gebilde durchaus von Bauten angeregt worden sein, wie sie in *Architecture Now!* vorkommen, stehen sie hier auch ohne bestimmbaren Ort und Zeit verloren in einem Meer aus urbanen Exkreten – inmitten von „Zerstörung und Verfall", um Norman Fosters Worte wieder aufzunehmen. Unverkennbar Schöpfungen der „Post-9/11-Ära", so Foster, liegen Costas Zukunftsvisionen möglicherweise näher an der Wirklichkeit, als er es selbst für möglich hält. Der größte Teil der hier wiedergegebenen Bilder liegt als C-Prints auf Aluminium mit einer Breite von bis zu drei Metern vor.

La récente monographie de Giacomo Costa, **THE CHRONICLES OF TIME** (Damiani, 2009), s'ouvre par une préface de Norman Foster qui écrit : « Je n'ai jamais discuté de l'imagerie contenue dans ces pages avec son auteur, mais elle évoque la science-fiction, des prophéties sinistres et des désastres dont l'homme serait responsable. Ces images au calme éthéré, sont en grande partie dénuées de toute vie. Bien que la destruction et la dégradation marquent un grand nombre de ces œuvres, on y trouve souvent en contrepoint la présence d'une sorte d'intervention venue d'un autre monde, traitée graphiquement dans une géométrie futuriste extra-terrestre, vestige d'une urbanité tardive idéalisée. La monumentalité de ces interventions rappelle les visions héroïques d'un Boullée ou d'un Soleri. » Costa mixe photographie et manipulations numériques de telle façon que l'on a du mal à séparer la fiction de la réalité, mais au milieu de ces ruines figurent des présences architecturales précises, assez inspirées de constructions que l'on pourrait trouver dans *Architecture Now !*, mais qui semblent déplacées, hors du temps, perdues dans un océan d'excrétions urbaines, « de destruction et de dégradation », comme le dit Foster. Comme le fait remarquer l'architecte britannique, ces visions « post 9/11 » du futur sont peut-être plus proches de la réalité qu'on ne le pense. Pour la plupart, ce sont des tirages C-print sur aluminium, qui mesurent jusqu'à trois mètres de long.

The astonishing verisimilitude of Costa's urban views is linked to his ability to portray both the forms of an existing city, and those of newer, more challenging structures.

Costas erstaunlich echt wirkenden Stadtansichten speisen sich aus seiner Fähigkeit, sowohl die in realen Städten vorzufindenden Formen nachzugestalten als auch neue, unbekannte Formen zu komponieren.

L'étonnante vraisemblance des visions urbaines de Costa tient à sa capacité à représenter à la fois le caractère formel d'une ville existante et celui d'une autre cité, encore à venir, qui incarne d'autres défis.

Ruins are an integral part of the worrisome images of Giacomo Costa, as though destruction and nature would and must inevitably take the upper hand over the dreams of architects.

Costas Ruinen, integraler Bestanteil seiner beunruhigenden Schöpfungen, wirken, als müssten Zerstörung und eine wiederkehrende Natur unabwendbar über die Träume der Architekten triumphieren.

Les ruines font partie intégrante des images troublantes de Giacomo Costa, comme si la destruction et la nature devaient inévitablement finir par s'imposer aux rêves des architectes.

Like an otherworldly Atlantis, this work carries spectators below the surface of their apprehensions, toward their fears of future collapse and decay.

Eine Darstellung von einer Art jenseitigem Atlantis, die den Betrachter an die Grenzen seiner Fassungskraft führt und ihn mit seiner Furcht vor künftigem Zusammenbruch und Verfall konfrontiert.

Comme une Atlantis mythique, cette œuvre entraîne le spectateur dans la profondeur de ses appréhensions, et la peur d'un futur fait d'effondrements et de décadence.

Ruins, or the encroachment of nature, are almost omnipresent in Costa's images, exposing the fragility of architecture, where most builders seek the reverse.

Während es den meisten Architekten um Beständigkeit zu tun ist, tauchen in fast jeder von Costas Arbeiten Ruinen oder eine sich die Zivilisation zurückerobernde Natur auf und legen die Fragilität von Architektur bloß.

Les ruines, ou les avancées de la nature, sont quasi omniprésentes dans les œuvres de Costa qui expose la fragilité de l'architecture alors que la plupart des bâtisseurs sont obnubilés par l'inverse.

RAND ELLIOTT

Elliott + Associates Architects
35 Harrison Avenue
Oklahoma City, OK 73104
USA

Tel: +1 405 232 9554
Fax: +1 405 232 9997
E-mail: design@e-a-a.com
Web: www.e-a-a.com

RAND ELLIOTT was born in 1950 in Clinton, Oklahoma. He received his B.Arch degree from Oklahoma State University in 1973. His firm has received 10 National AIA Honor Awards and is the only architecture firm in Oklahoma ever to receive this distinction. Michael Hoffner was the Project Architect for the Underground (Oklahoma City, Oklahoma, 2007, published here). He has been with Elliott + Associates since 1997, and was educated at the University of Oklahoma (B.Arch). Recent projects of the firm include the Chesapeake Boathouse (Oklahoma City, Oklahoma, 2006); ImageNet Houston (Houston, Texas, 2007); POPS Gas Station (Arcadia, Oklahoma, 2007); Car Park One at Chesapeake (Oklahoma City, 2009); Chesapeake Building 13 (Oklahoma City, 2010–); and a research project in progress called Turbinomics, all in the USA.

RAND ELLIOTT, geboren 1950 in Clinton im US-Bundesstaat Oklahoma, erwarb 1973 seinen B.Arch an der Oklahoma State University. Elliot + Associates erhielten zehn National Honor Awards des American Institute of Architects und sind das einzige Architekturbüro Oklahomas überhaupt, das mit dieser Auszeichnung geehrt wurde. Als Projekt-Architekt für das Tunnelnetzwerk Underground in Oklahoma City (Oklahoma, 2007, hier vorstellt) fungierte Michael Hoffner, der wie Elliott seinen B.Arch an der Oklahoma State University erwarb und seit 1997 zu dessen Büro gehört. Zu den jüngeren Projekten von Elliott + Associates zählen u. a. das Chesapeake Boathouse (Oklahoma City, Oklahoma, 2006), die Interieurgestaltung von ImageNet Houston (Houston, Texas, 2007), die POPS Gas Station (Arcadia, Oklahoma, 2007), das Car Park One, ein Parkhaus auf dem Gelände der Firma Chesapeake (Oklahoma City, USA, 2009), das Chesapeake Building 13 (Oklahoma City, Oklahoma, 2010–) und ein fortlaufendes Forschungsprojekt unter dem Titel Turbinomics, alle in den USA.

RAND ELLIOTT, né en 1950 à Clinton (Oklahoma), est B. Arch de la Oklahoma State University (1973). Son agence a reçu dix prix d'honneur nationaux de l'AIA, et est la seule de l'Oklahoma a avoir reçu cette distinction. Michael Hoffner est l'architecte projet de l'Underground (Oklahoma City, Oklahoma, 2007, publié ici). Il fait partie de Elliott + Associates depuis 1997, et a étudié à l'Université de l'Oklahoma (B. Arch). Parmi les réalisations récentes de l'agence : le garage à bateaux de Chesapeake (Oklahoma City, Oklahoma, 2006) ; ImageNet Houston (Houston, Texas, 2007) ; le poste d'essence POPS (Arcadia, Oklahoma, 2007) ; le parking One à Chesapeake (Oklahoma City, 2009) ; l'immeuble 13 à Chesapeake (Oklahoma City, Oklahoma, 2010–) et un projet de recherche en cours « Turbinomics ».

UNDERGROUND
Oklahoma City, Oklahoma, USA, 2007

Address: N Harvey Ave./N Broadway Ave. Oklahoma City, OK 73102, USA, www.downtownokc.com/Default.aspx?tabid=58
Area: 3902 m². Client: Downtown OKC, Inc. Cost: $1.277 million
Collaboration: Michael Hoffner (Project Architect), Joseph Williams

The nightclub atmosphere that permeates many images of Rand Elliott's Underground need not convey an impression of futility—these corridors and spaces are intended to link the spaces of Oklahoma City beneath the surface.

Die Nachtklubatmosphäre, die viele Aufnahmen von Rand Elliotts Underground beherrscht, sollte nicht den Eindruck erwecken, die Korridore und Räume hätten keine weitere Funktion – sie dienen dazu, eine Reihe von Gebäuden in Oklahoma City unterirdisch zu verbinden.

L'atmosphère de night-club qui imprègne de nombreuses vues de l'Underground ne doit pas être prise pour un effet futile. Ces corridors et ces volumes relient divers espaces souterrains du centre d'Oklahoma City.

The Conncourse (named after Jack Conn) is a system of tunnels and bridges built beginning in 1931 that connect 23 buildings in downtown Oklahoma City. The greater part of the complex was built between 1972 and 1984, but had not been properly maintained since that time. With the assistance of the City, the Conncourse Association and Downtown OKC, Inc., it was decided that the buildings connected to the system, whose name was changed to the **UNDERGROUND**, would contribute to its renovation. Music, colored lights, and historically themed photo galleries were part of the scheme to bring this practical web of connections back into use. Works of art have been commissioned for vacant storefronts and the architects also designed signage and a new logo for the Underground. Colors are used to assist in navigation but also are related to efforts to bring works of art into the space, as is the case in the so-called Light Gallery: "One of 11 different colored lighting installations that will provide users with the unique experience of walking through a permanent art installation."

Von 1931 an entstand unter dem Namen The Conncourse (benannt nach dem Initiator Jack Conn) in Oklahoma City ein weitläufiges System aus Tunneln und Brücken, das 23 Gebäude in Innenstadtbereich miteinander verbindet. Der größte Teil dieses Netzwerkes wurde zwischen 1972 und 1984 gebaut, in der Folgezeit jedoch nicht mehr richtig instand gehalten. Vor einigen Jahren fasste ein Konsortium aus den an die Tunnelsystem angeschlossenen Gebäuden den Beschluss, sich bei Unterstützung von städtischer Seite sowie durch die Conncourse Association und das Unternehmen Downtown OKC, Inc., an der Renovierung des Conncourse beteiligen. Der Name des Netzwerkes sollte künftig „**UNDERGROUND**" lauten. Das Konzept zur vollen Wiedernutzbarmachung des nützlichen Verbindungssystems umfasste auch Maßnahmen wie die Einbeziehung von Musik, farbigen Beleuchtungen und Fotogalerien mit historischen Stadtansichten. Ferner wurden Künstler beauftragt, Werke zur Dekoration leerer Ladenschaufenster anzufertigen. Die Architekten wiederum entwarfen ein neues Beschilderungssystem und ein neues Logo für den Underground. Besonders Farben kam eine große Bedeutung zu; einmal als Bestandteil des Leitsystems, aber auch im Zusammenhang mit den Kunstwerken, die in die unterirdischen Räume integriert werden sollten, etwa im Falle der sogenannten Light Gallery, „einer von elf verschiedenen farbigen Beleuchtungsinstallationen, die den Benutzern das besondere Gefühl vermitteln, durch eine permanente Kunstinstallation zu wandeln."

The Conncourse (ainsi nommé en hommage au banquier Jack Conn) est un système de tunnels et de ponts, dont la construction commença en 1931, destiné à relier vingt-trois immeubles du centre d'Oklahoma City. La plus grande partie de ce complexe a été édifiée entre 1972 et 1984, mais n'avait pas été correctement entretenue depuis cette époque. Avec l'aide de la ville d'Oklahoma City, de la Conncourse Association et de Downtown OKC, Inc., il a été décidé que les immeubles connectés devraient participer à la rénovation de ce qui était maintenant appelé l'**UNDERGROUND**. Afin de redonner de l'animation à ce réseau, des projets de musique, des projections colorées et des galeries de photographie à thème furent lancés. Des œuvres d'art ont été commandées pour les vitrines non occupées. Les architectes ont également mené à conçu la signalétique et le nouveau logotype du Underground. Les couleurs guident les passants, mais participent également à l'intégration des œuvres d'art dans l'espace, comme c'est le cas dans la Light Gallery, « l'une des onze installations lumineuses qui offriront aux visiteurs l'expérience unique de se déplacer à travers une œuvre d'art permanente ».

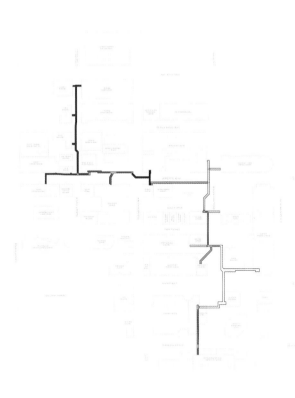

A map (above) shows the extent of the Oklahoma City Underground, while images of corridors demonstrate how the architect has played on saturated colors to bring these otherwise lightless spaces to life.

Die Karte oben zeigt die Ausdehnung des unterirdischen Verbindungsnetzwerkes. Die in den Passagen entstandenen Fotografien führen das Spiel des Architekten mit kräftigen Farben vor Augen, die die tageslichtlosen Räume lebendig werden lassen.

Une carte (ci-dessus) montre l'extension de l'Underground. L'architecte a joué de couleurs saturées pour insuffler un peu de vie dans ces espaces sans lumière naturelle.

SHUHEI ENDO

Shuhei Endo Architecture Institute
2–14–5 Tenma
Kita-ku
Osaka 530–0043
Japan

Tel: +81 6 6354 7456
Fax: +81 6 6354 7457
E-mail: endo@paramodern.com
Web: www.paramodern.com

Born in Shiga Prefecture, Japan, in 1960, **SHUHEI ENDO** obtained his Master's degree from the Kyoto City University of Art in 1986. He worked after that with the architect Osamu Ishii and established his own firm, the Shuhei Endo Architecture Institute, in 1988. His work has been widely published and he has received numerous prizes, including the Andrea Palladio International Prize in Italy (1993). He is currently Professor at the Graduate School of Architecture, Kobe University. His work includes Slowtecture S (Maihara, Shiga, 2002); Growtecture S (Osaka, 2002); Springtecture B (Biwa-cho, Shiga,2002); Bubbletecture M (Maihara, Shiga, 2003); Rooftecture C (Taishi, Hyogo, 2003); Rooftecture H (Kamigori, Hyogo, 2004); and Bubbletecture O (Maruoka, Fukui, 2004). Along with Bubbletecture H (Sayo-cho, Hyogo, 2006–07, published here), he completed Slowtecture M (Miki-city, Hygo) and Rooftecture M's (Habikino City, Osaka) in 2007, all in Japan.

SHUHEI ENDO wurde 1960 in der japanischen Präfektur Shiga geboren. Nach seinem Masterabschluss an der Städtischen Kunsthochschule Kyoto im Jahr 1986 arbeitete er zunächst für den Architekten Osamu Ishii. 1988 gründete er seine eigenes Büro, das Shuhei Endo Architecture Institute. Endo hat zahlreiche Publikationen veröffentlicht und ist vielfach ausgezeichnet worden, u. a. mit dem Premio internazionale di architettura Andrea Palladio (1993). Gegenwärtig lehrt Endo als Professor an der Graduiertenfakultät für Architektur der Universität Kobe. Zu Endos realisierten Projekten gehören Slowtecture S (Maihara, Shiga, 2002), Growtecture S (Osaka, 2002), Springtecture B (Biwa-cho, Shiga, 2002), Bubbletecture M (Maihara, Shiga, 2003), Rooftecture C (Taishi, Hyogo, 2003), Rooftecture H (Kamigori, Hyogo, 2004) und Bubbletecture O (Maruoka, Fukui, 2004). Parallel zum Bubbletecture H (Sayo-cho, Hyogo, 2006–07, hier vorgestellt) entstanden 2007 Slowtecture M (Miki-city, Hygo, Japan) und die Rooftecture M's (Habikino City, Osaka), alle Projekte in Japan.

Né dans la préfecture de Shiga au Japon en 1960, **SHUHEI ENDO** a obtenu son M.Arch de l'Université des arts de Tokyo en 1986. Il a ensuite travaillé pour l'architecte Osamu Ishii et fondé sa propre agence, Shuhei Endo Architecture Institute, en 1988. Son œuvre a été largement publiée et a reçu de nombreuses distinctions, dont le Prix Andrea Palladio International en Italie (1993). Il enseigne actuellement à l'École supérieure d'architecture de l'Université de Kobé. Parmi ses réalisations : Slowtecture S (Maihara, Shiga, 2002) ; Growtecture S (Osaka, 2002) ; Springtecture B (Biwa-cho, Shiga,2002) ; Bubbletecture M (Maihara, Shiga, 2003) ; Rooftecture C (Taishi, Hyogo, 2003) ; Rooftecture H (Kamigori, Hyogo, 2004) et Bubbletecture O (Maruoka, Fukui, 2004). Paralèlement à Bubbletecture H (Sayo-cho, Hyogo, 2006–07, publiée ici), il a achevé Slowtecture M (Miki-city, Hygo) et Rooftecture M's (Habikino City, Osaka) en 2007.

BUBBLETECTURE H

Sayo-cho, Hyogo, Japan, 2006–07

*Address: 679-5148, 1-chome, Hikarityou Sayo Sayo-gun 330-3, Hyogo, Japan, +81 79 158 20 65, www.eco-hyogo.jp/taikenkan/
Area: 968 m². Client: Hyogo Prefecture. Cost: not disclosed*

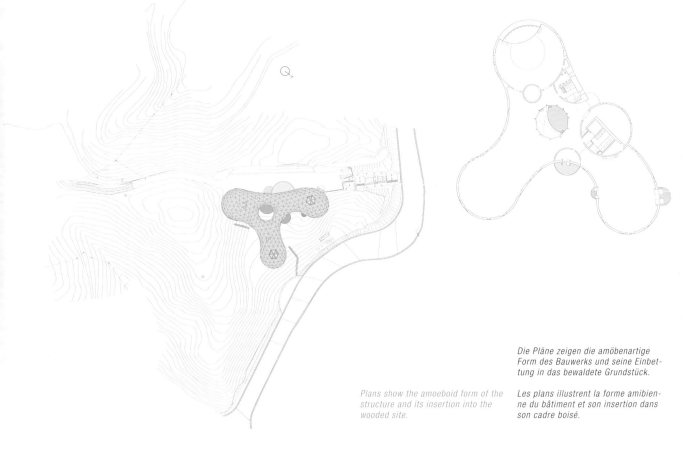

Die Pläne zeigen die amöbenartige Form des Bauwerks und seine Einbettung in das bewaldete Grundstück.

Plans show the amoeboid form of the structure and its insertion into the wooded site.

Les plans illustrent la forme amibienne du bâtiment et son insertion dans son cadre boisé.

This is a one-story structure located on a 5000-square-meter site in a mountainous region some two hours from Osaka. The program includes the education of adults and children on environmental issues and advances in "green" technology. Set on a steep slope near a forest, the structure was designed to have the minimum possible impact on the environment. A three-dimensional truss structure in Japanese cypress is covered with 1.2-millimeter-thick weather-resistant Corten-type steel that does not rust after the initial finishing process. The roof was designed to allow the growth of mosses. A waiting room and office are included in the structure, as well as the public exhibition or teaching space. The architect stresses that this unusual form is directly related to the program and also to his desire to protect the site as much as possible during and after construction.

Endos eingeschossiger Kuppelbau namens Bubbletecture H liegt auf einem 5000 m² großen Grundstück in einer bergigen Region zwei Fahrtstunden außerhalb von Osaka. Genutzt wird das Gebäude unter anderem für Lehrveranstaltungen, in denen Erwachsene und Kinder mit „grünen Technologien" vertraut gemacht werden. Der Architekt hat bei seinem Entwurf darauf geachtet, dass der auf einem steil abfallenden Gelände in unmittelbarer Waldnähe errichtete Bau die Natur so wenig wie möglich beeinträchtigt. Er entwickelte eine dreidimensionale Trägerstruktur aus japanischem Zypressenholz, die mit 1,2 mm dicken Stahlplatten mit ähnlichen Eigenschaften wie Corten-Stahl umhüllt wurde, die nach der Bewitterung nicht weiter rosten können. Dafür kann und soll auf dem Dach Moos anwachsen. Neben dem für Bildungsveranstaltungen und öffentliche Ausstellungen genutzten Raum umfasst das Gebäude außerdem einen Aufenthaltsraum und ein Büro. Wie der Architekt betont, hat sich die ungewöhnliche Form einerseits unmittelbar aus dem Nutzungskonzept ergeben, andererseits aus seinem Wunsch, das Gelände während und nach dem Bau so gut wie möglich zu schonen.

Cette construction d'un seul niveau a été édifiée sur un terrain de 5000 mètres carrés dans une région montagneuse à deux heures d'Osaka. Le programme portait sur un centre de formation d'adultes et d'enfants aux enjeux environnementaux et aux progrès des technologies « vertes ». Implanté sur un terrain très incliné à proximité d'une forêt, le projet a été conçu pour exercer le plus faible impact possible sur l'environnement. La structure porteuse tridimensionnelle en cyprès du Japon est recouverte d'une tôle d'acier de type Corten de 1,2 millimètre d'épaisseur dont l'oxydation se stabilise rapidement. Le toit a été conçu pour permettre la croissance de mousse. On trouve à l'intérieur du bâtiment une salle d'attente, un bureau, un espace destiné à l'enseignement et une salle d'expositions. L'architecte précise que la forme inhabituelle est une conséquence directe du programme et aussi de son désir de protéger le site autant que possible, aussi bien en cours du chantier qu'après.

Seen from ground level, the design seems to have a relation to the geodesic domes of Buckminster Fuller, albeit covered in this instance with pre-oxidized Corten steel.

Vom Boden aus gesehen scheint der Entwurf eine gewisse Verwandtschaft zu den geodätischen Kuppeln Buckminster Fullers zu besitzen, wobei Endos Werk mit einer Hülle aus voroxidiertem Stahl versehen ist.

Vus du sol, ces dômes semblent proches de ceux de Buckminster Fuller, mais sont en fait recouverts de panneaux en acier Corten.

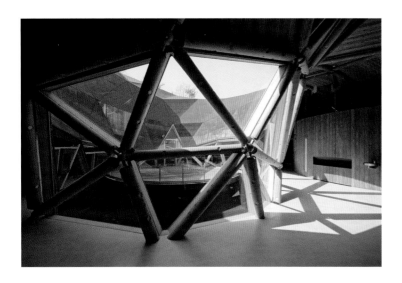

The bulbous forms of Endo's design are unexpected and surely make no effort to be fashionable in any traditional sense. Triangular windows bring natural light into this metal tent.

Die ungewöhnliche Knollenform ist sicherlich nicht darauf angelegt, im traditionellen Sinne „schick" zu sein. Durch dreieckige Fenster fällt Tageslicht in den metallenen Polyeder ein.

Les formes bulbeuses et inattendues du projet d'Endo ne font aucun effort pour être à la mode au sens traditionnel du terme. Des fenêtres triangulaires éclairent l'intérieur de cette tente de métal.

The triangulated space-frame used to support the building allows the architect to create a column-free interior space. Elevations show how it fits into its hilly site.

La structure porteuse tridimensionnelle a permis à l'architecte de créer un volume intérieur sans colonne. Les élévations montrent la manière dont elle est adaptée au terrain.

Die Verwendung eines aus vielen einzelnen Dreiecken zusammengesetzten Raumfachwerks ermöglichte dem Architekten die Schaffung eines säulenfreien Innenraums. Die Aufrisse führen die Einbettung des Gebildes in das abschüssige Gelände vor Augen.

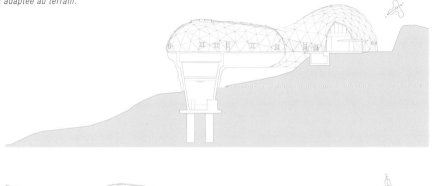

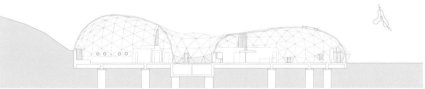

ALBERT FRANCE-LANORD

Albert France-Lanord Architecture
Rehnsgaten 3
11357 Stockholm
Sweden

Tel/Fax: +46 8 664 56 64
E-mail: info@af-la.com
Web: www.af-la.com

ALBERT FRANCE-LANORD was born in Nancy, France, in 1974. He attended the Paris-Villemin School of Architecture (1993–97), before doing postgraduate work at the Royal School of Fine Arts (KKH, Stockholm, 1998–99). He worked for Thomas Eriksson Arkitekter (Stockholm, 2002–03), before creating his own office in 2004. His work includes Teatron Nightclub (Stockholm, 2007); the Bahnhof Pionen (Stockholm, 2007–08, published here); J. Lindeberg Flagship Store (Stockholm, 2008); J. Lindeberg's Shop-in-Shop (Copenhagen, Oslo, London, 2009–); Stories Café and Restaurants (Stockholm, 2009–); and a Gym concept for Moscow (ongoing).

ALBERT FRANCE-LANORD wurde 1974 im französischen Nancy geboren. Nach seinem Studium an der École d'Architecture Paris-Villemin (1993–97) erwarb er ein zusätzliches Postgraduiertendiplom an der Königlichen Kunsthochschule in Stockholm (1998–99). Vor der Eröffnung seines eigenen Büros im Jahr 2004 arbeitete France-Lanord für Thomas Eriksson Arkitekter (Stockholm, 2002–03). Zu seinen Arbeiten gehören der Nachtklub Teatron (Stockholm, 2007), der Bahnhof Pionen (Stockholm, 2007–08, hier vorgestellt), der J. Lindeberg Flagship Store (Stockholm, 2008), mehrere J. Lindeberg-Shop-in-Shop-Filialen (Kopenhagen, Oslo, London, 2009–), das Café und die Restaurants Stories (Stockholm, 2009–) und ein fortlaufendes Konzept für Moskauer Fitnessstudios.

ALBERT FRANCE-LANORD, né à Nancy (France) en 1974, a étudié à l'École d'architecture de Paris-Villemin (1993–97), puis à la Royal School of Fine Arts (KKH, Stockholm, 1998–99). Il a travaillé pour Thomas Eriksson Arkitekter (Stockholm, 2002–03), avant de créer son agence en 2004. Parmi ses réalisations : le nightclub Teatron (Stockholm, 2007) ; la Bahnhof Pionen (Stockholm, 2007–08, publiée ici) ; le magasin amiral J. Lindeberg (Stockholm, 2008) ; la Shop-in-Shop J. Lindeberg (Copenhagen, Oslo, Londres, 2009–) ; le café et les restaurants Stories (Stockholm, 2009–) ainsi qu'un concept de gymnase pour Moscou (en cours).

BAHNHOF PIONEN

Stockholm, Sweden, 2007–08

Address: Bahnhof, Renstiernas Gata 37, 11631 Stockholm, Sweden, www.bahnhof.se
Area: 1200 m². Client: Bahnhof (CEO Jon Karlung). Cost: not disclosed

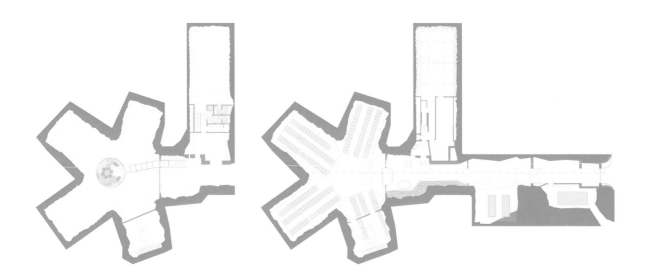

This project was carried out in a former atomic bomb shelter located 30 meters beneath the granite underlying Vita Berg Park in Stockholm. The client is an Internet service provider, and the space is used for server halls and offices. Albert France-Lanord states: "The starting point of the project was to consider the rock as a living organism. We created strong contrasts between rooms where the rock dominates and the human being is a stranger and rooms where the human being took over totally." The architect sought to bring as much variety to the lighting as possible in order to avoid the claustrophobic feeling that such a setting might easily have given. Albert France-Lanord states clearly that his influences include a number of James Bond films and the movie *Silent Running*. The architect concludes: "It has been very exciting to work with a space which at first didn't offer one square angle: the rock. The main room is not a traditional space limited by surfaces but, rather, is defined by the emptiness inside a mass."

Der **BAHNHOF PIONEN** befindet sich in einem ehemaligen Atomschutzbunker in 30 m Tiefe unter dem Granitfels, der sich unter dem Stockholmer Vita Berg Park hindurchzieht. Der Auftraggeber für das Projekt war ein Internetprovider, der Raum wird für seine Server und für Büros genutzt. Albert France-Lanord selbst erklärt zu dem Projekt: „Unser Ausgangspunkt bestand darin, den Fels als einen lebendigen Organismus zu betrachten. So haben wir gegensätzliche Arten von Räumen geschaffen: einmal solche, in denen der Fels dominiert und der Mensch wie ein Fremdkörper wirkt, und dann solche, in denen allein der Mensch im Vordergrund steht." Um eine klaustrophobischen Atmosphäre zu vermeiden, die in einer solche Kulisse nur allzu leicht entstehen könnte, hat der Architekt sich darum bemüht, ein möglichst abwechslungsreiches Beleuchtungssystem zu integrieren. Bezüglich der Einflüsse auf die Ästhetik des Projekts verweist Albert France-Lanord unumwunden auf die Szenerien aus James-Bond-Filmen und dem Film „Silent Running" (dt. „Lautlos im Weltraum"). France-Lanords Resümee: „Es war sehr spannend, mit einem Raum zu arbeiten, in dem es zunächst keinen einzigen rechten Winkel gab, nur Fels. Der Hauptsaal ist kein im üblichen Sinn durch klare Flächen begrenzter Raum, sondern wird vielmehr von der Leere im Innern einer Masse bestimmt."

Ces installations d'une entreprise de services pour l'Internet occupent un ancien abri atomique creusé dans le granit à 30 mètres de profondeur sous le parc de Vita Berg à Stockholm. Les lieux ont été affectés à des salles d'ordinateurs et des bureaux. Albert France-Lanord précise : « Le point de départ de ce projet est de considérer le rocher comme un organisme vivant. Nous avons créé de puissants contrastes entre les salles où le rocher domine et l'être humain se sent comme un étranger, et d'autres où il prend totalement le dessus. » L'architecte s'est efforcé de diversifier l'éclairage, afin d'éviter la sensation de claustrophobie qu'un tel cadre pourrait facilement susciter. Il avoue que parmi ses influences figurent un certain nombre de films de James Bond et le film de science-fiction *Silent Running*. Il conclut : « Ce fut une expérience passionnante de travailler sur un espace qui, au départ, n'offrait pas un seul angle droit, mais que du rocher. La salle principale n'est pas un volume traditionnel limité par des surfaces, mais plutôt un vide creusé dans une masse. »

With its cavernous interior forms, the Bahnhof Pionen might bring to mind the lair of an evildoer in a James Bond movie, an influence that the architect does not deny.

Das höhlenartige Innere des Bahnhofs Pionen lässt an das Versteck eines Bösewichts aus einem James-Bond-Film denken, ein Einfluss, den der Architekt gar nicht bestreitet.

Les caverneux intérieurs de la Bahnhof Pionen rappellent les repaires des personnages maléfiques des films de James Bond, influence que l'architecte ne rejette d'ailleurs pas.

Though bored into the rock, as is visible in the drawing below, the interior design calls on numerous green plants: somewhat of a contradiction in an environment devoid of natural light.

Wie in der Zeichnung unten zu sehen, wurden die Räume tief in den Fels hineingebohrt. Trotzdem finden sich zahlreiche Grünpflanzen in den Büros – ein gewisser Widerspruch in einer Umgebung, der es komplett an Tageslicht fehlt.

Bien que creusés dans le rocher, comme le montre le dessin ci-dessous, les aménagements intérieurs font appel à de nombreuses plantes vertes, ce qui n'est pas sans provocation dans un environnement dénué de tout éclairage naturel.

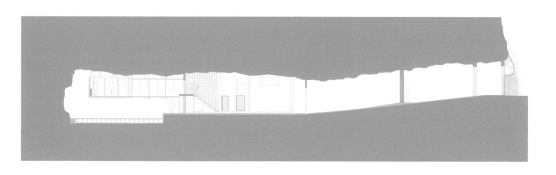

EDOUARD FRANÇOIS

Edouard François
136 rue Falguière
75015 Paris
France

Tel: +33 1 45 67 88 87
Fax: +33 1 45 67 51 45
E-mail: agence@edouardfrancois.com
Web: www.edouardfrancois.com

EDOUARD FRANÇOIS was born in Paris in 1957 and educated as an architect and urban designer. He attended the Beaux-Arts in Paris and the École National des Ponts et Chaussées, becoming an architect in 1983. He has taught at the École National Supérieure du Paysage in Versailles (1998–99), the Architectural Association (AA) in London (1997–98), and the École Spéciale d'Architecture in Paris the same year. The work of Edouard François emphasizes sustainable design and direct relations with nature. He completed the extension and renovation of the Buffon Primary School in Thiais (1996); an apartment building called "L'Immeuble qui pousse" (the Building that Grows—a structure covered in a mesh of steel cages containing loosely compacted stones in which plants can grow; Montpellier, 2000); Flower Tower (Paris, 2001–03); the covering for a ventilation tower in La Défense (Paris, 2004); Palace Fouquet's Barrière Hotel (Paris, 2006); the renovation and extension of the Ternes Parking facility (Paris, 2007); and Eden Bio (Paris, 2008, published here), all in France. Current projects include 114 housing units in Champigny-sur-Marne (Opac de Paris) and a further 70 housing units in Grenoble for the local rent-controlled housing office (Opac, 2008–).

EDOUARD FRANÇOIS, geboren 1957 in Paris, ist ausgebildeter Architekt und Stadtplaner. 1983 hat der Absolvent der École Nationale des Beaux-Arts in Paris und der École Nationale des Ponts et Chaussées erstmal als Architekt gearbeitet. 1997–98 lehrte François an der Architectural Association in London sowie an der École Spéciale d'Architecture in Paris, 1998–99 besaß er einen Lehrauftrag an der École National Supérieure du Paysage de Versailles. Edouard François legt in seinen Entwürfen großen Wert auf Nachhaltigkeit und eine direkte Beziehung zur Natur. Zu seinen realisierten Projekten gehören die Renovierung und Erweiterung der École maternelle Buffon in Thiais (1996), ein Apartmentgebäude in Montpellier mit Namen „L'Immeuble qui pousse" (das sprießende Haus – eine Konstruktion, die rundum von steingefüllten Stahlkörben eingefasst ist, in denen Pflanzen gedeihen können; 2000), der Flower Tower in Paris (2001–03), die Begrünung eines Belüftungsturmes in La Défense (Paris, 2004), Fouquets Hotel Barrière in Paris (2006), die Erneuerung und Erweiterung des Parking des Ternes, ein Pariser Parkhaus (2007), und die Sozialwohnanlage Eden Bio in Paris (2008, hier vorgestellt). Derzeit in der Umsetzungsphase befinden sich ein Projekt mit 114 Wohneinheiten in Champigny-sur-Marne für Opac de Paris sowie eines mit 70 mietpreisgebundenen Wohneinheiten im Auftrag des örtlichen Wohnungsamtes Grenoble (Opac, 2008–).

EDOUARD FRANÇOIS, né à Paris en 1957, est architecte et urbaniste depuis 1983. Il a étudié à l'École nationale des beaux-arts à Paris et à l'École nationale des ponts et chaussées. Il a enseigné à l'École nationale supérieure du paysage à Versailles (1998–99), à l'Architectural Association à Londres (1997–98) et à l'École spéciale d'architecture à Paris la même année. Son travail est axé sur un développement durable en relation directe avec la nature. Il a achevé l'extension et la rénovation de l'école primaire Buffon à Thiais (1996); un immeuble d'appartements, « L'immeuble qui pousse » (à la structure habillée de gabions à travers lesquels des plantes peuvent pousser, Montpellier, 2000); la tour Fleur (Paris, 2001–03); la couverture d'une tour de ventilation à La Défense (Paris, 2004); l'hôtel Fouquet's Barrière (Paris, 2006); la rénovation et l'extension du parking des Ternes (Paris, 2007) et l'Eden Bio (Paris, 2008, publié ici). Ses projets actuels comprennent 114 logements à Champigny-sur-Marne (Opac de Paris) et 70 à Grenoble pour l'office d'HLM local (Opac, 2008–).

EDEN BIO

Paris, France, 2008

Address: 27 rue des Vignoles, 75020 Paris, France
Area: 7700 m². Client: Paris Habitat. Cost: € 10.7 million

This project involved the construction of 98 rent-controlled apartments and 11 artist's ateliers, together with 52 parking spaces. The four-story structure differs radically from other buildings of this type, in particular because of the vegetal covering that should eventually grow on wooden supports on the façades. Models and drawings show this vegetal aspect better than the actual photos published here. Tightly inserted into the existing urban fabric of the 20th arrondissement, the structure's basic plan is rectangular. The architect has bowed to some extent to the form of older houses in the area, but he has completely avoided any sense of "pastiche" through the green aspect of the project, but also its innate modernity. The massing and juxtaposition of the complex gives it an apparently irregular appearance, as though several buildings had been inserted into the site over time, while plans make clear the highly rigorous alignment of the housing units.

Das Projekt umfasst den Bau von 98 Sozialwohnungen sowie elf Künstlerateliers und 52 Parkplätzen. Das viergeschossige Gebäude unterscheidet sich vor allem insofern radikal von ähnlichen Projekten dieser Art, als seine Fassaden mithilfe eines vorgebauten Holzgerüstes in einigen Jahren komplett von einem Pflanzenvorhang eingehüllt sein sollen. Vorläufig noch vermitteln allerdings Modelle und Zeichnungen eine bessere Vorstellung von der künftigen Begrünung als die aktuellen, hier gezeigten Fotos. Der rechteckige Grundriss der Anlage wurde exakt in die enge bestehende Bebauungsstruktur des 20. Arrondissements eingepasst. Der Architekt hat sich zwar bis zu einem gewissen Grad von der Bauform der älteren Wohnhäuser der Gegend anregen lassen, die Gefahr reiner „Pastiches" jedoch durch die grüne Ausrichtung und modernste Standards vollständig vermieden. Durch das dichte Nebeneinander der unterschiedlichen Einheiten entsteht ein unregelmäßiger Gesamteindruck der Anlage, so als seien die einzelnen Bestandteile peu à peu in das Grundstück eingefügt worden. Schaut man sich allerdings die zugrunde liegenden Pläne an, erkennt man an der strengen Einfluchtung einen Entwurf aus einem Guss.

Cet ensemble comprend 98 appartements à loyers modérés, 11 ateliers d'artiste et 55 emplacements de parking. Le bâtiment de quatre niveaux diffère radicalement des autres immeubles de ce type, en particulier dans sa couverture végétale qui devrait par la suite grimper sur les supports en bois des façades. Les maquettes et les dessins montrent mieux cet aspect végétal que les photos actuellement disponibles. Étroitement inséré dans le tissu urbain du XXᵉ arrondissement de Paris, le plan de l'ensemble est essentiellement rectangulaire. L'architecte fait une sorte de clin d'œil formel aux maisons anciennes du quartier, mais en évitant tout aspect de pastiche par la couverture végétale et une modernité indéniable. Le plan-masse et la juxtaposition des différents éléments créent une apparence irrégulière comme si ces immeubles avaient été édifiés au cours du temps. Cependant, les plans montrent clairement l'alignement très rigoureux des appartements.

Rather than producing a slick, continuous form, the architect has opted for something of a "village" atmosphere, and one surely related to the houses of the past.

Anstatt seiner Wohnanlage eine glatte, einheitliche Gestalt zu geben, hat sich der Architekt für eine eher „dörfliche" Atmosphäre entschieden, mit Bezug auf historische Häuserformen.

Plutôt qu'une forme continue et lissée, l'architecte a opté pour une atmosphère de « village » non sans lien avec le passé.

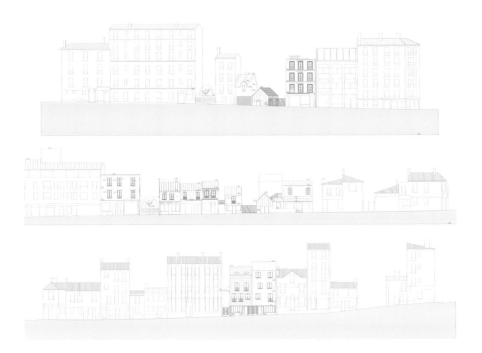

Varying surface treatments and an unexpected wooden outrigging give the housing an unexpected fragility or variety.

Variierende Oberflächengestaltungen und ungewöhnliche hölzerne Vorbauten verleihen der Anlage etwas ungewohnt Fragiles und zugleich Abwechselungsreiches.

La variété du traitement des surfaces et le curieux doublage de la façade par des longerons de bois créent un certain sentiment de fragilité.

Despite its apparent irregularity, the drawing below or even the image above do reveal the repetitive or "modern" basis for the houses.

Entgegen der scheinbaren Uneinheit-lichkeit der Häuser lassen die Zeichnung unten und sogar das Foto oben das ihnen zugrunde liegende repetitive oder „moderne" Schema erkennen.

Malgré son irrégularité apparente, le plan ci-dessous et même la photographie ci-dessus révèlent dans le plan des logements la mise en œuvre du principe « moderne » de répétitivité.

TERUNOBU FUJIMORI

Terunobu Fujimori, Professor, Institute of Industrial Science, University of Tokyo
4–6–1 Komaba, Meguro-ku, Tokyo 153–8505, Japan
Tel: +81 3 5452 6370 / Fax: +81 3 5452 6371 / E-mail: tanpopo@iis.u-tokyo.ac.jp

Born in Chino City, Nagano, Japan, in 1946, **TERUNOBU FUJIMORI** attended Tohoku University (1965–71) in Sendai, before receiving his Ph.D. in Architecture from the University of Tokyo (1971–78). He is currently a Professor at the University of Tokyo's Institute of Industrial Science. Although research on often long-forgotten Western-style buildings in Japan from the Meiji period onwards remains his main activity, he is also a practicing architect. "I didn't start designing buildings until my forties, so the condition I set for myself is that I shouldn't just repeat the same things that my colleagues or professors were doing," he has stated. He won the Japan Art Grand Prix (1997) for the Nira House, and the Architectural Institute of Japan Prize for Design (2001) for the Student Dormitory for Kumamoto Agricultural College. His first built work was the Jinchokan Moriya Historical Museum (Chino City, Nagano, 1990–91), which received mixed reviews for the use of local materials over a reinforced-concrete structure. Other completed projects include the Akino Fuku Art Museum (Hamamatsu, Shizuoka, 1995–97); Nira House (Leek House, Machida City, Tokyo, 1995–97); Student Dormitory for Kumamoto Agricultural College (Koshi City, Kumamoto, 1998–2000); Ichiya-tei (One Night Tea House, Ashigarashimo, Kanagawa, 2003); the Takasugi-an (Too-High Tea House, Chino City, Nagano, 2004), set six meters above the ground like a tree house; Chashitsu Tetsu (Tea House Tetsu, Musée Kiyoharu Shirakaba, Nakamaru, Hokuto City, Yamanashi, 2005); and Charred Cedar House (Nagano City, Nagano, 2006–07). He recently participated in the Sumika Project (Coal House, Utsunomiya, Tochigi, 2008) with Toyo Ito and other well-known architects; and completed Roof House (Omihachiman, Shiga, 2008–09, published here); and Copper House (Kokubunji City, Tokyo, 2009), all in Japan.

TERUNOBU FUJIMORI, geboren 1946 in Nagano, Japan, besuchte von 1965 bis 1971 die Universität Tohoku in Sendai, anschließend setzte er sein Architekturstudium an der Universität Tokio fort, an der er 1978 promoviert wurde. Derzeit ist Fujimori Professor am Institute of Industrial Science der Universität Tokio. Obgleich er sich nach wie vor hauptsächlich mit der Erforschung oftmals in Vergessenheit geratener japanischer Bauten, die ab der Meiji-Zeit in einem westlich geprägten Stil entstanden, beschäftigt, ist er auch praktizierender Architekt. „Als ich selbst mit dem Bauen anfing, hatte ich bereits die 40 überschritten. Deshalb nahm ich mir vor, nicht bloß das zu wiederholen, was schon meine Kollegen oder andere Professoren machen", sagte Fujimori einmal. Für das Haus Nira erhielt Fujimori 1997 den Großen Preis für Japanische Kunst, das Studentenwohnheim der landwirtschaftlichen Hochschule Kumamoto wurde 2001 mit dem Designpreis des Architectural Institute of Japan ausgezeichnet. Fujimoris erstes realisiertes Projekt war das Historische Museum Jinchokan Moriya (Chino, Nagano, 1990–91), das seinerzeit angesichts der Verwendung traditioneller Materialen über einem Tragwerk aus Stahlbeton auf ein geteiltes Echo stieß. Zu seinen in der Folge verwirklichten Projekten, allesamt in Japan, gehören das Akino Fuku Kunstmuseum (Hamamatsu, Shizuoka, 1995–97), das erwähnte Haus Nira (Haus Leek, Machida, Tokio, 1995–97), ein Studentenwohnheim für die landwirtschaftliche Hochschule Kumamoto (Koshi, Kumamoto, 1998–2000), das Teehaus Ichiya-tei (Ashigarashimo, Kanagawa, 2003), das wie ein Baumhaus sechs Meter über der Erde schwebende Teehaus Takasugi-an (Chino, Nagano 2004), das Chashitsu Tetsu, ebenfalls ein Teehaus (Museum Kiyoharu Shirakaba, Nakamaru, Hokuto, Yamanashi, 2005), und das Charred Cedar House (Nagano, 2006–07). In jüngerer Zeit beteiligte Fujimoro sich gemeinsam mit Toyo Ito und weiteren bekannten Architekten an einem Projekt namens Sumika, zu dem er das Coal House beitrug (Utsunomiya, Tochigi, 2008), 2008–09 realisierte er das Roof House (Omihachiman, Shiga, hier vorgestellt) und 2009 das Copper House (Kokubunji, Tokio).

Né à Chino City, Nagano (Japon), en 1946, **TERUNOBU FUJIMORI** a fait ses études à l'Université Tohoku (1965–71) à Sendaï. Il est docteur en architecture de l'Université de Tokyo (1971–78) et enseigne actuellement à l'Institut des sciences et techniques de cette université. Si ses recherches sur les bâtisses de style occidental au Japon, datant de l'ère Meiji et souvent longtemps oubliées, restent sa principale activité, il est également un praticien de l'architecture : « Je n'ai pas commencé à concevoir de construction avant la quarantine, aussi me suis-je donné comme condition de ne pas répéter ce que mes confrères ou professeurs faisaient. » Il remporté le Grand prix d'art du Japon (1997) pour la Maison Nira, et le prix de conception de l'Institut d'architecture du Japon (2001) pour le foyer d'étudiants du collège agricole de Kumamoto. Son premier projet réalisé a été le musée historique Jinchokan Moriya (Chino City, Nagano, 1990–91), diversement apprécié pour son recours à des matériaux locaux sur une structure en béton armé. Parmi ses autres réalisations : le musée d'art Akino Fuku (Hamamatsu, Shizuoka, 1995–97) ; la Maison Nira (la Maison du poireau, Machida City, Tokyo 1995–97) ; un foyer d'étudiants pour le collège d'agriculture de Kumamoto (Koshi City, Kumamoto, 1998–2000) ; Ichiya-tei (Maison de thé pour une nuit, Ashigarashimo, Kanagawa, 2003) ; Takasugi-an (Maison de thé trop haute, Chino City, Nagano 2004), installée à six mètres au-dessus du sol, comme une maison dans un arbre ; Chashitsu Tetsu (Maison de thé Tetsu, musée Kiyoharu Shirakaba, Nakamaru, Hokuto City, Yamanashi, 2005) et la Maison de thé carbonisée (Nagano City, Nagano, 2006–07). Il a récemment participé au projet Sumika (Maison de charbon, Utsunomiya, Tochigi, 2008) avec Toyo Ito et d'autres architectes connus ; et la Maison toit (Omihachiman, Shiga, 2008–09, publiée ici) et achevé la Maison de cuivre (Kokubunji City, Tokyo, 2009).

ROOF HOUSE

Omihachiman, Shiga, Japan, 2008–09

*Area: 458 m². Client: not disclosed. Cost: not disclosed
Collaboration: Hiroshi Nakatani, Akimura Flying-C (Builder)*

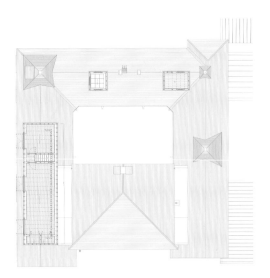

Set opposite Lake Biwa, the largest lake in Japan, this house continues Terunobu Fujimori's unexpected exploration of Japanese traditional architecture seen from a thoroughly contemporary point of view. There is also something of the humor that the architect often employs in his work evident here. With its multiple copper-sheathed roof pavilions, one of which appears to be entirely detached from the house, this residence looks like something out of *The Lord of the Rings* as much as it does more obviously contemporary structures. He explains: "The theme of this work is 'the roof.' The reason why I chose this theme is that the roofs match the surrounding scenery of mountains. Several oak trees are planted on the tops of the roofs so that the building and greenery unite with each other to make a whole built work." Essentially square, the house is set at an angle and off-center in its largely rectangular site, and features a large internal courtyard. The interior assumes the same kind of understated and oblique modernity, still linked to tradition or to such ideas of the home as a cave that have been seen in earlier work by the architect.

Mit diesem unweit des Biwa-Sees, des größten Sees Japans, errichteten Gebäude setzt Terunobu Fujimori seine aus einer durch und durch zeitgenössischen Perspektive erfolgende Auseinandersetzung mit der traditionellen japanischen Architektur fort. Einmal mehr ist hier der Humor unverkennbar, den Fujimori in viele seiner Werke einfließen lässt. Mit seinen kupferschindelgedeckten Dachpavillons, von denen einer wie völlig losgelöst von dem Baukörper wirkt, erscheint das Haus wie ein Domizil aus *Der Herr der Ringe*, während es ebenso viel mit Bauten gemeinsam hat, die offenkundig zeitgenössischer sind. Fujimori erklärt: „Das zentrale Thema dieses Hauses ist ‚das Dach'. Dahinter stand die Absicht, die Dächer in einen Zusammenhang mit der umgebenen Bergkulisse zu stellen. Die einzelnen Dachspitzen wurden mit Eichen bepflanzt, so dass sich eine direkte Verbindung zwischen dem Gebäude und dem Grün der Umgebung einstellt und ein gesamtes Bauwerk entsteht." Das mehr oder weniger quadratische Haus wurde mit einer Spitze in einem schrägen Winkel an den Rand des fast rechteckigen Grundstücks gesetzt und besitzt einen großzügigen Innenhof. Die Innengestaltung zeigt jene Art von subtiler und zugleich ausgefallener Modernität, die immer auch mit der Tradition oder der Vorstellung vom Wohnhaus als einer Höhle verbunden ist, wie sie schon in früheren Arbeiten des Architekten auszumachen war.

Face au lac Biwa, le plus grand lac du Japon, cette maison poursuit les explorations inattendues de Terunobu Fujimori dans le domaine de l'architecture traditionnelle japonaise analysée sous un angle très contemporain. On y retrouve un peu de l'humour dont l'architecte fait souvent preuve dans ses travaux. Avec ses multiples toits recouverts de cuivre, dont l'un semble s'être entièrement détaché, cette résidence fait autant penser à une maison tirée du *Seigneur des anneaux* qu'à des projets plus contemporains. « Le thème de cette réalisation est "le toit". La raison pour laquelle je l'ai choisi est que les toits s'accordent avec le cadre des montagnes environnantes. Plusieurs chênes sont plantés au sommet de ces toitures pour que le bâtiment et la verdure s'unissent et ne fassent qu'un », explique l'architecte. De plan essentiellement carré, la maison est décentrée et posée en biais par rapport à son terrain rectangulaire. Elle possède une grande cour interne. L'intérieur reprend le même principe de modernité détournée et sous-entendue, mais reste lié à la tradition ou à l'idée de maison caverne, précédemment abordée dans certaines réalisations antérieures de l'architecte.

Plans show the basic square form of the house and its underlying complexity.

Aufsicht und Grundriss (oben) lassen den komplexen Aufbau des im Grunde quadratischen Hauses erkennen.

Les plans montrent la complexité de l'organisation de la maison à l'intérieur d'une forme carrée.

The architect is given to a certain
sense of humor or incongruity, seen
here in the trees planted on each
pointed roof of the house.

Der dem Architekten zugeschriebene
Sinn für Humor und skurrile Einfälle
zeigt sich hier in Form von Bäumen,
die auf die Dachspitzen gepflanzt
wurden.

L'architecte est crédité d'un certain
sens de l'humour – ou de l'incongrui-
té – comme l'illustrent les arbres
plantés au sommet de la toiture.

Fujimori adds curious touches—such as the suspended pavilion seen in the image below—but, fundamentally, he is seeking a real fusion between deep traditions of Japan and an undeniable modernity.

Fujimori stattet seine Bauten gerne mit kuriosen Elementen aus – hier zum Beispiel den vom Rest des Daches losgelösten Pavillon –, dennoch geht es ihm letztlich um eine echte Verschmelzung von alter japanischer Tradition und bewusster Modernität.

Fujimori a ajouté quelques touches curieuses comme le pavillon suspendu (ci-dessous), mais cherche surtout une vraie fusion entre les traditions anciennes du Japon et son indéniable modernité.

SOU FUJIMOTO

Sou Fujimoto Architects
10-3 Ichikawa-Seihon Building 6F
Higashi-Enoki-cho Shinjuku
Tokyo 162-0807
Japan

Tel: +81 3 3513 5401
Fax: +81 3 3513 5402
E-mail: sosuke@tka.att.ne.jp
Web: www.sou-fujimoto.com

SOU FUJIMOTO was born in 1971. He received a B.Arch degree from the University of Tokyo, Faculty of Engineering, Department of Architecture (1990–94). He established his own firm, Sou Fujimoto Architects, in 2000. He is considered one of the most interesting rising Japanese architects, and his forms usually evade easy classification. He has been a lecturer at the Tokyo University of Science (2001–), Tokyo University (2004), and Kyoto University (2007–). His work includes Industrial Training Facilities for the Mentally Handicapped (Hokkaido, 2003); the Environment Art Forum for Annaka (Gunma, 2003–06); Treatment Center for Mentally Disturbed Children (Hokkaido, 2006); a Tokyo apartment (Tokyo, 2006–07); House O (Chiba, 2007); N House (Oita Prefecture, 2007–08); Final Wooden House (Kumamura, Kumamoto, 2007–08); and Namba and Hayashi (both in Tokyo, 2008). Other recent work includes his participation in Toyo Ito's Sumika Project (House Before House, Utsunomiya, Tochigi, 2008) and House H (Tokyo, 2008–09, published here), all in Japan.

SUO FUJIMOTO, geboren 1971, studierte von 1990 bis 1994 an der Universität Tokio, wo er am Architektur-Department der Fakultät für Ingenieurwesen seinen B.Arch erwarb. Im Jahr 2000 gründete er sein eigenes Architekturbüro, Sou Fujimoto Architects. Fujimoto, dessen Gebäudeformen sich oft nur schwierig einordnen lassen, gilt als einer der interessantesten kommenden Architekten Japans. 2004 besaß Fujimoto einen Lehrauftrag an der Universität Tokio, seit 2001 ist er Dozent an der Tokioter Universität der Wissenschaften, seit 2007 lehrt er an der Universität Kyoto. Zu seinen allesamt in Japan realisierten Arbeiten gehören eine Ausbildungseinrichtung für geistig Behinderte (Hokkaido, 2003), das Environment Art Forum for Annaka (Gunma, 2003–06), ein Behandlungszentrum für psychisch gestörte Kinder (Hokkaido, 2006), ein Apartment in Tokio (2006–07), das House O (Chiba, 2007), das House N (Präfektur Oita, 2007–08), das Final Wooden House (Kumamura, Kumamoto, 2007–08), das Haus Namba (Tokio, 2008), das Haus Hayashi (Tokio, 2008) und das House H (Tokio, 2008–09, hier vorgestellt). Außerdem nahm Fujimoto mit dem Beitrag House Before House an Toyo Itos Sumika-Projekt teil (Utsunomiya, Tochigi, 2008).

SOU FUJIMOTO, né en 1971, est B. Arch de l'Université de Tokyo, Faculté d'ingénierie, département d'architecture (1990–94). Il a fondé son agence, Sou Fujimoto Architects, en 2000. Il est considéré comme l'un des plus intéressants jeunes architectes japonais émergents, et ses formes échappent à toute classification aisée. Il a été lecteur à l'Université des sciences de Tokyo (2001–), à l'Université de Tokyo (2004) et à l'Université de Kyoto (2007–). Parmi ses travaux : des installations pour la formation des handicapés mentaux (Hokkaido, 2003) ; l'Environment Art Forum pour Annaka (Gunma, 2003–06) ; un Centre de traitement pour enfants mentalement perturbés (Hokkaido, 2006) ; un appartement à Tokyo (Tokyo, 2006–07) ; la Maison O (Chiba, 2007) ; la Maison N (préfecture d'Oita, 2007–08) ; la Maison de bois définitive (Kumamura, Kumamoto, 2007–08) et Namba et Hayashi (toutes deux à Tokyo, 2008). Il a participé récemment au projet Sumika de Toyo Ito (Maison d'avant la maison, Utsunomiya, Tochigi, 2008) et a réalisé la Maison H (Tokyo, 2008–09, publiée ici).

HOUSE H

Tokyo, Japan, 2008–09

Area: 142 m². Client: not disclosed. Cost: ¥45 million
Collaboration: Hiroshi Kato

This house for a family of three is located in a residential area of Tokyo. The architect compares living in multistory dwellings to being in a tree house, albeit a geometric one made of reinforced concrete in this instance. He seeks to create a network of interrelationships between the "branches" of the tree, in the sense that both individuality and "holistic coexistence" can exist in the same residence. Walls, ceilings, and floors are marked by holes in **HOUSE H**, allowing residents to see each other through the spaces. Fujimoto concludes: "Using artificial materials and geometric order, the succession of voids in connectivity engenders a greater field of relationships. This concept of a residence akin to a large tree, with a treelike ambiguity in its connectivity with the exterior, propounds a prototypical dwelling/city of the future."

Das House H für eine dreiköpfige Familie befindet sich in einem Tokioter Wohngebiet. Der Wohnraum setzt sich aus vielen einzelnen Ebenen zusammen, ein Konzept, das der Architekt mit dem Aufenthalt in einem Baumhaus vergleicht, wobei das **HOUSE H** freilich aus Stahlbeton besteht und streng geometrisch angeordnet ist. Fujimotos Absicht bestand darin, einen „Baum" zu entwerfen, dessen einzelne „Äste" in einer wechselseitigen Beziehung stehen, sodass man innerhalb ein und desselben Wohnhauses ganz für sich sein kann und doch gleichzeitig eine „ganzheitliche Koexistenz" möglich ist. Wände, Decken und Böden besitzen große Öffnungen, durch die die Bewohner sich von verschiedenen Räumen aus gegenseitig sehen können. „Mithilfe künstlicher Materialien und einer streng geometrischen Anordnung", erklärt Fujimoto, „ergab sich ein Schema aus miteinander korrespondierenden Durchlässen, die ein erweitertes Beziehungsgefüge entstehen lassen. Ein Haus, das wie ein großer Baum aufgebaut ist, dessen Eingebundenheit in sein direktes äußeres Umfeld sich nie eindeutig bestimmen lässt, könnte ein Prototyp für das Wohnen beziehungsweise die Stadt der Zukunft sein."

Cette maison destinée à une famille de trois personnes est située dans un quartier résidentiel de Tokyo. L'architecte compare la vie dans une maison à plusieurs niveaux avec l'expérience des maisons dans les arbres, en l'occurrence un arbre en béton armé. Il a cherché à créer un réseau de relations entre les diverses « branches », dans le sens où l'individualisme et la « coexistence holistique » peuvent exister en un même lieu. Les murs, les plafonds et les sols sont diversement découpés, ce qui permet aux résidents de se voir plus facilement à travers l'espace. Pour Fujimoto : « Grâce à des matériaux artificiels et à un ordre géométrique strict, cette succession de vides en connexion engendre un champ de relations plus proches. Ce concept de maison, comparable à un grand arbre, entretient son ambiguïté arboricole dans ses liens avec l'extérieur et propose un prototype de mode de logement urbain pour le futur. »

Beneath a geometric skin, the house hides as many spatial surprises as it does residents or visitors, seen here from above, below, and from the side.

Schaut man in die geometrische Hülle des Hauses hinein, trifft man nicht nur auf Bewohner und Gäste, sondern auch auf zahlreiche räumliche Überraschungen.

Derrière ses façades géométriques, la maison révèle de multiples surprises spatiales que découvrent ses visiteurs ou ses habitants.

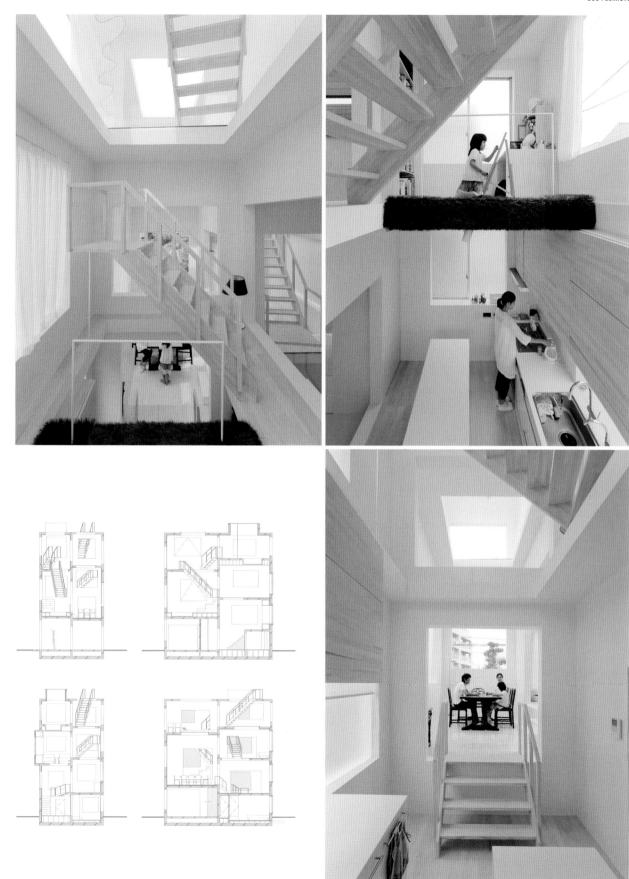

While incorporating many standard elements of a house, Fujimoto astonishes at every turn, as he does in the glass floor seen above and right in use.

Même s'il intègre dans ses projets tous les composants standard d'une maison, Fujimoto étonne à chaque fois, comme par exemple dans ce sol en verre (ci-dessus et à droite).

Natürlich finden sich im House H auch zahlreiche Standardelemente, das Besondere aber sind seine zahlreichen gestalterischen Clous, zum Beispiel der gläserne Fußboden (oben und gegenüberliegende Seite).

GUSTAFSON PORTER +
GUSTAFSON GUTHRIE NICHOL

Gustafson Porter Ltd.
Linton House, 39–51 Highgate Road
London NW5 1RS, UK
Tel: +44 20 72 67 20 05 / Fax: +44 20 74 85 92 03
E-mail: enquiries@gustafson-porter.com / Web: www.gustafson-porter.com

Gustafson Guthrie Nichol Ltd.
Pier 55, Floor 3, 1101 Alaskan Way
Seattle, WA 98101, USA
Tel: +1 206 903 6802 / Fax: +1 206 903 6804
E-mail: contact@ggnltd.com / Web: www.ggnltd.com

Kathryn Gustafson was born in 1951 in the US. She attended the University of Washington (Seattle, 1970), the Fashion Institute of Technology (New York, 1971), and the École National Supérieure du Paysage (Versailles, France, 1979). **GUSTAFSON PORTER** Ltd. was founded in 1997 by Kathryn Gustafson and Neil Porter. In 1999, Gustafson, with partners Jennifer Guthrie and Shannon Nichol, established the practice **GUSTAFSON GUTHRIE NICHOL** Ltd. in Seattle. Aside from having conceived *Towards Paradise* (Venice Architecture Biennale, Venice, Italy, 2008, published here), Kathryn Gustafson is working on the Marina East Gardens by the Bay (Singapore, 2006–); Mazyad Desert Park and Visitor Center (Abu Dhabi, UAE, 2007–); and the Hili Archeological Park (Al Ain, UAE, 2008–). Neil Porter was born in the UK in 1958. He attended Newcastle University School of Architecture (1977–80) and the Architectural Association (London, 1981–83). He is a joint Director and designer for Gustafson Porter. Mary Bowman was born in the US in 1958. She attended the University of Virginia (Charlottesville, Virginia, 1976–80), and the Architectural Association (AA; London, 1984–88). She has been a Director of the firm, with Gustafson and Porter, since 2002.

Kathryn Gustafson, geboren 1951 in den USA, besuchte die University of Washington in Seattle (1970), das Fashion Institute of Technology in New York (1971) und die École Nationale Supérieure du Paysage in Versailles (Frankreich, 1979). 1997 gründete sie mit Neil Porter die gemeinsame Firma **GUSTAFSON PORTER** Ltd. 1999 rief sie außerdem mit Jennifer Guthrie und Shannon Nichol als Partnerinnen das Büro **GUSTAFSON GUTHRIE NICHOL** Ltd. in Seattle ins Leben. Hier vorgestellt ist für die Architektur-Biennale Venedig entstandene Projekt *Towards Paradise* (2008). Derzeit arbeitet Kathryn Gustafson an den Marina East Gardens by the Bay in Singapur (2006–) sowie dem Wüstenpark und Besucherzentrum Mazyad in Abu Dhabi (VAE, 2007–) und dem Archäologiepark Hili in Al Ain (Abu Dhabi, VAE, 2008–). Der gebürtige Brite Neil Porter, Jahrgang 1958, studierte an der Newcastle University School of Architecture (1977–80) und der Architectural Association in London (1981–83). Er ist Mitglied der Gesamtgeschäftsführung und Designer bei Gustafson Porter. Mary Bowman, geboren 1958 in den USA, besuchte die University of Virginia (Charlottesville, Virginia, 1976–80) und die Architectural Association in London (1984–88). Seit 2002 leitet sie gemeinsam mit den namensgebenden Gründern die Firma Gustafson Porter.

Kathryn Gustafson est née aux États-Unis en 1951. Elle a étudié à l'Université de Washington (Seattle, 1970), au Fashion Institute of Technology (New York, 1971) et à l'École nationale supérieure du paysage (Versailles, France, 1979). L'agence **GUSTAFSON PORTER** Ltd. a été fondée en 1997 par Kathryn Gustafson et Neil Porter. En 1999, Gustafson et ses associées, Jennifer Guthrie et Shannon Nichol, ont fondé l'agence **GUSTAFSON GUTHRIE NICHOL** Ltd. à Seattle. En dehors de *Towards Paradise* (Vers le paradis, Biennale d'architecture de Venise, 2008, publié ici), Kathryn Gustafson travaille actuellement sur le projet des Marina East Gardens by the Bay (Singapore, 2006–) ; le parc et centre de visiteurs du désert de Mazyad (Abu Dhabi, EAU, 2007–) et le parc archéologique de Hili (Al Ain, EAU, 2008–). Neil Porter, né au Royaume-Uni en 1958, a étudié à l'École d'architecture de l'Université de Newcastle (1977–80) et à l'Architectural Association (Londres, 1981–83). Il est codirecteur et concepteur pour Gustafson Porter. Mary Bowman, née aux États-Unis en 1958, a fait ses études à l'Université de Virginie (Charlottesville, Virginie, 1976–80) et à l'Architectural Association (Londres,1984–88). Elle dirige l'agence avec Gustafson et Porter depuis 2002.

TOWARDS PARADISE

Venice Architecture Biennale, Venice, Italy, 2008

Area: 944 m². Client: Venice Biennale Foundation. Cost: not disclosed
Collaboration: Gustafson Guthrie Nichol

At the very end of the domain of the Arsenale in Venice, the designers created a totally unexpected, dream-like garden.

Auf dem hintersten Geländeabschnitt des Arsenale in Venedig schufen die Landschaftsarchitekten einen durch und durch verblüffenden Garten wie aus einem Traum.

Les architectes ont créé un jardin de rêve totalement inattendu à l'extrémité des installations de l'Arsenal de Venise.

Curving paths and a balloon-suspended expanse of white cloth contrast with the dense and overgrown exterior limits of this part of the Arsenale, more abandoned than contemporary in any sense.

Gewundene, klar verlaufende Pfade und ein an Ballons schwebendes Segel kontrastieren mit den dicht überwachsenen Randzonen dieses zuvor fast vergessenen Arsenale-Abschnitts.

Des allées en courbe et une voile suspendue en l'air par des ballons blancs contrastent avec l'environnement dense et luxuriant du parc.

One of the most surprising contributions to the 2008 Architecture Biennale in Venice was Gustafson Porter's **TOWARDS PARADISE**. Located at the exit of the Arsenale, along the Porta Nova and the Rio delle Vergini, this largely abandoned garden is located in the grounds of the former Convento delle Vergini, founded in 1239 and demolished in 1830. Historical maps show formal gardens and vegetable allotments on this site. Small buildings in a state of ruin surround the site and the garden itself emerged from an overgrown tangle of ivy and other dense vegetation. In their description of the project, the designers write: "'Towards Paradise' responds to the challenge of how to cultivate one's garden, or how to tend to our affairs. In an idealistic world to have that capacity, one needs wisdom and a desire to search for wisdom. In French one's *jardin secret* is the private and protected part of the soul." They created three main areas within the overgrown spaces at the end of the Arsenale, "Remember—The Store Room; Nourish—Abundance; and Enlighten—Contemplation." The Store Room includes oversized shelves with the Latin names of extinct flora and fauna, while the Nourishment: Abundance sequence is a colorful dense space for conversation and observation of "the plant world's earthly and aesthetic delights." The Enlightenment: Contemplation area is a "long oval sculpted land movement covered in grass…" with "cloudlike curtains" that hover above, held up by balloons.

Gustafson Porters **TOWARDS PARADISE** war einer der überraschendsten Beiträge zur Architektur-Biennale Venedig des Jahres 2008. Realisiert wurde die Arbeit an der Zufahrt zum Arsenale zwischen Porta Nova und Rio delle Vergini auf einem weitgehend ungenutzten Gartenareal, auf dem sich lange Zeit – von seinem Gründungsjahr 1239 bis zum Abriss im Jahr 1830 – der Convento delle Vergini befand. Historischen Karten kann man noch die frühere Verteilung der Anbauflächen für Nutzpflanzen entnehmen. Über das Gelände verteilt sind einige kleine, verfallene Gebäude, der Garten selbst war bis vor Kurzem von dichtem Efeugestrüpp und anderen Pflanzen überwuchert. In ihrer Projektbeschreibung führten die Gestalter aus: „'Towards Paradise' setzt sich mit der Frage auseinander, wie man seinen eigenen Garten bestellt oder mithin: wie man sich um seine persönlichen Angelegenheiten kümmert. Um in einer idealistischen Welt über diese Fähigkeit zu verfügen, bedarf es einer gewissen persönlichen Weisheit und des Wunsches, nach Weisheit zu suchen. Im Französischen gibt es den Begriff des *jardin secret*, mit dem der ganz private, geschützte Teil der Seele bezeichnet wird." Im hinteren Teil des überwachsenen Geländes an der Arsenalezufahrt richteten Gustafson Porter drei Hauptbereiche ein, denen sie die Namen „Erinnern – Der Vorratsraum", „Ernähren – Überfluss" und „Erleuchtung – Kontemplation" gaben. Im „Vorratsraum" befinden sich überdimensionierte Regale, in denen die Namen ausgestorbener Pflanzen und Tiere versammelt sind. Der Abschnitt „Ernähren – Überfluss" dagegen ist ein farbenfroher, enger Raum, in dem man „die von der Welt der Pflanzen ausgehenden sinnlich-stofflichen und ästhetischen Freuden" betrachten und sich über sie austauschen kann. Der Bereich „Erleuchtung – Kontemplation" besteht aus einer „langen, oval geformten und mit Gras bewachsenen Erdaufschüttung", über der „wolkenartige Vorhänge" an Ballons in der Luft schweben.

Signée Gustafson Porter, l'une des contributions les plus surprenantes de la Biennale d'architecture de Venise 2008 était intitulée **TOWARDS PARADISE** (Vers le paradis). À la sortie de l'Arsenal, près de la Porta Nova et du rio delle Vergini, s'étend un jardin en grande partie abandonné qui occupe la clôture de l'ancien couvent delle Vergini, fondé en 1239 et démoli en 1830. Les plans historiques montrent la présence sur ce site de jardins formels et de potagers. De petites constructions en ruine entourent le terrain, et le jardin a disparu dans une jungle de lierre et de mauvaises herbes. Dans leur description du projet, les architectes expliquent leur démarche : « *Towards Paradise* répond au défi de comment cultiver son jardin, ou comment se préoccuper de nos affaires. Dans un monde idéal, cette capacité nécessite une certaine sagesse et le désir d'une recherche de la sagesse. En français, le terme de "jardin secret" signifie la partie la plus personnelle et la plus protégée de l'âme. » Ils ont créé trois espaces principaux dans le jardin en friche : « Souvenir–le grenier ; Nourrir – abondance ; Éclairer – contemplation ». Le grenier est meublé de rayonnages surdimensionnés ornés du nom latin de plantes et d'animaux disparus, tandis que la séquence « Nourrir – abondance » est un espace coloré destiné à la conversation et à l'observation « des délices esthétiques et terrestres du monde des plantes ». L'espace « Éclairer – contemplation » est « un long mouvement de terrain, ovale, sculpté, recouvert d'herbe », avec des « rideaux de nuages » qui planent au-dessus du sol, maintenus par des ballons.

Alternating fairly open sequences with more intimate passages, which sometimes take in the decaying architecture of the Arsenale itself (left page, bottom), the landscape architects create truly new space.

Mit einem Wechselspiel aus offenen Bereichen und intimeren Passagen, die teilweise die verfallende Architektur des Grundstücks mit einbeziehen, haben die Architekten etwas komplett Neues geschaffen.

Alternant des séquences assez ouvertes avec des passages plus intimes qui intègrent parfois des éléments datant de l'Arsenal (en bas à gauche), les paysagistes ont réussi à créer un espace entièrement nouveau.

Lighting on elements of the Arsenale itself links the garden with this place, with an installation that rides the fine line between art, architecture, and landscape design.

Unter Einbeziehung von zufällig entdeckten Elementen des Arsenale-Geländes entstand eine Installation im Spannungsfeld von Kunst, Architektur und Landschaftsdesign.

L'éclairage de certains éléments de l'Arsenal crée un lien entre le jardin et ce lieu historique. L'installation est à la limite de l'art, de l'architecture et du paysage.

The designers inserted their garden into the existing space as though its allegorical presence could hardly be more natural, modern, and yet integrated into this unusual environment.

Die Landschaftsarchitekten haben ihren allegorischen Garten so in die bestehenden Gegebenheiten eingepasst, dass er völlig natürlich wirkt – zugleich modern und doch ganz in die ungewöhnliche Umgebung integriert.

Les paysagistes ont inséré le jardin dans l'espace existant comme si sa présence allégorique pouvait difficilement être plus naturelle, moderne et néanmoins intégrée à son curieux environnement.

A list of extinct species (Aplonis corvina, for example, is an extinct bird from the family of starlings) covers an interior wall in one of the existing garden structures.

Eine Liste ausgestorbener Tierarten bedeckt eine Innenwand eines der bestehenden Gartengebäude (Aplonis corvina, der Kosrae-Singstar, ist zum Beispiel ein ausgestorbener Singvogel aus der Familie der Stare).

Une liste d'espèces éteintes (Aplonis corvina est, par exemple, un oiseau disparu de la famille des étourneaux) occupe un mur entier à l'intérieur des anciennes constructions encore existantes.

ZAHA HADID

Zaha Hadid
Studio 9, 10 Bowling Green Lane, London EC1R 0BQ, UK
Tel: +44 20 72 53 51 47 / Fax: +44 20 72 51 83 22
E-mail: mail@zaha-hadid.com / Web: www.zaha-hadid.com

ZAHA HADID studied architecture at the Architectural Association (AA) in London beginning in 1972 and was awarded the Diploma Prize in 1977. She then became a partner of Rem Koolhaas in the Office for Metropolitan Architecture (OMA) and taught at the AA. She has also taught at Harvard, the University of Chicago, in Hamburg, and at Columbia University in New York. In 2004, Zaha Hadid became the first woman to win the coveted Pritzker Prize. Well-known for her paintings and drawings, she has had a substantial influence, despite having built relatively few buildings. She completed the Vitra Fire Station (Weil am Rhein, Germany, 1990–94); and exhibition designs such as that for "The Great Utopia" (Solomon R. Guggenheim Museum, New York, 1992). Significant competition entries include her design for the Cardiff Bay Opera House (1994–96); the Habitable Bridge (London, 1996); and the Luxembourg Philharmonic Hall (1997). More recently, Zaha Hadid has entered a phase of active construction with such projects as the Bergisel Ski Jump (Innsbruck, Austria, 2001–02); Lois & Richard Rosenthal Center for Contemporary Art (Cincinnati, Ohio, USA, 1999–2003); Phaeno Science Center (Wolfsburg, Germany, 2001–05); the Central Building of the new BMW Assembly Plant in Leipzig (Germany, 2005); Ordrupgaard Museum Extension (Copenhagen, Denmark, 2001–05); Home House (London, UK, 2007–08); and Mobile Art, Chanel Contemporary Art Container (various locations, 2007–). She has recently completed the MAXXI, the National Museum of 21st Century Arts (Rome, Italy, 1998–2009); Burnham Pavilion (Chicago, Illinois, USA, 2009, published here); and the JS Bach/Zaha Hadid Architects Music Hall (Manchester, UK, 2009, also published here). Current projects include the Guangzhou Opera House (Guangzhou, China, 2006–10) and the Sheik Zayed Bridge (Abu Dhabi, UAE, 2005–10).

ZAHA HADID studierte ab 1972 an der Architectural Association (AA) in London und erhielt 1977 den Diploma Prize. Anschließend wurde sie Partnerin von Rem Koolhaas im Office for Metropolitan Architecture (OMA) und unterrichtete an der AA. Darüber hinaus lehrte sie in Harvard, an der Universität von Chicago, in Hamburg sowie an der Columbia University in New York. 2004 wurde Zaha Hadid als erste Frau mit dem begehrten Pritzker-Preis ausgezeichnet. Hadid wurde besonders durch ihr malerisches und zeichnerisches Werk bekannt. Obwohl nur wenige ihrer Entwürfe realisiert wurden, zählt sie zu den einflussreichsten Vertreterinnen ihrer Zunft. Realisiert wurden u.a. die Feuerwache für Vitra (Weil am Rhein, Deutschland, 1990–94) und Ausstellungsarchitekturen wie „The Great Utopia" (Solomon R. Guggenheim Museum, New York, 1992). Zu ihren wichtigsten Wettbewerbsbeiträgen zählen der Entwurf für das Cardiff Bay Opera House (Wales, 1994–96), die Habitable Bridge (London, 1996) und die Philharmonie in Luxemburg (1997). In jüngerer Zeit begann eine Phase des aktiven Bauens für Hadid, etwa mit der Skisprungschanze Bergisel (Innsbruck, Österreich, 2001–02), dem Lois & Richard Rosenthal Center for Contemporary Art (Cincinnati, Ohio, 1999–2003), dem Phaeno Wissenschaftszentrum (Wolfsburg, 2001–05), dem Zentralgebäude des neuen BMW-Werks in Leipzig (2005), dem Anbau für das Museum Ordrupgaard (Kopenhagen, 2001–05), das Home House (London, 2007–08), sowie dem Mobile Art, Chanel Contemporary Art Container (verschiedene Standorte, 2007–). Unlängst fertiggestellt wurde das MAXXI Nationalmuseum für Kunst des 21. Jahrhunderts in Rom (1998–2009) sowie die beiden hier vorgestellten Projekte Burnham Pavilion (Chicago, Illinois, 2009) und JS Bach/Zaha Hadid Architects Music Hall (Manchester, 2009). Aktuell im Bau sind u.a. das Opernhaus in Guangzhou (Guangzhou, China, 2006–10) sowie die Scheich-Zajed-Brücke (Abu Dhabi, VAE, 2005–10).

ZAHA HADID a étudié à l'Architectural Association (AA) de Londres de 1972 à 1977, date à laquelle elle a reçu le Prix du diplôme. Elle devient ensuite partenaire de Rem Koolhaas, à l'Office for Metropolitan Architecture (OMA) et a enseigné à l'AA ainsi qu'à Harvard, à l'Université de Chicago, à Hambourg et à Columbia University. En 2004, elle a été la première femme à remporter le très convoité prix Pritzker. Connue pour ses peintures et dessins, elle a exercé une réelle influence, même si elle n'a construit que relativement peu pendant longtemps. Parmi ses réalisations : un poste d'incendie pour Vitra (Weil am Rhein, Allemagne, 1990–94), et des projets pour des expositions comme « La Grande Utopie » au Solomon R. Guggenheim Museum (New York, 1992). Elle a participé à de nombreux concours dont les plus importants sont le projet pour l'Opéra de la baie de Cardiff (Pays de Galles, 1994–96) ; le « Pont habitable » (Londres, 1996) ; et la salle de concerts philharmoniques de Luxembourg (1997). Plus récemment, elle est entrée dans une phase active de grands chantiers avec des réalisations comme le tremplin de ski de Bergisel (Innsbruck, Autriche, 2001–02) ; le Lois & Richard Rosenthal Center for Contemporary Art (Cincinnati, Ohio, 1999–2003) ; le musée scientifique Phaeno (Wolfsburg, Allemagne, 2001–05) ; le bâtiment central de la nouvelle usine BMW de Leipzig (2005) ; l'extension de l'Ordrupgaard Museum (Copenhague, Danemark, 2001–05) ; la Home House (Londres, 2007–08) ; et le pavillon Mobile Art pour Chanel (divers lieux, 2007–). Elle a récemment achevé le Musée national des arts du XXIe siècle (MAXXI, Rome, 1998–2009) ; le pavillon Burnham (Chicago, Illinois, 2009, publié ici) et le JS Bach/Zaha Hadid Architects Music Hall (Manchester, 2009, également publié ici). Parmi ses projets récents figurent l'Opéra de Guangzhou (Guangzhou, Chine, 2006–09) et le pont Cheikh Zayed (Abu Dhabi, EAU, 2005–10).

BURNHAM PAVILION

Chicago, Illinois, USA, 2009

Address: Millennium Park, Chicago, IL, USA, http://burnhamplan100.uchicago.edu
Area: 45 m². Client: Burnham Plan Centennial. Cost: not disclosed
Collaboration: Fabric Images (General Contractor & Fabricator), Dear Productions (Lighting), The Gray Circle (Media Content)

Though Zaha Hadid speaks of hidden references to Burnham's plan of Chicago, her pavilion seems most of all to stand out strikingly from the surrounding city.

Laut Zaha Hadid enthält ihr Pavillon zwar versteckte Anspielungen auf die stadtplanerischen Visionen Burnhams, trotzdem sticht er unübersehbar aus seiner städtischen Kulisse heraus.

Si Zaha Hadid parle de références cachées au plan de Burnham, son pavillon semble davantage cultiver le contraste avec la ville qui l'entoure.

One of a number of small structures commissioned to celebrate the 100th anniversary of the Burnham Plan for Chicago, this pavilion is made of bent aluminum. Each element was shaped and welded while inner and outer fabric skins were wrapped around this skeleton. The architect suggests that the structure contains "hidden traces of Burnham's organizational structure." The fabric serves as a screen for video installations within the pavilion. Intended to be easily dismantled or recycled, the pavilion is also meant to be assembled in another location in the future. Zaha Hadid Architects states: "The presence of the new structure triggers the visitor's intellectual curiosity whilst an intensification of public life around and within the pavilion supports the idea of public discourse."

Dieser Pavillon ist einer von mehreren Bauten, die anlässlich der 100-Jahr-Feier des Burnham-Masterplans der Stadt Chicago in Auftrag gegeben wurde. Der Pavillon besteht aus gebogenen Aluminiumelementen, die einzeln geformt und geschweißt wurden. Über dieses Skelett wurde eine Innen- und Außenhaut aus Textil gespannt. Der Architektin zufolge zeigen sich in der Konstruktion „unterschwellige Spuren der von Burnham entworfenen Organisationsstruktur". Die Textilbespannung dient zugleich als Leinwand für Videoinstallationen im Pavillon. Der leicht demontierbare und recycelbare Pavillon lässt sich in Zukunft auch an anderen Standorten installieren. Die Architektin erklärt: „Die Präsenz des neuen Baus weckt die intellektuelle Neugier der Besucher und belebt zugleich das öffentliche Leben im und um den Pavillon. So wird ein öffentlicher Diskurs gefördert."

Ce pavillon commandé dans le cadre d'un programme de petites constructions lancé à l'occasion des célébrations du centième anniversaire du Plan Burnham pour Chicago, a été réalisé en aluminium cintré. Ses éléments mis en forme et soudés constituent un squelette qui est enveloppé de « peaux » de toile à l'extérieur et à l'intérieur. L'architecte aime imaginer que cette structure contient des « traces cachées de la structure organisée de Burnham ». À l'intérieur, la toile tendue sert d'écran à des installations vidéo. Conçu pour être facilement démonté ou recyclé, le pavillon pourra être éventuellement transporté dans un autre lieu. « La présence d'une nouvelle construction suscite la curiosité intellectuelle du visiteur, tandis que l'intensification de la vie et des échanges autour du pavillon et à l'intérieur de celui-ci développe une idée de discours public », explique l'agence.

Like a glowing UFO, the pavilion does indeed challenge visitors to think again about space, and about the surrounding city.

Der wie ein leuchtendes UFO wirkende Pavillon hält seine Besucher unweigerlich dazu an, über Raumfragen und die gebaute Umwelt Chicagos nachdenken.

Comme un Ovni lumineux, le pavillon invite les spectateurs à repenser leur perception de l'espace et de la ville.

With its continuous curving forms and changing colors, the pavilion is in a sense all that the architecture around is not: non-geometric, challenging, and new.

Mit seinen geschwungenen Formen und der wechselnden Farbgebung ist der Pavillon gewissermaßen all das, was die umgebende Architektur nicht ist: winkellos, kontrovers, neuartig.

À travers ses courbes continues et ses couleurs changeantes, le pavillon est un peu tout ce que l'architecture environnante n'est pas : non orthogonal, provocateur et nouveau.

JS BACH / ZAHA HADID ARCHITECTS MUSIC HALL

Manchester, UK, 2009

Address: www.mif.co.uk/events/js-bach-zaha-hadid
Site Area: 17 x 25 m. Client: Manchester International Festival. Cost: not disclosed
Collaboration: Sandy Brown Associates (Acoustic Consultant), Tony Hogg Design Ltd. (Tensile Structural Engineer),
Base Structures (Fabricator)

 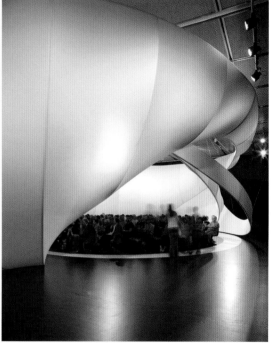

The swooping fabric membrane imagined by Hadid in this instance occupies and even re-creates the empty space surrounding the performance area.

Zaha Hadids textilbespannte Raumskulptur schlängelt sich quer durch den Saal und dynamisiert den leeren Raum rund um Bühne und Zuschauerbereich.

La membrane tendue imaginée par Hadid crée et occupe l'espace qui enserre le lieu du concert.

Zaha Hadid Architects created a space intended for solo performances of the work of Johann Sebastian Bach. The "voluminous ribbon" used for the installation "swirls within the room, carving out a spatial and visual response to the intricate relationships of Bach's harmonies." This ribbon, employed both for its spatial and acoustic qualities, swells and contracts in its movement through the existing space. Made up of a translucent fabric membrane around an internal steel structure, the ribbon is complemented by clear acrylic acoustic panels suspended above the stage. Programmed lighting and musical recordings outside the hours of performance are also part of the installation. This work is intended to be transportable and installable in similar locations.

Zaha Hadid Architects gestaltete einen Ort für Soloaufführungen mit Werken von Johann Sebastian Bach. Das „voluminöse Band", aus dem die Installation besteht, „schlängelt sich durch den Raum und wird zum räumlichem und visuellen Pendant der kunstvoll ineinandergreifenden Bach'schen Harmonien". Das Band, ausgewählt wegen seiner räumlichen und akustischen Eigenschaften, entfaltet und kontrahiert sich in seiner dynamischen Bewegung durch den Raum. Ergänzt wird das Band – eine transluzente Textilmembran, die auf eine Stahlkonstruktion gespannt wurde – durch transparente Akustiktafeln aus Acrylglas, die über der Bühne abgehängt sind. Außerhalb der Konzerttermine wird die Installation mit programmierten Lichteffekten und Musikaufnahmen bespielt. Sie ist transportfähig und kann an ähnlichen Standorten installiert werden.

Zaha Hadid Architects a créé ici un espace pour des concerts de solistes de l'œuvre de Johann Sebastian Bach. Le « volumineux ruban » qui constitue cette installation « tourbillonne dans la pièce, sculptant une réponse spatiale et visuelle aux relations complexes des harmonies de Bach ». Ce ruban aux qualités à la fois spatiales et acoustiques se gonfle et se contracte dans un mouvement à travers l'espace. Fait d'une membrane translucide tendue sur une structure interne en acier, il est complété par des panneaux d'acrylique transparent suspendus au-dessus de la scène. En dehors des heures de concert, des éclairages et des enregistrements programmés sont prévus dans le cadre de cette installation. L'ensemble pourrait être transporté et installé dans des lieux similaires.

While architecture generally remains static in the presence of music, this structure flows around the stage, enveloping spectators much as the sound of music does.

Während die meisten Aufführungsorte für Musik nur statische Hülle sind, umfließt Hadids Konstruktion die Bühne und hüllt den Besucher genauso ein wie der Klang der Musik.

Alors que l'architecture reste généralement statique en présence de la musique, cette structure enveloppe la scène et les spectateurs comme le ferait la musique elle-même.

HERREROS ARQUITECTOS

Herreros Arquitectos
c/Princesa 25, 5to. 7
28008 Madrid
Spain

Tel: +34 91 522 77 69
Fax: +34 91 559 46 78
E-mail: estudio@herrerosarquitectos.com
Web: www.herrerosarquitectos.com

Juan Herreros Guerra was born in San Lorenzo de el Escorial, Spain, in 1958 and studied in the school there. He was a founding partner of Ábalos & Herreros from 1984 to 2006. Their built work includes the notable Woermann Tower and Square (Las Palmas de Gran Canaria, 2001–05). Herreros is a Senior Professor and Head of Teaching Thesis Program at the School of Architecture of Madrid (ETSAM), where he was previously a Professor of Building Design (1984–88). The work of **HERREROS ARQUITECTOS** includes a House in the Countryside (Artá, Mallorca, Spain, 2007); the design of the collection layout in the Museum of Contemporary Art Reina Sofía (Madrid, Spain, 2008); Hispasat Satellite Control Center (Madrid, Spain, 2009–); Panama Tower (Panama City, Panama, 2008–); Social Housing, Retail and Parking Spaces (Sant Boi de Llobregat, Barcelona, Spain, 2009–); Olympiakwartier Almere (Amsterdam, The Netherlands, 2009–, with MVRDV); and the Munch Area, Munch Museum, and Stenersen Museum Collections (Oslo, Norway, 2009–, published here).

Juan Herreros Guerra wurde 1958 in San Lorenzo de el Escorial, Spanien, geboren, wo er auch studierte. Von 1984 bis 2006 war er Gründungspartner bei Ábalos & Herreros. Zu den namhaften realisierten Projekten des Büros zählen der Woermann-Turm und -Platz (Las Palmas de Gran Canaria, 2001–05). Herreros ist Professor und Leiter der Promotionsprogramme der Architekturfakultät an der ETSA in Madrid, wo er zuvor Professor für Konstruktion war (1984–88). Projekte von **HERREROS ARQUITECTOS** sind u.a. ein Haus auf dem Land (Artá, Mallorca, 2007), der Entwurf für die Raumgliederung der Sammlung zeitgenössischer Kunst am Museo Reina Sofía (Madrid, 2008), das Satellitenkontrollzentrum Hispasat (Madrid, 2009–), der Panama Tower (Panama City, Panama, 2008–), Sozialwohnungen, Ladenflächen und Parkplätze (Sant Boi de Llobregat, Barcelona, 2009–), das Olympiakwartier Almere (Amsterdam, 2009–, mit MVRDV) sowie das Munch-Quartier mit dem Munch Museum und Stenersen Museum (Oslo, Norwegen, 2009–, hier vorgestellt).

Juan Herreros Guerra est né à San Lorenzo de el Escorial (Espagne), en 1958. Il a été fondateur associé de l'agence Ábalos et Herreros (1984–2006). Parmi leurs réalisations, figurent la tour et place Woermann (Las Palmas de Gran Canaria, 2001–05). Herreros est professeur senior et dirige le programme des thèses à l'École d'architecture de Madrid (ETSAM) où il a antérieurement enseigné la conception architecturale (1984–88). Les travaux de l'agence **HERREROS ARQUITECTOS** comprennent entre autres : une maison de campagne (Artá, Mallorque, 2007) ; la présentation des collections du Musée de la reine Sophie (Madrid, 2008) ; le centre de contrôle de satellites Hispasat (Madrid, 2009–) ; la tour Panama (Panama City, Panama, 2008–) ; des logements sociaux, commerces et parkings (Sant Boi de Llobregat, Barcelone, 2009–) ; le quartier Olympiakwartier Almere (Amsterdam, 2009–, avec MVRDV) ainsi que le quartier Munch avec le Musée Munch et les collections du Musée Stenersen (Oslo, 2009–, publié ici).

MUNCH AREA, MUNCH MUSEUM, AND STENERSEN MUSEUM COLLECTIONS

Oslo, Norway, 2009–

Address: Munch Museum, Tøyengata 53, 0578 Oslo, Norway, +47 23 49 35 00, www.munch.museum.no
The Stenersen Museum, Munkedamsveien 15, 0250 Oslo, Norway, +47 23 49 36 00, www.stenersen.museum.no
Area: 16 000 m² (museum); 50 000 m² (Munch area). Client: HAV-EIENDOM. Cost: not disclosed
Collaboration: Jens Richter, Paola Simone

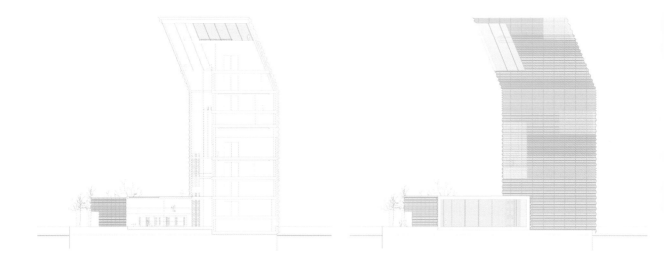

The architects were winners of an invited competition concerning the Bjørvika Area of Oslo, which includes the recently completed Opera House by Snøhetta, amongst other buildings of note. Herreros wrote: "We are not proposing a site with isolated phenomena. We propose a dynamic, fruitful conversation with the surroundings, a proposal that selects the appropriate uses, scales and densities that in turn articulate the spatial forms of occupation, the dimensions and treatment of the public space and its sustained growth toward the future." For the **MUNCH MUSEUM**, Herreros won another invited competition with a tilted design that brings to mind the form of their Woermann Tower. "The future complex formed by the Munch Museum and the **STENERSEN MUSEUM COLLECTIONS** is not only to safeguard and disseminate a basic heritage of the history and character of Norwegian culture; we find ourselves faced with a unique opportunity to develop a contemporary museum concept drawn from a transcendental urban role and a historical responsibility as a cohesive element for the community not only of Oslo but of all the nation," they conclude.

Die Architekten konnten sich in einem eingeladenen Wettbewerb für das Osloer Bjørvika-Viertel durchsetzen, in dem neben anderen bedeutenden Bauten auch das unlängst fertiggestellte Opernhaus von Snøhetta liegt. Herreros schrieb: „Wir schlagen kein Areal mit isolierten Einzelphänomenen vor. Stattdessen plädieren wir für einen dynamischen, fruchtbaren Dialog mit dem Umfeld. Unser Entwurf entscheidet sich für angemessene Nutzungen, Maßstäblichkeiten und Dichten. Dies wiederum bringt die räumlichen Nutzungsformen zum Ausdruck, ebenso wie die Dimensionen des öffentlichen Raums, den Umgang mit ihm und seine nachhaltige Entwicklung für die Zukunft." Einen weiteren Wettbewerb für das **MUNCH-MUSEUM** gewann Herreros Arquitectos mit dem Entwurf eines Turms mit gekippter Spitze, der an den Woermann-Turm des Büros erinnert. „Der geplante Komplex, zu dem das Munch-Museum und die **SAMMLUNGEN DES STENERSEN-MUSEUMS** gehören, wird nicht nur einen wichtigen, historischen und genuin norwegischen Kulturschatz hüten und präsentieren. Wir wollten darüber hinaus die einzigartige Gelegenheit nutzen, ein Konzept für ein zeitgenössisches Museum zu entwickeln – abgeleitet sowohl aus einer transzendenten urbanen Funktion, als auch aus historischer Verantwortung – als Element, das Bürger verbindet, nicht nur in Oslo, sondern im gesamten Land."

L'agence a remporté le concours sur invitation organisé pour le quartier de Bjørvika à Oslo qui comprend, entre autres réalisations intéressantes, l'opéra récemment achevé par Snøhetta. Herreros écrit : « Nous ne proposons pas un site et quelques événements architecturaux isolés. Nous proposons une conversation dynamique et fructueuse avec l'environnement, une proposition qui sélectionne les usages, les échelles et les densités appropriées, qui articule les formes d'occupation spatiale, le dimensionnement et le traitement de l'espace public et sa croissance durable dans le futur. » Pour le Musée Munch, Herreros a remporté un autre concours sur invitation. L'inclinaison du bâtiment rappelle la forme de la tour Woermann. « Le futur complexe formé par le **MUSÉE MUNCH** et les **COLLECTIONS DU MUSÉE STENERSEN** n'est pas seulement là pour sauvegarder et faire connaître le patrimoine historique et le caractère de la culture norvégienne : nous nous trouvons confrontés à une opportunité unique de développer un concept de musée contemporain inspiré par le rôle transcendantal de l'urbanité et de la responsabilité historique, élément de cohésion non seulement pour le quartier, non seulement pour Oslo, mais pour la nation tout entière », conclut l'architecte.

In the midst of a larger development district that involves other architects, the Munch project met with some controversy but takes into account the site and the larger concept of Oslo's intended ambitions.

Das Munch-Projekt im Zentrum eines größeren Erschließungsprojekts, an dem noch weitere Architekten beteiligt sind, nimmt zwar Rücksicht auf das Umfeld und die ehrgeizigen Pläne Oslos, trotzdem stieß es auch auf Vorbehalte.

Au centre d'une vaste zone de rénovation qui a fait appel à plusieurs architectes, le projet Munch a soulevé quelques controverses mais a pris en compte le site et plus généralement les ambitions urbanistiques d'Oslo.

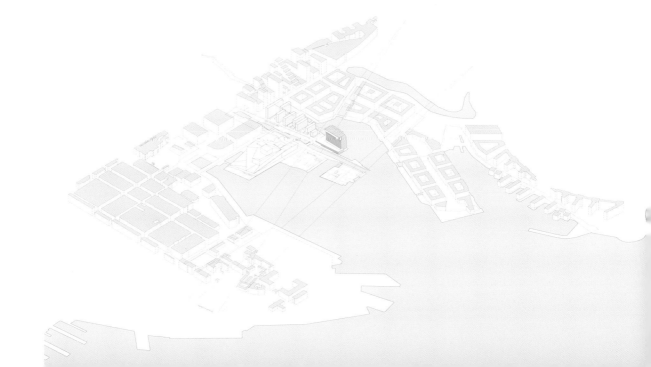

HERZOG & DE MEURON

Herzog & de Meuron
Rheinschanze 6, 4056 Basel, Switzerland
Tel: +41 61 385 57 57 / Fax: +41 61 385 57 58
E-mail: info@herzogdemeuron.com

JACQUES HERZOG and **PIERRE DE MEURON** were both born in Basel in 1950. They received degrees in architecture from the ETH, Zurich, in 1975, after studying with Aldo Rossi, and founded their partnership in Basel in 1978. Harry Gugger and Christine Binswanger joined the firm in 1991 and 1994, respectively, whereas Robert Hösl and Ascan Mergenthaler became partners in 2004. Stefan Marbach became a partner in 2006, followed by Wolfgang Hardt, David Koch, and Markus Widmer in 2009. Jacques Herzog and Pierre de Meuron won the 2001 Pritzker Prize, and both the RIBA Gold Medal and Praemium Imperiale in 2007. They were chosen to design Tate Modern in London (1995–2000). In 2005, Herzog & de Meuron were commissioned by the Tate to develop a scheme for the extension of the gallery and its surrounding areas (expected completion 2012). More recently, they have built the Forum 2004 Building and Plaza (Barcelona, Spain, 2001–04); Allianz Arena (Munich, Germany, 2002–05); the de Young Museum (San Francisco, California, USA, 2002–05); the Walker Art Center, Expansion of the Museum and Cultural Center (Minneapolis, Minnesota, USA, 2003–05); the CaixaForum (Madrid, Spain, 2001–08); the National Stadium for the 2008 Olympic Games in Beijing (China, 2003–08); and TEA, Tenerife Espacio de las Artes (Santa Cruz de Tenerife, Canary Islands, Spain, 2003–08). Current work includes VitraHaus, a new building to present Vitra's "Home Collection" on the Vitra campus in Weil am Rhein (Germany, 2010); 1111 Lincoln Road, a mixed-use building in Miami (Florida, USA, 2010); the Elbe Philharmonic Hall in Hamburg (Germany, 2007–11); the Head Office of Roche Basel (Switzerland, projected completion 2011); and the new Miami Art Museum (Florida, USA, projected completion 2012).

JACQUES HERZOG und **PIERRE DE MEURON** wurden beide 1950 in Basel geboren. 1975 schlossen sie ihr Architekturstudium bei Aldo Rossi an der ETH Zürich ab und gründeten 1978 in Basel ihr Büro Herzog & de Meuron. 1991 bzw. 1994 wurden Harry Gugger und Christine Binswanger Partner, 2004 folgten Robert Hösl und Ascan Mergenthaler, 2006 Stefan Marbach sowie 2009 Wolfgang Hardt, David Koch und Markus Widmer. 2001 wurden Jacques Herzog und Pierre de Meuron mit dem Pritzker-Preis ausgezeichnet, 2007 erhielten sie die RIBA Goldmedaille und den Praemium Imperiale. Zu ihren realisierten Bauten zählen u.a. die Tate Modern in London (1995–2000), wo sie inzwischen an einer Erweiterung des ursprünglichen Projekts arbeiten (Transforming Tate Modern, 2009–12). Unlängst realisiert wurden das Forum 2004, Gebäude und Vorplatz (Barcelona, 2002–04), die Allianz Arena (München, 2002–05), das De Young Museum (San Francisco, Kalifornien, 2002–05), die Erweiterung des Walker Art Center (Minneapolis, Minnesota, 2003–05), das Nationalstadion in Peking, Hauptaustragungsort der Olympischen Spiele 2008, das CaixaForum (Madrid, 2001–08) sowie das TEA, Tenerife Espacio de las Artes (Santa Cruz de Tenerife, Kanarische Inseln, Spanien, 2003–08). Aktuelle Projekte sind u.a. das VitraHaus, ein Neubau zur Präsentation der Vitra „Home Collection" auf dem Vitra-Campus, Weil am Rhein (2010, hier vorgestellt), 1111 Lincoln Road, ein Komplex mit gemischter Nutzung in Miami (Florida, 2010), die Elbphilharmonie in Hamburg (2007–11), der Firmenhauptsitz für Roche Basel (geplante Fertigstellung 2011) sowie das neue Miami Art Museum (Florida, geplante Fertigstellung 2012).

JACQUES HERZOG et **PIERRE DE MEURON**, tous deux nés à Bâle en 1950, sont diplômés en architecture de l'ETH de Zurich (1975) où ils ont étudié auprès d'Aldo Rossi. En 1978 à Bâle, ils fondent Herzog & de Meuron. Harry Gugger et Christine Binswanger les rejoignent en 1991 et 1994, ainsi que Robert Hösl et Ascan Mergenthaler qui deviennent partenaires en 2004, Stefan Marbach en 2006, puis Wolfgang Hardt, David Koch et Markus Widmer en 2009. Ils ont remporté le prix Pritzker en 2001, la médaille d'or du RIBA, ainsi que le Praemium Imperiale en 2007. Parmi leurs réalisations : la Tate Modern à Londres (1995–2000) dont ils construisent actuellement une extension (Transforming the Tate Modern, 2009–12). Ils ont fait partie des architectes sélectionnés dans la *short list* du concours du nouveau Museum of Modern Art à New York (1997). Plus récemment, ils ont construit le bâtiment et la place du Forum 2004 à Barcelone (2002–2004) ; le stade Allianz Arena (Munich, 2002–05) ; le De Young Museum (San Francisco, Californie, 2002–05) ; et l'extension du Museum and Cultural Center du Walker Art Center (Minneapolis, Minnesota, 2003–05) ; le Stade national, principal stade des Jeux olympiques 2008 de Pékin ; le CaixaForum (Madrid, 2001–08) ; et le TEA, Tenerife Espacio de las Artes (Santa Cruz de Tenerife, Iles Canaries, Espagne, 2003–08). Parmi leurs projets actuels figurent la VitraHaus, nouveau bâtiment de présentation de la « Collection Maison » sur le campus Vitra à Weil am Rhein (Allemagne, 2009, publiée ici) ; le 1111 Lincoln Road, un immeuble mixte à Miami (Floride, 2010) ; la Salle philharmonique de l'Elbe à Hambourg (2007–11) ; le siège de Roche Basel (Suisse, achèvement prévu pour 2011) et le nouveau Miami Art Museum (Floride, achèvement prévu pour 2012).

VITRAHAUS

Weil am Rhein, Germany, 2006–09

Address: Vitra Campus, Charles Eames Str. 2, 79576 Weil am Rhein, Germany, +49 7621 702 35 00, vitrahaus@vitra.com
Area: 4126 m² (gross). Client: Vitra Verwaltungs GmbH. Cost: not disclosed
Collaboration: Wolfgang Hardt, Guillaume Delemazure, Charlotte von Moos, Thomasine Wolfensberger

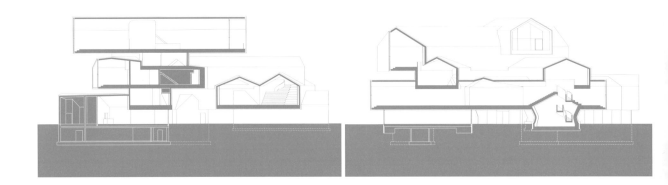

With its rotated and stacked forms, the VitraHaus brings to mind the typology of a house albeit in a largely sublimated incarnation.

Das VitraHaus besitzt zwar die typologischen Merkmale eines Hauses, mit seinen gestapelten und verdrehten Volumina ist es indes eine stark weiterentwickelte Variante.

Par ses formes empilées et tournées sur leur axe, la VitraHaus rappelle la typologie de la maison dans une incarnation en grande partie sublimée.

The **VITRAHAUS** on the Vitra Campus, opened in March 2010, has five stories above grade and one below. The ground floor includes the reception area, an 80-seat café, the Vitra Design Museum Shop, a business lounge, and display space. Showrooms for Vitra's "Home Collection" are located on levels one to four. The Vitra Campus, located near Basel, Switzerland, is noted for its numerous buildings by well-known architects, ranging from Frank Gehry (Vitra Design Museum) and Zaha Hadid to Tadao Ando. A new factory building by the Japanese architects SANAA was also completed in 2010. The addition of a Herzog & de Meuron structure to the complex is only fitting. The architects explained that the design of this building is a rendition of a type of house "found in the immediate vicinity of Vitra and, indeed, all over the world." Herzog & de Meuron further state: "By stacking, extruding and pressing—mechanical procedures used in industrial production—simply shaped houses become complex configurations in space, where outside and inside merge. The interior is designed as a spatial sequence with surprising transitions and views of the landscape." The stacked design reveals itself in floor-by-floor plans to be made up of a juxtaposition of essentially rectangular elements. The sloping roofs of the accumulated bars, together with full glazing looking out to the countryside and site, emphasize the "home-like" atmosphere intended for Vitra's collection of objects.

Das auf dem Vitra Campus gelegene **VITRAHAUS** wurde im März 2010 eröffnet und hat ein Untergeschoss sowie fünf oberirdige Niveaus. Im Erdgeschoss befinden sich ein Empfangsbereich, ein Café mit 80 Plätzen, der Vitra Design Museum-Shop, eine Businesslounge sowie Ausstellungsflächen. Die Ebenen 1 bis 4 sind Vitras „Home Collection" vorbehalten. Der unweit von Basel gelegene Vitra Campus ist bekannt für seine zahlreichen Bauten berühmter Architekten, etwa von Frank Gehry (Vitra-Designmuseum), Zaha Hadid oder Tadao Ando. Eine neue Werkshalle nach Entwürfen der japanischen Architekten SANAA wurde 2010 fertiggestellt. Die Erweiterung mit einem Bau von Herzog & de Meuron fügt sich ins Bild. Den Architekten zufolge ist der Entwurf die Interpretation eines Haustyps, der „in unmittelbarer Nachbarschaft von Vitra zu finden ist und im Grunde überall auf der Welt". Zudem merken Herzog & de Meuron an: „Durch Stapelungen, Extrusionen und Stauchungen – technische Verfahren aus der industriellen Fertigung – werden die einfachen Hausformen zu komplexen räumlichen Konfigurationen. Innen und Außen verschmelzen. Der Innenbau wurde als räumliche Sequenz mit überraschenden Übergängen und Ausblicken in die Landschaft entwickelt." In den Etagengrundrissen entpuppt sich der gestapelte Entwurf als Versatz von im Grunde rechteckigen Volumina. Die Spitzdächer der gebündelten Gebäuderiegel und die vollverglasten Fronten mit Blick über das Land und den Komplex lassen den „Home"-Charakter der Präsentationsflächen für Vitras Objektkollektion umso stärker hervortreten.

Construite sur le campus Vitra et inaugurée en mars 2010, la **VITRAHAUS** se développe sur six niveaux, dont un en sous-sol. Le rez-de-chaussée comprend le hall d'accueil, un café de 80 places, la boutique du Vitra Design Museum, un salon d'affaires et des espaces d'expositions. Les showrooms de la « Home Collection » Vitra occupent les quatre étages suivants. Le Vitra Campus, installé près de Bâle, est connu pour ses constructions signées par des architectes de renom comme Frank Gehry (Vitra Design Museum), Zaha Hadid ou Tadao Ando. Un nouveau bâtiment d'usine, conçu par les architectes japonais de l'agence SANAA, a également été achevé en 2010. Le nouveau bâtiment d'Herzog & de Meuron s'installe donc dans une continuité logique. Les architectes expliquent que l'idée de ce projet est la traduction d'un type de maison « que l'on trouve dans les environs immédiats de Vitra et, en fait, dans le monde entier. En empilant, extrudant et compressant – processus mécaniques utilisés en production industrielle – de simples maisons laissent émerger des configurations spatiales complexes, dans une fusion de l'intérieur et de l'extérieur. L'intérieur est conçu comme une séquence spatiale ponctuée de transitions surprenantes et de vues sur le paysage. » L'empilement tel qu'on le constate dans les plans des étages est une juxtaposition d'éléments essentiellement rectangulaires. Les toits à double pente et les pignons entièrement vitrés, qui ouvrent sur le terrain et la campagne, confirment l'atmosphère « domestique » recherchée pour ce bâtiment de présentation des collections Vitra.

The fully glazed ends of the stacked rectangular blocks that form the structure invite those outside to peer in and permits visitors inside to view the surroundings.

Mit ihren vollständig verglasten Fronten ermöglichen die übereinandergestapelten rechteckigen Gebäudeteile Einblicke von außen, während sie den Besuchern im Innern den Ausblick auf die Umgebung eröffnen.

Les parois entièrement vitrées des extrémités des blocs qui constituent le bâtiment invitent les passants à regarder ce qui se passe à l'intérieur et ses visiteurs à regarder l'environnement extérieur.

The products of Vitra are exhibited within the building as though they were indeed in a house—confirming the symbiotic relationship between the Herzog & de Meuron design and the concept of Vitra boss Rolf Fehlbaum.

Die im Innern des Gebäudes arrangierten Vitra-Produkte wirken, als befänden sie sich in einem richtigen Wohnhaus – mit anderen Worten: Der Entwurf von Herzog & de Meuron passt perfekt zum Konzept von Vitra-Chef Rolf Fehlbaum.

Les produits Vitra sont exposés dans le bâtiment comme dans une maison, illustration de la relation symbiotique entre le projet Herzog & de Meuron et le concept commercial du directeur de Vitra, Rolf Fehlbaum.

Interior volumes are not simply
stacked—they also allow for numerous points of penetration and views
from one space to another.

Die Innenräume wurden nicht einfach
übereinandergestapelt, sondern sind
an zahlreichen Stellen zueinander geöffnet, sodass man kreuz und quer in
verschiedene Bereiche blicken kann.

Les volumes intérieurs ne sont pas
simplement superposés, ils autorisent
de nombreuses liaisons et perspectives d'un espace à l'autre.

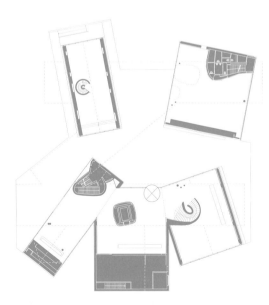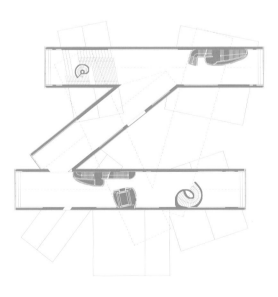

A curving stair is introduced between levels, contrasting with the apparently rectilinear design.

Ein Wendeltreppe verbindet die Geschossflächen und setzt einen visuellen Kontrapunkt zu dem betont schnörkellosen Design.

Un escalier en courbe introduit entre les niveaux contraste avec un plan d'esprit rectiligne.

HHF

HHF architekten GmbH
Allschwiler Str. 71A
4055 Basel
Switzerland

Tel: +41 61 756 70 10 / Fax: +41 61 756 70 11
E-mail: info@hhf.ch / Web: www.hhf.ch

HHF architects was founded in 2003 by Tilo Herlach, Simon Hartmann, and Simon Frommenwiler. Tilo Herlach was born in 1972 in Zurich. He studied architecture at the ETH Zurich and EPFL in Lausanne (1992–98). He subsequently worked with d-company in Bern (2001–03), and with Rolf Furrer Architekten (Basel, 2003). Simon Hartmann was born in 1974 in Bern, and studied architecture at the EPFL, at the Technical University of Berlin, and at the ETH (1994–2000). From 1997 to 2003, he worked with Nicola di Battista in Rome, A.B.D.R., Garofalo & Miura, Steuerwald + Scheiwiller Architekten in Basel, and Rolf Furrer Architekten in Basel. Simon Frommenwiler was born in London in 1972. He attended the ETH in Zurich (1994–2000), and worked subsequently with Bearth & Deplazes in Chur, ARchos Architecture in Basel, and Skidmore, Owings & Merrill in New York. Simon Hartmann has been a teaching assistant at the ETH Studio Basel, working with Jacques Herzog, Pierre de Meuron, Roger Diener, and Marcel Meili (2002–07), and Professor at the University of Applied Sciences of Fribourg, Switzerland, since 2009. Simon Frommenwiler has been a teaching assistant with Harry Gugger at the EPFL in Lausanne since 2005. Recent work of HHF includes the Jinhua Sculpture Park Baby Dragon (Jinhua, China, 2006); "Ono" Bar-Café-Lounge (Basel, Switzerland, 2006); SonVida Housing (Bottmingen, Switzerland, 2003–07); Cafeteria Kirschgarten High School (Basel, Switzerland, 2006–08); Tsai Residence (Ancram, New York, USA, 2006–08); Artfarm, a showroom and storage for art (Salt Point, New York, USA, 2007–08, published here); and Labels 2, a fashion center in Berlin (Germany, 2007–09).

HHF wurde 2003 von Tilo Herlach, Simon Hartmann und Simon Frommenwiler gegründet. Tilo Herlach, 1972 in Zürich geboren, studierte Architektur an der ETH Zürich und der EPFL in Lausanne (1992–98). Anschließend arbeitete er für d-company in Bern (2001–03) und Rolf Furrer Architekten (Basel, 2003). Simon Hartmann wurde 1974 in Bern geboren und studierte Architektur an der EPFL, der TU Berlin und der ETH Zürich (1994–2003). Von 1997 bis 2003 arbeitete er für Nicola di Battista in Rom, A.B.D.R., Garofalo & Miura, Steuerwald + Scheiwiller Architekten, Basel, und Rolf Furrer Architekten in Basel. Simon Frommenwiler wurde 1972 in London geboren. Nach seinem Studium an der ETH Zürich (1994–2000) war er für Bearth & Deplazes in Chur, ARchos Architecture in Basel, und Skidmore, Owings & Merrill in New York tätig. Simon Hartmann war Lehrassistent am ETH Studio Basel, wo er mit Jacques Herzog, Pierre de Meuron, Roger Diener und Marcel Meili zusammenarbeitete (2002–07). Seit 2009 ist er Professor an der Hochschule für Technik und Architektur Fribourg, Schweiz. Simon Frommenwiler ist seit 2005 Lehrassistent bei Harry Gugger an der EPFL in Lausanne. In letzter Zeit arbeitete HHF am „Baby Dragon" im Skulpturenpark Jinhua (Jinhua, China, 2006), der Bar-Café-Lounge „Ono" (Basel, 2006), dem Wohnbauprojekt SonVida (Bottmingen, Schweiz, 2003–07), der Kirschgarten Schulcafeteria (Basel, 2006–08), der Tsai Residence (Ancram, New York, 2006–08), der Artfarm, einem Ausstellungsraum und Lager für Kunst (Salt Point, New York, 2007–08, hier vorgestellt), sowie dem Modezentrum Labels 2 (Berlin, 2007–09).

L'agence **HHF** architects a été fondée en 2003 par Tilo Herlach, Simon Hartmann et Simon Frommenwiler. Tilo Herlach, né en 1972 à Zurich, a étudié l'architecture à l'ETH à Zurich et à l'EPFL à Lausanne (1992–98). Il a ensuite travaillé pour la d-company à Berne (2001–03) et Rolf Furrer Architekten à Bâle, (2003). Simon Hartmann, né en 1974 à Berne, a étudié l'architecture à l'EPFL, à l'Université technologique de Berlin et à l'ETH (1994–2000). De 1997 à 2003, il a travaillé pour Nicola di Battista à Rome, A.B.D.R., Garofalo & Miura, Steuerwald + Scheiwiller Architekten et Rolf Furrer Architekten, tous deux à Bâle. Simon Frommenwiler, né à Londres en 1972, a étudié à l'ETH à Zurich (1994–2000), puis travaillé pour Bearth & Deplazes à Chur, ARchos Architecture à Bâle et Skidmore, Owings & Merrill à New York. Simon Hartmann a été enseignant assistant à l'ETH à Bâle et a collaboré avec Jacques Herzog, Pierre de Meuron, Roger Diener et Marcel Meili (2002–07). Il est professeur à l'Université des sciences appliquées de Fribourg (Suisse). Simon Frommenwiler a été enseignant assistant, et travaille avec Harry Gugger à l'EPFL à Lausanne depuis 2005. HHF est récemment intervenue sur le Jinhua Sculpture Park, Baby Dragon (Jinhua, Chine, 2006) ; le "Ono" Bar-Café-Lounge (Bâle, 2006) ; les logements SonVida (Bottmingen, Suisse, 2003–07) ; la résidence Tsai (Ancram, New York, 2006–08) ; la cafétéria du collège du Kirschgarten (Bâle, 2006–08) ; le showroom et entrepôt d'art, Artfarm (Salt Point, New York, 2007–08, publié ici) et Labels 2, un Centre pour la mode à Berlin (2007–10).

ARTFARM

Salt Point, New York, USA, 2007–08

Address: Salt Point, NY, USA, +1 212 414 1169, www.chambersfineart.com
Area: 373 m². Client: Christophe W. Mao, Chambers Fine Art/New York/Beijing
Cost: $300 000. Collaboration: Ai Wei Wei

This project is located one and a half hours from New York City, on the property of an art collector and dealer specialized in Chinese art. The new building is divided into showrooms for the gallery owner. The architects employed a three-part steel structure, typical of local agricultural buildings. Each of the three volumes is set on a concrete slab that is situated within the existing grade of the site. A sloped ramp in the middle of the structures connects the different volumes and levels. The **ARTFARM** has few windows, but its white interior spaces are remarkably bright. The architects were challenged by the temperature extremes during the year in Salt Point (minimum and maximum temperatures: -25°C to +45°C), since the artworks require relatively constant conditions. The building is thus conceived as a hermetically closed volume, with white shiny PVC insulation. The maximum height of the structures from ground level is 5.8 meters.

Das Projekt liegt anderthalb Stunden von New York auf dem Grundstück eines auf chinesische Kunst spezialisierten Kunstsammlers und Galeristen. Der Neubau ist in Showrooms für den Galeristen unterteilt. Die Architekten arbeiten mit einer dreiteiligen Stahlkonstruktion, die typischerweise in der örtlichen Landwirtschaft zum Einsatz kommt. Jeder der drei Baukörper fußt auf einer Betonplatte, die in das Gefälle des Grundstücks eingelassen wurden. Eine mittig verlaufende, schräge Rampe verbindet die unterschiedlichen Baukörper und Niveaus. Obwohl die **ARTFARM** kaum Fenster hat, sind die weißen Innenräume erstaunlich hell. Eine Herausforderung für die Architekten war das extreme Temperaturgefälle in Salt Point (die Temperaturen schwanken im Laufe des Jahres zwischen -25°C und +45°C), denn die Kunstwerke erfordern vergleichsweise konstante Klimabedingungen. Entsprechend wurde der Bau als hermetisch abgeriegeltes Volumen mit glänzendweißer PVC-Dämmung entworfen. Die Maximalhöhe der Bauten über Bodenniveau beträgt 5,8 m.

Ce projet a été réalisé dans la propriété d'un collectionneur et marchand d'art chinois, située à une heure et demie de New York. Le nouveau bâtiment est divisé en salles d'expositions pour le galeriste. Les architectes ont réalisé une structure en acier tripartite, typique des bâtiments agricoles locaux. Chacun des trois volumes repose sur une dalle en béton coulée en fonction du dénivelé du terrain. Une rampe centrale relie les différents volumes et niveaux. L'**ARTFARM** ne possède que peu de fenêtres, mais son intérieur, entièrement blanc, est remarquablement lumineux. Les architectes devaient résoudre le défi de températures extrêmes dans la région de Salt Point (de -25 à +45°C), car les œuvres d'art requièrent des conditions de conservation relativement constantes. Le bâtiment est donc un volume hermétiquement clos, isolé par du PVC brillant blanc. La hauteur maximum des bâtiments est de 5,8 mètres.

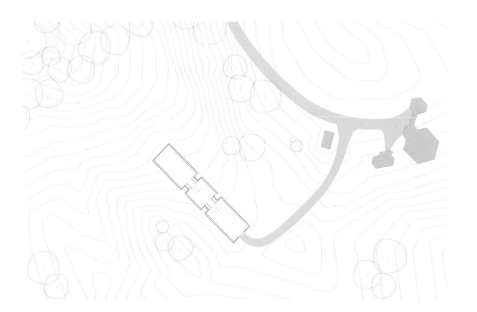

Industrial and farming buildings
appear to be the inspiration for these
shedlike designs, set here in a hilly
rural environment.

Anregung für den schuppenartigen
Entwurf der Artfarm, die in einer
hügeligen ländlichen Umgebung errichtet wurde, waren augenscheinlich
Bauten aus Industrie und Landwirtschaft.

Des bâtiments industriels et agricoles
semblent avoir inspiré ces projets de
constructions-hangars insérées dans
un environnement rural.

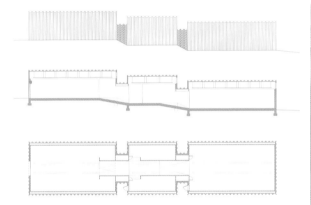

A plan shows the tripartite design, while section and elevation drawings make clear the stepped insertion into the site.

Die Grundrisszeichnung zeigt den dreigeteilten Aufbau, Querschnitt und Aufriss veranschaulichen die zur Anpassung an den Untergrund gewählte Stufung.

Plan de la répartition du projet en trois parties. Les coupes et les élévations illustrent l'insertion des bâtiments en gradins dans le terrain.

The industrial appearance of the exteriors is confirmed by the summary surface treatments seen in these interior views.

Das industrielle Erscheinungsbild der Außenseiten setzt sich im Innern in einer schlichten Gestaltung der Oberflächen fort.

L'aspect industriel de l'extérieur se renforce dans l'habillage sommaire des volumes intérieurs.

STEVEN HOLL

Steven Holl Architects, P.C.
450 West 31st Street, 11th Floor, New York, NY 10001, USA
Tel: +1 212 629 7262 / Fax: +1 212 629 7312
E-mail: nyc@stevenholl.com / Web: www.stevenholl.com

Born in 1947 in Bremerton, Washington, **STEVEN HOLL** obtained his B.Arch degree from the University of Washington (1970). He studied in Rome and at the Architectural Association (AA) in London (1976). He began his career in California and opened his own office in New York in 1976. Holl has taught at the University of Washington, Syracuse University, and, since 1981, at Columbia University. His notable buildings include: Void Space/Hinged Space, Housing (Nexus World, Fukuoka, Japan, 1991); Stretto House (Dallas, Texas, 1992); Makuhari Housing (Chiba, Tokyo, Japan, 1997); Chapel of Saint Ignatius, Seattle University (Seattle, Washington, 1997); Kiasma Museum of Contemporary Art (Helsinki, Finland, 1998); and an extension to the Cranbrook Institute of Science (Bloomfield Hills, Michigan, 1999). Winner of the 1998 Alvar Aalto Medal, Steven Holl's more recent work includes the Turbulence House in New Mexico for the artist Richard Tuttle (2005); the Pratt Institute Higgins Hall Center Insertion (Brooklyn, New York, 2005); the New Residence at the Swiss Embassy (Washington, D.C., 2006); and an Art and Art History Building for the University of Iowa (Iowa City, Iowa, 2006), all in the USA unless stated otherwise. He recently won the competition (2009) for the Glasgow School of Art (Glasgow, UK), and completed an expansion and renovation of the Nelson-Atkins Museum of Art (Kansas City, Missouri, USA, 2007); Linked Hybrid (Beijing, China, 2005–08); the Knut Hamsun Center (Hamarøy, Norway, 2006–09, published here); the Vanke Center (Shenzhen, China, 2006–09); and HEART: Herning Museum of Contemporary Art (Herning, Denmark, 2007–09, also published here). Current projects include Cité de l'Océan et du Surf (Biarritz, France, 2005–10, with Solange Fabião); the Nanjing Museum of Art and Architecture (China, 2008–10); and Beirut Marina and Town Quay (Beirut, Lebanon, 2009–).

STEVEN HOLL wurde 1947 in Bremerton, Washington, geboren. Er absolvierte seinen B.Arch an der University of Washington (1970) und studierte in Rom sowie der Architectural Association in London (1976). Er begann seine Laufbahn in Kalifornien und eröffnete sein erstes Büro 1976 in New York. Holl war Dozent an der University of Washington und der Syracuse University und lehrt seit 1981 an der Columbia. Zu seinen namhaften Bauten zählen: Wohnblock Void Space/Hinged Space (Nexus World, Fukuoka, Japan, 1991), Stretto House (Dallas, Texas, 1992), Wohnanlage in Makuhari (Chiba, Tokio, Japan, 1997), Kapelle St. Ignatius, Seattle University (Seattle, Washington, 1997), Kiasma Museum of Contemporary Art (Helsinki, Finnland, 1998) und die Erweiterung des Cranbrook Institute of Science (Bloomfield Hills, Michigan, 1999). Steven Holl, der 1998 mit der Alvar-Aalto-Medaille ausgezeichnet wurde, realisierte in letzter Zeit u.a. das Turbulence House in New Mexico für den Künstler Richard Tuttle (2005), das Higgins Hall Center am Pratt Institute (Brooklyn, New York, 2005), die neue Residenz der Schweizer Botschaft (Washington D.C., 2006) sowie ein Gebäude für das Institut für Kunst und Kunstgeschichte der Universität Iowa (Iowa City, 2006), alle in den USA, sofern nicht anders angegeben. Unlängst gewann Holl einen Wettbewerb (2009) für die Glasgow School of Art (Glasgow) und konnte die Erweiterung und Sanierung des Nelson-Atkins Museum of Art abschließen (Kansas City, Missouri, 2007). Weitere Projekte sind Linked Hybrid (Peking, 2005–08), das Knut Hamsun Center (Hamarøy, Norwegen, 2006–09, hier vorgestellt), das Vanke Center (Shenzhen, China, 2006–09) und HEART: Herning Museum of Contemporary Art (Herning, Dänemark, 2007–09, ebenfalls hier vorgestellt). Zu seinen aktuellen Projekten zählen die Cité de l'Océan et du Surf (Biarritz, 2005–10, mit Solange Fabião), das the Nanjing Museum für Kunst und Architektur (China, 2008–10) sowie die Marina mit Stadtkaianlage in Beirut (Libanon, 2009–).

Né in 1947 à Bremerton (Washington), **STEVEN HOLL** est B. Arch de l'Université de Washington (1970). Il a étudié à Rome et à l'Architectural Association de Londres (1976). Après avoir entamé sa carrière en Californie, il ouvre une agence à New York en 1976. Il a enseigné à l'Université de Washington, à Syracuse University et, depuis 1981, à Columbia University. Parmi ses réalisations les plus notables : les logements Void Space/Hinged Space (Nexus World, Fukuoka, Japon, 1991) ; la Maison Stretto (Dallas, Texas, 1992) ; l'immeuble de logements Makuhari (Chiba, Japon, 1997) ; la chapelle de Saint-Ignatius, Seattle University (Seattle, Washington, 1997) ; le Musée d'art contemporain Kiasma (Helsinki, Finlande, 1998) ; et une extension pour le Cranbrook Institute of Science (Bloomfield Hills, Michigan, 1999). Il obtient la médaille Alvar Aalto en 1998. Parmi ses réalisations plus récentes : la Maison turbulence pour l'artiste Richard Tuttle (New Mexico, 2005) ; le Higgins Hall Center du Pratt Institute (Brooklyn, New York, 1997–2005) ; une nouvelle résidence à l'ambassade de Suisse (Washington D.C., 2006) et un bâtiment pour l'art et l'histoire de l'art à l'Université de l'Iowa (Iowa City, Iowa, 1999–2006). Il a récemment remporté le concours pour l'École d'art de Glasgow (Glasgow, 2009) et achevé l'extension et la rénovation du Nelson-Atkins Museum of Art (Kansas City, Missouri, 2007) ; le Linked Hybrid (Pékin, 2005–08) ; le Knut Hamsun Center (Hamarøy, Norvège, 2006–09, publié ici) ; le Centre Vanke (Shenzhen, Chine, 2006–09) et HEART, Herning Museum of Contemporary Art (Herning, Danemark, 2007–09, également publié ici). Parmi ses projets actuels : la Cité de l'océan et du surf (Biarritz, 2005–10, avec Solange Fabião) ; le Musée d'art et d'architecture de Nankin (Chine, 2008–10) ; et la Marina et Town Quay à Beyrouth (Liban, 2009–).

HEART: HERNING MUSEUM OF CONTEMPORARY ART

Herning, Denmark, 2007–09

Address: Birk Centerpark 8, 7400 Herning, Denmark, +45 97 12 10 33, www.heartmus.com
Area: 5600 m². Client: Herning Center of the Arts. Cost: not disclosed

This center combines visual arts and music through the **HERNING MUSEUM OF CONTEMPORARY ART**, the MidWest Ensemble, and the Socle du Monde. The intention of Steven Holl was to "fuse landscape and architecture" in a single-story structure that includes temporary exhibition galleries, a 150-seat auditorium, museum rehearsal rooms, a restaurant, a library, and offices. The Museum features a collection of 46 works by Piero Manzoni and has an ongoing interest in textiles, given the fact that the corporate sponsor (Herning) is a shirt manufacturer. Holl states that the "roof geometry resembles a collection of shirt sleeves laid over the gallery spaces: the curved roofs bring balanced natural lights to the galleries. The loose edges of the plan offer spaces for the café, auditorium, lobby, and offices." Orthogonal gallery spaces are conceived as "treasure boxes," though lightweight internal gallery walls are movable. The unusual surface of the building's exterior adds interest, as the architect explains: "Truck tarps were inserted into the white concrete formwork to yield a fabric texture to the building's exterior walls." The scheme features a 3700-square-meter "bermed landscape of grass mounds and pools" that conceals parking and service areas.

Das Zentrum umfasst das **HERNING MUSEUM OF CONTEMPORARY ART**, das MidWest Ensemble sowie das Socle du Monde – und damit eine Verbindung aus bildenden Künsten und Musik. Steven Holl ging es darum, in seinem einstöckigen Bau „Landschaft und Architektur miteinander verschmelzen zu lassen". Hier befinden sich temporäre Ausstellungsräume, ein Auditorium mit 150 Plätzen, Probenräume des Museums, ein Restaurant, eine Bibliothek sowie Büros. Das vom Hemdenhersteller Herning geförderte Museum besitzt eine Sammlung mit 46 Werken des Künstlers Piero Manzoni und hat ein besonderes Interesse an Textilien. Steven Holl erklärt: „Die Geometrie des Dachs wirkt, als hätte man mehrere Hemdsärmel über den Ausstellungsraum gelegt: Die geschwungenen Dachflächen lassen ausgewogenes Tageslicht in die Galerien einfallen. Die frei gestalteten Konturen des Grundrisses bieten Platz für Café, Auditorium, Lobby und Büros." Die rechtwinkligen Ausstellungsräume wurden wie „Schatzkästchen" geplant; dabei sind die Leichtbautrennwände zwischen den Galerien beweglich. Auch die Oberfläche des Außenbaus wurde interessant gestaltet. Der Architekt führt aus: „In die Verschalung des weißen Betons wurden LKW-Planen eingebunden, wodurch die Außenfassaden des Baus eine textile Struktur erhalten." Zum Komplex gehören ein 3700 m² großes Grundstück, eine „Böschungslandschaft aus Grashügeln und Wasserbecken", die Parkplätze und Servicebereiche verbirgt.

Ce centre culturel qui réunit arts plastiques et musique regroupe le **MUSÉE HERNING D'ART CONTEMPORAIN**, le MidWest Ensemble et le Socle du Monde. L'intention de Steven Holl était de « fusionner le paysage et l'architecture » dans une structure d'un seul niveau comprenant des galeries d'expositions temporaires, un auditorium de 150 places, des salles de répétition, un restaurant, une bibliothèque et des bureaux. Le musée possède 46 œuvres de Piero Manzoni et s'intéresse aux textiles, le mécène institutionnel (Herning) étant un fabricant de chemises. Steven Holl précise que « la géométrie du toit fait penser à des manches de chemises posées sur les galeries : ces toitures incurvées régulent l'éclairage naturel qui arrive jusqu'aux salles. En bordure de celles-ci se trouvent un café, l'auditorium, le hall d'entrée et les bureaux. » Les galeries orthogonales sont pensées comme des « coffres aux trésors » à partitions intérieures mobiles. L'habillage extérieur inhabituel renforce encore plus l'intérêt de ce projet. Comme l'explique l'architecte : « Des bâches de camion ont été insérées dans le coffrage du béton blanc pour donner une texture textile aux murs extérieurs. » Le projet comprend également l'aménagement des 3700 mètres carrés d'un « paysage de levées de terre et de bassins », qui masque les parkings et les installations techniques.

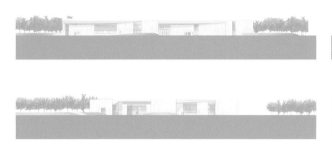

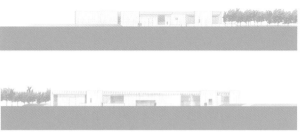

The long, low-lying structure is enlivened by irregular openings and angles, visible in the two pictures on this double page.

Wie auf den Fotos dieser Doppelseite zu sehen, wird das längliche niedrige Bauwerk durch unregelmäßige Öffnungen und Vorsprünge aufgelockert.

Le bâtiment long et surbaissé est animé par des ouvertures irrégulières et des articulations de plans visibles sur les photos de cette double-page.

Although the museum is made up in good part of two rectangular blocks, the architect, as always, makes intriguing use of openings, curves, and light to give visitors an unexpected experience.

Wie immer weiß der Architekt auch hier Öffnungen, Biegungen und Licht-führung so einzusetzen, dass der Besuch des im Prinzip nur aus zwei großen rechteckigen Kuben bestehenden Gebäudes zum Erlebnis wird.

Si le musée est en grande partie constitué de deux blocs rectangulaires, l'architecte a comme toujours fait un étonnant usage des ouvertures, des courbes et de la lumière pour offrir aux visiteurs une expérience architecturale originale.

KNUT HAMSUN CENTER
Hamarøy, Norway, 2006–09

Address: Presteid, Hamarøy, Norway, +47 75 50 35 00, www.hamsunsenteret.no
Area: 2508 m². Client: Nordland Fylkeskommune (County)
Cost: not disclosed

Set above the Arctic Circle, the Center is located on an isolated site at the water's edge, emphasizing its unusual forms.

Das Knut Hamsun Center liegt nördlich des Polarkreises; vor der Kulisse des einsamen Sees erscheint seine äußere Form umso ungewöhnlicher.

Le Centre se dresse en un lieu isolé au-delà du cercle arctique, au bord de l'eau, ce qui fait ressortir son aspect étrange.

Knut Hamsun, described as Norway's most inventive 20th-century writer, is attributed with the creation of a modern school of fiction. Located above the Arctic Circle, this new Center is near the farm where the writer grew up. The structure includes exhibition areas, a library and reading room, a café, and an auditorium equipped with the latest film-projection equipment. More than 17 films were based on Hamsun's literature. Steven Holl declares: "The building is conceived as an archetypal and intensified compression of spirit in space and light, concretizing a Hamsun character in architectonic terms. The concept for the museum, 'Building as a Body: Battleground of Invisible Forces,' is realized from inside and out." The stained black wood exterior of the building is inspired by wooden stave Norse churches, while a roof garden is linked to traditional Norwegian sod roofs. Rough, white-painted concrete interiors are calculated to allow natural light to "ricochet" into the structure on certain days of the year.

Knut Hamsun gilt als Norwegens schöpferischster Autor des 19. Jahrhunderts und Begründer eines modernen Schreibstils. Das nördlich des Polarkreises gelegene neue Zentrum liegt unweit des Bauernhofs, auf dem der Schriftsteller aufwuchs. Der Bau umfasst Ausstellungsbereiche, eine Bibliothek mit Lesesaal, ein Café und ein Auditorium, ausgestattet mit modernster Technik für Filmvorführungen. Hamsuns Werke wurden über 17-mal verfilmt. Steven Holl erklärt: „Das Gebäude wurde als archetypische, gesteigerte spirituelle Verdichtung konzipiert, die sich in Raum und Licht manifestiert, und ist damit die Verkörperung einer Hamsun'schen Figur in architektonischer Form. Das Konzept des Museums, ‚Gebäude als Körper: Schlachtfeld unsichtbarer Kräfte' wurde innen und außen konsequent umgesetzt." Das schwarz gebeizte Holz des Außenbaus knüpft an nordische Stabkirchen an, der Dachgarten wiederum an traditionelle norwegische Grassodenhäuser. Die rauen, weiß gestrichenen Betonwände des Interieurs wurden so platziert, dass das Tageslicht an bestimmten Tagen im Jahr durch den Bau „geistern" kann.

Knut Hamsun, l'écrivain norvégien le plus inventif du XXᵉ siècle, est à l'origine d'une école de fiction moderne. Situé au-dessus du cercle arctique, ce nouveau centre a été établi près de la ferme où a grandi l'écrivain. Le bâtiment comprend des espaces d'expositions, une bibliothèque, une salle de lecture, un café et un auditorium équipé des dernières techniques de projection (plus de 17 films ont été inspirés par les œuvres de Knut Hamsun). Steven Holl a déclaré : « Le bâtiment est conçu comme un archétype, une forme de compression spirituelle intense dans l'espace et la lumière, qui incarne en termes architectoniques un personnage de Hamsun. Le concept du musée, "un bâtiment comme un corps : champ de bataille de forces invisibles", est réalisé de l'intérieur vers l'extérieur. » L'habillage extérieur en bois teint en noir s'inspire de celui des églises locales, tandis que la toiture-jardin rappelle les toits d'herbe traditionnels du pays. L'intérieur en béton brut peint en blanc a été étudié pour que la lumière naturelle « ricoche » sur la structure à certains moments de l'année.

Balconies in different materials, a leaning structure, and the rooftop garden suggest an almost anthropomorphic design, confirmed by the "building as a body" concept.

Das anthropomorphe Design der aus unterschiedlichen Materialien bestehenden Balkone, des leicht geneigten Baukörpers und des Dachgartens verweist auf Holls Konzept des „Gebäudes als Körper".

Des balcons faits de divers matériaux, une partie du bâtiment inclinée et la toiture-jardin illustrent le concept de l'architecte de « bâtiment comme un corps ».

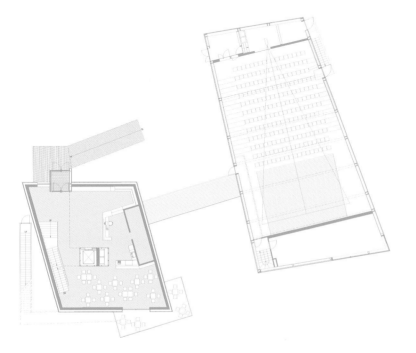

Steven Holl's masterly orchestration
of angles and light sources is visible
in these images.

Einige Beispiel für Steven Holls ge-
konnten Umgang mit Vorsprüngen und
dem von außen einfallenden Licht.

L'orchestration magistrale des plans
inclinés et des sources lumineuses
par Steven Holl ressort particulièrement sur ces images.

Elevations reveal the irregular external forms and extrusions. Below, an image of the rooftop garden.

Die Aufrisse führen die unregelmäßige Gebäudegestalt mit ihren außenseitigen „Auswüchsen" vor Augen. Unten ein Foto des Dachgartens.

Ces coupes montrent les formes extérieures irrégulières et la mise en projection de certains éléments. Ci-dessous, la toiture-jardin.

INFORMATION BASED ARCHITECTURE

Information Based Architecture
Stavangerweg 890/29
1013 AX Amsterdam
The Netherlands

Tel: +31 206 36 62 22
E-mail: office@iba-bv.com
Web: www.iba-bv.com

Mark Hemel was born in 1966 and received his Diploma in Architectural Design from the Technical University of Delft (1993), followed by an M.A. Graduate Design from the Architectural Association (AA) in London. He founded **INFORMATION BASED ARCHITECTURE** with Barbara Kuit in 1998. He is the Artistic Director of the firm. Barbara Kuit was born in 1968 and also holds a Diploma in Architectural Design from the Technical University of Delft (1994). She is the General Director of Information Based Architecture. Their work includes the Information Tower (Shenzhen, China, 2009); a guesthouse, Internet café, and student housing (Elmina, Ghana, 2006–09); the Guangzhou TV and Sightseeing Tower (Guangzhou, China, 2005–10, published here); and a Furniture Store Headquarters (Foshan, China, in progress).

Mark Hemel wurde 1966 geboren und absolvierte sein Diplom in Architektur an der Technischen Universität Delft (1993) sowie anschließend einen M.A. im Aufbaustudiengang Entwerfen an der Architectural Association (London). 1998 gründete er gemeinsam mit Barbara Kuit das Büro **INFORMATION BASED ARCHITECTURE**, wo er künstlerischer Leiter ist. Barbara Kuit wurde 1968 geboren und absolvierte ebenfalls ein Diplom in Architektur an der TU Delft (1994). Sie ist Generaldirektorin bei Information Based Architecture. Zu ihren Projekten zählen der Information Tower (Shenzhen, China, 2009), ein Gästehaus, Internetcafé und Studentenwohnheim (Elmina, Ghana, 2006–09), der Guangzhou TV and Sightseeing Tower (Guangzhou, China, 2005–10, hier vorgestellt) sowie der Hauptsitz eines Möbelgeschäfts (Foshan, China, in Arbeit).

Mark Hemel, né en 1966, diplômé de conception architecturale de l'Université polytechnique de Delft (1993), est M. A. en conception de l'Architectural Association (Londres). Il a fondé **INFORMATION BASED ARCHITECTURE** avec Barbara Kuit en 1998. Il est directeur artistique de l'agence. Barbara Kuit, née en 1968, est également diplômée en conception architecturale de l'Université polytechnique de Delft (1994). Elle est directrice générale d'Information Based Architecture. Parmi leurs réalisations : la tour d'information (Shenzhen, Chine, 2009) ; une maison d'hôtes, un café internet et des logements pour étudiants (Elmina, Ghana, 2006–09) ; la tour de télévision et plate-forme d'observation de Guangzhou (Guangzhou, Chine, 2005–10, publiée ici) et le siège d'une chaîne de magasins de meubles (Foshan, Chine, en cours).

GUANGZHOU TV AND SIGHTSEEING TOWER

Guangzhou, China, 2005–10

Address: Yuejiang Road West/Yiyuan Road, Haizhu District, Guangzhou GD, China, www.gztvtower.info
Area: 114 000 m². Client: Guangzhou Municipal Construction Commission. Cost: € 220 million
Collaboration: Arup (Engineering), GZDI (Local Design Institute)

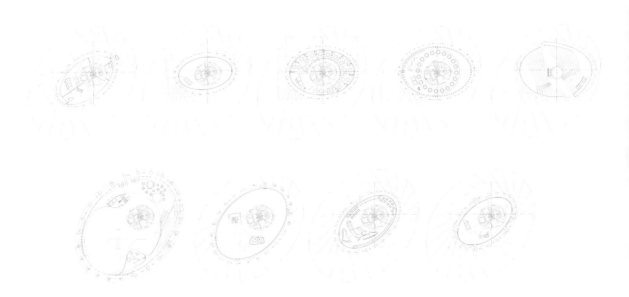

An international competition was held in 2004 for the design of the **GUANGZHOU TV TOWER** and the master plan for the 56-hectare park at its base, including an elevated plaza, a pagoda park, retail facilities, an office, a TV Station, and a hotel. Mark Hemel, IBA architect and Artistic Director, states: "Where most skyscrapers bear 'male' features, being introverted, strong, straight, rectangular, and based on repetition, we wanted to create a 'female' tower-complex, transparent, curvy and gracious." The 610-meter-high tower is a twisted, tapering tube. This form was derived from the interaction of two ellipses, one at the foundation level and another at a horizontal plane 450 meters above ground level. It is the rotation of these ellipses that generates the "waist" of this tower. Subway and bus stations are located in the base of the tower, as is a museum, a food court, commercial areas, and a 600-vehicle bus and car parking area. A two-story rotating restaurant is located near the upper observation decks. The tower is due to be fully operational for the 2010 Asian Games.

2004 wurde ein internationaler Wettbewerb für den Entwurf des **FERNSEHTURMS IN GUANGZHOU** ausgeschrieben, einschließlich eines Masterplans für den 56 ha großen Park zu seinen Füßen, zu dem ein erhöhter Vorplatz, ein Pagodenpark, Geschäfte, Büros, ein Fernsehsender und ein Hotel gehören. Mark Hemel, Architekt und künstlerischer Leiter bei IBA, führt aus: „Während sich die meisten Wolkenkratzer durch ‚männliche' Attribute auszeichnen – introvertiert, stark, geradlinig und rechtwinklig wirken und auf repetitiven Mustern basieren – wollten wir einen ‚weiblichen' Turm mit zugehörigem Komplex schaffen: transparent, geschwungen und anmutig." Der 610 m hohe Turm ist eine in sich gedrehte und sich verjüngende Röhre. Abgeleitet ist die Form aus zwei ineinandergreifenden Ellipsen, einer auf Ebene des Fundaments, einer zweiten auf einer horizontalen Ebene 450 m über dem Boden. Durch die Rotation der beiden Ellipsen entsteht die „Taille" des Turms. Im Sockel des Turms sind U-Bahn- und Busstationen, ein Museum, eine Gourmetmeile, Ladenflächen und ein Parkplatz mit 600 Stellplätzen für Busse und PKWs untergebracht. Unweit der Aussichtsplattformen an der Spitze des Turms liegt ein zweistöckiges rotierendes Restaurant. Bis zu Beginn der Asian Games 2010 soll der Turm voll in Betrieb sein.

Ce projet a été remporté à l'issue d'un concours international organisé en 2004 pour la conception de la **TOUR DE TÉLÉVISION DE GUANGZHOU** et le plan directeur du parc de 56 hectares qui s'étend à ses pieds. Celui-ci comprend une place surélevée, le parc de la Pagode, des commerces, une station de télévision et un hôtel. Mark Hemel, architecte et directeur artistique d'IBA précise : « Alors que la plupart des gratte-ciel qui affichent des caractéristiques "mâles" sont introvertis, forts, raides, rectangulaires et basés sur un principe de répétition, nous souhaitions créer une tour complexe aux caractéristiques "féminines", transparente, tout en courbes et gracieuse. » De 610 mètres de haut, cette tour est un tube tors et effilé. Cette forme résulte de l'interaction de deux ellipses, l'une au niveau de la base, l'autre à 450 mètres au-dessus du sol. Leur rotation génère géométriquement la « taille » de la tour. Une station de métro et une gare de bus sont situées à la base de la tour, ainsi qu'un musée, un multirestaurant, des commerces et un parking pour 600 voitures et bus. Un restaurant tournant à deux niveaux a été implanté près de la plate-forme d'observation. L'ensemble devrait être pleinement opérationnel pour les Jeux asiatiques de 2010.

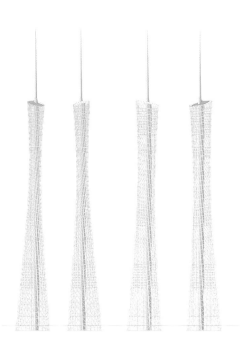

The subtly tapered and twisted form of the tower is revealed in the drawings on this page and in the plans opposite. The tower stands out as a new symbol of Guangzhou.

Die Konstruktionszeichnungen links und auf der gegenüberliegenden Seite machen die verdrehte Doppelkegel-struktur des Turmes, des künftigen Wahrzeichens von Guangzhou, nachvollziehbar.

La forme torse et subtilement effilée de la tour se révèle dans les dessins ci-contre et les plans de la page précédente. La tour est un nouveau monument symbolique pour Guang-zhou (Canton).

INTERNATIONAL POLAR FOUNDATION

The International Polar Foundation (IPF)
120A rue des Deux Gares
1070 Brussels
Belgium

Tel: +32 2 543 06 98
Fax: +32 2 543 06 99
E-mail: info@polarfoundation.org
Web: www.polarfoundation.org

THE INTERNATIONAL POLAR FOUNDATION (IPF) is a public utility foundation created in 2002 with the "objective of promoting polar research as a tool for raising public awareness and fostering understanding of the fundamental mechanisms of our climate." The IPF was responsible for the construction of the Princess Elisabeth Antartica station published here. Alain Hubert, born in 1953, is a Belgian polar explorer, civil engineer, entrepreneur, mountain guide (UIAGM), public speaker, good-will Ambassador for UNICEF, and cofounder and Chairman of the IPF. Hubert was the initiator of the Princess Elisabeth Station project and was responsible for construction coordination on site. Johan Berte, also Belgian, born in 1969, is the Project Manager of the Princess Elisabeth Station, and was responsible for the technical design. He has been with the IPF since 2004. Nighat Amin, environmental chemist, born in Kenya in 1959, was responsible for liaison with technical and construction teams, coordination, base-camp management, logistics, environmental management and impact assessment, and procurement issues related to the station. Philippe Samyn, born in Ghent in 1948 (MS in Civil Engineering from MIT, 1973), principal of Samyn and Partners, was responsible for the shell technology and the design of the support struts of the station.

Die 2002 gegründete **INTERNATIONAL POLAR FOUNDATION** (IPF) ist eine gemeinnützige Stiftung mit dem „Ziel, durch die Polarforschung ein öffentliches Bewusstsein und Verständnis für die grundlegenden Mechanismen unseres Klimas zu schaffen und zu fördern." Die IPF initiierte den Bau der hier vorgestellten Prinzessin-Elisabeth-Station in der Antarktis. Alain Hubert, geboren 1953, ist ein belgischer Polarforscher, Bauingenieur, Unternehmer, Bergführer (UIAGM), Redner, UNICEF-Botschafter und Mitbegründer und Leiter der IPF. Hubert war Initiator der Prinzessin-Elisabeth-Polarstation und verantwortlich für die Koordination der Bauarbeiten vor Ort. Johan Berte, ebenfalls Belgier und 1969 geboren, ist Projektmanager der Prinzessin-Elisabeth-Polarstation und betreute die technische Planung. Er ist seit 2004 für die IPF tätig. Nighat Amin, geboren 1959 in Kenia, ist Umweltchemikerin und war für Gesamtkoordination, Zusammenarbeit von Technikern und Bauteams, Management des Basecamps, Logistik, Umweltmanagement und Umweltverträglichkeitsprüfung sowie Beschaffungsfragen im Hinblick auf die Station zuständig. Philippe Samyn, 1948 in Gent geboren (1973 M.Sc./Bauingenieurwesen an der MIT), Direktor von Samyn and Partners, zeichnete für Rohbautechnik und den Entwurf der Druckstreben der Station verantwortlich.

La **FONDATION POLAIRE INTERNATIONALE** (FPI) est un organisme d'utilité publique créé en 2002 pour « promouvoir la recherche polaire, susciter une prise de conscience publique, et faire avancer la compréhension des mécanismes de notre climat ». La Fondation est responsable de la construction de la station antarctique Princesse Élizabeth publiée ici. Alain Hubert, né en 1953, est un explorateur polaire belge, ingénieur civil, entrepreneur, guide de montagne (UIAGM), conférencier ambassadeur de bonne volonté pour l'UNICEF et cofondateur et président de la FPI. Initiateur du projet, il a été responsable de la coordination sur place. Johan Berte, également belge, né en 1969, est le directeur du projet de la station et a été responsable de sa conception technique. Il travaille pour FPI depuis 2004. Nighat Amin, chimiste spécialisé en environnement, né au Kenya en 1959, a été responsable de la liaison avec les équipes techniques et de construction, de la coordination, de la gestion du camp de base, de la logistique, de la gestion de l'environnement et du contrôle de l'impact environnemental. Philippe Samyn, né à Gand en 1948 (MA en ingénierie civile du MIT en 1973), directeur de Samyn and Partners a été chargé de la technologie de la coque et du dessin de la structure de soutien de la station.

PRINCESS ELISABETH ANTARCTICA

Utsteinen, 71°57'S–23°20'E, Dronning Maud Land, East Antarctica, 2007–09

Address: Utsteinen, 71°57'S–23°20'E, Dronning Maud Land, East Antarctica, www.antarcticstation.org
Area: 440 m² (1440 m² with technical workshops, vehicle hangars, and additional accommodations)
Client: International Polar Foundation. Cost: not disclosed

Although its forms are largely dictated by the harsh climate, the ice station is both elegant and modern.

Obwohl ihre äußere Form in erster Linie durch das harsche Klima vorgegeben war, ist die Polarstation so modern wie elegant.

Bien que ses formes soient dictées par la dureté du climat, cette station antarctique est de lignes à la fois modernes et élégantes.

Isolated in Antarctica, the station imparts its rather alien presence on the landscape, suggesting by its very design that it is a temporary fixture.

Die Abgeschiedenheit der Antarktis und das fremdartige Erscheinungsbild der Station in der Eislandschaft erwecken den Eindruck, dass es sich um eine temporäre Einrichtung handelt.

Isolée dans l'Antarctique, la station impose une présence assez étrange dans le paysage tout en suggérant par sa conception même qu'elle n'est que temporaire.

In the context of the International Polar Year 2007–09, the International Polar Foundation was commissioned by the Belgian government to design and build a new research station in Antarctica. The IPF created a station that produces zero carbon emissions by operating on renewable energies and implementing advanced energy efficiency protocols. The station is set at an altitude of 1300 meters above sea level and is 684 kilometers from the Japanese Syowa Station and 431 kilometers from the Russian Novolazarevskaya Station. It is intended to house a maximum of 25 people and to have a lifespan of 25 years. Year round temperatures vary between -50°C and -5°C, with wind gusts that can reach 250km/hour. The Station was designed to research the Sør Rondane Mountains, glaciers, coast, and Antarctic Plateau. Though this structure is not typical of others in *Architecture Now!*, in that much of its form and substance is derived from considerations of survival and research, its remarkable design is certainly worthy of consideration as a work of truly contemporary architecture.

Anlässlich des Internationalen Polarjahrs 2007–09 beauftragte die belgische Regierung die International Polar Foundation mit dem Entwurf und dem Bau einer neuen Forschungsstation in der Antarktis. Die von der IPF realisierte Station ist dank erneuerbarer Energien und zukunftsweisender Energieeffizienzvorgaben emissionsfrei. Die Station liegt 1300 m.ü.N.N. und dabei 684 km von der japanischen Syowa-Station sowie 431 km von der russischen Nowolasarewskaja-Station entfernt. Das Stationsgebäude ist auf maximal 25 Personen und eine Lebensdauer von 25 Jahren ausgelegt. Die Temperaturen schwanken im Laufe des Jahres zwischen -50°C und -5°C, Windböen können eine Geschwindigeit von bis zu 250km/h erreichen. Zweck der Station ist die Erforschung des Sør-Rondane-Gebirges, der Gletscher, Küsten und des Polarplateaus. Obwohl dieser Bau untypisch für die sonst in *Architecture Now!* vorgestellten Bauten ist, da ein Großteil des Entwurfs von Faktoren wie Überlebensfähigkeit und Forschung diktiert wurde, ist seine bemerkenswerte Gestaltung Grund genug, ihn als höchst zeitgenössische Architektur zu würdigen.

Dans le contexte de l'Année polaire internationale 2007–09, la Fondation polaire internationale a été commissionnée par le gouvernement belge pour concevoir et construire une nouvelle station de recherche en Antarctique. La FPI a créé une base « zéro émission de carbone » qui fonctionne à partir d'énergies renouvelables, et met en œuvre des protocoles d'efficacité énergétique avancés. La station se trouve à 1300 mètres d'altitude, à 684 km de la station japonaise Syowa et 431 km de la station russe de Novolazarevskaja. Elle doit accueillir un maximum de vingt-cinq personnes et sa durée de vie prévue est de vingt-cinq ans. La température extérieure varie au long de l'année entre –5 et –50°C, les vents pouvant atteindre 250 km/h. La station a été conçue pour mener des recherches sur les glaciers des monts Sør Rondane, la côte et le plateau antarctique. Si cette structure n'est pas vraiment représentative des cas illustrés dans cet ouvrage, puisque sa forme et sa nature sont d'abord dictées par des considérations de survie et de recherche, sa remarquable conception permet de la classer valablement parmi les réalisations de l'architecture contemporaine.

Arrays of solar panels provide electrical power to the building, as seen in the image above.

Hier zu sehen die große Anzahl von Photovoltaikpanelen, die das Gebäude mit Strom versorgen.

Des batteries de panneaux solaires alimentent la station en électricité (ci-dessus).

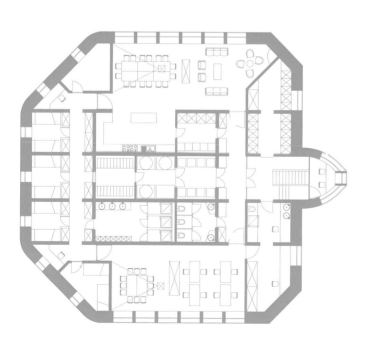

A main floor plan and a view of the
icy landscape taken from the roof of
the structure (above).

Links ein Raumverteilungsplan des
Hauptgeschosses, oben ein vom Dach
aus aufgenommenes Foto mit Blick in
die eisige Landschaft.

Plan du niveau principal et vue du
paysage désert et glacé prise du toit
du bâtiment.

IROJE KHM ARCHITECTS

IROJE KHM Architects
1805 Gardentower Building
98–78 Unni-dong, Jongro-gu
Seoul 110–795
South Korea

Tel: +82 2 766 1928
Fax: +82 2 766 1929
E-mail: iroman@unitel.co.kr
Web: www.irojekhm.com

HyoMan Kim is the principal of **IROJE KHM**. He graduated from the Department of Architecture of DanKook University (Seoul, 1978). Since 2004, he has been a Professor at the Graduate School of Architecture KyongGi University (Seoul) and at the Department of Architecture of DanKook University (now located in Yongin). His work includes Purple Whale (Paju Book City, Gyeonggi-do, 2008); Island House (Gapyung-gun, Gyeonggi-do, 2007–09, published here); Purple Hill House (Youngin, Gyeonggi-do, 2009); and BuYeonDang House (SungNam, Gyeonggi-do, 2009), all in South Korea. Ongoing work includes the PyeongChang Institute for Buddhism (PyeongChang-Gun, GangWonDo, 2009–) and Green Hill Village (Seoul, 2009–). "Concept is an ideal and abstract thought," says HyoMan Kim. "The concept does not hold value until the concept is embodied into a concrete building in reality."

HyoMan Kim, Direktor von **IROJE KHM**, schloss sein Studium 1978 an der Fakultät für Architektur der DanKook University in Seoul ab. Seit 2004 ist er Professor im Aufbaustudiengang Architektur der KyongGi University (Seoul) sowie an der Fakultät für Architektur der DanKook University (inzwischen in Yongin). Zu seinen Projekten zählen Purple Whale (Paju Book City, Gyeonggi-do, 2008), Island House (Gapyung-gun, Gyeonggi-do, 2007–09, hier vorgestellt), Purple Hill House (Youngin, Gyeonggi-do, 2009) und BuYeonDang House (SungNam, Gyeonggi-do, 2009), alle in Südkorea. Aktuelle Projekte sind u.a. das PyeongChang-Institut für Buddhismus (PyeongChangGun, GangWonDo, 2009–) sowie Green Hill Village (Seoul, 2009–). „Ein Konzept ist ein Ideal, eine abstrakte Idee", so HyoMan Kim. „Ein Konzept ist wertlos, solange es nicht tatsächlich als reales Bauwerk umgesetzt wurde."

Hyo Man Kim, diplômé du département d'architecture de l'Université Dankook (Séoul, Corée du Sud, 1978), dirige l'agence **IROJE KHM**. Depuis 2004, il est professeur à l'École supérieure d'architecture de l'Université Kyonggi à Séoul et au département d'architecture de l'Université Dankook (aujourd'hui relocalisée à Yongin). Parmi ses réalisations, toutes en Corée du Sud, figurent la Baleine pourpre (Purple Whale, Paju Book, Gyeonggi-do, 2008) ; la Maison île (Island House, Gapyung-gun, Gyeonggi-do, 2007–09, publiée ici) ; la Maison de la colline pourpre (Purple Hill House, Youngin, Gyeonggi-do, 2009) et la Maison BuYeonDang (Sungnam, Gyeonggi-do, 2009). Il travaille actuellement sur les projets de l'Institut du bouddhisme de PyeongChang (PyeongChang-Gun, GangWon-Do, 2009–) et le Village de la colline verte (Green Hill Village, Séoul, 2009–). « Le concept est un idéal, une pensée abstraite », écrit Hyo Man Kim. « Le concept n'a pas de valeur tant qu'il n'est pas incarné dans une construction concrète, issue de la réalité. »

ISLAND HOUSE

Gapyung-gun, Gyeonggi-do, South Korea, 2007–09

Area: 337 m². Client: Sung Hun Lee. Cost: not disclosed

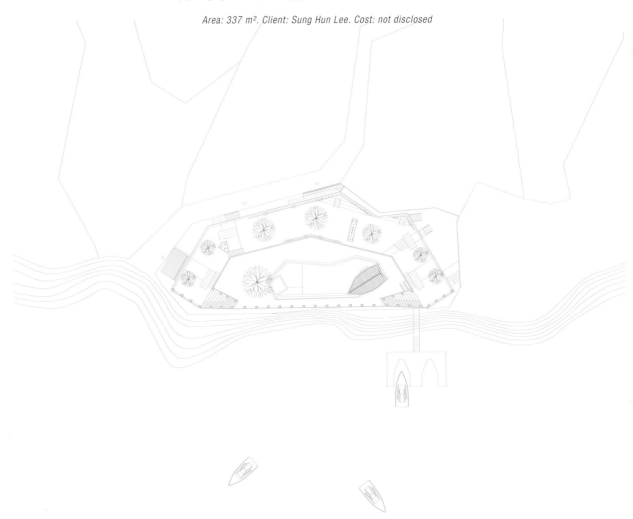

This surprising house is described by the architect in rather poetic terms: "I recognized this site, where the house is now floating on a river confronted with a graceful landscape, as a part of nature. From that point on, I started to visualize 'architectural nature' as a place of recreation." He sought a maximum efficiency of land use on this 955-square-meter site. The house has a gross floor area of 728 square meters. A water-filled courtyard is imagined as a central recreational space that creates a sense of communication between architecture and nature. A stepped roof garden links to the bedrooms on the upper floor, and to both sides of the inner court, where a swimming pool is located. All of the rooms are laid out with a view of the natural setting and the architect continuously emphasizes the connections between his design, the site, and nature, be it exterior or artificially continued into the residence in the courtyard and roof.

Der Architekt beschreibt das erstaunliche Haus auf geradezu poetische Weise: „Ich verstand das Grundstück, auf dem das Haus vis-à-vis der lieblichen Landschaft über dem Fluss schwebt, als Teil der Natur. Von diesem Moment an entstand vor meinem inneren Auge durch die ‚architektonische Beschaffenheit', ein Ort der Erholung." Das 955 m² große Grundstück wurde maximal ausgenutzt. Das Haus selbst hat eine Gesamtgrundfläche von 728 m². Ein Innenhof mit einem Pool ist zentraler Ort der Erholung und wirkt wie ein Zwiegespräch zwischen Architektur und Natur. Ein treppenförmiger Dachgarten verbindet die Schlafzimmer mit dem Obergeschoss, sowie beidseitig mit dem Innenhof mit Pool. Alle Zimmer haben Blick in die umgebende Natur. Immer wieder betont der Architekt die Verknüpfungen zwischen Entwurf, Grundstück und Natur – ob nun im Außenraum oder künstlich fortgesetzt im Haus, im Hof und auf dem Dach.

Cette maison étonnante est présentée par l'architecte en termes assez poétiques : « Pour moi, le site où la maison se trouve, flottant sur la rivière au sein d'un paysage plein de grâce, est une partie de la nature. Parti de là, j'ai commencé à visualiser "nature architecturale" qui serait un lieu de récréation. » Hyo Man Kim a cherché à utiliser au maximum les 955 mètres carrés du terrain, dont la maison occupe 728 mètres carrés. La cour-bassin est un lieu de détente central qui crée une communication entre l'architecture et la nature. Le jardin en escalier sur le toit fait lien avec les chambres de l'étage supérieur et entre les deux côtés de la cour intérieure où est installée une piscine. Toutes les chambres disposent de vues sur le cadre naturel, et l'architecte a particulièrement mis en valeur les connexions entre la maison, le terrain et la nature, qu'elles soient réelles ou artificielles, comme, par exemple, dans le traitement de la cour et du toit.

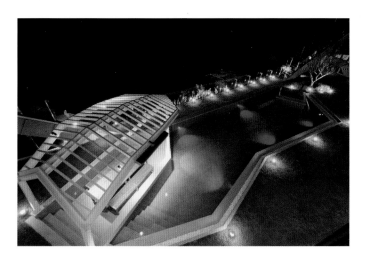

The unusual configuration and disposition of the house corresponds to its site, as seen in the site plan on the left page.

Wie der Grundstücksplan auf der gegenüberliegenden Seite zeigt, erklärt sich der ungewöhnliche Aufbau und Charakter des Hauses aus seiner exakten Anpassung die Inselform.

La configuration et la situation curieuses de la maison correspondent à son site très particulier, comme le montre le plan de la page de gauche.

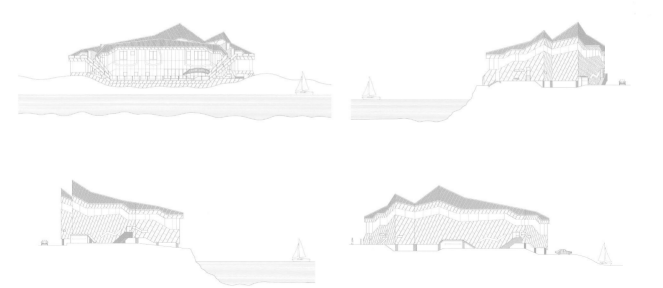

Drawings of the house emphasize its topographical design. Interior spaces continue the same forms and offer views out to a pool and the water beyond.

Die Zeichnungen verdeutlichen die Anpassung des Entwurfs an die Topografie. In den Innenräumen – mit Blick auf Pool und Fluss – setzt sich die „topografische" Gestaltung fort.

Ces dessins témoignent de l'importance de la topographie dans le projet. Les volumes intérieurs sont la continuation de ces formes. Ils offrent des vues sur une piscine et la rivière.

JUNYA ISHIGAMI

junya.ishigami+associates
1–2–6–5F Suido
Bunkyo-ku
Tokyo 112–0005
Japan

Tel: +81 3 5840 9199
Fax: +81 3 5840 9299
E-mail: ii@jnyi.jp
Web: www.jnyi.jp

JUNYA ISHIGAMI was born in Kanagawa, Japan, in 1974. He studied at the Tokyo National University of Fine Arts and Music in the Architecture Department, graduating in 2000. He worked in the office of Kazuyo Sejima & Associates (now SANAA) from 2000 to 2004, establishing Junya Ishigami + Associates in 2004. Given his age, his list of projects is not long, but he has designed a number of tables, including one 9.5 meters long and 3 millimeters thick made of prestressed steel, and a project for the Hotel Kaiyo and housing (2007). Aside from the Kanagawa Institute of Technology KAIT workshop (Japan, 2007–08), he has designed a New York store for Yohji Yamamoto (USA, 2008) in the so-called Meatpacking District, and participated in the 2008 Venice Architecture Biennale (Greenhouses for the Japanese Pavilion, Venice, Italy, published here). Despite his limited number of completed works Junya Ishigami has emerged as one of the more significant young Japanese architects.

JUNYA ISHIGAMI wurde 1974 in Kanagawa, Japan, geboren. Er studierte an der Fakultät für Architektur der Staatlichen Kunst- und Musikhochschule Tokio, wo er 2000 seinen Abschluss machte. Zwischen 2000 und 2004 arbeitete er für Kazuyo Sejima & Associates (inzwischen SANAA) und gründete 2004 sein Büro Junya Ishigami + Associates. Angesichts seines Alters ist seine Projektliste nicht lang, doch hat Ishigami bereits mehrere Tische entworfen, darunter den 9,5 m langen „Table" aus 3 mm starkem Spannstahl, sowie ein Projekt für die Kaiyo Hotel- und Wohnanlage (2007). Neben dem Werkstattgebäude für das Kanagawa Institute of Technology (KAIT; Japan, 2007–08) gestaltete er einen Yohji Yamamoto Store im New Yorker Meatpacking District (2008) und war 2008 auf der Architektur-Biennale in Venedig vertreten (Gewächshäuser für den japanischen Pavillon, Venedig, hier vorgestellt). Trotz der geringen Anzahl gebauter Projekte, hat sich Junya Ishigami als einer der maßgeblichen jungen japanischen Architekten etabliert.

JUNYA ISHIGAMI, né en 1974 à Kanagawa au Japon, a étudié au département d'architecture de l'Université nationale des beaux-arts et de musique de Tokyo, dont il est sorti diplômé en 2000. Il a travaillé chez Kazuyo Sejima & Associates (aujourd'hui SANAA) de 2000 à 2004, et a créé l'agence Junya Ishigami + Associates en 2004. Son jeune âge explique que sa liste de réalisations ne soit pas très longue, mais il a dessiné un certain nombre de tables, dont une de 9,5 mètres de long et 3 millimètres d'épaisseur en acier précontraint (Table), et un projet pour l'hôtel Kaiyo et des logements (2007). En dehors d'installations pour l'Institut de technologie Kanagawa (2007–08), il a conçu le magasin new-yorkais du couturier japonais Yohji Yamamoto (2008) dans le quartier du Meatpacking. Il a participé à la Biennale d'architecture de Venise en 2008 (serres pour le pavillon japonais, publiées ici). Malgré ce nombre limité de projets achevés, Ishigami apparaît comme l'un des jeunes architectes japonais les plus prometteurs.

GREENHOUSES, JAPANESE PAVILION

Venice Architecture Biennale, Venice, Italy, 2008

Area: 20 m², 6 m², 11 m², 6 m². Client: The Japan Foundation. Cost: not disclosed
Collaboration: Taro Igarashi (Commissioner), Hideaki Ohba (Botanist),
Jun Sato (Structural Engineer)

For the 2008 Venice Architecture Biennale, Junya Ishigami designed a series of small glass greenhouses that he set around the building in the *giardini*. Each of the greenhouses was conceived as an actual building, pushing the limits of structural soundness thanks to sophisticated calculations. His intention was to suggest "the future possibilities of architecture." Ishigami also refers to Joseph Paxton's Crystal Palace at the Great Exhibition in London (1851), which took the form of a greenhouse. Ishigami worked with the botanist Hideaki Ohba, who carefully selected varieties of plants that at first seemed to be native to the environment, but in fact represent a "slight disturbance in the landscape of the park." Wooden furniture was placed in the garden, suggesting the ambiguity or more precisely "simultaneity" of interior and exterior space, while the inside of the Pavilion itself was essentially empty except for delicate drawings on the white walls.

Für die Architektur-Biennale 2008 entwarf Junya Ishigami eine Reihe kleinerer Gewächshäuser, die er rund um den Pavillon in den Giardini platzierte. Jedes Gewächshaus war als eigenständiger Bau konzipiert und dank ausgeklügelter Berechnungen eben gerade in der Lage stabil aufrecht zu stehen. Seine Absicht war es, „künftige Möglichkeiten der Architektur" aufzuzeigen. Zugleich nimmt Ishigami auf Joseph Paxtons Kristallpalast Bezug, der 1851 zur Londoner Weltausstellung erbaut worden und ebenfalls wie ein Gewächshaus angelegt war. Ishigami arbeitete mit dem Botaniker Hideaki Ohba, der sorgsam Pflanzen auswählte, die zunächst einheimisch wirkten, tatsächlich aber „eine subtile Störung der Parklandschaft" darstellten. Außerdem wurden im Garten Holzmöbel aufgestellt, eine Anspielung auf die Mehrdeutigkeit, oder vielmehr „Simultaneität", von Innen- und Außenraum. Die Innenräume des Pavillons selbst waren bis auf wenige zarte Zeichnungen an den weißen Wänden so gut wie leer.

Junya Ishigami a conçu pour la Biennale de Venise 2008 une série de petites serres en verre disposées autour du pavillon japonais dans les Giardini. Chacune a été conçue comme une vraie construction, dont la stabilité a fait l'objet de calculs sophistiqués. Son intention était de suggérer « les possibilités futures de l'architecture ». Ishigami se réfère également au Crystal Palace construit par Joseph Paxton pour la grande exposition de Londres (1851), qui était aussi en forme de serre. Il a travaillé avec le botaniste Hideaki Ohba qui a sélectionné méticuleusement différentes plantes apparemment natives du lieu, mais qui, en fait, représentent un « léger dérangement dans le paysage du parc ». Le mobilier de bois a été disposé dans les jardins pour suggérer une ambiguïté, ou plus précisément une « simultanéité », entre l'intérieur et l'extérieur, tandis que l'intérieur du pavillon lui-même reste essentiellement vide, à part quelques délicats dessins sur ses murs blancs.

At first glance, the vegetation contained in Ishigami's greenhouses appears to be indigenous, but on closer examination reveals itself to be more exotic.

Die auf den ersten Blick einheimisch wirkenden Pflanzen in Ishigamis Gewächshäusern erweisen sich bei näherem Hinsehen als exotischere Gattungen.

À première vue, la végétation contenue dans les serres d'Ishigami semble indigène, mais elle est en fait plutôt exotique.

The inside space almost looks white in these images, but the walls are covered with delicate drawings. Below, a drawing of the outdoor structures in their natural setting.

Auch im Innern des Pavillons, der auf den Fotos fast weiß wirkt, erkennt man erst auf den zweiten Blick die ungemein feinen Wandzeichnungen. Unten eine Zeichnung der von Bäumen umstandenen Gewächshäuser.

Bien que l'espace intérieur semble presque blanc sur ces reproductions, les murs sont en fait recouverts de délicats dessins. Ci-dessous, une représentation des serres dans leur cadre naturel.

TOYO ITO

Toyo Ito & Associates, Architects
1–19–4 Shibuya, Shibuya-ku
Tokyo 150–0002
Japan

Tel: +81 33 409 58 22
Fax: +81 33 409 59 69

Born in 1941 in Seoul, South Korea, **TOYO ITO** graduated from the University of Tokyo in 1965 and worked in the office of Kiyonori Kikutake until 1969. He created his own office, Urban Robot (URBOT), in Tokyo in 1971, assuming the name of Toyo Ito & Associates, Architects in 1979. He was awarded the Golden Lion for Lifetime Achievement at the 8th International Venice Architecture Biennale in 2002 and the RIBA Gold Medal in 2006. His completed work includes the Silver Hut (Nakano, Tokyo, 1982–84); Tower of the Winds (Yokohama, Kanagawa, 1986); Yatsushiro Municipal Museum (Yatsushiro, Kumamoto, 1988–91); and the Elderly People's Home (1992–94) and Fire Station (1992–95), both located in the same city on the island of Kyushu. Other projects include his Nagaoka Lyric Hall (Nagaoka, Niigata, 1993–96); Odate Jukai Dome Park (Odate, 1993–97); and Ota-ku Resort Complex (Tobu-cho, Chiisagata-gun, Nagano, 1995–98). One of his most successful and widely published projects, the Sendai Mediatheque, in Sendai, was completed in 2001, while in 2002 he designed a temporary Pavilion for the Serpentine Gallery in London (UK). More recently, he has completed TOD'S Omotesando Building (Shibuya-ku, Tokyo, 2003–04); Island City Central Park Grin Grin (Fukuoka, Fukuoka, 2004–05); Tama Art University Library (Hachioji City, Tokyo, 2005–07); Za-Koenji Public Theater (Tokyo, 2006–08, published here); and the Main Stadium for the World Games 2009 (Kaohsiung, Taiwan, 2006–09), all in Japan unless stated otherwise. Toyo Ito was the curator of the Sumika Project (Utsunomiya, Tochigi Prefecture, Japan, 2008), a project he realized with architects Terunobu Fujimori, Sou Fujimoto, and Taira Nishizawa.

TOYO ITO wurde 1941 in Seoul, Korea, geboren und schloss sein Studium 1965 an der Universität Tokio ab. Bis 1969 arbeitete er im Büro von Kiyonori Kikutake. Sein eigenes Büro Urban Robot (URBOT) gründete er 1971 in Tokio, seit 1979 firmiert er unter dem Namen Toyo Ito & Associates, Architects. 2002 wurde er auf der 8. Architektur-Biennale in Venedig mit dem Goldenen Löwen für sein Lebenswerk ausgezeichnet, 2006 mit der RIBA-Goldmedaille. Zu seinen realisierten Bauten zählen Silver Hut (Nakano, Tokio, 1982–84), Tower of the Winds (Yokohama, Kanagawa, 1986), das Stadtmuseum Yatsushiro (Yatsushiro, Kumamoto, 1988–91), sowie ein Altenheim (1992–94) und eine Feuerwache (1992–95), beide in derselben Stadt auf der Insel Kyushu. Weitere Projekte sind die Nagaoka Lyric Hall (Nagaoka, Niigata, 1993–96), sein Odate Jukai Dome Park (Odate, 1993–97) und der Ota-ku Resort (Tobu-cho, Chiisagata-gun, Nagano, 1995–98), alle in Japan. Eines seiner bekanntesten und meistpublizierten Projekte, die Mediathek in Sendai, konnte 2001 fertiggestellt werden. 2002 entwarf er einen temporären Pavillon für die Serpentine Gallery in London. In jüngster Zeit realisierte er das Omotesando Building für TOD'S (Shibuya-ku, Tokio, 2003–04), den Island City Hauptpark Grin Grin (Fukuoka, Fukuoka, 2004–05), die Universitätsbibliothek der Tama Art University (Hachioji City, Tokio, 2005–07), das Za-Koenji Public Theater (Tokio, 2006–08, hier vorgestellt) sowie die Sportarena für die World Games 2009 (Kaohsiung, Taiwan, 2006–09), alle in Japan, sofern nicht anders angegeben. Darüber hinaus kuratierte Toyo Ito das Sumika-Projekt (Utsunomiya, Tochigi, Japan, 2008), ein Gemeinschaftsprojekt mit den Architekten Terunobu Fujimori, Sou Fujimoto und Taira Nishizawa.

Né en 1941 à Séoul (Corée du Sud), **TOYO ITO**, diplômé de l'Université de Tokyo en 1965, a commencé par travailler chez Kiyonori Kikutake jusqu'en 1969. Il a fondé sa propre agence, Urban Robot (URBOT), à Tokyo en 1971, qui a pris le nom de Toyo Ito & Associates, Architects en 1979. Il a reçu la médaille d'or du RIBA en 2006. Parmi ses œuvres réalisées : la Résidence de la hutte argentée (Silver Hut Residence, Nakano, Tokyo, 1984) ; la tour des vents (Tower of the Winds, Yokohama, Kanagawa, 1986) ; le musée municipal de Yatsushiro (Yatsushiro, Kumamoto, 1989–91) ; un foyer pour personnes âgées (1992–94) et un centre de secours (1992–95), tous deux dans une ville de l'île de Kyushu. D'autres projets incluent la salle de concerts lyriques de Nagaoka (Nagaoka, Niigata, 1993–96) ; le parc du Dôme de Jukai (Odate, 1993–97) et le complexe touristique d'Ota-ku (Tobu-cho, Chiisagata-gun, Nagano, 1995–98). L'un de ses projets les plus réussis et les plus publiés, la médiathèque de Sendaï, a été achevé en 2001. Il a conçu un pavillon temporaire pour la Galerie Serpentine à Londres (2002), et a reçu le Lion d'or pour l'ensemble de sa carrière à la VIIIe Biennale internationale d'architecture à Venise la même année. Plus récemment, il a construit l'immeuble TOD'S à Omotesando (Shibuya-ku, Tokyo, 2002–04) ; le Island City Central Park Grin Grin (Fukuoka, Fukuoka, 2004–05) ; la bibliothèque de l'université d'art Tama (Hachioji City, Tokyo, 2005–07) ; le théâtre Za-Koenji (Tokyo, 2006–08, publié ici) et le stade principal des Jeux mondiaux de 2009 (Kaohsiung, Taiwan, 2006–09). Toyo Ito est le commissaire du projet Sumika (Utsunomiya, préfecture de Tochigi, Japon, 2008), réalisé avec les architectes Terunobu Fujimori, Sou Fujimoto et Taira Nishizawa.

ZA-KOENJI PUBLIC THEATER

Tokyo, Japan, 2006–08

Address: 2–1–2 Koenji-Kita, Suginami-ku, Tokyo 166–0002, Japan, +81 3 3223 7500/7300, www.za-koenji.jp
Area: 4977 m². Client: Suginami-ku. Cost: not disclosed

This public theater replaced the former Koenji Hall, located five minutes' walk from the JR Koenji Station in Tokyo. The architect decided on a closed form that he compares to a "tent cabin." The walls and roof are made with steel-plate reinforced concrete—a solution that allows for substantial strength despite the thinness of the surfaces. The roof is made up of five elliptic cones and two cylinders, resulting from careful calculations related to the program of the theater and local zoning restrictions. A floating structural system has been created—with each floor slab, wall, and ceiling insulated from the main structural frame—for acoustic reasons, given the fact that there are several performance spaces in the building. The main small theater, cafeteria, and office are located above grade, while the rest of the program is set in the basement levels.

Der öffentliche Theaterbau ersetzte die ehemalige Koenji Hall in Tokio, nur fünf Gehminuten von der U-Bahn-Station JR Koenji entfernt. Der Architekt entschied sich für eine geschlossene Form, die er mit einer „zeltartigen Hütte" vergleicht. Wände und Dach wurden aus einem Verbund aus Beton und Stahlblech gefertigt – eine Lösung, die trotz dünnwandiger Flächen hohe Stabilität gewährleistet. Das Dach wurde aus fünf elliptischen Kegeln und zwei Zylindern gestaltet, eine Form, die sich aus sorgfältigen Berechnungen ergab, die das bauliche Programm des Theaters und die örtlichen Bebauungspläne berücksichtigten. Da mehrere Bühnen im Gebäude untergebracht sind, wurde aus akustischen Gründen eine „schwimmende Konstruktion" realisiert – jede Bodenplatte, Wand und Decke wurde separat vom Haupttragwerk gedämmt. Die kleine Hauptbühne sowie Cafeteria und Büros sind in den oberen Ebenen untergebracht, das übrige Programm in den Untergeschossen.

Ce théâtre a pris la place de l'ancien Koenji Hall, à cinq minutes de marche de la gare JR Koenji à Tokyo. L'architecte a opté pour une forme fermée qu'il compare à une « tente ». Les murs et la toiture sont en béton renforcé de tôle d'acier, solution qui permet des portées importantes malgré la minceur des plans. La toiture se compose de cinq cônes elliptiques et de deux cylindres, dessinés à partir de calculs poussés liés au programme du client et à la réglementation locale de la construction. Pour des raisons d'acoustique, puisque plusieurs lieux de spectacles sont regroupés dans ce bâtiment, chaque dalle du sol, les murs et le plafond sont indépendants de l'ossature principale grâce à un système structurel flottant. La salle principale, la cafétéria et les bureaux sont situés au-dessus du sol, le reste du programme est installé dans les sous-sols.

The dark, irregular form of the theater stands out from its urban environment, and yet seems somehow to be related to the neighboring architecture.

So deutlich sich die dunkle, unregelmäßige Gestalt des Theaters von seiner städtischen Umgebung abhebt, scheint sie doch auf eine Art mit der Bebauung der Nachbargrundstücke verwandt zu sein.

Les formes sombres et irrégulières du théâtre se détachent de son environnement urbain, tout en entretenant un certain rapport avec l'architecture des immeubles voisins.

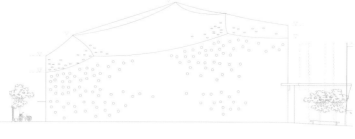

Toyo Ito was able to continue his work inside the theater, giving a real continuity to the architecture, a rare event in contemporary design.

Da Toyo Ito die Möglichkeit hatte, seine Arbeit im Innern des Theaters fortzusetzen – eine Seltenheit bei derartigen Projekten –, entstand eine durchweg homogene Architektur.

Toyo Ito a poursuivi son travail formel à l'intérieur du théâtre dans une continuité concrète avec l'architecture, pratique assez rare aujourd'hui.

Toyo Ito's presence is felt throughout
the theater. His mark is sometimes
relatively light, as in the image above,
yet the round lights and low, colorful
abstract furniture are sufficient to
demonstrate his mastery of the
space.

Toyo Itos Gegenwart ist in diesem
Theater förmlich zu spüren.
Manchmal hinterlässt er nur dezente
Spuren (wie im Bild oben zu sehen),
aber selbst die runden Leuchten
sowie niedrige, farbige abstrakte
Möbel genügen, um seinen meister-
haften Umgang mit dem Raum zu
verdeutlichen.

L'intervention de Toyo Ito se perçoit
dans la totalité du bâtiment. Sa marque est parfois relativement discrète,
comme dans l'image ci-dessus, mais
les luminaires en pastille et le
mobilier bas, minimaliste et coloré
démontrent sa maîtrise de l'espace.

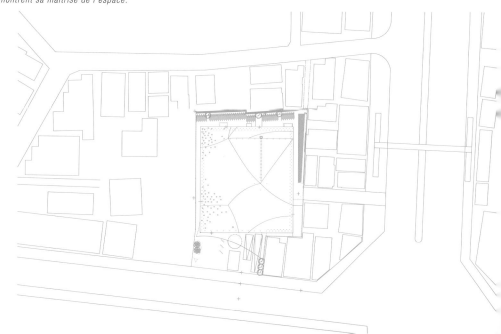

JAMES CORNER FIELD OPERATIONS / DILLER SCOFIDIO + RENFRO

James Corner Field Operations
475 10th Avenue, 10th Floor, New York, NY 10018, USA
Tel: +1 212 433 1450 / Fax: +1 212 433 1451
E-mail: info@fieldoperations.net / Web: www.fieldoperations.net

Diller Scofidio + Renfro
601 West 26th Street, Suite 1815, New York, NY 10001, USA
Tel: +1 212 260 7971 / Fax: +1 212 260 7924
E-mail: disco@dsrny.com / Web: www.dsrny.com

JAMES CORNER FIELD OPERATIONS is a landscape architecture and urban design firm based in New York. James Corner is a registered landscape architect and urban designer, and founder and Director of James Corner Field Operations, where he oversees the production of all design projects in the office. He is also Chair of and Professor in the Department of Landscape Architecture at the University of Pennsylvania School of Design. He was educated at Manchester Metropolitan University, UK (B.A. in landscape architecture with first class honors) and the University of Pennsylvania (M.L.A/U.D.). Lisa Tziona Switkin is an Associate Principal at James Corner Field Operations with a B.A. in Urban Planning from the University of Illinois and an M.L.A. from the University of Pennsylvania. Nahyun Hwang is a Senior Associate at James Corner Field Operations with a B.Arch from Yonsei University, Seoul, South Korea, and an M.Arch from Harvard University GSD. **DILLER SCOFIDIO + RENFRO** is an interdisciplinary firm based in New York. Elizabeth Diller is Professor of Architecture at Princeton University; Ricardo Scofidio is Professor Emeritus of Architecture at the Cooper Union in New York; and Charles Renfro is a Visiting Professor at Parsons the New School for Design. According to their own description: "The team is primarily involved in thematically driven experimental works that take the form of architectural commissions, temporary installations and permanent site-specific installations, multimedia theater, electronic media, and print." Matthew Johnson, a Senior Associate at DS+R, is a native of Michigan. He is a graduate of the University of Michigan and holds an M.Arch from Princeton University.

JAMES CORNER FIELD OPERATIONS ist ein Büro für Landschaftsarchitektur und Stadtplanung mit Sitz in New York. James Corner ist Landschaftsarchitekt und Stadtplaner sowie Gründer und Direktor von James Corner Field Operations, wo er leitend sämtliche Entwurfsprojekte des Büros betreut. Zudem war er Dekan und Professor an der Fakultät für Landschaftsarchitektur am Designinstitut der University of Pennsylvania. Seine Ausbildung absolvierte er an der Manchester Metropolitan University, Großbritannien (B.A. in Landschaftsarchitektur, mit Auszeichnung) und der University of Pennsylvania (Master in Landschaftsarchitektur und Stadtplanung). Lisa Tziona Switkin ist geschäftsführende Partnerin bei James Corner Field Operations und schloss ihr Studium an der University of Illinois mit einem B.A. in Stadtplanung ab, dem ein Master in Landschaftsarchitektur an der University of Pennsylvania folgte. Nahyun Hwang ist Seniorpartner bei James Corner Field Operations und schloss sein Studium mit einem B.Arch an der Yonsei University, Seoul, sowie einem M.Arch am Harvard University GSD ab. **DILLER SCOFIDIO + RENFRO** ist ein interdisziplinäres Büro mit Sitz in New York. Elizabeth Diller ist Professorin für Architektur in Princeton, Ricardo Scofidio Professor Emeritus für Architektur an der Cooper Union in New York und Charles Renfro Gastprofessor am Parsons The New School for Design. Sie schreiben: „Das Team beschäftigt sich in erster Linie mit thematisch ausgerichteten, experimentellen Projekten, wobei es sich um architektonische Aufträge, temporäre Installationen und permanente, ortsspezifische Installationen handeln kann, um Multimedia-Theater, elektronische Medien und Publikationen." Matthew Johnson, einer der Seniorpartner bei DS+R, kommt aus Michigan. Er schloss sein Studium an der University of Michigan ab und absolvierte seinen M.Arch in Princeton.

JAMES CORNER FIELD OPERATIONS est une agence d'urbanisme et d'architecture du paysage basée à New York. James Corner est architecte paysagiste, urbaniste, et dirige son agence et la conception de tous les projets. Il est également président et professeur du département d'architecture du paysage à l'École de conception de l'Université de Pennsylvanie. Il a fait ses études à la Manchester Metropolitan University au Royaume-Uni (B. A. en architecture du paysage, avec honneurs de première classe) et à l'Université de Pennsylvanie (M. L. A/U. D.). Lisa Tziona Switkin est directrice associée de James Corner Field Operations, B. A. en urbanisme de l'Université de l'Illinois et M. L. A. de l'Université de Pennsylvanie. Nahyun Hwang est associé senior chez James Corner Field Operations, B. Arch de l'Université Yonsei à Séoul, et M. Arch d'Harvard University GSD. **DILLER SCOFIDIO + RENFRO** est une agence multidisciplinaire basée à New York. Elizabeth Diller est professeur d'architecture à Princeton University, Ricardo Scofidio est professeur émérite d'architecture à Cooper Union à New York, et Charles Renfro est professeur invité à Parsons The New School for Design. Selon leur descriptif : « L'équipe travaille essentiellement sur des recherches thématiques expérimentales qui peuvent prendre la forme de commandes architecturales, d'installations temporaires, d'installations permanentes adaptées au site, de théâtres multimédia, de médias électroniques et d'édition. » Matthew Johnson, associé senior chez DS+R, né dans le Michigan, est diplômé de l'Université du Michigan. Il est également M. Arch de Princeton University.

THE HIGH LINE

New York, New York, USA, 2006–09 (Section 1)

Address: Gansevoort Street, New York, NY, USA, +1 212 500 6035, www.thehighline.org
Area: 1.1 hectares. Client: City of New York, Friends of the High Line. Cost: $86.2 million (Section 1)
Collaboration: Nahyun Hwang (Senior Associate JCFO), Matthew Johnson (Senior Associate DS+R),
Piet Oudlof (Planting)

THE HIGH LINE is an unused elevated railway running about 2.5 kilometers from West 34th Street near the Jacob Javits Convention Center in New York to Gansevoort Street in the Meatpacking District on Manhattan's Lower West Side. The West Side Improvement Project, including the High Line, built because of the number of accidents involving trains serving Manhattan's docks, was put into effect in 1929. Intended to avoid the negative effects of subway lines over crowded streets, the High Line cuts through the center of city blocks. Increasing truck traffic led to the demolition of parts of the High Line in the 1960s and a halt to train operations in 1980. Despite efforts to demolish the remaining structure to allow new construction, a good part of the High Line survived and a group called Friends of the High Line, created in 1999, eventually convinced authorities to renovate it rather than to allow its destruction. The landscape architects James Corner Field Operations have participated in a collective project for the High Line with Diller Scofidio + Renfro and a number of other parties to renovate and bring new life to a disused part of the city. As they say: "Inspired by the melancholic, unruly beauty of the High Line, where nature has reclaimed a once vital piece of urban infrastructure, the team retools this industrial conveyance into a post-industrial instrument of leisure reflection about the very categories of 'nature' and 'culture' in our time. By changing the rules of engagement between plant life and pedestrians, our strategy of agri-tecture combines organic and building materials into a blend of changing proportions that accommodate the wild, the cultivated, the intimate, and the hyper-social." The U.S. Senate voted a credit of $18 million for the project in July 2005.

THE HIGH LINE ist eine rund 2,5 km lange, nicht mehr genutzte Hochbahntrasse in New York. Sie verläuft zwischen West 34th Street, unweit des Jacob Javits Convention Center, und Gansevoort Street im Meatpacking District in der Lower Westside von Manhattan. Bereits 1929 war das West Side Improvement Project in Kraft getreten, in dessen Zuge die High Line gebaut wurde. Die Hochbahntrasse war aufgrund zahlreicher Unfälle erforderlich geworden, die durch den damals noch ebenerdigen Bahnverkehr an den Docks verursacht wurden. Um die Nachteile der Trassenführung über stark befahrene Straßen zu umgehen, wurde die High Line mitten durch Häuserblocks hindurchgeführt. Die Zunahme des LKW-Verkehrs in den 1960er-Jahren führte zum Abriss von Teilabschnitten der High Line und 1980 schließlich zur vollständigen Stilllegung des Bahnverkehrs. Obwohl manche den Abriss des gesamten Restabschnitts forderten, um Bauflächen zu erschließen, blieb ein Großteil der High Line erhalten. Die 1999 gegründete Initiative „Friends of the High Line" überzeugte die Behörden schließlich den Bau zu sanieren, statt ihn abzureißen. Neben den Landschaftsarchitekten James Corner Field Operations und Diller Scofidio + Renfro beteiligten sich weitere Akteure am kollektiven Projekt „High Line", das diesen ungenutzten Teil der Stadt sanieren und neu beleben will: „Inspiriert von der melancholischen, unbändigen Schönheit der High Line, an der sich die Natur ein ehemals unverzichtbares Stück urbaner Infrastruktur zurückerobert hat, rüstet das Team den industriellen Verkehrsweg um. Er wird zum postindustriellen Vehikel des Nachdenkens über Freizeitgestaltung und die Begriffe ‚Natur' und ‚Freizeit' in unserer Zeit. Unsere ‚Agri-Tektur'-Strategie definiert neue Regeln für die Interaktion von Vegetation und Fußgängern, kombiniert organisches Material mit Baumaterialien und gestaltet so abwechslungsreiche Proportionen, in denen Wildes, Kultiviertes, Intimes und Hypersoziales nebeneinander existiert." Der US-Senat bewilligte 2005 einen Kredit von 18 Millionen Dollar für das Projekt.

THE HIGH LINE est une ligne suspendue de chemin de fer urbain new-yorkais abandonnée, qui court sur 2,5 km environ entre la 34e rue Ouest près du Jacob Javits Convention Center jusqu'à Gansevoort Street, dans le quartier du Meatpacking du Lower West Side à Manhattan. Le « West Side Improvement Project », qui comprend la High Line, avait été lancé en 1929 pour diminuer le nombre d'accidents dus aux trains desservant les docks de Manhattan. Évitant les aspects négatifs des lignes souterraines, cette ligne était surélevée et passait même au centre de certains *blocks*. L'augmentation du nombre des camions a conduit à démolir certaines parties de la High Line dans les années 1960, puis à la désaffecter en 1980. Malgré les efforts déployés pour détruire ce qui en restait, une bonne partie subsistait encore lorsqu'un groupe appelé les « Amis de la High Line », créé en 1999, réussit à convaincre les autorités de préférer la rénovation à la destruction. Les architectes paysagistes de James Corner Field Operations ont participé à ce projet collectif en collaboration avec Diller Scofidio + Renfro et un certain nombre d'autres intervenants pour donner une nouvelle vie à cet élément urbain abandonné. « Inspirée par la beauté mélancolique et dérangeante de la High Line, où la nature avait déjà récupéré un élément jadis vital de l'infrastructure urbaine, l'équipe a reformulé cette structure industrielle en un instrument post-industriel de réflexion sur les loisirs et les catégories mêmes de " nature " et de " culture " de notre temps. Modifiant les règles des rapports entre le monde végétal et les piétons, notre stratégie d' " agri-tecture " combine des matériaux organiques et de construction en un mélange de proportions changeantes qui réunit le sauvage, le cultivé, l'intime et l'hypersocial. » Le Sénat américain a voté un crédit de 18 millions de dollars pour ce projet en juillet 2005.

As seen from above (left page) or below, the High Line adds a new element to urban life near the former Meatpacking District in Manhattan.

Ansichten von oben (gegenüberliegende Seite) und von unten zeigen, wie die umgestaltete High Line den ehemaligen Meatpacking District in Manhattan bereichert.

Vue d'un immeuble voisin (page de gauche) ou vue d'en bas, la High Line vient enrichir la vie quotidienne de ce quartier en rénovation du Meatpacking à Manhattan.

The High Line has a real legitimacy in the context because it has been there so long: the architects have played on this authenticity and added a modern spirit.

Nicht zuletzt ihre weit zurückreichende Geschichte hat den weiteren Fortbestand der High Line legitimiert. Mit der Umgestaltung hat die Anlage ein modernes Gesicht erhalten, ohne ihr authentisches Moment zu verlieren.

La longue présence de la High Line lui a assuré sa légitimité dans son contexte urbain. Les architectes se sont appuyés sur son authenticité mais lui ont donné un caractère moderne.

JENSEN & SKODVIN ARCHITECTS

Jensen & Skodvin Arkitektkontor AS
Fredensborgveien 11
0177 Oslo
Norway

Tel: +47 22 99 48 99
Fax: +47 22 99 48 88
E-mail: js@jsa.no
Web: www.jsa.no

JENSEN & SKODVIN was established in 1995 by Jan Olav Jensen and Børre Skodvin. The firm currently has nine architects. Born in 1959, Jan Olav Jensen received his degree from the Oslo School of Architecture in 1985. He has been a Professor at the Oslo School of Design and Architecture since 2004. He was the Kenzo Tange Visiting Critic at Harvard University (1998) and won a 1998 Aga Khan Award for Architecture for the Lepers Hospital in Chopda Taluka, India. Børre Skodvin was born in 1960 and received his degree from the Oslo School of Architecture in 1988. He has been a teacher at the Oslo School of Design and Architecture since 1998. Their built work includes the Storo Metro Station (Oslo, 2003); Headquarters and Exhibition Space for the Norwegian Design Council (Oslo, 2004); Sinsen Metro Station (Oslo, 2005); a Multipurpose City Block (Oslo, 2005); the Tautra Maria Convent (Tautra Island, 2004–06); and Thermal Bath, Therapy Center, and Hotel (Bad Gleichenberg, Austria, 2005–07). They have worked recently on the Gudbrandsjuvet Tourist project, viewing platforms, and bridges (Gudbrandsjuvet, Norway 2008); Giørtz Summer House (Valldal, 2008); and the Juvet Landscape Hotel (Gudbrandsjuvet, 2007–09, published here), all in Norway unless stated otherwise. Ongoing work includes a plan for a new town in south Oslo (2005–15).

JENSEN & SKODVIN wurde 1995 von Jan Olav Jensen und Børre Skodvin gegründet. Derzeit beschäftigt das Büro neun Architekten. Olav Jensen, geboren 1959, schloss sein Studium 1985 an der Architektur- und Designhochschule Oslo ab, wo er seit 2004 als Professor tätig ist. Er war Kenzo Tange Gastkritiker in Harvard (1998) und wurde 1998 für das Leprakrankenhaus in Chopda Taluka, Indien, mit dem Aga Khan Preis für Architektur ausgezeichnet. Børre Skodvin wurde 1960 geboren und schloss sein Studium 1988 an der Architektur- und Designhochschule Oslo ab, wo er seit 1998 lehrt. Zu ihren realisierten Projekten zählen die Metrostation Storo (Oslo, 2003), die Zentrale und ein Ausstellungsraum für den Norwegischen Designverband (Oslo, 2004), die Metrostation Sinsen (Oslo, 2005), ein Gebäude mit gemischter Nutzung (Oslo, 2005), das Mariakloster Tautra (Insel Tautra, 2004–06) sowie das Heilbad, Therapiezentrum und Hotel Bad Gleichenberg (Österreich, 2005–07). In letzter Zeit arbeitete das Büro an Aussichtsplattformen und Brücken für das Gudbrandsjuvet Tourismusprojekt (Gudbrandsjuvet, Norwegen 2008), dem Giørtz Sommerhaus (Valldal, 2008) und dem Juvet Landscape Hotel (Gudbrandsjuvet, 2007–09, hier vorgestellt), alle in Norwegen, sofern nicht anders angegeben. Laufende Projekte sind u.a. ein neues Stadtzentrum in Süd-Oslo (2005–15).

L'agence **JENSEN & SKODVIN** a été fondée en 1995 par Jan Olav Jensen et Børre Skodvin. Elle emploie aujourd'hui neuf architectes. Né en 1959, Olav Jensen est diplômé de l'École d'architecture d'Oslo (1985). Il est professeur à l'École de design et d'architecture d'Oslo depuis 2004. Il a été critique invité Kenzo Tange à Harvard (1998) et a remporté le prix Aga Khan d'architecture 1988 pour l'hôpital de lépreux de Chopda Taluka, en Inde. Børre Skodvin, né en 1960, est également diplômé de l'École d'architecture d'Oslo (1988). Il est enseignant à l'École de design et d'architecture d'Oslo depuis 1998. Parmi leurs réalisations : la station de métro Storo (Oslo, 2003) ; le siège et l'espace d'expositions du Conseil norvégien du design (Oslo, 2004) ; la station de métro Sinsen (Oslo, 2005) ; un bloc urbain mixte (Oslo, 2005) ; le couvent de Tautra Maria (Ile de Tautra, 2004–06) et des bains, un centre thérapeutique et un hôtel à Bad Gleichenberg (Autriche, 2005–07). Ils ont récemment travaillé sur le projet touristique du Gudbrandsjuvet comprenant des plates-formes d'observation et des ponts (Gudbrandsjuvet, Norvège, 2008) ; la Maison d'été Giørtz (Valldal, 2008) ; le Juvet Landscape Hotel (Gudbrandsjuvet, 2007–09, publié ici) et un plan pour une ville nouvelle au sud d'Oslo (2005–15).

JUVET LANDSCAPE HOTEL

Gudbrandsjuvet, Norway, 2007–09

Address: Alstad, 6210 Valldal, Norway, +47 95 03 20 10, www.juvet.com
Area: 800 m². Client: Knut Slinning. Cost: € 1 million

Sitting lightly in their natural setting, the pavilions that form the hotel are geometrically shaped and amply glazed.

Die Pavillons des Hotels greifen kaum in die landschaftliche Umgebung ein, sind geometrisch gestaltet und großzügig verglast.

L'hôtel se compose de pavillons de formes géométriques largement vitrées, délicatement déposés dans leur cadre naturel.

The **JUVET LANDSCAPE HOTEL** is located in northwestern Norway. Tourists are drawn here by a spectacular waterfall in a gorge near the "Gudbrandsjuvet" road. The client, Knut Slinning, is a local resident. The idea of the Juvet Landscape Hotel emerged as an opportunity to take advantage of the scenery with minimal architectural intervention. This approach permitted the architects to build in locations that would otherwise be prohibited for reasons of conservation. Instead of a conventional hotel, with guest rooms grouped together in one large building, the Landscape Hotel distributes rooms throughout the terrain as small individual houses. Through careful orientation, each room gets its own view of the landscape, and no room looks out at another. The rooms are built in massive wood with just 50 millimeters of exterior insulation, and are intended for summer use only. Each building rests on a set of 40-millimeter steel rods drilled into the rock, thus leaving the existing topography and vegetation almost untouched. The architects state: "Today's concern for sustainability in architecture focuses almost exclusively on reduced energy consumption in production and operation. We think that conservation of topography is another aspect of sustainability which deserves attention."

Das **JUVET LANDSCAPE HOTEL** liegt im Nordwesten Norwegens. Touristen kommen vor allem wegen des spektakulären Wasserfalls in der Gudbrandsjuvet-Schlucht. Bauherr Knut Slinning lebt selbst in der Gegend. Die Idee zum Juvet Landscape Hotel entstand aus dem Wunsch heraus, die landschaftliche Lage bei nur minimaler architektonischer Intervention optimal zu nutzen. Dieser Ansatz erlaubte den Architekten, an Orten zu bauen, wo dies aus Naturschutzgründen sonst nicht möglich gewesen wäre. Statt die Zimmer wie bei einem konventionellen Hotel in einem großen Haupthaus zu bündeln, verteilen sie sich beim Landscape Hotel über mehrere kleine, freistehende Häuser im gesamten Gelände. Dank sorgfältiger Ausrichtung hat jedes Zimmer Blick in die Landschaft, jedoch keinen Sichtkontakt zu den übrigen Zimmern. Die Häuser wurden aus Massivholz gebaut, sind lediglich außen mit einer 50 mm starken Dämmung versehen und als Sommerhäuser konzipiert. Alle Bauten sind auf 40 mm starken Stahlstangen aufgeständert, die in den felsigen Untergrund gebohrt wurden, sodass Topografie und Vegetation weitgehend unberührt blieben. Die Architekten erklären: „Bemühungen um Nachhaltigkeit in der Architektur konzentrieren sich fast ausschließlich auf die Reduzierung des Energieverbrauchs bei Fertigung und Nutzung. Wir sind der Ansicht, dass der Schutz der Topografie ein weiterer Aspekt von Nachhaltigkeit ist, der Aufmerksamkeit verdient."

Le **JUVET LANDSCAPE HOTEL**, qui appartient à un habitant de la région, Knut Slinning, se trouve dans le nord-ouest de la Norvège. Les touristes viennent admirer une cascade spectaculaire dans une gorge à proximité de la route de Gudbrandsjuvet. L'idée de cet hôtel est de profiter du spectacle de la nature, mais en minimisant l'intervention architecturale. Cette approche a permis aux architectes de construire sur des terrains qui auraient pu leur être interdits pour des raisons de conservation. Refusant le schéma conventionnel de l'hôtel regroupant des chambres dans un seul grand bâtiment, ils les ont réparties sur le terrain comme de petites maisons individuelles. Une orientation étudiée offre à chacune une vue sur le paysage et aucune ne peut voir les autres. Les constructions sont en bois massif doublé d'une couche d'isolant de 50 mm épaisseur. Elles ne servent qu'en été. Chaque unité repose sur des pilotis d'acier de 40 mm de diamètre forés dans le rocher, ce qui permet de ne pratiquement pas toucher à la topographie et à la végétation. « Les préoccupations actuelles de durabilité en architecture se concentrent presque exclusivement sur la réduction de la consommation d'énergie dans la consommation, la production et le fonctionnement. Nous pensons que conserver la topographie est un autre aspect de la durabilité qui mérite notre attention », commentent les architectes.

The full-height glazing and undisturbed natural setting almost give clients the impression that they are really in the midst of nature, even as they sit in a protected environment.

Dank der deckenhohen Verglasung und der naturbelassenen Umgebung haben die Gäste fast den Eindruck, draußen in der Natur zu sein, statt in einem geschützten Raum zu sitzen.

Le vitrage toute hauteur et le cadre naturel laissé intact donnent presque aux clients l'impression se trouver au milieu de la nature, même s'ils sont dans un environnement protégé.

KALHÖFER-KORSCHILDGEN

Kalhöfer - Korschildgen /// Architekten
Neusserstr. 26
50670 Cologne
Germany

Tel: +49 221 846 97 15
Fax: +49 221 846 97 16
E-mail: mail@kalhoefer-korschildgen.de
Web: www.kalhoefer-korschildgen.de

Gerhard Kalhöfer attended the RWTH Aachen (1984–92) and the Kunstakademie Düsseldorf (1990–92). He worked in the offices of Eisele+Fritz, and Jean Nouvel in Paris, before founding his firm, **KALHÖFER-KORSCHILDGEN**, in Paris and Aachen in 1995. The firm has been located in Cologne since 2000. Stefan Korschildgen did an apprenticeship as a carpenter (1982–84) before attending the RWTH Aachen (1984–92), the University of Washington (Seattle, 1989–90), and the Kunstakademie Düsseldorf (1990–92). He worked in architecture offices in Düsseldorf, Graz, and Seattle before jointly founding Kalhöfer-Korschildgen Architects. Recent and current work includes a Public Archive and a Permanent Exhibition at the Wedinghausen Monastery (Arnsberg, 2005); Diaphanous Space, also at Wedinghausen Monastery (Arnsberg, 2006–07, published here); conversion of a railway line to a "Route of Industrial Culture" (Remscheid, 2007); a Mobile Roof (Cologne, Lövenich, 2008); and One + One = One, Extension of the Zülpicher Tor (Nideggen, 2010), all in Germany.

Gerhard Kalhöfer studierte an der RWTH Aachen (1984–92) und der Kunstakademie Düsseldorf (1990–92). Er arbeitete bei Eisele+Fritz sowie bei Jean Nouvel in Paris und gründete 1995 das Büro **KALHÖFER-KORSCHILDGEN** in Paris und Aachen. Seit 2000 hat das Büro seinen Sitz in Köln. Stefan Korschildgen absolvierte eine Zimmermannslehre (1982–84), bevor er an der RWTH Aachen (1984–92), der University of Washington (Seattle, 1989–90) und der Kunstakademie Düsseldorf (1990–92) studierte. Er arbeitete in verschiedenen Büros in Düsseldorf, Graz und Seattle, ehe er Kalhöfer-Korschildgen Architekten mitgründete. Jüngere und aktuelle Projekte sind u.a. das öffentliche Archiv und die Dauerausstellung im Kloster Wedinghausen (Arnsberg, 2005), der Diaphane Raum, ebenfalls am Kloster Wedinghausen (Arnsberg, 2006–07, hier vorgestellt), der Umbau einer Bahntrasse zur „Route der Industriekultur" (Remscheid, 2007), eine mobile Dachterrasse (Köln-Lövenich, 2008) sowie eins + eins = eins, Erweiterungsbau Zülpicher Tor (Nideggen, 2010), alle in Deutschland.

Gerhard Kalhöfer a étudié au RWTH d'Aix-la-Chapelle (1984–92) et à la Kunstakademie de Düsseldorf (1990–92). Il a travaillé avec les agences Eisele + Fritz et Jean Nouvel à Paris, avant de fonder, avec Stefan Korschildgen, l'agence **KALHÖFER-KORSCHILDGEN** installée à Paris et Aachen en 1995, puis à Cologne depuis 2000. Stefan Korschildgen a été apprenti charpentier (1982–84) avant d'étudier au RWTH d'Aix-la-Chapelle (1984–92), à l'Université de Washington (Seattle, 1989–90) et à la Kunstakademie de Düsseldorf (1990–92). Il a travaillé dans diverses agences à Düsseldorf, Graz et Seattle, avant de fonder son agence. Parmi leurs réalisations récentes : des archives publiques et un Centre d'expositions permanent au monastère de Wedinghausen (Arnsberg, 2005) ; l'Espace diaphane dans ce même monastère (Arnsberg, 2006–07, publié ici) ; la transformation d'une voie ferrée en « Route de la culture industrielle » (Remscheid, 2007) ; un Toit mobile (Cologne, Lövenich, 2008) et One + One = One, extension de la Zülpicher Tor (Nideggen, 2010).

DIAPHANOUS SPACE

Wedinghausen Monastery, Arnsberg, Germany, 2006–07

Address: Kloster Wedinghausen, Klosterstr. 11, 59821 Arnsberg, Germany
+49 2932 201 12 41, www.kloster-wedinghausen.de
Area: 80 m². Client: Town of Arnsberg. Cost: €1.9 million

Though its form appears to be thoroughly modern, the structure echoes that of the older building and its long-since demolished parts.

Obwohl durch und durch modern, zitiert die Struktur die Form des älteren Gebäudes und seiner vor langer Zeit zerstörten Teile.

Bien que sa forme soit d'aspect résolument moderne, cette nouvelle construction évoque celle du bâtiment ancien en partie démoli.

The Wedinghausen Monastery closed in 1803 and parts of it were demolished. The demolition of the south wing in 1885 allowed for the opening of a 1500-square-meter courtyard. The **DIAPHANOUS SPACE** or Light Pavilion conceived by the architects is intended symbolically to replace the missing southern wing, marking the border of the former courtyard without blocking the visual continuity of the site. Visible like a sort of ghost of a long-demolished structure, the addition by Kalhöfer-Korschildgen has a certain ambiguity generated by the actual form of the building and also by the use of irregular patterns on the glazing. In the continuity of the axis of the space, climbing plants and an undulating ground plane are meant as a reference to "the forest and nature nearby." This green area forms a willful contrast to the rather austere courtyard itself.

Das Kloster Wedinghausen wurde 1803 aufgelöst und teilweise abgerissen, wobei der Abbruch des Südflügels 1885 auch zur Öffnung des 1500 m² großen Klosterhofs führte. Der von den Architekten entworfene **DIAPHANE RAUM** mit seinem Lichthaus vertritt symbolisch den verschwundenen Südflügel, ohne die visuelle Kontinuität des Raums zu brechen. Der Erweiterungsbau von Kalhöfer-Korschildgen, fast eine geisterhafte Präsenz des lang abgerissenen Bauwerks, ist von einer Mehrdeutigkeit, die sich zum einen der Form des Gebäudes, zum anderen der unregelmäßigen Verglasung verdankt. In Verlängerung der Achse des Neubaus wurden Kletterpflanzen auf einem wellenförmigen Hang angelegt, ein Ensemble, das formal an die „nahe gelegene Waldlandschaft" anknüpfen soll. Der begrünte Bereich ist zudem ein bewusst gewählter Kontrast zur eher strengen Hofanlage.

En partie démoli, le monastère de Wedinghausen avait fermé ses portes en 1803. La démolition de l'aile sud, en 1885, a permis d'ouvrir une cour carrée de 1500 m². L'**ESPACE DIAPHANE**, ou Pavillon de lumière, remplace symboliquement cette aile disparue et marque la limite de l'ancienne cour, sans bloquer la continuité visuelle avec le terrain. Sorte de fantôme de construction disparue depuis longtemps, cet ajout présente une certaine ambiguïté de forme, mais aussi dans la composition irrégulière de son vitrage. Dans la continuité de l'axe de ce pavillon, des plantes grimpantes et un sol ondulé font référence à la forêt et à la nature proches. Cette zone plantée forme également un contraste marqué avec l'austérité de la cour.

The form of the monastery is symbolically continued or rather completed by the new structure, seen to the right in the plan, above.

Die Klosteranlage wird durch den Neubau, im Grundriss oben rechts zu sehen, symbolisch fortgeführt oder vielmehr ergänzt.

La forme du monastère se poursuit symboliquement, ou plutôt se complète, dans la nouvelle construction, vue à droite sur le plan ci-dessus.

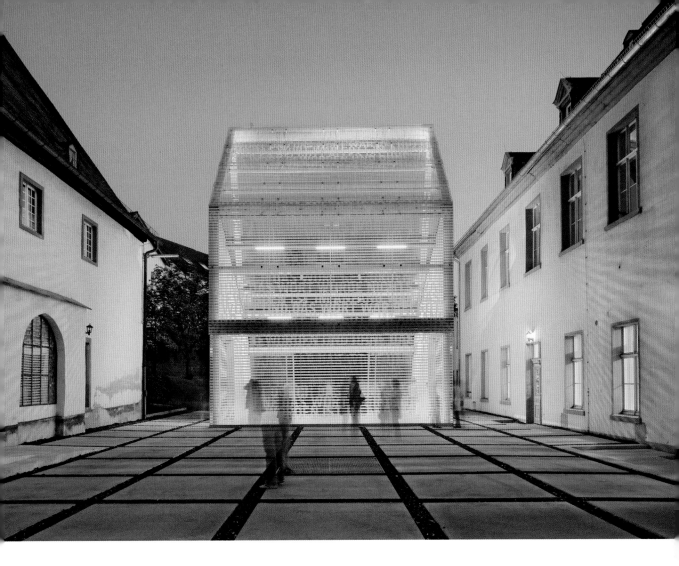

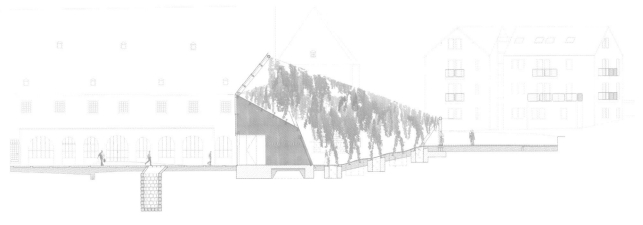

The diaphanous pavilion is intended to provide a sort of echo of the south wing of the monastery, demolished in 1885.

Der transparente Pavillon ist in gewisser Weise ein Echo des ehemaligen Südflügels des Klosters, der 1885 abgerissen wurde.

Ce pavillon diaphane rappelle l'aile sud du monastère, démolie en 1885.

KHR

KHR arkitekter AS
Kanonbaadsvej 4
1437 Copenhagen K
Denmark

Tel: +45 41 21 70 00
Fax: +45 41 21 70 01
E-mail: khr@khr.dk
Web: www.khr.dk

Jan Sondergaard was born in 1947. He attended the School of Architecture, Royal Academy of Fine Arts, Copenhagen (1979), the Copenhagen Advanced College of Building Technology (1972), and is a certified carpenter. He has been a partner of **KHR** architects since 1988. Nominated for the Mies van der Rohe European Award in both 1992 and 1994, he has designed the headquarters of Unicon Beton (Copenhagen, 1985–87); the Danish Pavilion, Expo '92 (Seville, Spain); the headquarters of Pihl & Son (Lyngby, 1994–96); the headquarters of Bayer Denmark (Lyngby, 1995–96); and an extension of the Royal Danish Embassy in Moscow (Russia, 1996–97). His more recent projects include the new main building of Fiberline Composites (Middelfart, 2004–06, published here) and the Holy Cross Church (Jyllinge, 2007–08, also published here). Ongoing projects include town planning for Klaksvik (Faroe Islands, 2004–); an Activity Center (Kristiansand, Norway, 2005–); the Herning Business School (Herning, 2011); and the Helleren School and Swimming Pool (Bergen, Norway, 2012), all in Denmark unless stated otherwise.

Jan Sondergaard wurde 1947 geboren. Er studierte an der Fakultät für Architektur der Königlichen Dänischen Kunstakademie in Kopenhagen (1979) sowie der Dänischen Technischen Hochschule, Kopenhagen (1972), und ist gelernter Zimmermann. Seit 1988 ist er Partner bei **KHR** Arkitekter. Sondergaard war 1992 und 1994 für den Mies van der Rohe Preis für Europäische Architektur nominiert und entwarf die Zentrale für Unicon Beton (Kopenhagen, 1985–87), den Dänischen Pavillon für die Expo '92 (Sevilla, Spanien), die Zentrale für Pihl & Son (Lyngby, 1994–96), die Zentrale für Bayer Dänemark (Lyngby, 1995–96) sowie einen Erweiterungsbau für die Königlich-Dänische Botschaft in Moskau (Russland, 1996–97). Zu seinen jüngeren Projekten zählen das neue Hauptgebäude für Fiberline Composites (Middelfart, 2004–06, hier vorgestellt) sowie die Kirche vom Heiligen Kreuz (Jyllinge, 2007–08, ebenfalls hier vorgestellt). Laufende Projekte sind u.a. die Stadtplanung für Klaksvik (Faröer Inseln, 2004–), ein Jugendzentrum (Kristiansand, Norwegen, 2005–), ein Wirtschaftskolleg in Herning (2011) und die Helleren Schule mit Schwimmbad (Bergen, Norwegen 2012), alle in Dänemark, sofern nicht anders angegeben.

Jan Sondergaard, né en 1947, a étudié à l'École d'architecture de l'Académie royale des beaux-arts de Copenhague (1979), au Collège supérieur des technologies de la construction de Copenhague (1972) et est charpentier qualifié. Il est partenaire de **KHR** Arkitekter depuis 1988. Nominé pour le prix européen Mies van der Rohe en 1992 et 1994, il a conçu le siège social de Unicon Beton (Copenhague, 1985–87); le Pavillon danois pour Expo '92 (Seville); le siège de Pihl & Son (Lyngby, 1994–96); celui de Bayer Denmark (Lyngby, 1995–96) et une extension de l'ambassade royale du Danemark à Moscou (1996–97). Parmi ses réalisations plus récentes : le nouveau bâtiment principal de Fiberline Composites (Middelfart, 2004–06, publié ici); et l'église de la Sainte-Croix (Jyllinge, 2007–08, également publiée ici). Il travaille actuellement sur des projets d'urbanisme pour Klaksvik (Iles Féroé, 2004–); un centre d'activité (Kristiansand, Norvège, 2005–); la Herning Business School (Herning, 2011) et l'école et piscine Helleren (Bergen, Norvège, 2012).

CHURCH OF THE HOLY CROSS

Jyllinge, Denmark, 2007–08

Address: Hellig Kors Kirke, Agerskellet 10, 4040 Jyllinge, Denmark
Area: 800 m². Client: Parochial Council of Jyllinge. Cost: €2.693 million
Collaboration: Emi Ishida Hatanaka, Mette Lysgaard

This unusual structure was built with fiberglass composites and appears to be translucent. The architect explains that it was conceived and designed as an abstraction in the open horizontal landscape around Jyllinge. Although the internal spaces are arranged according to the functions of the church and in terms of the light admitted into the interior, the "idea was to let homogeneous surfaces change in angles and planes and thereby create light, shadow, heaviness, lightness and transparency inside and outside," according to the architect. The procession aisle of the church extends outside the structure in order to make visitors aware of a continuity with the fjord where it is located, and the sky above. The project was nominated for the 2009 Mies van der Rohe Award.

Das ungewöhnliche Gebäude wurde aus glasfaserverstärkten Kunststoff-Bauteilen errichtet und ist lichtdurchlässig. Dem Architekten zufolge wurde es als Abstraktion inmitten der offenen, flachen Landschaft im Umland von Jyllinge entworfen. Zwar wurden die Bereiche im Innern des Kirchenbaus entsprechend ihrer Funktionen und des Lichteinfalls geplant, dennoch, betont der Architekt, „hatten wir den Gedanken, die homogenen Oberflächen durch schräge Linien und Ebenen zu variieren und dadurch innen wie außen Licht, Schatten, Schwere, Leichtigkeit und Transparenz entstehen zu lassen." Der Mittelgang der Kirche setzt sich außerhalb des Baus fort, um den Besuchern die Kontinuität zum Roskilde Fjord, an dem der Bau liegt, sinnfällig zu machen, ebenso wie seine Anbindung an den sich darüberspannenden Himmel. Das Projekt war für den Mies van der Rohe Preis 2009 nominiert.

Cette curieuse église, qui semble entièrement transparente, est construite en matériaux composites à base de fibre de verre. L'architecte explique qu'elle a été conçue comme une abstraction au milieu du paysage ouvert et plat des environs de Jyllinge. Bien que ses volumes internes s'articulent pour répondre aux diverses fonctions d'un lieu de culte et à la pénétration de la lumière, « l'idée était de laisser des surfaces homogènes se modifier selon leur inclinaison et leurs plans pour créer des jeux d'ombre et de lumière, de pesanteur, de légèreté et de transparence à l'intérieur comme à l'extérieur », explique l'architecte. La nef principale se prolonge à l'extérieur pour que les visiteurs prennent conscience de la continuité avec le fjord au bord duquel elle se dresse et du ciel immense. Le projet a été nominé pour le prix Mies van der Rohe 2009.

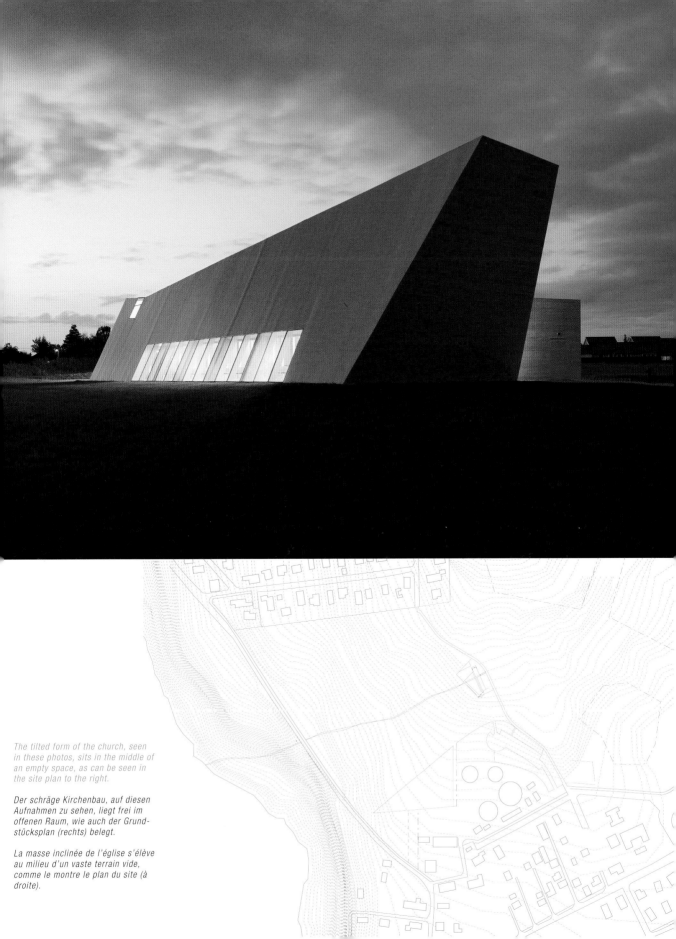

The tilted form of the church, seen
in these photos, sits in the middle of
an empty space, as can be seen in
the site plan to the right.

Der schräge Kirchenbau, auf diesen
Aufnahmen zu sehen, liegt frei im
offenen Raum, wie auch der Grundstücksplan (rechts) belegt.

La masse inclinée de l'église s'élève
au milieu d'un vaste terrain vide,
comme le montre le plan du site (à
droite).

The simple exterior forms of the church are echoed in its fairly austere interior (below, and right page).

Das schlichte Äußere des Kirchen-baus spiegelt sich auch im eher strengen Interieur (unten und rechte Seite).

Les formes extérieures simples de l'église se retrouvent en écho dans son intérieur assez austère (ci-dessous et page de droite).

The plans of the church reveal its essential simplicity, not based on traditional schemes. Above, opaque surfaces alternate with windows.

Die Grundrisse der Kirche veranschaulichen die beeindruckende Schlichtheit des Baus, der sich von traditionellen Vorbildern löst. Opake Oberflächen und Fenster wechseln einander ab (oben).

Les plans de l'église expriment une simplicité basique qui ne repose pas sur des schémas traditionnels. Ci-dessus, des parois opaques alternent avec des fenêtres.

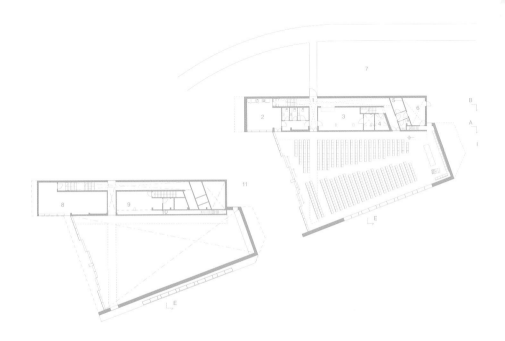

FIBERLINE FACTORY

Middelfart, Denmark, 2004–06

Address: Fiberline Composites A/S, Barmstedt Allé 5, 5500 Middelfart, Denmark
+45 70 13 77 13, www.fiberline.com
Area: 25 000 m². Client: Fiberline Composites. Cost: not disclosed

The surprising tilted shapes of the factory do not immediately bring to mind other industrial facilities, creating an iconic presence for the client.

Die überraschende Neigung des Werkgebäudes erinnert nicht sofort an übliche Industriebauten und verhilft dem Auftraggeber zugleich zu einem unverwechselbaren Auftritt.

L'étonnante forme inclinée de l'usine diffère de celle de la plupart des installations industrielles habituelles. Elle confère à l'entreprise une présence iconique.

FIBERLINE is a fiberglass manufacturer and this FACILITY contains production areas and administrative offices. The architect envisaged the building as being a work of "countryside art" growing out of the landscape on the highway near the city of Middelfart. A high bay warehouse or stock space is "integrated into the building's architecture as a dynamic and central installation." Overall, the architect's concern, together with the client, was to optimize production flow. Administrative, research, and marketing offices are located in a gallery on the building's east side. Three large slits in the building allow natural light to enter. The Fiberline Factory was nominated for the 2007 Mies van der Rohe Award.

Der KOMPLEX FÜR DIE FIRMA FIBERLINE, einen Hersteller für Bauteile aus Glasfaserverbundstoffen, umfasst Produktionshallen sowie die Büros der Verwaltung. Der Architekt konzipierte den Bau als „Landkunst", die gewissermaßen unmittelbar aus der Landschaft an der Autobahn bei Middelfart wächst. Ein Hochregallager bzw. Warenlager wurde „als dynamische, zentrale Installation in die Architektur des Gebäudes integriert". Insgesamt ging es Architekten und Auftraggeber darum, den Fertigungsablauf zu optimieren. Verwaltungs-, Forschungs- und Marketingbüros sind in einer Galerie an der Ostseite des Baus untergebracht. Drei lange Einschnitte in das Gebäude lassen Tageslicht herein. Das Fiberline Werk war 2007 für den Mies van der Rohe Preis nominiert.

L'USINE DE FIBERLINE, fabricant de fibres de verre, regroupe des ateliers de production et des bureaux administratifs non loin de la route principale qui mène à la ville de Middelfart. L'architecte a envisagé son projet comme une œuvre d'« art rural » qui aurait surgi dans le paysage. Un atelier à baies de chargement ou espace de stockage est « intégré dans l'architecture du bâtiment et devient l'installation dynamique centrale ». La préoccupation principale de l'architecte et de son client était d'optimiser le flux de la production. L'administration, la recherche et le marketing sont installés dans une galerie en partie est. Trois énormes ouvertures en longueur permettent à la lumière naturelle d'éclairer le bâtiment. L'usine Fiberglass a été nominée au prix Mies van der Rohe 2007.

The factory sits on the horizon in the image above, creating a rather enigmatic presence.

Auf der Aufnahme oben scheint das Werksgebäude geradezu auf dem Horizont zu liegen und wirkt ungewöhnlich mysteriös.

La présence énigmatique de l'usine qui se détache sur l'horizon (image ci-dessus).

A stairway creates a complex pattern of lines with the shadows generated by the ample, angled windows.

Vor dem Schattenriss der großen schrägen Fensterflächen bildet die Treppe ein komplexes Muster aus Linien.

Un escalier s'élève dans une composition complexe de lignes qui jouent avec les ombres provoquées par les grandes baies inclinées.

A meeting table is placed in the space formed by the dramatic tilting windows of the factory.

Ein Konferenztisch in einem Raum, der von den dramatisch geneigten Fenstern des Werksgebäudes definiert wird.

Une table de réunions a été installée dans l'espace aménagé sous de grandes verrières inclinées.

LAAC

LAAC Architects
Wilhelm Greil Str. 15
6020 Innsbruck
Austria

Tel: +43 512 89 03 35
Fax: +43 512 89 03 15
E-mail: info@laac.eu
Web: www.laac.eu

Kathrin Aste was born in 1969 in Innsbruck and received her diploma from the Faculty of Architecture of Innsbruck University in 2000. She cofounded **LAAC** with Frank Ludin, who was born in Weil am Rhein, Germany, in 1972. He also received his degree in Innsbruck in 2004. LAAC was founded in 2009 as the successor of astearchitecture, a firm founded in Innsbruck in 2004 "to provide an intersection point between teaching, research and realization." The research work is done in the design studios of the Technical Faculty of Innsbruck University. Under the name "Built by Velocity," the firm designs ski jumps, bob runs, and sprint toboggan runs, as well as panoramic platforms, such as the Mountain Platform published here (Top of Tyrol Mountain Platform, Stubai Glacier, Tyrol, 2007–08). They are currently working on a Roof Landscape SOHO II (Innsbruck, 2010); a Multifunction Hall and Rehearsal Room (Weissenbach am Lech, 2010); and a Ski Jump Center (Astana, Kazakhstan, 2008–11), all in Austria unless stated otherwise.

Kathrin Aste wurde 1969 in Innsbruck geboren und absolvierte ihr Diplom 2000 an der Fakultät für Architektur der Universität Innsbruck. Ihr Büro **LAAC** gründete sie gemeinsam mit Frank Ludin, 1972 geboren in Weil am Rhein. Ludin schloss sein Studium 2004 ebenfalls an der Universität Innsbruck ab. 2009 wurde LAAC Nachfolger des Vorgängerbüros astearchitecture, das 2004 als „Schnittstelle für Lehre, Forschung und Praxis" in Innsbruck gegründet worden war. Forschungsprojekte werden in den Studios für Entwerfen an der Fakultät für Bauingenieurwissenschaften verfolgt. Unter dem Namen „Built by Velocity" entwirft das Büro Skischanzen, Bobbahnen, Sprintrodelbahnen sowie Aussichtsplattformen, darunter auch die hier vorgestellte Gipfelplattform (Top of Tyrol, Aussichtsplattform am Stubaier Gletscher, Tirol, 2007–08). Derzeit arbeitet das Team an der Dachlandschaft SOHO II (Innsbruck, 2010), einem Mehrzwecksaal und Probenraum (Weissenbach am Lech, 2010) sowie einem Skischanzen-Zentrum in Astana (Kasachstan, 2008–11), alle in Österreich, sofern nicht anders angegeben.

Kathrin Aste, née en 1969 à Innsbruck, est diplômée de la Faculté d'architecture de l'Université d'Innsbruck (2000). Elle a fondé **LAAC** avec Frank Ludin, né à Weil-am-Rhein (Allemagne) en 1972, également diplômé d'Innsbruck (2004). LAAC a été fondée en 2009 pour succéder à astearchitecture, agence créée à Innsbruck en 2004, « point d'intersection entre l'enseignement, la recherche et la réalisation ». Le travail de recherche est effectué dans les ateliers de conception de la Faculté polytechnique de l'Université d'Innsbruck. Sous le label d'ensemble de « Built by Velocity », l'agence conçoit des tremplins de saut à ski, des pistes de bobsleigh et des toboggans de saut, ainsi que des plates-formes panoramiques comme la Gipfel Platform publiée ici (plate-forme du sommet du Tyrol, glacier du Stubai, Tyrol, 2007–08). Ils travaillent actuellement sur un projet d'aménagement paysager de toiture SOHO II (Innsbruck, 2010) ; un hall multifonction, une salle de répétitions (Weissenbach-am-Lech, 2010) et un centre de saut à ski (Astana, Kazakhstan, 2008–11).

TOP OF TYROL MOUNTAIN PLATFORM

Mount Isidor, Stubai Glacier, Tyrol, Austria, 2007–08

Area: 80 m². Client: Wintersport Tirol AG & CO Stubaier Bergbahnen KG. Cost: €300 000

The platform is visible to the left at the bottom of this panoramic mountain view.

Unten links auf diesem Bergpanorama ist die Plattform zu sehen.

À gauche, la plate-forme semble minuscule dans cette vue panoramique.

Located an hour's drive from Innsbruck, the Stubai Glacier is in the heart of a tourist area, and this platform aims to revive interest in summer hiking or mountain climbing. The platform is only open in winter when weather conditions permit. The architects were directly commissioned by the client. The structure is located near the Schaufelijoch station of the Stubai Gletscher Bahn (3180 meters above sea level). In clear weather, no less than 109 3000-meter peaks are visible from the platform. The architects say that their goal was to create a "situation in space more than a building." Weather-resistant Corten steel was chosen as a "contrast to the zinc-covered steel structures of the surrounding ski region." Handrails and a bench are made of larch, filled with stainless-steel netting. Nineteen tons of Corten steel were used for the structure, carried in appropriately sized pieces to the site by helicopter.

Nur eine Autostunde von Innsbruck liegt der Stubaier Gletscher mitten im Herzen eines Urlaaubsgebiets. Die Plattform soll Lust auf sommerliche Wanderungen oder Klettertouren wecken. Geöffnet ist sie nur im Winter bei geeigneten Witterungsverhältnissen. Die Architekten wurden direkt vom Bauherrn beauftragt. Das Bauwerk liegt unweit der Station Schaufeljoch der Stubaier Gletscherbahn (3180 m ü.N.N.). Bei klarem Wetter sind von der Plattform aus nicht weniger als 109 Dreitausendergipfel zu sehen. Den Achitekten ging es nach eigener Aussage eher darum, „eine Situation im Raum" als „ein Bauwerk" zu schaffen. Als „Kontrast zu den zinkverblendeten Stahlbauten des umliegenden Skigebiets" entschied man sich für wetterbeständigen Corten-Stahl. Handläufe und eine Bank wurden aus Lärchenholz gefertigt und mit einem Kern aus Edelstahldraht versehen. Um die Konstruktion zu realisieren wurden 19 Tonnen Corten-Stahl verbaut, die in entsprechend kleinen Segmenten per Hubschrauber zum Bauplatz transportiert wurden.

À une heure de voiture d'Innsbruck, le glacier du Stubai s'étend au cœur d'une vaste région touristique. Cette plate-forme a pour objectif de réveiller l'intérêt des touristes pour l'alpinisme ou la marche en montagne. Elle n'est ouverte en hiver que lorsque les conditions climatiques le permettent. Il s'agit d'une commande directe. Cet objet architectural se trouve près de la gare de Schaufeljoch du télécabine du glacier du Stubai, à 3180 mètres d'altitude. Par temps clair, on aperçoit pas moins de 109 sommets de plus de 3000 mètres d'altitude. Le propos des architectes a été plus de créer « une situation dans l'espace qu'une construction ». Un acier Corten résistant au climat a été choisi « qui contraste avec les constructions en acier recouvertes de zinc de la région touristique environnante ». Les garde-corps et la banquette sont en mélèze renforcé d'une structure en acier inoxydable. Dix-neuf tonnes d'acier Corten ont été nécessaires, réparties en éléments de dimensions et de poids adaptés à la capacité des hélicoptères de transport.

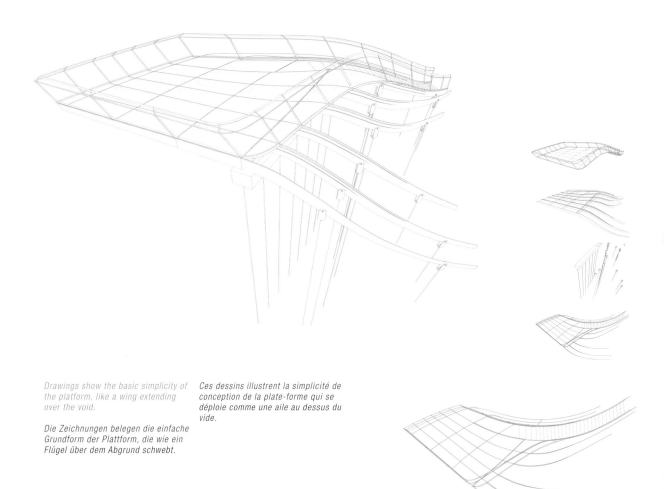

Drawings show the basic simplicity of the platform, like a wing extending over the void.

Ces dessins illustrent la simplicité de conception de la plate-forme qui se déploie comme une aile au dessus du vide.

Die Zeichnungen belegen die einfache Grundform der Plattform, die wie ein Flügel über dem Abgrund schwebt.

The platform juts out over the
mountain edge, allowing visitors to
participate in the vertiginous landscape more than if they were com-
fortably placed on the rock of
the mountain itself.

Die Plattform ragt über die Felskante
hinaus und macht die schwindelerregende Bergwelt für die Besucher viel
eindrücklicher erfahrbar, als würden
sie sicher auf dem felsigen Berggrund
stehen.

La plate-forme se projette par-dessus
l'arête de la montagne. Les visiteurs
ont davantage le sentiment de ne
faire qu'un avec le paysage vertigineux que s'ils étaient confortable-
ment assis sur un rocher.

EMILIANO LÓPEZ MÓNICA RIVERA

Emiliano López Mónica Rivera Arquitectos
C/Pintor Fortuny, 28 2do
08001 Barcelona
Spain

Tel/Fax: +34 93 317 69 02
E-mail: info@lopez-rivera.com
Web: www.lopez-rivera.com

MÓNICA RIVERA was born in Puerto Rico in 1972. She received a B.F.A. in 1993 and a B.Arch in 1994, both from the Rhode Island School of Design (RISD Scholarship). In 1999, she received an M.Arch from the Harvard University Graduate School of Design (GSD Scholarship). She has been a Guest Professor of Architecture at the Universitat Internacional de Catalunya (1999–2002) and Professor of a third-year Interior Design Studio focusing on domestic space at Elisava Escola de Disseny, Barcelona (2001–08). **EMILIANO LÓPEZ** was born in Argentina in 1971 and grew up in Barcelona. He received his degree in Architecture from the Universitat Politècnica de Catalunya, Vallès (1996). In 1997 He received a Master's in "History: Art, City and Architecture" from the UPC, Barcelona, and in 1999 an M.Arch from Harvard University GSD. He has taught at the Univesitat Rovira i Virgili School of Architecture, Reus, and at the Universitat Internacional de Catalunya, Elisava Escola de Disseny. He is currently an Assistant Professor of Architecture at the UPC, Vallès. He is now writing his doctoral thesis on Harvard's Married Students Dormitories by Josep Lluís Sert. Rivera and López began working together in 2001. Their recent work includes Social Housing for young people (Barcelona, 2003–07); the Hotel Aire de Bardenas (Tudela, Navarre, 2006–07, published here); a Public High School (Tona, Catalonia, 2003–08); Studio House (Barcelona, 2004–08); Social Housing (Gavá, Barcelona, 2004–08); a Public High School (Begues, Catalonia, 2006–); a Local Police Station (Gavá, Barcelona, 2008–); and a Housing development in Santiago de Compostela (2009–), all in Spain.

MÓNICA RIVERA wurde 1972 in Puerto Rico geboren. 1993 absolvierte sie einen B.F.A., 1994 einen B.Arch an der Rhode Island School of Design (RISD-Stipendium). 1999 folgte ein M.Arch an der Harvard University Graduate School of Design (GSD-Stipendium). Sie war Gastprofessorin für Architektur an der Universitat Internacional de Catalunya (1999–2002) und Professorin für einen Innenarchitekturkurs (drittes Studienjahr) mit Schwerpunkt privater Wohnraum an der Elisava Escola de Disseny, Barcelona (2001–08). **EMILIANO LÓPEZ** wurde 1971 in Argentinien geboren und wuchs in Barcelona auf. Er schloss sein Architekturstudium 1996 an der Universitat Politècnica de Catalunya, Vallès, ab. 1997 folgte ein Masterabschluss in „Geschichte: Kunst, Stadt und Architektur" an der UPC, Barcelona, sowie 1999 ein M.Arch an der GSD Harvard. Er lehrte an der Fakultät für Architektur der Universitat Rovira i Virgili, Reus, sowie der Universitat Internacional de Catalunya, Elisava Escola de Disseny. Zur Zeit ist er Assistenzprofessor für Architektur an der UPC, Vallès, und schreibt an seiner Doktorarbeit über die von Josep Lluís Sert entworfenen Studentenwohnheime für verheiratete Paare in Harvard. Rivera und López arbeiten seit 2001 zusammen. Unlängst realisierte Projekte sind u.a. Sozialwohnungen für Jugendliche (Barcelona, 2003–07), das Hotel Aire de Bardenas (Tudela, Navarra, 2006–07, hier vorgestellt), eine öffentliche Oberschule in Tona (Katalonien, 2003–08), das Studio House (Barcelona, 2004–08), Sozialwohnungen (Gavá, Barcelona, 2004–08), eine öffentliche Oberschule in Begues (Katalonien, 2006–), eine Polizeiwache (Gavá, Barcelona, 2008–) sowie ein Wohnbauprojekt in Santiago de Compostela (2009–), alle in Spanien.

MÓNICA RIVERA, née à Puerto Rico en 1972, est B.F.A. (1993) et B.Arch (1994) de la Rhode Island School of Design (bourse RISD). En 1999, elle a reçu son M.Arch de l'Harvard University Graduate School of Design (bourse GSD). Elle a été professeure invitée d'architecture à l'Universitat Internacional de Catalunya (1999–2002) et professeure d'un atelier d'architecture intérieure de troisième année axé sur l'espace domestique à la Elisava Escola de Disseny de Barcelone (2001–08). **EMILIANO LÓPEZ**, né en Argentine en 1971, a grandi à Barcelone. Il est diplômé d'architecture de l'Universitat Politècnica de Catalunya à Vallès (1996). En 1997, il passe un mastère « Histoire : art, ville et architecture » à l'UPC (Barcelone) et, en 1999, un M.Arch à Harvard. Il a enseigné à l'École d'architecture de Rovira i Virgili à Reus, à l'Universitat Internacional de Catalunya, et à l'Elisava Escola de Disseny. Il est actuellement professeur assistant d'architecture à l'UPC de Vallès. Il rédige en ce moment sa thèse de doctorat sur les foyers pour étudiants mariés d'Harvard conçus par Josep Lluís Sert. Rivera et López ont commencé à collaborer en 2001. Parmi leurs réalisations récentes : des logements sociaux pour jeunes (Barcelone, 2003–07) ; l'Hotel Aire de Bardenas (Tudela, Navarre, 2006–07, publié ici) ; un collège public (Tona, Catalogne, 2003–08) ; une maison atelier (Barcelone, 2004–08) ; des logements sociaux (Gavá, Barcelone, 2004–08) ; un collège public (Begues, Catalogne, 2006–) ; un poste de police (Gavá, Barcelone, 2008–) ; et des logements à Saint-Jacques-de-Compostelle (2009–).

HOTEL AIRE DE BARDENAS
Tudela, Navarre, Spain, 2006–07

Address: Ctra. de Ejea, Km. 1.5. 31500 Tudela, Navarre, Spain
+34 948 11 66 66, www.airedebardenas.com
Area: 1500 m². Client: Aire de Bardenas S.L.
Cost: not disclosed

This is a four-star hotel located three kilometers from the town center of Tudela. It is a one-story building with 22 rooms, 13 of which have private gardens. The plan is inspired by the riverbank area structures, with a central courtyard. The architects state: "The building is composed of a series of simple monochromatic cubic structures. Their dispersed arrangement allows views through the interstitial spaces, minimizing a massive appearance and generating an animated play of light and shadow." White cherry trees are planted near the main reception area, which also includes a hall, meeting room, bar, restaurant, and 10 rooms with private patios. The rest of the rooms are located in freestanding pavilions reached along an exterior walkway. Boulders extracted from the site and plants characteristic of the region were selected for the spaces around the hotel. Large recycled wooden crates, typically found in Tudela's crop fields for fruit and vegetable collection and transport, were employed as windbreakers for the hotel's outdoor spaces. The architects conclude: "From the exterior, the hotel intentionally blurs with the surroundings. It presents itself as a lightweight construction that can be dismantled and recycled, recalling local industrial and agricultural constructions, such as barns and vegetable coops found in the area."

Das 4-Sterne-Hotel liegt drei Kilometer außerhalb von Tudela. Das Hotel ist ein Bungalowkomplex mit 22 Zimmern, von denen 13 über einen eigenen Außenbereich verfügen. Der Grundriss ist von den typischen Bauten der vom Fluss geprägten Landschaft inspiriert und gliedert sich um einen zentralen Innenhof. Die Architekten erklären: „Das Gebäude wurde aus einer Reihe schlichter, monochromer Kuben komponiert. Die verstreute Anordnung schafft Sichtachsen durch die Zwischenräume hindurch, mindert den Eindruck von Massivität und sorgt für ein lebhaftes Spiel von Licht und Schatten." In der Nähe des Empfangsbereichs, zu dem eine Lobby, ein Konferenzraum, eine Bar, ein Restaurant und zehn Zimmer mit privaten Terrassen gehören, wurden weiße Kirschbäume gepflanzt. Die übrigen Zimmer liegen in freistehenden Pavillons, die über Wege erschlossen werden. Im Gelände geborgene Felssteine und regionaltypische Pflanzen wurden zur Gestaltung der Hotelumgebung genutzt. Große recycelte Holzkisten, üblicherweise in den Obst- und Gemüsefeldern um Tuleda als Ernte- und Transportkisten im Einsatz, dienen als Windschutz für die Außenbereiche des Hotels. Die Architekten fassen zusammen: „Von außen verschmilzt das Hotel absichtlich mit seinem Umfeld. Es präsentiert sich als Leichtbaukonstruktion, die sich demontieren und recyceln lässt, und erinnert damit an industrielle und landwirtschaftliche Bauten, etwa an die Scheunen und Gemüsekooperativen der Gegend."

Cet hôtel 4 étoiles se situe à trois kilomètres du centre de la ville de Tudela. Bâtiment d'un seul niveau, il compte 22 chambres, dont 13 sont prolongées par un jardin privé. Le plan à cour centrale s'inspire des constructions de cette zone du long de la rivière. « L'hôtel se compose d'une succession de structures cubiques simples et monochromes. Leur dispersion permet de créer des perspectives à travers les espaces interstitiels, minimise un aspect massif éventuel et génère un jeu animé d'ombre et de lumière », explique l'architecte. Des cerisiers blancs ont été plantés près de la réception principale, qui comprend un hall, une salle de réunions, un bar, un restaurant et dix chambres à patios privatifs. Le reste des chambres est implanté dans des pavillons autonomes accessibles par une allée extérieure. Des galets extraits du terrain même et des plantes caractéristiques de la région ont été mis en place autour de l'hôtel. De grands conteneurs en bois recyclés, typiques de cette région, habituellement utilisés pour le stockage et le transport de fruits et de primeurs, servent de coupe-vent et protègent les espaces extérieurs. « De l'extérieur, l'hôtel se fond volontairement dans le paysage. Il se présente comme une construction légère qui pourrait être démontée et recyclée, et rappelle les constructions agricoles et industrielles locales, comme les granges et les coopératives de la région », conclut l'architecte.

The unexpected forms of the hotel stand in the landscape almost like an industrial site with its piles of wooden crates.

Die formal ungewöhnlichen Hotelbauten mit den rundum aufgestapelten Holzkisten wirken in der Landschaft fast wie ein industrieller Komplex.

Les formes surprenantes de l'hôtel se détachent sur le fond du paysage et évoquent presque un site industriel par un amoncellement de caisses en bois.

A pool is enclosed, at ground level, by a wooden barrier that reveals the mountainous landscape beyond.

Der Pool wird im unteren Bereich von einer hölzernen Einfriedung umrahmt, hinter der sich die Berglandschaft abzeichnet.

La piscine est protégée au niveau du sol par une barrière en bois qui cadre le paysage de montagnes.

To the right, a room with an outdoor tub is placed in direct contact with the powerful natural setting.

Ein Zimmer mit Wanne unter freiem Himmel (rechts) ist direkt in die beeindruckende Landschaft eingebettet.

À droite, une chambre à baignoire extérieure en contact direct avec la brutalité du cadre naturel.

A bed, or a tub, faces the astonishing, arid landscape, contrasting the comfort of the hotel with the reality of nature.

Vom Bett oder der Wanne hat man Blick auf die eindrucksvolle, karge Landschaft – ein Kontrast zwischen Hotelkomfort und der umgebenden Landschaft.

Face à l'aridité du paysage, une baignoire et un lit cristallisent le contraste entre le confort de l'hôtel et la réalité de la nature.

GREG LYNN FORM

Greg Lynn FORM
1817 Lincoln Boulevard
Venice, CA 90291
USA

Tel: +1 310 821 2629
Fax: +1 310 8219729
E-mail: node@glform.com
Web: www.glform.com

GREY LYNN was born in 1964. He received his Bachelor of Philosophy and Bachelor of Environmental Design from Miami University of Ohio (1986), and his M.Arch from Princeton University (1988). He worked in the offices of Antoine Predock (1987) and Peter Eisenman (1987–91), before creating his present firm, FORM, in 1994. He has worked on the New York Korean Presbyterian Church (Long Island City, New York, 1997–99) with Garofalo Architects and Michael McInturf. His work includes "Predator," an exhibition with Fabian Marcaccio (Wexner Center for the Arts, Columbus, Ohio, USA); Visionaire Case Design (6250 custom cases for *Visionaire* magazine, 2000); PGLife.com Showroom, Stockholm, designed in collaboration with Dynamo Sthlm (Stockholm, Sweden, 2000); the Cincinnati Country Day School (Cincinnati, Ohio, USA, designed in collaboration with Michael McInturf Architects, Cincinnati, and GBBN Architects, Cincinnati, 1998–2000); "Imaginary Forces" exhibition design (Wexner Center for the Arts, Columbus, Ohio, USA, January 2001); and "Expanding the Gap," Rendel & Spitz Gallery (Cologne, Germany, January 2002). More recent work includes a proposal for Museum Pavilion No. 3 (Saadiyat Island Cultural Development, Guggenheim Foundation, Abu Dhabi, UAE, 2006); Blobwall and Toy Furniture (various locations, 2007–08, published here); Bloom House (southern California, USA, 2008); Ark of the World Museum (San José, Costa Rica, 2002–); and Slavin House (Venice, California, USA, 2004–).

GREG LYNN wurde 1964 geboren. Er schloss seinen Bachelor in Philosophie und Umweltdesign an der Miami University in Ohio ab (1986) und absolvierte anschließend einen M.Arch in Princeton (1988). Er arbeitete für Antoine Predock (1987) und Peter Eisenman (1987–91), bevor er 1994 sein Büro FORM gründete. Gemeinsam mit Garofalo Architects und Michael McInturf arbeitete er an der koreanisch-presbyterianischen Kirche in New York (Long Island City, New York, 1997–99). Zu seinen Projekten zählen „Predator", eine Ausstellung mit Fabian Marcaccio (Wexner Center for the Arts, Columbus, Ohio), ein Schuber für *Visionaire* (6250 individuell entworfene Schuber für die Zeitschrift *Visionaire*, 2000), ein Showroom für PGLife.com, Stockholm, entworfen in Kollaboration mit Dynamo Sthlm (Stockholm, 2000), die Cincinnati Country Day School (Cincinnati, Ohio, in Kollaboration mit Michael McInturf Architects, Cincinnati, und GBBN Architects, Cincinnati, 1998–2000), „Imaginary Forces", Ausstellungsarchitektur (Wexner Center for the Arts, Columbus, Ohio, January 2001) sowie „Expanding the Gap", Galerie Rendel & Spitz (Köln, Januar 2002). Weitere neuere Projekte sind u.a. der Entwurf für den Museumspavillon Nr. 3 (Kulturbezirk der Insel Saadiyat, Guggenheim-Stiftung, Abu Dhabi, VAE, 2006), Blobwall und Toy Furniture (verschiedene Standorte, 2007–08, hier vorgestellt), das Bloom House (Südkalifornien, 2008), Ark of the World Museum (San José, Costa Rica, 2002–) sowie das Slavin House (Venice, Kalifornien, 2004–).

GREG LYNN, né en 1964, est B.Ph et B.A. en design environnemental de la Miami University (Ohio, 1986), et M.Arch de Princeton University (1988). Il a travaillé dans les agences d'Antoine Predock (1987) et Peter Eisenman (1987–91), avant de créer sa structure actuelle, FORM, en 1994. Il est intervenu sur l'église presbytérienne coréenne de New York (Long Island City, New York, 1997–99) avec Garofalo Architects et Michael McInturf. Parmi ses réalisations : « Predator », une exposition avec Fabian Marcaccio (Wexner Center for the Arts, Columbus, Ohio) ; Visionaire Case Design (6250 étuis pour le magazine *Visionaire*, 2000) ; le showroom de PGLife.com, en collaboration avec Dynamo Sthlm (Stockholm, Suède, 2000) ; l'École Country Day à Cincinnati (Ohio, en collaboration avec Michael McInturf Architects, Cincinnati, et GBBN Architects, Cincinnati, 1998–2000) ; l'exposition « Imaginary Forces » (Wexner Center for the Arts, Columbus, Ohio, janvier 2001) ; et « Expanding the Gap », Rendel & Spitz Gallery (Cologne, Allemagne, janvier 2002). Plus récemment, il a fait une proposition pour le Pavillon musée n°3 (île de Saadiyat, Guggenheim Foundation, Abu Dhabi, EAU, 2006) ; le mobilier Blobwall et Toy (divers lieux, 2007–08, publié ici) ; la Maison Bloom (Californie, 2008) ; le musée Ark of the World (San José, Costa Rica, 2002–) ; et la Maison Slavin (Venice, Californie, 2004–).

BLOBWALL AND TOY FURNITURE
Various locations, 2007–08

Area, client, and cost vary

Between 2006 and 2008, Greg Lynn developed and exhibited two innovative concepts. The first of these featured his **TOY FURNITURE**, including four different-sized tables with plastic Panelite tops, a bench, storage wall, coat rack, and cylindrical shoe closet. He explains that since his father worked at the Container Corporation of America, he was surrounded by plastics as a child—and that he is now preoccupied with the reuse of his own children's plastic toys. This led him to the **BLOBWALL** system of construction based on plastic bricks (also with Panelite). Laser scanned, digitized, and arrayed like bricks, these pieces can be welded together with a tool used to repair car fenders. Lynn concludes: "In the Renaissance, palaces were designed to have a mixture of the opulent and the base, the elegant and the rustic. Stones were hewn so that they had planar faces for stacking and bonding but their outward faces expressed on their façades were left cloven and rustic. The recycled toy constructions are rustic, curvaceous, globular, molded, voluptuous, and playful; they are toys after all."

Zwischen 2006 und 2008 entwickelte und präsentierte Greg Lynn zwei innovative Konzepte. Zunächst seine Möbelserie **TOY FURNITURE**, zu der u.a. vier Tische verschiedener Größe mit Tischplatten aus Panelite, eine Bank, eine Wandregalkombination, ein Garderobenständer und ein zylindrisches Schuhregal gehören. Lynn erzählt, er sei als Kind von Kunststoff umgeben gewesen, da sein Vater bei der Container Corporation of America gearbeitet habe – und dass er sich deshalb heute damit beschäftige, wie sich die Plastikspielzeuge seiner Kindheit neu nutzen lassen könnten. So entstand die Idee zur **BLOBWALL**, einem Baukastensystem, das aus Kunststoffelementen besteht (ebenfalls aus Panelite). Die lasergescannten, digital gefertigten und wie Bausteine zusammengesetzten Einzelteile lassen sich mit einem Gerät verschweißen, das normalerweise zur Reparatur von Autokühlern eingesetzt wird. Lynn fasst zusammen: „In der Renaissance wurden Paläste als Kombination aus Opulenz und Schlichtheit gestaltet, aus Eleganz und Rustikalität. Steine wurden so behauen, dass einige Seiten flach waren, um sie stapeln und verbinden zu können. Die an der Fassade sichtbare Schauseite wurde jedoch grob und rustikal belassen. Die recycelten Spielzeugkonstruktionen sind derb, geschwungen, kugelig, thermisch geformt, üppig und verspielt – schließlich sind es Spielzeuge."

De 2006 à 2008, Greg Lynn a mis au point deux concepts novateurs qu'il a présentés lors d'expositions. Le premier, **TOY FURNITURE** (mobilier jouet), comprend quatre tables de dimensions différentes à plateau en plastique Panelite, une banquette, un mur de rangements, un casier à vêtements et un meuble à chaussures cylindrique. Il a expliqué qu'enfant il était entouré de plastiques, car son père travaillait pour la Container Corporation of America, et qu'il se sent préoccupé aujourd'hui par la réutilisation de ses propres jouets en plastique. Cette réflexion l'a conduit au **BLOBWALL**, un système constructif fait de briques de plastique (également en Panelite). Numérisés, découpés au laser et disposés comme des briques, ces éléments sont soudés grâce à un outil utilisé dans la réparation des pare-chocs en plastique. Lynn conclut : « À la Renaissance, les palais mélangeaient l'opulence et le basique, l'élégant et le rustique. Les pierres étaient taillées de façon à présenter vers l'intérieur des faces planes pour assurer un bon appareillage, mais leur face extérieure, exprimée en façade, était rustiquée. Ces constructions en jouets recyclées sont rustiques, tout en courbes, globuleuses, moulées, voluptueuses et ludiques. Ce sont des jouets après tout. »

Drawings and images show the variable configurations of the blobwall concept, creating an almost free-form architecture within more orthogonal walls.

Zeichnungen und Aufnahmen zeigen variable Konfigurationen des Blobwall-Konzepts, mit dessen Hilfe sich eine formal fast völlig freie Architektur zwischen den eher geradlinigen Wänden schaffen lässt.

Les dessins et les photos montrent la variété des configurations possibles du Blobwall qui permet de créer des architectures presque libres à l'intérieur d'espaces orthogonaux.

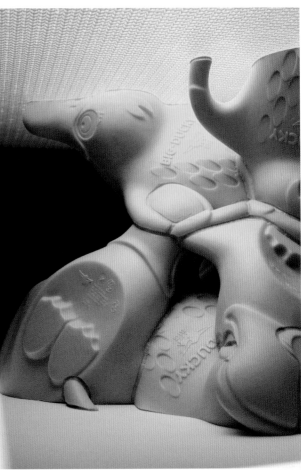

Although toys are at the origin of the furniture seen here, it takes on a presence that is not really linked to the world of childhood.

Zwar basieren die hier abgebildeten Möbel auf Spielzeug, vermitteln jedoch eine Atmosphäre, die nur wenig mit Kindheit zu tun hat.

Bieen que des jouets soient à l'origine de ce mobilier, celui-ci possède une présence qui va au-delà du monde de l'enfance.

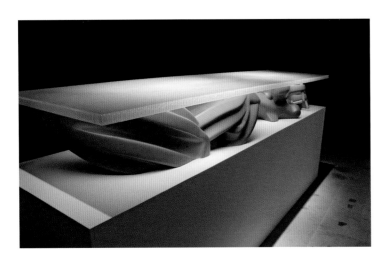

Where contemporary architecture has in good part rejected what might be called a figurative interpretation of objects and buildings, Greg Lynn makes use of the plastic presence of his enlarged toys.

Während die zeitgenössische Architektur überwiegend auf figurative Interpretationen von Objekten und Bauten verzichtet, arbeitet Greg Lynn mit der Präsenz dieser überdimensionierten Plastikspielzeuge.

Si l'architecture contemporaine a rejeté en grande partie ce que l'on pourrait appeler une interprétation figurative des objets et des constructions, Greg Lynn sait utiliser la présence plastique de ces jouets agrandis.

MADE IN SÀRL

Made in Sàrl
12 rue du Clos
1207 Geneva
Switzerland

Tel: +41 22 700 32 12
Fax: +41 22 700 32 13
E-mail: office@madein2003.ch
Web: www.madein2003.ch

François Charbonnet was born in Geneva, Switzerland, in 1972. He studied at the ETH Zurich under Hans Kollhoff (1994–99), worked in the office of Herzog & de Meuron (Basel, 2000–03), and participated in the creation of **MADE IN SÀRL** in Geneva in 2003. Patrick Heiz was born in Nyon, Switzerland, in 1973. He also studied at the ETH under Kollhoff (1993–99) and worked in the office of Herzog & de Meuron in Basel (2002–03), before jointly founding Made in Sàrl. They have participated in numerous competitions since creating their firm, including the New Jalisco Public Library (Guadalajara, Mexico, 2005); the National Library of the Czech Republic (Prague, 2006); and an extension of the Kunstmuseum Basel (2009). They have also worked on a project concerning the Château Cheval Blanc, a new 3800-square-meter winery and the reorganization of the existing estate (Saint-Emilion, France, 2006), and Villa Chardonne (Chardonne, Switzerland, 2007–08, published here).

François Charbonnet wurde 1972 in Genf geboren. Er studierte an der ETH Zürich bei Hans Kollhoff (1994–99), arbeitete im Büro von Herzog & de Meuron (Basel, 2000–03) und war 2003 einer der Mitbegründer von **MADE IN SÀRL** in Genf. Patrick Heiz wurde 1973 in Nyon, Schweiz, geboren. Auch er studierte an der ETH bei Kollhoff (1993–99) und war in Basel für Herzog & de Meuron tätig (2002–03), ehe er Made in Sàrl mitgründete. Das Büro beteiligte sich seit Gründung an zahlreichen Wettbewerben, darunter dem Wettbewerb für die New Jalisco Public Library (Guadalajara, Mexiko, 2005), die Tschechische Nationalbibliothek (Prag, 2006) und die Erweiterung des Kunstmuseum Basel (2009). Das Team arbeitete außerdem an einem Projekt am Château Cheval Blanc, einem neuen, 3800 m² großen Weingut sowie der Neugestaltung des alten Guts (Saint-Emilion, Frankreich, 2006), und der Villa Chardonne (Chardonne, Schweiz, 2007–08, hier vorgestellt).

François Charbonnet, né à Genève en 1972, a étudié à l'ETH à Zurich auprès d'Hans Kollhoff (1994–99), travaillé chez Herzog & de Meuron (Bâle, 2000–03) et participé à la création de **MADE IN SÀRL** à Genève en 2003. Patrick Heiz, né à Nyon (Suisse) en 1973, a également étudié à l'ETH auprès de Kollhoff (1993–99) et travaillé chez Herzog & de Meuron à Bâle (2002–03), avant de fonder Made in Sàrl avec Charbonnet. Depuis, ils ont participé à de nombreux concours, dont celui de la nouvelle bibliothèque publique de Jalisco (Guadalajara, Mexique, 2005) ; la Bibliothèque nationale de la République tchèque (Prague, 2006) et une extension du Kunstmuseum de Bâle (2009). Ils ont également travaillé sur un projet de chais de 3800 m² et la réorganisation du domaine du Château Cheval Blanc (Saint-Émilion, 2006), et ont réalisé la Villa Chardonne (Chardonne, Suisse, 2007–08, publiée ici).

VILLA CHARDONNE
Chardonne, Switzerland, 2007–08

Area: 145 m². Client: H. and S. Heiz. Cost: not disclosed

VILLA CHARDONNE was the winner of an Honorable Mention in the Prix Acier 2009 (European Steel Design Award). This house hovers over the Lake Geneva (Lac Léman) as though it had arrived in a single piece. Set up on struts, it touches the site as little as possible and leaves ample space for a garden, while views of the lake are offered from almost every angle. The owners of the house are familiar with the world of aviation and this appears evident in the final design. The house is entered via a suspended walkway. The architects used a Vierendeel beam structure with four modular sections. Two angled pillars hold up the strictly rectangular form. There are no load-bearing walls within the house. The jury of the Prix Acier 2009 noted that this "unusually simplified, yet refined concept for a house in the form of a bridge" is notable for the attention to details shown by the architects and the builders.

Die **VILLA CHARDONNE** fand ehrenhafte Erwähnung beim Prix Acier 2009 (Europäischer Preis für Stahldesign). Das Haus schwebt über dem Genfer See (Lac Léman), geradezu als sei es hier in einem Stück gelandet. Der auf Druckstreben ruhende Bau greift so minimal wie möglich in das Terrain ein und lässt viel Platz für einen Garten. Blick auf den See ist fast überall möglich. Die Eigentümer des Hauses haben Kontakte zur Luftfahrt, was der realisierte Entwurf deutlich zeigt. Erschlossen wird das Haus über eine Hängebrücke. Die Architekten arbeiteten mit einer Vierendeel-Konstruktion in vier modularen Abschnitten. Zwei schräge Träger stützen den streng rechteckigen Baukörper. Im gesamten Haus gibt es keine tragenden Wände. Die Jury des Prix Acier 2009 merkte an, dass das „ungewöhnlich einfache und doch raffinierte Konzept für ein Haus in Form einer Brücke" erwähnenswert sei wegen der Aufmerksamkeit zum Detail, die Architekten ebenso wie Baufirmen bewiesen hätten.

La **VILLA CHARDONNE** a remporté une mention honorable au prix Acier 2009. Suspendue au-dessus du lac Léman, elle semble avoir été livrée d'une pièce. Reposant sur des béquilles, ses contacts avec le sol sont réduits au minimum ce qui dégage toute la place pour le jardin. Le lac est visible de presque toutes les ouvertures. Les propriétaires sont des familiers de l'aviation, ce que l'on retrouve un peu dans l'esprit du plan final. On accède à la maison par une passerelle suspendue. Les architectes ont utilisé une structure en poutres Vierendeel à quatre modules. Deux béquilles supportent la structure de plan strictement rectangulaire. Aucun mur n'est porteur. Le jury du prix Acier 2009 a distingué « cette conception inhabituellement épurée, et en même temps raffinée, d'une maison d'habitation en forme de pont », remarquable par l'attention aux détails apportée par les architectes et les constructeurs.

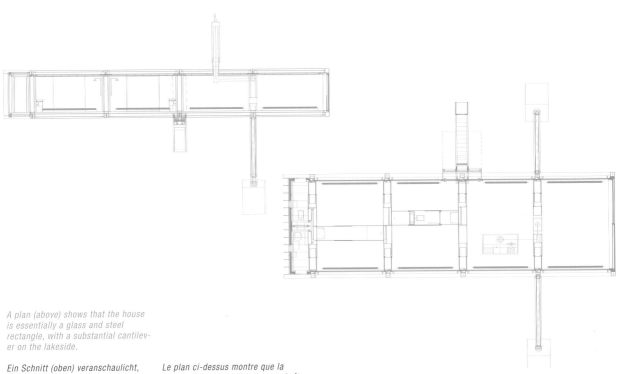

A plan (above) shows that the house is essentially a glass and steel rectangle, with a substantial cantilever on the lakeside.

Ein Schnitt (oben) veranschaulicht, dass das Haus im Prinzip ein Rechteck aus Glas und Stahl ist, wenn auch mit einem ausgeprägten Ausleger zur Seeseite.

Le plan ci-dessus montre que la maison est essentiellement une boîte de verre et d'acier qui se déploie en un important porte-à-faux du côté du lac.

The clean lines of the house and its ample glazing distinguish it, but it is the forward cantilever that makes it unusual.

Die klaren Linien des Hauses und die großzügige Verglasung zeichnen den Bau aus; doch ist es der Ausleger, der ihn zu etwas Ungewöhnlichem macht.

Si les lignes nettes de la maison et de ses immenses baies vitrées lui donnent son caractère, le substantiel porte-à-faux lui assure une réelle originalité.

The full glazing and simple lines of the interior of the house harmonize with its strict rectangular form.

Die Komplettverglasung und die schlichte Linienführung im Innern des Hauses sind ein ideales Pendant zur strengen Rechtecksform.

Les immenses vitrages et les lignes simples de l'architecture intérieure sont en accord parfait avec sa stricte forme rectangulaire.

The house is seen here in an unfurnished state, which surely emphasizes its strict simplicity.

Die Ansichten zeigen das Haus vor seiner Möblierung, was die konsequente Schlichtheit unterstreicht.

Vues de la maison non encore meublée, qui mettent en évidence sa rigoureuse simplicité.

FUMIHIKO MAKI

Maki and Associates, Hillside West Building C
13–4 Hachiyama-cho, Shibuya-ku, Tokyo 150–0035, Japan
Tel: +81 3 3780 3880 / Fax: +81 3 3780 3881

Born in Tokyo in 1928, **FUMIHIKO MAKI** received his B.Arch degree from the University of Tokyo in 1952, and M.Arch degrees from the Cranbrook Academy of Art (1953) and Harvard GSD (1954). He worked for Skidmore, Owings & Merrill in New York (1954–55) and Sert Jackson and Associates in Cambridge, Massachusetts (1955–58), before creating his own firm, Maki and Associates, in Tokyo in 1965. Notable buildings include the Fujisawa Municipal Gymnasium (Fujisawa, Kanagawa, 1984); Spiral (Minato-ku, Tokyo, 1985); National Museum of Modern Art (Sakyo-ku, Kyoto, 1986); Tepia (Minato-ku, Tokyo, 1989); Nippon Convention Center Makuhari Messe (Chiba, Chiba, 1989); Tokyo Metropolitan Gymnasium (Shibuya, Tokyo, 1990); and the Center for the Arts Yerba Buena Gardens (San Francisco, California, USA, 1993). The Hillside West buildings (completed in 1998) are part of his ongoing Hillside Terrace project. More recent and current work includes the TV Asahi Broadcast Center (Minato-ku, Tokyo, 2003); Niigata International Convention Center (Niigata, Niigata, 2003); National Language Research Institute (Tachikawa, Tokyo, 2004); Nakatsu City Museum (Nakatsu, Oita, 2005); the Shimane Museum of Ancient Izumo (Izumo, Shimane, 2003–06); and the Sam Fox School of Design and Visual Arts, Washington University (Saint Louis, Missouri, USA, 2006), all in Japan unless stated otherwise. Having recently completed the Mihara Performing Arts Center (Mihara, Hiroshima, 2005–07); the Delegation of the Ismaili Imamat (Ottawa, Ontario, Canada, 2006–08, published here); and the MIT Media Laboratory Expansion (Cambridge, Massachusetts, USA, 2009), Fumihiko Maki is currently working on a tower for the United Nations in New York; a second tower in the area of the former World Trade Center in New York; and a new museum of Islamic art for the Aga Khan in Toronto (Canada).

FUMIHIKO MAKI wurde 1928 in Tokio geboren und schloss sein Studium 1952 mit einem B.Arch an der Universität Tokio ab. Es folgten M.Arch-Abschlüsse an der Cranbrook Academy of Art (1953) und der Harvard GSD (1954). Er arbeitete für Skidmore, Owings & Merrill in New York (1954–55) und Sert Jackson and Associates in Cambridge, Massachusetts (1955–58), bevor er 1965 sein eigenes Büro, Maki and Associates, in Tokio gründete. Wichtige Bauten sind u.a. die städtische Sporthalle in Fujisawa (Fujisawa, Kanagawa, 1984), das Spiral Building (Minato-ku, Tokio, 1985), das Nationalmuseum für Moderne Kunst (Sakyo-ku, Kyoto, 1986), der Tepia-Pavillon (Minato-ku, Tokio, 1989), das Nippon Convention Center (Makuhari Messe; Chiba, Chiba, 1989), die städtische Sporthalle Tokio (Shibuya, Tokio, 1990) sowie das Kunstzentrum Yerba Buena Gardens (San Francisco, Kalifornien, USA, 1993). Die Hillside West Buildings (fertiggestellt 1998) entstanden im Zuge des noch andauernden Hillside Terrace-Projekts. Weitere neuere und aktuelle Projekte sind das Sendezentrum des Fernsehsenders Asahi (Minato-ku, Tokio, 2003), das Niigata International Convention Center (Niigata, Niigata, 2003), das National Language Research Institute (Tachikawa, Tokio, 2004), das Stadtmuseum in Nakatsu (Nakatsu, Oita, 2005) sowie das Shimane-Museum des Izumo-Schreins (Izumo, Shimane, 2003–06), die Sam Fox Fakultät für Design und Bildende Künste der Washington University (Saint Louis, Missouri, USA, 2004), alle in Japan, sofern nicht anders vermerkt. Nach der kürzlichen Fertigstellung des Zentrums für Darstellende Künste in Mihara (Mihara, Hiroshima, 2005–07, hier vorgestellt), der Delegation des Ismaili Imamat (Ottawa, Ontario, Kanada, 2006–08, hier vorgestellt) und der Erweiterung des MIT-Medienlabors (Cambridge, Massachusetts, USA, 2009), arbeitet Fumihiko Maki derzeit an einem Hochhaus für die Vereinten Nationen in New York, einem zweiten Hochhaus auf dem Gelände des ehemaligen World Trade Center in New York und einem neuen Museum für Islamische Kunst für die Aga-Khan-Stiftung in Toronto (Kanada).

Né à Tokyo en 1928, **FUMIHIKO MAKI** est B.Arch de l'Université de Tokyo (1952) et M.Arch de la Cranbrook Academy of Art (1953) et de l'Harvard GSD (1954). Il a travaillé chez Skidmore, Owings & Merrill à New York (1954–55) et Sert Jackson and Associates à Cambridge, Massachusetts (1955–58), avant de fonder sa propre agence, Maki and Associates, à Tokyo en 1965. Parmi ses réalisations notables figurent : le gymnase municipal de Fujisawa (Fujisawa, Kanagawa, 1984) ; le Spiral (Minato-ku, Tokyo, 1985) ; le Musée national d'art moderne (Sakyo-ku, Kyoto, 1986) ; Tepia (Minato-ku, Tokyo, 1989) ; le centre de congrès nippon Makuhari Messe (Chiba, Chiba, 1989) ; le gymnase métropolitain de Tokyo (Shibuya, Tokyo, 1990) et le Centre des arts des Yerba Buena Gardens (San Francisco, Californie, 1993). Les immeubles Hillside West (achevés en 1998) font partie du projet en développement de l'Hillside Terrace. Plus récemment, il a construit le centre de télédiffusion Asahi (Minato-ku, Tokyo, 2003) ; le Niigata International Convention Center (Niigata, Niigata, 2003) ; le National Language Research Institute (Tachikawa, Tokyo, 2004) ; le musée de la Ville de Nakatsu (Nakatsu, Oita, 2005) ; le Musée Shimane de l'ancien Izumo (Izumo, Shimane, 2003–06) et l'École Sam Fox de design et d'arts plastiques de Washington University (Saint Louis, Missouri, 2006). Après avoir récemment achevé le Centre des arts de la scène de Mihara (Mihara, Hiroshima, 2005–07) ; la Délégation de l'imamat ismaélien (Ottawa, Ontario, Canada, 2006–08, publiée ici) et l'extension du laboratoire des médias du MIT (Cambridge, Massachusetts, 2009), Fumihiko Maki travaille actuellement sur un projet de tour pour les Nations unies à New York ; également sur une autre tour dans la zone de l'ancien World Trade Center, toujours à New York et un nouveau musée d'art islamique pour l'Aga Khan à Toronto (Canada).

DELEGATION OF THE ISMAILI IMAMAT
Ottawa, Ontario, Canada, 2006–08

Address: 199 Sussex Drive, Ottawa, Ontario K1N 1K6, Canada, +1 613 237 2532, www.akfc.ca
Area: 6600 m². Client: Imara Sussex Drive Ltd. Cost: not disclosed
Collaboration: Moriyama & Teshima Architects

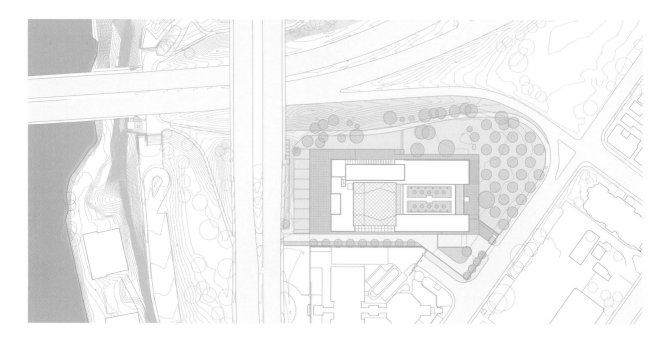

The **DELEGATION OF THE ISMAILI IMAMAT** building establishes a formal and symbolic presence in Canada, on Sussex Drive, a ceremonial route into the capital city where Parliament Hill and the residences of the Governor General and Prime Minister are located. The structure is a secular facility that houses the Aga Khan Foundation Canada, an institution that fosters education and understanding between Islamic countries and populations and the West. The institutional part of the structure includes a research library, seminar rooms, and office space, as well as exhibition areas and assembly zones. A planted grove creates the immediate setting. Within the building, interior spaces connect to the landscape through framed views of the Ottawa River, City Hall, or Gatineau Mountains. The elongated, rectangular structure surrounds an atrium and a courtyard that "recalls the traditional Persian-Islamic garden called a *chahar-bagh.*" Discussions between the architect and the Aga Khan led to the use of the aesthetic properties of rock crystal for the design inspiration. The north and south façades of the building are clad with crystallized glass panels (Neoparies). The glazed atrium structure, forming a faceted glass dome with a suspended inner membrane of woven glass fiber, marks the presence of the building from a distance. A network of geometrically patterned aluminum lattice screens further recalls Islamic tradition without any hint of pastiche.

Das Gebäude der **DELEGATION DES ISMAILI IMAMAT** behauptet sich als formelle und symbolische Präsenz in Kanada. Der Bau liegt am Sussex Drive, einer in die Hauptstadt hineinführenden Paradestraße in Richtung Parliament Hill und zu den Wohnsitzen der Generalgouverneurin und des Premierministers. Der Komplex ist ein Säkularbau und Sitz der kanadischen Aga-Khan-Stiftung, deren Anliegen die Förderung von Bildung und Verständnis zwischen islamischen Ländern und Bürgern und denen des Westens ist. Einrichtungen der Institution im Komplex sind u.a. eine Forschungsbibliothek, Seminarräume und Büros sowie Ausstellungs- und Versammlungsräume. Unmittelbares Umfeld bildet ein eigens angepflanztes Wäldchen. Die Räume im Gebäude sind durch Ausblicke zum Ottawa River, zum Rathaus oder zu den Gatineau Mountains in ihren landschaftlichen Kontext eingebunden. Der längliche, rechteckige Bau umschließt ein Atrium und einen Innenhof, der an eine „traditionelle persisch-islamische Gartenform, den sogenannten *Tschahar Bagh* erinnert". Gespräche zwischen dem Architekten und der Aga-Khan-Stiftung führten dazu, dass die ästhetischen Eigenschaften von Quarz zum Ausgangspunkt des Entwurfs wurden. Nord- und Südfassaden des Gebäudes sind mit Glaskeramikplatten (Neoparies) verblendet. Dominiert wird der Bau von Weitem durch das verglaste Atrium, eine Glaskuppel aus facettiertem Glas, in der eine Innenmembran aus Glasfasergewebe abgespannt ist. Auch ein geometrisches Gitterwerk aus Aluminiumsegmenten ist Verweis auf islamische Bautraditionen, ohne dabei in irgendeiner Weise ins Pastischehafte abzugleiten.

La **DÉLÉGATION DE L'IMAMAT ISMAÉLIEN** affirme la présence concrète et symbolique de la communauté ismaélienne à Ottawa, sur Sussex Drive, principale voie d'accès à la colline du Parlement où se trouvent également les résidences du Gouverneur général et du Premier ministre. Le bâtiment abrite la Fondation Aga Khan-Canada, institution qui promeut l'éducation et la compréhension entre les pays islamiques et les populations occidentales. La partie institutionnelle de l'immeuble comprend une bibilothèque de recherche, des salles de séminaires, des bureaux et des espaces d'expositions ou de réunions. Un bosquet en forme l'environnement immédiat. À l'intérieur, les volumes s'ouvrent sur le paysage par des perspectives cadrées sur l'Ottawa River, l'hôtel de ville ou les Monts de Gatineau. La construction de plan rectangulaire allongé entoure un atrium et une cour qui «rappelle le jardin persan-islamique traditionnel, le Chahar-bagh». Les discussions entre l'Aga Khan et l'architecte ont abouti au choix esthétique du cristal de roche qui inspire certaines formes. Les façades nord et sud sont habillées de panneaux de verre cristallisé (Neoparies). L'atrium vitré, dont la couverture en forme de coupole de verre sous laquelle est tendue une membrane de fibre de verre tissée, signale de loin la présence du bâtiment. Un réseau d'écrans en lattis à motifs géométriques évoque également la tradition islamique, sans pour autant tomber dans le pastiche.

The clean lines of the structure culminate in the unusual, asymmetrically slanted dome.

Die klaren Linien des Baus kulminieren in der ungewöhnlichen Kuppel mit ihren asymmetrischen Schrägen.

Les lignes bien définies du bâtiment culminent dans la coupole à inclinaisons asymétriques.

Large, open spaces allow for assembly. Light is the constant theme of the structure, a sublimated interpretation of texts from the Koran.

Große, offene Räume bieten Platz für Versammlungen. Licht ist im gesamten Bau ein kontinuierliches Thema und eine indirekte Interpretation von Texten aus dem Koran.

De vastes espaces ouverts sont prévus pour les assemblées. La lumière est un thème omniprésent dans ce projet, dans une interprétation sublimée de textes du Coran.

Though strict geometric forms are the rule, the architect has used a honeycomb-shaped screen (right) that filters incoming light and provides a counterpoint to the smoother cladding surfaces.

Obgleich strenge geometrische Formen hier dominieren, setzt der Architekt einen Wandschirm mit Wabenmuster (rechts) ein, um einfallendes Licht zu filtern. Zudem kontrastiert der Schirm mit den glatteren Oberflächen der Wandverkleidung.

Une rigoureuse géométrie est de mise, y compris dans l'écran en nid d'abeille (à droite) qui filtre la lumière extérieure et vient en contrepoint à des plans habillés de matériaux plus doux.

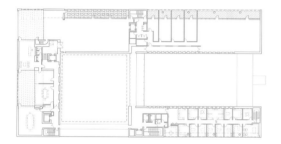

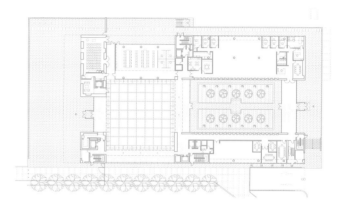

MORPHOSIS

Morphosis
2041 Colorado Avenue
Santa Monica, CA 90404, USA

Tel: +1 310 453 2247
Fax: +1 310 829 3270
E-mail: studio@morphosis.net
Web: www.morphosis.net

MORPHOSIS Principal Thom Mayne, born in Connecticut in 1944, received his B.Arch in 1968 from the University of Southern California, Los Angeles, and his M.Arch degree from Harvard GSD in 1978. He created Morphosis in 1979 with Michael Rotondi, who left to create his own firm, RoTo. Mayne has taught at UCLA, Harvard, Yale, and SCI-Arc, of which he was a founding Board Member. Thom Mayne was the winner of the 2005 Pritzker Prize. Some of the main buildings by Morphosis are the Lawrence House (Hermosa Beach, California, 1981); Kate Mantilini Restaurant (Beverly Hills, California, 1986); Cedar's Sinai Comprehensive Cancer Care Center (Beverly Hills, California, 1987); Crawford Residence (Montecito, 1987–92); Yuzen Vintage Car Museum (project, West Hollywood, 1992); the Blades Residence (Santa Barbara, California, 1992–97); and the International Elementary School (Long Beach, California, 1997–99). More recent work includes the University of Cincinnati Student Recreation Center (Cincinnati, Ohio, 1999–2005); NOAA Satellite Operation Facility in Suitland (Maryland, 2001–05); San Francisco Federal Building (San Francisco, California, 2003–07); 41 Cooper Square (New York, New York, 2006–09, published here); a proposal for the 2012 Olympics in New York City made prior to the selection of London; and the Phare Tower (Paris, France, 2006–12). They are also participating in Brad Pitt's Make it Right initiative in New Orleans with their "Floating Prototype House," and are working on the Museum of Nature and Science (Dallas, Texas) and the Alexandria Bay Port of Entry (Alexandria Bay, New York), all in the USA unless stated otherwise.

Thom Mayne, Direktor von **MORPHOSIS**, wurde 1944 in Connecticut geboren. Seine Studien schloss er 1968 mit einem B.Arch an der University of Southern California, Los Angeles, sowie 1978 mit einem M.Arch in Harvard ab. 1979 gründete er mit Michael Rotondi sein Büro Morphosis. Rotondi machte sich später mit seiner eigenen Firma RoTo selbstständig. Mayne lehrte an der UCLA, in Harvard, Yale und am Sci-Arc, zu dessen Gründungsmitgliedern er zählt. 2005 wurde Mayne mit dem Pritzker-Preis ausgezeichnet. Zu den wichtigsten Bauten von Morphosis zählen das Lawrence House (Hermosa Beach, Kalifornien, 1981), Kate Mantilini Restaurant (Beverly Hills, Kalifornien, 1986), Cedar's Sinai Krebsklinik (Beverly Hills, Kalifornien, 1987), Crawford Residence (Montecito, 1987–92), Yuzen Oldtimermuseum (Projekt, West Hollywood, 1992), Blades Residence (Santa Barbara, Kalifornien, 1992–97) sowie die International Elementary School (Long Beach, Kalifornien, 1997–99). Jüngere Arbeiten sind das Freizeitzentrum für Studenten der University of Cincinnati (Cincinnati, Ohio, 1999–2005), das NOAA-Satellitenzentrum in Suitland (Maryland, 2001–05), das San Francisco Federal Building (San Francisco, Kalifornien, 2003–07), 41 Cooper Square (New York, 2006–09, hier vorgestellt), ein Entwurf für die Olympiade 2012 in New York (entstanden vor der Entscheidung für London aus Austragungsort), sowie das Hochhaus Phare (Paris, Frankreich, 2006–12). Darüber hinaus ist das Büro mit seinem „Floating Prototype House" an Brad Pitts Initiative „Make it Right" in New Orleans beteiligt und arbeitet an einem Museum für Naturkunde (Dallas, Texas) sowie am Importhafen Alexandria Bay (Alexandria Bay, New York), alle in den USA, sofern nicht anders vermerkt.

Le directeur de **MORPHOSIS**, Thom Mayne, né dans le Connecticut en 1944, est B. Arch de l'Université de Californie du Sud à Los Angeles (1968) et M. Arch d'Harvard (1978). Il fonde l'agence Morphosis en 1979 avec Michael Rotondi, qui la quitte ensuite pour créer sa propre structure, RoTo. Il a enseigné à UCLA, Harvard, Yale, et SCI-Arc, dont il est un des fondateurs. Thom Mayne a reçu le prix Pritzker en 2005. Parmi ses principales réalisations : la Maison Lawrence (Hermosa Beach, Californie, 1981) ; le restaurant Kate Mantilini (Beverly Hills, Californie, 1986) ; le centre anticancéreux de Cedar's Sinai (Beverly Hills, Californie, 1987) ; la Résidence Crawford (Montecito, Californie, 1987–92) ; le Musée historique de l'automobile Yuzen (projet, West Hollywood, 1992) ; la Résidence Blades (Santa Barbara, Californie, 1992–97) et l'École élémentaire internationale de Long Beach (Californie, 1997–99). Plus récemment, il a construit le centre de sports des étudiants de l'Université de Cincinnati (Ohio, 1999–2005) ; les installations de suivi de satellites de NOAA (Suitland, Maryland, 2001–05) ; l'immeuble fédéral de San Francisco (San Francisco, 2003–07) ; l'immeuble du 41 Cooper Square (New York, 2006–09, publié ici) ; une proposition pour la candidature de New York aux Jeux olympiques 2012 et le projet de la tour Phare (Paris-La Défense). Morphosis participe à l'initiative de Brad Pitt « Make it Right » à la Nouvelle-Orléans à travers une proposition de « maison flottante prototype », et travaille sur les projets du Musée de la nature et des sciences (Dallas, Texas) et sur celui de l'entrée du port d'Alexandria Bay (Alexandria Bay, New York).

41 COOPER SQUARE

New York, New York, USA, 2006–09

Address: 41 Cooper Square (3rd Avenue between 6th and 7th Streets), Lower Level 1, New York, NY 10003, USA, www.cooper.edu
Area: 9755 m². Client: The Cooper Union for the Advancement of Science and Art. Cost: not disclosed
Collaboration: Gruzen Sampton (Associate Architect), F. J. Sciame Construction Company (Construction Management),
Jonathan Rose Companies (Project Management)

41 COOPER SQUARE is a new academic building for the Cooper Union, a privately funded college founded in 1859. The architects state: "41 Cooper Square aspires to reflect the institution's stated goal to create an iconic building—one that reflects its values and aspirations as a center for advanced and innovative education in Art, Architecture and Engineering." The college's three schools, previously housed in separate buildings, are brought together in this new structure that is intended to promote a dialogue between them. A six-meter wide grand stairway runs up four stories of the structure in a central atrium. A glazed double-height student lounge overlooking the city is located at the top of these stairs. Sky lobbies and meeting places are arranged near the central atrium on the fifth to ninth floors. The architects have sought to make the building transparent to the city, for example at street level. An exhibition gallery and 200-seat auditorium are located one level below grade. The exterior double skin has a semitransparent layer of perforated stainless steel over the glazing. 41 Cooper Square was built to LEED Gold standards and is "likely to achieve a Platinum rating."

41 COOPER SQUARE ist ein neues akademisches Lehrgebäude für die Cooper Union, eine 1859 gegründete Privatuniversität. Die Architekten führen aus: „41 Cooper Square ist der Versuch, den erklärten Anspruch der Institution einzulösen, ein Bauwerk zu schaffen, das zugleich eine Ikone ist – eine Ikone, die ihre Werte und Ziele als herausragendes und innovatives Bildungszentrum in den Künsten, der Architektur und den Ingenieurwissenschaften widerspiegelt." Die drei bis dato in verschiedenen Gebäuden untergebrachten Fakultäten werden im neuen Gebäude zusammengelegt, das den Austausch der Disziplinen fördern will. Eine sechs Meter breite Haupttreppe zieht sich im zentral gelegenen Atrium vier Stockwerke in die Höhe. Am Ende der Treppe liegt eine verglaste Studentenlounge mit doppelter Geschosshöhe und Blick über die Stadt. Von der fünften bis zur neunten Etage wurden in Nähe des zentralen Atriums *sky lobbies* und Treffpunkte angelegt. Den Architekten ging es darum, das Gebäude zur Stadt hin transparent zu gestalten, so auch auf Straßenniveau. Im ersten Untergeschoss sind Ausstellungsräume und ein Auditorium mit 200 Plätzen untergebracht. Die doppelte Außenhaut des Gebäudes besteht aus Glas und einer darübergelagerten, semitransparenten Schicht aus perforiertem Edelstahl. 41 Cooper Square wurde nach den Standards eines LEED Goldzertifikats gebaut und wird „vermutlich eine Platin-Auszeichnung erhalten".

Le **41 COOPER SQUARE** est un immeuble universitaire construit pour la Cooper Union, institution privée fondée en 1859. « 41 Cooper Square aspire à exprimer l'objectif de l'institution de créer un immeuble iconique, reflétant ses valeurs et ses aspirations de centre avancé et innovateur de formation à l'art, à l'architecture et à l'ingénierie. » Les trois écoles de Cooper Union, préalablement logées dans des bâtiments séparés, sont réunies dans cette structure, ce qui favorisera leur dialogue. Un escalier principal de six mètres de large dessert quatre étages à partir de l'atrium central. Tout en haut, une salle pour étudiants à vitrage double-hauteur domine la ville. De vastes paliers et des salles de réunions sont disposés autour de l'atrium central du 5e au 9e niveau. L'agence a cherché à rendre l'immeuble transparent vers la ville, par exemple au niveau de la rue. Une galerie d'expositions et un auditorium de 200 places se trouvent au sous-sol. La double-peau externe contient une strate semi-transparente en acier inoxydable perforé qui protège les vitrages. Le 41 Cooper Square a été édifié selon les règles LEED Or, et « atteindra probablement le niveau Platine. »

Interior spaces are in harmony with
the unexpected fractured exterior
forms of the building.

Die Innenräume harmonieren mit den
erstaunlichen, fragmentierten Formen
des Außenbaus.

Les volumes intérieurs sont en
harmonie avec la forme extérieure du
bâtiment, curieusement fracturée.

Though it has an essentially rectangular volume, as seen in the drawings to the right, the building has many unexpected features, such as the stairway seen below.

Obwohl der Bau im Grunde ein rechteckiges Volumen ist (siehe Zeichnungen rechts), hat er zahlreiche ungeahnte Besonderheiten, wie etwa die Treppe unten im Bild.

Bien qu'occupant un volume essentiellement rectangulaire (dessins de droite), le bâtiment présente des éléments architecturaux inattendus comme l'escalier ci-dessous.

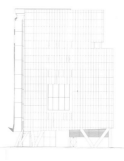
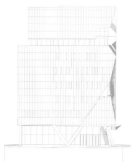
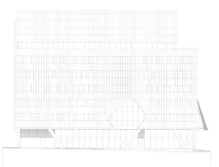
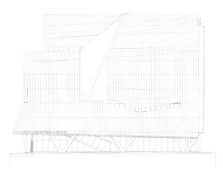

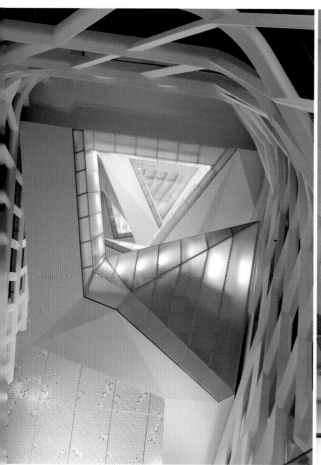

ERIC OWEN MOSS

Eric Owen Moss Architects
8557 Higuera Street
Culver City, CA 90232
USA

Tel: +1 310 839 1199
Fax: +1 310 839 7922
E-mail: mail@ericowenmoss.com
Web: www.ericowenmoss.com

Born in Los Angeles, California, in 1943, **ERIC OWEN MOSS** received his B.A. degree from UCLA in 1965, and his M.Arch from UC Berkeley in 1968. He also received an M.Arch degree at Harvard in 1972. He has been a Professor of Design at the Southern California Institute of Architecture since 1974. He opened his own firm in Culver City in 1973. His built work includes the Central Housing Office, University of California at Irvine (Irvine, 1986–89); Lindblade Tower (Culver City, 1987–89); Paramount Laundry (Culver City, 1987–89); Gary Group (Culver City, 1988–90); The Box (Culver City, 1990–94); I.R.S. Building (Culver City, 1993–94); and Samitaur (Culver City, 1994–96), all in California. Other more recent work includes projects for the Queens Museum of Art (Queens, New York, 2001); the Beehive (Culver City, California, 2002); Stealth (Culver City, California, 2002); the Mariinsky and New Holland Cultural Center (Saint Petersburg, Russia, 2001–03); 3555 Hayden (Culver City, California, 2007); and the Gateway Art Tower (Culver City, California, 2007–09, published here), all in the USA unless stated otherwise. Ongoing projects are the Glass Tower, a high-rise office building (Los Angeles, California, 1998/2006–); Sunset Doheny Hotel (West Hollywood, California); and 3585 Hayden (Culver City, California, 2008–).

ERIC OWEN MOSS wurde 1943 in Los Angeles geboren und absolvierte seinen B.A. 1965 an der UCLA, sowie 1968 einen M.Arch an der UC Berkeley. 1972 erwarb er zudem einen M.Arch in Harvard. Seit 1974 ist er Professor für Entwerfen am Southern California Institute of Architecture. Sein eigenes Büro eröffnete er 1973 in Culver City. Zu seinen realisierten Bauten zählen das Central Housing Office auf dem Campus der University of California in Irvine (1986–89), der Lindblade Tower (Culver City, 1987–89), der Paramount Waschsalon (Culver City, 1987–89), die Gary Group (Culver City, 1988–90), The Box (Culver City, 1990–94), das I.R.S. Building (Culver City, 1993–94) sowie Samitaur (Culver City, 1994–96), alle in Kalifornien. Jüngere Arbeiten sind u.a. das Queens Museum of Art (New York, 2001), der Beehive (Culver City, 2002), Stealth (Culver City, 2002), die Erweiterung des Mariinskij-Theaters (St. Petersburg, Russland, 2001–03), 3555 Hayden (Culver City, 2007) und der Gateway Art Tower (Culver City, 2007–09, hier vorgestellt), alle in den USA, sofern nicht anders vermerkt. Aktuelle Projekte sind der Glass Tower, ein Bürohochhaus (Los Angeles, 1998/2006–), das Sunset Doheny Hotel (West Hollywood) und 3585 Hayden (Culver City, 2008–).

Né à Los Angeles en 1943, **ERIC OWEN MOSS** est B.A. de UCLA (1965) et M.Arch de UC Berkeley (1968). Il est également M.Arch d'Harvard (1972). Il a ouvert son agence à Culver City en 1973 et enseigne la conception architecturale au Southern California Institute of Architecture depuis 1974. Parmi ses réalisations, toutes en Californie : le Bureau central du logement de l'Université de Californie à Irvine (Irvine, 1986–89) ; la tour Lindblade (Culver City, 1987–89) ; la blanchisserie Paramount (Culver City, 1987–89) ; le Gary Group (Culver City, 1988–90) ; The Box (Culver City, 1990–94) ; les immeubles de l'I.R.S. (Culver City, 1993–94) ; et Samitaur (Culver City, 1994–96). Plus récemment, il est l'auteur de projets pour le Queens Museum of Art (Queens, New York, 2001) ; la Beehive (Culver City, 2002) ; Stealth (Culver City, 2002) ; le théâtre Mariinsky et le centre culturel du quartier de la Nouvelle-Hollande (Saint-Pétersbourg, Russie, 2001–03) ; l'immeuble 3555 Hayden (Culver City, 2007) ; et la tour Gateway Art (Culver City, 2007–09, publiée ici). Ses projets en cours sont la tour Glass, un immeuble de bureaux de grande hauteur (Los Angeles, 1998/2006–) ; le Sunset Doheny Hotel (West Hollywood) ; et un immeuble 3585 Hayden (Culver City, 2008–).

GATEWAY ART TOWER

Culver City, California, USA 2007–09

Address: Hayden Avenue/National Boulevard, Culver City, CA 90232, USA
Area: 139 m². Client: Samitaur Constructs. Cost: not disclosed
Collaboration: Dolan Daggett, Pegah Sadr, Eric McNevin

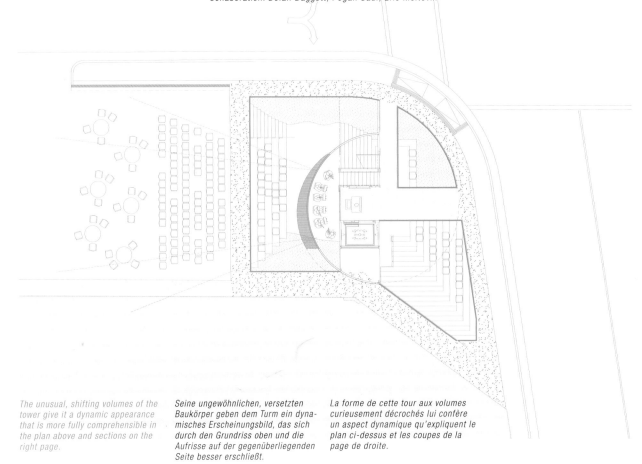

The unusual, shifting volumes of the tower give it a dynamic appearance that is more fully comprehensible in the plan above and sections on the right page.

Seine ungewöhnlichen, versetzten Baukörper geben dem Turm ein dynamisches Erscheinungsbild, das sich durch den Grundriss oben und die Aufrisse auf der gegenüberliegenden Seite besser erschließt.

La forme de cette tour aux volumes curieusement décrochés lui confère un aspect dynamique qu'expliquent le plan ci-dessus et les coupes de la page de droite.

The **ART TOWER**, an information facility, is located at the busy intersection of Hayden Avenue and National Boulevard at the entry to the area of Culver City that Eric Owen Moss has done much to redevelop over the years. The Tower is meant to display cultural and local event information. The building is 22 meters high, exceeding the usual 17-meter height limitation in the area, thus contributing to its iconic presence. Made up of five, stacked, circular steel rings about nine meters in diameter, the Tower has translucent acrylic projection screens and viewing decks for visitors at each level. The building has an enclosed glazed elevator and an open stairway for access to each floor. Because of earthquake regulations, the Tower is supported by a deep foundation of concrete piles with a "continuous grade beam tying the piles together."

Der **ART TOWER**, ein Informationszentrum, liegt an der vielbefahrenen Kreuzung Hayden Avenue und National Boulevard, an der Grenze zum Bezirk Culver City, zu dessen Neugestaltung Eric Owen Moss im Laufe der Jahre entscheidend beigetragen hat. Der Turm soll über kulturelle Ereignisse und lokale Veranstaltungen informieren. Mit seinen 22 m übersteigt er die übliche Höhenbegrenzung von 17 m in dieser Gegend, was ihn umso mehr zu einem Wahrzeichen macht. Der Tower besteht aus fünf gestapelten, runden Stahlringen mit einem Durchmesser von je rund neun Metern. Jede Etage wurde mit Infoscreens aus mattem Acrylglas und Aussichtsplattformen für die Besucher versehen. Erschlossen werden die einzelnen Etagen des Gebäudes durch einen Glasaufzug und eine offene Treppe. Aufgrund von Bauvorschriften zur Erdbebensicherheit fußt der Turm auf einer Tiefgründung aus Betonpfählen. Ein „durchgängiger Fundamentträger hält die Pfähle zusammen".

L'**ART TOWER**, tour support d'informations, se dresse au carrefour d'Hayden Avenue et du National Boulevard, à l'entrée de la zone de Culver City qu'Eric Owen Moss rénove depuis des années. Elle affiche des informations sur des événements locaux et culturels. D'une hauteur de 22 mètres, elle dépasse de 5 mètres la hauteur autorisée dans cette zone, ce qui renforce sa présence iconique. Composée d'une superposition de cinq anneaux d'acier de 9 mètres de diamètre environ, elle est équipée d'écrans de projection en acrylique translucide et, à chaque niveau, de plates-formes d'observation pour les visiteurs. Un ascenseur de verre et un escalier ouvert desservent chaque niveau. Pour respecter les normes antisismiques, l'ensemble repose sur des pieux de béton profondément enfoncés dans le sol, « reliés par une poutre de sol continue qui les solidarise ».

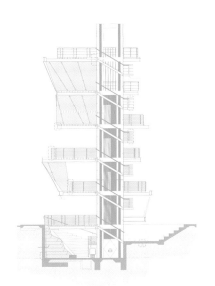
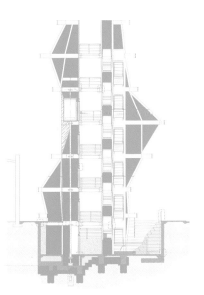
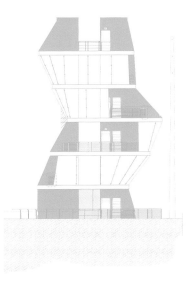

SUSANNE NOBIS

Susanne Nobis
Am Fichtenhain 9
82335 Berg
Germany

Tel: +49 8151 95 91 87
Fax: +49 8151 95 91 86
E-mail: su.nobis@t-online.de

SUSANNE NOBIS was born in Munich, Germany, in 1963. She attended the Architecture Polytechnic of Central London (1991–92) and obtained her diploma in architecture from the University of Applied Sciences (Munich, 1987–92). She received a further diploma in Architecture from the Technical University Berlin (1996–99). She worked in the Renzo Piano Building Workshop (Genoa, 1992–93), with Herzog + Partner (Munich, 1994–95), and with Ackermann und Partner (Munich, 1995–96), before creating her own office in 2000. Her work includes House D_Residential (Ulm, 2000–05); House N_Residence with Office (Lake Starnberg, 2003–06); House RW (Wörthsee, 2006–08); Architektouren Traveling Exhibition (2008); House H, a residence with an exhibition area (Walls in the Landscape, Grossburgwedel, 2007–09, published here); and the design of the Ecological Architecture Exhibition (Starnberg, 2009), all in Germany.

SUSANNE NOBIS wurde 1963 in München geboren. Sie studierte an der Architecture Polytechnic of Central London (1991–92) und schloss ihr Architekturstudium mit einem Diplom an der Fachhochschule München ab (1987–92). Ein weiteres Diplom in Architektur absolvierte sie an der TU Berlin (1996–99). Bevor sie 2000 ihr eigenes Büro gründete, arbeitete sie für Renzo Piano Building Workshop (Genua, 1992–93), Herzog + Partner (München, 1994–95) sowie für Ackermann und Partner (München, 1995–96). Zu ihren Projekten zählen Haus D, Wohnhaus (Ulm, 2000–05), Haus N, Wohnhaus mit Büro (Starnberger See, 2003–06), Haus RW (Wörthsee, 2006–08), Architektouren Wanderausstellung (2008), Haus H, Wohnhaus mit Galerie (Walls in the Landscape, Großburgwedel, 2007–09, hier vorgestellt) sowie die Architektur für eine Ausstellung über ökologische Architektur (Starnberg, 2009), alle in Deutschland.

SUSANNE NOBIS, née à Munich en 1963, a étudié au département d'architecture de la Polytechnic of Central London (G.-B., 1991–92) et obtenu son diplôme d'architecture de l'Université des arts appliqués de Munich, (1987–92). Elle est également diplômée en architecture de l'Université polytechnique de Berlin (1996–99). Elle a travaillé au Renzo Piano Building Workshop (Gênes, 1992–93), chez Herzog + Partner (Munich, 1994–95) et Ackermann und Partner (Munich, 1995–96), avant de créer sa propre structure en 2000. Parmi ses réalisations, toutes en Allemagne : la Maison D (Ulm, 2000–05) ; la Maison N, résidence et bureaux (lac de Starnberg, 2003–06) ; la Maison RW (Wörthsee, 2006–08) ; l'exposition itinérante Architektouren (2008) ; la Maison H, résidence avec galerie d'expositions (murs dans le paysage, Grossburgwedel, 2007–09, publiée ici) et la conception de l'Exposition d'architecture écologique (Starnberg, 2009).

WALLS IN THE LANDSCAPE

Grossburgwedel, Germany, 2007–09

Area: 343 m². Client: not disclosed. Cost: not disclosed
Collaboration: Björn Siedke

With its rhythmic Corten-steel walls, the house appears like a cross between a contemporary sculpture and a work of architecture.

Mit seinen rhythmisch bewegten Corten-Stahl-Wänden wirkt das Bauwerk wie eine Kreuzung aus zeitgenössischer Skulptur und Architektur.

Par ses murs en acier Corten rythmant sa composition, la maison se trouve au croisement de la sculpture et de l'architecture contemporaines.

Set in a large green space, the house opens out onto its environment as much as local weather permits.

Das auf einem weitläufigen grünen Grundstück gelegene Haus öffnet sich zu seinem Umfeld, soweit es das regionale Wetter zulässt.

Implantée dans un vaste espace vert, la maison s'ouvre sur son environnement autant que le climat local le permet.

The meadow site of this residence with an exhibition area is in the town of Grossburgwedel, in Lower Saxony, about 15 kilometers from Hanover. An oak-lined avenue marks the landscape. The structure is defined by walls made of Corten steel. According to the architect, these "make a colorful analogy with the old trees in the landscape." The single-story structure "arranges itself very gently in the park" and floor-to-ceiling glazing allows residents to have a full view of the natural setting. A gallery area, mostly for photography, receives indirect natural lighting through a narrow skylight over a rear wall. Walls on both sides of the north-south axis of the building allow for further exhibition space with overhead lighting provided by a large skylight. Susanne Nobis comments: "The inner workings of the house are enhanced by emerging variations in the light." A partially covered terrace marks one end of the house. One might be tempted to call this architecture "minimal," yet the massive presence of Corten-steel walls gives it a more complex, sculptural character.

Das Wiesengrundstück dieses Wohnhauses mit Galerie liegt in Großburgwedel in Niedersachsen, rund 15 km von Hannover entfernt. Eine Eichenallee zieht sich durch die Landschaft. Der Bau selbst wird von Wandelementen aus Corten-Stahl geprägt. Der Architektin zufolge sind sie „eine farbige Analogie zu den alten Bäumen in der Landschaft". Der Bungalow „fügt sich höchst einfühlsam in den Park". Deckenhohe Verglasung ermöglicht den Bewohnern uneingeschränkten Ausblick in die Umgebung. Eine Galerie, in erster Linie für Fotografie, wird durch ein schmales Oberlicht indirekt mit Tageslicht erhellt. Wände entlang der Nord-Süd-Achse des Hauses bieten zusätzliche Präsentationsfläche. Dort fällt das Tageslicht durch ein großes Oberlicht ein. Susanne Nobis erläutert: „Das Innenleben des Hauses wird durch die sich wandelnde Lichtsituation zusätzlich belebt." Eine teilweise überdachte Terrasse bildet den Gebäudeabschluss. Man mag versucht sein, diese Architektur „minimalistisch" zu nennen – doch die massive Präsenz der Corten-Stahl-Wandelemente verleihen ihr einen eher komplexen, skulpturalen Charakter.

Cette résidence et sa galerie d'expositions ont été construites dans une prairie sur la commune de Großburgwedel en Basse-Saxe, à quinze kilomètres environ de Hanovre. Une allée bordée de chênes structure le paysage. La maison se définit par des murs en acier Corten, qui, selon l'architecte, « établissent une analogie colorée avec les arbres anciens que l'on trouve dans le paysage ». La structure d'un seul niveau « s'insère très délicatement dans le parc » et le vitrage toute hauteur permet à ses occupants une vue globale du cadre naturel. Une galerie, essentiellement consacrée à la photographie, reçoit un éclairage naturel de façon indirecte et par une étroite verrière ouverte en bordure du mur de fond. Des deux côtés de l'axe Nord-Sud, les murs permettent des accrochages sous un éclairage zénithal fourni par une grande verrière. Pour Susanne Nobis : « Les aménagements intérieurs de la maison sont mis en valeur par les variations de la lumière. » Une terrasse partiellement couverte marque l'extrémité de la maison. On pourrait être tenté de parler de « minimalisme », mais la présence massive de parois en acier Corten confère à cette réalisation un caractère complexe plus sculptural.

A canopied exterior terrace allows residents to dine outside in warmer months (above).

Eine überdachte Terrasse erlaubt den Bewohnern, in warmen Monaten draußen zu essen (oben).

Une terrasse abritée par un auvent permet de dîner dehors à la belle saison (ci-dessus).

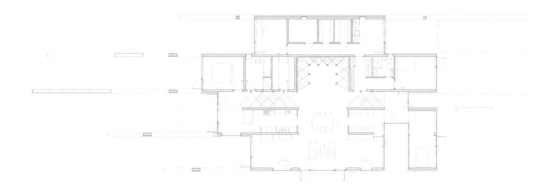

Although rectilinearity is the rule in this house, the disposition of volumes and voids provides for ample variety.

Zwar sind rechte Winkel in diesem Haus die Regel, doch die Anordnung der Baukörper und Zwischenräume bietet jede Menge Abwechslung.

Bien que l'orthogonalité soit de règle ici, la disposition des volumes et des vides offre une grande variété de composition.

NOX

NOX/Lars Spuybroek
Groothandelsgebouw D8.122
Conradstraat 38
3013 AP Rotterdam
The Netherlands

Tel/Fax: +31 10 477 28 53
E-mail: nox@luna.nl
Web: www.nox-art-architecture.com

Lars Spuybroek is the principal of **NOX**. Since the early 1990s, he has been involved in research on the relationship between architecture and media, often more specifically between architecture and computing. He was the editor-publisher of one of the first magazines on the subject, and has made videos and interactive electronic artworks, and is known for his theoretical work on digital design. Since 2006, he has been a Professor at the Georgia Institute of Technology in Atlanta. NOX completed HtwoOexpo (Neeltje Jans Island, 1994–97); V2_lab (Rotterdam, 1998); wetGRID, exhibition design (2000, Nantes, France); an interactive tower for the Dutch city of Doetinchem, D-tower (1999–2004); Son-O-house, "a house where sounds live" (Son-en-Breugel, 2000–04); Maison Folie, a complex of cultural buildings (Lille, France, 2001–04); and the NAMOC-field (Beijing, China, 2008); as well as working on competitions for the Centre Pompidou in Metz (France, 2003; competition won by Shigeru Ban) and the Silk Road West (Xi'an, China, 2007–, first prize), all in the Netherlands unless stated otherwise. Recent and ongoing work includes the Three Graces (Dubai, UAE, 2008–, first prize); The Ladies of the Lake Residences (Milan, New York, USA, 2009–11, published here); and The Beacon of Amsterdam (Amsterdam, the Netherlands, 2009–12, also published here).

Lars Spuybroek ist leitender Architekt bei **NOX**. Seit den frühen 1990er-Jahren beschäftigt er sich mit Forschungen zum Verhältnis von Architektur und Medien, oft insbesondere von Architektur und Computertechnik. Er war Herausgeber und Verleger einer der ersten Zeitschriften zum Thema, realisierte Videos und interaktive elektronische Kunstprojekte und ist bekannt für seine theoretischen Arbeiten zum computergestützten Entwerfen. Seit 2006 ist er Professor am Georgia Institute of Technology in Atlanta. NOX realisierte die Projekte HtwoOexpo (Neeltje Jans, 1994–97), V2_lab (Rotterdam, 1998), wetGRID, Ausstellungsarchitektur (2000, Nantes, Frankreich), D-tower, einen interaktiven Turm für die niederländische Stadt Doetinchem (1999–2004), Son-O-house, „ein Haus, in dem Klänge wohnen" (Son-en-Breugel, 2000–04), den Kulturkomplex Maison Folie (Lille, Frankreich, 2001–04) sowie das NAMOC-field (Peking, China, 2008). Darüber hinaus arbeitete das Büro an Wettbewerbsentwürfen für das Centre Pompidou in Metz (Frankreich, 2003, den Wettbewerb gewann Shigeru Ban) und die Silk Road West (Xi'an, China, 2007–, erster Preis), alle in den Niederlanden, sofern nicht anders angegeben. Jüngere und aktuelle Projekte sind u.a. Three Graces (Dubai, VAE, 2008–, erster Preis), Ladies of the Lake, Wohnbauten (Milan, New York, USA, 2009–11, hier vorgestellt) und schließlich der Beacon of Amsterdam (Amsterdam, 2009–12, ebenfalls hier vorgestellt).

NOX est dirigée par Lars Spuybroek qui, depuis le début des années 1990, s'intéresse aux recherches sur les relations entre l'architecture et les médias, et plus spécifiquement entre l'architecture et l'informatique. Il a été le rédacteur en chef-éditeur de l'un des premiers magazines sur le sujet, a réalisé des vidéos et des œuvres artistiques interactives numériques, et est aussi connu pour son travail théorique sur la conception numérique. Depuis 2006, il enseigne au Georgia Institute of Technology à Atlanta. NOX a réalisé HtwoOexpo (île de Neeltje Jans, 1994–97) ; V2_lab (Rotterdam, 1998) ; wetGRID, une conception d'exposition (2000, Nantes, France) ; la D-tower, tour interactive pour la ville néerlandaise de Doetinchem (1999–2004) ; la Son-O-house, « la maison où vivent les sons » (Son-en-Breugel, 2000–04) ; la Maison Folie, un complexe de bâtiments culturels (Lille, 2001–04) ; le NAMOC-field (Pékin, 2008) ; des participations à des concours comme le Centre Pompidou à Metz (2003 ; concours remporté par Shigeru Ban) et la Route de la Soie Ouest (Xi'an, Chine, 2007–, premier prix). Actuellement, il travaille sur les projets des Trois Grâces (Dubaï, EAU, 2008–, premier prix) ; les Résidences des dames du lac (Milan, New York, 2009–11, publiées ici) et le phare d'Amsterdam (Amsterdam, 2009–12, également publié ici).

THE BEACON OF AMSTERDAM

Amsterdam, The Netherlands, 2009–12

Area: 18 750 m². Client: De Alliantie, Amsterdam. Cost: not disclosed
Collaboration: Thomas Wortmann, Joseph Corsi, Emilie Meaud

Located in Amsterdam, this tower has something of a Romantic ruin about it. As Lars Spuybroek, principal of NOX, puts it: "**THE BEACON OF AMSTERDAM** uses our interest in variation and the picturesque to create a signature residential tower on the banks of the wide water north of Amsterdam." Seen from another angle, the structure uses industrial panel and prefabrication techniques that have very little to do with the stone tower evoked in some of the renderings published here. Just three different panels are used, creating irregular patterns on a relatively small scale—a scale that is contrasted with the rather monumental outline of the tower. The Beacon of Amsterdam is to contain a variety of different apartment types, three floors of office space, and a ground-floor lobby and restaurant, together with parking located below grade.

Der in Amsterdam gelegene Turm hat etwas von einer romantischen Ruine. Lars Spuybroek, leitender Architekt bei NOX, formuliert es so: „**DER LEUCHTTURM VON AMSTERDAM** macht sich unsere Faszination für Abwechslung und unsere Liebe zum Idyllischen zunutze. So entsteht ein Wohnhochhaus als Wahrzeichen am offenen Wasser nördlich von Amsterdam". Aus anderen Blickwinkeln zeigt sich, dass der Bau industrielle Verblend- und Fertigbautechniken nutzt, die nur wenig mit der Optik eines gemauerten Turms zu tun haben, was einige der hier vorgestellten Renderings vermuten lassen. Insgesamt kommen nur drei verschiedene Verblendpaneele zum Einsatz, durch die ein relativ kleinteiliges, unregelmäßiges Muster entsteht. Diese Kleinteiligkeit kontrastiert mit der eher monumentalen Gesamtsilhouette des Turms. Im Beacon of Amsterdam sollen verschiedene Wohnungstypen entstehen, drei Etagen mit Büroflächen, Lobby und Restaurant im Erdgeschoss sowie ein unterirdisches Parkhaus.

Cette tour, qui s'élèvera bientôt à Amsterdam, n'est pas sans évoquer une ruine romantique. Comme l'explique Lars Spuybroek qui dirige NOX : « **LE PHARE D'AMSTERDAM** joue de notre intérêt pour les variations et le pittoresque pour créer un tour résidentielle remarquable au bord des grands plans d'eau du nord d'Amsterdam. » La tour, qui fait appel à des panneaux industriels et des techniques de préfabrication, n'a cependant pas grand-chose à voir avec la tour de pierre à laquelle pourraient faire penser certaines perspectives numériques publiées ici. Trois types de panneaux permettent de créer des compositions irrégulières de relativement petite échelle qui contraste avec l'aspect assez monumental de l'immeuble. Le phare contiendra divers types d'appartements, trois étages de bureaux et, au rez-de-chaussée, un hall d'accueil et un restaurant. Les parkings seront en sous-sol.

  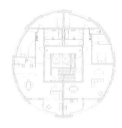

The articulated surface of the tower and its tapering form give it an almost ancient appearance, especially as seen in the rendering on the left page.

Die strukturierte Oberfläche des Turms und seine sich verjüngende Form erinnern fast an Bauten des Altertums, besonders auf dem Rendering auf der linken Seite.

La façade articulée de la tour et sa forme effilée font presque penser à des constructions anciennes, en particulier dans la perspective de synthèse de la page de gauche.

THE LADIES OF THE LAKE

Milan, New York, USA, 2009–11

Area: 150–350 m². Client: Marlof Maks, Haarlem. Cost: not disclosed
Collaboration: Thomas Wortmann, Megan Ng, Thomas Buseck

Located two hours from Manhattan in Dutchess County, this project concerns a total of three houses of different sizes set around a lake. The houses are lifted up and have no garden or terrace. The architect explains: "Each house is covered by a large, heavily decorated structure that creates such outdoor spaces around and in between the rooms, and provides a form of camouflage, blending the houses with the environment." The decoration is a computer-generated pattern that is inspired, unexpectedly, by the writing of John Ruskin. Lars Spuybroek evokes the "wall-veil" seen in the Ca d'Oro in Venice. "In the Mediterranean," says the architect, "one believes skin should cover structure by cladding, the other believes structure can be projected outward and turn into ornament by becoming filigree. By combining these two, the shiplike nave and skinlike tracery are merged, which has a substantial effect on people walking in the house because they are constantly offered the possibility of seeing out in the lateral direction, with the still lake and the trees."

Das zwei Stunden von Manhattan entfernte Projekt liegt in Dutchess County und umfasst drei Häuser unterschiedlicher Größe an einem See. Die aufgeständerten Hausbauten haben keinerlei Gärten oder Terrassen. Der Architekt führt aus: „Jedes der Häuser wird von einer monumentalen, auffällig ornamentierten Konstruktion umfangen, durch die Außenbereiche um die Räume und zwischen den Räumen entstehen. Zugleich bilden sie eine Art Tarnhülle, die die Häuser mit der Umgebung verschmelzen lässt." Das Ornament basiert auf einem computergenerierten Muster, das erstaunlicherweise von den Schriften John Ruskins inspiriert wurde. Lars Spuybroek erinnert an „Wand-Schleier" wie man sie vom Ca d'Oro in Venedig kennt. „Im Mittelmeerraum", so der Architekt, „glauben die einen, die Gebäudehaut müsse ein Bauwerk als Verkleidung umhüllen, die anderen, man könne die Struktur nach außen projizieren, indem man sie zum Filigranornament werden lässt. Durch eine Kombination dieser beiden Ansätze verschmelzen der schiffsartige Baukörper und das hüllenartige Maßwerk zu einer Einheit. Dies hat erhebliche Auswirkung auf alle, die sich im Haus bewegen – sie haben uneingeschränkt die Möglichkeit, seitlich aus dem Bau zu blicken, hinaus zum stillen See und den Bäumen."

Ce projet porte sur trois maisons de dimensions différentes disposées autour d'un lac, sur un terrain situé à deux heures de voiture de Manhattan dans le comté de Dutchess. Reposant sur des pilotis, elles ne possèdent ni jardin ni terrasse. Selon l'architecte : « Chaque maison est recouverte d'une grande structure fortement décorée qui crée des espaces extérieurs autour des pièces, mais aussi entre elles, dans une sorte de camouflage qui aide les maisons à se fondre dans l'environnement. » Le motif de cette superstructure composé par ordinateur est inspiré de façon inattendue des écrits de John Ruskin. Lars Spuybroek évoque le « mur voile » vu sur la Ca d'Oro à Venise. « Dans l'espace méditerranéen », explique l'architecte, « certains croient que la peau doit recouvrir la structure comme un habillage, d'autres que la structure peut se projeter vers l'extérieur et se transformer en ornement par effet de filigrane. En combinant ces deux approches, le volume en nef et les découpes de la peau fusionnent, ce qui affecte substantiellement l'existence des habitants de cette maison puisqu'en se déplaçant, ils ont en permanence la possibilité d'apercevoir sur les côtés le lac et les arbres. »

The architect describes the exterior web that covers these houses as a sort of "camouflage" that permits the creation of intermediate spaces, between interior and exterior.

Der Architekt beschreibt die netzähnliche Außenhaut, die die Bauten umfängt, als eine Art „Tarnhülle". Durch sie entstehen Zonen zwischen Innen- und Außenraum.

L'architecte présente la résille qui recouvre les maisons comme une sorte de « camouflage » qui permet de créer des espaces intermédiaires entre l'intérieur et l'extérieur.

The vegetally inspired exterior panels allow light in and enable residents to take in the view of the wooded site.

Die von Pflanzenformen inspirierten Außenpaneele lassen Licht in das Haus und gestatten den Bewohnern zugleich Ausblick auf die waldige Umgebung.

L'habillage extérieur inspiré de la végétation permet le passage de la lumière et laisse aux résidents une vue sur l'environnement boisé.

SHINRO OHTAKE

SHINRO OHTAKE was born in Tokyo in 1955. After graduating from high school, he went to work on a ranch on the northern island of Hokkaido, before living briefly in London (1977–78). He graduated from the Department of Painting of Musashino Art University (1980), and had his first solo exhibition in 1982. He spent 1989 in New York at the invitation of USIA and the Artist Colony Foundation. In 1995, he stayed in Atlanta, Georgia, for two months at the invitation of the Atlanta Committee for the Olympic Games (ACOG) Cultural Olympiad. The Museum of Contemporary Art Tokyo staged a monographic exhibition of the work of Shinro Ohtake in 2006. He has been involved in a number of exhibitions and other work on the island of Naoshima. Ohtake has stated that his work is influenced by David Hockney and Adolf Wölfli (1864–1930, one of the first artists to be associated with the Art Brut movement). Another source of inspiration for the Japanese artist is Ferdinand Cheval (1836–1924), also known as the Facteur Cheval, who spent 33 years of his life building a remarkable work of naive art and architecture called Le Palais Idéal ("The Ideal Palace") in Hauterives, France.

SHINRO OHTAKE wurde 1955 in Tokio geboren. Nach seinem Schulabschluss arbeitete er auf einem Bauernhof auf der nordjapanischen Insel Hokkaido und lebte anschließend kurze Zeit in London (1977–78). Sein Studium der Malerei schloss er an der Musashino Art University ab (1980), seine erste Einzelausstellung folgte 1982. Auf Einladung der USIA und der Artist Colony Foundation verbrachte Ohtake das Jahr 1989 in New York. 1995 lebte er auf Einladung der Kulturabteilung des Komitees zur Vorbereitung der Olympischen Spiele in Atlanta (ACOG) zwei Monate lang in Atlanta, Georgia. 2006 veranstaltete das Museum für zeitgenössische Kunst in Tokio eine Retrospektive zum Werk von Shinro Ohtake. Darüber hinaus war er an verschiedenen Ausstellungen und Projekten auf der Insel Naoshima beteiligt. Ohtake zufolge wurde sein Werk von David Hockney und Adolf Wölfli (1864–1930, einem der ersten Künstler, den man mit der Art Brut in Zusammenhang brachte) beeinflusst. Eine weitere Inspirationsquelle des japanischen Künstlers ist Ferdinand Cheval (1836–1924), auch bekannt als Facteur Cheval, der im französischen Hauterives über 33 Jahre lang an einem erstaunlichen Werk naiver Kunst und Architektur arbeitete, dem sogenannten Palais Idéal (den „Idealen Palast").

SHINRO OHTAKE est né à Tokyo en 1955. À sa sortie du collège, il a travaillé dans un ranch de l'île d'Hokkaïdo, avant de séjourner brièvement à Londres (1977–78). Il est diplômé du département de peinture de l'Université d'art Musashino (1980), et a tenu sa première exposition personnelle en 1982. Il a séjourné en 1989 à New York à l'invitation de l'USIA et de l'Artist Colony Foundation. En 1995, il s'est installé à Atlanta (Georgie) pendant deux mois, invité par le Comité d'organisation des Jeux olympiques d'Atlanta (ACOG) pour l'Olympiade culturelle. Le Musée d'art contemporain de Tokyo lui a consacré une exposition monographique en 2006. Il a eu plusieurs expositions et réalisé divers travaux sur l'île de Naoshima. Ohtake précise que son œuvre est influencée par David Hockney et Adolf Wölfli (1864–1930), l'un des premiers artistes associé au concept d'art brut. Une autre de ses sources est Ferdinand Cheval (1836–1924), dit le Facteur Cheval, qui consacra trente-trois années de sa vie à construire une remarquable œuvre d'art naïf et d'architecture appelée Le Palais idéal à Hauterives (France).

NAOSHIMA PUBLIC BATHS

Naoshima, Kagawa, Japan, 2009

Address: 2252–2, Naoshima, Kagawa Prefecture, Japan, +81 87 892 2626, www.naoshimasento.jp
Area: 214 m². Client: Naoshima Fukutake Art Museum Foundation. Cost: not disclosed
Collaboration: graf, Osaka

The **NAOSHIMA PUBLIC BATHS** opened in July 2009 near the port of the Miyanoura district. The single-story reinforced-concrete building was completely decorated by Shinro Ohtake using colored tiles and various objects collected by the artist all over Japan. These objects include an aircraft cockpit, the bottom of a ship, a statue of a small elephant from a museum of erotica, and pine trees planted on the roof. The point of the facility is that it can function as a normal public bathhouse even as it retains its status as a work of art. As is the custom in Japan, there is one bath area for women, and one for men, and baths are taken in the nude. They are each 1.6 meters wide and 4.4 meters long. Called a *sento*, this type of bathhouse is considered a place of meeting and community togetherness, though the principle dates from before the time when each house had its own bath. Ohtake collaborated with the Osaka-based design studio graf on this project.

Die **ÖFFENTLICHEN BÄDER NAOSHIMA** wurden im Juli 2009 in der Nähe des Hafens, im Stadtviertel Miyanoura eröffnet. Der einstöckige Stahlbetonbau wurde vollständig von Shinro Ohtake dekoriert, mit farbigen Fliesen und den verschiedensten Objekten, die der Künstler in ganz Japan gesammelt hatte. Hierzu zählen u.a. ein Flugzeugcockpit, der Kiel eines Boots, die Skulptur eines kleinen Elefanten aus einem Museum für Erotica und Pinien, die auf dem Dach gepflanzt wurden. Die Besonderheit des Projekts ist, dass es als normales öffentliches Bad funktioniert und zugleich ein Kunstwerk ist. Wie in Japan üblich, gibt es getrennte Badebereiche für Frauen und Männer, gebadet wird nackt. Die Bäder sind je 1,6 m breit und 4,4 m lang. Diese Art von Badehaus, genannt *sento*, gilt als Treffpunkt und Ort der Gemeinschaft. Dieses Prinzip geht auf Zeiten zurück, als nicht jedes Haus ein eigenes Bad hatte. Ohtake arbeitete bei diesem Projekt mit dem Designstudio graf aus Osaka zusammen.

Les **BAINS PUBLICS DE NAOSHIMA** ont ouvert en juillet 2009 à proximité du port du district de Miyanoura. Le bâtiment en béton armé d'un seul niveau a été entièrement décoré par Shinro Ohtake à l'aide de carrelages de couleur et de multiples objets trouvés par l'artiste dans diverses régions du Japon. On identifie ainsi un cockpit d'avion, le fond de la coque d'un bateau, une petite statue d'éléphant trouvée dans un musée d'art érotique et quelques pins plantés en toiture. Ces installations sont réellement des bains publics opérationnels, même si elles affichent un statut d'œuvre d'art. Comme de coutume au Japon, les bains, que l'on prend nu, sont séparés pour les hommes et les femmes. Chaque salle mesure 4,4 mètres de long par 1,6 mètre de large. Appelé *sento*, ce type de Bains est un lieu de rencontre, une occasion d'être ensemble. Son principe remonte à une époque où chacun n'avait pas encore sa salle de bains. Ohtake a collaboré pour ce projet avec gaf, un studio de design d'Osaka.

Perhaps more a work of art than a piece of architecture in the more traditional sense, the Naoshima Public Baths are an assembly of found objects and themes developed by Shinro Ohtake.

Die öffentlichen Bäder in Naoshima sind vermutlich eher ein Kunstwerk als Architektur: eine Collage aus Fundstücken und Motiven, zusammengestellt von Shinro Ohtake.

Peut-être davantage œuvre d'art que d'architecture au sens traditionnel du terme, les Bains publics de Naoshima sont un assemblage d'objets trouvés autour de thématiques développées par Shinro Ohtake.

A kind of kitsch that the Japanese would not find unfamiliar occupies the interiors, where cacti and a model elephant are neighbors.

Une sorte de kitsch qui ne peut déplaire aux Japonais a envahi l'intérieur où des cactus voisinent avec une sculpture d'éléphant.

Eine Art von Kitsch, den Japaner nicht ungewöhnlich finden dürften, prägt die Innenräume. Hier leben Kakteen und nachgebildete Elefanten in trauter Nachbarschaft.

A painted overhead window and other details give a kind of luxuriant atmosphere to the bath interior.

Ein bemaltes Dachfenster und andere Details verleihen dem Interieur des Bads eine geradezu luxuriöse Atmosphäre.

Une verrière peinte et de multiples autres détails créent une atmosphère luxuriante.

OMA*AMO/REM KOOLHAAS

OMA Office for Metropolitan Architecture
Heer Bokelweg 149, 3032 AD Rotterdam, The Netherlands
Tel: +31 10 243 82 00 / Fax: +31 10 243 82 02
E-mail: office@oma.com / Web: www.oma.com

REM KOOLHAAS created the Office for Metropolitan Architecture in 1975 together with Elia and Zoe Zenghelis and Madelon Vriesendorp. Born in Rotterdam in 1944, Koolhaas tried his hand as a journalist for the *Haagse Post* and as a screenwriter, before studying at the Architectural Association (AA) in London. He became well known after the 1978 publication of his book *Delirious New York*. OMA is led today by six partners: Rem Koolhaas, Ole Scheeren, Ellen van Loon, Reinier de Graaf, Shohei Shigematsu, and Managing Partner Victor van der Chijs. Koolhaas was named head architect of the Euralille project in Lille in 1988. He won the 2000 Pritzker Prize and, in 2003, the Praemium Imperiale Award. OMA's built work includes the Villa dall'Ava, Saint-Cloud (Paris, France, 1985–91); Guggenheim Las Vegas (Nevada, USA, 2001); the McCormick Tribune Campus Center at the Illinois Institute of Technology (Chicago, Illinois, USA, 2000–03); the Dutch Embassy in Berlin (Germany, 2003); and Prada boutiques in New York (USA, 2001) and Los Angeles (USA, 2004). OMA completed the Seattle Public Library in 2004 (Washington, USA). Their work includes the 1850-seat Porto Concert Hall (Portugal, 2005) and the New City Center for Almere, for which the firm has drawn up the master plan (The Netherlands, 2007). Recent and current projects include Prada Catwalk Man SS 2010 (Milan, Italy, 2009); Prada Lookbook SS 2009 (worldwide, 2009); Prada Catwalk Man FW 2009 (Milan, Italy, 2009); Prada Transformer (Seoul, South Korea, 2009, published here); a 2009 competition for the Ile Seguin (Paris, France); MahaNakhon (Bangkok, Thailand, 2009–, commission); the 575 000-square-meter Headquarters and CCTV Television Station and Headquarters (Beijing, China, 2005–08, also published here); The Interlace (Singapore, 2009–, construction documentation); and Taipei Performing Arts Center (Taipei, Taiwan, 2009–14).

1975 gründete **REM KOOLHAAS** mit Elia und Zoe Zenghelis und Madelon Vriesendorp das Office for Metropolitan Architecture. Koolhaas, 1944 in Rotterdam geboren, arbeitete als Journalist für die *Haagse Post* und als Drehbuchautor, bevor er sein Studium an der Architectural Association in London aufnahm. Bekannt wurde er 1978 nach der Veröffentlichung seines Buchs *Delirious New York*. Heute wird OMA von sechs Partnern geführt: Rem Koolhaas, Ole Scheeren, Ellen van Loon, Reinier de Graaf, Shohei Shigematsu und Victor van der Chijs als geschäftsführendem Partner. 1988 wurde Koolhaas zum Chefarchitekten des Euralille-Projekts in Lille ernannt, 2000 gewann er den Pritzker-Preis, 2003 den Praemium Imperiale. Zu OMAs realisierten Bauten zählen die Villa dall'Ava, Saint-Cloud (Paris, Frankreich, 1985–91), das Guggenheim Las Vegas (Nevada, USA, 2001), das McCormick Tribune Campus Center am Illinois Institute of Technology (Chicago, Illinois, USA, 2000–03), die Niederländische Botschaft in Berlin (Deutschland, 2003), Prada Stores in New York (USA, 2001) und Los Angeles (USA, 2004). Darüber hinaus realisierte OMA 2004 die Zentralbibliothek in Seattle (Washington, USA). Zu den Projekten des Büros zählen auch das Konzerthaus Porto mit 1850 Plätzen (Portugal, 2005) oder der Masterplan für das neue Stadtzentrum von Almere (Niederlande, 2007). Jüngere und aktuelle Projekte sind u.a. der Prada Catwalk Man SS 2010 (Mailand, Italien, 2009), das Prada Lookbook SS 2009 (weltweit, 2009), der Prada Catwalk Man FW 2009 (Mailand, 2009), der Prada Transformer (Seoul, Südkorea, 2009, hier vorgestellt), ein Wettbewerb für die Ile Seguin (Paris, 2009), das MahaNakhon (Bangkok, Thailand, 2009–, Auftrag), eine 575 000 m² große Zentrale mit Kulturzentrum für das chinesische Staatsfernsehen (CCTV, Peking, China, 2005–08, ebenfalls hier vorgestellt), The Interlace (Singapur, 2009–, Baudokumentation) sowie das Taipei Performing Arts Center (Taipei, Taiwan, 2009–14).

REM KOOLHAAS a fondé l'Office for Metropolitan Architecture en 1975 en compagnie d'Elia et Zoe Zenghelis et de Madelon Vriesendorp. Né à Rotterdam en 1944, il a débuté comme journaliste pour le *Haagse Post*, et a été scénariste, avant d'étudier à l'Architectural Association de Londres. Il se fit connaître par la publication, en 1978, de son livre *Delirious New York*. OMA est dirigé aujourd'hui par six partenaires : Rem Koolhaas, Ole Scheeren, Ellen van Loon, Reinier de Graaf, Shohei Shigematsu, et pour la gestion par Victor van der Chijs. Koolhaas a été nommé architecte en chef du projet Euralille à Lille en 1988. Il a remporté le prix Pritzker en 2000 et le Praemium Imperiale en 2003. Les réalisations d'OMA comprennent : la Villa dall'Ava (Saint-Cloud, près de Paris, 1985–91) ; le Guggenheim-Las Vegas (Nevada, 2001) ; le Centre du McCormick Tribune Campus à l'Illinois Institute of Technology (Chicago, Illinois, 2000–03) ; l'ambassade néerlandaise à Berlin (2003) et les magasins Prada à New York (2001) et Los Angeles (2004). OMA a achevé la bibliothèque publique de Seattle en 2004 (Washington) ; la salle de concerts de Porto (Portugal, 2005) et le plan directeur du nouveau centre d'Almere (Pays-Bas, 2007). Parmi les réalisations récentes figurent le podium homme Prada SS 2010 (Milan, 2009) ; le Lookbook SS 2009 Prada (2009) ; le podium homme Prada FW 2009 (Milan, 2009) ; le Prada Transformer (Séoul, Corée du Sud, 2009, publié ici) ; un concours pour l'Île Seguin (Paris, 2009) ; MahaNakhon (Bangkok, Thaïlande, 2009–, commande) ; le siège et centre culturel de la télévision centrale de Chine (CCTV, Pékin, 2005–08, publié ici) ; l'Interlace (Singapour, 2009–, documentation de construction) et le Centre des arts du spectacle de Taipei (Taïwan, 2009–14).

PRADA TRANSFORMER

Seoul, South Korea, 2008–09

Area: not disclosed. Client: Prada. Cost: not disclosed
Collaboration: Alexander Reichert (Design Architect)

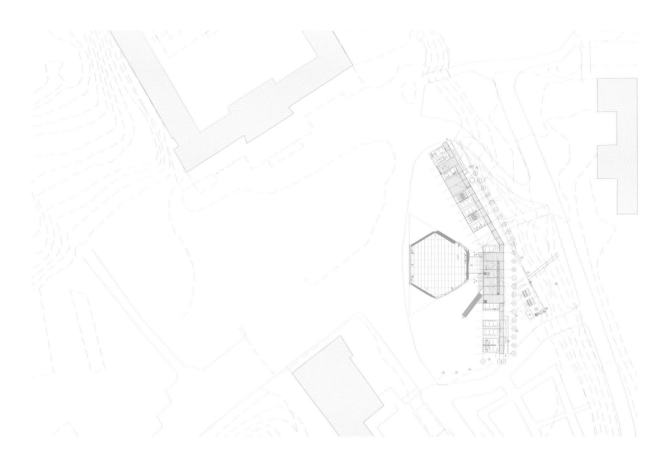

This temporary exhibition pavilion is part of an ongoing collaboration between the office of Rem Koolhaas/OMA and the Italian fashion company Prada. The form of the Transformer is derived from a Tetrahedron and, when rotated, each side accommodates a different program. In order to accommodate a range of different fashion, art, and movie events in 2009, cranes rotated, and then flipped the pavilion into four different façade-and-floor-plate configurations. Thus, over the course of the exposition, floors become walls and walls will become ceilings. The structure is wrapped in a translucent membrane incorporating an LED display showing movies of the transformation and advertisements. In its Seoul location, the Transformer was erected adjacent to the 16th-century Gyeonghui Palace, adding a modern element to the historic context.

Der temporäre Ausstellungspavillon entstand im Rahmen der andauernden Zusammenarbeit von Rem Koolhaas/OMA mit dem italienischen Modehaus Prada. Formal leitet sich der Transformer von einem Tetraeder ab – wird er gedreht, bietet jede Seite ein anderes Programm. Um 2009 eine ganze Bandbreite verschiedener Mode-, Kunst- und Filmevents im Pavillon stattfinden lassen zu können, wurde er mithilfe von Kränen gedreht und auf eine jeweils andere Seite gelegt. Insgesamt ergaben sich vier verschiedene Fassaden- und Bodenkonfigurationen. Im Laufe der Ausstellung wurden Böden zu Wänden und Wände zu Decken. Umhüllt war die Konstruktion von einer lichtdurchlässigen Membran mit integrierter LED-Anzeige, die Filme des Transformationsprozesses ebenso wie Werbespots zeigten. Errichtet wurde der Transformer in Seoul in unmittelbarer Nachbarschaft zum Gyeonghuigung Palast, einem Bau aus dem 16. Jahrhundert. Der Pavillon bereicherte den historischen Kontext des Standorts um ein modernes Element.

Ce pavillon, destiné à des expositions temporaires, illustre la longue collaboration entre l'agence de Rem Koolhaas et le groupe de mode italien Prada. La forme du Transformer dérive de celle d'un tétraèdre. Chacune de ces faces répond à un programme différent. Pour s'adapter à différents types de manifestations des univers de la mode, de l'art ou du cinéma en 2009, des grues faisaient pivoter le pavillon selon quatre configurations différentes de façade et de sols. Au cours de l'exposition, les sols pouvaient se transformer en murs et les murs en plafonds. La structure est enveloppée d'une membrane translucide incorporant un dispositif à Leds présentant des films sur la transformation du pavillon et de publicités. À Séoul, le Transformer a été installé à côté du palais de Gyeonghui (XVIᵉ siècle), apportant une touche de modernité dans ce contexte historique.

Neighboring a 16th-century palace, the Prada Transformer is a rather alien presence in its Korean setting. The interior of the structure remains enigmatic from the outside.

Neben einem Palast aus dem 16. Jahrhundert wirkt der Prada Transformer recht fremdartig an seinem koreanischen Standort. Der Innenraum des Baus ist von außen nicht auszumachen und gibt sich enigmatisch.

À quelque pas d'un palais du XVIᵉ siècle, le Prada Transformer impose sa présence assez étrange dans ce cadre traditionnel coréen. Vu de l'extérieur, l'intérieur reste assez énigmatique.

The vertiginous interior design appears to sweep visitors up in a rotating movement. The structure is both temporary and transformable, as its name implies.

Die schwindelerregende Interieurgestaltung scheint die Besucher in einen rotierenden Sog zu ziehen. Wie der Name verrät, ist der Bau temporär und umwandelbar.

L'intérieur vertigineux semble entraîner les visiteurs dans un mouvement de rotation. Le pavillon est à la fois temporaire et transformable, d'où son nom.

Interior spaces are given over to the display of Prada clothes and accessories, displayed in unexpected ways and locations.

Der Innenraum ist ganz der Präsentation von Kleidung und Accessoires von Prada gewidmet. Diese werden auf ungewöhnliche Weise an überraschenden Orten ausgestellt.

Les volumes intérieurs sont consacrés à l'exposition de vêtements et d'accessoires Prada présentés de façon inattendue dans des situations souvent originales.

The interior of the structure as seen in the image to the right (seen with more light on the left page, bottom) allows for seating and group viewing.

Rechts das Innere der Konstruktion (unten links mit mehr Licht). Hier gibt es Möglichkeiten zum Sitzen und für Gruppenvorführungen.

L'intérieur du pavillon – à droite et plus éclairé à gauche – permet aussi d'organiser des visites de groupe et de donner des conférences.

The surprising and rather complex appearance of the interior announces a different way of looking at both temporary architecture and structures destined to fashion.

Das erstaunliche und recht komplexe Interieur zeugt von einer neuen Art, zeitgenössische Architektur und Bauten für Mode zu interpretieren.

L'aspect étonnant et assez complexe de l'intérieur annonce une façon nouvelle de considérer à la fois l'architecture temporaire et les structures destinées à la mode.

Drawings show how the structure can be mounted using cranes.

Die Zeichnungen unten illustrieren die Montage des Baus mithilfe von Kränen.

Dessins montrant comment la structure est mise en place à l'aide de grues.

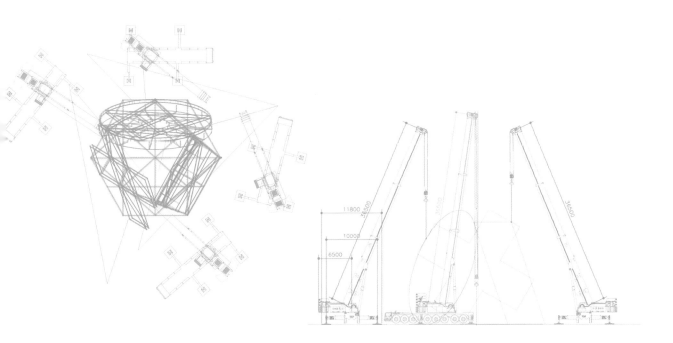

CCTV TELEVISION STATION AND HEADQUARTERS

TVCC Television Cultural Center, Beijing, China, 2005–08

Address: CCTV Headquarters, Guanghua Lu, Chaoyang, Beijing, China, www.cctv.com
Site: 20 ha in new Central Business District. Area: 575 000 m². Client: China Central Television (CCTV)
Cost: € 495 million. Collaboration: Ole Scheeren and Rem Koolhaas (Partners in Charge),
Inside/Outside, Amsterdam (Landscape), Ma Qingyun Shanghai (Strategic Advisor), ECADI-East China Architecture and Design Institute,
Shanghai (Associate Architects and Engineers)

OMA and Rem Koolhaas have approached the **CCTV HEADQUARTERS** in Beijing with a radically different way than other designers might have employed. As they write: "Instead of competing in the hopeless race for ultimate height … the project proposes an iconographic constellation of two high-rise structures that actively engage the city space: CCTV and TVCC." A common production platform is the base for the two linked towers, and they are joined at the top, creating a "cantilevered penthouse for the management." "A new icon is formed…" say the designers, "not the predictable 2-dimensional tower 'soaring' skyward, but a truly 3-dimensional experience, a canopy that symbolically embraces the entire population… The consolidation of the TV program in a single building allows each worker to be permanently aware of the nature of the work of his co-workers—a chain of interdependence that promotes solidarity rather than isolation, collaboration instead of opposition. The building itself contributes to the coherence of the organization." The CCTV tower is partially open to the public, who are admitted to a dedicated "loop" allowing views of the production process and the city itself. The Television Cultural Center (TVCC) is entirely open to the public and includes a 1500-seat theater, a ballroom, cinemas, recording studios, and exhibition areas. A broadcasting center and a five-star hotel are also accommodated in the building. Much as they did in the case of the Seattle Central Library, the architects have taken on not only the specific functions requested in this instance, but also the very idea of the building typology involved.

Die Herangehensweise von OMA und Rem Koolhaas an die **CCTV-ZENTRALE** in Peking unterscheidet sich radikal davon, was andere Architekten womöglich getan hätten. Das Team schreibt: „Statt in den aussichtslosen Wettlauf um ultimative Höhenmarken einzusteigen … geht es bei diesem Projekt darum, eine Konstellation aus zwei Hochhausbauten zu entwerfen, die das Format zur Ikone haben und sich aktiv auf den Stadtraum einlassen: CCTV und TVCC." Basis der zwei miteinander verbundenen Türme ist eine gemeinsam genutzte Produktionsplattform. Auch oben sind die Türme verbunden, wodurch ein „auskragendes Penthouse für das Management" entsteht. „Ein neues Wahrzeichen entsteht…", so die Gestalter, „kein vorhersagbarer, zweidimensionaler Turm, der den Himmel ‚stürmt', sondern ein wahrhaft dreidimensionales Erlebnis, ein Dach, unter dem sich symbolisch die gesamte Bevölkerung versammelt… Die Zusammenlegung eines kompletten Fernsehsenders in ein einzelnes Gebäude ermöglicht jedem einzelnen Mitarbeiter, sich permanent der Tätigkeit seiner Kollegen bewusst zu sein – in einer Kette gegenseitiger Abhängigkeit, die Solidarität statt Isolation fördert, Kollaboration statt Opposition. Das Gebäude selbst trägt zum Zusammenhalt der Organisation bei." Das CCTV-Hochhaus ist teilweise öffentlich zugänglich, Besucher erhalten durch einen speziellen *loop* (Rundgang) Einblicke in den Produktionsprozess und Ausblick auf die Stadt. Das Television Cultural Center (TVCC) ist uneingeschränkt öffentlich und umfasst eine Bühne mit 1500 Plätzen, einen Ballsaal, Kinos, Aufnahmestudios und Ausstellungsbereiche. Ebenfalls im Bau untergebracht sind das Funkhaus sowie ein 5-Sterne-Hotel. Ähnlich wie bei der Zentralbibliothek in Seattle griffen die Architekten hier nicht nur spezifische Funktionen auf, die von ihnen gefordert waren, sondern setzten sich grundsätzlich mit der konkreten Gebäudetypologie auseinander.

OMA et Rem Koolhaas ont traité le problème du **SIÈGE DE LA CCTV** à Pékin selon une approche radicalement différente de celle qu'auraient pu employer d'autres architectes. «Au lieu de participer à la course sans espoir pour la plus grande hauteur … le projet propose la fusion iconographique de deux structures de grande hauteur qui participent activement au paysage urbain : CCTV et TVCC.» Les deux tours reliées reposent sur une plate-forme commune et se rejoignent à leur sommet par un «penthouse en porte-à-faux, occupé par la direction». «Une nouvelle icône est ainsi constituée … », poursuivent les architectes, «non pas la tour prévisible en deux dimensions qui s'élève vers le ciel, mais une authentique expérience tridimensionnelle, un auvent qui recouvre symboliquement toute la population … La consolidation des programmes de télévision dans un bâtiment unique permet à chaque collaborateur d'être conscient en permanence de la nature du travail des autres … une chaîne d'interdépendance qui promeut la solidarité plutôt que l'isolement, la collaboration plutôt que l'opposition. L'immeuble lui-même contribue à la cohérence de l'organisation.» La tour CCTV est en partie ouverte au public, admis à suivre un circuit précis qui lui permet de découvrir le processus de production et diverses perspectives sur Pékin. Le centre culturel de la télévision (TVCC) est, lui, entièrement ouvert au public. Il comprend une salle de spectacles de 1500 places, une salle de bal, des cinémas, des studios d'enregistrements et une galerie d'expositions. Un centre de diffusion et un hôtel 5 étoiles sont également installés dans l'immeuble. En grande partie comme pour la Bibliothèque centrale de Seattle, les architectes ont traité non seulement les fonctions du programme, mais également la typologie constructive elle-même.

A colorful axonometric drawing and the images on these pages show the segment linking the towers in the process of completion.

Eine bunte Axonometrie und die Aufnahmen auf diesen Seiten zeigen den verbundenen Hauptbau während der Bauarbeiten am Verbindungsstück zwischen den Türmen.

Un éclaté axonométrique et les photographies de ces deux pages montrent le chantier pendant la construction de la liaison entre les deux parties verticales.

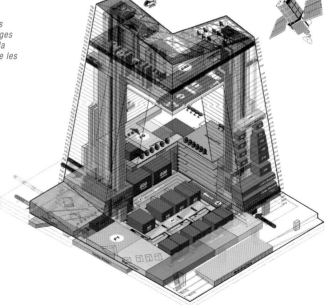

The 159-meter-high Television Cultural Center was damaged by a fire set off by fireworks on February 9, 2009. The building is seen before the fire, above right and left.

Das 159 m hohe Television Cultural Centre wurde bei einem Brand beschädigt, der am 9. Februar 2009 durch einen Feuerwerksunfall ausgelöst wurde. Links und oben das Gebäude vor dem Brand.

Le 9 février 2009, le Centre culturel de la télévision de 159 mètres de haut a été endommagé par un incendie provoqué par des feux d'artifice. L'immeuble avant l'incendie, ci-dessus à droite et à gauche.

PAREDES PEDROSA ARQUITECTOS

Paredes Pedrosa Arquitectos
Nervión 12
28002 Madrid
Spain

Tel/Fax: +34 91 411 20 17
E-mail: correo@paredespedrosa.com
Web: www.paredespedrosa.com

IGNACIO GARCÍA PEDROSA was born in Madrid, Spain, in 1957. He graduated from the Madrid School of Architecture (ETSAM) in 1983, and has taught Project Design there since 1995. He has also been an Invited Professor at the ETSA in Pamplona. **ANGELA GARCÍA DE PAREDES** was born in Madrid in 1958. She also graduated from the ETSAM in 1983, and has been a Guest Professor at the Barcelona ESARQ and Pamplona ETSA. They have been lecturers in Rome, Mexico, Münster, Santo Domingo, Buenos Aires, at the City University of New York (CCNY), and at the Politecnico di Milano. They created their firm in Madrid in 1990. Their work includes a Public Library in Madrid (2003); Auditorium and Convention Center (Peñíscola, 2003); Archeological Museum (Almería, 2004); Faculty of Psychology (Madrid, 2004); Torner Museum (Cuenca, 2005); and the Valle Inclán Theater (Madrid, 2005). Recent projects include Social Housing in Madrid (2005–06); wine cellars, Bodegas Real (Valdepeñas, 2004–07); and La Olmeda Roman Villa (Pedrosa de la Vega, Palencia, 2006–09, published here), all in Spain.

IGNACIO GARCÍA PEDROSA wurde 1957 in Madrid geboren. 1983 schloss er sein Studium an der Madrider Hochschule für Architektur (ETSAM) ab, wo er seit 1995 Entwurfsplanung lehrt. Darüber hinaus war er Gastprofessor an der ETSA in Pamplona. **ANGELA GARCÍA DE PAREDES** wurde 1958 in Madrid geboren. Auch sie absolvierte ihren Abschluss 1983 an der ETSAM und lehrte zudem als Gastprofessorin an der ESARQ in Barcelona und der ETSA in Pamplona. Beide hatten Lehraufträge in Rom, Mexiko, Münster/Westfalen, Santo Domingo, Buenos Aires, an der City University of New York (CCNY) sowie der Politecnico di Milano. 1990 gründeten sie in Madrid ihr eigenes Büro. Zu ihren Projekten zählen eine Stadtbibliothek in Madrid (2003), ein Auditorium und Messezentrum in Peñíscola (2003), ein Archäologisches Museum in Almería (2004), die Fakultät für Psychologie der Autonomen Universität Madrid (2004), das Torner Museum (Cuenca, 2005) sowie das Valle Inclán Theater (Madrid, 2005). Jüngere Projekte sind u.a. soziale Wohnbauten in Madrid (2005–06), Weinkeller für die Bodegas Real (Valdepeñas, 2004–07) und die Villa Romana de La Olmeda (Pedrosa de la Vega, Palencia, 2006–09, hier vorgestellt), alle in Spanien.

IGNACIO GARCÍA PEDROSA, né à Madrid en 1957, est diplômé de l'École d'architecture de Madrid (ETSAM) en 1983, où il enseigne la conception de projet depuis 1995. Il a également été professeur invité à l'ETSA de Pampelune. **ANGELA GARCÍA DE PAREDES**, née à Madrid en 1958, est elle aussi diplômée de l'ETSAM (1983) et a été professeure invitée à l'ESARQ de Barcelone et à l'ETSA de Pampelune. Ils ont donné des conférences à Rome, Mexico, Munster, Santo Domingo, Buenos Aires, à la City University de New York (CCNY) et au Politecnico de Milan. Ils ont créé leur agence à Madrid en 1990. Parmi leurs réalisations : une bibliothèque publique à Madrid (2003) ; un auditorium et centre de congrès (Peñíscola, 2003) ; un musée archéologique (Almería, 2004) ; la Faculté de psychologie (Madrid, 2004) ; le Musée Torner (Cuenca, 2005) et le théâtre Valle Inclán (Madrid, 2005). Récemment, ils ont réalisé des logements sociaux à Madrid (2005–06) ; des chais pour les Bodegas Real (Valdepeñas, 2004–07) et la Villa romaine d'Olmeda (Pedrosa de la Vega, Palencia, 2006–09, publiée ici).

LA OLMEDA ROMAN VILLA

Pedrosa de la Vega, Palencia, Spain, 2006–09

Address: Apdo. Correos no. 13, Pedrosa de la Vega, 34100 Saldaña, Palencia, Spain,
+34 97 911 99 97 / 67 045 01 43, www.villaromanalaolmeda.com
Area: 6083 m². Client: Diputación de Palencia. Cost: € 7.836 million
Collaboration: Luis Calvo (Civil Engineer), Alfonso G. Gaite (Structure), Clemens Eichner (Architect)

It was the accidental discovery of a Roman bronze in 1968 that was at the origin of an archeological dig on the site of the Olmeda. The dig brought to light the ruins of a villa dating from the late Roman Empire. The significance of this discovery led authorities to plan the construction of a roof and protection for the mosaics found *in situ*, and a visitor's center and study building for archeologists. The architects designed a metallic structure with four roof modules with a maximum span of 25 meters, supported by four freestanding pillars. Set outside the polycarbonate façade of the structure are 110 pilasters. The exterior of the building is also marked by a concrete plinth topped by folding screens made of perforated Corten steel panels that serve in part to attenuate solar gain inside. Within, elevated walkways guide visitors in their tour of the mosaics. The outline of the Roman villa covers no less than 4479 square meters with some 1648 square meters of mosaics to be seen. The total site area is 28 000 square meters.

Es war der zufällige Fund einer römischen Bronze 1968, der den Anstoß zu archäologischen Grabungen in Olmeda gab, in deren Zuge man die Ruinen einer Villa aus dem späten römischen Reich entdeckte. Die Bedeutung des Funds veranlasste die Behörden zur Planung eines Daches zum Schutz für die vor Ort gefundenen Mosaike sowie eines Besucherzentrums und Forschungsgebäudes für die Archäologen. Die Architekten entwarfen eine Metallkonstruktion aus vier Dachmodulen mit einer maximalen Spannbreite von 25 m, die auf vier freistehenden Stützen ruhen. Vor die Außenfassade aus Polycarbonat wurden 110 Pilaster gesetzt. Dominiert wird der Außenbau von einem Sockel aus Beton und beweglichen Wandschirmen aus perforiertem Corten-Stahl, welche die Sonneneinstrahlung im Gebäude abschwächen. Im Innern des Baus werden die Besucher in einem Rundgang auf aufgeständerten Stegen über die Mosaike geführt. Die Außengrenzen der römischen Villa umschließen eine Fläche von nicht weniger als 4479 m², auf der rund 1648 m² Mosaikflächen zu sehen sind. Die Fläche des Gesamtgrundstücks beträgt 28 000 m².

La découverte accidentelle d'un bronze romain en 1968 est à l'origine de fouilles archéologiques sur le site d'Olmeda, qui ont mis au jour les ruines d'une villa datant de la fin de l'empire romain. L'importance de cette découverte a conduit les autorités à prévoir la construction d'une toiture de protection pour les mosaïques in situ, un centre d'accueil pour les visiteurs, et un bâtiment de recherche pour les archéologues. Les architectes ont conçu une structure métallique composée de quatre modules de toiture d'une portée maximum de 25 mètres, soutenus par quatre piliers. La façade en polycarbonate est précédée de 110 pilastres. L'extérieur se caractérise par une importante plinthe surmontée d'écrans dépliables en panneaux d'acier Corten perforés, qui servent en partie à réguler le gain solaire. À l'intérieur, des coursives surélevées guident les visiteurs dans leur découverte des mosaïques. Le périmètre de la villa ne couvre pas moins de 4479 m² dont 168 m² de mosaïques visibles. La totalité du site couvre 28 000 m².

*The long, elegant profile of La Olme-
da Roman Villa is seen in photos and
elevation drawings on this double
page.*

*Auf den Fotos und Zeichnungen
dieser Doppelseite wird das gestreckte,
elegante Profil der Villa Romana de
La Olmeda sichtbar.*

*Le profil allongé et élégant de la
Villa Olmeda saisi par les photographies et les élévations (à droite).*

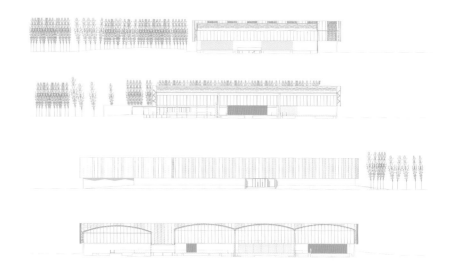

The broad, open interior spaces
cover the archeological site, allowing
visitors to view the results of the dig.

Die weitläufigen offenen Räume
wurden über der archäologischen
Grabungsstätte errichtet und ermöglichen den Besuchern, den Fortgang
der Grabungen zu beobachten.

Les vastes volumes intérieurs ouverts
qui recouvrent le site archéologique
laissent au visiteur toute liberté pour
observer le résultat des fouilles.

The structure forms an elegant,
geometric shell around the dig,
protecting it and opening it to the
public.

Der Bau bildet eine elegante,
geometrische Hülle über der
Grabungsstätte, die sie zugleich
schützt und der Öffentlichkeit
zugänglich macht.

Le bâtiment forme une élégante
coque de protection par-dessus les
fouilles, tout en permettant son
ouverture au public.

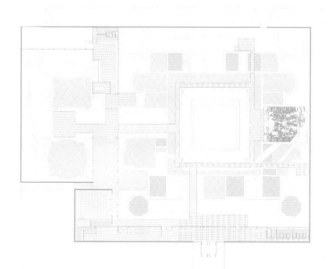

DOMINIQUE PERRAULT

Dominique Perrault Architecture
6 rue Bouvier
75011 Paris
France

Tel: +33 1 44 06 00 00 / Fax: +33 1 44 06 00 01
E-mail: dpa@d-p-a.fr / Web: www.perraultarchitecte.com

DOMINIQUE PERRAULT was born in 1953 in Clermont-Ferrand, France. He studied in Paris and received his diploma as an architect from the École des Beaux-Arts in 1978. He received a further degree in Urbanism at the École nationale des Ponts et Chaussées in 1979, as well as a Master's in History at the EHESS (École des hautes études en sciences sociales) in 1980. He created his own firm in 1981 in Paris. His most significant projects include the French National Library in Paris (1989–95); and the Velodrome and Olympic Swimming Pool (Berlin, Germany, 1992–99). Recent buildings include the Media Library in Vénissieux (France, 1997–2001); the design of several supermarkets for the MPreis chain in Austria (1999–2003); the master plan for Donau City in Vienna (Austria, 2002–03); and the refurbishment of Piazza Gramsci (Cinisello Balsamo, Milan, Italy, 1999–2004). More recent projects include the new Mariinsky Theater (Saint Petersburg, Russia, 2003–); the ME Barcelona Hotel Tower (Barcelona, Spain, 2002–07); an extension of the Court of Justice of the European Communities (Luxembourg, 2004–08); the EWHA Womans University in Seoul (South Korea, 2004–08, published here); Priory Park Pavilion (Reigate, UK, 2007–08); the NH–Fieramilano Hotel (Milan, Italy, 2006–09); the Arganzuela Footbridge in Madrid (Spain, 2005–10); and the Fukoku Tower (Osaka, Japan, 2008–10). Recent ongoing projects include the DC Towers in Vienna (Austria, 2004–12); the new Grand Albi Theater (France, 2009–13); the extension of the Dobrée Museum in Nantes (France, 2010–15); the development of the new FFS station district at Locarno (Switzerland, 2009–); and the city center redevelopement of Sofia (Bulgaria, 2009–).

DOMINIQUE PERRAULT wurde 1953 in Clermont-Ferrand geboren. Er studierte in Paris und absolvierte sein Architekturdiplom 1978 an der École des Beaux-Arts. 1979 folgte ein weiterer Abschluss in Städtebau an der École nationale des Ponts et Chaussées, sowie 1980 ein Master in Geschichte an der EHESS (École des hautes études en sciences sociales). 1981 gründete er sein eigenes Büro in Paris. Seine bedeutendsten Projekte sind u.a. die Französische Nationalbibliothek in Paris (1989–95) und die Schwimm- und Sprunghalle Velodrom (Berlin, 1992–99). Unlängst realisierte Bauten sind u.a. die Mediathek in Vénissieux (Frankreich, 1997–2001), Gestaltung mehrerer Filialien der Supermarktkette MPreis in Österreich (1999–2003), der Masterplan für die Donau City in Wien (2002–03) sowie die Sanierung der Piazza Gramsci (Cinisello Balsamo, Mailand, 1999–2004). Zu den noch jüngeren Projekten zählen das neue Mariinskij-Theater (St. Petersburg, Russland, 2003–), der ME Barcelona Hotel Tower in Barcelona (2002–07), die Erweiterung des Europäischen Gerichtshofs (Luxemburg, 2004–08), die EWHA Womans University in Seoul (Südkorea, 2004–08, hier vorgestellt), der Priory-Park-Pavillon (Reigate, Großbritannien, 2007–08), das NH–Fieramilano Hotel (Mailand, 2006–09), die Fußgängerbrücke Arganzuela in Madrid (2005–10) und der Fukoku Tower (Osaka, Japan, 2008–10). Laufende Projekte sind u.a. die DC Towers in Wien (Österreich, 2004–12), das neue Grand Theater in Albi (Frankreich, 2009–13), die Erweiterung des Dobrée Museums in Nantes (Frankreich, 2010–15), die Planung des neuen FFS Bahnhofsareals in Locarno (Schweiz, 2009–) sowie die Umgestaltung der Innenstadt von Sofia (Bulgaria, 2009–).

DOMINIQUE PERRAULT est né en 1953 à Clermont-Ferrand (France). Il est diplômé d'architecture de l'École des beaux-arts de Paris – UP 6 – (1978), et d'urbanisme de l'École nationale des ponts et chaussées (Paris, 1979). Il est également titulaire d'une maîtrise d'histoire à l'École des hautes études en sciences sociales (Paris, 1980). Il crée son agence en 1981 à Paris. Parmi ses principales réalisations figurent la Bibliothèque de France (Paris, 1989–97) ; le vélodrome et la piscine olympique de Berlin (1992–99) ; la médiathèque de Vénissieux (France, 1997–2001) ; plusieurs supermarchés pour la chaîne M-Preis en Autriche (1999–2003) ; le plan directeur de Donau City à Vienne (Autriche, et 2002–03) et la rénovation de la Piazza Gramsci (Cinisello Balsamo, Milan, 1999–04). Ses projets actuels comprennent le nouveau théâtre Mariinsky (Saint-Pétersbourg, 2003–) ; la tour de l'hôtel ME Barcelona Hotel (Barcelone, 2002–07) ; une extension de la Cour de justice des Communautés européennes (Luxembourg, 2004–08) ; l'université féminine EWHA à Séoul (Corée du Sud, 2004–08, publiée ici) ; le pavillon de Priory Park (Reigate, G.-B., 2007–08) ; l'hôtel NH–Fieramilano (Milan, 2006–09) ; la passerelle de l'Arganzuela à Madrid (2005–10) et la tour Fukoku (Osaka, 2008–10). Actuellement, il travaille sur les projets des tours DC à Vienne (Autriche, 2004–12) ; le nouveau Grand théâtre d'Albi (2009–13) ; l'extension du musée Dobrée à Nantes (France, 2010–15) ; le plan de développement du nouveau quartier de la gare FFS station à Locarno (Suisse, 2009–) et le plan de rénovation du centre de Sofia (Bulgarie, 2009–).

EWHA WOMANS UNIVERSITY

Seoul, South Korea, 2004–08

Address: 11–1 Daehyungdong, Seodaemun-gu, Seoul 120–750, South Korea, www.ewha.ac.kr
Area: 70 000 m². Client: EWHA Womans University. Cost: not disclosed
Collaboration: Baum Architects, Seoul

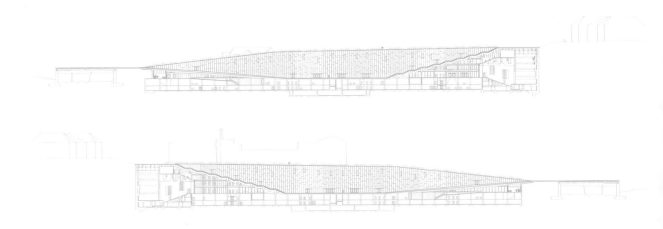

Drawings of the structure show its slightly angled form, following the lines of the topography of the site.

Auf Zeichnungen des Gebäudes ist seine leicht schräge Form zu erkennen, die der Topografie folgt.

Les plans ci-dessus montrent la forme légèrement inclinée de l'université, qui suit la topographie.

Founded in 1886, **EWHA** has 22 000 female students. Dominique Perrault won the international competition to design these new facilities in 2003, inaugurating the building on April 29, 2008. The program includes spaces for study, sports, including outdoor areas, offices, a cinema, and parking. A great emphasis was put on the energy efficiency of the structure, with its green roof, water-use efficiency, and renewable energy sources. In winter fully 80% and in summer 70% of the power demands are provided by natural resources, such as geothermal energy or natural ventilation. The project resembles a work of landscape architecture as much as it does more traditional structures—with its long avenue slicing through the middle of the site and revealing the academic spaces below the green roof. The architect calls the main spaces the Sports Strip and the Campus Valley—emphasizing the landscape elements of the design. As he wrote at the beginning of the project: "A new seam slices through the topography revealing the interior of the EWHA campus center. A void is formed, a hybrid place, in which a variety of activities can unfold. It is an avenue, gently descending, controlling the flow of traffic, leading to a monumental stair carrying visitors upwards, recalling the Champs Elysees or the Campidoglio in Rome."

Die 1886 gegründete **EWHA** Universität hat 22 000 weibliche Studierende. Dominique Perrault gewann den Wettbewerb für die neuen Einrichtungen 2003, eingeweiht wurde der Bau am 29. April 2008. Das Programm umfasst Räume für Lehre und Studium, Sport (einschließlich Außenanlagen), Büros, ein Kino sowie Parkplätze. Besondere Aufmerksamkeit wurde der Energieeffizienz des Komplexes gewidmet, was durch ein begrüntes Dach, effiziente Wassernutzung und den Einsatz erneuerbarer Energien unterstützt wurde. Im Winter werden gut 80%, im Sommer 70% des Energieverbrauchs durch natürliche Ressourcen gedeckt, etwa durch Erdwärme oder natürliche Belüftung. Das Projekt wirkt teilweise wie Landschaftsarchitektur und erinnert zugleich an traditionelle Bauten – eine lange Schneise zieht sich mitten durch das Gelände, unter den begrünten Dächern liegen die akademischen Einrichtungen. Der Architekt nennt die Hauptzonen des Komplexes „Sportstreifen" und „Campustal" und betont damit die landschaftlichen Aspekte des Entwurfs. Zu Beginn des Projekts formulierte er: „Eine neue Nahtstelle verläuft quer durch die Topografie und enthüllt das Innenleben des EWHA-Campuszentrums. Es entsteht ein Leerraum, ein hybrider Raum, in dem sich die verschiedensten Aktivitäten entfalten können. Eine sanft abfallend Chaussee, regelt den Verkehrsfluss und mündet in einer monumentalen Treppe, die die Besucher nach oben führt und an die Champs-Élysées oder den Campidoglio in Rom erinnert."

Fondée en 1886, l'université d'**EWHA** compte 22 000 étudiantes. Dominique Perrault a remporté, en 2003, le concours international lancé pour ce nouveau bâtiment, dont l'inauguration a eu lieu le 29 avril 2008. Le programme comprend des installations pour l'étude, le sport, y compris de plein air, des bureaux, un cinéma et des parkings. La consommation énergétique a été particulièrement étudiée, ce qui se traduit entre autres par une toiture végétalisée, une gestion efficace de l'eau et l'appel à des sources d'énergie renouvelables. En hiver, 80 % de la consommation électrique, pour 70 % en été, sont fournis par des ressources naturelles, comme la géothermie ou la ventilation naturelle. Le projet fait penser à une œuvre d'architecture paysagère par sa longue avenue centrale en tranchée sur laquelle donnent les salles d'étude protégées par une toiture végétalisée. Dans cet esprit, l'architecte a appelé les deux éléments principaux « Boucle des sports » et « Vallée du campus ». Il explique : « L'université féminine s'organise autour d'une clôture géométrique modelée à partir d'une faille naturelle, et cette profonde incision dans le terrain, qui sert aussi d'axe de circulation piétonne, est complétée par une bande horizontale à usage sportif. Comme une peinture suprématiste, le projet se résout ainsi en deux gestes topographiques catégoriques [...] qui font disparaître l'architecture dans un paysage violemment altéré par la géométrie ... »

Images of the central walkway and the site show how the architect has inserted the buildings into the earth, almost like a piece of functional land art.

Ansichten der zentralen Wegschneise und des Geländes verdeutlichen, wie der Architekt die Bauten in den Boden integriert hat – beinahe wie eine funktional nutzbare Land-Art-Installation.

Les images de l'avenue centrale et du site montrent comment l'architecte a intégré les bâtiments dans le profil du terrain, un peu comme une œuvre de land art fonctionnel.

Because of the way it is cut into the earth, the university complex allows daylight to penetrate interior areas. Below, a site plan, showing the long rectangular path of the main walkway.

Dank der Art, wie der Universitätskomplex in den Boden eingelassen wurde, fällt Tageslicht in die Innenräume. Unten ein Grundstücksplan, auf dem die längliche Wegschneise zu erkennen ist.

La profonde tranchée dans le sol permet à la lumière naturelle de pénétrer dans tous les volumes intérieurs. Ci-dessous, un plan montrant la longue tranchée centrale.

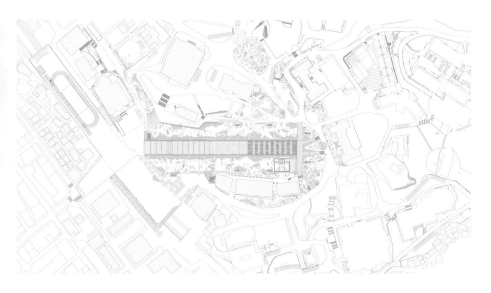

RENZO PIANO

Renzo Piano Building Workshop
34 rue des Archives, 75004 Paris, France
Tel: +33 1 42 78 00 82 / Fax: +33 1 42 78 01 98
E-mail: info@rpbw.com / Web: www.rpbw.com

RENZO PIANO was born in 1937 in Genoa, Italy. He studied at the University of Florence and at the Polytechnic Institute (Milan, 1964). He formed his own practice (Studio Piano) in 1965, then associated with Richard Rogers (Piano & Rogers, 1971–78). Piano completed the Pompidou Center in Paris in 1977. From 1978 to 1980, he worked with Peter Rice (Piano & Rice Associates). He created the Renzo Piano Building Workshop in 1981 in Genoa and Paris. Piano received the RIBA Gold Medal in 1989. His built work includes the Menil Collection Museum (Houston, Texas, 1981–86; San Nicola Stadium (Bari, Italy, 1987–90); the 1988–90 extension for the IRCAM (Paris, France); Kansai International Airport Terminal (Osaka, Japan, 1988–94); Cité Internationale de Lyon (Lyon, France, 1985–96); Beyeler Foundation Museum (Riehen, Basel, Switzerland, 1991–97); Jean-Marie Tjibaou Cultural Center (New Caledonia, South Pacific, 1991–98); Mercedes-Benz Center (Stuttgart, Germany, 1993–98); reconstruction of a section of Potsdamer Platz (Berlin, Germany, 1992–2000); Parma Auditorium (Italy, 1997–2001); Maison Hermès (Tokyo, Japan, 1998–2001); Rome Auditorium (Italy, 1994–2002); conversion of the Lingotto Factory Complex (Turin, Italy, 1983–2003); the Padre Pio Pilgrimage Church (San Giovanni Rotondo, Foggia, Italy, 1991–2004); Woodruff Arts Center Expansion (Atlanta, Georgia, USA, 1999–2005); Renovation and Expansion of the Morgan Library (New York, New York, USA, 2000–06); and the New York Times Building (New York, New York, USA, 2005–07). Recently completed and ongoing work includes the California Academy of Sciences (San Francisco, California, USA, 2000–08); the Chicago Art Institute Expansion (Chicago, Illinois, USA, 2005–09); the Emilio and Annabianca Vedova Foundation (Venice, Italy, 2008–09, published here); and London Bridge Tower (London, UK, 2000–).

RENZO PIANO wurde 1937 in Genua, Italien, geboren. Er studierte an der Universität Florenz und der Polytechnischen Hochschule Mailand (1964). Sein Büro Studio Piano gründete er 1965, gefolgt von einer Partnerschaft mit Richard Rogers (Piano & Rogers, 1971–78). Die Arbeiten am Centre Pompidou in Paris konnte Piano 1977 abschließen. Von 1978 bis 1980 arbeitete er mit Peter Rice (Piano & Rice Associates). 1981 gründete er sein Büro Renzo Piano Building Workshop mit Sitz in Genua und Paris. 1989 wurde Piano mit der RIBA-Goldmedaille ausgezeichnet. Zu seinen realisierten Bauten zählen u.a.: Menil Collection Museum (Houston, Texas, 1981–86), San Nicola Stadium (Bari, Italien, 1987–90), Erweiterungsbau IRCAM (Paris, 1988–90), Flughafenterminal Kansai International (Osaka, Japan, 1988–94), Cité Internationale de Lyon (Lyon, Frankreich, 1985–96), Fondation Beyeler (Riehen, Schweiz, 1991–97), Jean-Marie Tjibaou Kulturzentrum (Neukaledonien, Südpazifik, 1991–98), Mercedes-Benz Design Center (Stuttgart, 1993–98), Rekonstruktion eines Abschnitts des Potsdamer Platzes (Berlin, 1992–2000), Auditorium in Parma (Italien, 1997–2001), Maison Hermès (Tokio, 1998–2001), Auditorium in Rom (1994–2002), Umgestaltung des Lingotto-Werkskomplexes (Turin, 1983–2003), Padre Pio Pilgerkirche (San Giovanni Rotondo, Foggia, Italien, 1991–2004), Erweiterung des Woodruff Arts Center (Atlanta, Georgia, 1999–2005), Renovierung und Erweiterung der Pierpont Morgan Library (New York, 2000–06) sowie das New York Times Building (New York, 2005–07). Unlängst realisierte und aktuelle Projekte sind u.a. die California Academy of Sciences (San Francisco, Kalifornien, 2000–08), die Erweiterung des Chicago Art Institute (Chicago, Illinois, 2005–09), die Stiftung Emilio und Annabianca Vedova (Venedig, 2008–09, hier vorgestellt) und die London Bridge Tower (London, 2000–).

RENZO PIANO, né en 1937 à Gênes en Italie, étudie à l'Université de Florence et à l'Institut polytechnique de Milan (1964). Il crée son agence, Studio Piano, en 1965, puis s'associe à Richard Rogers (Piano & Rogers, 1971–78). Ils achèvent le Centre Pompidou à Paris en 1977. De 1978 à 1980, il travaille avec Peter Rice (Piano & Rice Associates). Il fonde le Renzo Piano Building Workshop en 1981 à Gênes et Paris. Il a reçu la médaille d'or du RIBA en 1989 et le prix Pritzker en 1998. Parmi ses réalisations : le Ménil Collection Museum (Houston, Texas, 1981–86) ; le stade San Nicola (Bari, Italie, 1987–90) ; l'extension de l'IRCAM (Paris, 1988–90) ; le terminal de l'aéroport international du Kansai (Osaka, Japon, 1988–94) ; la Cité internationale (Lyon, France, 1985–96) ; le musée de la Fondation Beyeler (Riehen, Bâle, Suisse, 1991–97) ; le centre culturel Jean-Marie Tjibaou (Nouvelle-Calédonie, 1991–98) ; le Centre Mercedes-Benz (Stuttgart, 1993–98) ; la reconstruction d'une partie de la Potsdamer Strasse (Berlin, 1992–2000) ; l'auditorium de Parme (Italie, 1997–2001) ; la Maison Hermès, Tokyo (1998–2001) ; l'auditorium de Rome (Italie, 1997–2001) ; la reconversion de l'usine Fiat du Lingotto (Turin, 1983–2003) ; l'église de pèlerinage du Padre Pio (San Giovanni Rotondo, Foggia, Italie, 1991–2004) ; l'extension du Woodruff Arts Center (Atlanta, Géorgie, 1999–2005) ; la rénovation et l'agrandissement de la Morgan Library (New York, 2000–06) ; la tour du New York Times (New York, 2005–07). Parmi ses projets récents, ou en cours : la California Academy of Sciences (San Francisco, 2000–08) ; l'extension du Chicago Art Institute (Chicago, 2005–09) ; la Fondation Emilio et Annabianca Vedova (Venise, 2008–09, publiée ici) et le London Bridge Tower (Londres, 2000–)

Senza titolo – Rosso '83,

EMILIO AND ANNABIANCA VEDOVA FOUNDATION

Venice, Italy, 2008–09

Address: Dorsoduro 46, 30123 Venice, Italy, +39 41 241 37 90, www.fondazionevedova.org
Area: 500 m². Client: Fondazione Emilio e Annabianca Vedova. Cost: not disclosed
Collaboration: Alessandro Traldi (Architect), Germano Celant (Artistic Consultant),
Favero & Milan (Lead Consultants)

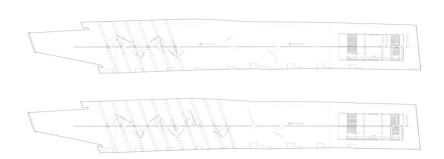

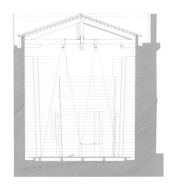

The casual visitor first sees the Magazzino del Sale, a series of nine 14th-century warehouses located on the Zattere overlooking the shipping canal that separates the city from the Giudecca. "One enters from the Zattere," says Piano, "that is, from the water and full sunlight, through a wooden, rather heavy door—an important detail, like all that follow, which helps shape this adventure." Within, the light is low, and a great sloped floor leads up from the entrance, allowing visitors to penetrate the great, open, brick-walled space that the architect has seemingly left untouched. Works of the painter Emilio Vedova are rotated throughout the space, occasionally being taken out of storage from the back of the warehouse. Piano carried on discussions with the artist over many years, leading finally to this unusual, technically sophisticated solution. "I don't believe that Emilio and I ever discussed it, but this idea of not having a static museum, but rather a true warehouse from which one could take out one piece at a time, was an idea that he had in mind.... The point was not to make a museum in one way or another; in fact the word 'museum' was never used. But the idea was in the air, and let us not forget that the Magazzini are narrow and long, and thus it made sense to imagine that down at the far end, a bit hidden in the shadow, would be the storage facility." Working with the Milan architect Alessandro Traldi, Piano has devised a solution that steps aside and allows visitors to see the painter's work, but also to admire the remarkable, ancient space. Emilio Vedova said to Renzo Piano: "I, a Venetian—you, a Genovese… light-movement-water into the open… we are people of the open sea."

Zufällige Passanten sehen zunächst das Magazzino del Sale, eine Reihe von neun Lagerhäusern aus dem 14. Jahrhundert, die an der Zattere-Promenade liegen, mit Blick über den Schiffskanal, der die Stadt von der Giudecca trennt. „Beim Eintritt in das Gebäude kommt man von der Zattere-Promenade", so Piano, „tritt also vom Wasser und hellen Sonnenlicht durch eine recht schwere Holztür – ein wichtiges Detail, das wie alle folgenden dieses Erlebnis prägt." Das Licht im Innern des Baus ist gedämpft, ein breiter, sanft ansteigender Boden führt den Besucher vom Eingang nach oben und ist Zugang zum weitläufigen, offenen Raum mit seinen Backsteinwänden, die wirken, als hätte der Architekt sie unberührt gelassen. Werke des Malers Emilio Vedova bewegen sich langsam rotierend durch den Raum, laufen ohne jede Eile aus einem Magazin am Ende des Lagerhauses. Piano war jahrelang im Gespräch mit dem Künstler, was schlussendlich zu dieser ungewöhnlichen, technisch aufwändigen Lösung führte. „Ich glaube nicht, dass Emilio und ich je darüber gesprochen haben, aber die Idee, kein statisches Museum zu schaffen, sondern eher ein veritables Lager, aus dem sich ein Werk nach dem anderen zeigen lässt, war durchaus etwas, das er im Sinn hatte... Der springende Punkt war, nicht einfach eine beliebige Form von Museum zu realisieren, im Grunde fiel der Begriff ‚Museum' nie. Dennoch lag die Idee in der Luft, und vergessen wir nicht, dass die Magazzini schmal und lang sind. Deshalb machte es Sinn sich vorzustellen, dass dort hinten, im Schatten, ein Lager liegen könnte." Mit dem Mailänder Architekten Alessandro Traldi entwickelte Piano eine Lösung, die in den Hintergrund tritt und den Besuchern erlaubt, das Werk des Künstlers zu betrachten und dabei zugleich den bemerkenswerten, alten Raum zu bewundern. Emilio Vedova hatte zu Renzo Piano gesagt: „Ich, ein Venezianer – du, ein Genueser... Licht – Bewegung – Wasser, ins Weite hinaus... wir sind Menschen der offenen See."

Le visiteur perçoit d'abord le Magazzino del Sale, une succession de neuf entrepôts datant du XIVe siècle sur les Zattere, au bord du canal qui sépare Venise de la Giudecca. « On entre par les Zattere », explique Piano, « c'est-à-dire à partir de l'eau, en plein soleil, par une porte de bois assez lourde, détail important [...] qui aide à mettre en forme cette aventure. » À l'intérieur, l'éclairage est réduit. Le sol en pente qui part de l'entrée conduit les visiteurs vers le grand volume aux murs de brique auquel l'architecte n'a apparemment pas touché. Les œuvres du peintre Emilio Vedova se déplacent lentement dans l'espace, pivotent, et vont se ranger dans un espace de stockage au fond de l'entrepôt. Piano a discuté pendant de nombreuses années avec l'artiste avant d'arriver à cette solution étonnante et techniquement sophistiquée. « Je ne pense pas qu'Emilio et moi n'en ayons jamais parlé, mais cette idée de ne pas avoir un musée statique, mais plutôt un véritable entrepôt dans lequel on pouvait aller prendre une œuvre à la fois, était quelque chose que nous avions en tête ... Il ne s'agissait pas de faire un musée quelconque, en fait le mot de musée n'a même jamais été prononcé. Mais l'idée était dans l'air et n'oublions pas que les Magazzini sont longs et étroits, et qu'il était donc logique d'imaginer que le stockage se fasse à une extrémité un peu cachée dans l'ombre. » Collaborant avec l'architecte milanais, Alessandro Traldi, Piano a mis au point cette solution discrète qui permet aux visiteurs de voir les œuvres du peintre, mais aussi d'admirer ce remarquable bâtiment ancien. Emilio Vedova a dit à Renzo Piano : « Moi, un Vénitien, toi un Génois ... la lumière, le mouvement l'eau, tout ouvert ... nous sommes des gens de la haute mer. »

Works are automatically moved from the reserves at the back of the space into the public viewing area, where the circular work is seen above.

Die Kunstwerke werden automatisch aus den Magazinen im hinteren Teil des Gebäudes gefahren und im öffentlichen Ausstellungsbereich präsentiert, wo auch das runde Gemälde oben zu sehen ist.

Les œuvres sont automatiquement acheminées des réserves, situées au fond du bâtiment, vers la zone où les visiteurs peuvent les regarder comme dans le cas de ce tableau circulaire, ci-dessus.

PLASMA STUDIO

Plasma Studio
Unit 51 – Regents Studios
8 Andrews Road, London E8 4QN, UK

Tel: +44 20 78 12 98 75 / Fax: +44 87 04 86 55 63
E-mail: mail@plasmastudio.com
Web: www.plasmastudio.com

PLASMA STUDIO was founded by Eva Castro and Holger Kehne in London in 1999. Eva Castro studied architecture and urbanism at the Universidad Central de Venezuela and subsequently completed the Graduate Design program under Jeff Kipnis at the Architectural Association (AA) in London. She is Director of the AA Landscape Urbanism Program. Holger Kehne studied architecture at the University of Applied Sciences in Münster, Germany, and at the University of East London. He is a Unit Master for Diploma Unit 12 at the AA. Ulla Hell is an Associate Partner, and she studied at the University of Innsbruck, Austria, and the Technical University Delft and Technical University Eindhoven (The Netherlands). The office made its reputation through a number of small residential and refurbishment projects in London. The architects say: "The studio is best known for its architectural use of form and geometry. Shifts, folds and bends create surface continuities that are never arbitrary but part of the spatial and structural organization." They won the Corus/Building Design "Young Architect of the Year Award" in 2002. They participated in the Hotel Puerta America project with architects like Jean Nouvel and Zaha Hadid (Madrid, Spain, 2005), and their recent work includes the Strata Hotel (Alto Adige, 2007); Cube House (Sexten, 2005–08); Tetris House, a multi-family residential compound (San Candido, 2007); and Esker House (San Candido, 2006), all in Italy. An ongoing project is Flowing Gardens, Xi'an World Horticultural Fair 2011 (Xi'an, China, 2009–11, published here).

PLASMA STUDIO wurde 1999 von Eva Castro und Holger Kehne in London gegründet. Eva Castro studierte Architektur und Stadtplanung an der Universidad Central de Venezuela und schloss einen Aufbaustudiengang Entwerfen bei Jeff Kipnis an der Architectural Association (AA) in London an. Inzwischen leitet sie das Landschaftsplanungsprogramm der AA. Holger Kehne studierte Architektur an der Fachhochschule Münster/Westfalen und der University of East London. Er ist Unit Master für den Diplombereich 12 an der AA. Ulla Hell ist Partnerin und Teilhaberin des Büros und studierte an der Universität Innsbruck sowie der Technischen Universität Delft und der Technischen Universität Eindhoven (Niederlande). Einen Namen machte sich das Büro mit einer Reihe kleinerer Wohnbau- und Sanierungsprojekte in London. Die Architekten erklären: „Das Studio ist besonders für seinen architektonischen Umgang mit Formgebung und Geometrie bekannt. Materialverschiebungen, -faltungen und -biegungen schaffen Oberflächenkontinuitäten, die nie zufällig sind, sondern Teil der räumlichen und konstruktiven Organisation." 2002 erhielt das Büro den Corus/Building Design „Young Architect of the Year Award". Darüber hinaus waren sie neben Architekten wie Jean Nouvel und Zaha Hadid am Hotel Puerta America beteiligt (Madrid, Spanien, 2005). Zu ihren jüngeren Projekten zählen das Strata Hotel (Alto Adige, 2007), das Cube House (Sexten, 2005–08), das Tetris House, ein Mehrfamilienwohnkomplex (San Candido, 2007) und das Esker House (San Candido, 2006), alle in Italien. Ein aktuelles Projekt ist Flowing Gardens, Xi'an Weltgartenschau 2011 (Xi'an, China, 2009–11, hier vorgestellt).

L'agence PLASMA STUDIO a été fondée par Eva Castro et Holger Kehne à Londres en 1999. Eva Castro a étudié l'architecture et l'urbanisme à l'Universidad Central de Venezuela, puis à l'Architectural Association (AA) à Londres (Graduate Design Program, sous la direction de Jeff Kipnis). Elle est directrice du mastère d'urbanisme paysager à l'AA. Holger Kehne a étudié l'architecture à l'Université des sciences appliquées de Münster (Allemagne) et à l'Université de l'est de Londres. Il est responsable de l'Unité de diplôme 12 à l'AA. Ulla Hell est partenaire associée. Elle a étudié à l'Université d'Innsbruck (Autriche) ainsi qu'à l'Université polytechnique de Delft et à celle d'Eindhoven (Pays-Bas). Plasma s'est fait remarquer par un certain nombre de petits projets résidentiels et de rénovation à Londres. « L'agence est surtout connue pour l'utilisation architecturale de la forme et de la géométrie. Glissements, plis et courbures créent des continuités de surface qui ne sont jamais arbitraires, et font partie de l'organisation spatiale et structurelle », expliquent les architectes. Ils ont remporté le Corus/Building Design « Prix du jeune architecte de l'année » 2002, et ont participé au projet de l'Hotel Puerta America aux côtés d'architectes comme Jean Nouvel et Zaha Hadid (Madrid, 2005). Parmi leurs réalisations récentes, toutes en Italie : la Maison Esker (San Candido, 2006) ; le Strata Hotel (Haut- Adige, 2007) ; la Maison Tetris, complexe résidentiel plurifamilial (San Candido, 2007) ; et la Maison Cube (Sexten, 2005–08, publiée ici). Ils travaillent actuellement sur un projet en cours, les Flowing Gardens (Jardins en flux), Floralies internationales de Xi'an 2011 (Xi'an, Chine, 2009–11, publiée ici).

FLOWING GARDENS

Xi'an World Horticultural Fair 2011, Xi'an, China, 2009–11

Area: 12 000 m². Client: Chang'an Ecological District Cost: not disclosed
Collaboration: Ulla Hell (Architect), Arup (Structural and Civil Engineering),
Groundlab (Landscape Design)

Blending into its site, the structure also evokes the very plants that are the subject of the World Horticultural Fair.

Der mit dem Gelände verschmelzende Komplex erinnert von seiner Formgebung her an die Pflanzen, die Mittelpunkt der Internationalen Gartenausstellung sind.

Fondu dans son site, le bâtiment évoque aussi les plantes qui sont le thème du Festival international d'horticulture.

This project includes a 5000-square-meter exhibition hall, a 4000-square-meter greenhouse, a 3500-cubic-meter gate building, and 37 hectares of landscaped areas. The architects state: "The project, titled **FLOWING GARDENS**, was generated as a synthesis of horticulture and technology where landscape and architecture converge at a sustainable and integral vision." The Horticultural Fair scheduled for 2011 is expected to attract no less than 200 000 visitors a day. The overall plan of the complex is "strikingly similar to an estuary." The architects employ "flowing forms" to create an obvious continuity between the gardens and the buildings. Located at the top of the South Hill, the greenhouse allows visitors to see the Flowing Gardens and at the same time to view plants and flowers from four different climatic zones.

Zu diesem Projekt gehört eine 5000 m² große Ausstellungshalle, ein 4000 m² großes Gewächshaus und ein 3500 m³ großes Torgebäude, sowie 37 ha landschaftlich gestaltete Freiflächen. Die Architekten erklären: „Das Projekt **FLOWING GARDENS** (Fließende Gärten) wurde als Synthese aus Gartenbaukunst und Technologie konzipiert, als eine Schnittstelle, an der Landschaft und Architektur zu einer nachhaltigen und ganzheitlichen Vision verschmelzen." Die für 2011 geplante Gartenausstellung rechnet mit nicht weniger als 200 000 Besuchern pro Tag. Der Gesamtgrundriss „hat erstaunliche Ähnlichkeit mit einem Flussdelta". Die Architekten arbeiten mit „fließenden Formen", um sichtliche Kontinuität zwischen Gärten und Bauten zu schaffen. Die auf dem südlichen Hügel gelegenen Gewächshäuser bieten den Besuchern Ausblick über die Flowing Gardens und versammeln zugleich Pflanzen und Blumen aus vier verschiedenen Klimazonen.

Ce projet comprend un hall d'expositions de 5000 m², une serre de 4000 m², un bâtiment d'entrée de 3500 m³ et 37 hectares de terrain paysagé. « Le projet intitulé "**FLOWING GARDENS**" est une synthèse d'horticulture et de technologie au sein de laquelle le paysage et l'architecture convergent en une vision intégrée et durable », expliquent les architectes. Les Floralies, programmées pour 2011, devraient attirer pas moins de 200 000 visiteurs par jour. Le plan d'ensemble du complexe est « étonnamment similaire à celui d'un estuaire ». Les architectes ont utilisé ces formes « fluides » pour créer une continuité entre les jardins et les bâtiments. Implantée au sommet de South Hill, la serre permet aux visiteurs d'avoir une vue d'ensemble des jardins, tout en découvrant des plantes et des fleurs de quatre zones climatiques différentes.

The architects explain that their design evokes an estuary, a concept that is visible in the renderings on this page and opposite (top).

Den Architekten zufolge ist der Entwurf einem Flussdelta nachempfunden – ein Konzept, das an den Renderings auf dieser Seite und gegenüber (oben) deutlich wird.

Les architectes expliquent que leur projet évoque un estuaire, concept illustré par les images de synthèse de cette page et la page ci-contre (en haut).

An interior rendering with a shelf-like ceiling that echoes the exterior forms of the building.

Rendering eines Innenraums mit einer Decke, die an ein Regal erinnert und die Formen des Außenbaus aufgreift.

Vue intérieure. Le plafond en coque évoque la structure extérieure du bâtiment.

Villa Navarra

RUDY RICCIOTTI

Agence Rudy Ricciotti Architecte
17 Bd Victor Hugo
83150 Bandol
France

Tel: +33 4 94 29 52 61
Fax: +33 4 94 32 45 25
E-mail: rudy.ricciotti@wanadoo.fr
Web: www.rudyricciotti.com

Born in 1952 in Algiers, Algeria, **RUDY RICCIOTTI** moved to the south of France as a child. He attended the École Supérieure Technique in Geneva, from which he graduated as an engineer in 1975, and the Architecture School of Marseille, from which he graduated in 1980. He created his office in Bandol, France, in 1980. Ricciotti won the 2006 Grand Prix National for Architecture, the highest French award in the field. His early work includes a number of private villas in the south of France. His first large-scale work was the Stadium in Vitrolles (1994). In 1997, he completed the College 600 secondary school in Saint-Ouen; and in 1999 a new building for the Luminy Science Faculty in Marseille. Recent work includes the Philharmonic Concert Hall in Potsdam (Germany, 2000); the Tanzmatten Concert and Sports Hall near Strasbourg (2001); the Peace Footbridge in Seoul (South Korea, 2003); the National Choreographic Center (Aix-en-Provence, 1999–2005); and the "Passerelle des Anges" (Hérault, 2009), all in France unless stated otherwise. Rudy Ricciotti recently won competitions for the Mucem in Marseille (European and Mediterranean Civilizations Museum, France, 2009 completion); for the Islamic Arts Department of the Louvre Museum in Paris (France, 2005–); and for the new building of the Venice Film Festival (Italy, 2005).

RUDY RICCIOTTI, 1952 in Algiers, Algerien geboren, zog als Kind nach Südfrankreich. Er besuchte die École Supérieure Technique in Genf, an der er 1975 seinen Abschluss als Ingenieur machte, sowie die Hochschule für Architektur in Marseille, wo er 1980 sein Studium abschloss. Im gleichen Jahr gründete er auch sein Büro in Bandol, Frankreich. 2006 wurde Ricciotti mit dem Grand Prix National d'Architecture ausgezeichnet, dem prestigeträchtigsten französischen Architekturpreis. Zu seinen frühen Werken zählen verschiedene Privatvillen in Südfrankreich. Sein erstes Großprojekt war das Stadion Vitrolles (1994). 1997 konnte er das Collège 600, eine Oberschule in Saint-Ouen fertigstellen, 1999 einen Neubau für die naturwissenschaftliche Fakultät Luminy in Marseille. Jüngere Projekte sind der Nikolaisaal der Philharmonie Potsdam (Deutschland, 2000), die Konzert- und Veranstaltungssäle Les Tanzmatten unweit von Straßburg (2001), die Friedensbrücke in Seoul (Südkorea, 2003), das Nationale Choreografiezentrum (Aix en Provence, 1999–2005) sowie die „Passerelle des Anges" (Hérault, 2009), alle in Frankreich, sofern nicht anders angegeben. Kürzlich gewann Ricciotti Wettbewerbe für das Mucem in Marseille (Museum der europäischen und Mittelmeerkulturen, Frankreich, Fertigstellung 2011), die Abteilung für Islamische Kunst des Louvre in Paris (Frankreich, 2005–) sowie ein neues Gebäude für die Filmfestspiele in Venedig (Italien, 2005).

Né en 1952 à Alger, **RUDY RICCIOTTI** est arrivé en France encore enfant. Il est ingénieur diplômé del'École supérieure technique de Genève (1975) et diplômé de l'École d'architecture de Marseille (1980). Il a créé son agence à Bandol (France) la même année. Il a remporté, en 2006, le Grand Prix national d'architecture, la plus haute distinction française. Il entame sa carrière par un certain nombre de villas dans le Sud de la France. Sa première réalisation d'importance est le stade de Vitrolles (1994). En 1997, il achève le College 600 à Saint-Ouen et, en 1999, un nouveau bâtiment pour la Faculté des sciences de Luminy à Marseille. Parmi ses réalisations récentes : une salle de concerts philharmoniques à Potsdam (Allemagne, 2000) ; la salle de sports et de concerts de Tanzmatten près de Strasbourg (2001) ; le pont de la Paix à Séoul (Corée du Sud, 2003) ; le Centre chorégraphique national (Aix-en-Provence, 1999–2005) et la passerelle des Anges (Hérault, 2009). Rudy Ricciotti a récemment remporté le concours pour le Musée des civilisations de l'Europe et de la Méditerranée, MUCEM (2009, en cours de chantier) ; pour les aménagements du département des arts islamiques au Musée du Louvre (2005–) et pour le nouveau bâtiment du Festival du cinéma à Venise (2005).

VILLA NAVARRA

Le Muy, France, 2007

Area: 220 m². Client: Enrico Navarra. Cost: not disclosed
Collaboration: Romain Ricciotti (Structural Engineer, Concrete Design),
Lafarge (Cement), Bonna Sabla (Precast Concrete)

The house is integrated into the hillside in such a way as nearly to disappear.

Das Haus wurde so in den Abhang integriert, dass es geradezu verschwindet.

La maison est insérée au flanc d'une colline au point de presque disparaître.

The house actually consists in
good part of its technically remarkable roof.

Tatsächlich besteht das Haus zu
einem Großteil aus dem technisch
bemerkenswerten Dach.

C'est en grande partie sa toiture
d'une réelle originalité technique qui
constitue cette maison.

The architect lists the materials for this house as "concrete + concrete + concrete." Designed for a well-known figure in the Paris art world, the dealer Enrico Navarra, the Villa makes use of a special fiber-reinforced concrete developed by Lafarge called Ductal. Ricciotti had already employed this material in his Peace Bridge (Seoul, South Korea, 2003), and in his more recent "Passerelle des Anges" in the Valley of the Hérault (France, 2009, also designed with his son, the engineer Romain Ricciotti) with a 67.5-meter span. Ricciotti explains: "Villa Navarra is intended as a gallery that can be visited on the Internet; it will not be open to the public. It is an abstract place that is intentionally enigmatic." With a 7.8-meter cantilever, the roof of the house, made up of 17 panels (each 9.25 x 2.35 meters in size), is just three centimeters thick. Designed to account for thermal expansion, wind resistance, and size restrictions due to transportation, these panels were precast by Bonna Sabla in Montpellier using metal molds supplied by an aviation industry firm.

Dem Architekten zufolge lautet die Liste der Baumaterialien für dieses Haus wie folgt: „Beton + Beton + Beton". Die Villa für eine bekannte Persönlichkeit der Pariser Kunstwelt, den Galeristen Enrico Navarra, wurde mit Ductal realisiert, einem von der Firma Lafarge entwickelten, faserverstärkten Spezialbeton. Ricciotti arbeitete bereits bei der Friedensbrücke (Seoul, Südkorea, 2003) mit diesem Material, ebenso wie bei seiner unlängst realisierten „Passerelle des Anges" im Tal von Hérault (Frankreich, 2009), einer Brücke mit einer Spannweite von 67,5 m, die er ebenfalls mit seinem Sohn, dem Ingenieur Romain Ricciotti, entworfen hatte. Ricciotti erklärt: „Die Villa Navarra wurde als Galerie geplant, die im Internet besucht werden kann, sie wird nicht öffentlich zugänglich sein. Sie ist ein abstrakter Raum, der bewusst enigmatisch ist." Das 7,8 m auskragende Dach ist aus 17 Segmenten (zu je 9,25 x 2,35 m) zusammengesetzt und nur 3 cm stark. Die Segmente wurden mithilfe von Gussformen aus Metall, die eine Luftfahrtfirma zur Verfügung stellte, bei Bonna Sabla in Montpellier vorgegossen. Sie wurden so berechnet, dass sie Wärmeausdehnung, Windbelastung und transportbedingten Größenvorgaben gerecht werden.

Rudy Ricciotti dresse rapidement la liste des matériaux de cette maison : « béton + béton + béton ». Conçue pour une personnalité du milieu de l'art parisien, le marchand Enrico Navarra, la Villa Navarra a été construite à l'aide d'un béton spécial renforcé de fibres, le Ductal, du cimentier Lafarge. Ricciotti avait déjà employé ce matériau pour le pont de la Paix à Séoul et pour la récente passerelle des Anges de 67,5 mètres de portée dans la vallée de l'Hérault (2009, en collaboration avec son fils, l'ingénieur Romain Ricciotti). Ricciotti explique que « la Villa Navarra est conçue comme une galerie qui peut se visiter par Internet, elle ne sera pas ouverte au public. C'est un lieu abstrait, volontairement énigmatique. » De trois centimètres d'épaisseur seulement, le toit en porte-à-faux de 7,8 mètres se compose de dix-sept panneaux de 9,25 x 2,35 mètres chacun. Conçus pour absorber la dilatation thermique, la résistance au vent, les contraintes dimensionnelles liées au transport des éléments, ces panneaux ont été fabriqués par Bonna Sabla à Montpellier à l'aide de moules métalliques fournis par une entreprise de construction aéronautique.

Quite intentionally, Rudy Ricciotti shows only very selected views of the Villa Navarra—it is almost as though the house only exists on the Internet.

Durchaus beabsichtigt zeigt Rudy Ricciotti nur sehr ausgewählte Ansichten der Villa Navarra – fast scheint es, als existiere der Bau nur im Internet.

Volontairement, Rudy Ricciotti ne montre que quelques vues très choisies de la Villa Navarra au point que cette maison semble n'exister que sur Internet.

A drawing below and an image above show the extremely long and thin nature of the design, which opens out onto the natural setting and a pool.

Zeichnung (unten) und Aufnahme (oben) veranschaulichen die extrem lange und schmale Form des Entwurfs, der sich zur umgebenden Landschaft und zum Pool hin öffnet.

Le dessin ci-dessous et l'image ci-dessus montrent le profil extrêmement allongé de ce projet et l'immense ouverture donnant sur la piscine et l'environnement naturel.

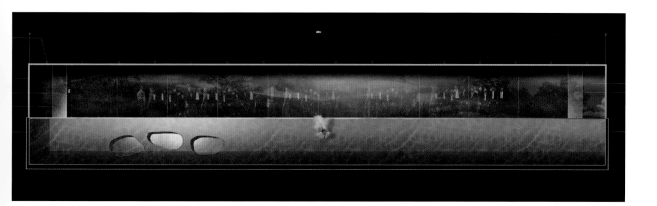

PETER RICH

Peter Rich Architects
9 Escombe Avenue
Parktown, 2193, Johannesburg, Gauteng
South Africa

Tel: +27 11 726 6151
Fax: +27 11 726 2892
E-mail: peter@peterricharchitects.co.za
Web: www.peterricharchitects.co.za

PETER RICH was born in 1945 in Johannesburg, South Africa. He obtained his B.Arch and M.Arch degrees from the University of the Witwatersrand. He has been a Professor at the University of the Witwatersrand for 30 years. He has studied indigenous African iconography and architecture, in particular that of the Ndebele. Heinrich Kammeyer is a Project Architect working with Peter Rich. He was born in 1942 in Pretoria, South Africa, and received his M.Arch and Ph.D degrees from the University of Pretoria. Robert Rich was born in 1978 and graduated from the University of Pretoria in 2006. He is a Senior Designer working with his father in the practice. Others involved were Anne Fitchett, a Consultant who has focused on the history of African architecture, and Lineo Lerothol-Mosoeunyane, who works in Community Empowerment and was born in 1966 in Lesotho. The firm's work includes Westridge House and Garden (Gauteng, 1986); Elim Shopping Center (Limpopo Province, 1986); Kemp House (Evenhuis, Natures Valley, 1991); Mennel Pavilion (Melrose, Gauteng, 1992); River Park Housing Project (Johannesburg, 1998); Bwanari Lodge Project (Madikwe Game Reserve, Northwest Province, 2000); Thulumtwana Children's Facility (Gauteng, 2000); Makuleke Cultural Project, Limpopo, 2001); House Kennedy (George, Western Cape, 2003); Bopitikelo Community and Cultural Center (Molatedi, Northwest Province, 2005); Alexandra Heritage Center (Johannesburg, Gauteng, 2004–09, published here); and the Mapungubwe Interpretation Center, Mapungubwe National Park (Limpopo, 2007–09, also published here), all in South Africa.

PETER RICH wurde 1945 in Johannesburg, Südafrika, geboren. Seine B.Arch- und M.Arch-Abschlüsse absolvierte er an der Universität Witwatersrand, wo er 30 Jahre lang Professor war. Er studierte traditionelle afrikanische Ikonografie und Architektur, insbesondere die der Ndebele. Heinrich Kammeyer ist Projektarchitekt und arbeitet mit Peter Rich. Er wurde 1942 in Pretoria, Südafrika, geboren, absolvierte seinen M.Arch und promovierte an der Universität Pretoria. Robert Rich wurde 1978 geboren und schloss sein Studium 2006 an der Universität Pretoria ab. Er ist im Büro seines Vaters als leitender Architekt im Entwurf tätig. Weitere Mitarbeiter sind Anne Fitchett, Beraterin mit Schwerpunkt afrikanische Architekturgeschichte, sowie Lineo Lerothol-Mosoeunyane, geboren 1966 in Lesotho, die sich für die Stärkung von Gruppen und Gemeinden engagiert. Projekte des Büros sind u. a.: Haus Westridge mit Garten (Gauteng, 1986), Elim Einkaufszentrum (Provinz Limpopo, 1986), Haus Kemp (Evenhuis, Natures Valley, 1991), Mennel-Pavillon (Melrose, Gauteng, 1992), Wohnungsbauprojekt River Park (Johannesburg, 1998), Bwanari-Lodge-Projekt (Wildreservat Madikwe, Provinz North-West, 2000), Kinderzentrum Thulumtwana (Gauteng, 2000), Kulturprojekt Makuleke (Limpopo, 2001), Haus Kennedy (George, Western Cape, 2003), Gemeinde- und Kulturzentrum Bopitikelo (Molatedi, Provinz North-West, 2005), Kulturerbe-Zentrum Alexandra (Johannesburg, Gauteng, 2004–09, hier vorgestellt) sowie das Mapungubwe Interpretation Center, Nationalpark Mapungubwe (Limpopo, 2007–09, ebenfalls hier vorgestellt), alle in Südafrika.

PETER RICH, né en 1945 à Johannesburg (Afrique du Sud), est B. Arch et M. Arch de l'Université du Witwatersrand. Il y enseigne depuis trente ans. Il a étudié l'iconographie et l'architecture indigènes, en particulier celle des Ndebele. Heinrich Kammeyer est architecte de projet travaillant avec Peter Rich. Né en 1942 à Pretoria, il est M. Arch et Ph. D de l'université de cette ville. Robert Rich, né en 1978, est diplômé de l'Université de Pretoria (2006). Il est concepteur senior et collabore avec son père. Parmi les autres collaborateurs figurent Anne Fitchett, consultante en histoire de l'architecture africaine et Lineo Lerothol-Mosoeunyane, né en 1966 au Lesotho, qui travaille pour des services de développement communautaire. Parmi les réalisations de l'agence, toutes en Afrique du Sud : la maison et le jardin Westridge (Gauteng, 1986) ; le centre commercial Elim (province du Limpopo, 1986) ; la Maison Kemp (Evenhuis, Natures Valley, 1991) ; le pavillon Mennel (Melrose, Gauteng, 1992) ; le projet de logements du River Park (Johannesburg, 1998) ; le projet de la Bwanari Lodge (Madikwe Game Reserve, province du Nord-Ouest, 2000) ; des installations pour des enfants de Thulumtwana (Gauteng, 2000) ; le projet culturel de Makuleke (Limpopo, 2001) ; la Maison Kennedy (George, Western Cape, 2003) ; le centre culurel et communautaire de Bopitikelo (Molatedi, province du Nord-Ouest, 2005) ; le Centre du patrimoine d'Alexandra (Johannesburg, Gauteng, 2004–09, publié ici) et le centre d'interprétation de Mapungubwe (Parc national de Mapungubwe, Limpopo, 2007–09, également publié ici).

ALEXANDRA HERITAGE CENTER
Johannesburg, Gauteng, South Africa, 2004–09

Address: www.southafrica.info/mandela/mandelacentre-alexandra.htm
Area: 811 m². Client: Gauteng Tourist Authority, Department of Environment and Tourism, Alexandra Renewal Program
Cost: $1.525 million. Collaboration: Walter Martins

This structure is located opposite a site known as Mandela's Yard, a shack inhabited by the former South African President in the 1940s. Peter Rich writes: "The project builds a sense of community and provides poverty relief through training inhabitants in tourism and heritage; nurturing small enterprises; and by showcasing the arts, culture and heritage of Alexandra." Ramps rising from street level allow visitors to reach the upper exhibition space and library, and also to survey the neighborhood. New public areas for entrepreneurial activity and training can also be used for political and social events. Rich declares: "Just as the 'spaces between' the yards are active, so there is no residual space in the Center. Uses overlap and interact: a fifth dimension is created under the building; space becomes street and street is reconfigured as space." The architect has made a clear effort to give dignity to this modest community and to encourage its development in ways related to local habits and customs.

Dieser Bau liegt gegenüber von Mandela's Yard, einer Hütte, die in den 1940er-Jahren Wohnort des ehemaligen südafrikanischen Präsident war. Peter Rich schreibt: „Das Projekt ist gemeinschaftsstiftend und trägt zur Armutsminderung bei, indem es die Anwohner in den Bereichen Tourismus und Kulturerbe ausbildet, kleine Unternehmen fördert und auch der Kunst, der Kultur und dem kulturellen Erbe von Alexandra ein Forum bietet." Rampen führen von der Straßenebene hinauf zum Obergeschoss, in dem Ausstellungsräume und eine Bibliothek untergebracht sind und von wo aus man Ausblick auf das Stadtviertel hat. Neu eingerichtete öffentliche Räume für unternehmerische Aktivitäten und Ausbildung stehen auch für politische und gesellschaftliche Veranstaltungen zur Verfügung. Rich erklärt: „Ebenso wie die ‚Zwischenräume' zwischen den Höfen aktiv genutzt werden, gibt es im gesamten Zentrum keinen ‚Rest'-Raum. Es nutzt Überschneidungen und schafft Interaktion: unter dem Gebäude ensteht eine fünfte Dimension – Raum wird zu Straße und Straße wird zu Raum umkonfiguriert." Ganz offensichtlich ging es dem Architekten darum, diesem bescheidenen Stadtviertel Würde zu geben und Entwicklungen zu fördern, die an lokale Traditionen und Bräuche anknüpfen.

Cette construction s'élève face au site de Mandela's Yard, une cabane habitée par l'ancien président sud-africain dans les années 1940. Peter Rich écrit : « Le projet participe à la constitution d'un sentiment communautaire et apporte des solutions à la pauvreté en proposant aux habitants des formations au tourisme et au patrimoine, en encourageant de petites entreprises, et en présentant les arts, la culture et le patrimoine d'Alexandra. » Des rampes qui s'élèvent à partir de la rue permettent aux visiteurs d'atteindre l'espace d'expositions et la bibliothèque situés à l'étage, mais aussi d'avoir une vue sur le quartier. Les salles destinées aux activités d'entreprises ou de formation peuvent également servir à des réunions sociales ou politiques. « De même que les espaces "entre-deux" existant entre les cabanes sont actifs, il n'y a pas d'espace résiduel dans ce Centre. Les usages se superposent et interagissent : une cinquième dimension a été créée sous le bâtiment. L'espace devient la rue et la rue se reconfigure en espace », précise Rich. L'architecte s'est efforcé de donner une dignité nouvelle à cette modeste communauté et d'encourager son développement en accord avec les habitudes et coutumes locales.

In its township setting, the Alexandra Heritage Center stands out as a well adapted piece of contemporary architecture.

Das Alexandra Heritage Center fällt in seinem Township-Umfeld als besonders gelungen integrierte zeitgenössische Architektur auf.

Projet pour une township, l'Alexandra Heritage Center s'en détache comme une œuvre architecturale contemporaine mais s'y est adapté.

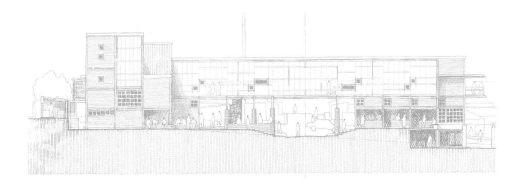

The building is quite simple in its conception, functional, and above all dignified and attractive.

Das Gebäude ist konzeptionell recht einfach, funktional und vor allem würdevoll und ansprechend.

Le bâtiment est de conception assez simple mais fonctionnel, digne et attirant.

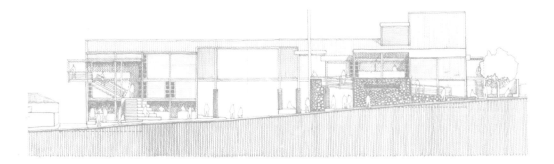

A section drawing shows (above) how the structure adapts to the slightly sloping terrain. Below, the cheerful and open interior of the building. With its steps opening onto the street (opposite) the Center is inviting and open by design as well as by function.

Die Schnittzeichnung (oben) belegt, wie der Bau an das leicht abfallende Terrain angepasst wurde. Unten die fröhlichen und offenen Innenräume des Komplexes. Gegenüber: Mit den Stufen, die sich zur Straße hin öffnen, wirkt das Zentrum einladend und offen – in gestalterischer wie funktioneller Hinsicht.

La coupe ci-dessus montre comment le bâtiment s'adapte au terrain légèrement incliné. Ci-dessous, l'intérieur ouvert et chaleureux. Grâce à des escaliers qui descendent directement dans la rue, le Centre paraît ouvert et accueillant aussi bien dans sa fonction que dans ses plans.

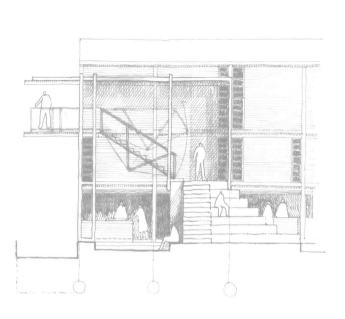

MAPUNGUBWE INTERPRETATION CENTER

Mapungubwe National Park, Limpopo, South Africa, 2007–09

Address: Mapungubwe National Park, Limpopo, South Africa, mapungubwe.com
Area: 1797 m². Client: SAN Parks. Cost: $1.875 million

With a more rural setting than the Alexandra Heritage Center, the Mapungubwe Interpretation Center takes on the profile of local architecture, albeit in a modern mode.

Das Mapungubwe Interpretation Center liegt in einem erheblich ländlicheren Umfeld als das Alexandra Heritage Center. Sein Profil erinnert an regionale Bauten, wenngleich in einer modernen Variante.

Dans un cadre plus rural que l'Alexandra Heritage Center, le Mapungubwe Interpretation Center reprend les caractéristiques de l'architecture locale, mais dans un mode moderne.

The appearance of this structure immediately makes clear that it is directly related to local traditions. The architect states: "The Mapungubwe National Park celebrates the site of an ancient trading civilization in the context of a natural setting. The complex landscape was both the inspiration for the design and the source of the materials for the construction of the new Interpretation Center, resulting in a composition of structures that are authentically rooted to their location." The thin shell vaults seen here evoke the "archeological revelation of past cultures." Local people were trained to produce the stabilized earth tiles and to build the vaults that are the most visible architectural element of the **MAPUNGUBWE INTERPRETATION CENTER**. Though designs of this sort might seem incongruous in the midst of the contemporary architecture of Japan, the United States, or Europe, it is a fact that good architecture in these circumstances can make a tangible difference to lives and cultures, a success that "first world" architects rarely achieve.

Schon von außen wird deutlich, dass dieser Bau unmittelbar Bezug auf lokale Traditionen nimmt. Der Architekt erläutert: „Der Nationalpark Mapungubwe würdigt den Standort einer uralten Handelszivilisation im Kontext eines landschaftlichen Umfelds. Die komplexe Landschaft war sowohl Inspiration für den Entwurf als auch Lieferant für die Baumaterialien des neuen Interpretation Center. Dies führte zu einer baulichen Komposition, die authentisch an ihrem Standort verwurzelt ist." Die abgebildeten dünnwandigen Schalengewölbe greifen die „archäologische Enthüllung vergangener Kulturen" auf. Anwohner wurden angelernt, um Blocksteine aus verdichtetem Lehm zu fertigen und die Gewölbe zu bauen, die das auffälligste architektonische Element des **MAPUNGUBWE INTERPRETATION CENTER** sind. Selbst wenn Entwürfe wie diese inmitten zeitgenössischer Bauten aus Japan, den USA oder Europa überraschen mögen, ist es zweifellos so, dass gelungene Architektur unter solchen Bedingungen spürbare Auswirkungen auf Leben und Kulturen haben kann – ein Erfolg, den Architekten der „ersten Welt" selten für sich verbuchen können.

L'aspect de cette construction affirme ses liens directs avec les traditions locales. Comme l'explique l'architecte : « Le Parc national de Mapungubwe célèbre le site d'une ancienne civilisation commerçante dans un contexte de cadre naturel. Le paysage complexe est la source à la fois de l'inspiration et des matériaux de construction de ce nouveau centre d'interprétation, ce qui produit une composition de petits bâtiments authentiquement enracinés dans leur site. » Les voûtes à coque mince sont « une révélation des cultures du passé ». Les habitants ont été formés à la production de briques de terre stabilisée et à la construction de ces voûtes qui sont l'élément architectural le plus caractéristique du **MAPUNGUBWE INTERPRETATION CENTER**. Bien que des réalisations de ce type puissent sembler incongrues comparées à l'architecture contemporaine du Japon, des États-Unis et de l'Europe, il n'en est pas moins vrai qu'une bonne architecture peut apporter une différence sensible dans la vie et la culture des habitants des pays moins développés, ce que ne réussissent pas toujours les architectes des pays riches.

An arching dome defines the
presence of the Center in the hilly
site.

*Die gewölbte Kuppel prägt das
Erscheinungsbild der Centers in der
hügeligen Landschaft.*

*L'arc élégant d'une coupole
indique la présence du Centre
dans les collines.*

An elegant, arching brick roof allows light to enter and generates ample interior space.

Ein elegantes Ziegelgewölbe lässt Licht in den Bau und schafft großzügige Innenräume.

Une élégante toiture voûtée en brique laisse entrer la lumière et protège un généreux volume intérieur.

Drawings show the site and the insertion of the Center into the sloping site. Below, an oculus admits overhead natural light.

Zeichnungen zeigen das Grundstück und die Integration des Centers in das abschüssige Terrain. Unten ein Kuppelauge, durch das Tageslicht einfällt.

Dessins illustrant le site et l'insertion du Centre dans le terrain incliné. Ci-dessous, un oculus à la verticale laisse pénétrer l'éclairage naturel.

ROTOR

Rotor vzw-asbl
Laekensestraat 101
1000 Brussels
Belgium

Tel: +32 485 87 57 63
E-mail: rotorasbl@gmail.com
Web: www.rotordb.org

The principals of the non-profit organization **ROTOR** call it "a platform for the endorsement of industrial waste reuse. Rotor wants, among other things, to encourage contacts between producers of 'interesting' waste and potential reusers from the field of industry, design or architecture." Maarten Gielen was born in Aalst, Belgium, in 1984. He is a founding member of Rotor, created in 2005. Tristan Boniver was born in Brussels in 1976 and his currently finishing his M.Arch at La Cambre Architecture Institute, Brussels. He is another founding member of the team. Lionel Devlieger was born in Rwamagana, Rwanda, in 1972. He obtained his Master's in Architecture and Urbanism degree from Ghent University (1996) and a Ph.D in Engineering Sciences—Architecture from the same university in 2005. He has been an active member of Rotor since 2006. Mia Schmallenbach was born in Canberra, Australia, in 1982. She received her Master's in Industrial Design from La Cambre Art Institute, Brussels (2008), and was an active member of Rotor from 2006 to 2008. Their recent projects include RDF181, temporary offices (Brussels, Belgium, 2007, published here); "Deutschland im Herbst" exhibition at the Ursula Blickle Stiftung (Kraichtal, Germany, 2008); and the Kunstenfestivaldesarts 2009 (Festival Center, Brussels, Belgium, 2009).

Die Partner der gemeinnützigen Organisation **ROTOR** definieren sich als „Plattform für die Wiederverwertung von Industriemüll. Rotor will, unter anderem, Kontakte zwischen den Produzenten ‚interessanter' Abfälle und potenzieller Wiederverwender in Industrie, Design und Architektur fördern". Maarten Gielen wurde 1984 in Aalst, Belgien, geboren. Er war eines der Gründungsmitglieder von Rotor. Tristan Boniver wurde 1976 in Brüssel geboren und absolviert derzeit seinen M.Arch am Architekturinstitut der Kunsthochschule La Cambre in Brüssel. Auch er zählt zu den Gründungsmitgliedern des Teams. Lionel Devlieger wurde 1972 in Rwamagana, Ruanda, geboren. Er absolvierte seinen Master in Architektur und Stadtplanung an der Universität Gent (1996) und promovierte 2005 in Ingenieurwissenschaften/Architektur an derselben Universität. Er ist seit 2006 aktives Mitglied bei Rotor. Mia Schmallenbach wurde 1982 in Canberra, Australien, geboren. Sie absolvierte ihren Master in Industriedesign an der Kunsthochschule La Cambre, Brüssel (2008), und war zwischen 2006 und 2008 aktives Mitglied bei Rotor. Ihre jüngsten Projekte sind u.a. RDF181, temporäre Büros (Brüssel, 2007, hier vorgestellt), „Deutschland im Herbst" Ausstellung der Ursula Blickle Stiftung (Kraichtal, Deutschland, 2008) sowie das KunstenfestivaldesArts 2009 (Festival Center, Brüssel, 2009).

Les responsables de **ROTOR**, association à but non lucratif créée en 2005, la présentent comme une « plate-forme pour la défense de la réutilisation des déchets industriels. Rotor souhaite, entre autres, encourager les contacts entre les producteurs de déchets "intéressants" et leurs réutilisateurs potentiels dans le domaine de l'industrie, du design et de l'architecture ». Maarten Gielen, né à Aalst (Belgique) en 1984, est membre fondateur de Rotor. Tristan Boniver, né à Bruxelles en 1976, termine actuellement son M. Arch à l'Institut d'architecture de La Cambre à Bruxelles, et a également participé à la fondation de Rotor. Lionel Devlieger, né à Rwamagana (Rwanda) en 1972, a obtenu son mastère en architecture et urbanisme de l'Université de Gand (1996), et son Ph. D en sciences de l'ingénierie-architecture de la même université, en 2005. Il est membre actif de Rotor depuis 2006. Mia Schmallenbach, née à Canberra (Australie) en 1982, a passé son mastère en design industriel à l'Institut d'art de La Cambre Art (2008), et a été membre actif de Rotor de 2006 à 2008. Leurs projets récents comprennent RDF181, les bureaux temporaires du groupe (Bruxelles, 2007, publié ici) ; « Deutschland im Herbst », exposition à la Fondation Ursula Blickle (Kraichtal, Allemagne, 2008) et le KunstenfestivaldesArts 2009 (Centre des festivals, Bruxelles, 2009).

RDF181
Brussels, Belgium, 2007

Address: 181, rue de Flandre,1000 Brussels, Belgium
Area: 60 m² (plus 60 m² terrace). Client: Rotor Vzw
Cost: €3000 + 500 hours of voluntary work

This "parasite" structure was designed as an office for Rotor. It was entirely made of waste materials: "A rejected lot of plastic film, old exhibition material and transparent sailcloth for the windows, EVA1 foam to insulate the roof, plastic van cladding as terrace paving, and materials they have borrowed from building firms for the structure: props, struts, and formwork beams." Located on a site where a developer intended to build a new structure, **RDF181** was built without any application for planning permission, but with the permission of the owner, a situation Rotor calls "legal squatting." The owner required the use of the ground level for parking, thus the structure is lifted off the ground. RDF181 was in place for one year and served as a demonstration of the group's thesis that other methods of construction and occupation of cities are possible. Similar efforts exist in other countries, such as Recetas Urbanas in Spain (Santiago Cirugeda).

Die „parasitäre" Konstruktion wurde als Büroraum für Rotor geplant. Sie besteht vollständig aus Abfallmaterialien: „Ein ausgemusterter Posten Plastikfolie, alte Ausstellungsmaterialien und transparentes Segeltuch für die Fenster, EVA-1-Schaumstoff zur Dämmung des Dachs, Kunststoff-LKW-Plane als Terrassenbelag und Materialien, die von Baufirmen leihweise zur Verfügung gestellt wurden: Stützen, Druckstreben und Schalungsgerüstelemente." **RDF181** wurde auf einem Grundstück errichtet, auf dem ein Neubau in Planung war. Ohne Baugenehmigung, jedoch mit Genehmigung des Eigentümers, war das Vorgehen Rotor zufolge eine „legale Hausbesetzung". Der Eigentümer nutzte die Straßenebene als Parkplatz, weshalb der Bau aufgeständert wurde. RDF181 bestand ein Jahr und ist ein Beleg für die These der Gruppe, dass alternative Bau- und Nutzungsmodelle in der Stadt möglich sind. Ähnliche Initiativen gibt es auch in anderen Ländern, etwa Recetas Urbanas (Santiago Cirugeda) in Spanien.

Cette structure « parasite » a été conçue pour servir de bureaux à Rotor. Elle a été entièrement réalisée en matériaux de récupération : « Un lot de film plastique rejeté, une vieille toile transparente, du vieux matériel d'exposition et de la toile de voile pour les fenêtres, de la mousse EVA1 pour isoler le toit, de l'habillage plastique de caravanes pour servir de pavement en terrasse et des matériaux obtenus auprès d'entreprises de construction pour la structure : poteaux, étrésillons et poutres de coffrage. » Implanté sur un terrain sur lequel un promoteur projetait un nouvel immeuble, **RDF181** a été construit sans demande de permis de construire, mais avec l'autorisation du propriétaire – situation qualifiée de « squat légal » par Rotor. Le propriétaire souhaitait conserver l'utilisation du sol pour garer des voitures, ce qui explique que la structure soit suspendue. RDF181 est resté en place pendant un an et a servi à démontrer la thèse du groupe qui veut que d'autres méthodes de construction et d'occupation sont possibles dans les villes. Des expériences similaires ont été tentées dans d'autres pays, comme celle de Recetas Urbanas en Espagne (Santiago Cirugeda).

An intentionally temporary extrusion above an empty lot, RDF181 is a commentary on the voids that populate modern cities.

RDF181 ist ein bewusst temporärer Anbau über einem ungenutzten Baugrundstück und zugleich ein Kommentar zu den Brachflächen, die sich durch die modernen Städte ziehen.

Bâtiment temporaire qui se projette au-dessus d'une parcelle vide, le RDF181 est aussi un commentaire sur les vides urbains dans les villes modernes.

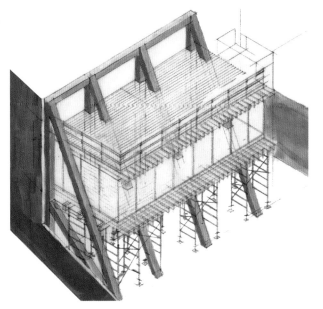

Materials and spaces are in keeping
with the ephemeral nature of the
structure. Rough materials echo the
external appearance of the office.

Materialien und Räume spiegeln die
kurzlebige Natur des Baus wider. Die
groben Materialien korrespondieren
mit dem äußeren Erscheinungsbild
des Büros.

Les matériaux et les volumes sont
en accord avec la nature éphémère
de cette construction. Les matériaux
bruts s'harmonisent avec l'aspect
extérieur de ces bureaux.

The office grafts itself onto the existing elements of the site—a building wall or a leaning support column.

Les bureaux se greffent sur des éléments existants : le mur d'un immeuble ou des étais de soutien.

Das Büro schreibt sich in die bestehenden architektonischen Elemente des Grundstücks ein – sei es eine Brandmauer oder eine Druckstrebe.

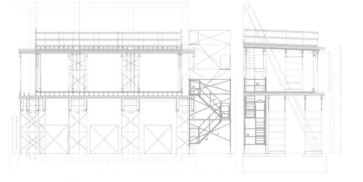

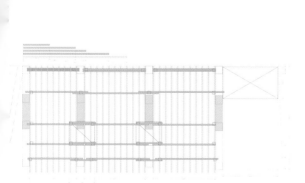

HIROSHI SAMBUICHI

Hiroshi Sambuichi Architects
8–3–302 Nakajima naka-ku
730–0811 Hiroshima
Japan

Tel: +81 82 544 1417
Fax: +81 82 544 1418
E-mail: samb@d2.dion.ne.jp

HIROSHI SAMBUICHI was born in 1968. He graduated from the Department of Architecture in the Faculty of Science and Technology at Tokyo University of Science. After working for Shinichi Ogawa and Associates, he established Hiroshi Sambuichi Architects and began design work in Hiroshima. His work includes the Running Green Project (Yamaguchi, 2001); Air House (Yamaguchi, 2001); Miwa-gama (Yamaguchi, 2002); Sloping North House (Yamaguchi, 2003); Stone House (Shimane, 2005); and the Inujima Art Project Seirensho (Okayama, 2006–08), a museum located on a small island in the Inland Sea of Japan, carried out for the client responsible for Tadao Ando's work on the nearby island of Naoshima. In 2008, Hiroshi Sambuichi completed the Hiroshima Project offices, Miyajima Office (Hatsukaichi, Hiroshima, published here). Work currently in its final phase includes Miwa-Storage (Hagi, Yamaguchi, 2009–), and the Rokko Observation Platform (Kobe, Hyogo, 2010), all in Japan.

HIROSHI SAMBUICHI wurde 1968 geboren. Sein Architekturstudium schloss er an der Fakultät für Naturwissenschaften und Technik an der Tokyo University of Science ab. Nachdem er zunächst für Shinichi Ogawa & Associates gearbeitet hatte, gründete er sein Büro Hiroshi Sambuichi Architects und begann in Hiroshima zu praktizieren. Zu seinen Projekten zählen u.a.: Running Green Project (Yamaguchi, 2001), Air House (Yamaguchi, 2001), Miwa-gama (Yamaguchi, 2002), Sloping North House (Yamaguchi, 2003), Stone House (Shimane, 2005) und das Inujima Art Project Seirensho (Okayama, 2006–08), ein Museum auf einer kleinen Insel in der Seto-In-landsee, für denselben Bauherrn, für den Tadao Ando auf der nahe gelegenen Insel Naoshima Projekte realisiert hatte. 2008 konnte Hiroshi Sambuichi das Hiroshima-Projektbüro, das Miyajima-Büro, fertigstellen (Hatsukaichi, Hiroshima, hier vorgestellt). In der Abschlussphase befinden sich derzeit Projekte wie ein Lagergebäude für Miwa (Hagi, Yamaguchi, 2009–) oder die Rokko-Beobachtungsplattform (Kobe, Hyogo, 2010), alle in Japan.

Né en 1968, **HIROSHI SAMBUICHI** est diplômé du département d'architecture de la Faculté des sciences et technologies de l'Université des sciences de Tokyo. Après avoir travaillé pour Shinichi Ogawa and Associates, il a fondé l'agence Hiroshi Sambuichi Architects et commencé à travailler à Hiroshima. Parmi ses réalisations, toutes au Japon : le Running Green Project (Yamaguchi, 2001) ; la Maison Air (Yamaguchi, 2001) ; Miwa-gama (Yamaguchi, 2002) ; la Maison Sloping North (Yamaguchi, 2003) ; la Maison Stone (Shimane, 2005–) et le projet artistique d'Inujima Seirensho (Okayama, 2006–08), musée situé sur une petite île de la Mer intérieure du Japon, réalisé à la demande du client à l'origine des interventions de Tadao Ando sur l'île voisine de Naoshima. En 2008, Hiroshi Sambuichi a achevé le projet des bureaux Miyajima (Hatsukaichi, Hiroshima, publié ici). Il achève actuellement les entrepôts Miwa (Hagi, Yamaguchi, 2009–) et la plate-forme d'observation de Rokko (Kobe, Hyogo, 2010).

MIYAJIMA OFFICE

Hatsukaichi, Hiroshima, Japan, 2007–08

Address: Miyajima-cho, Hatsukaichi, Hiroshima Prefecture 739-0500, Japan
Area: 78 m². Client: Funakura Accountants Office. Cost: not disclosed

For this project, the architect sought to make maximum use of the topography and the "latent energy" of the site to reduce carbon emissions to a strict minimum. Located 500 meters from a Unesco World Heritage Site (Itsukushima-jinja Shrine), the office is powered in good part by solar and convection energy. The most visible feature of the building is a "chimney of glass" that brings to mind the wind towers seen in Middle Eastern countries such as Iran, although the architect does not make reference to these traditions. Continuing along the same lines, Sambuichi found a stock of wood that had been left unused for 40 years in a local warehouse, employing the wood to give character to the new building. "I gave idle materials new life and created a rich space while drawing out the charm of the materials," he states. With his characteristic modesty and humor, the architect concludes: "I think that a new endemic species suitable for this area was born."

Bei diesem Projekt ging es dem Architekten darum, die Topografie und „latente Energie" des Geländes maximal zu nutzen, um die CO_2-Emissionen auf ein absolutes Minimum zu reduzieren. Das nur 500 m von einer Unesco-Weltkulturerbestätte (dem Itsukushima-Schrein) entfernte Büro wird zum Großteil mit Sonnen- und Konvektionsenergie versorgt. Auffälligstes Merkmal des Gebäudes ist sein „gläserner Kamin", der an Windfänger erinnert, wie sie in Ländern des Mittleren Ostens wie dem Iran verbreitet sind, obwohl der Architekt sich nicht explizit auf solche Traditionen bezieht. Nach demselben Prinzip entdeckte Sambuichi einen Holzbestand, der seit 40 Jahren ungenutzt in einem örtlichen Lagerhaus gelegen hatte, und setzte das Holz ein, um dem Neubau besonderen Charakter zu geben. „Ich habe ungenutzten Materialien neues Leben gegeben, einen facettenreichen Raum geschaffen und zugleich den Charme der Materialien zur Geltung gebracht", erklärt er. Mit der für ihn typischen Bescheidenheit und Ironie folgert der Architekt: „Ich glaube, hier wurde eine neuartige einheimische Spezies geboren, die dieser Gegend entspricht."

Pour ce projet, l'architecte a cherché à utiliser au maximum la topographie et « l'énergie latente du site » pour réduire au strict minimum les émissions de carbone. Situé à 500 mètres d'un site répertorié au Patrimoine de l'humanité de l'Unesco (le mausolée Itsukushima-jinja), ce petit immeuble de bureaux est en grande partie alimenté par l'énergie solaire et par convection. L'élément le plus caractéristique du projet est une « cheminée de verre » qui rappelle les tours de vent de certains pays du Moyen-Orient comme l'Iran, bien que l'architecte ne se réfère pas à ces traditions. Selon la même approche, Sambuichi a trouvé un stock de bois abandonné pendant quarante ans dans un entrepôt local et l'a utilisé pour renforcer le caractère qu'il voulait donner à son projet. « J'ai offert une nouvelle vie à des matériaux inutilisés, et créé un espace plus riche en m'appuyant sur leur charme », explique l'architecte. Avec l'humour et la modestie qui le caractérisent, il conclut : « Je pense qu'une nouvelle espèce endémique adaptée à cette région vient de naître. »

The surprisingly tall, tapered,
wood-clad tower of the office is its
most visible exterior feature.

Der erstaunlich hohe, leicht konische,
holzverkleidete Turm des Büros ist
von außen das auffälligste Merkmal.

Étonnement élevée et effilée, la tour
habillée de bois est la caractéristique
extérieure la plus visible du projet.

The wooden interior of the tower creates a light-well of sorts, an unoccupied, high space that redefines the interior.

Das Innere des Holzturms wirkt wie eine Art Lichtschacht, ein ungenutzter hoher Raum, der den Innenraum neu definiert.

L'intérieur vide de la tour doublé de bois fait office de puits de lumière et personnalise l'intérieur.

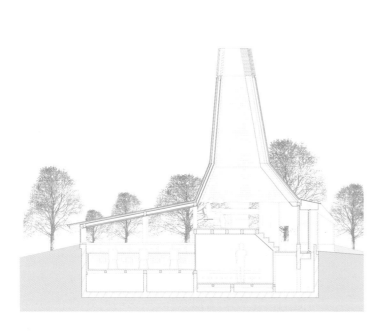

SANAA/
KAZUYO SEJIMA + RYUE NISHIZAWA

SANAA/Kazuyo Sejima + Ryue Nishizawa
1-5-27 Tatsumi, Koto-ku, Tokyo 135-0053, Japan
Tel: +81 3 5534 1780 / Fax: +81 3 5534 1757
E-mail: press@sanaa.co.jp

Born in Ibaraki Prefecture, Japan, in 1956, Kazuyo Sejima received her M.Arch from the Japan Women's University in 1981 and went to work in the office of Toyo Ito the same year. She established Kazuyo Sejima and Associates in Tokyo in 1987. She has been a Visiting Lecturer at Japan Women's University and at Waseda University since 1994. Ryue Nishizawa was born in Tokyo in 1966, and graduated from the National University in Yokohama in 1990. He has been a Visiting Professor at the Harvard School of Design and at the National University in Yokohama. They began working together in 1990, and created the new firm **SANAA/KAZUYO SEJIMA + RYUE NISHIZAWA** in 1995. In 2010, SANAA was awarded the Pritzker Prize. The built work of Kazuyo Sejima includes the Saishunkan Seiyaku Women's Dormitory (Kumamoto, 1990–91); Pachinko Parlor I (Hitachi, Ibaraki, 1992–93); Pachinko Parlor II (Nakamachi, Ibaraki, 1993); Villa in the Forest (Tateshina, Nagano, 1993–94); Chofu Station Police Box (Tokyo, 1993–94); Pachinko Parlor III (Hitachi, Ibaraki, 1995), all in Japan. The work of SANAA includes the 21st Century Museum of Contemporary Art (Kanazawa, Ishikawa, Japan, 2002–04); Moriyama House (Tokyo, Japan, 2002–05); the Glass Pavilion of the Toledo Museum of Art (Ohio, USA, 2003–06); a theater and cultural center in Almere (The Netherlands, 2004–07); a building for the New Museum of Contemporary Art in New York (New York, USA, 2005–07); the Serpentine Pavilion (London, UK, 2009, published here); and an extension of the Valencia Institute of Modern Art (IVAM) in Spain (2002–). SANAA completed the Rolex Learning Center of the EPFL in Lausanne (Switzerland, 2007–09, also published here), and won the competition to design the new building of the Louvre-Lens (Lens, France, 2009–12).

Die 1956 in der Präfektur Ibaraki geborene Kazuyo Sejima erhielt 1981 den M.Arch der Japanischen Frauenuniversität und begann noch im selben Jahr für Toyo Ito zu arbeiten. 1987 gründete sie in Tokio ihr Büro Kazuyo Sejima and Associates. Seit 1994 ist die als Gastprofessorin an der Frauenuniversität und an der Universität Waseda tätig. Ryue Nishizawa wurde 1966 in Tokio geboren und schloss sein Studium 1990 an der Nationaluniversität in Yokohama ab. Nishizawa hatte eine Gastprofessur an der Harvard School of Design und der Nationaluniversität in Yokohama. 1990 begann er, mit Sejima zusammenzuarbeiten und 1995 gründete das Duo die Firma **SANAA/KAZUYO SEJIMA + RYUE NISHIZAWA**. 2010 wurde SANAA mit dem Pritzker-Preis ausgezeichnet. Kazuyo Sejima realisierte u.a. das Frauenwohnheim Saishunkan Seiyaku (Kumamoto, 1990–91), Pachinko Parlor I (Hitachi, Ibaraki, 1992–93), Pachinko Parlor II (Nakamachi, Ibaraki, 1993), die Villa im Wald (Tateshina, Nagano, 1993–94), Polizeistation Bahnhof Chofu (Tokio, 1993–94), Pachinko Parlor III (Hitachi, Ibaraki, 1995), alle in Japan. Zum Werk von SANAA zählen das Museum für Kunst der 21. Jahrhunderts (Kanazawa, Ishikawa, Japan, 2002–04), Haus Moriyama (Tokio, 2002–05), der Glaspavillon am Toledo Museum of Art (Ohio, USA, 2003–06), Theater und Kulturzentrum in Almere (Niederlande, 2004–07), das New Museum of Contemporary Art in New York (2005–07), der Pavillon für die Serpentine Gallery (London, 2009, hier vorgestellt) sowie eine Erweiterung des Instituts für Moderne Kunst (IVAM) in Valencia (Spanien, 2002–). Kazuyo Sejima und Ryue Nishizawa gewannen die Wettbewerbe zum Bau des Rolex Learning Center der EPFL in Lausanne (Schweiz, 2007–09, ebenfalls hier vorgestellt) und für das neue Gebäude des Louvre in Lens (Frankreich, 2009–12).

Née dans la préfecture d'Ibaraki en 1956, Kazuyo Sejima obtient son M. Arch de l'Université féminine du Japon en 1981, et est engagée par Toyo Ito la même année. Elle crée l'agence Kazuyo Sejima and Associates à Tokyo en 1987. Elle est chargée de cours invitée à l'Université féminine et à l'Université Waseda depuis 1994. Ryue Nishizawa, né à Tokyo en 1966, est diplômé de l'Université nationale de Yokohama en 1990. Il a été professeur invité à la Harvard School of Design et à l'Université nationale de Yokohama. Il a commencé à travailler avec Sejima en 1990, avant qu'ils ne fondent ensemble **SANAA/KAZUYO SEJIMA + RYUE NISHIZAWA** en 1995. En 2010, SANAA a reçu le prix Pritzker. Les réalisations de Kazuyo Sejima, toutes au Japon, comprennent : le foyer pour jeunes filles Saishunkan Seiyaku (Kumamoto, 1990–91) ; la salle de jeux Pachinko Parlor I (Hitachi, Ibaraki, 1992–93) ; Pachinko Parlor II (Nakamachi, Ibaraki, 1993) ; la Villa en forêt (Tateshina, Nagano, 1993–94) ; le poste de police de Chofu (Tokyo, 1993–94) et Pachinko Parlor III (Hitachi Ibaraki, 1995). Parmi les références de SANAA figurent aussi le Musée d'art contemporain du XXIᵉ siècle (Kanazawa, Ishikawa, 2002–04) ; la Maison Moriyama (Tokyo, 2002–05) ; le pavillon de verre du Toledo Museum of Art (Toledo, Ohio, 2003–06) ; un théâtre et centre culturel à Almere (Pays-Bas, 2004–07) ; le New Museum of Contemporary Art (New York, 2005–07) ; le pavillon de la Serpentine (Londres, 2009, publié ici) et une extension de l'Institut d'art moderne de Valence, IVAM (Espagne, 2002–). Kazuyo Sejima et Ryue Nishizawa ont remporté les concours du Learning Center de l'EPFL à Lausanne (Suisse, 2007–09) et les nouvelles installations du Louvre à Lens (France, 2009–12).

SERPENTINE PAVILION

Kensington Gardens, London, UK, 2009

Area: 557 m². Client: The Serpentine Pavilion.
Cost: not disclosed

This Pavilion is essentially a continuous 26-millimeter-thick aluminum roof supported by random 50-millimeter-diameter steel columns. It is the latest in a series of summer pavilions erected in the gardens of London's Serpentine Gallery, designed by such notable architects as Frank O. Gehry, Oscar Niemeyer, Toyo Ito, and Álvaro Siza. An event space, a café, a music area, and a rest space are placed beneath this graceful canopy. Although there are some curved acrylic partitions, the work of SANAA is as close to being truly evanescent in every sense of the word as possible. In this sense, it is perfectly related to other work by these gifted designers that challenges the limits of perception, inviting visitors to enter a kind of floating world where appearances can change in the blink of an eye. The architects state: "The Pavilion is floating aluminum, drifting freely between the trees like smoke. The reflective canopy undulates across the site, expanding the park and sky. Its appearance changes according to the weather, allowing it to melt into the surroundings. It works as a field of activity with no walls, allowing views to extend uninterrupted across the park and encouraging access from all sides."

Der Pavillon besteht im Grunde aus einem durchgängigen, 26 mm starken Aluminiumdach, das auf unregelmäßig platzierten, 50 mm starken Stahlstützen ruht. Es ist der jüngste in einer andauernden Serie von Sommerpavillons der Londoner Serpentine Gallery, die von so namhaften Architekten wie Frank O. Gehry, Oscar Niemeyer, Toyo Ito oder Álvaro Siza entworfen wurden. Unter dem eleganten Dach wurden ein Veranstaltungsbereich, ein Café, ein Bereich für Musik und eine Ruhezone eingerichtet. Obwohl es einige geschwungene Trennwände aus Acrylglas gab, war dieses Projekt von SANAA in jeder Hinsicht so flüchtig wie nur möglich. In diesem Sinne ist der Pavillon klar mit anderen Arbeiten dieser talentierten Architekten verwandt, die mitunter bis an die Grenzen der Wahrnehmung gehen und Besucher in eine Art fließende Welt einladen, in der sich der äußere Schein von einem Augenblick zum nächsten ändern kann. Die Architekten erklären: „Der Pavillon ist fließendes Aluminium, das wie Rauch frei zwischen den Bäumen schwebt. Das reflektierende Dach windet sich durch das Gelände, dehnt sich aus in Park und Himmel. Je nach Wetterlage verändert sich sein Erscheinungsbild, was ihm erlaubt, mit seinem Umfeld zu verschmelzen. Der Pavillon funktioniert als Aktionsfeld ohne Wände: Der Blick kann ungehindert durch den Park schweifen, Zugang ist von allen Seiten möglich."

Ce pavillon est essentiellement un plan continu d'aluminium de 26 mm d'épaisseur soutenu par des colonnes d'acier de 50 mm de diamètre disposées de façon aléatoire. Il est le dernier-né de cette série de pavillons d'été érigés chaque année dans les jardins de la Serpentine Gallery de Londres, conçus par des architectes de renom comme Frank Gehry, Oscar Niemeyer, Toyo Ito ou Álvaro Siza. Un espace de réceptions et un lieu de repos étaient aménagés sous cet auvent plein de grâce. Bien que l'on y trouve quelques cloisons incurvées en acrylique, il n'est pas loin de l'évanescence, dans tous les sens du terme. C'est d'ailleurs cette qualité qui le relie à d'autres réalisations de ces architectes doués qui remettent en question les limites de la perception, en invitant les visiteurs à pénétrer dans une sorte de monde flottant où les apparences peuvent changer en un instant. « Le pavillon Serpentine est de l'aluminium en suspension, qui progresse librement entre les arbres comme un nuage de fumée. Cet auvent réfléchissant ondule au-dessus du terrain, et dilate la perception du parc et du ciel. Son aspect change en fonction du temps et il se fond dans son environnement. Il fonctionne comme un lieu d'activité mais sans murs, qui laisse le regard se glisser sans rupture à travers le parc, et lance de tous côtés une invitation à venir le découvrir. »

event
space

cafe

table

The reflective surfaces of the Pavilion
make its flowing form into a constant
reflection of the park, passersby, and
the Serpentine itself.

Durch seine reflektierenden Oberflächen werden die fließenden Formen
des Pavillons zum kontinuierlichen
Spiegelbild des Parks sowie der
Passanten und der Serpentine Gallery
selbst.

Les plans horizontaux en métal
poli du pavillon réfléchissent aussi
bien le parc que les passants ou
la Serpentine elle-même.

With its extremely thin columns and rather incongruous potted plants, the pavilion is more of a canopy than it is a real building.

Mit seinen extrem schmalen Stützen und den unpassenden Topfpflanzen ist der Pavillon eher nur ein Dach als ein tatsächliches Gebäude.

Par ses colonnes extrêmement fines et ses plantes en pot un peu incongrues, le pavillon est plus une sorte d'auvent qu'une vraie construction.

Night views show the Serpentine in the background (right) and the almost evanescent substance of the reflective roof.

Nächtliche Ansichten zeigen die Serpentine Gallery im Hintergrund (rechts) und die geradezu flüchtige Materialität des spiegelnden Dachs.

Vues nocturnes montrant la Serpentine dans le fond (à droite) et le toit réfléchissant dont la substance semble parfois quasi évanescente.

ROLEX LEARNING CENTER

EPFL, Lausanne, Switzerland, 2007–09

Address: EPFL, 1015 Lausanne, Switzerland, +41 21 693 11 11, www.rolexlearningcenter.ch
Area: 37 000 m². Client: EPFL École Polytechinque Fédérale de Lausanne.
Cost: € 75.096 million (total cost)

The undulating roof of the EPFL Rolex Learning Center appears in this view to echo the forms of the mountains on the opposite side of Lake Geneva.

Das geschwungene Dach des Rolex Learning Center der EPFL wirkt auf dieser Aufnahme wie ein Echo der Berge auf der gegenüberliegenden Seite des Genfer Sees.

Les ondulations de la toiture du Rolex Learning Center de l'EPFL semblent ici faire écho aux montagnes de l'autre rive du lac Léman.

The EPFL in Lausanne is one of two federal polytechnic institutes in Switzerland (the other is the ETH in Zurich). The wide gamut of subjects taught at the EPFL's lakeside campus includes various engineering sciences, but also architecture. It is the home of the modern computer mouse but also of the America's Cup winning boat, *Alinghi*. It is fitting that the institution's President Patrick Aebischer firmly backed the choice of SANAA as the architects for the innovative **ROLEX LEARNING CENTER**, which was inaugurated in February 2010. The structure, described by Ryue Nishizawa as a "landscape" building, has almost no internal walls but numerous slopes and arches. The external façades are almost entirely glazed, which did not keep the architects from designing a low-energy structure that bears the Swiss Minergie label. Numerous exterior courtyards are nestled beneath and between the building's arches. The Rolex Learning Center contains a multimedia library (500 000 volumes), 860 student work seats, a 600-seat auditorium, an 80-seat restaurant together with a café, bar, and food court seating a further 180 people, a Career Center, bookshop, and other facilities, including 500 parking spaces. It will indeed be interesting to see how this wide-open building functions for the student body, with its lack of walls and often steeply sloped floors. It is rare that a piece of architecture can be truly called "revolutionary," but the Rolex Learning Center certainly represents a bid for that qualification.

Die EPFL Lausanne ist (neben der ETH Zürich) eine der zwei polytechnischen Bundeshochschulen der Schweiz. Das breite akademische Spektrum der EPFL mit ihrem Campus am See umfasst verschiedene Ingenieurstudiengänge ebenso wie Architektur. Hier wurde die moderne Computermaus entwickelt und auch die *Alinghi*, Siegerin der America's Cup. So überrascht es nicht, dass sich Patrick Aebischer, Präsident der EPFL, für SANAA als Architekten für das innovative **ROLEX LEARNING CENTER** stark machte, das im Februar 2010 eingeweiht wurde. Das Gebäude, laut Ryue Nishizawa ein „Landschafts"-Bau, verzichtet fast gänzlich auf Innenwände, hat dafür jedoch zahlreiche Bodenneigungen und Bögen. Die Außenfassaden sind fast vollständig verglast, was die Architekten nicht daran hinderte, einen Niedrigenergiebau zu planen, der mit dem schweizerischen Minergie-Zertifikat ausgezeichnet wurde. Unterhalb und zwischen den Bögen des Gebäudes sind zahlreiche Innenhöfe verteilt. Das Rolex Learning Center verfügt über eine multimediale Bibliothek (mit 500 000 Bänden), 860 Arbeitsplätze für Studierende, einen Hörsaal mit 600 Plätzen, ein Restaurant mit 80 Plätzen sowie ein Café, eine Bar und einen Speisesaal mit zusätzlichen 180 Plätzen, ein Career Center, eine Buchhandlung, weitere Einrichtungen sowie 500 Parkplätze. Es wird höchst interessant sein zu beobachten, wie sich das überaus offene Gebäude mit seinen fehlenden Wänden und teilweise steilen Bodenschrägen in der Praxis bei den Studierenden bewährt. Nur selten kann man Architektur mit Fug und Recht „revolutionär" nennen, doch das Rolex Learning Center ist zweifellos ein Anwärter auf diesen Titel.

L'EPFL de Lausanne est l'un des deux grands instituts polytechniques de Suisse (l'autre étant l'ETH à Zurich). Parmi la grande diversité des matières enseignées sur le campus de l'EPFL installé en bordure du lac Léman figurent l'ingénierie, mais aussi l'architecture. L'École est le lieu de naissance de la souris d'ordinateur, mais aussi du bateau vainqueur de l'America's Cup, l'*Alinghi*. Il est donc assez logique que le président de l'institution, Patrick Aebischer ait fermement soutenu le choix de SANAA pour ce très novateur **ROLEX LEARNING CENTER**, inauguré en février 2010. La structure, conçue par Ryue Nishizawa en forme d'« immeuble paysage », ne possède pratiquement pas de murs internes, mais de nombreux arcs et rampes. Les façades extérieures sont presque entièrement vitrées, ce qui n'a pas empêché les architectes de réussir à construire un bâtiment à faible consommation énergétique qui a reçu le label suisse Minergie. De nombreuses cours sont nichées sous et entre les arcs du bâtiment. Ce centre contient une bibliothèque multimédia de 500 000 volumes, 860 postes de travail pour étudiants, un auditorium de 600 places, un restaurant de 80 places, un café, un bar, un food-court pour 180 personnes, un centre d'orientation professionnelle, une librairie et d'autres installations, dont 500 places de parking. Il sera intéressant de voir comment ce vaste immeuble ouvert fonctionne une fois les étudiants installés. Il est rare qu'une œuvre d'architecture puisse être vraiment qualifiée de « révolutionnaire », mais le Rolex Learning Center peut certainement prétendre à ce titre.

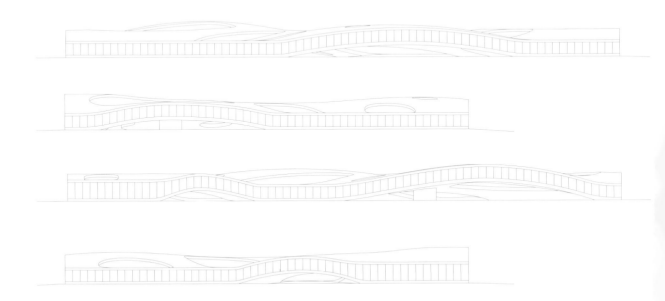

The long, serpentine form of the building is seen clearly in the elevations above and in the image (top right). A more aerial view shows the roof and its amoeboid openings.

Auf Aufrissen (oben) und der Aufnahme oben rechts ist die gestreckte, sich windende Form des Baus deutlich zu sehen. Ein Luftbild zeigt das Dach und seine amöbenförmigen Öffnungen.

Le profil serpentin du bâtiment s'exprime clairement dans les élévations ci-dessus et la photo de droite (en haut). Une vue aérienne montre la toiture et ses ouvertures de forme organique.

Described by the architects as a landscape in itself, the EPFL Rolex Learning Center also takes on the appearance of a bridge from certain angles.

Das Rolex Learning Center der EPFL, von den Architekten als Landschaft an sich bezeichnet, wirkt aus manchen Blickwinkeln wie eine Brücke.

Présenté par les architectes comme un paysage en soi, le Centre peut aussi prendre une apparence de pont vu sous certains angles.

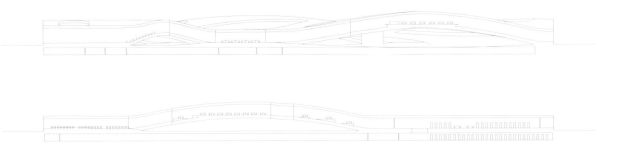

Internal openings allow for sheltered exterior space where students can sit or gather in warmer months.

Aussparungen im Gebäudekörper lassen geschützte Außenbereiche entstehen, in denen Studenten in wärmeren Monaten sitzen oder sich treffen können.

Les ouvertures internes créent aussi des espaces extérieurs protégés où les étudiants peuvent se retrouver pendant les mois plus chauds.

The interior has unusual sloping floors that were the object of some discussion animated by associations for handicapped persons. Below, left, the auditorium, and, right a glazed wall looking out into an interior courtyard.

Die Böden im Innern des Baus sind ungewöhnlich abschüssig. Die recht umstrittenen Schrägen wurden auch von Behindertenverbänden lebhaft diskutiert. Unten links ein Hörsaal, rechts eine Fensterfront mit Blick in einen der Innenhöfe.

L'intérieur présente de curieux sols inclinés qui ont été l'objet de discussions animées dans les associations d'handicapés. Ci-dessous, à gauche, l'auditorium et, à droite, un mur de verre qui donne sur une cour intérieure.

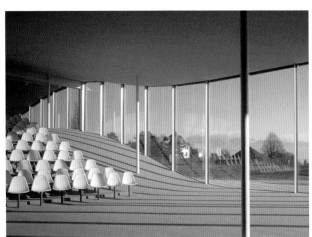

A basic plan reveals the strict, rectangular outer limits of the building, with its numerous irregular openings and flowing space.

Ein vereinfachter Grundriss illustriert die strengen, rechteckigen Außengrenzen des Gebäudes, seine zahlreichen unregelmäßigen Öffnungen sowie den fließenden Raumeindruck.

Ce plan montre les nombreuses ouvertures de forme irrégulière et les espaces traités en flux mais circonscrits dans un cadre rectangulaire.

GERMÁN DEL SOL

Germán del Sol, Architecto
Camino Las Flores 11 441
Las Condes, Santiago
Chile

Tel: +56 2 214 12 48
Fax: +56 2 214 20 20
E-mail: contacto@entelchile.net
Web: www.germandelsol.cl

GERMÁN DEL SOL GUZMÁN was born in Santiago de Chile in 1949. He graduated in 1973 from the ETSAB of Barcelona, Spain. He created his own firm in Barcelona (1973–79), before returning to Santiago, where he worked on his own (1980–83) and then spent two years in the office of R. Elmore in Palo Alto, California (1984–86). He then returned to his own practice in Santiago, where he has been based since 1986. Between 1988 and 1998, he created and directed explora, a company dedicated to promoting new travel destinations in remote places in South America. Between 1995 and 1998, he created and directed "Viña Gracia," a new Chilean vineyard. Germán del Sol then created and directed a new Hot Springs Complex, next to the Villarrica Volcano, in Pucón (Chile, 2001–05). He won the National Association of Chilean Architects Award in 2006. His built work includes the Hotel explora en Atacama (San Pedro de Atacama, 1998); Horse Stables (San Pedro de Atacama, 1999); Saunas and Pools (Atacama, 2000); Puritama Hot Springs Complex (Atacama, 2000); Hotel Remota (Patagonia, 2005–06); Remota Spot (Patagonia, 2007); and Termas Geométricas Hot Springs Complex, Coñaripe (Villarrica National Park, Chile, 2004, Phase 1, 2008, Phase 2, also published here), all in Chile. Also in 2008, he completed an apartment building in Vallecas, Spain.

GERMÁN DEL SOL GUZMÁN wurde 1949 in Santiago de Chile geboren. Sein Studium schloss er 1973 an der Escuela Técnica Superior de Arquitectura de Barcelona in Spanien ab. Nachdem er zunächst in Barcelona ein eigenes Büro betrieb (1973–79), kehrte er nach Santiago zurück, wo er selbstständig arbeitete (1980–83), bevor er zwei Jahre lang für R. Elmore in Palo Alto, Kalifornien, tätig war (1984–86). Schließlich kehrte er zu seinem eigenen Büro in Santiago zurück, von wo aus er seit 1986 praktiziert. Von 1988 bis 1998 leitete er die von ihm gegründete Agentur Explora, die sich auf die Erschließung neuer Reiseziele an abgelegenen Orten Südamerikas spezialisiert hatte. Von 1995 bis 1998 führte er das von ihm gegründete chilenische Weingut „Viña Gracia". Schließlich baute und leitete Germán del Sol auch eine Hotelanlage an den Thermalquellen am Vulkan Villarrica in Pucón (Chile, 2001–05). Er gewann den National Association of Chilean Architects Award im Jahr 2006. Zu seinen realisierten Projekten zählen das Hotel Explora en Atacama (San Pedro de Atacama, 1998), Pferdeställe (San Pedro de Atacama, 1999), Saunen und Pools (Atacama, 2000), die Thermalquellen Puritama (Atacama, 2000), das Hotel Remota (Patagonia, 2005–06), Remota Spot (Patagonia, 2007), sowie der Thermalquellenkomplex Geometricas, Coñaripe (Nationalpark Villarrica, Chile, 2004: Bauabschnitt 1, 2008: Bauabschnitt 2, hier vorgestellt), alle in Chile. 2008 konnte außerdem ein Apartmentgebäude in Vallecas, Spanien, fertiggestellt werden.

GERMÁN DEL SOL GUZMÁN, né à Santiago du Chili en 1949, est diplômé de l'ETSAB de Barcelone. Il a fondé une agence à Barcelone (1973–79), avant de revenir à Santiago où il a travaillé pour son compte (1980–83) et a passé deux années chez R. Elmore à Palo Alto (Californie, 1984–86). Il est ensuite revenu à Santiago où son agence est basée depuis 1986. Entre 1988 et 1998, il a créé et dirigé « explora », une société de promotion de nouvelles destinations de voyages dans des lieux mal connus d'Amérique du Sud. Entre 1995 et 1998, il a créé et dirigé « Viña Gracia », un nouveau vignoble chilien, puis un nouveau complexe thermal, près du volcan de Villarrica à Pucón (Chili, 2001–05). Il a remporté le prix de l'Association nationale des architectes chiliens en 2006. Parmi ses réalisations : l'hôtel explora à Atacama (San Pedro de Atacama, 1998) ; des écuries (San Pedro de Atacama, 1999) ; des saunas et piscines (Atacama, 2000) ; le complexe thermal de Puritama (Atacama, 2000) ; l'hôtel Remota (Patagonie, 2005–06) ; le Remota Spot (Patagonie, 2007) ; le complexe des Termas Geométricas de Coñaripe (Parc national de Villarrica, Chili, 2004, Phase 1, 2008, Phase 2, publié ici) et un immeuble d'appartements à Vallecas (Espagne, 2008).

TERMAS GEOMÉTRICAS
HOT SPRINGS COMPLEX

Coñaripe, Villarrica National Park, Los Lagos Region, Chile, 2004 (Phase 1), 2008 (Phase 2)

Area: 10 000 m². Client: Termas Geométricas. Cost: € 1.5 million
Collaboration: José Luis Ibañez (Architect), Carlos Venegas (Architect)

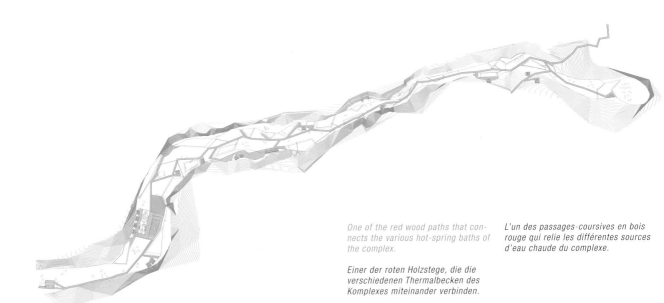

One of the red wood paths that connects the various hot-spring baths of the complex.

Einer der roten Holzstege, die die verschiedenen Thermalbecken des Komplexes miteinander verbinden.

L'un des passages-coursives en bois rouge qui relie les différentes sources d'eau chaude du complexe.

Located 725 kilometers south of Santiago in Chile's southern Lake Country, this bath complex includes 17 slate-covered pools fed by hot spring waters that emerge from the earth as a mountain stream. Native coigüe wood is used for the paths that connect these pools, and the same material is used for the wooden conduits that direct the water into the pools from beneath the walkway. Each pool has a wood pavilion and private bathrooms or locker rooms. A large, covered, and secluded space with an open fire invites guests to relax with a cup of tea or a glass of water. The roof of this structure is planted with wild grass. The architect states: "They are named Termas Geométricas because it is a work of architecture built with strong primitive geometric elements that allow one to be captivated again by natural elements in the midst of wild, brutal nature."

Der 725 km südlich von Santiago de Chile im südlichen Seengebiet gelegene Thermalquellenkomplex umfasst 17 Wasserbecken aus Schiefer, die von Thermalquellen gespeist werden, die als Fluss aus dem Boden treten. Die Stege zwischen den Becken sind aus regionalem *coigüe*-Holz gefertigt, dasselbe Material wurde für die hölzernen Wasserrinnen genutzt, die das Wasser unter den Stegen in die einzelnen Becken leiten. Zu jedem Becken gehört ein Holzpavillon mit Toiletten und Umkleiden. Ein großzügiger überdachter und geschützter Bereich mit einem offenen Feuer lädt Besucher zu einer Tasse Tee oder einem Glas Wasser ein. Das Dach ist mit wilden Gräsern begrünt. Der Architekt führt aus: „Die Termas Geométricas verdanken ihren Namen der Architektur aus markanten, allereinfachsten geometrischen Elementen, die möglich machen, sich wieder von den Naturwundern gefangen nehmen zu lassen, und das inmitten einer wilden, ungezähmten Natur."

Situé à 725 kilomètres au sud de Santiago dans le pays des lacs, ce complexe thermal compte 17 bassins en ardoise alimentés par des sources chaudes qui débouchent dans un torrent. Un bois local, le coigüe, a servi à construire des coursives qui relient ces bassins, mais aussi à acheminer l'eau dans les bassins. Chacun d'eux est accompagné d'un petit pavillon de bois et de toilettes privées ou de vestiaires. Un vaste espace couvert et isolé, équipé d'une cheminée à feu ouvert, permet aux hôtes de se détendre autour d'un thé ou d'un verre d'eau. Le toit de cette construction est recouvert d'herbes sauvages. « Nous avons appelé ces installations "Thermes géométriques", parce qu'elles sont vraiment une œuvre d'architecture réalisée à l'aide de composants géométriques puissants, voire primitifs, qui permettent de se laisser captiver par les éléments naturels au milieu d'une nature sauvage et brutale », explique l'architecte.

Channels carry both visitors and water amidst the spectacular natural setting.

Inmitten der spektakulären Landschaft dienen Stege und Wasserläufe als Transportweg für Besucher und das Wasser.

Ces « canaux » facilitent la circulation de l'eau et des visiteurs au milieu d'un cadre naturel spectaculaire.

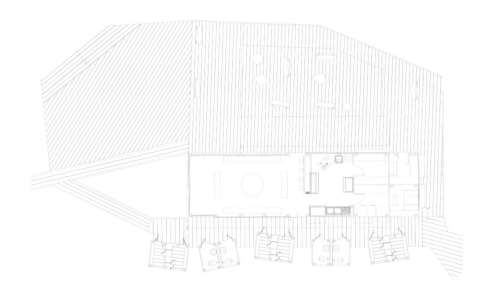

Bathhouses are also made of red wood, like the meandering paths that lead visitors to their destinations.

Auch die Badehäuser wurden aus rotem Holz gebaut, ebenso wie die mäandernden Stege, auf denen die Besucher ihr Ziel erreichen.

Les maisons de bains sont également en bois teinté en rouge, comme les coursives qui les desservent.

SKIDMORE, OWINGS & MERRILL

Skidmore, Owings & Merrill LLP
224 South Michigan Avenue, Suite 1000, Chicago, IL 60604, USA /
Adrian Smith (Associated Architect)

Tel: +1 312 554 9090 / Fax: +1 312 360 4545
E-mail: somchicago@som.com / Web: www.som.com

SKIDMORE, OWINGS & MERRILL LLP (SOM) is one of the largest architecture firms in the United States. Founded in Chicago in 1936 by Louis Skidmore and Nathaniel Owings (John Merrill joined the firm in 1939), they have worked on some of the best-known skyscrapers in the US, including Lever House (New York, 1952); John Hancock Center (Chicago, 1969); and the Sears Tower (Chicago, 1973). Some of the more famous partners of the firm have included Gordon Bunshaft, Bruce Graham, and more recently David Childs, who has taken over the Freedom Tower project from Daniel Libeskind on the Ground Zero site in Lower Manhattan, New York, and **ADRIAN SMITH**, lead designer of the Burj Khalifa tower published here (Dubai, UAE, 2004–10). Other recent work includes the 420-meter Jin Mao Tower in Pudong (Shanghai, China, 1998); Time Warner Center at Columbus Circle in New York (New York, USA, 2003); and Terminal 3 at Ben Gurion Airport (Tel Aviv, 2004, in association with Moshe Safdie). Other current projects include the Trump International Hotel and Tower (Chicago, USA, 2009); Nanjing Greenland Financial Center (Nanjing, China, 2010, with Gordon Gill); and Pearl River Tower (Guangzhou, China, completion due 2010, with Gordon Gill). Adrian Smith, who studied Architecture at Texas A&M and the University of Illinois, Chicago, and was with SOM for 40 years, becoming a partner in 1980, the designer of the Trump Hotel, left SOM in October 2006 to create his own firm, Adrian Smith + Gordon Gill Architecture. Whatever the plans of Smith, the identity of SOM has long since evolved beyond the question of specific architects. It is the quintessential large, quality architectural firm that many have tried to imitate.

SKIDMORE, OWINGS & MERRILL LLP (SOM) ist eines der größten Architekturbüros der Vereinigten Staaten. 1936 von Louis Skidmore und Nathaniel Owings in Chicago gegründet (John Merrill schloss sich dem Büro 1939 an), arbeitete die Firma an einigen der bekanntesten Wolkenkratzer der USA, darunter dem Lever House (New York, 1952), dem John Hancock Center (Chicago, 1969) und dem Sears Tower (Chicago, 1973). Zu den berühmtesten Partnern des Büros zählen u.a. Gordon Bunshaft, Bruce Graham und in jüngerer Zeit David Childs, der das Freedom Tower-Projekt auf dem Ground-Zero-Gelände in Manhattan von Daniel Libeskind übernahm, sowie **ADRIAN SMITH**, der den hier vorgestellten Burj Khalifa entwarf (Dubai, VAE, 2004–10). Andere jüngere Projekte sind u.a. der 420 m hohe Jin Mao Tower in Pudong (Shanghai, China, 1998), das Time Warner Center am Columbus Circle in New York (2003) und das Terminal 3 am Flughafen Ben Gurion (Tel Aviv, 2004, in Zusammenarbeit mit Moshe Safdie). Weitere aktuelle Projekte sind das Trump International Hotel und Tower (Chicago, 2009), das Nanjing Greenland Finanzcenter (Nanjing, China, 2010, mit Gordon Gill) und der Pearl River Tower (Guangzhou, China, geplante Fertigstellung 2010, mit Gordon Gill). Adrian Smith, der Architektur an der Texas A&M und der University of Illinois, Chicago, studiert hatte und 40 Jahre lang bei SOM tätig war (seit 1980 als Partner), plante auch das Trump Hotel. Im Oktober 2006 verließ er SOM, um sein eigenes Büro Adrian Smith + Gordon Gill Architecture zu gründen. Doch was immer die Pläne von Smith sein mögen, SOM ist schon lange nicht mehr an bestimmte Architekten gebunden. SOM ist der Prototyp des anspruchsvollen Architektur-Großbüros, an das schon viele versucht haben heranzureichen.

SKIDMORE, OWINGS & MERRILL LLP (SOM) est l'une des plus grandes agences d'architecture du monde. Fondée à Chicago en 1936 par Louis Skidmore et Nathaniel Owings (John Merrill les rejoignit en 1939), elle a réalisé certains des plus célèbres gratte-ciel américains, comme la Maison Lever (New York, 1952) ; le John Hancock Center (Chicago, 1969) ; et la tour Sears (Chicago, 1973). Parmi les plus célèbres partenaires de l'agence figurent Gordon Bunshaft, Bruce Graham, et plus récemment David Childs, qui a repris le projet de la tour de la Liberté de Daniel Libeskind sur le site de Ground Zero à Manhattan, et **ADRIAN SMITH**, concepteur de la tour Burj Khalifa présentée ici (Dubaï, EAU, 2004–10). D'autres réalisations récentes comprennent la tour Jin Mao de 420 mètres à Pudong (Shanghaï, 1998) ; le Time Warner Center à Columbus Circle à New York (2003) ; et le Terminal 3 de l'aéroport Ben Gourion (Tel Aviv, 2004, en association avec Moshe Safdie). Parmi les projets récents figurent la Trump International Hotel and Tower (Chicago, 2009) ; le Centre financier Nanjing Greenland (Nankin, Chine, 2010) ; et la tour de la rivière des Perles (Guangzhou, achèvement prévu en 2010). Adrian Smith, qui a fait ses études d'architecte à l'Université Texas A&M et à l'Université de l'Illinois à Chicago, a travaillé chez SOM pendant quarante ans, en est devenu partenaire en 1980, a conçu le Trump Hotel, quitté SOM en octobre 2006 pour créer son agence, Adrian Smith + Gordon Gill Architecture. En dehors du cas de Smith, l'identité de SOM dépasse depuis longtemps la personnalité de ses architectes. Elle représente aujourd'hui la quintessence de la grande agence de qualité que beaucoup ont essayé d'imiter.

BURJ KHALIFA
Dubai, UAE, 2004–10

*Address: 1 Emaar Boulevard, Downtown Dubai, Dubai, UAE, +971 4 366 1655, www.burjkhalifa.ae
Area: 334 000 m². Height: 828 meters. Client: Emaar Properties PJSC, Dubai
Cost: not disclosed*

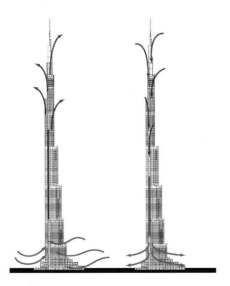

The extraordinarily slim form of the tower stands out from the large neighborhood of housing, offices, retail, and landscape space at its base.

Die außergewöhnlich schmale Silhouette des Turms hebt sich von der weitläufigen Nachbarschaft aus Wohnbauten, Büros, Einzelhandelsflächen und landschaftlich gestalteten Zonen zu seinen Füßen ab.

La forme extraordinairement élancée de la tour se détache de son environnement d'immeubles de bureaux, d'appartements, de centre commerciaux et d'espaces paysagés.

Part of the appeal of the massive **BURJ KHALIFA** in Dubai is that it was billed from the outset as the tallest building in the world, and yet its exact height was made an absolute secret. Work started on the tower in January 2004 and the building opened on January 4, 2010. At a final height of 828 meters, it is by far the tallest man-made structure ever built. "Burj Khalifa is not a mere vertical conquest or a race for fame; it is an icon for the collective aspiration of the people of Dubai, who have been led to dream of the impossible and attain it," said Mr. Mohamed Ali Alabbar, Chairman or Emaar Properties. Clearly, in a time of economic difficulties, Burj Khalifa also assumes the symbolic onus of architectural excess, but the building will surely survive the downturn that struck Dubai in late 2008. The tower includes 1000 residences, commercial spaces, leisure facilities, and the Armani Hotel, Dubai, developed with the Italian fashion designer. Burj Khalifa is the centerpiece of the ($20 billion) Downtown Burj Khalifa, "a mixed-use project in the heart of Dubai featuring residences, commercial space, hospitality projects, and several retail outlets including the Dubai Mall, the world's largest shopping and entertainment destination." Adrian Smith, the designer of Burj Khalifa, admits that he was thinking of the towers of the Emerald City in the film version of *The Wizard of Oz*. "That was in my mind as I was designing Burj Khalifa," Smith says, "although in a subliminal way." "I didn't research the way it looked. I just remembered the glassy, crystalline structure coming up in the middle of what seemed like nowhere. The funny thing is, I didn't remember it being green." Emaar Properties originally wanted a tower of approximately 550 meters in height, but the designer persuaded them to go higher still. "At the very top, it didn't feel like it was resolved properly," Smith said. "I kept adding height, and got to a point where it could be a more continuous extrusion of elements of the building below it, instead of feeling like a base and a top with no middle," he says.

Der gewaltige **BURJ KHALIFA** in Dubai faszinierte vermutlich auch deshalb so viele, weil er von Anfang an als größtes Gebäude der Welt gehandelt wurde, obwohl seine exakte Höhe bis Bauabschluss streng geheim gehalten wurde. Die Arbeiten am Turm begannen im Januar 2004, eröffnet wurde das Bauwerk am 4. Januar 2010. Mit seiner endgültigen Höhe von 828 m ist er das bei weitem höchste, je von Menschenhand errichtete Bauwerk. „Der Burj Khalifa ist nicht bloß eine vertikale Bezwingung oder ein Wettlauf um Ruhm, er ist eine Ikone der kollektiven Ambitionen der Bürger Dubais, die den Traum vom Unmöglichen geträumt und erreicht haben", betont Mohamed Ali Alabbar, Vorstandschef von Emaar Properties. Natürlich hat der Burj Khalifa damit zu leben, in wirtschaftlich schwierigen Zeiten als Symbol eines architektonischen Exzesses zu gelten, doch zweifellos wird das Gebäude die Krise überstehen, die Dubai Ende 2008 traf. Untergebracht sind im Turm 1000 Wohnungen, Gewerbeflächen, Freizeiteinrichtungen sowie das Armani Hotel Dubai, das mit dem italienischen Modedesigner entwickelt wurde. Burj Khalifa ist das Herzstück des 20-Milliarden-Dollar-Projekts Downtown Burj Khalifa, „einem Projekt mit gemischter Nutzung im Herzen von Dubai mit Wohnungen, Gewerbe, Hotels und verschiedenen Einzelhandelsflächen, darunter der Dubai Mall, der größten Einkaufs- und Unterhaltungsmeile der Welt". Adrian Smith, der den Burj Khalifa entwarf, räumt ein, dass er die Türme der Smaragdstadt aus dem Film *Der Zauberer von Oz* vor Augen hatte. „Das hatte ich im Kopf, als ich am Entwurf für den Burj Khalifa arbeitete", erzählt Smith, „wenn auch eher unterbewusst". „Ich habe nicht recherchiert, wie [die Smaragdstadt] aussieht. Ich erinnere mich nur an die gläserne, kristalline Struktur, die scheinbar aus dem Nichts heraus in die Höhe wuchs. Das Seltsame ist, dass ich mich offenbar nicht daran erinnert habe, dass die Stadt grün war." Emaar Properties wollte ursprünglich ein 550 m hohes Hochhaus, doch der Architekt überzeugte sie davon, noch höher zu gehen. „Oben an der Spitze hatte ich nicht den Eindruck, dass das Ganze wirklich schlüssig war", sagt Smith. „Ich ging immer höher und kam an den Punkt, wo alles eher eine kontinuierliche Extrusion der daruntergelegenen Ebenen des Gebäudes zu sein schien, statt ein Sockel mit Spitze, dem eine Mitte fehlte."

Une partie de l'attrait de l'énorme tour **BURJ KHALIFA** à Dubaï vient de ce qu'elle a été annoncée, dès le départ, comme l'immeuble le plus haut du monde, même si sa hauteur exacte est restée longtemps secrète. Le chantier a débuté en janvier 2004 et l'immeuble a été inauguré le 4 janvier 2010. D'une hauteur de 828 mètres, cette tour est de loin le plus haut édifice jamais construit par l'homme. « Burj Khalifa n'est pas seulement une conquête de la verticalité ou une course de prestige, c'est une icône des aspirations collectives du peuple de Dubaï qui a su rêver l'impossible et l'atteindre », a déclaré Mohamed Ali Alabbar, président d'Emaar Properties, son promoteur. En une période de crise économique, Burj Khalifa symbolise également les excès architecturaux de l'époque, mais l'immeuble survivra aux déconvenues financières de l'émirat à la fin de 2008. La tour comprend 1000 appartements, des locaux commerciaux, des installations de détente, et l'Armani Hotel réalisé en collaboration avec le couturier italien. Elle est l'élément central d'un programme urbain de vingt milliards de dollars, appelé Downtown Burj Khalifa, « un projet mixte au cœur de Dubaï offrant des logements, des locaux commerciaux, des hôtels et plusieurs centres commerciaux, dont le Dubai Mall, plus grand centre commercial et de divertissement du monde ». Adrian Smith, concepteur de la tour, admet qu'il a pu être inspiré par celles de la Cité d'émeraude vue dans le film *Le Magicien d'Oz* : « J'avais cette image en tête en dessinant Burj Khalifa », dit-il, « mais de façon subliminale [...] je ne suis pas allé voir à quoi tout cela ressemblait. Je me souvenais seulement de constructions cristallines s'élevant au milieu de nulle part. La chose amusante est que je ne me rappelais pas la couleur verte. » Emaar Properties souhaitait à l'origine une tour de 550 mètres de haut, mais l'architecte a persuadé son client de viser encore plus haut. « Je n'avais pas le sentiment que le problème avait été résolu correctement tout en haut », ajoute Smith, « je ne cessais d'ajouter des niveaux, et j'en suis arrivé à une solution où la tour devenait davantage l'extrusion continue d'éléments issus du bas, plutôt qu'une base et un sommet sans milieu. »

The exact height of the tower was a closely guarded secret until the time of its opening. Left, the Burj Khalifa tower standing out from other structures in Dubai.

Die exakte Höhe des Turms war bis zur Eröffnung des Baus ein streng gehütetes Geheimnis. Links der Burj Khalifa, der sich deutlich von den übrigen Bauten Dubais abhebt.

La hauteur précise de la tour est restée un secret bien gardé jusqu'à son inauguration. À gauche, le Burj Khalifa dominant les constructions avoisinantes.

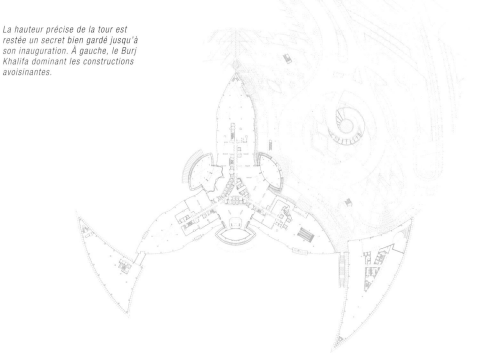

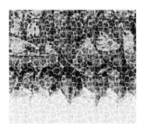

SPLITTERWERK

SPLITTERWERK
St. Peter Pfarrweg 30/56
8042 Graz
Austria

Tel: +43 316 81 05 98
Fax: +43 316 81 05 98 40
E-mail: splitterwerk@splitterwerk.at
Web: www.splitterwerk.at

SPLITTERWERK is a fine-art studio established in Austria in 1988 that works in the fields of painting, installations, architecture, and new media. From the outset, their work has revolved around cross-disciplinary projects, for example, the combination of art and architecture seen in the Frog Queen building published here (Graz, Austria, 2006–07). The studio's projects have been exhibited at the Vienna Secession, the Ars Electronica Festival in Linz, the Venice Biennale, the São Paulo Biennial, Documenta in Kassel, and the National Art Museum of China in Beijing, amongst other locations. Their work includes the Science Vision Filmstudios (Graz, 2002–03); Orangerie d'Or, Banquet, Concert and Exhibition Hall (Graz, 2004–05); and Froschkönig, Seminar House for the Landesverwaltungsakademie des Landes Steiermark (Graz, 2007–08), all in Austria. They have worked with the Stadtmuseum Graz since 2005, and have been involved in the International Building Exhibition (IBA, Hamburg, Germany, 2009–).

SPLITTERWERK ist ein 1988 in Österreich gegründetes Künstler-Studio, das auf den Gebieten Malerei, Installation, Architektur und Neue Medien arbeitet. Von Anfang an konzentrierte sich das Team auf Disziplinen übergreifende Projekte, etwa auf die Verbindung von Kunst und Architektur, wie bei dem hier vorgestellten Frog-Queen-Projekt (Graz, Österreich, 2006–07). Arbeiten des Studios waren u.a. bei Ausstellungen in der Wiener Sezession, dem Ars Electronica Festival in Linz, der Biennale von Venedig, der Biennale von São Paulo, der Documenta in Kassel sowie am National Art Museum of China in Peking zu sehen. Zu ihren Projekten zählen: Science Vision Filmstudios (Graz, 2002–03), Orangerie d'Or, Veranstaltungsort für Bankette, Konzerte und Ausstellungen (Graz, 2004–05), und Froschkönig, Seminarhaus für die Landesverwaltungsakademie des Landes Steiermark (Graz, 2007–08), alle in Österreich. Seit 2005 kooperiert das Team mit dem Stadtmuseum Graz und beteiligte sich außerdem an der Internationalen Bauausstellung (IBA Hamburg, Deutschland, 2009–).

SPLITTERWERK est un studio de création artistique fondé en Autriche en 1988, qui intervient dans les domaines de la peinture, des installations, de l'architecture et des nouveaux médias. Dès le départ, son travail a tourné autour de projets multidisciplinaires, par exemple la combinaison d'art et d'architecture dans l'immeuble Frog Queen (Graz, Autriche, 2006–07, publié ici). Les projets du studio ont été exposés à la Vienna Secession, au festival Ars Electronica Festival à Linz, à la Biennale de Venise, la Biennale de São Paulo, la Documenta à Kassel et le Musée national d'art de Chine à Pékin, entre autres lieux. Parmi ses réalisations, toutes en Autriche : les studios de cinéma Science Vision (Graz, 2002–03) ; l'Orangerie d'Or, une salle de banquets, de concerts et d'expositions (Graz, 2004–05) et le centre de séminaires de Froschkönig pour la Landesverwaltungsakademie des Landes Steiermark (Graz, 2007–08). Le studio travaille avec le Stadtmuseum de Graz depuis 2005, et a participé à l'Exposition internationale de la construction (IBA, Hambourg, 2009–).

FROG QUEEN

Graz, Austria, 2006–07

Address: Liebenauer Hauptstr. 82c, 8041 Graz, Austria
Area: 1060 m². Client: Prisma Engineering Maschinen- und Motorentechnik GmbH.
Cost: not disclosed

This building is intended as the headquarters of a mechanical engineering company called Prisma. The decorated façades of the building stand out from a distance. Made of silkscreen aluminum boards, these façades have ornamental motifs generated by the arrangement of different sized dots. Windows are placed at irregular intervals in this essentially cubic structure, making it difficult to perceive the different floor levels from the exterior. The mirrored entrance of the building leads to an elevator and the upstairs reception area. A foyer in a closed atrium is coated with epoxy resin with blown-in silver chips. Wall murals with scenes representing nature are a feature of the interiors. The architects state: "Extended installations of artworks with landscape images in combination with the colors of the floors, walls, ceilings, and furniture create different micro-atmospheres in every working room."

Das Gebäude ist die Hauptniederlassung der Maschinenbaufirma Prisma Engineering. Die mit grafischen Ornamenten versehene Fassade ist von Weitem sichtbar. Die Fassaden aus siebbedruckten Aluminiumpaneelen zeigen Ornamente, die aus der Anordnung verschieden großer Pixelpunkte entstehen. Die Fenster des im Grunde kubischen Baukörpers wurden unregelmäßig positioniert, weshalb sich die Gebäudeebenen von außen kaum ausmachen lassen. Der verspiegelte Eingangsbereich ist zugleich Aufzug, der in die Rezeption im darüber gelegenen Stockwerk fährt. Das Foyer im geschlossenen Atrium ist rundum mit einer Beschichtung aus Epoxidharz versehen, in die Silberchips eingeblasen wurden. Auffälliges Gestaltungsmerkmal der Innenräume sind die Landschaftsmotive an den Wänden. Die Architekten erklären: „Künstlerische Installationen aus Landschaftsbildern im ganzen Bau sorgen – neben der Farbpalette von Böden, Wänden, Decken und Möbeln – für das Entstehen verschiedener Mikro-Atmosphären in jedem einzelnen Arbeitsraum."

Ce bâtiment, dont les façades se remarquent de loin, est le siège de Prisma, entreprise d'ingénierie mécanique. Habillés de panneaux d'aluminium sérigraphiés, les murs extérieurs sont parés de motifs ornementaux formés de « pixels » de dimensions variées. Les fenêtres sont percées à intervalles irréguliers tout autour de la structure de nature essentiellement cubique, ce qui rend difficile la perception des niveaux de l'extérieur. De l'entrée en miroirs, on accède à un escalier mécanique qui conduit à la réception à l'étage. Le hall d'accueil est un atrium fermé aux murs enduits de résine d'époxy à éclats argentés insufflés. Diverses salles sont décorées de panneaux muraux représentant la nature. « L'installation très présente d'œuvres d'art à base d'images de paysages, comme la couleur des sols, des murs, des plafonds et du mobilier, crée une micro-atmosphère dans chaque salle de travail », expliquent les architectes.

The architects controlled the size and density of the ornamental motifs to create a pixilated pattern that leaves the function of the building entirely enigmatic.

Die Architekten variierten Größe und Dichte der Ornamente, sodass ein gepixeltes Muster entstand, das nichts über die Funktion des Gebäudes aussagt.

Les architectes ont calculé les dimensions et la densité des panneaux pour créer un motif pixellisé qui ne laisse rien deviner de la fonction de cet immeuble.

A very basic cubic structure,
Frog Queen is made unusual by its
irregular and unexpected façades.

Frog Queen, ein schlichter kubischer
Baukörper, wird erst durch die
unregelmäßigen, überraschenden
Fassaden ungewöhnlich.

Structure tout simplement cubique,
la Frog Queen tire son originalité de
ses surprenantes façades.

The irregular window placement and a generous ceiling height link the space seen on the left page with the building's exterior. Landscape images on interior walls also create unusual perceptions of space.

Die unregelmäßige Platzierung der Fenster und die großzügige Deckenhöhe lassen Bezüge zwischen dem Raum links und dem Außenbau erkennen. Auch die Landschaftsmotive auf den Innenwänden sorgen für ein ungewöhnliches Raumerlebnis.

Le positionnement irrégulier des fenêtres et de généreuses hauteurs de plafonds relient ce volume intérieur (page de gauche) avec la vision extérieure de l'immeuble. Les reproductions de paysages sur les murs jouent aussi dans la perception de l'espace.

HIROSHI SUGIMOTO

New Material Research Laboratory
3–1–15 Shirogane, Minato-ku
Tokyo 108–0072
Japan

Tel: +81 3 5422 9125 / Fax: +81 3 5422 9126
E-mail: sugimoto@shinsozai.com

HIROSHI SUGIMOTO was born in Tokyo, Japan, in 1948, attended Saint Paul's University in Tokyo (1966–70), and then studied photography at the Art Center College of Design in Los Angeles, receiving a B.F.A. in 1972. He moved to New York, where he currently resides, in 1974. Six main photographic series characterize his work thus far: his pictures taken of *Dioramas* and *Wax Museums* (both since 1976); his *Theaters* (since 1978); the *Seascapes* (since 1980); and his images of *Sanjusangendo, Hall of Thirty-Three Bays* (sculptures of the Buddhist temple Sanjusangendo, 1995); and *Architecture* (since 1997). His large, usually black-and-white, images have been presented in numerous art galleries, such as White Cube in London and the Sonnabend Gallery in New York. Sugimoto has had one-man exhibitions at the Museum of Contemporary Art, Los Angeles (1994); Metropolitan Museum of Art, New York (1995); Contemporary Arts Museum, Houston (1996); Hara Museum of Contemporary Art, Tokyo (1996); and Museum of Contemporary Art, Chicago (2003), among others. The Hirshhorn Museum and Sculpture Garden, Washington, D.C., and the Mori Art Museum, Tokyo, were joint organizers of a 2005 Sugimoto retrospective. Hiroshi Sugimoto has shown a consistent interest in architecture, first in his photography, but also in actual works of architecture, such as his Go-Oh Shrine (Naoshima, 2002); *Colors of Shadow* (Shirogane Apartment, Tokyo, 2004–06); and the Izu Photo Museum (Nagaizumi, Shizuoka, 2009, published here), all in Japan. In August 2009, the Koyanagi Gallery in Tokyo jointly showed the work of Hiroshi Sugimoto and of the architect Junya Ishigami. Sugimoto won the 2009 Praemium Imperiale Award.

Der 1948 in Tokio geborene **HIROSHI SUGIMOTO** besuchte von 1966 bis 1970 die Saint Paul's University in Tokio und studierte dann am Art Center College of Design in Los Angeles Fotografie, wo er 1972 den Grad eines B.F.A. erwarb. 1974 zog er an seinen heutigen Wohnort New York. Bisher wird sein Werk von sechs Fotografieserien geprägt: *Dioramas* und *Wax Museums* (beide seit 1976), *Theaters* (seit 1978), *Seascapes* (seit 1980) *Sanjusangendo, Hall of Thirty-Three Bays* (Skulpturen des buddhistischen Tempels Sanjusangendo, 1995) und *Architecture* (seit 1997). Seine großformatigen, in der Regel schwarz-weißen Fotografien wurden in zahlreichen Galerien, darunter dem White Cube in London und der Sonnabend Gallery in New York, ausgestellt. Sugimoto hatte Einzelausstellungen am Museum of Contemporary Art, Los Angeles (1994), am Metropolitan Museum of Art, New York (1995), Contemporary Arts Museum, Houston (1996), Hara Museum of Contemporary Art, Tokio (1996) sowie dem Museum of Contemporary Art, Chicago (2003), u. a. Das Hirshhorn Museum and Sculpture Garden, Washington, D.C., initiierte 2005 mit dem Mori Art Museum, Tokio, eine Sugimoto-Retrospektive. Der Künstler hat ein beständiges Interesse an Architektur, das sich zunächst in seinen Fotografien spiegelt, jedoch auch in tatsächlich realisierten Architekturprojekten, wie dem Go-Oh Shrine (Naoshima, 2002) oder *Colors of Shadow* (Shirogane Apartment, Tokio, 2004–06) sowie dem Izu Photo Museum (Nagaizumi, Shizuoka, 2009, hier vorgestellt), alle in Japan. Im August 2009 präsentierte die Koyanagi Gallery in Tokio Arbeiten von Hiroshi Sugimoto neben Arbeiten des Architekten Junya Ishigami. 2009 wurde Sugimoto mit dem Praemium Imperiale ausgezeichnet.

HIROSHI SUGIMOTO, né à Tokyo en 1948, a étudié à l'Université Saint-Paul (Tokyo, 1966–70), puis s'est spécialisé en photographie à l'Art Center College of Design à Los Angeles (B.F.A. en 1972). En 1974, il s'est installé à New York où il réside actuellement. Son œuvre est marquée jusqu'à présent par cinq séries de photographies : *Dioramas* et *Wax Museums* (depuis 1976) ; *Theaters* (depuis 1978) ; *Seascapes* (depuis 1980) ; ses images du *Sanjusangendo, Hall of Thirty-Three Bays* (sculptures du temple bouddhiste de Sanjusangendo, 1995) et *Architecture* (depuis 1997). Ses grands tirages, généralement en noir et blanc, ont été exposés dans de nombreuses galeries telles que la White Cube à Londres et la Sonnabend Gallery à New York. Sugimoto a été l'objet d'expositions personnelles au Museum of Contemporary Art de Los Angeles (1994) ; au Metropolitan Museum of Art à New York (1995) ; au Contemporary Arts Museum de Houston (1996) ; au Musée d'art contemporain Hara à Tokyo (1996) ; au Museum of Contemporary Art, Chicago (2003), parmi d'autres. Le Hirshhorn Museum and Sculpture Garden, à Washington, et le Mori Art Museum de Tokyo, ont organisé ensemble une rétrospective de son œuvre en 2005. Hiroshi Sugimoto a toujours montré un grand intérêt pour l'architecture, d'abord dans sa photographie, mais aussi dans des réalisations architecturales, comme son mausolée Go-Oh Shrine (Naoshima, 2002) ; *Colors of Shadow* (Couleurs de l'ombre, Shirogane Apartment, Tokyo, 2004–06) et le Musée de la photographie d'Izu (Nagaizumi, Shizuoka, 2009, publié ici). En août 2009, la galerie Koyanagi à Tokyo a présenté concurremment l'œuvre d'Hiroshi Sugimoto et de l'architecte Junya Ishigami. Sugimoto a remporté le Praemium Imperiale 2009.

IZU PHOTO MUSEUM

Nagaizumi, Shizuoka, Japan, 2009

Address: 347–1 Higashino Clematis no Oka, Nagaizumi-cho Sunto-gun, Shizuoka-ken 411–0931, Japan
+81 55 989 8780, www.izuphoto-museum.jp
Area: 490 m². Client: Izu Photo Museum. Cost: not disclosed
Collaboration: Tomoyuki Sakakida / New Material Research Laboratory

One of a series of architectural initiatives undertaken by the photographer Hiroshi Sugimoto, the new **IZU MUSEUM OF PHOTOGRAPHY** is part of a "multicultural" facility called Clematis-No-Oka. This institution opened in April 2002 and features "Flowers, Art Museums, and Slow Food." It is located two hours by train from Tokyo. Also on the grounds are the Bernard Buffet Museum, the Literary Museum for Yasushi (opened in 1973), and the Vangi Sculpture Garden Museum. Located near this Garden Museum, which features clematis flowers, the Izu Photo Museum opened in October 2009 and was inaugurated with a show of the artist's most recent works. As has usually been the case, Sugimoto has created very subtle spaces, with galleries that he photographed himself to emphasize their control of light.

Das neue **IZU MUSEUM FÜR FOTOGRAFIE** ist eines von mehreren Architekturprojekten des Fotografen Hiroshi Sugimoto. Das Museum ist Teil einer „multikulturellen" Einrichtung, dem Clematis-No-Oka, die im April 2002 eröffnet wurde und nach eigener Aussage unter dem Motto „Blumen, Kunstmuseen und Slow Food" steht. Der Komplex liegt zwei Zugstunden von Tokio entfernt. Auf dem Gelände liegen auch das Bernard Buffet Museum, das 1973 eröffnete Yasushi-Inoue-Literaturmuseum sowie das Vangi Skulpturen- und Gartenmuseum. Unweit des Gartenmuseums mit seiner Clematisausstellung wurde das Izu Museum für Fotografie im Oktober 2009 mit einer Ausstellung neuerer Arbeiten Sugimotos eröffnet. Wie auch sonst schuf Sugimoto überaus zurückhaltende Räume. Er fotografierte die Ausstellungsräume persönlich, um die kontrollierte Lichtführung hervorzuheben.

Incursion du photographe Hiroshi Sugimoto dans le domaine de l'architecture, ce nouveau **MUSÉE DE LA PHOTOGRAPHIE D'IZU** fait partie d'un ensemble d'installations « multiculturelles » appelé Clematis-No-Oka. Cette institution, qui a ouvert ses portes en avril 2002, se trouve à deux heures de train de Tokyo. Elle travaille sur les thématiques des « fleurs, des musées d'art et de la nourriture authentique ». Dans le même ensemble se trouvent le Musée Bernard-Buffet, le Musée littéraire de Yasushi (ouvert en 1973), ainsi que le Musée et jardin de sculptures Vangi qui présente des clématites. Édifié non loin, le Musée de la photographie, qui a ouvert en octobre 2009, a été inauguré par une exposition des œuvres les plus récentes de l'artiste. Comme toujours, Sugimoto a créé des espaces très subtils et des galeries qu'il photographie lui-même pour mettre en évidence leur éclairage contrôlé.

Although his primary work is as a
photographer, Hiroshi Sugimoto has
made several forays into the domain
of architecture.

Zwar ist Hiroshi Sugimoto in erster
Linie Fotograf, dennoch hat er sich
bereits mehrfach in den Bereich der
Architektur vorgewagt.

Bien que photographe avant tout,
Hiroshi Sugimoto a mené plusieurs
explorations dans le domaine de
l'architecture

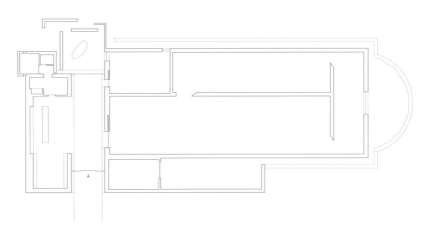

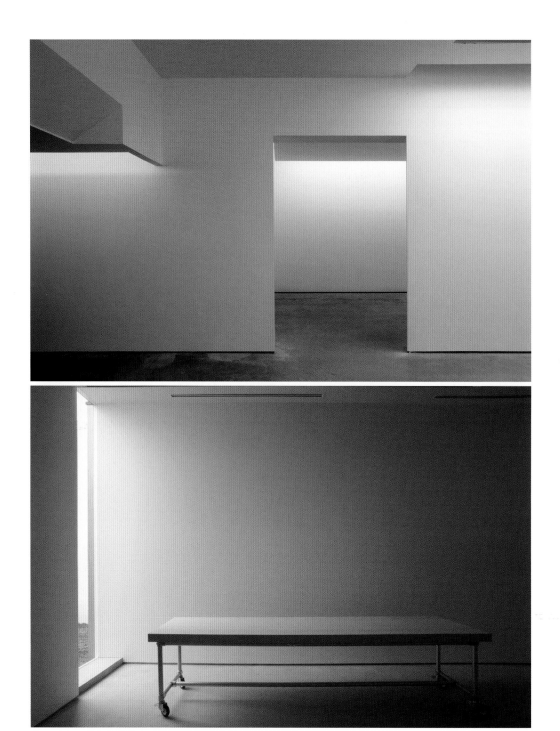

The artist has carefully studied the lighting effects in these spaces. The photos are by Hiroshi Sugimoto.

Der Künstler studierte die Wirkung der Raumbelichtung sehr aufmerksam. Die Aufnahmen sind von Hiroshi Sugimoto.

L'artiste a soigneusement étudié les effets de la lumière dans ces espaces. Les photos sont d'Hiroshi Sugimoto lui-même.

SUPERSUDAKA

Juan Pablo Corvalán Hochberger
c/o Escuela de Arquitectura, Universidad de Talca
2 Norte 685
Talca
Chile

Web: www.supersudaka.cl / www.supersudaca.org
E-mail: info@supersudaka.cl / info@supersudaca.org

SUPERSUDAKA was founded by Juan Pablo Corvalán Hochberger and Gabriel Vergara. Juan Pablo Corvalán Hochberger received his architecture degree from the École d'Ingénieurs de Genève (1996), and Master's degree from the Berlage Institute, Rotterdam (2002). Gabriel Vergara graduated as an architect from the Universidad de Talca (2006). Supersudaka has a sister organization called Supersudaca, which bills itself as a "think tank for architecture and urban investigation." The website of Supersudaka starts with the phrase: "We don't want to change the world with architecture, we want to change architecture with the world." Other members of Supersudaka are Pablo Abdala, Natalia Gajardo, José Miguel Mardones, and Ingrid Sepúlveda. Their project list includes Bonachón (Puente Alto, 2003); MAAM (Linares, 2004); Lumineda (Linares, 2005); Hot Spot (Talca, 2005); Moto House (Talca, 2006); Canoe Club (Talca, 2006); Mirage House (Santiago, 2007); Multihouse (Talca, 2007); Patio Vicinity (La Serena, 2007); Kiltro House (Talca, 2006–08, published here); and Church(ita) (Talca, 2006–09), all in Chile.

SUPERSUDAKA wurde von Juan Pablo Corvalán Hochberger und Gabriel Vergara gegründet. Juan Pablo Corvalán Hochberger schloss sein Architekturstudium an der École d'Ingénieurs de Genève (1996) ab und erwarb einen Masterabschluss am Berlage Institute, Rotterdam (2002). Gabriel Vergara absolvierte sein Architekturstudium an der Universidad de Talca (2006). Supersudaka hat eine Schwesterorganisation, Supersudaca, die sich als „Thinktank für Architektur und Stadterforschung" versteht. Die Website von Supersudaka ist mit dem Satz überschrieben: „Wir wollen die Welt nicht durch Architektur verändern, wir wollen die Architektur durch die Welt verändern." Weitere Mitarbeiter von Supersudaka sind Pablo Abdala, Natalia Gajardo, José Miguel Mardones und Ingrid Sepúlveda. Zu ihren Projekten zählen Bonachón (Puente Alto, 2003), MAAM (Linares, 2004), Lumineda (Linares, 2005), Hot Spot (Talca, 2005), Moto House (Talca, 2006), Canoe Club (Talca, 2006), Mirage House (Santiago, 2007), Multihouse (Talca, 2007), Patio Vicinity (La Serena, 2007), Casa Kiltro (Talca, 2006–08, hier vorgestellt) sowie Church(ita) (Talca, 2006–09), alle in Chile.

L'agence **SUPERSUDAKA** a été fondée par Juan Pablo Corvalán Hochberger et Gabriel Vergara. Juan Pablo Corvalán Hochberger est diplômé en architecture de l'École d'Ingénieurs de Genève (1996), et M.Arch de l'Institut Berlage à Rotterdam (2002). Gabriel Vergara est diplômé en architecture de l'Universidad de Talca (2006). Supersudaka possède une société-sœur appelée Supersudaca, qui se présente comme un « groupe de réflexion pour l'architecture et l'investigation urbaines ». Le site web de Supersudaka explique : « Nous ne voulons pas changer le monde par l'architecture, nous voulons changer l'architecture par le monde. » Les autres membres de Supersudaka sont Pablo Abdala, Natalia Gajardo, José Miguel Mardones et Ingrid Sepúlveda. La liste de leurs projets, tous au Chili, comprend : Bonachón (Puente Alto, 2003) ; MAAM (Linares, 2004) ; Lumineda (Linares, 2005) ; Hot Spot (Talca, 2005) ; la Maison Moto (Talca, 2006) ; le Canoe Club (Talca, 2006) ; la Maison Mirage (Santiago, 2007) ; la Multihouse (Talca, 2007) ; le Patio Vicinity (La Serena, 2007) ; la Maison Kiltro (Talca, 2006–08, publiée ici) ; et Church(ita) (Talca, 2006–09).

KILTRO HOUSE

Talca, Chile, 2006–08

Area: 103 m². Client: Oscar Corvalán. Cost: € 65 000

This house was built on a fairly wild natural site in Talca, a city of about 250 000 people located 250 kilometers south of Santiago. According to the architects: "This project is almost a statement of how to accomplish architecture in Latin America. The process was so unsteady that all possible architectural design resources available were exercised to cope with the challenge of this house in the Chilean Central Valley. Everything was in constant change: the program, the surface, building permits, the contractors, even the view…. The result: a mix, a bastardized design, a fusion, like a crossbreed dog, in Chilean: a *kiltro.*" Lifted up off the ground, and folded in form and plan, the structure has ample terrace space and generous glazing that allow residents to take in the scenery. With its nearly empty ground level and fuller, slatted wood cladding above, the house, especially seen with its roof line, seems to be in a state of symbiosis with the neighboring mountains.

Das Haus wurde auf einem vergleichsweise wilden Naturgrundstück in Talca erbaut, einer Stadt mit 250 000 Einwohnern 250 km südlich von Santiago. Die Architekten erklären: „Dieses Projekt ist fast so etwas wie ein Paradebeispiel für die Realisierung von Architektur in Lateinamerika. Der gesamte Prozess war so unsicher, dass alle nur möglichen architektonischen Gestaltungsressourcen aktiviert werden mussten, um die Herausforderung, dieses Haus im chilenischen Valle Central zu bauen, zu bewältigen. Alles änderte sich ständig: das Programm, die Geländeoberfläche, die Baugenehmigungen, die Baufirmen, sogar der Ausblick… Das Ergebnis: eine Mischung, ein Zwitterentwurf, eine Fusion – wie ein Mischlingshund oder, auf chilenisch, ein *kiltro.*" Der über dem Boden aufgeständerte Bau wurde formal „gefaltet", dasselbe trifft auf den Grundriss zu. Die großzügig bemessenen Terrassen und Fensterflächen ermöglichen den Bewohnern Aussicht auf die Umgebung. Mit seinem baulich fast ungenutzten Erdgeschoss und dem prominenteren, mit Holzlatten verblendeten Obergeschoss wirkt das Haus – besonders wenn die Dachlinie sichtbar ist – als wolle es sich symbiotisch in die angrenzende Berglandschaft fügen.

Cette maison a été construite dans un cadre naturel presque sauvage près de Talca, ville de 250 000 habitants à 250 kilomètres au sud de Santiago. Selon les architectes : « Ce projet est presque un manifeste sur l'architecture en Amérique latine. Le processus était si délicat que toutes les ressources de conception architecturale disponibles ont dû être utilisées pour répondre au défi de cette maison implantée dans la vallée centrale du Chili. Tout changeait en permanence : le programme, la surface, les permis de construire, les enreprises et même la vue … Le résultat : un projet mixte, bâtard, une fusion, comme un chien croisé, en chilien un *kiltro.* » Suspendue au-dessus du sol, de forme et de plan pliés, la maison offre de vastes terrasses et de généreuses baies vitrées qui permettent à ses résidents de profiter pleinement du spectacle de la nature. Par sa surélévation sur pilotis et son habillage en lattes de bois, elle semble en symbiose avec le paysage des montagnes environnantes, en particulier quand on peut percevoir la ligne de sa toiture.

The house is lifted off the ground on pilotis and has a faceted roof form, as seen in the drawing on this page.

Das Haus ist auf pilotis über dem Boden aufgeständert und hat ein facettiertes Dach, wie auch die Zeichnung auf dieser Seite belegt.

La maison repose sur des pilotis et possède une toiture à facettes, comme le montrent les plans de cette page.

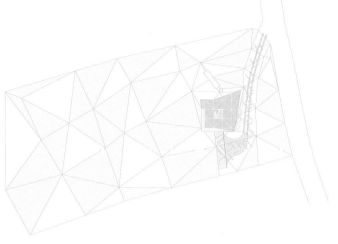

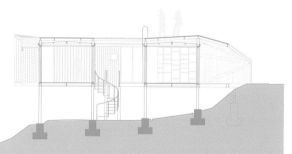

The house with its large windows,
unusual openings, and surprising
forms is nothing short of spectacular
in this natural setting.

Das Haus mit seinen großen Fensterflächen, ungewöhnlichen Öffnungen
und überraschenden Formen ist ein
spektakuläres Ereignis in der natürlichen Umgebung.

La maison aux vastes fenêtres,
aux ouvertures inhabituelles et aux
formes surprenantes prend un aspect
spectaculaire dans ce cadre naturel.

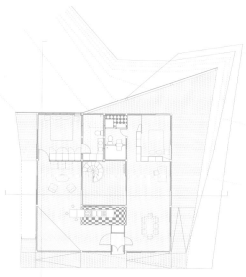

Sitting above the ground, the Kiltro House seems like an ephemeral point of observation in an ever-changing landscape.

Das über dem Boden schwebende Kiltro House wirkt wie ein flüchtiger Aussichtspunkt in der sich ständig wandelnden Landschaft.

Surplombant le sol, la Maison Kiltro est comme une plate-forme d'observation suspendue au-dessus d'un paysage en perpétuel changement.

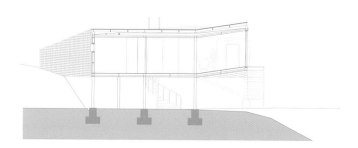

MASAHARU TAKASAKI

Takasaki Architects
1–42–22 Kamoike
Kagoshimashi
Japan

Tel: +81 99 284 0081
Fax: +81 99 284 0082
E-mail: ta@takasaki-architects.co.jp
Web: www.takasaki-architects.co.jp

MASAHARU TAKASAKI was born in Kagoshima in 1953. He studied at the Technical University of Graz, Austria, under Peter Cook, and at the University of Stuttgart, Germany. He created the Takasaki Monobito Institute in 1982, and his firm Takasaki Architects in 1990. He is an Honorary Fellow of the Royal Institute of British Architects, a Professor at the Kyoto University of Art and Design, and a Professor at Innsbruck University. His built work includes the Kuju National Park Restaurant (Kumamoto, Oita, 1994); Kihoku Astronomical Museum (Kihoku, Kagoshima, 1996); Shomyo Kindergarten (Mizobe, Kagoshima, 1996); Nanohanakan, Kagoshima Community Center for Seniors (Nanohanakan, Kagoshima, 1996–98); and Tenchi House, Mono Cosmology (Nagoya, 2009, published here), all in Japan.

MASAHARU TAKASAKI wurde 1953 in Kagoshima geboren. Er studierte an der Technischen Universität Graz bei Peter Cook und an der Universität Stuttgart. 1982 gründete er das Takasaki Monobito Institute, 1990 dann sein Büro Takasaki Architects. Er ist Ehrenmitglied des Royal Institute of British Architects, Professor an der Kyoto University of Art and Design, sowie Professor an der Universität Innsbruck. Zu seinen realisierten Bauten zählen das Restaurant im Nationalpark Kuju (Kumamoto, Oita, 1994), das Kihoku Astronomie-Museum (Kihoku, Kagoshima, 1996), der Shomyo Kindergarten (Mizobe, Kagoshima, 1996), ein Seniorenzentrum in Nanohanakan (Kagoshima, 1996–98) sowie das Tenchi House, Mono Cosmology (Nagoya, 2009, hier vorgestellt), alle in Japan.

MASAHARU TAKASAKI, né à Kagoshima en 1953, a étudié à l'Université polytechnique de Graz en Autriche, auprès de Peter Cook, et à l'Université de Stuttgart. Il a fondé l'Institut Takasaki Monobito en 1982 et son agence Takasaki Architects en 1990. Il est membre honoraire du Royal Institute of British Architects, professeur à l'Université d'art et de design de Kyoto et professeur à l'Université d'Innsbruck. Parmi ses réalisations, toutes au Japon : le restaurant du Parc national de Kuju (Kumamoto, Oita, 1994) ; le Musée d'astronomie de Kihoku (Kihoku, Kagoshima, 1996) ; le jardin d'enfant de Shomyo (Mizobe, Kagoshima, 1996) ; le centre communautaire pour personnes âgées de Kagoshima (Nanohanakan, Kagoshima, 1996–98) et la Maison Tenchi, Mono Cosmology (Nagoya, 2009, publiée ici).

TENCHI HOUSE
Mono Cosmology, Nagoya, Japan, 2009

Area: 151 m². Client: Keiko Ito.
Cost: not disclosed

The entrance to this unusual house is located at its center. A front gate is formed to resemble the word "mind" in Japanese. Masaharu Takasaki states: "This entrance has the shape of a sculptural circle that suggests 'architecture becomes human.' It is a symbol leading to the time of art space." He states that the house is an "unfinished entity" that "absorbs the energy of the natural universe through metamorphosis reflecting seasonal changes." Suggesting that his architecture "embraces chaos," Takasaki also states that the **TENCHI HOUSE** is "an artificial organic space serving as a mind art house." The house is a surprising mixture of apparently organic forms with shapes that seem more mechanical than human. Materials also underline this dichotomy. The house occupies its site almost fully, standing out sharply from the more conventional buildings around it.

Der Eingang zu diesem ungewöhnlichen Haus liegt in seiner Mitte. Ein Gartentor wurde so gestaltet, dass es an das japanische Zeichen für „Geist" erinnert. Masaharu Takasaki erklärt: „Der Eingang hat die Form eines skulpturalen Kreises, der zu sagen scheint: ‚Architektur wird menschlich'. Er ist ein Symbol, der in die Zeit eines Kunstraums führt." Er bezeichnet ds Haus als „unfertiges Gebilde", das „die Energie des natürlichen Universums durch Metamorphose in sich aufnimmt und die Veränderungen der Jahreszeiten spiegelt." Takasaki deutet an, seine Architektur „bejahe das Chaos", und meint zugleich, das **TENCHI HOUSE** sei „ein künstlich-organischer Raum, der als Geist-Kunst-Haus dient". Das Haus ist eine überraschende Kombination aus augenscheinlich organischen Formen und solchen, die eher mechanisch als menschlich wirken. Auch die Baumaterialien unterstreichen diese Dichotomie. Das Haus nutzt das Grundstück fast vollständig aus und kontrastiert scharf mit den eher konventionellen Bauten in der Nachbarschaft.

L'entrée de cette étonnante maison se trouve en son centre. Le portail d'entrée évoque l'idéogramme signifiant « esprit » en japonais. Pour l'architecte : « Cette entrée a la forme d'un cercle sculptural qui suggère que "l'architecture devient humaine". C'est un symbole qui introduit au temps de l'espace conçu comme un art. » Il explique que sa maison est une « entité non finie » qui « absorbe l'énergie de l'univers naturel par une métamorphose reflétant le changement des saisons ». Suggérant que son architecture « étreint le chaos », Takasaki pense également que sa **MAISON TENCHI** est « un espace organique artificiel, une maison de l'art et de l'esprit ». C'est un surprenant mélange de formes apparemment organiques et d'autres qui semblent plus mécaniques qu'humaines. Les matériaux mettent également en évidence cette dichotomie. La maison occupe la quasi-totalité de son terrain, et se détache avec violence de son environnement bâti.

Although the architect has been designing unusually shaped structures for many years, it would seem that his extravagance may once again be fashionable.

Obwohl der Architekt bereits seit Jahren formal ungewöhnliche Bauten entwirft, scheint es jetzt, als würde diese Extravaganz wieder in Mode kommen.

L'architecte conçoit des structures assez étonnantes depuis des années et ce type d'extravagance semble revenir à la mode.

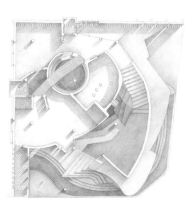
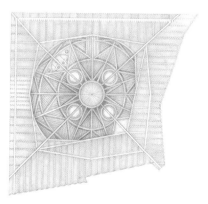

The interior is just as complex as the outside of the house, echoing and developing the designer's cosmological view of architecture.

Die Innenräume des Hauses sind ebenso komplex wie der Außenbau und zugleich ein Spiegel und eine Weiterentwicklung des kosmologischen Architekturverständnisses des Architekten.

Exprimant la vision cosmologique de l'architecture de son auteur, l'intérieur est aussi complexe que l'extérieur.

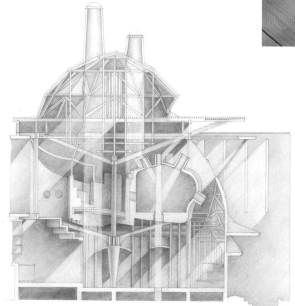

Remarkable detailed drawings, which also seem as though they are from another era, show the complexity of the design, also visible in the image above.

Auch die erstaunlichen, detaillierten Zeichnungen wirken, als stammten sie aus einer anderen Zeit und illustrieren die Komplexität des Designs, die sich auch in der Aufnahme oben zeigt.

Des dessins remarquablement détaillés, qui semblent dater d'une autre époque, montrent la complexité du projet, également perceptible dans la photographie ci-dessus.

Swarovski Ginza ▶

YOSHIOKA TOKUJIN

Tokujin Yoshioka Design
9–1 Daikanyama-cho
Shibuya-ku
Tokyo 150–0034
Japan

Tel: +81 3 5428 0830
Fax: +81 3 5428 0835
E-mail: tyd@tokujin.com
Web: www.tokujin.com

YOSHIOKA TOKUJIN was born in 1967 in Saga, Japan. He graduated from the Kuwasawa Design School and worked under the celebrated designer Shiro Kuramata (1987), and then with Issey Miyake from 1988. He established his own studio, Tokujin Yoshioka Design, in 2000 in Tokyo. His work for Issey Miyake over a period of 20 years included extensive shop design and installations. His work is represented at the Museum of Modern Art (MoMA) in New York, the Centre Pompidou in Paris, the Victoria & Albert Museum in London, Cooper Hewitt National Design Museum in New York, and Vitra Design Museum in Germany. He has collaborated with companies such as Hermès, BMW, and Toyota. Among other things, he designed Yamagiwa's lighting "ToFU" (2000); the paper chair "Honey-pop" (2000–01); Driade's "Tokyo-pop" (2002); "Water Block" made of special glass (2002); "Media Skin" cell phone (2005); "Stardust" chandelier for the Swarovski Crystal Palace (2005); the polyester "Pane Chair" (2003–06); Waterfall (Tokyo, 2005–06, published here); "Venus–Natural crystal chair" (2008); and the flagship store of Swarovski in Ginza (Tokyo, 2006–08, also published here). In 2009, Yoshioka Tokujin worked on an exhibition concerning the archives of Cartier.

YOSHIOKA TOKUJIN wurde 1967 in Saga, Japan, geboren. Sein Studium schloss er an der Kuwasawa Design School ab. Er arbeitete für den bekannten Designer Shiro Kuramata (1987) und ab 1988 für Issey Miyake. Sein eigenes Studio, Tokujin Yoshioka Design, gründete er 2000 in Tokio. Zu seinen im Laufe von rund 20 Jahren entstandenen Arbeiten für Issey Miyake zählen zahlreiche Ladengestaltungen und Installationen. Zu sehen ist sein Werk auch im Museum of Modern Art (MoMA) in New York, dem Centre Pompidou in Paris, dem Victoria & Albert Museum in London, dem Cooper Hewitt National Design Museum in New York sowie dem Vitra Design Museum in Weil am Rhein. Tokujin kooperierte mit Firmen wie Hermès, BMW oder Toyota. Er gestaltete unter anderem die Leuchte „ToFU" für Yamagiwa (2000), die Stühle „Honey-pop" aus Papier (2000–01), „Tokyo-pop" für Driade (2002) und „Water Block" aus Spezialglas (2002), das „Media Skin" Mobiltelefon (2005), den Kronleuchter „Stardust" für den Swarovski Crystal Palace (2005), den „Pane Chair" aus Polyester (2003–06), Waterfall (Tokio, 2005–06, hier vorgestellt), den Stuhl „Venus" aus Kristall (2008) sowie den Swarovski-Flagship-Store im Ginza-Viertel (Tokio, 2006–08, ebenfalls hier vorgestellt). 2009 war Yoshioka Tokujin mit einer Ausstellung über die Archive von Cartier beschäftigt.

YOSHIOKA TOKUJIN, né en 1967 à Saga (Japon), est diplômé de l'École de design Kuwasawa et a travaillé auprès du célèbre designer Shiro Kuramata (1987), puis avec Issey Miyake à partir de 1988. Il a fondé son agence, Tokujin Yoshioka Design, en 2000 à Tokyo. Ses réalisations pour Issey Miyake pendant plus de vingt années comprennent de multiples créations de magasins et des installations. Son œuvre est représentée au Musée d'art moderne de New York (MoMA), au Centre Pompidou à Paris, au Victoria & Albert Museum à Londres, au Cooper Hewitt National Design Museum à New York et au Vitra Design Museum à Weil am Rhein. Il a travaillé pour des entreprises comme Hermès, BMW et Toyota. Entre autres projets, il a conçu la lampe ToFU pour Yamagiwa (2000) ; le siège en papier Honey-pop (2000–01) ; le canapé Driade Tokyo-pop (2002) ; le siège Water Block en verre spécial (2002) ; le téléphone cellulaire Media Skin (2005) ; le lustre Stardust pour le Swarovski Crystal Palace (2005) ; le siège en polyester Pane (2003–06) ; le bar Waterfall (Tokyo, 2005–06, publié ici) ; le siège en cristal Venus–Natural (2008) et le magasin amiral de Swarovski à Ginza (Tokyo, 2006–08, également publié ici). En 2009, Yoshioka Tokujin a travaillé sur un projet d'exposition pour les archives de Cartier.

SWAROVSKI GINZA
Tokyo, Japan, 2006–08

Address: Jewel Box Ginza 1, 2F, Ginza 8–9–15, Chuo-ku, Tokyo, Japan, +81 3 3289 3700, www.swarovski.com
Area: 256 m² (commercial space). Client: Daniel Swarovski Corporation AG
Cost: not disclosed

Part of a worldwide effort on the part of the Austrian glass and luxury-goods purveyor Swarovski, this is also one of a series of projects undertaken by Yoshioka Tokujin for the firm. The Japanese designer was selected to create and develop a new Swarovski retail concept subsequent to a 2006 competition. The store in Ginza is the first new flagship facility completed. Tokujin calls his concept "Crystal Forest," and explains it in the following terms: "When I pondered how to express the intimate relationship between crystals and nature, I looked to the forest as a key element of my inspiration. I intended to design a new retail architecture, which makes the visitor wonder, from the moment of stepping into the boutique, whether he/she is in the forest, jeweled with crystals and pieces of jewelry, rather than proposing an ordinary interior design." The façade incorporates 1500 stainless-steel mirrors, and, within, visitors discover a waterfall-like chandelier and a crystal staircase. Crystals are embedded in the floor stone "like fossils." A second-floor installation called *Shooting Star* arrays 28 000 crystals "like a fall of shooting stars."

Im Zuge einer internationalen Kampagne des österreichischen Glas- und Luxusgüterherstellers realisierte Yoshioka Tokujin verschiedene Projekte für Swarovski, von denen dies ein Beispiel ist. Der japanische Designer hatte nach einem Wettbewerb 2006 den Auftrag erhalten, ein neues Konzept für die Verkaufsräume von Swarovski zu entwickeln. Der Laden an der Ginza ist der erste Flagship-Store, der fertiggestellt werden konnte. Tokujin nennt sein Konzept "Crystal Forest" (Kristallwald) und erklärt: "Als ich mich damit befasste, wie man die enge Beziehung von Kristall und Natur zum Ausdruck bringen könnte, war der Wald ein Schlüsselelement für meine Inspiration. Mir ging es darum, eine neue Art von Einzelhandelsarchitektur zu gestalten. Die Besucher sollten sich beim Betreten des Geschäfts verwundert fragen, ob sie in einem mit Kristallen und Schmuckstücken geschmückten Wald geraten waren. Ich wollte keine gewöhnliche Innenarchitektur." An der Fassade kamen 1500 Edelstahlspiegel zum Einsatz, im Laden selbst können die Kunden einen wasserfallartigen Kronleuchter und eine Treppe aus Kristall entdecken. Selbst in den Boden wurden "wie Fossilien" Kristalle eingearbeitet. Im zweiten Stock formieren sich 28 000 Kristalle "wie ein Sternenregen" zur Installation *Shooting Star*.

Dans le cadre de sa politique d'expansion internationale, le fabricant de cristaux et d'articles de luxe autrichien Swarovski a chargé Yoshioka Tokujin de créer et développer un nouveau concept de magasin à l'occasion d'un concours organisé en 2006. Le magasin amiral de Ginza est le premier à avoir été réalisé. Tokujin a intitulé son concept « Forêt de cristal » qu'il explique ainsi : « Lorsque j'ai étudié comment exprimer la relation intime entre les cristaux et la nature, j'ai recherché dans les forêts l'élément clé de mon inspiration. J'ai voulu créer une architecture commerciale nouvelle qui fait qu'au moment où il entre dans la boutique, le visiteur se demande s'il ne se trouve pas dans une forêt ornée de cristaux et de pièces de joaillerie, plutôt qu'à l'intérieur d'une boutique ». Quelque 1500 miroirs en acier inoxydable ont été utilisés pour la façade. À l'intérieur, le visiteur découvre un chandelier-cascade et un escalier de cristal. Des cristaux sont incrustés dans le sol, « comme des fossiles ». À l'étage, une installation intitulée Shooting Star déploie 28 000 cristaux « comme une pluie d'étoiles filantes ».

Tokujin uses the trademark crystal of Swarovski and stainless-steel mirrors to create an unusual forest of stalactite-like forms.

Tokujin arbeitet mit den für Swarovski typischen Kristallen und mit Edelstahlspiegeln, um einen ungewöhnlichen Wald aus stalaktitenähnlichen Elementen zu gestalten.

Tokujin a utilisé le cristal de Swarovski et des miroirs en acier inoxydable poli pour créer cette forêt de stalactites.

Crystal is present throughout, even embedded here in the stone floors.

Kristalle sind überall zufinden, wurden sogar in die steinernen Bodenplatten eingelassen.

Le cristal est omniprésent, y compris dans le pavement.

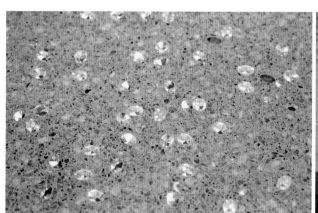

An astonishing waterfall of "shooting stars" made of 28 000 crystals marks the second floor of the shop.

Une étonnante cascade d'« étoiles filantes » composée de 28 000 cristaux illumine l'étage de la boutique.

Der atemberaubende Wasserfall aus „Sternschnuppen" besteht aus 28 000 Kristallen und dominiert das Obergeschoss des Stores.

WATERFALL
Tokyo, Japan, 2005–06

Address: not disclosed
Area: 33 m². Client: not disclosed. Cost: not disclosed

The private gallery of a collector of contemporary art in which Yoshioka Tokujin's **WATERFALL** bar is located was designed by Tadao Ando, with a work by Olafur Eliasson installed on a courtyard wall. The designer used a massive block of glass usually used as a material for space shuttles. 4.2 meters in length, the bar "creates miraculous space like a large block of ice refracts light." Yoshioka Tokujin relates this work to a piece he designed for Roppongi Hills between 2002 and 2003, the "Chair that disappears in the rain." Since it is part of a private residence, this bar is not open to the public, but it has already been extensively published.

Die Privatgalerie für einen Sammler zeitgenössischer Kunst, in der Yoshioka Tokujins Bar **WATERFALL** liegt, wurde von Tadao Ando entworfen. Im Hof ist eine Wandinstallation von Olafur Eliasson zu sehen. Der Designer arbeitete mit einem massiven Glasblock, einem Material, das normalerweise beim Bau von Spaceshuttles zum Einsatz kommt. Die 4,2 m lange Bar „lässt einen rätselhaften Raum entstehen, der das Licht bricht wie ein riesiger Eisblock." Yoshioka Tokujin bringt den Entwurf in Zusammenhang mit einem Projekt, das er zwischen 2002 und 2003 für Roppongi Hills realisierte, einen „Stuhl, der im Regen verschwindet". Da sich die Bar in einem privaten Wohnhaus befindet, ist sie nicht öffentlich zugänglich, wurde jedoch vielfach publiziert.

La galerie du collectionneur d'art contemporain dans laquelle est installé ce bar **CASCADE** a été conçue par Tadao Ando. Elle possède une œuvre d'Olafur Eliasson, qui recouvre un des murs de la cour. Le designer s'est servi du bloc massif d'un verre habituellement utilisé pour les navettes spatiales. D'une longueur de 4,2 mètres, le bar « crée un espace miraculeux, comme un gros bloc de glace réfractant la lumière ». Yoshioka Tokujin fait le lien entre cette œuvre et une pièce qu'il a conçue pour les Collines de Roppongi entre 2002 et 2003, « Le Fauteuil qui disparaît sous la pluie ». Ce bar n'est pas ouvert au public, mais a déjà été largement publié.

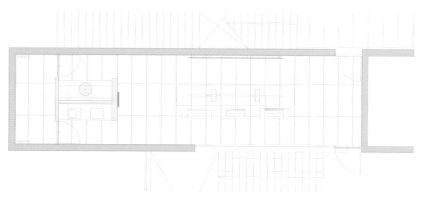

. This private bar is made with an enormous piece of optical-quality glass. The designer manipulates the impression of space through the choice of unusual materials.

Die private Bar wurde aus einem monumentalen Block aus optischem Glas gefertigt. Durch die Wahl ungewöhnlicher Materialien gelingt es dem Designer, das Raumerleben zu manipulieren.

Ce bar privé est fait d'un énorme morceau de verre de qualité optique. Le designer intervient ainsi sur l'espace par le choix de matériaux inusités.

*Production Facilities for
Les Ballets C de la B and LOD* ▶

DE VYLDER VINCK TAILLIEU

*architecten de vylder vinck taillieu
Recollettenlei 36
9000 Ghent
Belgium*

*Tel: +32 9 233 83 45
Fax: +32 9 233 83 47
E-mail: mail@jandevylderarchitecten.com
Web: www.jandevylderarchitecten.com*

JAN DE VYLDER was born in St Niklaas, Belgium, in 1968 and received his Architecture degree from Sint Lucas Ghent in 1992. He worked in the offices of Stephane Beel (1997–2006). A first firm he created, Jan De Vylder en Trice Hofkens Architecten, also existed during this period (2000–07). **INGE VINCK** was born in Ghent, Belgium, in 1973 and received her degree in Architecture from Sint Lucas Ghent in 1997. She worked with Patrice Mottini (Paris, 1997–2001), and then with Stephane Beel (2001–07), before joining Jan De Vylder Architecten. **JO TAILLIEU** was born in Menen, Belgium, in 1971 and received his degree in Architecture from Sint Lucas Ghent in 1995. He worked in the office of Stephane Beel and Xaveer De Geyter (1997–2006). Their built work includes House Jef (Gentbrugge, 2007); House H (Oosterzele, 2007); House 43; offices for 'het toneelhuis" in Antwerp; Malpertuus veterinary clinic in Heusden; and the production facilities for Les Ballets C de la B and LOD (Ghent, 2008, published here), all in Belgium. Ongoing work includes the extension of the Museum for Contemporary Art SMAK, in Ghent, with a department for the collection of Marcel Broodthaers; the conversion of an old townhouse in the Ledeberg district of Ghent into a theater and service center; and a study for social housing, a service center and a master plan for the city of Aarschot in Belgium.

JAN DE VYLDER wurde 1968 in St. Niklaas, Belgien, geboren, schloss sein Architekturstudium 1992 am Sint Lucas Gent ab und arbeitete für Stephane Beel (1997–2006). Während dieser Zeit bestand auch sein erstes Büro, Jan De Vylder en Trice Hofkens Architecten (2000–07). **INGE VINCK** wurde 1973 in Gent, Belgien, geboren und machte ihren Abschluss 1997 am Sint Lucas Gent. Sie arbeitete für Patrice Mottini (Paris, 1997–2001) und danach für Stephane Beel (2001–07), bevor sie zu Jan De Vylder Architecten kam. **JO TAILLIEU** wurde 1971 in Menen, Belgien, geboren und schloss sein Studium 1995 ebenfalls am Sint Lucas Gent ab. Er arbeitete für Stephane Beel und Xaveer De Geyter (1997–2006). Zu den gebauten Projekten des Büros zählen Haus Jef (Gentbrugge, 2007), Haus H (Oosterzele, 2007), Haus 43, Büros für „het toneelhuis" in Antwerpen, die Tierklinik Malpertuus in Heusden sowie Studios, Probenräume und Bühnen für Les Ballets C de la B und LOD (Gent, 2008, hier vorgestellt), alle in Belgien. Laufende Projekte sind u.a. das Museum für zeitgenössische Kunst (SMAK) in Gent, mit einer Abteilung für die Sammlung Marcel Broodthaers, der Umbau eines alten Stadthauses im Genter Stadtteil Ledeberg zu einem Theater und Servicezentrum, eine Studie für Sozialwohnungen, ein Servicezentrum sowie ein Masterplan für die Stadt Aarschot in Belgien.

JAN DE VYLDER, né à St Niklaas en Belgique en 1968, est diplômé en architecture de l'École des arts appliqués de Sint Lucas à Gand (1992). Il a travaillé dans l'agence de Stephane Beel (1997–2006). Sa première agence, Jan De Vylder en Trice Hofkens Architecten, a été opérationnelle de 2000 à 2007. **INGE VINCK**, née à Gand en 1973, est diplômée en architecture de la même école (1997). Elle a travaillé chez Patrice Mottini (Paris, 1997–2001) et Stephane Beel (2001–07), avant de rejoindre Jan De Vylder Architecten. **JO TAILLIEU**, né à Menen en Belgique en 1971, est également diplômé de Sint Lucas (1995). Il a travaillé dans les agences de Stephane Beel et de Xaveer De Geyter (1997–2006). Parmi leurs réalisations, toutes en Belgique : la Maison Jef (Gentbrugge, 2007) ; la Maison H (Oosterzele, 2007) ; la Maison 43 ; des bureaux pour « het toneelhuis » à Anvers ; la clinique vétérinaire Malpertuus à Heusden et les installations de production pour les Ballets C de la B et LOD (Gand, 2008, publiée ici). Ils travaillent actuellement à l'extension du Musée d'art contemporain SMAK à Gand qui comprend un département consacré à la collection de Marcel Broodthaers ; la reconversion en théâtre et centre de services d'une ancienne maison de ville dans le quartier du Ledeberg à Gand ; une étude pour des logements sociaux ; un centre de services et le plan directeur de la ville d'Aarschot en Belgique.

PRODUCTION FACILITIES FOR LES BALLETS C DE LA B AND LOD

Ghent, Belgium, 2008

Address: Bijlokekaai 1, 9000 Ghent, Belgium, +32 9 221 75 01, www.lesballetscdela.be
Area: 680 m². Client: HeL (Les Ballets C de la B and LOD). Cost: € 2.75 million
Collaboration: Trice Hofkens (Design)

Haphazardly positioned awnings and an irregular glass façade make the building stand out, despite its essentially rectilinear forms.

Dank der unregelmäßig angeordneten Markisen und der unregelmäßigen Glasfassade fällt das Gebäude trotz seiner Geradlinigkeit auf.

Des auvents disposés irrégulièrement et des façades de composition complexe personnalisent le bâtiment malgré ses formes relativement simples et rectilignes.

Window placement and surface décor are used in the structures seen above to differentiate them from simple cubes.

Durch Fensteranordnung und dekorative Fassadenelemente (oben) unterscheidet sich der Bau vom schlichten Kubus.

La position des fenêtres ou le décor des murs font échapper ces structures à leur statut de simples parallélépipèdes rectangles.

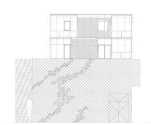

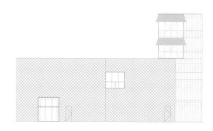

This is a **PRODUCTION FACILITY FOR THE DANCE COMPANY LES BALLETS C DE LA B AND THE MUSIC THEATER LOD**. The city of Ghent assigned both institutions to the site in 2003, wishing to create an art and culture center. As Jan De Vylder explains: "We were asked to design a single building with six theater venues. After reconsidering the entire project, we ended up with three buildings with one theater venue each. At this moment, two have been built, and the third building obtained a new function as foyer." The architects opted for two buildings rather than a single large one, although from certain angles, the two elements look like they are part of the same structure. Unlike the theaters within, the two main façades are transparent, revealing aspects of the interior forms and colors. The architects state: "The result is a poetic combination of building materials, window settings, staircases, and concrete floors, with only a glass curtain separating private from public." Slate was used for closed façade areas, with gaps where plants are meant to grow. Strong colors, awnings that match a number of windows, and an overall sense of movement are generated by the design, where budgetary considerations were a significant element in guiding the design.

Das Projekt umfasst **STUDIOS, PROBENRÄUME UND BÜHNEN FÜR DAS TANZENSEMBLE LES BALLETS C DE LA B UND DAS MUSIKTHEATER LOD**. Die Stadt Gent hatte den beiden Institutionen 2003 einen Standort zugewiesen, an dem ein Kunst- und Kulturzentrum entstehen sollte. Jan De Vylder führt aus: „Man beauftragte uns, ein Gebäude mit sechs Theaterbühnen zu entwerfen. Nachdem wir das ganze Projekt noch einmal überdacht hatten, entschieden wir uns schließlich für drei Gebäude mit je einer Bühne. Bis dato wurden zwei gebaut, das dritte Gebäude erhielt eine neue Funktion als Foyer." Die Architekten entschieden sich für zwei Gebäude statt eines großen, obwohl die Bauten aus bestimmten Blickwinkeln wie Teile ein und desselben Gebäudes wirken. Anders als die Bühnen im Innern sind die beiden Hauptfassaden transparent und lassen Einblicke in die Form- und Farbgebung des Interieurs zu. Die Architekten erklären: „Das Ergebnis ist eine poetische Kombination verschiedener Baumaterialien, Fensterrahmen, Treppen und Betonböden. Nur ein Glasvorhang trennt private und öffentliche Bereiche." Die geschlossenen Fassaden wurden mit Schiefer verblendet, wobei Aussparungen eingeplant wurden, in denen Pflanzen wachsen sollen. Kräftige Farben, Markisen für jedes Fenster und ein dynamischer Gesamteindruck zeichnen den Entwurf aus, bei dem finanzielle Überlegungen eine maßgebliche Rolle spielten.

Ce bâtiment abrite les **INSTALLATIONS DE PRODUCTION DE LA COMPAGNIE LES BALLETES C DE LA B ET DU THÉÂTRE MUSICAL LOD**. La ville de Gand qui souhaitait créer un centre d'art et de culture avait accordé ce terrain aux deux institutions en 2003. Comme l'explique Jan de Vylder : « On nous a demandé de concevoir un bâtiment unique avec six salles. Après avoir revu le projet tout entier, nous avons fini par proposer trois bâtiments équipés chacun d'une salle de théâtre. Actuellement deux ont été construits et le troisième fera fonction de foyer. » Les architectes ont opté pour deux bâtiments plutôt qu'un seul, bien que sous certains angles les deux éléments semblent faire partie de la même structure. À la différence des théâtres qu'elles contiennent, les deux façades sont transparentes et révèlent les formes et les couleurs des aménagements intérieurs. « Le résultat est une combinaison poétique de matériaux de construction, de composition de fenêtres, d'escaliers et de sols en béton et d'un rideau de verre qui sépare le domaine public du domaine privé. » Les façades fermées sont en ardoise avec des interstices dans lesquels des plantes devraient pousser. Des couleurs fortes, des auvents qui protègent un certain nombre de fenêtres et un sens général du mouvement caractérisent ce projet très lié à des considérations budgétaires.

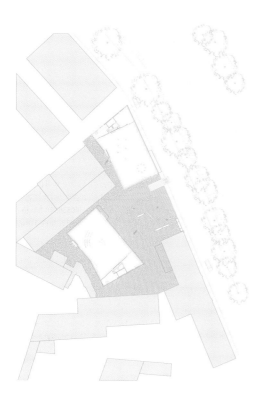

A site plan shows the disposition of the buildings. Generous interior spaces with bright colors provide an echo to the lively exterior of the structures.

Ein Grundstücksplan verdeutlicht die Anordnung der Bauten. Großzügige Innenräume mit kräftigen Farben präsentieren sich als Pendant zu den lebhaften Fassaden.

Le plan du terrain montre l'implantation des divers bâtiments. Les généreux volumes intérieurs de couleurs vives rappellent l'animation des façades.

INDEX OF ARCHITECTS, BUILDINGS, AND PLACES

CREDITS

P 480

PHOTO CREDITS — 2 © Oliver Schuh / **8** © Giacomo Costa **11** © Iwan Baan / **12** © Luke Hayes / **13** © Robert Shimer © Hedrich Blessing / **14–15** © JongOh Kim / **16** © Roland Halbe / **17** © Alex Fradkin courtesy Advanced Geometry Unit, Arup / **19** © Iwan Baan / **21** © Jensen & Skodvin / **22** © Architektur & Landschaft / **24** © Grant Smith/VIEW / **25** © Greg Lynn / **26** © Iwan Baan / **27** © Christian Richters / **28** © Åke E:son Lindman / **29** © Mitsuo Matsuoka / **30** © Iwan Baan / **31** © Tom Bonner / **32–33** © Iwan Baan / **37** © René Robert/IPF / **39** © Eric Mairiaux / **40** © Tadashi Kawamata, courtesy the artist and Kamel Mennour, Paris / **41** © Osamu Watanabe / **42–43** © Nacása & Partners Inc. / **45** © Iwan Baan / **46** © Roland Halbe / **47** © Iwan Baan / **48** © Philippe Ruault / **49** © Supersudaka / **50** © Oliver Schuh / **52** © Iwan Baan / **53** Robert Shimer © Hedrich Blessing / **54** © Emilio Ambasz / **55–63** © Enrico Cano / **64** © Víctor Oddó / **65–69** © Cristobal Palma / **70–75** © Architektur & Landschaft / **76** © Asymptote Architecture / **77** © Hani Rashid / **78–81** © Björn Moerman / **78** © Hideya Tanaka/Ken Inahara / **79–83, 85–87** © Hideya Tanaka / **84** © Sueo Kai / **88–91** © Alex Fradkin courtesy Advanced Geometry Unit, Arup / **92** © Charles Barclay Architects / **93–97** © David Grandorge / **98** © Corinne Rose / **99–101 top** © Tom Harris / **101 bottom** © Kyle Talbott / **102** © Baumschlager Eberle / **103–107** © Eduard Hueber/archphoto.com / **108** © Jakob Galtt / **109** © Jakob Boserup/MAKWERK / **110** © Dragor Luftfoto / **111, 115** © Bjarke Ingels Group / **112–113** © Matteo Sartori / **114** © Ulrik Jantzen / **116** © Stefano Boeri Architetti / **117–118, 120–121** © Iwan Baan / **119** © Paolo Rosselli / **122** © BCHO Architects / **123–127** © Kim Yongkwan / **128–131** © Wooseop Hwang / **132** © Giorgio von Arb / **133–139** © Oliver Schuh / **140** © Giacomo Costa / **146** © Elliott + Associates Architects / **147–151** © Robert Shimer © Hedrich Blessing / **152–157** © Shuhei Endo Architecture Institute / **158** © Daniel Sahlberg / **159–163** © Åke E:son Lindman / **164** © Edouard Francois / **165–169** © David Boureau / **170** © Terunobu Fujimori / **171–175** © Akihisa Masuda / **176** © David Vintiner / **177–181** © Iwan Baan / **182** © Gustafson Porter + Gustafson Guthrie Nichol / **183–189** © Grant Smith/VIEW / **190** © Gautier Deblonde / **191–195** © Michelle Litvin / **196–197** © Luke Hayes / **198** Monica Patxot / **202** © Adriano A. Biondo / **203–209** © Roland Halbe / **210** © HHF architekten GmbH / **211–215** © Iwan Baan / **216** © Mark Heitoff / **217–218, 221** © Roland Halbe / **219–220** © Steen Gyldendal / **222-226** © Christian Richters/VIEW / **227** © Iwan Baan / **228** © Information Based Architecture / **232–237** © René Robert/IPF / **238** © HyoMan Kim / **239–242** © JongOh Kim / **243** © Hiroshi Hatate / **244–249** © Iwan Baan / **250** © Toyo Ito & Associates, Architects / **251–255** © Iwan Baan / **256** courtesy JCFO/Diller Scofidio + Renfro / **257–261** © Iwan Baan / **262–267** © Jensen & Skodvin / **268** © Kalhöfer-Korschildgen / **269–273** © Jörg Hempel / **274** © KHR arkitekter AS / **275–283** © Torben Eskerod / **284–289** © LAAC Architects / **290** © Emiliano López Mónica Rivera Arquitectos / **291–295** © José Hevia Blach / **296–301** © Greg Lynn / **302** © Made in Sàrl / **303–307** © Walter Mair / **308–309, 311** © Maki and Associates / **314** © Morphosis / **315–319** © Roland Halbe / **320** © Eric Owen Moss Architects / **321–323** © Tom Bonner / **324** © Susanne Nobis / **325–329** © Roland Halbe / **330** © NOX / **338** © Shinro Ohtake / **339–343** © Takako Urabe / **344** © OMA*AMO/Rem Koolhaas / **345–357** © Iwan Baan / **358** © Paredes Pedrosa Arquitectos / **359–363** © Roland Halbe / **364** © Dominique Perrault Architecture / **365–371** © André Morin / **372** © Renzo Piano Building Workshop / **373–377** © Attilio Maranzano / **378** © Plasma Studio / **374** © Agence Rudy Ricciotti Architecte / **385–389** © Philippe Ruault / **390** © Peter Rich Architects / **391–399** © Iwan Baan / **400** © Rotor vzw-asbl / **401–405** © Eric Mairiaux / **406** © Hiroshi Sambuichi Architects / **407–411** © Katsuhisa Kida/FOTOTECA / **412** © Takashi Okamoto / **413–415, 416 bottom, 417 bottom, 421 top, 422–423 top and bottom left, 424 bottom left** © Christian Richters / **416 top** © Iwan Baan / **417 top, 418, 423 bottom right, 424 bottom right** © Roland Halbe / **421 bottom, 424 top** © Hisao Suzuki / **426–431** © Germán del Sol, Architectos / **432** © Adrian Smith / **433–437** © James Steinkamp Photography / **434–435** © AP Photo/Kamran Jebreili / **438** © SPLITTERWERK / **439–443** © paul ott photografiert / **444–449** © Hiroshi Sugimoto / **450–455** © Supersudaka / **456** © Takasaki Architects / **457–461** © Hiroyasu Sakaguchi AtoZ / **462** © Masahiro Okamura / **463–469** © Nacása & Partners Inc. / **470** © edwin koster / **471–475** © filip dujardin/OWI

CREDITS FOR PLANS / DRAWINGS / CAD DOCUMENTS — 7 © Emaar Properties / **35** © Information Based Architecture / **57, 59, 61–63** © Emilio Ambasz / **67** © Alejandro Aravena Architects / **73–75** © Architektur & Landschaft / **81** © Asymptote Architecture / **85** © Atelier-Den/Inahara Archi-Lab / **90–91** © Advanced Geometry Unit, Arup / **94–97** © Charles Barclay Architects / **100–101** © Barkow Leibinger Architects / **111, 114–115** © Bjarke Ingels Group / **119** © Stefano Boeri Architetti / **125–130** © BCHO Architects / **137** © Santiago Calatrava SA / **141–145** © Giacomo Costa / **151** © Elliott + Associates Architects / **154, 157** © Shuhei Endo Architecture Institute / **160, 163** © Albert France-Lanord Architecture / **166–169** © Edouard François / **172** © Terunobu Fujimori / **179–180** © Sou Fujimoto Architects / **186** © Gustafson Porter + Gustafson Guthrie Nichol / **194** © Zaha Hadid Architects / **199** © Mir/Herreros Arquitectos / **200–201** © Herreros Arquitectos / **204, 208–209** © Herzog & de Meuron / **213–215** © HHF architekten GmbH / **219–220, 226–227** © Steven Holl Architects / **229–231** © Information Based Architecture / **237** © The International Polar Foundation / **240, 243** © IROJE KHM Architects / **248–249** © junya.ishigami+associates, courtesy of Gallery Koyanagi / **253, 255** © Toyo Ito & Associates, Architects / **264** © Jensen & Skodvin / **272–273** © Kalhöfer-Korschildgen / **276–281** © KHR arkitekter AS / **288** © LAAC Architects / **292** © Emiliano López Mónica Rivera Arquitectos / **299** © Greg Lynn / **304** © Made in Sàrl / **310, 313** © Maki and Associates / **319** © Morphosis / **322–323** © Eric Owen Moss Architects / **327, 329** © Susanne Nobis / **331–337** © NOX / **346–353** © OMA*AMO/Rem Koolhaas / **361, 363** © Paredes Pedrosa Arquitectos / **366, 371** © Dominique Perrault Architecture / **376** © Renzo Piano Building Workshop / **379–383** © Plasma Studio Images / **389** © Agence Rudy Ricciotti Architecte / **393–399** © Peter Rich Architects / **403, 405** © Rotor vzw-asbl / **410** © Hiroshi Sambuichi Architects / **415–425** © SANAA/Kazuyo Sejima + Ryue Nishizawa / **428, 430** © Germán del Sol, Architectos / **434, 437** © Adrian Smith + Gordon Gill Architect / **441–442** © SPLITTERWERK / **447** © New Material Research Laboratory /**453, 455** © Supersudaka / **459, 461** © Takasaki Architects / **469** © Tokujin Yoshioka Design / **473, 475** © architecten de vylder vinck taillieu